endorsed for
BTEC

Pearson
BTEC National
Health and
Social Care

Student Book 2

Carolyn Aldworth
Elizabeth Haworth
Sue Hocking
Peter Lawrence
Nicola Matthews
Marjorie Snaith
Mary Whitehouse

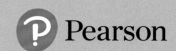
P **Pearson**

Published by Pearson Education Limited, 80 Strand, London, WC2R 0RL.

www.pearsonschoolsandfecolleges.co.uk

Copies of official specifications for all Edexcel qualifications may be found on the website: www.edexcel.com

Text © Pearson Education Limited
Designed by Andy Magee
Typeset by Tech-Set Ltd
Original illustrations © Pearson Education Ltd
Illustrated by Tech-Set Ltd
Cover design by Vince Haig
Cover photo/illustration © Getty Images: Michelle McMahon

First published 2016

19 18 17

10 9 8 7 6 5 4

British Library Cataloguing in Publication Data
A catalogue record for this book is available from the British Library

ISBN 978 129212 602 9

Printed in Slovakia by Neografia

Acknowledgements
We would like to thank Andy Ashton for his invaluable help in reviewing this book.

The publisher would like to thank the following for their kind permission to reproduce their photographs:

(Key: b-bottom; c-centre; l-left; r-right; t-top)

123RF.com: 207t, Cathy Yeulet 505; **Alamy Images:** 67Photo 21, André Quillien 357, Angela Hampton Picture Library 238, Art Directors & Trip 398, Blend Images 492, blickwinkel 340 (d), Bob Ebbessen 454, Brian Light 478, BSIP SA 64, 381, Carolyn Jenkins 490, Cultura Creative RF 259, 269br, Custom Medical Stock Photo 336, David Burton 297, david pearson 181, David Taylor 387, Enigma 393, Granger NYC 338, Image Source 17, Images-USA 16, Jeff Rotman 477, Jeffrey Blacker 116, Jochen Tack 280, Joerg Boethling 366, Marmaduke St John 243, Monkey Business Images 125, Paula Solloway 203, 206, 409, RGB Ventures 439, Richard Newton 488, senior images 129, SIBSA Digital Pvt. Ltd 426, Tom Wang 400, Transport for London 249, WILDLIFE GmbH 333; **Department of Health Publications:** 187; **Fotolia.com:** Antonioguillem 134, Ashwin 570, Danielle Bonardelle 422, didesign 446, Frank Boston 141, goodluz 142, Grafvision 118, lisovoy 432, Michaeljung 482, Monkey Business 99, 457, Monkey Business 99, 457, natali1991 463, Simon Greig 507, WavebreakmediaMicro 489, Zdenka Darula 137; **Getty Images:** Education Images 234, Edward G Malidine 147, JGI / Jamie Grill 104tl, John Moore 158, Johnny Greig 242, leesnow 278, McIninch 390, Noah Seelham 179, Oli Scarff 442, ParkerDeen 404, Pasieka 269cr, 294, PeopleImages 391, Peter Dazeley 380, Phil Boorman 461, Robert Neidring 92, Solstock 106, Stockbyte 386, sturti 5, VisitBritain / Daniel Bosworth 417, Yellow Dog Productions 34, YinYang 462, ZOOMDOSSO 358; **Pearson Education Ltd:** Gareth Boden 273, Jules Selmes 411, Lord and Leverett 107, Rob Judges 254, Studio 8 67; **PhotoDisc:** Kevin Peterson 207b; **Photofusion Picture Library:** John Birdsall 497l, 497r; **Public Health England:** 194t, 194b, 467; **Rex Shutterstock:** Ken McKay / ITV 405; **Science Photo Library Ltd:** 269l, animate4.com 516, 517, CNRI 272, 285, 291, 323l, Cordelia Molloy 362, Daniela Beckmann 282, David M Phillips 319b, 329, 346, Dr Jeremy Burgess 315, Dr Keith Wheeler 330, Dr P Marazzi 355, Eye of Science 321t, 321b, GUSTOIMAGE 323r, James Cavallini 271r, 319t, Jerry Mason 296, John Durham 290, Martin Shields 566, Merlin Tuttle / Bat Conservation International 340r, Monica Shroeder 562, Paul Rapson 407, Peter Gardiner 327, Science Source 331, 341l, Sinclair Stammars 363, Steve Gschmeissner 320, Visual Science 531, Zephyr 324; **Shutterstock.com:** 230, Alan Bailey 437, angellodeco 509, Anna Lurye 231, auremar 219, CandyBox Images 143, Cosmin Mancii 340 (b), D. Kucharski / K. Kucharska 340 (c), dafra 340 (a), Dariusz Gora 322, Darren Baker 313, Dennis Kuvaev 218, Digital Storm 1, Dmitry Lobanov 493, Felix Mizioznikov 370, Flashon Studio 410, goodluz 131, iordani 369, Jim Barber 403, Kerry Garvey 202, kurhan 24, Levant Konuk 271l, Lisa F Young 371, mangostock 246, Martin Noval 448, Monkey Business Imaegs 226, PT Images 508, R. Gino Santa Maria 257, Radu Razvan 569, Sebastian Kaulitzki 224, Susan Santa Maria 293, Vladimir Mucibabic 245, WavebreakmediaMicro 201, ZouZou 314; **WaterAid:** 354; **www.imagesource.com:** Nigel Riches 258

All other images © Pearson Education

This book contains information which is © Crown copyright. Contains public sector information licensed under the Open Government Licence v3.0.

The publisher would like to thank the following organisations for their kind permission to reproduce their materials:

p.6 Text on Francis, R (2013) Report of the Mid Staffordshire NHS Foundation Trust Public Inquiry, the Stationery Office. Crown Copyright; **p.22** Table 4.2 Dementia care in homes and hospitals - is used by the kind permission of Care Quality Commission (CQC). Copyright (c) Care Quality Commission; **p.61** Nuremburg Code was taken from: http://www.ncbi.nlm.nih.gov/pmc/articles/PMC3121268/ - US National Library of Medicine and National Institutes of Health; **p.75** Table 4.10 Selected statistics regarding smoking habits in England, as a percentage was taken from: Health & Social Care Information Centre, Statistics on Smoking, England 2015. Crown Copyright; **p.78**

Text from: BTEC Level 3 National Health and Social Care: Student Book 1, by: 'Stretch, B. and Whitehouse, M. (eds) Copyright 2010. Published by Pearson Education Limited. Used by permission; **p.79** HSCISC (2015) National Child Measurement Programme, England 2014/15: http://www.hscic.gov.uk/searchcatalogue?productid=19405&q=t itle%3a%22national+child+measurement+programme. Crown Copyright; **p.79** Unit 4. Public Health England came from GOV.UK. Crown Copyright; **p.90** Assessment Practice 4.3 In 2016, the Stroke Association reported that 1.2 million people in the UK were living as stroke survivors. Data provided by the Stroke Association and used by permission; Unit 6. Table 6.3 NHS core care values - taken from: www.nhs.uk. Crown Copyright; **p.112** Updated report Dementia UK from 2014.Prince M, Knapp M et al (2014). Dementia UK: Update. London: Alzheimer's Society. Used by permission; **p.121** Table 6.5 The NHS Constitution - taken from www.nhs.uk. Crown Copyright; **p.146** Data from Public Health England. Measles - taken from: www.gov.uk/government/ publications/measles-deaths-by-age-group-from-1980-to-2013-ons-data/measles-notifi cations-and-deaths-in-england-and-wales-1940-to-2013. Crown Copyright; Unit 8. Figure 8.2: Key health and safety statistics, Great Britain (2014/15) taken from: www.hse.gov.uk/statistics. Crown Copyright; **p.155** Figure 8.2: Syphilis, Tees Valley, 2012-2014 taken from: Public Health England. Crown Copyright; **p.159** Can cancer be prevented was found at: http://www.cancerresearchuk.org/about-cancer/causes-of-cancer/can-cancer-be-prevented (accessed September 2016) and is used by the kind permission of Cancer Research UK; **p.160** Figure 8.3: Life expectancy, England and Wales, 1992-2014 taken from the Office for National Statistics (ONS) Crown Copyright; **p.163** Public Health England's Alcohol and drugs prevention, treatment and recovery: why invest? (2013) taken from Public Health England. Crown Copyright; **p.167** Life expectancy and quality of life - taken from the Office for National Statistics (ONS) Crown Copyright; **p.171** Text on Unemployment - taken from the Office for National Statistics (ONS) Crown Copyright; **p.171** Text on Older People - taken from the Office for National Statistics (ONS) Crown Copyright; **p.174** Text on Tuberculosis (TB) was reprinted from the World Health Organization. Copyright (c) WHO. Used by permission of the World Health Organization; **p.177** Food production, preparation, storage and sales was taken from the Food Standards Act. Crown Copyright; **p.191** Figure 8.4: The theory of reasoned action. Taken from: Nebraska Symposium on Motivation, 1979: beliefs, attitudes and values by Monte M. Page, Herbert E. Howe. Published by University of Nebraska Press. Copyright (c) 1980; **p.199** Figure 8.12: Number of alcohol-related hospital admissions in 2013-14, in England taken from Public Health England. Crown Copyright; **p.218** Information on Down's Syndrome is reproduced from the DOWNS'S SYNDROME ASSOCIATION website: www.downs-syndrome.org.uk; **p.233** The Equality Act 2010 taken from: http://www.legislation. gov.uk/ukpga/2010/15/contents. Crown Copyright; **p.235** Health and Safety at Work Act etc (1974) (HASWA) taken from: http://www.hse.gov.uk/legislation/hswa. htm. Crown Copyright; **p.377** Golden Rice - taken from: The International Rice Research Institute (IRRI); **p.392** The Equality Act 2010 taken from: http://www. legislation.gov.uk/ukpga/2010/15/contents. Crown Copyright; **p.452** Every Child Matters, taken from: http://www.everychildmatters.co.uk/aims/. Crown Copyright; **p.452** The Early Years Foundation Stage (EYFS) (England) taken from: https://www. gov.uk/government/uploads/system/uploads/attachment_data/file/335504/ EYFS_framework_from_1_September_2014__with_clarification_note.pdf. Crown Copyright; **p.469** Food Supplements (England) (Amendment) Regulations 2007. Taken from: https://www.gov.uk/government/uploads/system/uploads/attachment_data/ file/204324/Supplements_SI_guidance__Jan_2012__DH_FINAL.pdf. Crown Copyright; **p.471** Figure 19.2 Chart for weight and height was taken from: NHS Choices 2015. Crown Copyright;**p.501** 'Malnutrition Universal Screening Tool' ('MUST') or weight loss chart] is reproduced here with the kind permission of BAPEN (British Association for Parenteral and Enteral Nutrition). For further information on 'MUST' see www. bapen.org.uk'; **p.501** Figure 19.8 Measuring demispan is reproduced here with the kind permission of BAPEN (British Association for Parenteral and Enteral Nutrition). For further information see www.bapen.org.uk

Websites
Pearson Education Limited is not responsible for the content of any external internet sites. It is essential for tutors to preview each website before using it in class so as to ensure that the URL is still accurate, relevant and appropriate. We suggest that tutors bookmark useful websites and consider enabling students to access them through the school/college intranet.

A note from the publisher
In order to ensure that this resource offers high-quality support for the associated Pearson qualification, it has been through a review process by the awarding body. This process confirms that this resource fully covers the teaching and learning content of the specification or part of a specification at which it is aimed. It also confirms that it demonstrates an appropriate balance between the development of subject skills, knowledge and understanding, in addition to preparation for assessment.

Endorsement does not cover any guidance on assessment activities or processes (e.g. practice questions or advice on how to answer assessment questions), included in the resource nor does it prescribe any particular approach to the teaching or delivery of a related course.

While the publishers have made every attempt to ensure that advice on the qualification and its assessment is accurate, the official specification and associated assessment guidance materials are the only authoritative source of information and should always be referred to for definitive guidance.

Pearson examiners have not contributed to any sections in this resource relevant to examination papers for which they have responsibility.

Examiners will not use endorsed resources as a source of material for any assessment set by Pearson.

Endorsement of a resource does not mean that the resource is required to achieve this Pearson qualification, nor does it mean that it is the only suitable material available to support the qualification, and any resource lists produced by the awarding body shall include this and other appropriate resources.

Contents

How to use this book

Welcome to your BTEC National Health and Social Care course.

You are joining a course that has a 30-year track record of learner success, with the BTEC National widely recognised within the industry and in higher education as the signature vocational qualification. Over 62 per cent of large companies recruit employees with BTEC qualifications and 100,000 BTEC learners apply to UK universities every year.

There are many roles available in the Health and Social Care sector, providing varied opportunities to make a difference to people's lives in a positive way – and the demand for skilled people is growing. Whether you are thinking of pursuing a career in nursing, healthcare science or social work, the BTEC National in Health and Social Care includes pathways that will help you to fulfil your ambition. Once you have completed your studies, whatever you choose to do you will be doing a job that is varied, rewarding and worthwhile.

You will be studying a range of units which will help you to gain skills that will be valuable in your chosen profession or future study. You will learn about the human body and how it changes over time. You will also learn about what it means to work in the sector and what skills and behaviours you will need to demonstrate. If you are studying the larger qualification sizes such as the Foundation Diploma or one of the Extended Diplomas, you will also learn about the principles of safe practice when working in the sector, and the importance of respecting the individual differences and needs of service users.

How your BTEC is structured

Your BTEC National is divided into **mandatory units** (the ones you must do) and **optional units** (the ones you can choose to do). The number of units you need to do and the units you can cover will depend on the type and size of qualification you are doing.

This book covers **units 4, 6, 8, 12, 13, 15, 17, 18, 19 and 24**. This book is designed to be used together with the *Pearson BTEC National Health and Social Care Student Book 1*, which includes further mandatory and optional units. The table below shows how each unit in this book maps to the BTEC National Health and Social Care qualifications.

Unit title	Mandatory	Optional
Unit 4 Enquiries into Current Research in Health and Social Care	Diploma and Extended Diplomas only	
Unit 6 Work Experience in Health and Social Care	Extended Diplomas only	Foundation Diploma and Diploma only
Unit 8 Promoting Public Health	Diploma and Extended Diplomas only	
Unit 12 Supporting Individuals with Additional Needs		All sizes except Certificate and Extended Diploma for Health Studies pathway
Unit 13 Scientific Techniques for Health Science		Extended Diploma Health Studies pathway only
Unit 15 Microbiology for Health Science		Extended Diploma Health Studies pathway only
Unit 17 Caring for Individuals with Dementia		Extended Diplomas only
Unit 18 Assessing Children's Development Support Needs		Extended Diploma general pathway only
Unit 19 Nutritional Health		All sizes except Certificate and Extended Certificate
Unit 24 Biochemistry for Health		Extended Diplomas only

Your learning experience

You may not realise it but you are always learning. Your educational and life experiences are constantly shaping you, your ideas, your thinking, and how you view and engage with the world around you.

You are the person most responsible for your own learning experience so it is really important you understand what you are learning, why you are learning it and why it is important both to your course and your personal development.

Your learning can be seen as a journey which moves through four phases.

Phase 1	Phase 2	Phase 3	Phase 4
You are introduced to a topic or concept; you start to develop an awareness of what learning is required.	You explore the topic or concept through different methods (e.g. research, questioning, analysis, deep thinking, critical evaluation) and form your own understanding.	You apply your knowledge and skills to a task designed to test your understanding.	You reflect on your learning, evaluate your efforts, identify gaps in your knowledge and look for ways to improve.

During each phase, you will use different learning strategies. As you go through your course, these strategies will combine to help you secure the core knowledge and skills you need.

This student book has been written using similar learning principles, strategies and tools. It has been designed to support your learning journey, to give you control over your own learning and to equip you with the knowledge, understanding and tools to be successful in your future studies or career.

Features of this book

In this student book there are lots of different features. They are there to help you learn about the topics in your course in different ways and understand it from multiple perspectives. Together these features:

▶ explain what your learning is about

▶ help you to build your knowledge

▶ help you understand how to succeed in your assessment

▶ help you to reflect on and evaluate your learning

▶ help you to link your learning to the workplace.

In addition, each individual feature has a specific purpose, designed to support important learning strategies. For example, some features will:

▶ get you to question assumptions around what you are learning

▶ make you think beyond what you are reading about

▶ help you make connections across your learning and across units

▶ draw comparisons between your own learning and real-world workplace environments

▶ help you to develop some of the important skills you will need for the workplace, including team work, effective communication and problem solving.

Features that explain what your learning is about

Getting to know your unit

This section introduces the unit and explains how you will be assessed. It gives an overview of what will be covered and will help you to understand *why* you are doing the things you are asked to do in this unit.

Getting started

This appears at the start of every unit and is designed to get you thinking about the unit and what it involves. This feature will also help you to identify what you may already know about some of the topics in the unit and acts as a starting point for understanding the skills and knowledge you will need to develop to complete the unit.

Features that help you to build your knowledge

Research

This asks you to research a topic in greater depth. Using these features will help to expand your understanding of a topic as well as developing your research and investigation skills. All of these will be invaluable for your future progression, both professionally and academically.

Worked example

Our worked examples show the process you need to follow to solve a problem, such as a maths or science equation or the process for writing a letter or memo. This will also help you to develop your understanding and your numeracy and literacy skills.

Theory into practice

In this feature you are asked to consider the workplace or industry implications of a topic or concept from the unit. This will help you to understand the close links between what you are learning in the classroom and the affects it will have on a future career in your chosen sector.

Discussion

Discussion features encourage you to talk to other students about a topic in greater detail, working together to increase your understanding of the topic and to understand other people's perspectives on an issue. This will also help to build your teamworking skills, which will be invaluable in your future professional and academic career.

Safety tip

This provides advice around health and safety when working on the unit. It will help build your knowledge about best practice in the workplace, as well as make sure that you stay safe.

Key terms

Concise and simple definitions are provided for key words, phrases and concepts, allowing you to have, at a glance, a clear understanding of the key ideas in each unit.

Link

This shows any links between units or within the same unit, helping you to identify where the knowledge you have learned elsewhere will help you to achieve the requirements of the unit. Remember, although your BTEC National is made up of several units, there are common themes that are explored from different perspectives across the whole of your course.

Step by step:

This practical feature gives step-by-step descriptions of particular processes or tasks in the unit, including a photo or artwork for each step. This will help you to understand the key stages in the process and help you to carry out the process yourself.

Further reading and resources

This contains a list of other resources – such as books, journals, articles or websites – you can use to expand your knowledge of the unit content. This is a good opportunity for you to take responsibility for your own learning, as well as preparing you for research tasks you may need to do academically or professionally.

Features connected to your assessment

Your course is made up of a series of mandatory and optional units. There are two different types of mandatory unit:

▶ externally assessed
▶ internally assessed.

The features that support you in preparing for assessment are below. But first, what is the difference between these two different types of units?

Externally assessed units

These units give you the opportunity to present what you have learned in the unit in a different way. They can be challenging, but will really give you the opportunity to demonstrate your knowledge and understanding, or your skills in a direct way. For these units you will complete a task, set directly by Pearson, in controlled conditions. This could take the form of an exam or it could be another type of task. You may have the opportunity in advance to research and prepare notes around a topic, which can be used when completing the assessment.

Internally assessed units

Internally assessed units involve you completing a series of assignments, set and marked by your tutor. The assignments you complete could allow you to demonstrate your learning in a number of different ways, from a written report to a presentation to a video recording and observation statements of you completing a practical task. Whatever the method, you will need to make sure you have clear evidence of what you have achieved and how you did it.

Assessment practice

These features give you the opportunity to practise some of the skills you will need when you are assessed on your unit. They do not fully reflect the actual assessment tasks, but will help you get ready for doing them.

Plan – Do – Review

You'll also find handy advice on how to plan, complete and evaluate your work after you have completed it. This is designed to get you thinking about the best way to complete your work and to build your skills and experience before doing the actual assessment. These prompt questions are designed to get you started with thinking about how the way you work, as well as understand why you do things.

Getting ready for assessment

For internally assessed units, this is a case study from a BTEC National student, talking about how they planned and carried out their assignment work and what they would do differently if they were to do it again. It will give you advice on preparing for the kind of work you will need to for your internal assessments, including 'Think about it' points for you to consider for your own development.

Getting ready for assessment

This section will help you to prepare for external assessment. It gives practical advice on preparing for and sitting exams or a set task. It provides a series of sample answers for the types of questions you will need to answer in your external assessments, including guidance on the good points of these answers and how these answers could be improved.

Features to help you reflect on and evaluate your learning

⏸ PAUSE POINT   Pause Points appear after a section of each unit and give you the opportunity to review and reflect upon your own learning. The ability to reflect on your own performance is a key skill you'll need to develop and use throughout your life, and will be essential whatever your future plans are.

Hint
Extend   These also give you suggestions to help cement your knowledge and indicate other areas you can look at to expand it.

Reflect

This allows you to reflect on how the knowledge you have gained in this unit may impact your behaviour in a workplace situation. This will help not only to place the topic in a professional context, but also help you to review your own conduct and develop your employability skills.

Features which link your learning with the workplace

Case study

Case studies are used throughout the book to allow you to apply the learning and knowledge from the unit to a scenario from the workplace or the industry. Case studies include questions to help you consider the wider context of a topic. This is an opportunity to see how the unit's content is reflected in the real world, and for you to build familiarity with issues you may find in a real-world workplace.

THINK ▶FUTURE

This is a special case study where someone working in the industry talks about the job role they do and the skills they need. This comes with a *Focusing your skills* section, which gives suggestions for how you can begin to develop the employability skills and experiences that are needed to be successful in a career in your chosen sector. This is an excellent opportunity to help you identify what you could do, inside and outside of your BTEC National studies, to build up your employability skills.

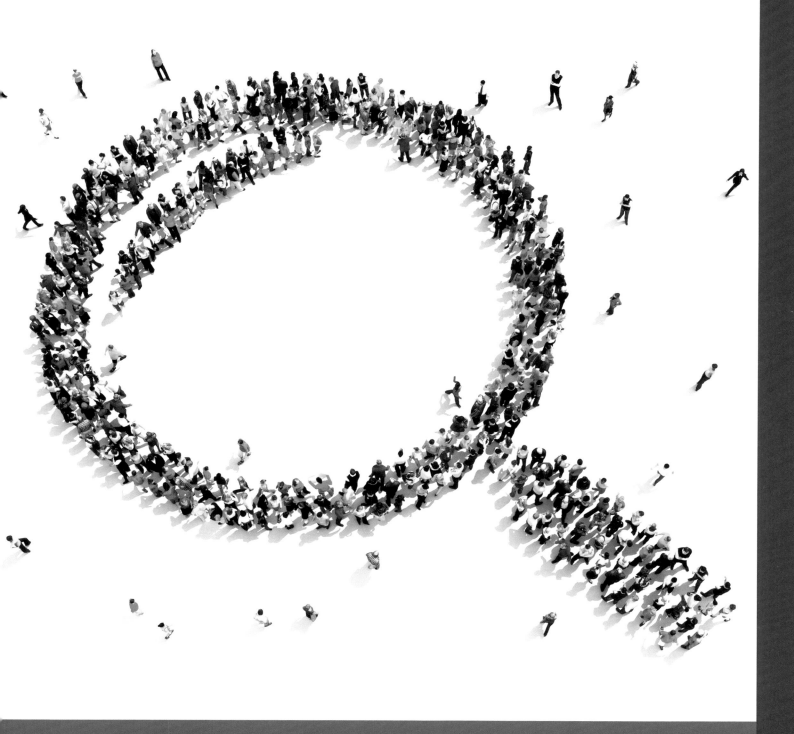

Enquiries into Current Research in Health and Social Care

4

Getting to know your unit

Assessment
You will be assessed by a controlled assessment in two parts set and marked by Pearson.

This unit will enable you to investigate a current issue in health and social care using a literature search methodology. You will investigate the possible purposes of research in health and social care and the methods that may be used in such research.

How you will be assessed

You will be assessed by a controlled assessment, which will have two parts. Part A will be issued to you a set period of time before the date of the Part B assessment. Part B will be a written assessment completed under supervised conditions.

Part A will consist of two articles about research on an issue relevant to health and social care. You should carry out secondary research based on one of the articles, using a literature search. During this time, you will be working independently, under supervised conditions and without conferring with other learners. Your tutor will be unable to give you any feedback on your research activity during the Part A assessment, although they will advise you of the schedule for the supervised sessions.

The first task for you to complete in the supervised sessions will be to read both articles carefully. You will then choose one on which to base your secondary research. You will then need to analyse your chosen article in depth, and find and use at least two further secondary sources for your research, focusing on an aspect of the issue explored in the article, as prompted by the qualitative and quantitative data it provides. You will be able to take notes but not take these away from the supervised room. Your tutor will tell you what your notes may, and may not, contain, and how long they may be. You will need to schedule time to prepare a) a list of all the secondary sources you use and b) some A4 notes, which you will be allowed to take into the Part B written assessment.

Part B will also take place under supervised conditions and you will be presented with a taskbook containing questions about the research article you have chosen, and about your secondary research. You will write your answers to the questions in this taskbook. You will have no access to the internet or other resources during the controlled assessment. However, the Part B taskbook will include a copy of the two articles issued in Part A and you will also have the notes you prepared in advance during Part A.

▶ The Part B paper will be presented in two sections, one for each of the two articles presented in Part A.

▶ The questions in each section are different so you will need to take great care that you complete the correct section for the article you have chosen to research.

▶ For each question, you will be provided with two to three pages of blank, lined paper to enter your responses. The first box of each section does not relate to a question and you should enter the details of the sources you have used in your secondary research.

▸ The questions will necessitate responses that are related both to the original Part A article and to the additional secondary sources you have accessed during Part A.

▸ Each of the questions will require you to demonstrate that you know and understand the knowledge and concepts specified in the unit specification for all of the assessment outcomes. To achieve a higher grade, you will need to be able to demonstrate effective use of the knowledge and understanding gained from both the article and the secondary sources you have selected during Part A.

▸ As the guidelines for assessment can change, you should refer to the official assessment guidance on the Pearson Qualifications website for the latest definitive guidance.

▸ **Table 4.1:** Command words or terms used in this unit

Command or term	Definition
Article	The pre-released account of a piece of recent research relating to an aspect of health or social care. Could be based on a longer research report.
Ethical issue	Ethically related aspects that may have affected how the research was carried out.
Health and social care practice	Used in relation to how health and social care professionals carry out their work or job roles.
Health and social care services	May be used in relation to how services are provided and/or made available to the individuals that need them.
Issue	May be used on its own to describe the subject of the research that the article is describing.
Literature review	An assessment of existing research around a particular issue or area of study.
Primary research	Research compiled directly from the original source, which may not have been compiled before. You are not expected to carry out primary research, but you are expected to understand the advantages and disadvantages of different primary research methods.
Qualitative research	Descriptive data, such as data drawn from open-ended questions in questionnaires, interviews or focus groups.
Quantitative research	Data in numerical form that can be categorised and used to construct graphs or tables of raw data, such as data drawn from results of experiments, hospital data showing admissions of individuals with certain health conditions, closed questions in questionnaires.
Research methods	Refers to how the research described in the article was carried out, for example through quantitative methods such as analysis of figures drawn from hospitals or GP surgeries; or qualitative based on focus groups, questionnaires.
Secondary sources/research	Published research reports and data, likely to be based on analysis of primary research.

Getting started

Research in health and social care potentially affects the health and wellbeing of everyone at each phase of their lives. List ten ways in which research in the sector has benefitted your health and wellbeing. Share your list with a friend, adding to your lists the items you had not included and add to it again by sharing your joint list with others. Discuss in groups the type of research required to achieve the benefits you have identified.

A Types of issues where research is carried out in the health and social care sector

A large amount of all the **research** carried out in the UK is either directly or indirectly related to the health and social care sector and much of this research contributes significantly to the country's economy. Although much research focuses on the diagnosis and treatment of specific health conditions, it is expected that all aspects of practice in health and social care should be evidence-based. Therefore, research has a direct or indirect effect on all who work in the sector, as well as on those using health and social care services.

Purpose of research in the health and social care sector

Research in the health and social care sector has a wide range of purposes and is carried out by people who have a very wide range of backgrounds in terms of knowledge, skills and practice expertise. Research in the sector is almost always collaborative, involving those from different specialisms working together to pool their collective expertise to make advances in knowledge and understanding that may affect individuals, communities and national policies, as well as potentially bringing benefits to the health and wellbeing of individuals across the globe.

Purpose of research
Improving outcomes for people using services
Person-centred care involves continual review of the care received by individuals, to ensure that it is tailored specifically to meet their needs to the fullest extent possible, to ensure the maximum benefit to their health and social care outcomes. While some needs may be met solely by those caring directly for the individuals, more complex and specialist knowledge and services may be necessary to meet all needs fully. A service provider may conduct research to help it identify how best to meet the needs of its service users, so it can make improvements to the services offered; providing more benefit to service users or providing the benefit to more service users. When an individual accesses a health or social care service for the first time, healthcare professionals conduct informal research, by asking questions to find out about the individual's health, wellbeing and circumstances, to establish an accurate and detailed understanding of the individual's health and/or social care needs. A GP questions a patient during a surgery appointment, before making decisions about treatment. A residential care manager questions a new resident, possibly with a relative present, to help ensure the home meets the resident's needs, and to help them settle in to their new surroundings.

▸ Person-centred care

Even though a professional care worker may deliver care to an individual service user, they work within a larger organisation providing services to many individuals. Professionals in the organisation may carry out research to investigate the extent to which its services benefit all the people using them. Other research may be carried out to monitor the pattern of diseases, so that the incidence of the disease across a population can be reduced. For example, Public Health England monitors the incidence of certain infectious diseases to better target appropriate prevention strategies, such as seasonal vaccination against influenza.

The health and social care outcomes sought by service users will vary, but most health and social care services are organised according to the type of service they provide. A hospital provides a range of specialist investigative services such as X-rays and scans, complex tissue or physiological tests in clinical specialties; for example, in endocrinology, orthopaedics, thoracic medicine or paediatrics. Service users access these specialist services after formal referral by their GP and a planned attendance at an outpatient appointment. However, a hospital's accident and emergency (A&E) service provides immediate services for anyone, at any time of the day or night, to support a very wide range of needs. In each case, the health service offered differs because the needs of the service users differ.

These types of questions can be a starting point for research. Health and social care services cost money to provide, even in the UK where a founding principle of the National Health Service (NHS) is to provide most health services free at the point of delivery. In times of economic constraint, the cost of services is an influential aspect of judging their effectiveness. The NHS, and some social care services, are paid for by the government from its taxation income. Governments have to balance the cost of health and social care services with their spending on their other responsibilities such as education, welfare and the environment. In contrast, social care services are often paid for directly by the individuals using the service, for example purchasing the social care they receive in their own homes. However health or social care services are funded, research into ways to ensure that their provision is as efficient as possible (gives maximum benefit in terms of outcomes for individuals within reasonable cost boundaries) is currently a significant issue in the UK.

Link

You can find more information about person-centred care in *Unit 2: Working in Health and Social Care*, learning aim A.

Discussion

What criteria would you consider makes a health and social care service effective? In a small group, discuss whether any of the criteria you identify provide a basis for research regarding how effective a service is in your locality.

Research

How effective is your local hospital in ensuring the best outcomes possible for its patients? How do you know this? How does it perform compared to other hospitals? What could improve outcomes for patients? Where could you find more information relating to these questions? Would it be feasible for you to research how effective hospitals are in improving patient outcomes?

Informing policy and practice

The best policies, be they at national, local or organisational levels, are evidence-based, which means they are developed as a consequence of evidence from reliable and valid research. National policies are usually enshrined in national legislation, sometimes with associated regulations and codes of practice.

In the 1990s, there was concern about the increasing amount of evidence indicating the low standards of care provided by social care providers. This led to the Care Standards Act of 2000, which introduced, for example the concept of National Minimum Standards for Care and Induction Training for all staff.

Research may sometimes be carried out specifically to investigate practice. A recent, high-profile example is the judge-led public inquiry into the reasons behind an exceptionally high death rate among hospital patients, between 2005 and 2009, within the Mid-Staffordshire Foundation Trust. The investigation was commissioned by the government and many individuals, including staff, patients and their relatives, gave evidence to the public inquiry. In 2013, the Francis Report was produced as a result of this inquiry, and it has already led to changes in policy and practice, including:

▶ more ward nurses on duty in hospitals at any one time

▶ patient or public representatives taking part in Care Quality Commission inspections of health provision

▶ a scheme for training nurses in which student nurses train as health care assistants before starting their nurse training

▶ introduction of the NHS Friends and Family Test – a customer-service type questionnaire to gather feedback from those using NHS services.

The Francis Report made many recommendations for improving the quality of patient care. One of these was a recommendation to review the training of health care assistants and led to the publication of the Cavendish Review in 2013, which made further recommendations regarding the training of health care assistants, making comparisons to the work of social care assistants. A key outcome from the Cavendish Review was that from April 2015 all care workers are now expected to achieve a Care Certificate.

Figure 4.1 shows possible ways in which provision and practice might be extended and, therefore, suggest themes to explore in a literature search.

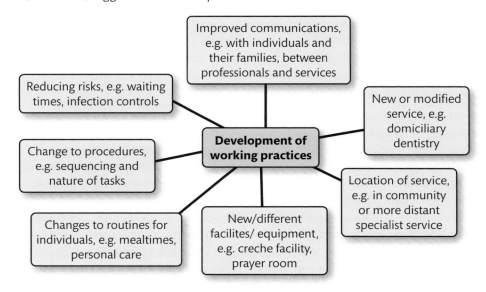

▶ **Figure 4.1:** Possible ways in which provision and working practices might be extended to improve health or social care services to benefit service users

Changes to policy and practice take time to develop, especially if they require legislative change leading to an Act of Parliament. Changes to working practices can be effected through the introduction of new legally binding regulations, if existing legislation gives the powers to do so. For example, a new regulation, introduced in response to a small selection of the recommendations of the 2013 Francis Report, includes hospitals being required, since April 2014, to publish monthly data relating to staffing levels on each ward (in accordance with NICE requirements), and for a named doctor and named nurse responsible for the overall care of each patient to be visibly displayed above the patient's bed.

Extending knowledge and understanding

Numerous scientific discoveries have transformed medicine so that many people now survive formerly fatal diseases, or their disease is managed to enable them to live a full and rewarding life. Research in all branches of science, medicine, nursing and care has an impact on health and social care.

Research has led to a far greater understanding of the physiology of the human body, particularly in the last 20 years or so following discoveries about the details of the human genome and how different genes work to influence the likelihood of specific diseases occurring. Such detailed knowledge is leading to the development of new treatments, which are highly specific in action, particularly for the benefit of individuals affected by inherited or rare conditions.

Technological research, involving physicists and engineers, has led to advances in health care that include:

▶ development of MRI scanners, for gathering information about the body's soft structures and how they behave as living tissue

▶ increasingly sophisticated equipment for hospital pathology and haematology laboratories, to speed up routine investigations allowing for earlier diagnosis of disease

▶ digital devices for continuous monitoring of physiological activity in the body, providing detailed information that enables better management of disease in individual patients

▶ using increasingly smaller devices to replace more intrusive investigations.

Research involving biochemists working with clinicians is essential to develop new drugs that are increasingly targeted at specific conditions, and even specific tissues. This approach has led to notable improvements in outcomes for patients, particularly perhaps, with regards to cancer outcomes. Cancer Research UK has reported that survival rates from some cancers have improved considerably in recent years.

Improvements in health care have been made because research has vastly increased the knowledge and understanding of the physiology of the body, the behaviour of microorganisms causing infections and led to the development of effective treatments for disease and disorders. Research over the last 100 years or so has also led to a better understanding of the social and psychological factors affecting health and wellbeing, so that there is now a better understanding of how to support ill, frail or vulnerable people, lessening the negative effects on their health. See also Figure 4.1.

Research

In groups, identify landmark discoveries that have transformed health and social care. Create a timeline to sequence them chronologically, and note their impact on the health and social care of individuals.

Identifying gaps in provision

Communities change over time for a variety of reasons, such as changes in local employment opportunities bringing new people to an area, families moving in and growing up, and young adults eventually moving on and leaving older adults in the family home. These changes alter the population profile of a community. For example, the health and social care provision originally planned to meet the needs of families with young children may no longer be appropriate 30 years later when most people remaining in the area are older and have different health and social care needs.

Other examples of how research might identify gaps in provision could include:

▶ patient and relative perception surveys (perhaps involving the Patient Advice and Liaison Service (PALS))

▶ monitoring the level of demand from those needing a health or social care service, to highlight whether the amount or scale of provision needs to be changed

▶ comparing the location of those requiring the provision to the actual location of the services

▶ data gathered by support networks working with those affected by specific diseases, disorders and social issues

▶ assessing the impact of innovations in treatments and care on the type of provision available

▶ assessing the impact of changes in population for health and social care services, e.g. building a large housing development.

> ### Research
>
> Scan recent news headlines and identify one news item relating to recent research into a health and social care issue. What was the purpose of the research? How might the research affect health and social care provision in the future, for example in five or ten years' time?

Gaps in provision tend to arise when there is an increased demand for services, for example a new policy initiative can give rise to a need for a new service. Examples of how gaps in services may arise include the following.

▶ In 2013, the government agreed that family doctors in England could pay other doctors to provide out-of-hours services on their behalf. This policy change now means that in most areas in England out-of-hours health care is provided by a team of doctors covering a far larger geographical area than local GP practices cover. This means that the doctors on call are highly unlikely to know the service users they visit.

▶ A gap in provision may arise because of an increase in the incidence of a particular disorder that means specialist services to manage that disorder are required to a greater extent than formerly.

▶ In recent years, there has been a trend in England for accident and emergency services to be concentrated in fewer but larger centres. This means that whether individuals live in a city or a rural area, they have to travel further to access this service. Hospitals formerly providing emergency services may now only provide cover for 'minor injuries' as this type of care needs lower levels of expertise. This results in the highly skilled and trained experts in acute emergency care moving to the new, more distant, emergency care hospitals.

Research in health and social care can identify the scale of gaps in provision and help to indicate how the gap could be addressed. Figure 4.2 shows a range of different types of health and social care and potential ways in which the provision might relate to the health and wellbeing of individuals using health and social care services.

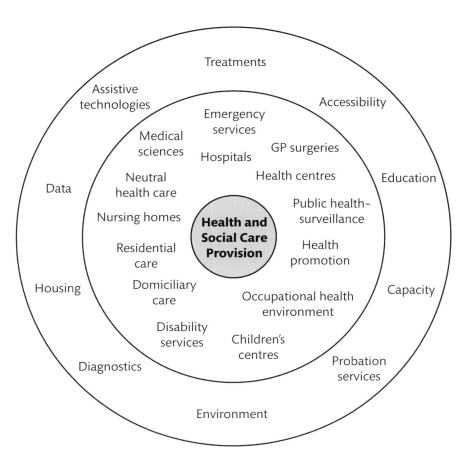

▶ **Figure 4.2:** Ways in which health and social care services might be developed to fill gaps in provision and so benefit service users

As the examples suggest, making changes to address gaps in provision can be controversial, and the issues involved are likely to make local news headlines. Clinical Commissioning Groups (CCGs), local authorities, local residents and patients' groups may all be involved. Each local health area has a CCG that decides how NHS money allocated by central government will be spent on local health services. Health and care professionals may contribute to the planning of the new or changed provision, but their personal work schedule and practices and their work team are likely to also be affected.

Examples of research that have improved practice and policy

A large amount of research carried out in the UK, and in other economically developed countries, is focused on health. Governments are concerned that tax-payers money is used as effectively as possible to maintain the health and wellbeing of individuals and communities. In relation to health and social care, some of the practices that have been changed in recent years as a result of research include:

▶ use of antiseptic gel by all clinical staff and visitors on entry to clinical areas, e.g. a hospital ward, an outpatient area, care home or dental practice, to reduce risk of infection

▶ hospital doctors no longer wear white coats or ties, and cannot wear sleeves below the elbow, again, to reduce the risk of spreading infection

▶ transferring responsibility for public health from the NHS to local authorities, so that policy can be more effectively targeted for local circumstances

- closer co-operation between speech and language therapists and teachers, to assist the communication and language development of young children who have speech and language difficulties

- provision of intermediate care to help individuals who have been hospitalised for a long period regain their confidence, to cope with a return to independent life in their own homes.

PAUSE POINT

What have you learned in this section about the purpose of research in the health and social care sector?

Hint

Draw three mind maps, one for each of the four main purposes discussed in the section, to show examples of current issues in each category. (It might be helpful to include these in the notes you pre-prepare for Part B).

Extend

What are the challenges of carrying out research in the health and social care sector?

Issues

People are likely to have health and social care needs at some stage in their lives. This means that at any one time, many people are likely to be interested in one or more issues relating to some aspect of health and social care. They might be parents concerned that their young children grow up healthily, or middle-aged people concerned about their care as they age. Many of the issues of interest to members of the public have some element of controversy associated with them. Controversy can arise when professionals and experts hold different opinions about the issues or see them from different perspectives.

Examples of how an issue may be controversial could include:

- an individual using a health and social care service perceives the care received differently from the people providing the service

- nurses may perceive the effectiveness of a change to a new care procedure differently from doctors

- doctors working with one group of patients may observe different effects of a new health intervention than other doctors working with a different patient group

- health risks that affect individuals directly, or those close to them, may be perceived differently from how the professionals responsible for the health of the whole population perceive them

- scientists working in a government agency or department interpret research evidence differently from a business looking to make a new product as a result of the research, or from a pressure group representing a specific socio-political perspective.

Figure 4.3 indicates some of the issues in the health and social care sector that are current at the time of writing. You could explore some of these as examples to develop your understanding of research processes, and how they are applied to research in the health and social care sector.

Researching into a health or social care issue involves exploring different aspects of the issue. The information gathered from any research is known as **data**. The articles and other sources you look at when researching issues will present several pieces of data about an issue and synthesise arguments from this data to reach a conclusion. Your task as a researcher is to undertake a literature search to explore their research in more detail.

Discussion

In small groups, explore and discuss the possible different perspectives around these issues:

- the effects on children of playing computer games
- caring for older people living alone.

What are the different perspectives? Why do the different perspectives on an issue arise? How might the different perspectives affect individuals? What research evidence can you find to support any of the perspectives you identify?

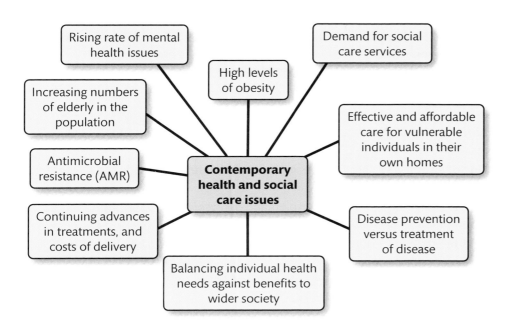

▶ **Figure 4.3:** Examples of contemporary issues in the health and social care sector

The data you collect is likely to be a mix of factual information, abstract concepts or theories and opinions. Your task as a researcher is to gather data from different sources, relevant to the issue you are researching. You will then need to analyse and evaluate the data from each source you have gathered separately. You will then be in a position to select and blend the data together to synthesise your own arguments about the issue and draw your own conclusions, based on the arguments you have developed.

All researchers need to be aware of the quality of the data they collect and take this into account when analysing and evaluating it. The **validity** and **reliability** of data are two particularly important factors when determining the quality of data.

Key terms

Data – information that could be measurements, opinions or concepts. It is a plural word, but its singular, datum, is rarely used.

Validity – a measure of the quality of data, information and concepts and how well any claims made are supported by evidence.

Reliability – a measure of the quality of the methods used to obtain data, and the extent to which the same result would be obtained if someone else repeated the research using an identical method.

It is important to define a clear **aim** for a research study, to ensure that it is purposeful and focused. How many different issues are researched in any one study will vary according to the purpose of the study. Each aspect of an issue investigated in research is referred to as a **line of enquiry**. A literature search should aim to identify several possible lines of enquiry that lead to the development of new **lines of reasoning**. After detailed analysis of each source in relation to the line of enquiry, the researcher should use the lines of reasoning to develop contrasting **arguments**, which are evaluated against the overall aims of the research and the evidence gathered, leading to **conclusions**.

Good research will reveal other lines of enquiry for investigation, leading to the need for further research in another study. A good researcher will identify these as **recommendations** for further investigation. Figure 4.4 provides a visual representation of the thought processes you will need to go through.

> **Key terms**
>
> **Aim** – an overall goal or target to be achieved. An aim should relate to a defined purpose.
>
> **Line of enquiry** – a specific focus for research that relates directly to a larger topic or issue.
>
> **Line of reasoning** – systematic exploration of reasons to support the development of an argument or point of view.
>
> **Arguments** – contrasting lines of reasoning that are synthesised systematically to develop a conclusion.
>
> **Conclusion** – a concise statement based on evidence and reasoned arguments that summarises key findings from an investigation.
>
> **Recommendations** – specific suggestions for future action.

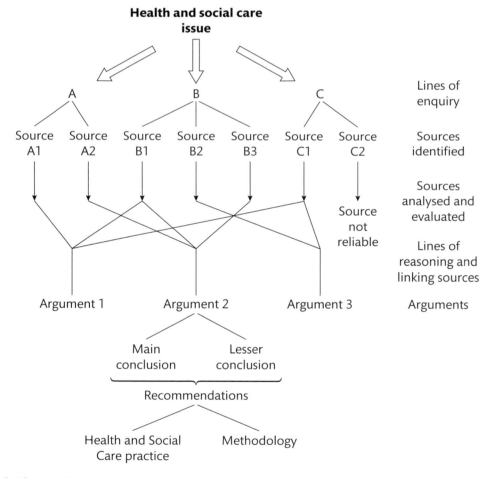

▶ **Figure 4.4:** A generic overview of a literature search relating to a health and social care issue, representing the relationship between the issue and possible lines of enquiry, lines of reasoning or argument that might be developed from them, leading to recommendations for health and social care practice and further research

Health conditions

Much research relates to specific health conditions, in order that those affected by the condition can benefit. Research over the last few decades has, for example, led to:

▶ greatly increased survival rates from several types of cancer

▶ treatments for infertility

▶ key-hole surgery techniques, reducing the need for more invasive (serious/risky) surgical operations

▶ new vaccinations to prevent harmful infectious diseases, e.g. meningitis C, Ebola, Zika virus

▶ increased survival following HIV infection.

An issue relating to research into specific health conditions is that the cost of, for example, developing new treatments for one condition can be very high indeed. The benefit to individuals affected by the condition may be considerable, and even life-changing. However, the issue that then emerges is how the costs associated with the new treatment will be paid for if the treatment is only of benefit to a relatively small proportion of the population.

Effectiveness of treatments

Issues relating to specific health conditions are likely to focus on the effectiveness of possible treatments, patterns in the incidence of the condition and the possible ways in which the risk of being affected by the disorder can be reduced. The specific needs of one individual with the same health condition may be similar to those of others but, before a new treatment or care routine is introduced for everyone, it is necessary to carry out a specific study, or research project, to investigate whether there are benefits to others.

Many organisations, often charities, are dedicated to improving the care of individuals with specific diseases and disorders through research. Their research may focus on better diagnosis so that needs can be identified earlier or more specifically, such as through screening, or by researching physiological aspects of the disease to enable better targeting of treatment in body systems. For example, 2.5 million people in the UK have type 2 diabetes. Diabetes UK spent over £6 m on research in 2009. Its website provides considerable information about its diabetes research. Healthcare professionals, commercial companies and others who work in the NHS frequently contribute to this type of research.

Some homeopathic remedies may be prescribed under the National Institute for Health and Care Excellence (**NICE**). However, many medical experts question the reliability and validity of research into the effectiveness of homeopathic remedies, so the use of homeopathic remedies, and other alternative therapies, to treat serious illnesses, such as cancer or diabetes, remains controversial.

Research to investigate the effectiveness of medical treatments is subject to strict rules issued by NICE. New drugs are subject to **double blind clinical trials** with patients, only after they have been tested comprehensively on animals. Such trials involve measuring patient responses to the trial drug against responses from patients given a **placebo** and are conducted, as far as is possible using a scientific method (see the section on Research methodologies).

Even if research trials prove that a new drug is effective in helping to treat a disease, it may not be approved by NICE for prescription by the NHS because of its cost, or because of the risk of undesirable side effects. The decisions made by NICE can sometimes in themselves become a current issue.

Research

Investigate the incidence of a common disorder such as lung cancer, type 2 diabetes, heart disease or dental decay. What are the trends in the incidence of the disorder? What information can you gather from secondary sources that might explain the changing trends in the incidence of the disorder?

Key terms

NICE – the National Institute for Health and Care Excellence; the government organisation that defines the standards expected for health and social care.

Double blind clinical trial – a research technique for testing the effectiveness of a new drug in which patients taking part are allocated at random to one of two groups: one given the test drug and the other a placebo. Neither the patients taking part in the trial, nor the doctors and professionals caring for them, know whether they are receiving the placebo or the test drug.

Placebo – a medical prescription deliberately made to look like, and be administered identically to, a real drug but which contains no medically active ingredients.

Health trends and reasons for trends observed

The incidence of specific diseases varies over time. For example, death from infectious diseases was very common before the introduction of antibiotic treatments in the 1940s and many people died from infectious diseases that are extremely rare now. When the NHS was established in 1948, people did not expect to live more than a few years beyond retirement age (65 for men and 60 for women). Research has produced treatments for many common diseases and disorders, so average life expectancy in the early twenty-first century in the UK is now more than 80 years. However, as a result of living longer, people living in the developed world are now affected more by different diseases, particularly those that are slow to develop and usually only become evident in later life. Dementia and most cancers, for example, are more prevalent in old age.

Diseases that previously led to premature death are now successfully managed with medication and have become chronic rather than acute diseases. In 1948 Type 2 Diabetes was relatively uncommon but Diabetes UK (2015) predicts that over 4.75 million people will be affected by it by 2025.

However, it is increasingly the case that individuals with diabetes may also be affected by other chronic conditions such as hypertension, early-stage dementia, chronic obstructive pulmonary disease (COPD). This has an impact on the type of services an individual might need and, therefore, how services might best be organised to be efficient for both providers of the service and users of it.

It takes several years to develop major health and social care services, such as building a new hospital or nursing home. Reorganising services to adjust to changing needs of communities also takes considerable time. Health and social care services are expensive because they are labour-intensive. The government, local authorities and private organisations (who tend to own and operate residential care provision), have to plan in advance so that they have the finance available to pay for developing new services.

Those responsible for planning service provision, such as the NHS and local authorities, need to predict the demand for services several years ahead, so that they have sufficient time to make the changes needed to meet future demand. Pharmaceutical companies also want to know what the demand for any new drug they develop is likely to be. For example, will there be sufficient demand to justify the extremely high cost involved in developing a new drug?

Gathering data regularly to monitor the incidence of different diseases and disorders is essential to enable the government, industry and private care providers to forecast the needs of a community and deliver appropriate services where they are most needed.

This highlights the importance of long-term planning, to ensure that the healthcare needs of individuals that are not currently evident, but which research indicates may develop at some time in the future, can be met when they do develop.

 **PAUSE POINT**

What is a health and social care issue? Can you give some examples of current issues?

Hint   Consider the examples mentioned in this section.

Extend   Choose one current issue of relevance to health and social care and develop possible lines of enquiry that you might use to investigate the issue in more detail.

Strategies for reducing likelihood of health risks, and their effectiveness

The NHS is responsible for providing healthcare services for those living in the UK. Local authorities (county unitary authorities) currently provide some social care services and local councils (district and town councils) have responsibilities for environmental health, such as refuse collection and pest control. Each of these public organisations is responsible for providing specified information to monitor trends in the health and wellbeing of the population it serves, to enable appropriate services to be planned to meet the projected demand.

A **strategy** is concerned with long-term planning. Knowing which disorders are increasing in prevalence, which groups are most likely to be affected and where people likely to develop a disorder are geographically, helps the authorities target their activity where it will have greatest impact on health and wellbeing. In addition, scientific, technological and clinical research is developing better understanding of the causes of a wide range of diseases and disorders so that the risks associated with each are better understood.

Health risks can be reduced by reducing the severity of the effects of the disease or disorder, through better treatment or management of symptoms, or by reducing the risk of getting the disease or disorder in the first place.

> **Key term**
>
> **Strategy** – a statement of key priorities for change, with associated outcomes that will result from the changes to be achieved within defined timescales.

> **Link**
>
> Go to *Unit 8: Promoting Public Health* to explore different strategies for reducing the public health risks associated with various common disorders.

An example is the longer-term strategic planning necessary to reduce the risk of people being infected by dangerous infectious diseases that can cause permanent harm to individuals or even death. Many infectious diseases of childhood are now largely controlled by the programme of vaccinations young babies receive against, for example, whooping cough, mumps, measles and polio. Vaccination programmes are a key strategy for protecting children from several of these diseases (see also the Wakefield case study in the section on Use and misuse of results).

> **Link**
>
> Go to *Unit 1: Human Lifespan Development* to find out about vaccination programmes for young children and the possible risks associated with measles, mumps or rubella if a child is not vaccinated.

Strategies are usually developed by the senior managers in an organisation. They provide a framework for staff in the organisation to contribute to the strategy in the context of their own job role and responsibilities. Local health and government authorities have ongoing strategic plans that are reviewed annually and updated to adapt to emerging factors, for example changing policies or environmental circumstances. Large and complex change will also be part of a longer-term strategy, perhaps as part of a five- or even ten-year plan. Planning for and constructing a new hospital, for example, is likely to be part of a longer-term plan.

Lifestyle factors

Most people are aware from the media, if not also from their doctor, that lifestyle factors may influence their health and wellbeing. Diet, exercise, recreational drugs, alcohol, and stress levels are factors over which individuals may have some choice and control. Individuals may have less control regarding some other lifestyle factors such as housing/where they live, or the type of work they do.

▶ What health issues might affect this man?

One of the most famous studies carried out in the 1940s and 1950s by Richard Doll and others (1965) provided convincing evidence that smoking was a strong risk factor for lung cancer. Survival times for lung cancer are still relatively short. Since the 1960s, there have been many active campaigns to discourage smoking and Cancer Research UK reports that the incidence of lung cancer is now declining. Government statistics show that the number of people who smoke is now far lower than it was fifty years ago. Many lifestyle factors have been acknowledged as having an effect on health and wellbeing.

The effects of lifestyle factors on health and wellbeing have been a major focus of research in recent times. However, because lifestyle factors may change over time, they are often interrelated and there is considerable natural variation in the way individuals are affected by any one lifestyle factor, research studies need to be carefully designed if they are to provide convincing evidence of the effect of any one lifestyle factor on health. Because there are many lifestyle factors that can affect health, and it can take decades for the effects of the lifestyle choices made by an individual to become apparent, research in this area necessitates long-term monitoring of individuals and is, therefore, difficult and expensive to carry out. To overcome this problem, some researchers have adopted highly sophisticated statistical techniques to pool comparable quantitative data from multiple, previously published research reports, and re-analysed the data to demonstrate more strongly the links between health and lifestyle. This process is called meta-analysis, and you may encounter reference to this technique in your reading for this unit about research studies. You are not expected to know any more about this technique than is outlined here.

The secondary sources you will be expected to access and make use of in your literature search for this unit may refer to meta-analysis but they are most likely to be reporting on primary and secondary research, in which the research methodologies used are either those of scientific method or social science methods. Your literature search should indicate that you are aware of the multifactorial influences of lifestyle factors and how that might affect the validity and reliability of any results and conclusions drawn from the research.

Age groups affected by different lifestyle factors

Some diseases affected by lifestyle are more common in different age groups. Diseases that usually take a long time to develop, such as heart disease or type 2 diabetes, tend to be more prevalent in older age groups. This is because they develop only after the lifestyle factor, for example lack of exercise or a poor diet, has been in place over many years. However, Diabetes UK (2015) reports that type 2 diabetes is beginning to appear in younger adults and older children, almost always because the young person is obese.

Some lifestyle related disorders are more common in children, perhaps because of childcare practices. A Public Health England (PHE) report in 2014 found that up to 19 per cent of 3 year olds in the East Midlands had some dental decay, in the South East the figure was lower, with only between 5–9 per cent of 3 year olds showing signs of dental decay. The PHE report suggested that the high incidence of dental decay in such young children was linked to the consumption of sugary drinks.

The mental health condition of depression has long been recognised in adults, perhaps associated with bereavement or living alone. Depression is now also being recognised with increasing frequency in younger age groups, possibly because children and young people experience more stress than they used to.

Case study

National Child Measurement Programme (NCMP)

The NCMP takes place in England and the Health and Social Care Information Service and PHE publish an annual report for each academic year. Primary school children in reception year and in year 6 have their height and weight measured to calculate their body mass index, to determine the extent to which some children may be overweight or obese.

The NCMP report for the academic year 2014/15, published in November 2015, involved more than a million children. Results showed that more than a fifth (21.9 per cent) of children in reception year are overweight or obese, and that in year 6, a third (33.2 per cent) of children are overweight or obese. Data is analysed by local authority area and the report indicates considerable variations in different areas, with almost double the proportion of children being obese or overweight in schools serving the most deprived neighbourhoods compared with those serving the most affluent areas.

The effect of deprivation is even more marked in the figures for obesity alone, where in reception year only 4.2 per cent of children from affluent areas are obese, compared with 13.6 per cent of children living in deprived areas. Similarly for year 6 children, the figures were 10.5 per cent from affluent areas and 27.8 per cent from deprived areas.

Check your knowledge

1 Why might it be useful to routinely monitor the BMI of children at the start and end of their time in primary school?

2 How might the data generated by the NCMP benefit children currently in primary school?

3 What might be the implications for health and social care service provision in the future if the children's BMIs remain the same or increase as they grow into adulthood?

4 What further research could be carried out to investigate reasons for the differences in the incidence of obesity and overweight in affluent and deprived areas?

Impact of lifestyle factors on health and social care needs

Health conditions most often associated with lifestyle factors include:

▸ endocrine disorders such as type 2 diabetes, pancreatic cancer

▸ respiratory disorders such as congestive pulmonary failure, lung cancer

▸ cardiovascular diseases such as high blood pressure (hypertension), heart disease, stroke

▸ dietary disorders such as being overweight, obesity, anaemia, vitamin deficiencies

▸ alcohol related disorders such as cirrhosis, Lewy body dementia, oesophageal varices

▸ addictions leading to mental health disorders, self-neglect, neglect of other family members particularly children

▸ skin disorders such as melanoma

▸ musculo-skeletal injuries such as fractures and soft-tissue damage from reckless driving, sports and other high risk leisure pursuits.

Individuals affected by any one of the conditions listed will require healthcare advice in the first instance; and most will require at least medication, probably long-term. Some conditions may require planned surgical procedures and in some cases, the health condition may involve sudden-onset symptoms, which require emergency treatment in hospital. In 2014, Diabetes UK claimed that treating diabetes cost the NHS £10 bn each year and that this cost was largely due to treating the complications of diabetes such as amputations and renal dialysis.

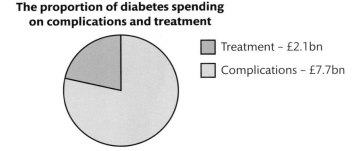

The proportion of diabetes spending on complications and treatment

Treatment – £2.1bn
Complications – £7.7bn

▶ **Figure 4.5:** Complications of diabetes lead to increasing healthcare needs

The issues associated with the impact of lifestyle factors on healthcare are based on the assumption that an individual makes an active decision to follow a particular type of lifestyle. This may be true for some individuals, but usually individuals who make active choices about their lifestyle choose healthy ways of living their lives – perhaps making healthy choices about diet or deliberately building regular exercise into their daily routines. Counterarguments could be put, however, regarding individuals whose lifestyle is less healthy – they perhaps do not make an active choice to pursue an unhealthy lifestyle. Instead their circumstances mean they are more vulnerable to making less healthy lifestyle choices. Therefore, the negative effects of these choices are not really choices at all, but consequences of the factors giving rise to their vulnerability. For example, people with limited incomes are more likely to buy cheaper food, but cheap food can be less healthy, or maybe their living accommodation has limited cooking facilities and it is easier to choose a fat-rich, ready meal than to cook a meal from raw ingredients.

Effect of lifestyle on demand for services

Given that lifestyle affects health and wellbeing, it is not surprising that the lifestyle choices made by individuals can affect that individual's need for health and social care services. The effects will depend on whether their lifestyle choices are more likely to promote greater health and wellbeing, or whether their lifestyle choices lead to a decline in health and/or social wellbeing.

The overall trend in the UK is that the lifestyle choices of many individuals are such that they are leading to greater ill health and, therefore, to a significant increase in the demand for health and social services. For example, the increase of type 2 diabetes in middle-age – and which continues into older age. More people are in need of mental health services, which is partly associated with the increased expectations of contemporary life leading to higher stress levels.

Discussion

As a class group, discuss a range of perspectives or opinions relating to the entitlement of people affected by disorders associated with their lifestyle choices to receive health and social care services on the NHS (free at the point of delivery), especially if it disadvantaged (for example, delayed treatment for) individuals considered to be ill through no choice of their own.

Research

Investigate trends in the incidence of foetal alcohol syndrome over the last 20–30 years. What are the implications for the needs of individuals affected by this syndrome? What are the implications for health and social care service provision?

The implications of lifestyle choices and possible strategies for mitigating service provision

When the NHS was founded in 1948, its priority was to enable everyone to receive treatment for unavoidable diseases. Now, over sixty years on, research has found ways of treating many of these diseases successfully, or of managing them so that affected individuals can lead more active and longer lives. Now that some diseases are much more attributable to avoidable lifestyle factors, treating the health consequences of lifestyle choices is a major issue. For individuals, the effects of these diseases can severely limit their quality of life, so more social care is required. For the NHS, the complications of disorders of a poor lifestyle are considerable and expensive to treat.

Strategies for reducing the consequences of lifestyle factors for health and social care service provision focus on reducing the likelihood of individuals being affected by them. Examples of strategies that are used include:

▶ health education programmes in schools and community centres, for example for parents expecting their first child

▶ specific public health campaigns, for example to raise awareness of the dangers of prolonged exposure to sunlight

▶ legislation, for example to limit the use of sunbeds to adults only, banning of smoking in indoor public spaces

▶ targeted provision of key information for consumers, for example labelling foods with nutritional information, labelling wine and beer with alcohol strength, placing photographs of the health consequences of smoking on cigarette packaging

▶ providing reliable, impartial and evidence-based information about health matters through the internet, for example websites from government, health and social care professional bodies, regulators, not-for profit organisations and charities

▶ educating individuals with a specific condition to better understand their condition, so they can manage their signs and symptoms more independently, for example finger-prick blood glucose testing and self-administration of insulin for treating diabetes

▶ empowering pharmacists in retail outlets to take a more active role in advising individuals about their health

▶ collecting statistical data about the population on a regular basis and analysing it to identify trends in health, so that services can be reconfigured to meet changing needs, for example community-based provision rather than hospital-based; or changing policy such as health promotion targeting dental care for weaning babies and toddlers, and school-aged children

▶ taxation to limit lifestyle choices that are harmful to health, for example taxes on alcoholic drinks, tobacco products and the sugar tax announced in the budget in March 2016, which will apply in 2018.

Investigation into the effectiveness of any one of these strategies could form the basis of a literature review research.

PAUSE POINT What are the issues likely to be encountered when researching lifestyle factors in relation to health and social care?

> Hint Focus on two or three lifestyle factors, their potential consequences for health and care needs and, therefore, for health and social care services.

> Extend How could research be used to reduce the negative effects of lifestyle choices on the health and social care sector?

Social care and welfare needs

All health or social care workers involved in care planning use research principles routinely to identify the needs of individuals. The medical 'history' of a patient, taken by a doctor during an initial consultation, requires the doctor to apply medical knowledge to identify the cause of the patient's problem so that their needs can be met effectively. The doctor may gather more quantifiable evidence from laboratory investigations such as blood tests or visual evidence from X-rays or scans. A healthcare assistant conducts research by measuring pulse rate or blood pressure at predetermined intervals to check on variations in a patient's wellbeing, as well as observing the patient for visible signs of any symptoms, for example pain or discomfort. A care home manager observing an individual resident may identify that they may need more assistance with personal care and discuss this with the individual and care staff. The information gathered enables professionals to make decisions about treatment or care to better meet an individual's needs.

Care and support practices for individuals

Since 2012, NICE has been responsible for defining the standards relating to social care as well as to health care. NICE is developing a set of quality standards for a wide range of specific aspects of health care, public health and social care. Each quality standard defines how different aspects of the care process should be carried out. The quality standards are reviewed annually and referred for revision or amendment, according to the evidence supplied by key stakeholders such as patient/service user organisations and regulators (CQC, Ofsted). The stakeholders provide evidence about practices that are particularly effective. NICE invites comments from the public and key stakeholders on the draft standards it produces before they are finally published. NICE quality standards are, therefore, evidence-based.

While the quality standards set by NICE are not mandatory, the intention is that they define a higher standard of care practice than the Care Quality Commission's Essential Standards. The aims of the standards include:

▶ supporting the provision of care that has been shown to work and to be cost-effective

▶ ensuring a more consistent approach to social care provision across the country

▶ supporting the development of joined-up working between agencies and professionals

▶ helping the social care sector demonstrate its importance as a key partner in the provision of care

▶ raising the profile of social care.

At the time of writing, the majority of the published standards relate to health care and very few relate to social care. However, over time, NICE is likely to publish more quality standards relating to social care. It will also update existing standards and publish new standards for health care. It could be useful to ensure that you are aware of the standards that are current at the time of your studies.

Success of care and support practices in promoting individuals' independence and wellbeing

Care and support practices are continually changing as new technology and treatments emerge. The professional codes underpinning health and social care practice in the UK increasingly expect that any new practice introduced is formally assessed with regards to its effectiveness. This is usually done through research, often carried out in the first instance on a small scale, in a particular health or social care context. Changes to procedures, modifications to job roles, introducing a different skill mix to a team, development of a new protocol for assessing a particular need should each be systematically assessed to gauge the extent to which the change introduced is helpful or not. By reporting the research in a practice journal or magazine, the research is made available to others and provides evidence on which others working elsewhere – possibly in different professional contexts, with different service users, or in different care environments or service provision – can justify adopting the same change. Studies such as these are examples of **action research**, which has a valuable role in contributing to health and social care research. If a practice innovation becomes widespread, then a much larger research study may be useful for a more formal assessment of its value.

> **Key term**
>
> **Action research** – systematic study, usually on a small-scale, that investigates the impact of a specific activity that is carried out as part of a normal work role. Action research is particularly practiced in education and in health and social care contexts.

Care and support practices that promote an individual's independence might involve action research such as:

▸ After research to investigate a service user's physical needs for day-to-day living, a care worker will make sure that the service user has various aids to enable her to continue to live independently in her own home

▸ how and where clothes are laid out or presented to an individual affected by painful arthritis, to enable them to dress with greater independence

▸ changing the time of day when residents of a nursing home are asked to make their meal choices for the next day, so that they are more alert and responsive when making a choice independently

▸ developing a routine for ensuring the availability of a potty to a toddler in nursery who is being toilet trained

▸ changing the arrangement of furniture around a hospital bed, so the patient is always able to reach a drink

▸ testing an improved technique in using a new slip sheet, so that post-operative patients can be transferred from a trolley to a bed more smoothly

▸ changing the layout of a day room, so that the increased number of residents using walking frames have more space to move about without disturbing others, while still enabling communication between the residents.

Services provided for individuals with specific needs and the effect of these on individuals' wellbeing

NICE has also published a quality standard for the support of individuals with specific needs. This follows particularly from the Winterbourne View scandal, in which abuse was inflicted routinely on adults with learning disabilities living in a residential care home near Bristol. The abuse was filmed undercover and then broadcast in a BBC Panorama programme, which brought the abuse to public attention. Staff were prosecuted and received prison sentences, the company running the home was fined and the home closed down.

Individuals with specific needs can often be particularly vulnerable members of society and the Protection of Vulnerable Adults (POVA) regulations recognise this. Having specific needs indicates that these individuals have more difficulty than most people in coping with everyday activities. Children, especially those with multiple and profound disabilities, and adults with learning disabilities and/or physical disabilities will have specific needs. They need special assistance with some or all activities of daily living, possibly throughout each day, especially if they need help with personal care such as bathing, toileting and dressing, which can add to their vulnerability.

Link

Refer to *Unit 7: Principles of Safe Practice in Health and Social Care* to find more information about care for vulnerable adults, children and young people.

Ⅱ PAUSE POINT

Develop a mind map to summarise possible issues relating to social care and welfare needs.

Hint

Make use of any work experience you may have had in working with individuals with specific needs.

Extend

Add notes to your mind map in the form of questions, to suggest possible lines of enquiry you might develop in relation to issues relating to social care and welfare needs.

Assessment practice 4.1

In 2014, a Care Quality Commission report reviewed dementia care in care homes and in hospitals by examining the quality of care received by individuals with dementia. The investigation found that 90 per cent of the providers reviewed showed aspects of variable or poor care delivery. Other findings are summarised in Table 4.2

▶ **Table 4.2:** Dementia care in homes and hospitals (source: www.cqc.org.uk/sites/default/files/20141009_cracks_in_the_pathway_final_0.pdf)

Aspect of care provision	Care homes (%)	Hospitals (%)
Providers working together	27	22
Involvement of families and carers	33	61
Staffing	27	56
Monitoring the quality of care	37	28

1 Select two other secondary sources relevant to the data in this report.

2 Explain how three recommendations you select from the report relate to the evidence presented in the report.

3 Analyse the issues associated with caring for those with dementia, referring to the additional sources as well as the report above.

4 Evaluate how findings from the report might lead to improved care for those affected by dementia, using other sources you have researched independently to support your arguments.

B Research methods in health and social care

Being able to undertake research is an essential part of the work of all healthcare professionals. Research is included in the undergraduate training that healthcare professionals must undertake to gain their professional status, as it is in all undergraduate programmes. As part of your BTEC Level 3 National in Health and Social Care, you are also required to research issues for your assignments. Gaining an understanding of some aspects of research methodology will equip you with skills that you will find both helpful for your studies now and also useful preparation for higher education, training or employment in health and social care.

This part of the unit introduces the principles of research methodology appropriate for your BTEC National studies by equipping you with the knowledge, understanding and skills needed to undertake a literature search into a current health and social care issue, which forms the basis of the assessment for this unit.

Research methodologies

As you have established in the previous section, research in the health and social care sector has a wide range of purposes. It is carried out by people who similarly have a wide range of backgrounds, in terms of knowledge, skills and practice expertise. Research in the sector is, therefore, almost always collaborative. It involves professionals from different specialisms working together to pool their collective expertise to make advances in knowledge and understanding that may affect individuals, communities and national policies, as well as bringing benefits to health and wellbeing worldwide. However, even if working alongside others, each individual researcher will need to be fully aware of the current body of knowledge in their own subject specialism, as it is relevant to their involvement in research projects.

Research in health and social care is planned and carried out by professionals who are experts in research methodology as well as in health and social care. It often involves research in which data is obtained directly from patients and users of health or social care services, their relatives and from other professionals working in the sector. Such research is **primary research** and generates primary data from observation, measurement or experiences, enabling it to be verified. Such data is known as **empirical data**. However, there are issues around primary research in health and social care. For example, it is expensive, it may need to be drawn out over several years and it may interfere with an individual's treatment or the service they receive. Additionally, ethical considerations that apply in many advanced countries means that primary research can only be carried out by professionally qualified researchers. Also, the field of knowledge relevant, especially in the healthcare sector, is vast. As a result in recent years, research that is based entirely on accessing published data, but which makes new connections to draw new conclusions about one aspect of health and social care practice, has become a valuable approach. Such research is known as **secondary research** as it uses secondary sources.

You will only be required to carry out secondary research as part of your BTEC National in Health and Social Care. For ethical reasons, you will be unable to carry out primary research in health and social care. The focus of your research will be on how research informs health and social care services and provision. You are not required to undertake secondary research involving technical or complex science-based research reports, though you may use them if you are confident about understanding them.

Key terms

Primary research – data contributing to the conclusions drawn is generated as a consequence of scientific method, or by the researcher obtaining personal information directly from individuals.

Empirical data – verifiable data obtained by observation, measurement or from experiences.

Secondary research – data contributing to the conclusions drawn is retrieved from previously published sources.

It would be appropriate and relevant if one of your lines of enquiry focused on the extent to which the issue is relevant to your home country; given that the organisation of health and social care services in England, Wales, Northern Ireland and Scotland is different, even though the NHS operates throughout the UK and some legislation applies in all four countries.

Qualitative and quantitative data

Research involves the formal collection of information. The information gathered is known as data. Research methodologies tend to generate data that is either qualitative or quantitative and both types of data are valuable in health and social care.

Qualitative data

Information that can only be described using words is known as qualitative data. Several research methodologies that are used routinely as part of health and social care delivery are qualitative. A health professional's preliminary perspective about the nature of a patient's health problem will be partly informed by observation of the individual's appearance such as whether they look flushed and sweaty, pale or bluish coloured, drawn and strained. The simplest laboratory investigations to prove or disprove the presence of an infection rely on observing a specimen taken from the patient, for example a sample of urine, or tissue gathered on a throat swab, and viewing it under the microscope for the presence of bacteria. Health and social care research that involves investigating events, behaviour or emotions is likely to adopt research methods such as interviews and observations to generate qualitative data. These methods, if carried out on a large enough scale involving many participants, may generate data that can be quantified for analysis, for example recording the frequency with which a particular behaviour is exhibited.

▶ Observation in a laboratory can have a valuable place in research, such as looking at changes to cell structure in a tissue sample

Few research projects are established on a sufficiently large scale to enable processing of large amounts of qualitative data, though the National Child Development Study (NCDS), which has been ongoing since a group of children were born in one week in March 1957, is sufficiently large to enable some quantitative analysis of qualitative data.

Obtaining qualitative data is time intensive. One in-depth unstructured interview involving one participant may take several days to carry out, and observations may involve a sequence spread over months, or even years, as in the NCDS project. In both cases organising and analysing the data collected is also time-consuming. Nonetheless, research in health and social care often includes gathering qualitative data.

Quantitative data

Quantitative data is based on numbers and physical measurements that can be quantified objectively using a measuring device, for example weight scales, height rules, thermometers, blood pressure monitors or other specifically designed measuring instrumentation. 'TPR' measurements (temperature, pulse rate and respiration rate), blood pressure, weight and height are probably the most common quantitative data used routinely in health and social care environments. Other examples of quantitative measures that are valuable in health and social care include:

▶ population statistics showing, for example birth, morbidity and mortality rates

▶ chemical analysis of body fluids, such as urine and blood plasma, carried out in a hospital biochemistry laboratory

▶ cell counts, such as the proportion of different blood cells in a sample of blood, carried out in a haematology laboratory.

Unless measuring a simple number, for example the number of people in a population, every quantitative measure is incomplete unless it is also presented with the units of measurement. For example, stating deaths per 1000 means nothing unless it is put within a time scale, for example 1000 deaths per year, or 1000 deaths per 100,000 population. A 'rate' is a measure of a change over time, so 1000 deaths per year. Physiological measurements are usually recorded as breaths per minute, pulse beats per minute, passing 200 ml of urine per hour and so on. Blood pressure measurements are usually presented in mm of mercury (mm Hg).

Quantitative data can be presented visually in tables, graphs and charts. Presenting quantitative data visually is convenient for large data sets (measurements of the same variable from a large number of samples) and can assist with interpreting the data by revealing patterns and trends. (See Figure 4.6)

Research

Got to www.cls.ioe.ac.uk and investigate the data generated by the National Child Development Study. What sort of data has been generated from the research study? How are the results being used to inform policy and practices in the health and social care sector?

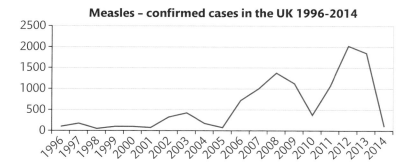

Measles – confirmed cases in the UK 1996-2014

▶ **Figure 4.6:** Line graph showing variations in the incidence of measles since 1996

The units of measurement for quantitative data will always be stated in a published source, for example numbers per year, deaths per 100,000 per year, percentage of adults with learning disability living independently. However, when interpreting charts and graphs, you should note the scales used for the *x* and *y* axes. If one scale is greatly enlarged, it can exaggerate a difference, which in reality is very small, or if the scale is reduced it could hide/mask a difference that could be important. In Figure 4.6, the *x*-axis scale starts at zero so the trends seen in the graph have not been artificially exaggerated.

For your literature search, it may be more useful to note and remember, for example, the trends shown in graphs, or the proportion of the pie chart for the variable you are interested in.

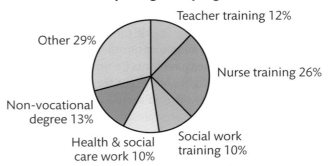

What BTEC Level 3 learners at Sidson College do after completing their programme

Teacher training 12%
Nurse training 26%
Social work training 10%
Health & social care work 10%
Non-vocational degree 13%
Other 29%

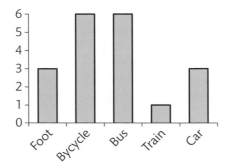

Bar graph to show the form of transport members of a BTEC class use to travel to college

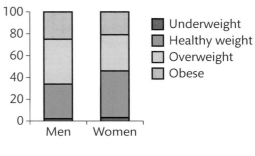

Graph to compare prevalence of underweight, healthy weight, overweight and obese men and women in a sample

- Underweight
- Healthy weight
- Overweight
- Obese

▶ **Figure 4.7:** Different formats for presenting quantitative data

⏸ PAUSE POINT   Look at the charts in Figure 4.7. Explain what each chart or graph is telling you about the data it presents.

Hint   What patterns are revealed in each chart or graph? What is the scale? Close your book and mind map the different purposes of research in health and social care. Add the examples you identified above to categorise each example.

Extend   Why is it important that research has a clear purpose?

Organisations involved in research

Organisations may be involved in health and social care research through:

▶ providing the funding to pay for the research

▶ providing specialist information

▶ enabling access to patients and other individuals using services

▶ providing specialist resources, such as expertise, equipment, data-handling facilities

▶ other reasons.

The usefulness of a piece of research, particularly relating to the physical world, may not be immediately apparent. Much technological research may be carried out in the first instance for industrial purposes and its health or care related uses may take some while to emerge. The development of silicone non-stick surfaces came about as part of the research for early space missions but now the unique properties of silicon surfaces are utilised in a range of medical products such as wound dressings and flexible tubing for infusions.

Government

The government is responsible for all areas of its citizens' lives such as health, employment, agriculture, education, arts, sports, the environment, defence. If the government is to produce effective policies in each of the areas of its responsibility, it requires reliable information about the country's population, its industry and the economy. The government, therefore, gathers a large amount of statistical data about the country so that it can plan how to allocate its resources across its areas of responsibility. The Office for National Statistics collects vast quantities of statistics about different aspects of activity across the UK, which it publishes. Statistics produced by each government department are available online. You should be aware that the names and organisation of government departments change from time to time, particularly when a new government is elected. Statistics relating to past years tend to be archived so may require a more detailed search to locate.

Government departments usually only initiate research, rather than carry it out themselves. Most government research is put out to tender. Organisations interested in carrying out the research have to bid, by presenting a detailed research proposal, and a panel of experts will select the proposal judged to be the most appropriate for their purpose. Cost-effectiveness will also be a consideration, because the cost of any government research has to be accountable to UK taxpayers. The Department of Health may pay for research by funding an academic team based in a university, or jointly with a university and healthcare providers. The government may also fund research carried out by charities or, sometimes, by private industry.

Health authorities

Health authorities are responsible for the health provided in their region. Legislation requires health authorities to be fully informed about the healthcare activity being undertaken in their region. In order to do this, they collect a range of data regarding the health care provided. Examples of the data routinely gather by health authorities include:

▸ the number of patients the authority is responsible for, categorised into age groups, social class groups, how long each patient stays in hospital etc

▸ statistics relating to hospital care such as the range of investigations carried out, diagnoses made according to predetermined categories, outcomes of treatment

▸ other data such as the uptake of vaccinations, or time between referral by a GP to being seen by a hospital consultant.

The data gathered by health authorities may be recorded annually, or more frequently. Collectively, the data is collated by the Office for National Statistics and made publicly available when published on government websites. NHS Digital is a specific source of statistics that could be helpful for your work on this unit.

Local authorities

Local authorities may be county, district or town councils, metropolitan boroughs or unitary authorities. County, metropolitan and unitary authorities are now responsible for public health matters, working with Public Health England (PHE). Different structures apply in Wales, Northern Ireland and Scotland.

Research

Investigate the JSNA for your local authority. What are its priorities? How does it intend to achieve them? What aspects of the JSNA have implications for the health and social care sector?

Currently, local authorities have a statutory responsibility for a Health and Wellbeing Board, which must put a Joint Health and Wellbeing Strategy in place based on their local Joint Strategic Needs Assessment (JSNA). The purpose of the JSNAs is to improve health and reduce inequalities, they involve health and local authorities in the council area who gather a range of data about the area. The Health and Wellbeing Board is required to publish a draft strategy document for public consultation.

Social service departments

Currently, social services in England are the responsibility of local government at county, metropolitan borough or unitary authority level. Responsibilities are separated into:

▸ Children's Services Departments, which focus on the needs of all children and young people up to the age of 18, and those with learning disability up to the age of 21

▸ services for adults, which are responsible for all individuals of 18 and over.

Charities and community groups

A charity must be registered with the Charities Commission and relies on money gifted by individuals and organisations. Apart from their activities to raise money, a high proportion of UK charities exist to support individuals with specific health and social care needs. Some charities are very important sponsors of research into health and social care such as Cancer Research UK, Diabetes UK, the Wellcome Trust, the Kings Fund and Action for Children.

Office for National Statistics (ONS)

The ONS is the government agency responsible for collating the data gathered from a variety of sources, such as the Census, local authorities, the NHS and all government departments. The ONS publishes quantitative data online, as summaries, publications, statistical bulletins and in other formats, with open access and which can be downloaded. Some types of data may be updated at regular intervals such as monthly, quarterly or annually. Table 4.3 shows the themes used to organise data on the ONS website.

▸ **Table 4.3:** The range of statistics potentially relating to health and social care available from the ONS

Theme	Data available concerning...
Environment	Air quality, use of antibiotics in agriculture, food production
Economy and business	Government expenditure, e.g. on public services, employment, investment in research and development
	Employment
Children and education	Children's mental health
	Education expenditure, young people not in education, training or employment
Health, wellbeing, health and social care	Alcohol abuse, smoking, drug use
	Incidence of specific diseases, e.g. cancers, infectious diseases
	Disability
	Mental health, including loneliness in older people
Population, people and communities	Demography, e.g. birth rates, death rates
	Living costs, household expenditure, food survey
	Census
	Crime

The statistics indicated in Table 4.3 are only a tiny proportion of those available from the ONS but they illustrate the different themes in which the ONS may categorise data. You can also access statistical data limited to your locality to compare with national data.

The ONS website also provides information about how it gathers and analyses its data and a calendar for publication of its regular reports, so you can check whether more up-to-date data is about to be published. Some data is also available from government departments.

Research

Using an issue related to your studies, investigate publications, bulletins and summaries for each theme on the ONS website.

What examples of statistics did you find within each theme? Which of the statistics that you found have provided you with a new perspective to your previous knowledge and understanding? Could any of the statistical data you encountered be relevant to your literature search for this unit?

⏸ **PAUSE POINT**   Review the organisations involved in research mentioned in this section.

Hint   Have you learned about the research interests of any of these organisations in your research for other units of the programme?

Extend   To what extent is data obtained from these organisations likely to be reliable and valid? What enables you to judge this?

Research methods

Several different methods can be used to undertake research. Understanding the advantages and disadvantages of each method is important, to ensure that the information gathered from the research will help provide data that is relevant to the research question being investigated. Even if you are not carrying out the research yourself, you need to be aware of the characteristics of different methodologies. The methodology used may be an important factor when determining the quality of the research and, therefore, to judging the weight or value of the results from any research study. Researchers should publish the details of their methods so that others can replicate the study (see the section on Issues). Being able to compare research methods, and to identify similarities and differences across different studies, is an important consideration when analysing and evaluating research in a literature review.

Sampling

Much research in health and social care involves obtaining information directly from individuals, especially when the information cannot be easily retrieved by any other means, for example measured directly using physical instruments or by observing the individual. Most research gathers information from a selected group of individuals who share some characteristic, for example people who have had a stroke, or experience such as people who have used services available in health centres. This group is known as the **sample population**. Sometimes the sample population may be only small, for example individuals affected by a rare disease. In these circumstances, the researcher may choose to **survey** everyone in the group. Alternatively, as is frequently the case, researchers may select a research methodology appropriate to investigating particularly small numbers, for example interviews or case studies. However, when the sample population is large, it is not practical for a researcher to include everyone in the sample population, so they select a smaller number of eligible individuals, the research **sample**, to include in the research.

Key terms

Sample population – group of individuals targeted for investigation on the basis that they share the characteristics being investigated.

Survey – systematic process of gathering information from several individuals, often using a questionnaire.

Sample – group of individuals selected to participate in a particular health and social care research investigation.

Some frequently used sampling techniques include:

▶ random sampling, in which individuals are selected randomly; researchers may use random numbers selected by a computer, or from a table of random numbers

▶ systematic sampling, which involves selection of the individual at a regular intervals, e.g. distributing a questionnaire to every other service user on an attendance list for a day centre, or every sixth service user with diabetes attending a GP practice

▶ quota sampling, which requires the researcher to select a predetermined number of individuals from representative groups (e.g. according to age, area of the country, socio-economic profile, male and/or female etc); opinion pollsters use this method

▶ opportunity sampling, which involves researchers handing out questionnaires to individuals who happen to be passing by at the time. For example, standing outside the entrance to a hospital on a particular day and handing out questionnaires to anyone who will take a copy would be opportunity sampling.

The sampling technique and sample size chosen for a research study affect the validity of the research and the conclusions that may be drawn from it.

> ### Key terms
>
> **Respondents** – individuals from the selected sample who submit a completed questionnaire to the researcher.
>
> **Open question** – allows the respondent to provide an answer in their own words.
>
> **Closed question** – requires the respondent to select a response from a given menu of possible answer options.
>
> **Response frame** – menu of answer options provided for a closed question.

Defining the sample population and selecting the sample is an important aspect of the planning of research, because these two aspects of the survey influence what information can be obtained and the quality of the data collected. Selection of the research sample may involve complex statistical processes, which are not of concern for this unit, but you should understand some of the core methods of sample selection so that when reviewing, analysing and evaluating the research for your literature search you can consider the potential impact of the sampling process on the outcomes from the research. Researchers working with large sample populations take care to select a sample of individuals to be as representative of the whole group as possible including similar age group, gender mix and spread across different parts of the country.

Questionnaires

Questionnaires are a convenient way of obtaining information from many individuals in a survey. Individuals who respond and submit a completed questionnaire are known as **respondents**.

A questionnaire is a pre-set series of questions compiled by a researcher to gather information, usually from individuals, or an individual responding on behalf of an organisation.

▶ A question that expects the respondent to provide a free response is known as an **open question**.

▶ A question that provides a menu of possible responses from which the respondent selects the most appropriate response is known as a **closed question**.

▶ The menu of response options provided by the researcher is known as the **response frame**, which may use a variety of formats (but you are unlikely to be required to know the detail).

However, health and social care researchers using a questionnaire as a means of obtaining qualitative data should have a clear understanding of whether information relevant to their research can be obtained using this technique.

Other factors to consider when constructing a questionnaire include:

▶ whether to use open questions, closed questions or a combination of both

▶ the capabilities of the individuals in the sample frame, particularly their ability to follow the instructions, read and understand the questions and responses offered, so the responses they select are reliable

▶ questions need to be short and free from any ambiguous meaning

▶ response frames need careful construction so that there is an answer option available to every respondent

▶ questions on sensitive issues may need to be asked indirectly rather than directly, or use response frames that elicit less precise information such as age as a series of age ranges rather than expecting an exact age

▶ leading questions – any questions that indicate there is an expected response should be avoided

▶ the sequencing of questions within the questionnaire may influence the respondents' responses

▶ information the researcher needs to know about the respondent that might affect the responses they make, e.g. their age, sex, employment or level of education.

Figure 4.8 shows an example of a structured question that might be included in a questionnaire.

Question   **How often do you engage in the following forms of exercise?**
Instructions: Enter one tick per line for each statement

	Daily	3–4 times per week	Once a week	Once a fortnight	Once a month
Walk for 20 minutes continuously	☐	☐	☐	☐	☐
Walk briskly without stopping for 1 hour or more	☐	☐	☐	☐	☐
Practice yoga or simular gentle exercise for 1 hour	☐	☐	☐	☐	☐
Participate in specific moderate exercise inducing mild sweating for at least an hour	☐	☐	☐	☐	☐
Engage in organised strenuous activity eg aerobics, field sports, tennis etc	☐	☐	☐	☐	☐

▶ **Figure 4.8:** An example of a response frame that might be included in a questionnaire

The construction of a questionnaire requires careful consideration, if it is to generate reliable data. Inappropriately constructed questions and response frames can result in respondents failing to answer questions, becoming confused and so not providing answers that reflect their actual situation, deliberately giving a false answer (note that 'Never' is not an option in the above response frame, so respondents may be forced to give a false response), especially one they think the questioner may want to hear, or simply not returning the questionnaire. All of these eventualities will reduce the validity of the data generated from the survey.

Questionnaires may be distributed by hand, in the post or online, provided the researcher has appropriate contact details for all individuals in the sample. However, the researcher only benefits from any of the data provided by the **participants** if the questionnaire is returned. The **response rate** is an important indicator of the validity and reliability of the data generated by the survey. The method of distributing the questionnaires in a survey can affect the response rate, so opportunistic sampling of patients waiting in a hospital outpatients department might elicit a high return rate of, say 60–80 per cent, whereas when distributing questionnaires by post, a 30 per cent response rate would be considered good.

It is now relatively easy to construct a questionnaire using online software. However, in health and social care research, completing surveys online may still be a barrier for some participants. This could introduce a bias in the data generated from the survey as data from the non-respondents would be excluded.

Reports of research based on self-completed questionnaire surveys should always state the response rate. A low response rate may not fairly represent the sample population, for example older people may not have responded because the survey was online. In contrast, if some participants are highly motivated to respond, because they want to express a particular point of view, the data generated may also be unreliable. Either way, the data could be skewed or biased and, therefore, reduce the validity of the conclusions drawn from the data. These issues may mean that it is better to adopt a different methodology for the research. A smaller number of good quality interviews, or a well-conducted focus group could generate more reliable data and increase the validity of the conclusions, even though the number of participants was lower.

> ### Key terms
>
> **Participant** – an individual who contributes data to research, for example by submitting responses to a questionnaire, taking part in an interview or focus group or by agreeing that their personal data can be used by researchers for a particular research project.
>
> **Response rate** – percentage representing the proportion of completed questionnaires returned to the researcher relative to the total number of questionnaires distributed. A high response rate increases the reliability and validity of the data gathered from the questionnaire.

Interviews

An interview involves an interviewer interacting directly with an individual to obtain information about that person, which will be included in the analysis of all data gathered in the research, to draw conclusions. Interviews can sometimes involve more than one interviewer, or two or three interviewees interviewed together. Interviews may take place:

- face-to-face
- over the telephone/voice over the internet enabled
- using text messaging
- online
- using video-enabled software, so those involved can see each other even though they are in different locations
- via social networking websites
- in a focus group of several interviewees.

An interview is a useful research method when, for example:

▸ detailed information is required

▸ knowledge and understanding are being sought from a specialist

▸ the sample population is very small

▸ participants may have difficulties completing a questionnaire

▸ a wide range of experience is being investigated

▸ the information being sought is not sufficiently predictable to be gathered using a structured questionnaire

▸ the information to be elicited from the interview is complex.

Interviews may be structured, semi-structured or unstructured (see Table 4.4). Whatever the form of the interview, the detail of what was said in the interview needs to be converted into a format that makes it readily accessible to the researcher when they are analysing it to draw conclusions from their research. The entire interview can be audio recorded, but it is usual to convert the spoken words to a text format to produce a **transcript**. Software is now available that can convert recorded sound into text, which can then be saved as a written document.

> **Key term**
>
> **Transcript** – exact, word-for-word written record ('ums' and 'ers' are included) of what is said by both the interviewee and the interviewer, usually taken from an audio or video recording.

▸ **Table 4.4:** Features of different types of interview

Type of interview	Characteristics of each type
Unstructured	• Particularly used to obtain in-depth and holistic information about the interviewee's experiences. • Open questions are carefully constructed to encourage the interviewee to respond freely, often at length. • Open questioning from the interviewer is used to elicit detailed information, often by adapting the questioning according to the information revealed in the interviewee's responses to preceding questions. • Follow-up questions may be used to probe detail from the interviewee's narrative, or to keep the interviewee on track for the information being sought by the interviewer. • Requires the interviewer to establish a good rapport with the interviewee, to build trust so that the information revealed in the interview is reliable, and as accurate as possible. • Several interviews with the same interviewee may be necessary to obtain all the information being sought by the researcher. • Data obtained is purely qualitative, may be difficult to analyse and requires considerable interviewing skills to ensure the interview remains focused.
Semi-structured	• Interviews are structured by an interview schedule, with a list of predetermined questions about a specific issue or experience being researched. • Each interview generates qualitative data. If the research involves interviewing many individuals, then analysis of qualitative responses across the sample may generate quantitative data. • The interview schedule enables greater reproducibility, so that the schedule can be used with several individuals, better enabling comparisons between the responses from all interviewees.
Structured	• Usually involves a questionnaire. • The interviewer poses questions orally, reads out the predetermined menu of possible responses and then ticks the response selected by the interviewee. • May be completed face-to-face, by telephone or online. • Often used for market research interviews surveys and customer satisfaction surveys.

▶ Researcher administering questionnaire

Focus groups

A focus group involves interviewing a group of individuals, usually no more than 20. It is a special sort of interview technique. Similar to a semi-structured format, an interviewer poses questions and facilitates discussion among the participants, to gather the different opinions and perspectives of the participants. The participants are usually selected to be representative of the sample population. The qualitative data gathered from the discussion is recorded by a note-taker, ideally someone who is neither the chairperson nor a participant in the discussion.

Case studies

A case study is a real example, explored in some depth, relevant to the issue being researched. To be worthy of specific study, a case study should relate to a clearly defined issue that can be studied independently of its context. When reporting on health and social care research based on case studies, it is important to define the boundaries of the study and its time context, so that the data generated can be reviewed and analysed within the context of the appropriate social policy environment. Case studies are useful for exploring complex situations such as issues relating to a family encountering difficulties, the dynamics of how a group of professionals work together or new approaches to supporting individuals with mental health issues.

Case study research may involve gathering specific data, which would not normally be obtained. It may also involve analysing data gathered routinely as part of an individual's care, or of an organisation's procedures, provided the participants were informed and had given their consent. New research could involve interviews, perhaps with an individual, their relatives and carers, and the professionals involved in their support. Records of quantitative data, for example clinical laboratory reports or case notes held on file, could contribute to the case study, provided the data are relevant to the research.

The value of a case study in research is that it can enable a wide range of data, which may only be considered separately – for example by different specialists, to be collated together. This provides a more holistic perspective that could be valuable to improving practice and policy. A case study generates qualitative data, which may be highly detailed but is specific only to the particular case studied. Preparing the data for a case study is time consuming, so only a small number of case studies are likely to be involved in any piece of research. This may limit the usefulness of the understanding gained, but useful insights may be generalised to wider contexts and can be valuable on a 'lessons learned' basis, especially if they relate to unforeseen or unusual events or situations. When reporting case study research, the report should always identify the context of place, time and other key information relevant to understanding the case study and its role in the research. If contextual information is not provided within the research report, then any insights gained from analysing the case study will be limited.

Your literature search may include case study data as it is a frequently used methodology, particularly in social care research.

Scientific experiments

The scientific method is used to investigate different physical **phenomena** in the natural world. Much scientific research takes place in laboratory conditions and often involves a large team of scientists and technicians, each contributing a specific expertise. For example, a doctor of emergency medicine may work with dermatologists, biochemists, physiologists, cytologists and chemists to develop a technique for lessening the lasting damage to skin following a burn injury.

However, research based on scientific methodology is not always carried out in laboratories. Most health research is conducted in clinical settings, using scientific principles. For example, the clinicians (doctors and nurses) involved in the example of burns injury research given above, will apply scientific methodology to their part of the research as much as the biochemists and cytologists culturing tissues for skin grafts in laboratory surroundings.

The scientific method involves testing a **hypothesis**, a statement about a phenomenon. The statement is based on prior knowledge and is an 'educated guess' about the relationship between factors influencing the observed phenomenon. Factors that influence a phenomenon are called **variables**.

Scientific research involves 'testing' the hypothesis by carrying out a series of carefully designed experiments to test the effect of each variable on the phenomenon. The results from the experiments may either prove or disprove the hypothesis, but either outcome is equally valuable. If an experiment proves a hypothesis, scientists can apply the hypothesis to new situations and contexts, to advance their understanding of the phenomenon. If a hypothesis is disproved, scientists will analyse and evaluate the results and construct a modified hypothesis based on their analysis, and then conduct further experiments to test it.

Scientists involved in medical research, for example developing new drugs or the better understanding of specific diseases, need to explore a large number of different hypotheses around the multiple variables affecting human physiology. Scientists break down the main hypothesis into individual hypotheses, investigating a single pair of variables for each of these in turn, so that the main hypothesis is not fully tested until a series of experiments is completed. A single report of scientific research can be very technical, exploring only a tiny detail of physiology. While this is not the focus of this unit, the principles of scientific method underpin much research in the health and social care sector, so an overall understanding of the methodology is important.

In a single scientific **experiment** meeting 'fair test' rules, only two variables are investigated at a time. The experiment is specifically designed to measure the influence of the **independent variable** on the **dependent variable**. The results will show how the dependent variable changes when exposed to the independent variable. However, it is important in scientific methodology to include a **control test** in the experiment in order to confirm that neither variable on its own can bring about the changes observed. Each variable needs to be measurable, preferably using instrumentation that provides an objective, quantitative reading.

> **Key terms**
>
> **Phenomenon** (plural is **phenomena**) – event or observation in relation to the physical world.
>
> **Hypothesis** – statement that predicts the relationship between two variables.
>
> **Variable** – entity or factor that can have a range of measurable values, a factor that will affect the results.

> **Key terms**
>
> **Experiment** – specifically designed test to assess the validity (truthfulness) of a hypothesis.
>
> **Independent variable** – a phenomenon not dependent on the value of another variable, for example time or temperature.
>
> **Dependent variable** – a variable relating to a phenomenon whose value is dependent on the value of another variable, for example respiration rate and pulse rate.
>
> **Control test** – a scientific test in which each variable is tested alone, without the influence of the variables being investigated, to check that any change observed in the experiment is not due to either the independent variable or the dependent variable on its own.

However, human beings are complex organisms and their behavioural and physiological responses are influenced by many variables, which cannot be easily controlled or investigated individually within living animal or human bodies. Application of scientific principles to health and social care research tends to be restricted by ethical issues. While it is usually acceptable to investigate the behaviour of chemicals and non-animal tissues by systematically controlling each variable in a laboratory, similar investigation of human and animal tissue, and the involvement of live animals in research, is governed by codes of ethics.

Research into specific diseases and treatments eventually needs to involve testing of physiological and psychological responses in patients and individuals, thus involving clinicians and care professionals as well as scientists. In healthcare research investigating the impact of a healthcare intervention such as a new drug or a wound dressing routine, it is usual to have a **control group**. Participants are randomly allocated to one of two groups and only one of the groups receives the intervention, the other group becomes the control group. Data will be collected and analysed in exactly the same way from both groups to identify the extent to which the results obtained are sufficiently different, which will demonstrate a benefit of the intervention. Participants should know that they may be allocated to a group that may or may not receive the intervention before giving consent to participate in the research. Although the focus of this unit is on health and social care policy, practice and needs, your literature search may involve you reading reports about scientific research.

The social science methodologies already explored are likely, for ethical reasons, to be more acceptable. Sometimes the research strategy mixes scientific method and social research. For example, an investigation into the effect of an exercise routine on individuals' health could measure some physical aspects of health (for example, changes in pulse rate, respiration rate and blood pressure) under scientific conditions, but would then need to adopt a social science methodology, such as a questionnaire, to investigate how the exercise made the individuals feel about their health.

> **Key term**
>
> **Control group** – group of individuals participating in research, but who are not exposed to the health or care intervention being investigated.

> **Reflect**
>
> In small groups, review experiments you have carried out. Select two or three and answer the following questions.
>
> What was the hypothesis? What were the variables investigated and which was the independent variable?
>
> What control tests were included? Why? What type of data was generated in the experiment? Was it qualitative or quantitative? What conclusions did you draw from the experiment?

Checklists

A checklist consists of a list of predetermined statements or features against which the presence or absence of the feature is recorded. The items in the checklist may be used to:

▶ monitor that each stage of a complex or important procedure is being followed, for example when preparing an organ and the patient for transplant surgery

▶ demonstrate the frequency of a given feature of behaviour taking place, for example in event sampling observations

▶ check that particular items are present or in the correct location, for example an operating department practitioner counts the number of clean swabs issued to surgeons during an operation, and counts back the number of used swabs received to ensure that no swabs are left inside the patient at the end of the operation

▶ record the time or day when a repeated action took place, for example the temperature of a fridge in a care home kitchen is measured and recorded every four hours

▶ routinely check on emergency equipment, for example testing fire alarms weekly.

The design of a checklist needs careful thought, to ensure the statements generate data that is relevant and sufficient for the overall aim of the research. However, once finalised, it can be a relatively quick and convenient technique to use when observing behaviours in a busy working environment, such as a hospital ward or a children's nursery, where the priority must always be the needs of the individuals being cared for rather than the research.

Observation

In the context of health and social care, an observation is probably primarily thought of as a technique for observing the behaviour of people and individuals. However observation is also important in relation to physical objects and spaces, for example:

▶ careful scrutiny, in effect close observation, of, for example, X-ray, CAT and MRI scan images by a radiologist and other experts is a critical part of diagnosis and health care

▶ assessing the extent to which a day room in a residential care home provides an environment that will encourage residents to relax and enjoy the company of others, and so contribute to maintaining their social wellbeing

▶ assessing features of a particular environment that have the potential to be hazards for those with health and social care needs

▶ analysing reasons why, when using a particular piece of health and social care equipment, the operators experience discomfort or find the equipment does not perform the intended task as well as it should.

Observations may be carried out with the observer as a **participant observer** or as a **non-participant observer**. The relationship between the observer and the situation and individuals being observed is an important factor to consider when judging the reliability and objectivity of any interpretation made of the data gathered from the observation.

Techniques for making formal observations include **narrative**, **time sampling**, checklists, **event sampling** and **sociograms**. Which observation method is adopted for a research study will depend on the overall objectives of the research and the contribution the observation inquiry is making towards these.

Key terms

Participant observer – an observer who actively engages in the activity context of the observation, alongside the individual or individuals who are being observed, for example a play therapist stimulating play in order to observe the behaviour of an emotionally disturbed child.

Non-participant observer – an observer removed from the context of the activity in which the participant behaviour is being observed. The observer is an onlooker only, for example an early years practitioner observing how a group of 3 year olds play with each other.

Narrative – verbal description (written or oral) of events in the order in which they happen, for example recording the details where the events occurred, who was involved, what was said, what happened.

Key terms

Time sampling – series of observations made at a regular, predetermined time interval for a predetermined fixed amount of time, for example every hour, for the duration of a particular finite activity.

Event sampling – recording behaviours at a specific moment in time, for example the key features of a child's behaviour during their first week attending a nursery.

Sociogram – record the interactions one individual makes with other people, for example they are used in childcare to document a child's social development as they learn to play with other children and interact with adults. Sociograms are often recorded as a chart.

A behavioural observation involves recording what is happening, as it occurs, so it is very important to record the date of the observation. Contextual details that may affect the behaviours being observed include, for example:

- the time of day, which could influence the observed behaviour of a young child or an elderly adult
- what has happened immediately preceding the observation, such as an event that might have disturbed or distracted the individual being observed
- who else, apart from the participant(s) being observed, is present during the observation
- the extent to which the physical needs of the individuals being observed have been met, for example hunger, fear or needing to use the toilet could result in distracting behaviours.

Observations generate qualitative data, so there is potential for considerable variation arising from, for example different perceptions, attention to different details or differences in how the each observation is recorded. Variation in using a particular observation technique may be less if every observation is being carried out by the same observer, or the observer is very experienced. Even so, there is still potential for each observation to vary according to the actual context of each observation. Radiographers and doctors are trained in reading radiographic and scanner images, but still confer about scans before making a diagnosis.

To minimise variations in the data that could arise from using the methodology itself, observers should understand the **standardisation** of the methodology before carrying out the observations. In health and social care research incorporating observations, the observation method will be carefully selected and the observations will be carried out according to a planned protocol to fit the contribution the observations are making to the research outcomes. If the research involves a team of observers, there is greater potential for variation. In the best quality research, the observers will have been trained and standardised for using the observation protocol. The research report should indicate what standardisation of the observation method has taken place. Standardisation processes would also be expected for interview and focus group methodologies when there is more than one interviewer or chairperson involved, for example because they are taking place in different locations.

> **Key term**
>
> **Standardisation** – formal process to ensure that individuals performing the same qualitative task in different situations do so as far as is possible in exactly the same way. Standardisation involves the individuals being trained for the task then completing an identical task under the same controlled conditions. A standardisation process should be repeated regularly if the task is being performed repeatedly over a long period of time.

Informal observations are a routine aspect of health and social care practice and could be a trigger for a more formal investigation using action research. Under safeguarding requirements, all carers and practitioners have a duty to be watchful of the wellbeing of individuals in their care, and also of their colleagues. For instance, a person might be uncharacteristically aggressive, or quiet and not participating in a group activity, or look pale and unwell. Ignoring these signs could be regarded as negligence. Informal observation is often the only means of gathering information about unplanned events or critical incidents, such as a violent outburst or a service user collapsing.

Observation is routinely used by those working in early years childcare environments, because it is an important tool for assessing a child's learning and development. It enables the early years practitioner to plan activities to promote the next stage of development for a child. The recording method used, when working with the spontaneity and fleeting nature of a young child's actions, needs to be straightforward in order to capture the moment where the child suddenly demonstrates a newly acquired skill. In a research report, informal observation may be referred to as 'anecdotal' evidence or as 'personal experience'. The data from such evidence has less value than that generated from research based on a planned observation protocol, because of the lack of standardisation. However, it could still have validity, especially if the person making the observation is a health or social care professional as their experience of using observation techniques makes the data more reliable.

Reflect

Think about the occasions where you have been observed by a professional.

When did the observations take place? You may or may not have been aware of them at the time, for example when you were a baby. What was their purpose? What (in general terms) do you think was learned from the observation; what was the outcome? What was the consequence of the outcome for you at the time of the observation? Has the outcome had a longer-term impact for your development, health and wellbeing?

If you have had a work placement in an early years environment, you will be aware that observation is an important aspect of assessing a young child's development. It is a routine task for an early years practitioner, which informs the planning of activities to stimulate further development of the children. Those working with adults will routinely use observation to detect discomfort or emotional change.

 **PAUSE POINT**   With your book closed, list each of the research methods explored in this section. Identify one advantage and one disadvantage of each method.

 Hint   Think of examples of research methods you have experienced, not necessarily in a health and social care context.

 Extend   What methods might be appropriate when researching the anxieties of older adults about their care when they are no longer able to care from themselves without assistance?

Analysis of data

So far, you have explored the different methodologies available to researchers carrying out primary research. It is increasingly easy and relatively quick, using digital devices and the internet, to collect data through automatic monitoring of activity. Generating data because it can be done is not a reason on its own to collect data. (Given that research is a planned process and is also subject to ethical considerations there must be a valid rationale to justify gathering the data.)

Raw data, such as that captured on or in observation records, interview transcripts or schedules, returned questionnaires or experimental results, are unwieldy, making it difficult to identify what has been/could be learned from it. Therefore, researchers organise raw data by collating it systematically, perhaps using spreadsheets, tables, graphs and charts; enabling the data to be analysed in relation to the original purpose of the research.

Analysis may identify trends, which may be small but consistent changes, for example the small but steady increase in the percentage of primary school children affected by obesity and being overweight revealed over several years of data from the NCMP (see the case study on the National Child Measurement Programme).

Health and care interventions to support patients and service users may not produce sudden and dramatic benefits that are easily observed and identified. Instead, changes may be imperceptible on a daily basis but may become apparent over a longer period of time. Monitoring these changes and analysis of the data generated is essential to reveal the full impact of the treatment or intervention. For example, psychological therapies, treatments for depression, chronic pain or dietary and insulin regimes for regulation of blood glucose in diabetics may all only produce detectable change over a long period of time.

Local authority data

Local authorities are responsible for provision of health and social care services for vulnerable individuals including:

▶ all children and young people under the age of 18

▶ adults with learning disabilities

▶ older people in need of assistance with personal care.

In order to ensure its services are in place and sufficient for the local population it serves, a local authority needs to know its local population well in terms of, for example:

▶ the number of people requiring the services

▶ where the people needing services are located within the local authority area

▶ how the needs of the population may change over the next few years

▶ whether the nature of the needs of the local population is changing.

Research

Explore the website of your local authority and retrieve data relating to health and social care provision in your local area. How does the data in your local area compare with the equivalent national data available? (You should note the URLs and access date, so that you can return to the data, if necessary, when carrying out your literature search.)

As indicated earlier, local authorities have statutory obligations to make certain data available to members of the public. They usually do this on their websites and also in public consultation meetings, so that members of the public can express their views. Some aspects of their activities must involve members of the public more closely, through having appointed representatives of the community who are not already elected councillors, for example, health and wellbeing boards.

Data from GP practices

In England, GPs are required by law to inform the local Health Protection Team (HPT) when they see an individual whom they suspect may be infected with any one of the 39 communicable (infectious) diseases. The process is called Notification of Infectious Diseases (NOIDs). Notification must be made within 24 or 48 hours of the person being seen. The HPT reports each case of suspected infection to Public Health England (PHE). Doctors in other parts of the UK are similarly obliged to report suspected cases of infection to their own health authorities. PHE publishes the statistics weekly by region and also by local authority. Trends in the incidence of these diseases are important indicators of potential epidemics. Monitoring their incidence helps to prompt appropriate precautions to reduce the risk of spread in communities.

Table 4.5 shows how other sources of information regarding health and social care in localities can be accessed.

National data

In the UK, national data is primarily published by the ONS (see the section on Office for National Statistics (ONS)). However, when conducting a literature search, you may find it useful to access more specialist data. Table 4.5 shows useful sources of information that may be relevant to research in the health and social care sector.

▶ **Table 4.5:** Sources of national data

Organisation	Website link	Examples of data available
NHS Digital	www.hscic.gov.uk	• Clinical Commissioning Groups (CCG), e.g. allocation of funding to community and secondary care in an area. • Adult social care outcomes framework (ASCOF), provides information on outcomes for people using social care services, and for their carers.
Health and Wellbeing Boards (HWB)	www.local.gov.uk/health	• Admissions to hospital • Serious case review reports
Public Health England (PHE)	www.gov.uk/government/organisations/public-health-england	• Health improvement and public health issues, including infectious diseases • Publishes statistics regularly (weekly/monthly/quarterly/annually) depending on the data
Health Research Authority (HRA)	www.hra.nhs.uk	• Health and social care research ethics

National data is useful to compare with local data, which may be very local, such as a local authority area or the area covered by a single Clinical Commissioning Group, or may be available for each region of the country. Comparisons between national and more local data are valuable and might be a line of enquiry to follow in your literature search depending on the health and social care issue you are investigating.

Conducting effective literature searches

In the twenty-first century, the quantity of text-based and visual information available is colossal, mainly because of the internet and online access. The problem for researchers is finding the sources that are relevant, and that have verifiable origins, from among the far greater number of sources that do not meet these criteria. A **literature search** is a systematic process in which a range of published material relevant to a specific issue is analysed, to extend knowledge and understanding of the issue, but not necessarily accessing all there is to know about the issue. A literature search is a useful preliminary step to any advanced study or research. It tells you the kind of sources available on the chosen issue and what the key issues may be. For this course, at least some of the sources accessed in a literature review should include references to enable you to extend your research into the issue further, if appropriate and if there is sufficient time. In contrast, a literature review is a more substantial process that involves a comprehensive and evaluative scrutiny of all sources relevant to a specific issue.

All learners need to learn the skills associated with a literature search, as this technique is essential for successful study at further and higher education. A literature review is usually carried out by specialists and experts researching for professional purposes. Systematic literature reviews make a valuable contribution in health and social care and may be influential in effecting changes in policy and practices.

Key term

Literature search – a process involving a planned, thorough and systematic exploration of a range of published material in order to gain a broader understanding of an issue.

Literature searches are an essential aspect of the work of professionals in the health and social care sector to enable them to keep up to date with new developments in the sector, which appear continually across the very wide range of specialisms carrying out research relevant to the sector. The more systematic and critically evaluative processes associated with a literature review are useful for generating an overview of an issue. This can be useful to a wider audience of professionals so that they can adapt their practice to take account of the research. The advantage of a literature search, or a literature review, is that they enable researchers to bring together, or collate, into a single source, a wide body of published research. This research has probably been carried out in several different locations by researchers working independently of each other, and it may otherwise not have been brought together.

No primary research is carried out in either a literature search or a literature review. Therefore, some of the ethical issues associated with primary research involving patients, service users, their families or other professionals are avoided. It is now considered inappropriate for those without professional training and status, such as learners studying a BTEC National in Health and Social Care course, to interview or use data retrieved directly from such individuals. However, you will still need to consider ethical issues when carrying out a literature search.

A feature of a literature search is that it includes a wide range of sources. Table 4.6 shows some of the sources you might access in your literature search.

▶ **Table 4.6:** Secondary sources

Secondary source	Examples, topics	Focus, key features
Textbooks	Health and social care Early years Human physiology	Should be Level 3 equivalent standard; often include lists for wider reading useful for more detail. Academic textbooks will include references, but assume advanced literacy skills of the reader.
Specialist books	Learning disability Mental health Dementia	Written for care workers, professionals and academics.
Journals	*Health Service Journal* *The Lancet*	May only be accessible via an academic search engine. May require login to access information.
Sector magazines	*Community Care* *Nursing Times* *Early Years Educator* *New Scientist* *Nursery World*	Published regularly and available at some newsagents or from a college library; online versions may include extra content, but there may be a charge for access.
Commissioned reports	Francis Report 2013 Cavendish Review 2013	Often commissioned by government for a specific purpose, e.g. to investigate failings, to update, to improve, assess impact of new technologies.
Regulator reports	Ofsted Care Quality Commission (CQC) NICE	Inspection reports on service provider organisations, each publishes an annual report.
Government organisation websites	Food Standards Agency PHE ONS Local authorities	Nutritional information, food safety. Data on immunisations, screening programmes, health and wellbeing.
Google Scholar search engine (**https://scholar.google.co.uk/**)	Abstracts of academic papers published in large number of academic journals	All sources are from peer-reviewed journals but you may have to pay to access the full research report; fewer recent sources, many are old (10+ years) which limits currency of information.

▶ **Table 4.6:** *continued*

Secondary source	Examples, topics	Focus, key features
The internet (via general search engines)	Several well-known websites provide specific information about health issues, conditions, disorders and diseases	Content is of unknown origin, so accuracy, objectivity and so on are unclear; such sources are not usually acceptable for referencing purposes but may enable access to reliable sources.
Health and social care organisations, including charities	Internally produced documents such as policies and procedures	Useful for action research, and as examples to illustrate the impact of legislation and standards on actual practice in a health or social care workplace, for example.
Leaflets, bulletins, fact sheets	May be available in doctors' surgeries, health centres and other outlets	Publisher should be stated in small print – important to identify to establish the reliability of the information provided.
Social media	Facebook Twitter YouTube etc	Reliability, validity and ethical issues need to be considered carefully regarding all data from these sources; unacceptable as a credible source for study purposes.
Images	Photographs Charts Objects associated with delivering care, such as physical aids Video	May have a place in research but reliability of photographs is difficult to ascertain, given the technical ease with which images can now be artificially constructed or modified.

This unit aims to develop your own literature search skills in the context of exploring an issue of current interest in health or social care. Developing literature search skills will assist you to be more effective in the research you carry out for other units in your BTEC National Health and Social Care studies. Additionally, developing these skills will be valuable when studying at higher levels, or if you intend to work in a supervisory role.

However, a literature search is only one method of carrying out research, even if it is likely to be used as part of every piece of research you do. Understanding the advantages and limitations of each research method is essential, to enable you to assess the extent to which the research methods used in the sources you include in your research affect the reliability or validity of the data they generated.

A focused form of literature search is usually carried out at the start of any primary research project to establish what is already known about the topic being researched. The findings from this type of literature search help establish the rationale for the primary research being undertaken. These are usually presented in the introduction section of a report of research, although they may also be referred to again in the discussion section. As a preliminary step in conducting primary research, a literature search can help researchers to avoid the problems encountered by others in their methodology, replicate findings to confirm them, or trigger new lines of enquiry.

For the literature search that you must carry out for this unit, the choice of issue will be limited. Additionally, you will only have a short time in which to complete it, so you will also be limited in the number of sources that you can access and analyse in the time available. However, the skills you develop in this unit should increase your ability to:

▶ find secondary sources relevant to a particular issue

▶ manage your literature search through keeping records appropriately, so that your sources can be accessed reliably and repeatedly, as required, and fully acknowledged formally

- analyse and evaluate the data within each source in relation to your issue, using identified lines of enquiry
- synthesise new thinking about the issue, using evidence from your sources based on your lines of enquiry
- draw conclusions relevant to your lines of enquiry regarding the issue, which you justify from your analysis of the evidence selected from your sources
- outline ways, based on your conclusions, in which the knowledge and understanding acquired from your own literature search could benefit health and social care, particularly in relation to one of more of the four purposes explored earlier.

Step by step: Stages of a literature search

`10 Steps`

1 Draw up a plan for the search, with timescales.

6 Analyse each source individually, evaluating the reliability and validity of the data presented in each to develop your own lines of reasoning in relation to your search.

2 Analyse the article that triggered your search thoroughly, to ensure you understand it fully.

7 Synthesise new arguments, developed from your lines of reasoning based on evidence from several of the sources (you must use at least two sources).

3 Identify possible lines of enquiry for your literature search that will extend the research presented in the article.

8 Evaluate your arguments in the context of the reliability of the data in the sources you use, taking into account any limitations in your own methodology used to conduct your literature search.

4 Select two to three initial lines of enquiry, to establish an overall aim for your search.

9 Draw conclusions from the arguments you present.

5 Search, using key words, for secondary sources, and select those that seem most relevant to your lines of enquiry.

10 Make recommendations for further research.

For the unit assessment, you should make notes of the data, lines of reasoning, arguments and conclusions that you have drawn from your literature search.

You might find it useful to refer back to Figure 4.4 at this stage. You are not expected to produce an overall report of your literature review for this unit, but should look at questions such as the following.

- What was the process you undertook in your literature search? What did you do and in what sequence?
- What was your thinking in selecting and developing your lines of enquiry? How did you use the sources you accessed as evidence to support, or counter argue, these lines of enquiry?

The step-by-step process outlined is the same for any literature search, and could be applied to research you undertake for any unit of your BTEC National course, or whenever you need to research information when undertaking higher-level study or as part of a future job role.

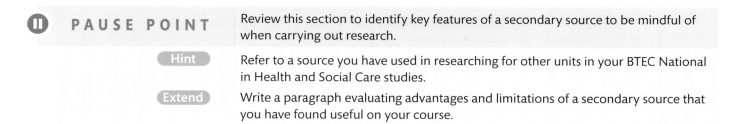

Review this section to identify key features of a secondary source to be mindful of when carrying out research.

Hint   Refer to a source you have used in researching for other units in your BTEC National in Health and Social Care studies.

Extend   Write a paragraph evaluating advantages and limitations of a secondary source that you have found useful on your course.

Identifying, analysing and evaluating source material

Identifying source material

As a well-recognised method of research, a literature search is a planned activity. Finding relevant source material relating to the topic or issue you are researching is an early step in the search process. However, you should be aware that you may need to find additional sources later in your literature search. This may be to find further specific evidence to support the arguments you develop based on the data from the sources you examined at the start of your search and to strengthen the validity of the conclusions you draw from the research.

Table 4.6 indicates a range of secondary sources that you could access for your literature search. There are vast numbers of sources available online on a wide range of health and social care issues. You may be very used to using a smart phone, notepad or computer to search for the information you want for your personal life – instantly and when you want it. However, a literature search needs to be planned and systematic, and not spontaneous or haphazard.

Almost all sources you access for your literature search are likely to be available in digital form, so retrievable online from government, local authority and charity websites, and those of other organisations. Data from these sources is usually freely available to the public. Textbooks are probably the sources you are most likely to access as printed copy. Journals, periodicals, newspapers and the content of broadcast media can be downloaded, although they may be subject to specialist access on a subscription basis. Your school or college may provide access to journals through specialist academic search engines, and you are expected to be aware of these and how they operate, but access to academic journals is not mandatory for your literature search for this unit. You should be able to access some of the most widely used health and social care magazines, such as those listed in Table 4.6.

An important starting point for any literature search is to identify a few **key words** that are specific to the subject you are researching. Key words will help you identify potential sources that may be relevant. However, given the large number of sources published relating to health and social care, you will almost certainly need to search using phrases or search filters, to narrow down the number of sources to a manageable number. Ideally, you will want to narrow down your initial search to perhaps 10–15 sources.

> **Key term**
>
> **Key words** – a single word, or a short string of words (a phrase) that indicate the content of a piece of text, for example 'health and social care.'

As an example, Figure 4.9 illustrates possible lines of enquiry for a literature search about a specific health and social care issue.

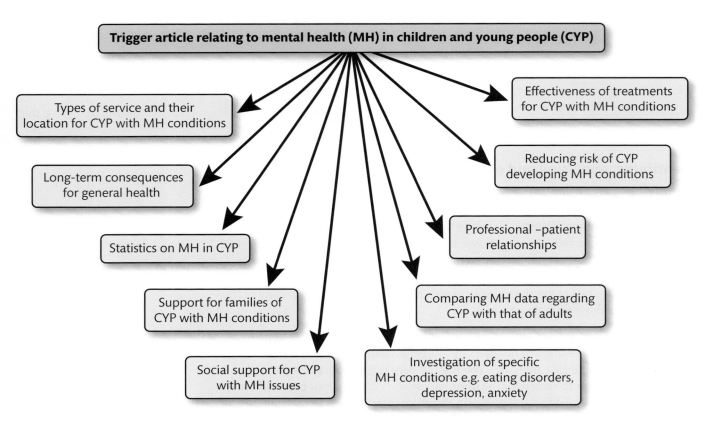

▶ **Figure 4.9:** Possible lines of enquiry that might be explored in relation to mental health in children and young people (CYP)

Research

Research one of the lines of enquiry suggested in Figure 4.9, experimenting with suitable key words to help you narrow down your search. Identify two sources to explore in more detail.

Analysing source material

An important influence on the quality of your findings from a literature search will be the quality of the sources you find. A researcher is likely to select a source because its subject matter or content seems relevant to their research issue. However, an essential aspect of a literature search is that the researcher takes into account any information available about the source of the accessed literature. Information gathered from a source that indicates who has written it and whether the authors are likely to have been guided by core principles of integrity, honesty, professionalism and objectivity, has greater worth than information gained from a source that you know nothing about. You may have no means of verifying that the information from such a source is truthful, free from bias, is accurate or has errors, is reliable or has not caused individuals to be harmed or exploited.

In this digital era, it is all too easy to deceive; for example by copying text from others or inventing or falsifying data, including falsified visual images by altering them digitally. Such practices would be regarded as unacceptable malpractice and unethical. In most health and social care professional organisations, and in UK universities, such malpractice could result in disciplinary action, including withdrawal of professional registration, and thus the legal licence to practice as a professional.

A schema to help you analyse a secondary source is shown in Figure 4.10.

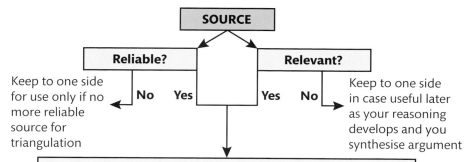

READ the source:
1. **Abstract/summary** (if present) to gain an overview
2. **Conclusions** and/or **Recommendations** for key outcomes
3. **Discussion** for reasoning and arguments
4. **Introduction** for context and purpose of writing
5. **Methods/evidence** how data was gathered
6. **References**/acknowledgement of sources for possible further sources to follow up

INTERROGATE the source:
- What was the purpose of the writing?
- What lines of enquiry were investigated?
- What arguments were synthesised?
- Are the conclusions drawn valid, ie based on the evidence and arguments presented?
- To what extent is the data evidence based or theoretical/conceptual?
- To what extent do the recommendations relate to health and social care?
- What limitations relating to the reliability and validity are there?

LINK the data in the source to your own research
- What aspects of the source are relevant to my lines of enquiry?
- To what extent are the lines of reasoning useful for my lines of reasoning?
- To what extent does this source provide relevant and valid evidence to support the arguments I am developing?
- What are the limitations of the source that I need to consider before drawing any conclusions or making recommendations?

Triangulate this source with other sources
- To support my lines of lines of enquiry
- To provide more evidence for my lines of reasoning
- To increase the validity of my conclusions and/or recommendations

▶ **Figure 4.10** Schema for analysing a secondary source

When studying this unit in particular, you will be expected to access a range of sources and not to rely solely on those you can access via the internet. Examples of other sources that could be relevant to your literature search may be a policy developed by your work placement, or information available from a local special-interest charity.

Sources written for an academic or specialist audience, such as teachers and researchers working in universities, may contain continuous and complex prose, with long sentences. However, complex texts can be read with greater ease by following a few simple steps:

▶ ask yourself what the heading tells you

▶ skim read to identify the type of text – whether it is a research report, a critical analysis, a review article – and its structure, such as headings, in-text signposting, referencing and sources

▶ scan-read for any key words you have already identified, to enable a preliminary judgement about the relevance of the source for your literature search

▶ target more detailed reading on the abstract/summary (if there is one, it may be in a feature box or sub-heading), conclusions (at the end), discussion (towards the end), introduction (start of main text), results and method, in that order

▶ make notes

▶ record all details of the source that you will need for referencing purposes.

Evaluating source material

Evaluation requires making a reasoned judgement regarding worth or value. You will only need to evaluate each source that you access for your literature search. An evaluation involves critically examining all aspects of the source. The critical examination, or assessment, of each source will involve you searching the source to:

▶ identify the authors

▶ identify the source organisation and country of origin (health and social care policy differs in different parts of the UK, as well as between the UK and other countries, so sources from other countries exploring health and care issues may be considerably less relevant)

▶ identify the currency of the source, by identifying the date it was first published – many sources may be citing the research of others that was done years ago; for example, many learners cite Maslow's theory of the hierarchy of needs, but rarely from the original description written by Maslow and published in 1943

▶ identify whether the source relates to health and social care provision, diagnosis or treatment, delivering care, the same or different, groups of individuals using health and social care services

▶ gain an overview of the key messages the source is communicating

▶ decide whether, in relation to your literature search – the issue you are investigating and your lines of enquiry – the source is relevant, irrelevant, or possibly relevant.

This evaluation is an essential part of a literature search because the critical review of each source will enable you to recognise the extent to which the evidence it provides is reliable, valid and has been gathered with full respect for ethical principles. In addition you will need to form an opinion about the relevance of the sources to your search.

 **PAUSE POINT**   Review this section in relation to the following health issue: provision of prescribed treatment programmes for obese patients who have received a medical referral for weight reduction.

Hint   Define obesity appropriately. This question is about provision, not obesity.

Extend   Under what circumstances will weight reduction treatment be prescribed? Find secondary sources to support your answer.

Planning Research

Planning is a key feature of research and takes place before any research project starts. The planning makes the research a deliberate and formal process. The care and thoroughness of planning a research project is a critical factor for its success in meeting the intended research outcomes. In the UK, it is also essential to comply with the ethical frameworks, legislation and codes of conduct that govern research. Results from research conducted without compliance to the ethical frameworks are immediately invalidated and are, therefore, worthless. They could not be used to justify changes to health and social care practices or provision.

Rationale for research

All valid research is undertaken for a reason or purpose, otherwise it would be unethical (see the section on Ethical issues). You have already looked at the possible purposes for research in the health and social care sector and the importance of defining a clear aim for research (see the section on Issues).

The **rationale** provides the reason for the aim of the research and justifies the research (see also the section on The purpose of research). The aim might be in the form of a research question or a hypothesis that can be tested. Research always takes place in the context of what is already known and understood about an issue from previous research and/or established knowledge. Professional researchers justify their rationale by placing it in the context of what is already known about the issue they are researching. They carry out a literature search and summarise their findings, usually in the introductory section of their published report of the research. You will need to be able to explain the reasons why you have chosen to focus on a specific aspect of health and social care when you carry out your literature search. The main rationale should be based on the data presented in the article but the specific lines of enquiry you choose to pursue could be influenced by for example, a job role, a work placement experience, personal experience or interests, or some other factor. Once you complete your literature search, you should be able to support your rationale by referring to some secondary data that you found.

You could choose to explore how the data in a source from your literature search might be relevant to, for example:

▶ a different health and social care environment, such as home care or residential care

▶ a different group using the same services, such as elderly people or young adults

▶ a similar group but a sub-group within it, such as young people and young people with mental disabilities.

Deciding objectives

An **objective** is what you aim to achieve as a consequence of deliberate, planned action or actions. In order to make your literature search manageable, so that you can meet the requirements of this unit, you will need to establish clear boundaries for your study. This will require you to define what aspect you will investigate and this, in turn, will be determined by two main factors:

▶ the time you have available

▶ the accessibility of relevant secondary sources.

An objective is a specific statement that relates to the overall aim, but which defines how you will achieve the aim. Objectives are set at the start of a project. Often a single aim involves setting several objectives. The actual achievements from the project may differ from the intended aims set at the start – ranging from complete

> **Key term**
>
> **Rationale** – a statement justifying a course of action.
>
> **Objective** – a statement of the intended outcome from an action. An objective should relate to an overall aim but be more specific.

non-achievement of the aim, partial achievement, full achievement and possibly, to achievement of unforeseen objectives. The actual achievements are known as **outcomes** or **findings**. Research outcomes will be based on the evidence gathered, such as the results from experiments or surveys or relevant statistical data, but they also take account of data gathered from secondary sources, such as ideas, concepts, arguments and conclusions.

> **Key terms**
>
> **Outcome** – the actual outcome from an activity.
>
> **Findings** – the knowledge and understanding gained from a piece of research, or a research study.

Objectives should always be SMART (specific, measurable, achievable, relevant and timely), as indicated in Table 4.7.

▶ **Table 4.7:** SMART objectives

S	**Specific**	Each action is identified as a short, clear statement of what is to be done.
M	**Measurable**	The outcome or result of each action can be measured in some way.
A	**Achievable**	Each action can be put into practice (any one action may require breaking down into several smaller actions to enable achievement of the main action).
R	**Relevant**	Each action should be contributing to the overall objective.
T	**Timely**	A deadline is set for each action and sub-action, so that the objective can be attained by the overall deadline set.

Clear definition of the boundaries of research early on, at the planning stage, will make it much easier to maintain the focus required. As with any research study, clearly defined objectives provide a clear focus for the research, which makes it more likely to be successful in contributing positively to knowledge and understanding in relation to people using services, informing policies and practice or identifying gaps in provision. The success of any research is measured against the objectives for it set at the beginning. Objectives that lack clear definition are unlikely to generate meaningful results that will meet those objectives.

Sometimes, considering what you cannot investigate can help you consider what will be feasible for you to research through your literature search. Fewer, smaller and less ambitious targets could well advance knowledge and understanding faster overall than larger, less clearly defined objectives. Less defined objectives are likely to generate data that only relates vaguely to the objectives, making analysis and evaluation of the data much more difficult.

Selecting appropriate research methods

Verifiable empirical data generated from observation, scientific experiments and from measurable experiences is likely to generate data that is more reliable and so generate research findings that have greater validity. Research data generated through primary research, therefore, tends to be held in high regard, provided it is carried out ethically and all steps possible have been taken to minimise the risk of errors and bias. As indicated earlier, the data generated from empirical research is more likely to be quantitative and health research tends, therefore, to use empirical or scientific methodology.

In contrast, social care research methodologies such as interviews, generate qualitative data. This time-consuming methodology usually only involves a small sample size, limiting the extent to which any findings can be generalised to the wider population. Only when it is feasible to gather quantitative data from a large number of participants, perhaps through a survey involving participant-completed questionnaires, can social care research generate reliable quantitative data that could be meaningfully applied more widely, for example to develop social policy, or improve services. Government statistics are usually gathered at a regional level. They tend to be reliable because they are based on a large population and, therefore, can be valuable in providing data against which smaller-scale research can be compared, increasing the validity of arguments developed in the research and the conclusions drawn.

In contrast to empirical data generated from primary research, a literature search or a literature review in which all data is gathered only from secondary sources, can be useful to develop abstract concepts and theories by bringing together published data from a variety of sources. It may subsequently be feasible to design appropriate tests for such theories and concepts using more empirical methods.

Other determinants of the choice of research methods can include the following.

▸ The research objectives – for the results to be valid, the methods used must be appropriate for the data that is being sought from the research. Table 4.8 suggests potential methods for researching topics in health and social care.

▸ Access to appropriate sources of data – these may be secondary sources, such as access to academic journals or to appropriate participants, for example a GP interested in the early diagnosis of motor neurone disease may see only a handful of patients with this condition in decades of working in a GP practice.

▸ Time available for research – there is a cost for time. Research by health and social care professionals and clinical scientists working in the UK may be carried out as action research within their main job, where the main priority must always be the needs of the patients and individuals using the service they provide. Time for conducting the research and writing it up for publication is, therefore, likely to be very limited. Research conducted in association with a university is often dependent on specific grants from, for example the NHS, charities or other not-for-profit organisations. Such funding is usually time-limited, for example for up to five years. A postgraduate student studying for a PhD research degree is only likely to receive an income to do so, including time for writing their thesis, for three to four years.

▸ Funding for research – required to meet the costs of the researchers' time and any other costs involved in carrying out the research, such as specialist equipment or expenses involved in travelling to meet participants. Research methods that depend on highly sophisticated equipment that is expensive to develop or purchase are likely to require very generous research grants. Exploration of some of the research charity websites such as Diabetes UK or Cancer Research UK will give you some idea of the costs associated with research in health and social care.

Reflect

What factors affect the choice of research methods available for you to use as a learner on a BTEC Level 3 National course?

▶ **Table 4.8:** Possible research methods to use in health and social care research

Research question/topic	Possible research methods
What are patients' preferences for support when being discharged from hospital following a stroke?	• Literature search to investigate the different approaches to support being used in different areas. • Interviews with patients and their families. • A survey of community-based occupational therapists and rehabilitation teams working with patients recovering from stroke.
What policy initiatives are required to reduce the rate of 'bed blocking' by patients no longer requiring hospital care or treatment following a stroke, but who require care and support to be able to return to their own home?	• Review of data from all hospital trusts where there is a dedicated hospital stroke unit. • Interviews with clinical managers of stroke units. • Interviews with hospital administrators. • Survey of local authority directors of adult social services. • Focus group meetings with patient representatives.
Investigating treatments to reduce the brain damage and, therefore, impairment of body functions caused by stroke.	• Laboratory experiments exploring the biochemical and physiological effects of potential pharmacologically active interventions for strokes. • Microscopic observations of cellular changes in tissues exposed to a simulated stroke. • Literature search to identify possible known pharmacological agents that might be predicted to have an appropriate mitigating effect on potential brain damage following a stroke. • Observation of radiographic scans, to ascertain how the stroke has affected the physiology of an individual's brain. • Eventual double-blind trial of any new drug developed.
Why are so few individuals affected by stroke accessing specialist support services?	• Literature search of statistics to ascertain the extent of the problem. • Interviews with those affected by strokes and their families. • Survey of the quality of the services currently available.

Selecting a target group and sample

The concept of sampling has already been discussed (see the section on Sampling). In health or social care research, the target group may be self-selecting, for example in Table 4.8 the target group is formed of individuals who have had a stroke. Within that there may be sub-groups, for example those whose stroke has left them well enough to be rehabilitated to an independent life in their own home, and another group whose stroke has left them with disabilities that mean they can no longer live independently.

However, even within a sub-group, a researcher may need to make decisions as to who would be appropriate to participate in the research. Individuals may be excluded for practical/logistical reasons such as they live a long distance from the research base and this should be made explicit in the research report as it may bias results because the group is less representative than it could be. Research groups may include:

▶ children and young people, for example children in their early years, adolescents, looked after children

▶ those with disabilities, for example learning/intellectual, physical, acquired brain injury

▶ adults, for example of working age, in old age

▶ those affected by specific disorders, for example diabetes, mental health issues, strokes

▶ workers in health and social care, for example health professionals, care workers.

Within each of these groups, a researcher might identify sub-groups, which will often distinguish between males and females and age (perhaps using an age range 0–5 years, 11–18 years or over 65 years). Other ways in which it may be important to differentiate sub-groups of participants might relate to their past experience or professional knowledge.

In a research project investigating knowledge and understanding, perhaps of how to deliver first person on scene assistance (first aid), it could be relevant to know whether the participant's background meant they would be likely to have greater knowledge than usual. In this scenario, it could be relevant for the researcher to gather information regarding whether the participant was a health professional or was a trained first responder/first aider. If the research focus were on perceptions of health or care workers, then defining the specialism of the worker more closely could be appropriate, for example speech and language therapists working with language delay in young children, a counsellor for mental health or nurses working in the community or in hospital provision.

Once a researcher has identified the target population on which to base their research, they will need to decide which individuals in the target group they will actually invite to be participants in the research. They can then select an appropriate method for selecting their sample.

Deciding realistic timescales

Most research projects are time-limited. This may be because there is urgency to obtain the outcomes from the research, so that patients and service users can benefit as soon as possible. Or maybe because a professional has been seconded from care responsibilities or a job role in order to carry out a piece of research, but has to return to their role within a defined timescale. The cost of research will always be a factor that defines when a project needs to be completed.

You will be very familiar with deadlines. Just as managing your time is a key aspect of managing your life, so it is critical to the success of a research study. If an end date has been defined for you, then you have to work backwards from that date. This involves:

▸ the action plan – identifying in detail all the activities/tasks that need to be done before the deadline, including preparing any research instruments, such as questionnaires, interview schedules or ordering laboratory materials

▸ time planning – identifying how much time will be required to complete each activity task

▸ creating a schedule of activities – recognising how the tasks need to be sequenced, which tasks need to be done first or where one task requires another task to be completed before it can commence

▸ scheduling – considering the extent to which longer tasks could be ongoing in parallel to shorter tasks, for example an interviewer could not be in two different locations on the same day

▸ being aware of and apportioning the total time available to all the tasks and presenting the time plan/schedule on an easily understood grid or template.

A Gantt chart, similar to that shown in Figure 4.11, is an example of a planning template that could be used for planning your literature search. For complex research projects there may be a series of different plans over different timescales, one for each of the different professionals involved in the research study. In your literature search, if just one of the activities you have identified in your plan takes longer to complete than you predicted, then the scheduling of all the other activities will be affected. The more detailed the breakdown of tasks you put into your plan/Gantt chart, the lower the likelihood that your planning schedule will be put off track. A possible strategy for planning your literature search might include time allocated for the following activities:

Tasks	Weeks	1	2	3	4	5	6
Read articles 1 and 2		■					
Brief analysis of both articles		■					
Identify possible lines of enquiry for each article		■					
Preliminary search for sources		■	■				
Choose article and detailed analysis of it			■				
Decide lines of inquiry			■				
Keep records of all sources accessed		■	■	■	■	■	■
Search for further sources for chosen lines of inquiry			■		■	■	
Evaluation of sources for reliability, relevance			■	■			
Analysis of source to develop lines of reasoning				■			
Establish clear focus of lines of reasoning				■	■		
Synthesise arguments relating to health and social care (individuals/policy/practice/new knowledge)					■	■	
Prepare notes for Part B						■	■
Prepare refernce list						■	■
Print notes and reference it							■

▶ **Figure 4.11** Gantt chart, used for planning and scheduling tasks in a project

▶ reading, re-reading and annotating your source, so that you understand it fully

▶ drawing up a time plan that includes all the activities in this list

▶ drawing a mind map of possible aspects of the issue to explore

▶ deciding which aspects of the issue will hold your interest and enable you to meet your objectives

▶ setting two to three objectives and allowing further time later in your schedule, in case you need to modify these as your search progresses

▶ deciding your measures of success

▶ following up secondary sources

▶ searching for other sources on the aspect(s) of the issue you select from your mind map

▶ reading and re-reading to understand the new sources fully

▶ keeping records of your literature search.

You will note that this list is more detailed and specific than the overall literature search process given in the Step-by-step process featured in the section on Conducting effective literature searches.

Deciding how research will be monitored and modified

An important aspect of any research project is to monitor your progress continually against your original research plan. There are two reasons for this:

▶ to keep focused on the purpose of the research as stated in the research question or hypothesis

▶ to monitor your progress against your action plan, so that you complete the different stages of the project by the deadlines set.

The range of secondary sources and their use in a literature search have already been discussed. As you read more sources in your literature search, so you will gain a better understanding of the issue and whether the lines of enquiry you chose will enable you to answer your original question. Re-reading your sources will enhance your understanding and help you assimilate more of the detail and, therefore, will probably result in you adjusting your interpretation of it. This process may also lead to you returning to sources that you judged to be less relevant initially but which you now realise are indeed relevant to the lines of enquiry you have explored, or support the lines of reasoning you develop. Other sources that you initially perceived as relevant may similarly end up as less relevant. If you have time, you may wish to find new sources to support the lines of reasoning you developed from your research of the issue.

Monitoring

Research rarely proceeds exactly as planned, so monitoring the progress made against the timescale available for your literature search will be important. Professional researchers will monitor their progress regularly, possibly by providing a progress report to their managers, or publishing it more widely in a journal. Although you might make some adjustments to your plan two or three weeks into your literature search, perhaps by adjusting your lines of enquiry, it would be unwise to make any significant changes to your lines of enquiry much later than this. Regular monitoring of your progress against your literature search plan should enable you to identify whether you are on target to complete this within your original time frame (by the end of studying this unit). Another important function of monitoring your progress is to check that you are maintaining an appropriate focus to enable you to meet the objectives you have set for your literature search.

Modification

Even when researchers set very clear objectives for their research and develop detailed plans, the nature of research is such that they cannot take account of all eventualities. Their objectives and planning are based on their knowledge and understanding of their issue before they started the research study. Once the research study is underway, the new data they generate as a consequence may make it appropriate to modify their initial objectives and plan. Some of the reasons why you may need to modify your objectives for your literature search might include:

▶ revising the order/sequencing of tasks

▶ adjusting the timescales for individual tasks (although you do not have scope to extend the overall time)

▶ adding new tasks, probably reading of new/different sources, to gather more data to support your objectives

▶ modifying/adjusting the exact focus of your objectives

▶ amending the scope of your literature search to make it more manageable within your time frame (deadline date).

Deciding measures for success

All research projects need to define what they aim to achieve with the resources at their disposal. Professionals involved in action research, which is very much based on their practice in their day-to-day job role, may decide on measures for success that seem very small, but which may make a difference for their service users. Some projects may have their measures for success defined for them in written terms of reference or broad goals, such as doing things more efficiently, so they are less costly or more effective. Measures of success in primary research may simply be the empirical data obtained and its interpretation in the context of the aims of the research.

Ethical considerations for carrying out research

All research in the UK and EU is governed by ethical principles, and all health and social care professions are governed by these principles. Throughout your literature search, you should be mindful of the ethical issues that might arise and take active steps to avoid any activity that could be considered unethical.

❚❚ PAUSE POINT   How will you apportion your time during your literature search?

Hint   What activities will you need to allocate time for and in what sequence/order will you need to do them?

Extend   What extra activities might you need to undertake in this time? How much time, and when, do you think you should allocate for these activities?

Ethical issues

Ethical considerations are an essential underpinning of all research carried out in a large number of countries around the world. **Ethics** are written statements, often referred to as ethical codes, which reflect the **morals** of a society. Both morals and ethics relate to what a society considers to be acceptable or unacceptable behaviours. Morals tend to be modified over time, so ethical codes also tend to evolve over time to reflect the changes in society's morals.

Maintaining confidentiality

Researchers must ensure that data from participants is stored securely and cannot be traced back to specific individuals. Personal data that can be directly, or indirectly, linked to an individual or can be accessed by those who do not have formal permission to view the data, could result in the data being misused and the participants being harmed in some way. In order to protect participants, researchers in health and social care need to establish appropriate systems to ensure the **confidentiality** of all the data about individuals that they collect in their research.

For many participants, the concept of **anonymity** is also important, because they want to be sure that any intimate data about themselves, which they may be prepared to share with a professional researcher in a health or social care context, is not going to be seen by others who are not subject to an ethical code of conduct.

Maintaining confidentiality and anonymity of data protects participants and guards against data about individuals being accessed by unauthorised people, meaning those who do not have formally agreed permission to view the data. You should be mindful that maintaining confidentiality and anonymity in research is not confined to the individuals who are participants in the research. It also applies to any health or social care providers, other organisations associated with the participants, and those involved in other ways in any research. This means the researchers should not name the setting or provider; instead only a general description of the size, type of organisation or provider, age group of users and similar non-specific data is provided. Only information relevant to the context of the research should ever be documented as part of a research project (see also the section on Data protection).

However, maintaining anonymity is about more than just not identifying an individual or organisation by name. It also means that you cannot provide information that might enable an individual or organisation to be identified indirectly, for example from a description that enables others to deduce the names.

Key terms

Ethics – written statements, relating to what is acceptable and unacceptable, that reflect the morals of a society.

Morals – unwritten codes of what a society considers to be acceptable or unacceptable behaviours.

Confidentiality – ensuring that personal information relating to any individual, including all data collected for a research study, is shared only with those whom the individual has consented to being informed.

Anonymity – ensuring that any data associated with an individual collected for research purposes is documented and stored in such a way that it cannot be traced back to the individual by name.

Any research report should explain how the confidentiality of the participants was maintained. One way of maintaining anonymity is to establish a system for collection, processing and storage of data gathered for research purposes that does not reveal the identity of the participants, yet enables all the data from any one participant to be linked. Usually, this involves representing each participant by a unique reference number, rather than by name, so ensuring all data relating to that individual is anonymous. Various techniques can be used, such as representing individuals by a name that is not their actual name, or coding the participants for example as Patient A or Service User 5.

Electronically stored data can be transferred easily and unintentionally. However, digital data can be stored more securely than paper-based data if it is correctly protected by robust firewall software, and secure logins and passwords are issued only on a selective basis to those in the research team with formal authorisation to access it.

Maintaining anonymity is important for maintaining the integrity of a research study, because it helps to reduce the risk of bias. If data were linked to specific individuals if could result in the analysis and interpretation of the data from the project being less objective, and so affect the validity and reliability of any conclusions drawn from that research.

Gaining consent from participants in research

Under human rights conventions and legislation, all participants in a research project should expect to have the opportunity to give their formal consent to being a participant. Consent is always required from research participants being observed as well as from the organisation on whose property the observation is being made. Observations made in public spaces may not need consent, on the grounds that anyone can observe others as a passer-by. However, recording events and activities for research purposes (for example, on mobile phones or video cameras) would require explicit consent from participants.

Researchers are required to provide every potential participant with sufficient information before they agree to participate. The information given to participants will include:

▶ the overall purpose of the research

▶ what is expected of the participants if they take part in the research

▶ what, if any, risks are involved in participating, such as possible side effects, how severe these might be, and how data generated from participation will contribute to the research

▶ the entitlement to withdraw from the research at any time.

Researchers should tell potential participants explicitly about their rights. It is important that the necessary information is made available to every participant in a form that each can understand it fully. Participants should be free to use their personal judgement about whether to participate, according to their own perception of the risks associated with participation. Once an individual agrees to participate, they will be required to provide formal consent to become a participant, usually by signing a form to this effect. This is known as informed consent. Participants may withdraw from the research while the research study is in progress, or request that their own data is withdrawn from any report of the study.

Occasionally, it may be necessary to withhold some information from participants, in order to avoid knowledge about the research affecting how participants respond. This is particularly the case in behavioural studies, when knowledge of what behaviour is being studied might affect how participants respond in the research. Another example

> **Reflect**
>
> Have you, a member of your family or a friend ever been involved as a participant in any kind of research? If so, what information were you/they given before participating? Did you/they have the opportunity to ask questions about the research? Did the information provided by the researcher influence your/their decision to participate, or not?

would be the double-blind trials that are used to test the effectiveness of new drugs. Neither the doctors administering the test nor the patients receiving the drug know whether it is the new drug or a placebo. This ensures that the doctor remains totally objective when monitoring the patient's progress in response to the new drug being tested. It also ensures that the patient is more likely to report actual rather than perceived effects or side effects.

Consent from vulnerable individuals

Extra precautions are required when gaining consent from vulnerable individuals to participate in research and additional considerations are likely to be needed to ensure that safeguarding requirements are maintained. The needs of vulnerable individuals may be such that factors giving rise to their vulnerability are a barrier to them giving informed consent independently. In this situation, a researcher would need to consider an alternative means of obtaining data from these individuals. Vulnerable individuals include:

▶ all children and young people under the age of 18, even if they are fully healthy and free from disability and are not using health and social care services

▶ adults who lack capacity, for example individuals with intellectual impairments, individuals who are confused, individuals with dementia or any individual who is unable to understand what is going on around them, perhaps because they have additional language needs.

Other adults may also be vulnerable, for example if they:

▶ have a disability or they are infirm

▶ are using health and social care services

▶ have recently been affected by bereavement

▶ are affected by a disease or a long-term health condition, including mental health issues or addictions

▶ are involved with the criminal justice system.

Link

Refer to *Unit 12: Supporting Individuals with Additional Needs, Unit 17: Caring for Individuals with Dementia* or *Unit 20: Understanding Mental Wellbeing* for more information about vulnerable individuals.

Research

Investigate the factors a researcher would need to consider when seeking informed consent from potential participants in each of these circumstances:
- participation in a drug trial of older adults with moderate dementia
- testing the use of an anaesthetic specifically for use in children under 10 years old undergoing major operations
- a young adult with moderate learning disability, who has a domineering relative with power of attorney from the Office of the Public Guardian for the individual's health
- participation of a recently bereaved adult in research about care of the terminally ill.

How might barriers to gaining informed consent in each of these circumstances be overcome?

Safeguarding considerations affecting participants in research might include:

▸ whether the individual can understand the nature of the research itself, and so understand what they are agreeing to when giving consent to participate

▸ the individual's intellectual capacity to understand the concept of risk, and any risks involved in participating in a particular research project

▸ whether the individual has the capacity to be a reliable participant, if the research involves qualitative methods

▸ any potential consequences of the research for a vulnerable individual, which might not be an issue, or might potentially have different consequences, for less vulnerable participants.

The Mental Health Act 2007 requires that research involving those who lack capacity has to be approved under the conditions set by the act. In the UK, the National Social Care Research Ethics Committee is delegated to grant approval for research involving adult social care. Ethical approval for a research project should always consider the possibility that the research process could make all participants vulnerable, and that the research protocols ensure that this risk is minimised. However, particular care would be needed if the research specifically involved those already recognised as vulnerable before the start of the project. For children and young people, consent is required from a parent or their legal guardian. In your placements, particularly in early years environments, you would probably need to follow a specific procedure should you need to observe one of the service users as part of your BTEC course.

Research

In your placement or workplace, investigate the policy and procedures relating to gaining consent to participate in any activity that involves observing a service user, or discussing the care of a service user.

In what way does the policy and procedure protect the vulnerable individual?

Research conduct

All professional bodies associated with health and social care will have **codes of practice** that govern the behaviour of their individual members. Each of the professions (currently 16) that are represented on the Health and Care Professions Council (HCPC) are governed by the Standards of Conduct, Performance and Ethics of the HCPC, which were published in January 2016. The Nursing and Midwifery Council Code was updated in 2015. Any researcher in health and social care is expected to comply with the code of practice of their professional body.

These professional codes of conduct expect individual professionals to respect the code whenever and wherever they are carrying out their professional duties, which includes involvement in conducting research. Carrying out research in health and social care may require professionals to spend more time with individuals using services, or to access more information about an individual than they would in their day-to-day role. However, respecting and abiding by their professional code of conduct means they must maintain a distinct boundary between themselves and the participants in their research. This is usually referred to as maintaining a professional distance.

A professional who exploits their position as a researcher to manipulate or take advantage of a participant, or who acts in an unethical way when conducting their research, could be struck off their professional register and barred from practice.

Key term

Code of practice – written statements that set out how members of a particular profession should conduct themselves.

Organisations that regularly undertake research in health and social care, such as universities, will have their own ethical codes for the conduct of research carried out within, or in association with, their organisation.

Ethical codes for research are only guidelines, they are not legislation. Research ethics committees (RECs) exist to approve research proposals. In England, ethical approval for health research, and all research involving the NHS, is the responsibility of Health RECs, which consider proposals at a regional level. From April 2015, the National Social Care REC has been the responsibility of the Health Research Authority (HRA).

Research

Go to www.hra.nhs.uk (the Health Research Authority website) and investigate the information it provides. Find out ways in which you, as a member of the public, could become involved in health and social care research.

Key term

Dilemma – a situation requiring a difficult choice to be made between two or more alternatives because the advantages and disadvantages between each of the alternatives is finely balanced.

While it may be straightforward to make a judgement about what is or is not acceptable for much research in health and social care, the ethical judgement for other areas of research may be less clear. Sometimes it is a matter of balancing one risk against another. When faced with this situation, there is an ethical **dilemma**. For example, researchers develop a powerful new treatment for people with a type of cancer that does not respond to other treatments. Human trials are required. However, the researchers suspect, from the evidence of earlier animal trials, that there could be serious and unpleasant side effects for humans. The researchers will have to balance the likelihood that people may die from this type of cancer and that there is a possibility of a cure against that of inflicting harm to patients in the trial.

Over time, the boundaries of medical knowledge and the ever-advancing range of techniques that become available tend to expand society's understanding of what is acceptable. However, balancing the potential of new technological advances with existing boundaries of knowledge, also creates an ethical dilemma.

Examples of dilemmas relating to research that have arisen in recent years include:

▶ using stem cells in research, to better understand certain diseases

▶ investigating genetically modified crops, as a way of increasing food production to support the increasing human population

▶ gene therapy, where specific genes are modified in order to reduce the harm arising from an inherited condition.

Dilemmas such as these make news headlines, because they affect society. Resolution of the dilemma may involve changes in the law, and in the interpretation of the ethical codes governing research.

Data protection

Any information held about an individual, by other individuals or organisations, is subject to the Data Protection Act (DPA) 1998. There are greater restrictions about holding sensitive information, such as about ethnicity, beliefs, health or sexual life. Organisations that hold personal information about individuals, such as employers, have to register with the Information Commissioner's Office, the public body that enforces the DPA. The DPA means that if information is held, it can only be used for specific, declared purposes; and the information can only be held for a specified period of time. For a researcher, this means that under the DPA:

▶ only data relevant to the project can be collected

▸ the data can only be processed according to the stated purpose, so a researcher could not use the data collected for one project in another project, unless specific consent for the second project had also been obtained from each participant

▸ it would be illegal to alter the information, so that it is no longer accurate

▸ information must be processed in such a way that it does not breach an individual's legal rights, or cause them harm or distress – this would include revealing the person's identity either directly or indirectly and thus it would contravene the DPA if, in a case study using a pseudonym, the information given still enabled the individual to be identified

▸ all information gathered from participants should be kept securely

▸ after the data is analysed, each individual's personal records must be destroyed

▸ individual data cannot be taken outside the UK, unless it is protected (for example, encrypted).

Any participant in research has the right to see the data collected from them, under the principle of 'right of subject access' laid out in the DPA. All organisations collecting and using personal information are legally required to comply with these principles. Participants are also entitled to request that their data be excluded from the analysis of the data.

Human rights and research

Research involving vulnerable individuals is important, if health and social care services and practice are to meet their needs. Vulnerability may arise due to an individual being affected by a learning disability or an acquired cognitive impairment, such as a brain injury, stroke or dementia. As participants in research, such individuals may find it difficult to understand the information given about the research, to ask questions about it or to answer questions in a questionnaire, for example, without help. There is a risk that anyone helping the participant to answer such questions could deliberately or unintentionally influence the responses given, or change them. Also, researchers could exploit the vulnerability of the participants by omitting to check that the participant has understood the information they have been given, or possibly by not being truthful about the research. Omitting individuals from a sample because they are vulnerable is also not ethical. Researchers should make provision to avoid exploitation or abuse of vulnerable people when they participate in research.

After the Second World War, the Nuremberg trials of Nazi medical accomplices who had conducted cruel and often fatal experiments on inmates of the concentration camps, led to the development of the Nuremberg Code of 1947 regarding human experimentation. The Universal Declaration of Human Rights (UDHR) was approved by the United Nations General Assembly in 1948 and, in 1953, all 47 members of The European Council (which involves many more countries than the European Union) signed The European Convention on Human Rights (ECHR). Since 1947, the ethical considerations relating to research and other aspects of human endeavour have led to further development of some aspects of the original Nuremberg Code. The UK enshrined the ECHR into British law in the Human Rights Act 1998. Ethical principles embedded in these conventions and the Human Rights Act govern the conduct of research in the present day and include:

▸ protecting individuals

▸ ensuring that individuals only participate voluntarily

▸ ensuring that any personal information gathered in the course of the research is treated confidentially

▸ requiring that the plan for any research project is subject to external scrutiny by subject experts who are independent of the research project.

In small groups investigate the:
- role of the Human Tissue Authority (HTA), particularly in relation to research
- European Convention on Human Rights (ECHR) and the Human Rights Act 1998 (HRA).

Discuss how the principles underpinning the ECHR and HRA are taken into account by the HTA in its role in governing research involving human tissues.
Has the HTA's attitude to aspects of its work changed since it was formed in 2005? If so, what reasons could you suggest for the changes identified?

Because a society's morals and, therefore, its codes of ethics change over time, research studies carried out many years ago may now be considered unacceptable. You could critique some of the studies carried out many years ago by considering changes in societal attitudes, and the ethical codes that govern current research practice.

Research

Research Milgram's psychology experiments on obedience/conformity, carried out in the early 1960s. In what ways would current ethical codes restrict similar experiments if they were to be carried out at the current time?

Organisations such as governments, universities, health authorities, businesses and pharmaceutical companies developing new medical treatments are likely to be involved in one or more research projects at any one time. Any organisation involved in research must gain approval to conduct their research from an appropriate ethical committee. These committees are made up of individuals with considerable appropriate experience in research, with knowledge of the relevant areas of law, the subject area of the research and so on. They also include representatives of participant groups, for example patients or advocates.

As you are aware from earlier in this unit, research is a planned activity. One aspect of the planning of a research project is for the researcher(s) to submit a research proposal to the ethical committee for its approval. The committee scrutinises the proposal and may ask for further information, or set certain conditions, before agreeing that the research project may proceed. An ethical committee might also require regular reports on the progress of the research throughout the project.

When reading secondary sources, you should always pay attention to the steps the researchers have taken to comply with the relevant ethical codes. Data from sources that are not likely to be underpinned by these principles should be regarded with great caution in the context of health and social care research.

Research

Find out about the codes of conduct for members of the Health and Care Professions Council.

Use and misuse of results

It is not ethical to use data gathered from research in any way other than that for which it was intended when the research commenced and consent was obtained from the research participants. To use the data in a different way, such as in another piece of research, would be to misuse the data. If the data was considered valuable for later research, then new consent would have to be obtained from the original participants for its use.

As already mentioned, statistical data is gathered routinely by the government and by local authorities, to monitor changes that could affect their activities and the communities they are responsible for. Most data is gathered as part of the routine activities of all public services, to help ensure that taxes paid by the public and businesses are being used wisely and for the benefit of individuals, communities and the population as a whole. Most statistical data is not linked to a specific individual and in health and social care it could relate to numbers of people living in an area, or with a recognised specific need such as a disability or the waiting times for treatment. Additional personal data may be collected by the government only if it is authorised by legislation, for example GPs being required to notify Public Health England when they suspect an individual has a specified infectious disease such as measles or meningitis.

It is only by gathering such statistics that the government and local authorities can plan health and social care services, which in the UK are still largely public sector services. Within the NHS, statistics are invaluable to inform managers and clinicians about the effectiveness of the health care provided. By revealing differences in outcomes for patients in relation to, perhaps, how long they spend in hospital, whether their illness recurs and they need to be readmitted, how soon they are well enough to return to work and so on it is possible for professionals to identify the practices that result in the best outcomes for patients and individuals using services.

All research in the developed world is carried out in accordance with the Nuremberg Code. There are ten core principles to the code.

1 Every individual participating must give, voluntary, well-informed consent.

2 Any experiment must have a beneficial aim, which cannot be measured in any other way.

3 Research should be based on previous knowledge.

4 The design of the research should avoid all unnecessary physical or mental suffering for participants.

5 Research that might result in the death or disability of participants should not be carried out.

6 The risks associated with the research should not be greater than the potential benefits.

7 The researchers must plan and prepare to ensure that all participants are protected from risks.

8 The researchers must be trained and scientifically qualified.

9 Any participant should be free to withdraw from the research at any time that they feel unable to carry on.

10 The researcher must cease their research project immediately there is any evidence to indicate that it has become dangerous for participants.

Researchers have a duty not only to protect participants from harm but also to ensure that the project is carried out with integrity. Integrity in research involves:

▶ carefully considering the methods used to carry out the research

▶ ensuring the accuracy of the data

▶ ensuring the accuracy of any generalisations derived from the results and the analysis

> ▶ ensuring that the contributions of participants are not wasted because the research is of poor quality due to flawed methodology. (This is not the same as research that does not prove its underlying hypothesis or does not provide an answer to the question posed by the research.)

The case study is about fraudulent research that has had major implications for the incidence of childhood infectious diseases, particularly measles, in recent years.

Case study

Fraudulent research – the Andrew Wakefield case

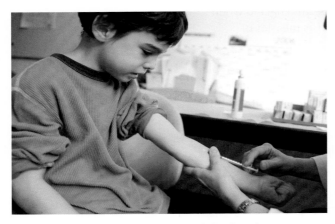

In 1998, a research paper was published in the highly reputable medical journal, *The Lancet*, written by Andrew Wakefield, at that time a surgeon and researcher. In the article, Wakefield claimed that there was a link between the measles, mumps and rubella (MMR) vaccine and autism and bowel disorders in children. The report received a great deal of attention in the press and broadcast media and, as a consequence, many parents of young children refused to let their children receive the MMR vaccine.

Andrew Wakefield's co-researchers were so unhappy about the interpretations put on the data in the published report that they publically withdrew their support for the report. Also, other independent researchers were unable to reproduce the research data, so other doctors doubted the validity and reliability of the data and the conclusions that Wakefield had drawn from it.

In 2007, the General Medical Council (GMC) began an investigation of the research. The GMC is.the professional organisation with which all doctors working in the UK must register. They must also comply with its professional code of conduct. This investigation led to Andrew Wakefield being charged on 30 counts of unethical research practice. In 2010, *The Lancet* published a statement from the editors retracting the report. Later in the same year, the GMC barred Andrew Wakefield from practising as a doctor in the UK. The many improprieties associated with the research he had published included falsifying results, inflicting invasive investigative procedures on young children that were unnecessary, and conflicts of financial interest.

The uptake of MMR vaccinations plummeted after 1998, when Wakefield's report was published. By 2005, the number of incidents of measles in children had risen dramatically. In 2013, there was a major measles epidemic in Wales, more than 1400 cases of the disease reported – of which over 600 were in Swansea, and one person died.

Despite considerable publicity being given to the fact that Wakefield's research conclusions were invalid, some parents still refuse to have their children vaccinated with MMR. However, the main consequence is that the low MMR vaccination rates since 1998 have increased the risks to the population as a whole of contracting measles and of individuals, particularly children, being affected by the lifelong damage that can result from measles infection.

Check your knowledge

1 Explain how the Wakefield research case exposed individuals to harm.

2 In what ways were the results of this study misused?

3 How might the misuse have been avoided?

Conflicts of interest

It is important to understand the nature of an organisation's involvement in a research project, in order to judge whether the research undertaken may have been influenced unduly by its involvement. For example, an organisation may be seeking a specific outcome from the research to suit its own purposes, rather than to obtain evidence that is totally objective and free of bias.

Research carried out by professionals, such as clinical staff, scientists and social scientists, is an expensive process and it is usual for researchers to seek sponsorship, or funding, to support their research. In the UK, much research takes place in university departments, often supported by grants from the government's own research organisations (currently the Research Councils), charities such as Cancer Research UK, the British Heart Foundation and many others.

Research in health and social care often involves a multidisciplinary team, with each member contributing their professional expertise to the research. For example, a research project on diabetes may involve physicians, endocrinologists, dieticians, community nurses, GPs, ophthalmologists and others. In addition, smaller organisations may sponsor others to undertake research on their behalf. Competition between organisations, research teams, and the need to produce successful outcomes from research in order to sustain the flow of research funding, may influence the research carried out and the interpretation of the research data. Research carried out by, or paid for by, an organisation is likely to reflect that organisation's interests. This could influence the research in several ways, including by:

- setting up the research methodology so that it deliberately only investigates a selected aspect of the subject, which will show the organisation in a favourable light, or benefit the market for the products it makes/sells

- only comparing findings with those from other research projects that also support the arguments in favour of the organisation's interests, but ignores any contradictory evidence

- suppressing, by not making public, any research findings that are against the organisation's interests in promoting its activities.

Commercial companies sponsoring research may only be interested in the findings of the research if they promote the company positively, for example if they boost sales or enhance the public's perception of the organisation. Many commercial companies are dependent on their shareholders. Shareholders invest their money in the company in anticipation that the profits the company makes will reward them (the shareholder) by paying a dividend on their investment. This may mean a commercial company makes decision based on wishing to please its shareholders rather than on meeting the needs of its customers. In health and social care, the customer purchasing the drugs or equipment produced from the research may be the NHS (so the tax payer) or individuals paying for their social care.

Research by private companies is essential for some types of health and social care research, particularly for developing the new, increasingly complex and expensive diagnostic equipment, and also in developing new drugs. Pharmaceutical companies may develop many drugs, but few may be successful and approved for clinical use by NICE. The companies use the profits they make from these few successful drugs to pay for the expensive research involved in developing more, potentially beneficial pharmaceutical substances. In the UK, testing a new drug involves regulated protocols, specified by NICE. The test protocols may take a decade or more to gather sufficient research evidence to ensure the new drugs are safe to use with patients. Some patients' groups now want protocols for safety testing of new drugs for human use to be speeded up, so that patients with life-threatening illnesses can benefit from them sooner.

Other examples where the role of organisations in sponsoring research can give rise to ethical concerns include:

▶ the food industry, which is expert in promoting sales of many food products, even when they are known to be unhealthy and perhaps increase the risk of dental decay or diabetes

▶ campaigning groups, which may be not-for-profit organisations, but may wish to overemphasise research that supports their particular agenda for change, and underplay any research data that contradicts their agenda. For example, the drinks industry using their own research to argue against the health benefits of taxing alcoholic or sugary drinks, or tobacco companies denying that smoking bans and warnings on cigarette packaging affect people's smoking habits.

Much research carried out by private companies and by non-governmental organisations is of a high quality. However, when reading secondary sources, you should consider the extent to which the research might have been influenced by its sponsors. Assessing this potential source of bias in research is one of the reasons why, when conducting a literature search, you should always seek to access two or more sources that have researched the same issue. You should then compare the extent to which the conclusions drawn about the issue are similar or different in each source. Several processes can reduce the influence of potential conflicts of interest in research.

▶ Disclosure is a process whereby a participant is invited to declare any potential conflict of interest before participating in the research. The researchers may then make a judgement as to whether it is appropriate for that individual to be a participant in the research.

▶ Peer review of a research report prior to it being published in a journal. A peer-reviewed research report has greater credibility than a research report that has not been peer-reviewed. Peer review involves an expert in the same field of research, who is completely independent of any member of the research team, scrutinising the report closely, to check that the research complies with ethical guidelines, that conclusions drawn are justified by the results presented and so on. The peer reviewer may recommend minor amendments to the report, or if there are serious weaknesses in any aspect of the research, they may recommend that the journal rejects the research report and does not publish it.

▶ Participant review enables the participants who have contributed data to review or comment on the research report. Under Health Research Authority guidelines, an individual could request that their data is excluded from any analysis included in the report, or request that statements relating to their data are withdrawn. Organisational participants may comment on any statements pertaining to their organisation in the report that are inaccurate.

▶ Mentoring, where an individual, either a researcher or a participant, is supported by another expert to discuss any difficulties that engagement with the research may cause, and thus help them to maintain their objectivity.

▶ Professional distance is a means of ensuring that personal influences on the researcher do not lead to a loss of objectivity when conducting the research.

▶ Whistle-blowing procedures are available in public organisations in the UK, and in some other organisations. They enable any single individual who has concerns about ethical matters relating to health or social care research to report them to a neutral third party. These concerns can then be investigated by others, who are neither participants nor researchers, nor from the organisations in which they work.

▶ Research misconduct includes failure to reveal any form of conflict of interest and issues such as making up results, falsifying results and plagiarism. (See the case study: Fraudulent research – the Andrew Wakefield case.)

Role of organisations

In the UK and Europe, the ethics of research is influenced by key organisations, which have responsibility for ensuring that research in health and social care is carried out in accordance with the Nuremberg Code. Some of the organisations that govern health and social care research in the UK include:

▶ Health Research Authority (HRA)

▶ National Research Ethics Advisors Panel (NREAP)

▶ National Institute for Health Research (NIHR)

▶ Human Fertilisation and Embryology Authority (HFEA)

▶ Human Tissue Authority (HTA)

The professional bodies such as the General Medical Council (GMC), the Nursing and Midwifery Council (NMC) and the Health and Care Professions Council (HCPC) are organisations that also influence research through their professional codes of conduct, as already discussed.

▶ Members of an ethics committee discussing approval of a research proposal

❚❚ PAUSE POINT   Create a spidergram that shows the ethical issues you should consider when reviewing a source as part of your literature search.

　　　Hint　　Think about what is meant by ethical issues in relation to research in health and social care.

　　　Extend　　In a research report, what clues would indicate how the researchers had taken account of the potential ethical issues associated with their research?

Research skills

Organisational skills and time management

As you have already seen individuals carrying out research need to be organised. They need to know what they need to do, how they will do it, keep accurate records of what they actually do (so they can refer back to them later) and plan their time to achieve the necessary outcomes in the time available.

Research is almost always time-limited. In health and social care, staff may be conducting the research on a fixed period of secondment from their usual professional role. Research project financing is usually allocated for a defined period of time, or there may be urgency to obtain results so that individuals at risk can benefit from the outcomes from the research sooner, for example developing vaccines for controlling the 2014–15 outbreak of Ebola in West Africa, or for the outbreak in Brazil of the Zika virus in 2016.

A third-year undergraduate may have a period of six to eight months to complete their undergraduate project, whereas a PhD (doctoral) student will usually have three to four years to complete their research, and write up their thesis. However long the period of time allowed for the research, the researcher needs to plan their time. As already discussed, this will usually involve:

▶ an action plan identifying key activities
▶ time planning to estimate how long each activity will take to complete
▶ creating a schedule of activities to sequence the activities appropriately, so that an activity is not held up because another activity that must be completed first has not been carried out
▶ building in some time to allow for unforeseen delays or interruptions
▶ being aware of the total time available, allowing enough time to prepare the formal research report.

One way of organising your time for your literature research period would be to use project management software or perhaps more practically, a time plan such as a Gantt chart.

An important discipline when carrying out any form of research, including a literature search, is to keep detailed records. You should keep your notes in one place so that you can access them easily and at any time. You might choose to use a small, perhaps A5-sized, notebook that you can keep in a pocket or bag. Alternatively, you could use the notes facility on your e-notebook or smart phone.

All entries you make should:

▶ be dated (the advantage of using e-notes is that every entry you make would be automatically dated)
▶ record the details of what you did and the data you obtained
▶ include the full reference details for every source you access, for example the broadcast programme, channel, date and time.

Non-judgemental practice

Non-judgemental practice is a key value underpinning health and social care. Being non-judgemental in research means that you should not allow any of your personal perceptions, prejudices, beliefs, political opinions and so on to influence the methods you adopt in your research, or the way in which you analyse the data or the conclusions you draw from evaluation of that analysis. Being non-judgemental also means that you should not be critical of an individual because of their actions, their thoughts or beliefs, or the attitudes you may encounter when conducting research. A researcher in health and social care should always maintain **objectivity**, both in relation to gathering the data and in analysing and evaluating it.

Connections between sources

As indicated in previous sections, interpreting the data you gather from your literature search should be based on rigorous analysis and evaluation of each source. However,

Key term

Objectivity – maintaining a neutral or open-minded perspective to ensure that any conclusions are based on impartially obtained evidence, which takes full account of all the data collected in the research.

some of the sources you use may be less relevant to the aspect of the issue you have chosen to investigate for your literature search. One skill you will need to develop is to identify potential links between the sources you access. Doing so could enable you to identify evidence that corroborates other findings from another source, so providing additional support for any conclusions you may draw.

Comparing sources for similarities and differences is a process known as **triangulation**; it strengthens any arguments you present in your literature search. An example of triangulation to support a study examining a new treatment for a disease might be to relate the risk of the new treatment to the possible side effects, issues associated with a similar treatment but for a different disease and statistics regarding the incidence of the disease.

> **Key terms**
>
> **Triangulation** – the circumstance where two or more sources agree with regard to trends in data gathered and/or conclusions drawn.
>
> **Collation** – the process of systematically organising data from research, in preparation for analysis and evaluation of the data.

Methods of analysis and drawing conclusions

The **collation** of data gathered from your literature search will help you to organise the data you have obtained from the individual sources you accessed. It should enable you to identify:

▶ similarities and differences between findings, such as between different service user groups

▶ agreements and disagreements between conclusions drawn from otherwise similar studies

▶ where a source not directly related to your line of inquiry includes data that is relevant/useful for the arguments you are developing

▶ where there are gaps or weaknesses in your data that you could address in the time you have available, for example demographic statistics, knowledge of a key report or policy document.

Collectively, your organised and collated data forms the results from your literature search. After analysing each source separately for relevance, reliability and validity, you can discuss all the data together, by developing lines of reasoning that integrate data and concepts from any or all of the sources, to synthesise arguments from which you draw your conclusions from the overall study. Your conclusions will form the outcome from the research and should relate back to the original aims and objectives you set for the search.

The process of developing lines of reasoning and synthesising arguments is an essential part of the research process in which you assess the extent to which your research has, or has not (a negative argument can be valid), extended understanding against the success criteria and purpose of the research defined at the start of the research. The researcher discusses, or analyses, all the evidence by comparing and contrasting their own data with that published by others, noting the extent to which the data is similar or differs from other evidence. In a technical report, such as might be used to present health or scientific research, there may be an explicit discussion section. In social research reports, discussion should be included; however, it may be less obvious because such research tends to be presented as continuous prose with few, if any, sub-headings.

In a literature search, when arguments are being synthesised, it is almost always necessary for the researcher to re-examine the secondary sources they have already accessed to seek specific data to add stronger support to their arguments. It may also be necessary to search for new sources for this purpose. This triangulation phase is important. If the researcher is unable to find other sources that triangulate the arguments being proposed in their findings, then the conclusions drawn may need to be more tentative than if the arguments could have been triangulated with other sources. However, the fact that the arguments cannot be triangulated will also signify the way in which the research is contributing new data (knowledge, understanding, concepts etc) that makes the research unique. In primary research, this triangulation phase will involve the researchers comparing the empirical data they have gathered from their experiments, observations interviews and so on, and relevant secondary sources.

The conclusions are more powerful and have greater validity if they are drawn up only after thorough exploration of all the available evidence. It is the responsibility of a professional researcher to ensure they do this. In primary research, the available evidence will be a combination of the unique empirical data the researchers have gathered. In secondary research, such as a literature search, data is only secondary data resulting from the researcher's investigation of an issue. However, it is the lines of reasoning and arguments that the researcher develops from these secondary sources that will form the 'new' or unique contribution to knowledge and understanding, which is necessary to make it a piece of meaningful research with well-validated conclusions.

Potential sources of bias and error

In the UK, research conduct expectations are that researchers have a duty of care to ensure that they avoid errors in their methodology, the presentation of their data, its analysis and the conclusions then drawn.

Researchers should plan their methodology to minimise the risk of errors. Ethical committee approval for research should be vigilant regarding critically evaluating the methodology being proposed to ensure that there is a minimal risk of potential errors. Peer review prior to publication of the research report can help remove many errors in the content of the report, including weaknesses in the analysis of the data or the conclusions being presented. Wakefield's colleagues (who were to be named as co-researchers) reviewed the research report and disassociated themselves from the report before it was published (see the case study in the section on Use and misuse of results).

Sources of bias

Another way in which research data can be distorted is through bias, where a particular perspective is explored to the exclusion of other perspectives. Examples of how research may be biased include:

▶ ignoring rogue data (data that does not fit the pattern evident from the rest of the data)

▶ designing the research methodology so that it intentionally, or unintentionally, favours a particular outcome, for example by asking leading questions, or the profile of the sample studied not being representative of the sample population

▶ only considering a limited number of interpretations of the data in the conclusions.

This list is not exhaustive, and you may encounter other sources of bias in sources you access in your literature search.

Sources of error

Sources of error in research can arise for a variety of reasons, for example through limitations in the equipment or the research tools used, from a poorly thought through research plan design or through insufficient standardisation. As part of the analysis of any research, all researchers should always acknowledge potential sources of bias or error in their own methodology, as well as any in the sources they use. In scientific experiments, equipment is calibrated for errors. In social science research, it is usual to carry out a small scale, preliminary **pilot study** to test that any interview schedule or questionnaire is likely to yield reliable data.

Bias and error may be an unintended consequence of the research design, which only becomes apparent when the research is in progress, or when the data is analysed. If bias or error is recognised at an early stage of the research, the researchers may be able to adapt their methodology to minimise the impact on their results, or to quantify the influence.

> **Key term**
>
> **Pilot study** – small scale, preliminary study used prior to undertaking a research project, to evaluate whether the proposed study will be feasible, and also to improve its design.

The extent to which bias or error may have influenced the results is an important determinant of the validity and reliability of the research findings. A researcher failing to consider possible sources of bias or error in their data analysis would be unethical. When you are carrying out your literature search, if you only have time to focus your analysis on one aspect of the data collected, you should make this explicit in your research report. Otherwise, you could be vulnerable to the accusation that you are introducing bias into your search by ignoring some of the data you have searched. In primary research in health and social care involving participants, it would be unethical not to analyse all the data collected, because it would mean you had collected personal data from participants unnecessarily, and you would be contravening the Data Protection Act.

Distinguishing between fact and opinion

In the UK, decisions about health and social care are expected to be based on **evidence-based practice (EBP)**. As explored earlier, the focus of all research in health and social care is to provide the evidence on which to base health and social care policy, practice and provision, as well as to acquire new knowledge and understanding. Health and social care research aims to establish information based on **facts** through the application of rigorous research principles.

> **Key terms**
>
> **Evidence-based practice (EBP)** – in health and social care, practice that is informed by reliable research data that enables the most appropriate care to be provided in the specific context of the circumstances.
>
> **Fact** – a phenomenon that is known, for example children grow into adults; or can be proven to be true, for example people affected by dementia lose aspects of their memory.

As already stated, research is a planned process and in order to plan, researchers need to have a clear understanding of the purpose of their research and what they are going to investigate. To do this, they define specific lines of enquiry, or the themes they will investigate. Their lines of enquiry will influence what their sample population will be, how they select their participants, what methodology they will use, what questions they may ask in interviews and/or questionnaires etc. There may be several possible lines of enquiry but for research to remain focused, a researcher in health and social care will probably investigate more than one, but probably no more than five, in any one study or project. Other lines of enquiry could be included in the recommendations for further research made at the end of the project.

When carrying out a literature search or review, where the researcher is only looking at secondary sources, you have to be careful to distinguish between the evidence in each source, which is based on fact, and the evidence which may only be a matter of **opinion**.

> **Key term**
>
> **Opinion** – a personal judgement, perspective or interpretation, which is not necessarily based on fact or knowledge, for example private health care is better than the health care provided by the NHS.

In health and social care research that has been well planned and structured, the researcher explores each of their lines of enquiry into the issue they are investigating by systematically analysing the data presented in each source. Then, based on logical reasoning, the researchers bring together, or synthesise, their own unique arguments based on the evidence from each of their sources to develop new, original thinking about the issue, and to draw conclusions as to how that new knowledge and understanding benefits health and social care. All conclusions drawn from the literature search should take into account any sources of error and bias in their methods, and any uncertainties not proven by their evidence. Research rarely results in absolute certainty, so researchers often use tentative language such as 'supports the concept', or the evidence 'suggests' that X has a beneficial effect on Y, rather than stating it 'proves the concept'. Conclusions should relate back to the original aims of the research but sometimes research can reveal unforeseen benefits that were not identified at the research planning stage.

In health and social care research, because of the difficulties associated with multiple variables – only some of which can be controlled – aspects of the conclusions drawn may incorporate opinion as well as fact.

The issue about practice, however, is that every individual is different and unique – both biologically and because of their past experiences and current circumstances. This means that evidence from even the best health and social care research is not necessarily going to provide the perfect care solution for any single individual. Evidence-based practice should blend the knowledge and understanding gained from good quality research with the unique circumstances of the individual, to derive the most appropriate care for that individual.

Interpreting graphs and tables produced by others

Tables are a useful way of organising data systematically. There are several examples in this unit. Each table should have a heading, and each column within it should have a suitable heading, indicating the units of measurement if appropriate, for example height in metres or weight in kilograms.

Graphs and charts can take a variety of different forms (see Table 4.9) and when exploring secondary sources in a literature search, you need to ensure that you have accurately understood the data in each graph and chart and used it effectively to develop lines of reasoning, arguments and your conclusions.

▶ **Table 4.9:** Features of different formats for presenting numerical data

Format	Features of the format
Tables	• Suitable for quantitative and qualitative data. • Enables systematic and compact presentation of data. • Enables sequencing in ascending or descending order, especially if entered on a spreadsheet. • Useful for recording measurements as they are made, or presenting several different measures in a systematic and compact format.
Line graphs	• Only suitable for plotting continuous data. Plot the dependent variable (e.g. weight) on the y axis against the independent variable (e.g. time) on the x axis. Each point on the graph can be joined by a straight line. • Useful for identifying trends (change over time).
Bar charts	• Used for discrete data. Each bar is separate from other bars, bars have identical widths, varying only in height (or length if horizontal bars). Complex bar charts, e.g. Figure 4.17, can represent sub-categories within the same bar. • Useful for presenting data relating to different categories, e.g. age groups.
Pie charts	• Used to present proportions of a whole, e.g. a population and its sub-groups. The size of each segment is proportionate to the percentage of a 360° circle, the pie. • The size of each sub-group in the data is presented very clearly, but does not represent absolute values unless these are stated separately.
Histograms and distribution curves	• Histograms are only useful for plotting continuous data. Plots a frequency distribution, where each measure is categorised into a class representing a specified range of measures. Each class covers an identical range, e.g. 0–4.9, 5.0–9.9, 10.0–14.9 etc. Each bar is presented with no gaps (unless none of the measures fall into one of the classes). Frequency is shown on the y axis and the classes on the x axis. • In a distribution curve, the frequency values are represented by a curved line. A normal distribution will have a 'bell' shape. • Both provide a visual presentation of an 'average' value, showing the range or spread of values in a data set.

When reading and interpreting graphs and tables, the important points to focus on include:

▶ the title of each chart, table or graph, which should tell you in words what it is illustrating, such as the two variables being measured against each other

▶ the units of measurement of each variable that are used on the x and y axes

▶ the scale used on each axis, particularly noting whether the scale starts at zero

▶ any patterns evident in the chart or graph, for example erratic/consistent trends in a line graph or bar chart, even/uneven split between different segments of a pie chart, normal/skewed distribution of data

▶ any specific notes that might indicate variations recognised by the authors of the article.

You will be expected to analyse some quantitative data and to interpret tables, graphs and charts. Where data is presented in a tabulated format, you could convert it to a suitable graph or chart – and this would make it unique to your search. You can also develop your graph electronically. Figure 4.12 shows ways of presenting large **data sets**, which can have any value, such as measures of height and weight.

Key term

Data set – a large number of values of the same measure from different individuals/tests.

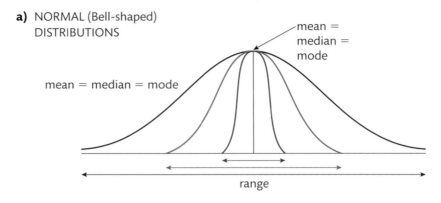

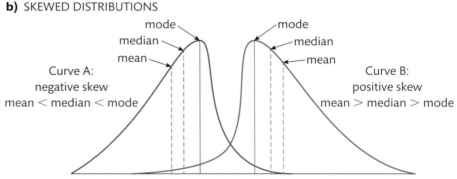

▶ **Figure 4.12:** Distribution curves illustrating different concepts of average for large sets of continuous data

Selecting relevant numerical data

Understanding a research report will involve interpretation of the numerical data it is likely to contain. You should expect to locate and select appropriate numerical data as part of your literature search. As you have seen, visual formats for presenting data help to reveal patterns in the data, which may be difficult to identify just by looking at the tables of the numerical data collected in the research.

Analysis of results

Analysis involves a detailed examination of the data you collect from all your sources and, in addition, being able to make links between the different data from all the sources.

Compilation of data

As part of your literature search, you will probably look at several sources before you find maybe between three and five that are the most relevant to your lines of enquiry. Some articles may contain more qualitative data, while others will have more quantitative data, and some may include both. Some may be more relevant and some less so. You may find one source that includes specific data that is useful evidence to support the arguments you might want to develop. You will need to analyse each article carefully and separately in the first instance, identifying the methodology used in each and the lines of enquiry investigated, the results obtained and the conclusions the researchers drew from their research results.

Your lines of enquiry will help you structure your analysis so that you can interrogate each source for each line of enquiry in turn. You will explore where there are similarities and differences regarding the data each contains about the issue you are investigating. Similarities will enable you to triangulate the data from two or more sources. The differences may reveal interesting points to discuss.

Once you have analysed each source for each line of enquiry separately, you can then start to develop your own arguments, bringing together relevant strands of data and opinion to develop a new understanding, or a different perspective on the issue.

Results and findings

When carrying out primary research, a researcher may be measuring large quantities of data or collecting data over a long period of time. It is, therefore, essential that the measurements made are recorded systematically and clearly, so there is no uncertainty later regarding what was being measured and the actual values measured. Digital devices are helpful but the researcher must be disciplined in keeping records of all the raw data gathered during experiments and observations.

In your literature search, the quantitative data you will be processing is likely to be from published statistical data. You will need to keep full records of the source of each piece of statistical data you find because you will need to list the source in your reference list for the written assessment. However, if you are collating quantitative data from your secondary sources, you still need to take care that you note what the source was actually measuring. For example, the data included in the National Child Measurement Programme case study (see the case study on the National Child Measurement Programme), relates to the incidence of overweight and obesity, which means the number of children with a BMI that indicated they were overweight or obese; the published report includes data separately for overweight and for obesity.

Collating qualitative data also requires discipline and care. You might find it useful to develop a mind map for each source to capture key features of the source, such as the methods used. Alternatively, you might develop a mind map for each line of enquiry that you are investigating, and use colour coding to differentiate the source of the entries you make on each mind map. Mind maps are particularly useful because they enable you to bring together a considerable quantity of qualitative data on a single page.

Methods of analysis valid for the data collected

Sequencing data in numerical order can be helpful, for example statistics relating to different years. Tables can be useful for organising data so it is easier to make comparisons to highlight similarities or differences, perhaps to contrast statistical data local to your area with the equivalent national data. Tables are also useful at a preliminary stage, before presenting quantitative data as a chart or graph; using spreadsheet software will aid this process. One way of avoiding plagiarism is to present data from a source in a different format. For example, if it was presented in the text, create a table, or convert data presented in a table to a chart or graph.

Use of percentages

A percentage enables you to consider numerical data as a proportion of a larger whole. The whole has a numerical value of 100, and sub-sets within that total are expressed as a proportion of 100. Many statistics are expressed as a percentage of the total population, or as a percentage of a smaller population, such as pupils aged 11–15 years old.

▶ **Table 4.10:** Selected statistics regarding smoking habits in England, as a percentage (source: Health & Social Care Information Centre, Statistics on Smoking, England 2015)

Percentage	2013	2003
Smokers among all individuals aged 16 and over	19	26
Pupils aged 11–15 years who have tried smoking	22	42

Table 4.10 illustrates the usefulness of using percentages. The concept of a smaller number is easier to understand than the much larger number of smokers in each of the two categories. Also it enables comparisons to be made between the figures for 2003 and 2013, even though the number of individuals in each group is different.

Use of statistical averages

'**Average**' is a valuable concept to understand in the context of both health and social care research. In statistical contexts, there are three different measures of average: **mean**, **median** and **mode**. Each provides useful information about a data set, but in combination they describe the data set more fully.

The mean is calculated from all the individual values, but it does not provide an indication of the spread of the individual values. If one of the values is much larger or much smaller than the majority of other values, then the mean will be distorted because it will be raised, or lowered, by the one rogue value. In contrast, the median value gives a clearer idea of the spread of individual values, because it means that half the values are bigger and half the values are smaller than the median. The mode, or modal value, provides information about the size of the most commonly found value.

If the values in the data set follow a normal distribution when plotted, then the mean, median and mode have the same value – however deep or shallow the bell curve (see Figure 4.12). The difference between the highest and lowest value in a data set is the range of values. Data generated from individuals is likely to show a considerable **range** because every individual is different.

In health research, the data collected is more likely to be measurable through using instrumentation and chemical analysis, for example analysis of blood or urine samples, so variations in the methodology are likely to be lower. However, in social care research, where the social science methodologies used are less easily controlled and standardised, there may be more variation. The different measures of average then become useful tools to describe the data generated more accurately. For example, if the value of the mode and median is lower than the mean, it suggests that the majority of the values lie towards the lower end of the range. Conversely, if the median and mode are larger than the mean, the majority of the values are higher so there must be some very low values reducing the value of the mean. The researcher might then investigate why their data did not fit.

Making notes and keepings records from source material

Keeping detailed records of all activities carried out in a research project is essential, especially as a formal research project may continue for many years. Your literature search will be completed in a relatively short time, but it is still essential to keep full records of the research you undertake during that period. Unless you keep full records, you are likely to forget the details you need to return to sources that you accessed early on, or thought processes sparked by a discussion about another unit in your study programme. Your record keeping should include:

▶ dates of all actions

▶ reading and thinking relevant to your literature search

▶ notes about the information, concepts, data and so on that you consider might be useful – whether written as text or as visuals, such as mind maps

▶ full details of every source you access, so that if you need to you can return to the same source later.

You will probably access many of your sources electronically. Those that you may want to scrutinise closely might be worth saving, or bookmarking for ease of later access. It will be essential to store any sources you access systematically, so you that you can access them again at a later date. For example, you might use a Word folder to file e-documents or, if you are working from print copies, you will need to file them safely.

Reading techniques

Reading many pages of dense text with few headings, which use sophisticated jargon and are written in an academic style, may contrast considerably with the format of text you are used to reading in this textbook, for example. Additionally, many people have become used to reading just short snippets of text online or on a mobile device, for example social media messages. When searching for sources, you will want to ascertain fairly quickly whether a source is relevant to your search or not. You will need to develop reading techniques, which are valuable in research to ensure that you are accessing the sources you need without wasting time on irrelevant sources. When used in combination, they can speed up a literature search by enabling judgements about the relevance of a source and whether it is worth closer scrutiny.

Searching for key words

Key words (see the section on Identifying, analysing and evaluating source material) are very useful for research purposes, and can help you narrow down your literature search more quickly, to locate relevant sources more effectively. As a starting point when scrutinising the research reports or articles you are going to use for your literature search, you could look for suitable key words.

Scan reading

Once you have identified a few key words, and have started to search for secondary sources, you will then need to scan read each source to see whether it includes the key words you have selected. Scan reading involves passing your eyes over the text quickly, and only for the purpose of locating the key words you are looking for.

Skim reading

If the text includes the key words you are seeking, then you can proceed to skim read it as a quick means of gaining an outline of the information in the text. Skim reading involves passing your eyes quickly, from left to right and top to bottom, over a piece of text to gain an overview of what the whole text is saying.

Scrutiny of text

If after scanning and skimming you consider the text could be relevant and useful to your literature search, then you may choose to scrutinise the text more closely. Scrutiny is a slower process, involving detailed reading of the text to examine the full meaning of its content. You could possibly delay your close scrutiny until you are collating the data from your search and preparing for analysis and evaluation.

▶ Scan reading – Passing your eyes over the text only for the purpose of locating key words.

▶ Skim reading – Passing your eyes quickly from left to right and top to bottom over a piece of text so that you gain an overview of what the whole text is saying.

▶ Scrutiny – A slower process involving detailed reading of a text to examine the full meaning of its content.

These reading techniques are valuable in research because used in combination, they can speed up a literature search by enabling judgements to be made quickly about the relevance of a source and whether it is worth closer scrutiny.

Referencing conventions

By now, you should be aware that you should acknowledge the sources of information you have used when researching for your assignment tasks.

Creating a bibliography

For assignment work, it is sufficient to list the sources you use in a **bibliography** (see Table 4.11). However, in the context of formal research, whether primary or secondary research, acknowledgement of sources is particularly important, because it enables all who are interested in the research reports to know what informed the decisions behind doing the research.

Creating a reference list

A **reference** to a source, to a specific article or data, must be precise. Acknowledgement of your reference source is required whenever you quote facts, knowledge, opinions, new terminology, statistics or use visual images that you have taken specifically from a particular source. This process is known as **citation**.

> **Key terms**
>
> **Bibliography** – a list of published sources relevant to a topic that have been read to increase knowledge and understanding, but which are not necessarily specifically referred to in an essay or research paper.
>
> **Reference** – a source referred to in an essay or research paper.
>
> **Citation** – the process of quoting evidence from other sources.

When citing material, you must first acknowledge this within your own text, immediately after you have cited the information from the source, for example:

'It has been said that research is a planned process in which information is collected systematically for a specific purpose, analysed and reported. (Stretch and Whitehouse, 2010).

In this example, the book has two authors, but if your source has three or more authors, then the convention is that you provide the name of only the first author followed by et al. (Et al. is a Latin term (et alia) meaning 'and others'.) You should then provide a reference list at the end of the text in which you give the full details of all the authors of the sources cited, for example:

'Stretch, B. and Whitehouse, M. (eds) (2010) *BTEC Level 3 National Health and Social Care: Student Book 1*, Harlow: Pearson Education Limited.'

Ways of acknowledging sources used in research have been established over time, and the conventions usually adopted are based on those prevalent in academic communities. The referencing technique most used in health and social care research is known as Harvard referencing, which you may already have been introduced to. Although there are some variations of detail, the key information you should provide for some of the most common types of source is presented in Table 4.11, which shows only a small selection of sources. Universities publish very detailed instructions regarding how they expect learners to present their reference list for a large number of different types of source, including social media.

> **Research**
>
> Use the internet to find out what guidance different universities give to their learners about acknowledging sources in their written work.

▶ **Table 4.11:** Conventions for presenting the details of sources used in a research report or in academic writing

Type of source	Details you should provide and the order in which they should be presented	Example
Book	Author 1, Author 2, Author 3 [or Author 1 followed by 'et al.' if there are many], (Year of publication), Title of book, Publisher.	Stretch, B. and Whitehouse, M. (2010) *Health and Social Care, Book 1*, Pearson Education Ltd.
Journal article	Author 1, Author 2, Author 3 [all authors even if there are many], (Year of publication), Title of article, Title of journal, Volume, (Issue number), Page number(s)	Scobbie, L. Duncan, E.A. Brady, M.C and Wyke, S. (2014) Goal Setting in services delivering community-based stroke rehabilitation: a United Kingdom (UK) wide survey. *Disability and Rehabilitation* 37 (14), 1291–8
Newspaper	Author(s) of article being cited, (year) Title of article, Name of newspaper, date of edition as DD/MM/YYYY	Broomfield, M. (2016) 'Cancer sufferers should lose weight to beat disease, Harvard scientists believe', Independent, 06/06/2016
Government report	Author 1 [if stated] or title of government department, (Year of publication), Title of report, The Stationery Office	Francis, R (2013) Report of the Mid Staffordshire NHS Foundation Trust Public Inquiry, The Stationery Office
Internet source	Author 1, Author 2, Author 3 [if stated], Title of article, full URL, access date DD/MM/YYYY	HSCISC (2015) National Child Measurement Programme, England 2014/15 http://www.hscic.gov.uk/searchcatalogue?productid=19405&q=title%3a%22national+child+measurement+programme access date DD/MM/YYYY

If you have accessed sources to acquire general knowledge and understanding, but you are not using specific pieces of information from that source, then you do not need to mention these sources within the text itself. Instead, you should provide a bibliography at the end of the text, listing these sources using the same technique used in your reference list. In both a bibliography and a reference list, sources are usually listed in alphabetical order of the surname of the first author of each source. The exact sequencing and font styling of the other details will depend on the publisher of the article, but the key details are usually the same.

Assessment practice 4.2

In 2015, the World Health Organization reported on the increasing concern regarding the global phenomenon of antimicrobial resistance (AMR). Infections caused by viruses, bacteria, fungi and parasites have been found to be untreatable, which could mean that in the near future people may die of infections that have become rare since the introduction of antibiotics in the 1950s. Evidence indicates that the treatment of tuberculosis, pneumonia, gonorrhoea and hospital-acquired infections, such as methicillin-resistant staphylococcus aureus (MRSA) and *Clostridium difficile*, is being affected. In 2015, Public Health England reported that antibiotic use in England had increased by 6.5 per cent over four years, and that there were marked differences in the number of antibiotic prescriptions issued in different parts of the country.

Find a minimum of two sources relating to AMR and analyse them.

1 Identify five possible lines of enquiry for a literature search relating to AMR and prepare a formal reference list.

2 Explain the causes of AMR, referring to the sources you have accessed.

3 Based initially on the two sources you have accessed relating to AMR, discuss the difficulties in restricting the use of antibiotics in the UK health and social care sector.

4 Evaluate the effectiveness of possible strategies for limiting the further development of AMR in the UK population.

C Carrying out and reviewing relevant secondary research into a contemporary health and social care issue

For this unit, you will be required to carry out a small research project in the form of a literature search. You will be using secondary sources only. However, you need to be fully aware of a range of research methodologies used to generate primary data, so that you can take these into account when analysing and evaluating any research reports carried out by others.

Your literature search will involve you posing a research question relating to a contemporary issue. Figure 4.3 shows some of the issues that are of public interest and have made recent news headlines. The issues identified are not exhaustive and new issues of similar interest are likely to emerge in the future.

Selecting appropriate secondary sources

You will need to find sources that publish reports of reliable research. You will be seeking to locate and effectively use sources that are authoritative, objective, factual or based on measurable evidence. There are many such sources but the following types of source will probably be most useful for your literature search.

Professional journals

Professional journals publish full reports of original research for an audience of academics and health and social care professionals. Readers are usually also researchers, who may wish to replicate the methods to test the reliability of the results reported. These reports will be written in an academic style. They will give considerable detail about methodology and sophisticated analyses, often using statistical methods to calculate the statistical significance of the results reported. You should be aware of such journals but you are not expected to include such advanced sources in your literature search.

Professional bodies

Professional bodies in health and social care include organisations such as the Health and Care Professions Council (HCPC) and the Nursing and Midwifery Council (NMC). Professional bodies can be a potentially useful source, especially if you are exploring the role of professionals in your literature search. Their websites will include useful information about the professions they regulate or represent, and some interesting reports particularly relating to the work done by their members.

Textbooks

Textbooks are specialist texts written to support individuals studying, for example for a GCSE or a BTEC, or for a higher level medical specialism. Textbooks published in the last ten years are likely to be available in both print and digital formats. A textbook appropriate for BTEC Level 3 National learners is likely to focus on factual information about a specific subject area, such as health and social care or children's play, learning and development.

Textbooks written for specific qualifications, such as this book, provide information focused for that qualification. Some textbooks are written more generally. Textbooks on specific topics that relate to undergraduate modules of study, perhaps for a nursing or social work degree, may provide more detailed information than a BTEC Level 3 National textbook. They may be useful as sources for this unit.

Factual texts written for the general public can also include valid and useful data. Topics such as dementia care, ageing or living with mental health issues may produce texts that fall into both of these categories.

Academic textbooks tend to be more expensive to purchase than books written for a wider audience so the price may be an indicator of how sophisticated and advanced the text is. It is possible to read sample pages of textbooks online before purchasing them, to check whether the text is understandable at your level of study and experience.

With all secondary sources, the authorship and publishing details are important because they may indicate a particular bias or opinion that would reduce a text's objectivity or its content. Another indicator of the objectivity of a book may be the extent to which it includes references to other sources of information, either in specific references (usual in academic texts at level 4 and above) or in a suggested reading list, which is more usual for lower level study and for wider reading by non-specialist members of the public.

Periodicals

Periodicals are magazines published on a regular basis, usually monthly. Examples might be *Community Care, Nursing Times, The Health Service Journal, Early Years Practitioner*. These publications provide reports and opinion that is highly vocational in nature. They may also advertise jobs in the vocational area in which they specialise, which can provide a clue as to the vocational specialism they represent. Articles in periodicals may consider the impact of new or pending legislation or policy changes on their vocational context, reports of action research and more substantial research projects, or they may review new textbooks or equipment. Most periodicals now have social media facilities where subscribers can contribute their own point of view to ongoing debates.

Websites

The internet can be a valuable source of information about a wide range of issues (see the section on Conducting electronic searches). Information about current and past research can be found on many charity websites, for example Diabetes UK or Cancer Research UK and from the websites of government agencies such as the Food Standards Agency or the Care Quality Commission. There are millions of websites. However, when you are doing a literature search, you will be expected to use only the websites of organisations that are likely to be reliable. For example, an 'ac.uk' ending to the organisation's domain name indicates that it is a UK university, or a related academic institution, so the research undertaken and the results produced will comply with UK ethical standards.

Research organisations

Specialised research organisations publish reports of research, for example:

▶ the Wellcome Trust is a leading promoter of medical research

▶ the Medical Research Council is a government funded organisation with a strong reputation in medical research.

Whatever type of source you access, you should always be mindful of its relevance to health and social care in the UK, which is the focus of this unit.

The country of origin of the source, and the date of the research, can mean that the data it is reporting on may not relate well to health and social care provision and practice in the UK.

Country of origin of a source

When using search engines to locate sources, you may encounter secondary sources that relate to countries other than the UK. If the article is about a disease or disorder that is common in the UK as well as in other countries, the content of the article may still be useful. However, health and social care services are often very specific to each country. Even within the UK, the health and social care systems are different across England, Wales, Northern Ireland and Scotland. Therefore, you should focus on data that relates to your own home country and how it makes a difference for health and social care provision in that country.

A source that refers to American departments of government or the American healthcare system will have minimal relevance. Articles using American spellings and vocabulary should warn you that they will be written from an American perspective.

Date of publication of a source

Any data relating to health and social care that is more than a few years old is likely to be out of date for current health and social care provision, services and practice, as they are continuously changing. Even if researching a specific health disorder, an article that was published ten years ago is unlikely to be providing the most up-to-date data.

Conducting electronic searches

You will be familiar with using electronic search engines in your everyday lives to retrieve information quickly. In contrast to this type of spontaneous use of a search engine, as a form of research, your literature search should be a planned process and a part of the planning will be to adopt a systematic procedure for conducting any electronic searches you undertake for this unit.

Using a search engine

The first step in using a search engine is to select appropriate key words from the article you have chosen to research. Entering the selected key word into a search engine will produce a list of sources that use that key word. If the word chosen is part of everyday vocabulary, this may produce millions of 'hits'.

Refining search data to manageable size

You will need to change (refine) your key words to narrow down the number of hits to a more manageable number, say 20–30. There are various techniques to help you, such as those shown in Table 4.12.

▶ **Table 4.12:** Possible techniques for narrowing down an electronic search

Technique	Effect
Key word 1	A large number of hits because the search will include every text that uses the key word.
Key word 1 + Keyword 2	A smaller number of hits because the text will need to contain both words.
Key word 1 + Keyword 2 + Keyword 3	A smaller number of hits.
(Key phrase of 4–6 words)	An even smaller number of hits because the brackets will mean the search will only include sources that use the full phrase.

Unfortunately in terms of narrowing an electronic search, the very large number of sources on the internet about all topics related to health and social care may mean that you will need to experiment with finding key phrases that will reduce the number of hits to a manageable number for your purposes.

Using advanced search tools

The lines of enquiry you select for researching an issue will be the first stage of planning for your literature search. Each line of enquiry should enable you to narrow down your search more specifically, and also to identify more specific key words and phrases. Apart from using key words, in more advanced searches such as those available through academic databases, you may have options to narrow the search more precisely. Examples of criteria that can be used include:

▸ sources only published after a certain date, for example from 2010 onwards

▸ sources relating to the UK only

▸ sources that relate only to a specific aspect of the issue, for example children and young people might be defined more narrowly to 16–18 year olds.

Apart from considering the aspects of the issue you do want to search for, more advanced search tools enable you to set exclusion criteria (aspects you actively do not want to explore). You will not have time to explore many sources for your literature search for this unit. However, if you are using advanced tools, you should be aware of the impact that setting inclusion or exclusion criteria may have on the validity of your literature search, in relation to the aims and success criteria that you set for your search.

When you get to the triangulation phase of your literature search and are seeking specific data to support the arguments you develop, then you may need to modify your selection criteria. However, at this stage, your preliminary reading should have equipped you with better knowledge, understanding and some useful key terminology to use in refining your literature search.

Consideration of the suitability of sources

Not all the sources that an electronic search produces will be appropriate for your literature search. Academic reading techniques (see the section on Reading techniques) are useful to ascertain quickly where a source is likely to be reliable and relevant to the lines of enquiry and arguments that you are developing. It might also help you to classify sources into categories, for example:

▸ very relevant ▸ possibly relevant

▸ marginally relevant/useful single statistic, argument or recommendation.

This will help you to prioritise your reading. You should prioritise those sources that are reliable and draw valid conclusions over those that may be based on personal opinion or that could be biased. You should always consider the extent to which the source is likely to be writing objectively, with due regard to confidentiality or participants, has reported conflicts of interest, whether it is a research report, and whether measures were taken to ensure ethical codes were followed.

Free software is available to download that enables you to keep a record of the sources you have accessed, and some will also automatically generate a reference list. Although you may access a large number of sources, you will only have time to analyse a few of them, so you will not have time to enter a long list, nor can you make use of a large number of sources.

Selecting relevant numerical data [to include graphs, tables and statistics]

You should ensure that you access at least one source that includes numerical data. You will need to demonstrate your ability to describe and analyse quantitative data, and to support your line of enquiry and the conclusions you draw from your analysis of all your sources. You may be able to locate data that helps you identify the scale of the issue, and where and how to incorporate it in your analysis of the issue.

> **Reflect**
>
> Consider how each of the selection criteria for secondary sources might impact on the outcomes of a literature search. How might the impact inform the conclusions you could draw and any recommendations you might make regarding an issue explored in a literature search?

Examining and interpreting graphs [and tables produced by others]

You should refer back to the section on Interpreting graphs and tables produced by others to refresh your understanding of how to examine and interpret graphs.

Recognising bias

Again, this has been explored already in the section on Potential sources of bias and error. Remember that potential sources of bias in presenting graphs, tables and statistics may arise from:

▶ an extended scale on an axis, so it exaggerates a difference that may be very small

▶ a small scale on an axis, so a difference is made to appear smaller than it really is

▶ omission of data, so that unexpected or 'outlying' values (ones that distort the mean/median/mode) are ignored, because the value reduces the size of a difference that would otherwise be more marked, or establishes a difference that does not fit with the conclusions that could otherwise be drawn

▶ only selecting sets of quantitative data that support the arguments and conclusions you want to draw from the study, and ignoring other data that is contrary to that position.

You should consider any of these possibilities when analysing visual representations of quantitative data.

Evaluation of research

Examining the content of secondary materials [including introduction, body of text, conclusion]

To read this and any other source you will need to analyse the text of each source you access in detail.

▶ Use academic reading skills as outlined in the section on Reading techniques.

▶ Assess the advantages and disadvantages of the research methodologies used in the article and each source.

▶ Make links between the recommendations made in each source and ways in which the research could be used to benefit people who use health and social care services.

Many of these points have been covered in detail earlier in this unit so brief summaries only are provided here.

Academic reading [to include surveying structure of source materials]

Academic reading differs from reading for pleasure, in that you do not necessarily start reading the source at the beginning and continue until you have reached the end. Generally, you will use your key words to start to look for the information of interest to you.

You can then select the chapter of the book, the article in the journal or the section of the government report that seems most relevant to your literature search. In a book, you can use the chapter titles listed in the contents page for broad topics, and the index at the back of the book to locate information relating to your key words. For a government report, there may be an executive summary at the start of the document, which provides some detail and an overview of the conclusions and any recommendations.

Advantages and limitations of research sources and methodologies [e.g. access to data]

For your literature search, a source that is investigating the same phenomenon in the same sample population as your line of enquiry will be of particular interest to you. No single source will provide all the information available, and in your literature search you should aim to triangulate (see the section on Methods of analysis and drawing conclusions) aspects of the data in one source with data in another source. If you are unable to find another source that presents similar results and conclusions, then you will need to make a judgement about the reliability and validity of the data and the arguments developed in the source. Any weakness in the reliability of a source should be recognised explicitly when writing about your literature search. Arguments presented in the source may still be useful, but they will be based on less secure evidence, so any conclusions you draw can be less certain and will need to be stated more tentatively/cautiously.

Validity and reliability of data researched

All researchers should take into account the reliability and validity of each their sources, be it secondary data from published sources or their data gathered from primary research. Researchers should explicitly recognise any limitations of their methodology in their analysis and evaluation so that the conclusions and recommendations they make are as valid as possible. For example, a source that you consider to be reliable and which contains a well-argued analysis, based on empirical evidence or thoroughly researched secondary sources, should carry more weight when you develop your own arguments than a source for which these characteristics are less clearly present.

Validity depends on what claims are made about a piece of research and how well the claims are supported by the evidence or results from the research. Validity should be considered in relation to various aspects of research. You might use the questions in Table 4.13 when you are analysing your own method/approach to your literature search and to any secondary sources that you use.

▶ **Table 4.13:** Suggestions for assessing the validity of a secondary source

Validity in the context of different aspects of the research	Possible questions to interrogate a source to test its validity
Research methodology used	• Are the methods appropriate for the purpose of the research? • Do the methods actually measure what is being claimed they are measuring? • What steps were taken to ensure their methods gave reliable results? Were these sufficient? • How did the researchers take account of ethical considerations in designing the research?
Results from research	• Is the data presented based on measurable evidence? • Have the results been presented objectively? • To what extent have the researchers presented arguments that are based on the evidence in their results? • Have the researchers considered all the results from their research? • Are their arguments logical?
Recommendations from the research	• To what extent are the recommendations related to the original stated purpose of the research? • Have the researchers considered all their evidence in making their recommendations? • Have the researchers taken account of any potential bias or errors in their data when making their recommendations?

A secondary source or a literature search that does not consider the extent to which the methods adopted are appropriate, or bases any recommendations that do not take account of all the data available from the research, will have limited validity.

Reliability is about the extent to which the research can be reproduced. Reliable research should produce the same results when repeated by another researcher using exactly the same methods. In a scientific experiment, the scientist must test the reliability of their equipment so they can be sure it is operating consistently, before they commence experiments.

Scientific methods and social science methods involve controls to check that the variable being investigated is not caused by the research itself. In an experiment, results may be carried out in duplicate or triplicate with an average value calculated, in order to eliminate unavoidable variations in each test. If a large number of measurements are taken of the same variable, it is possible to apply statistical analysis to assess the degree of probability of the accuracy of their results. See Figure 4.13.

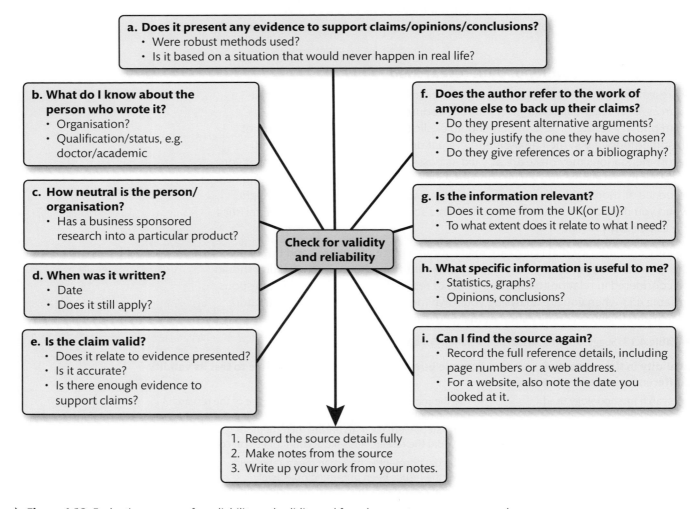

a. Does it present any evidence to support claims/opinions/conclusions?
- Were robust methods used?
- Is it based on a situation that would never happen in real life?

b. What do I know about the person who wrote it?
- Organisation?
- Qualification/status, e.g. doctor/academic

c. How neutral is the person/ organisation?
- Has a business sponsored research into a particular product?

d. When was it written?
- Date
- Does it still apply?

e. Is the claim valid?
- Does it relate to evidence presented?
- Is it accurate?
- Is there enough evidence to support claims?

Check for validity and reliability

f. Does the author refer to the work of anyone else to back up their claims?
- Do they present alternative arguments?
- Do they justify the one they have chosen?
- Do they give references or a bibliography?

g. Is the information relevant?
- Does it come from the UK(or EU)?
- To what extent does it relate to what I need?

h. What specific information is useful to me?
- Statistics, graphs?
- Opinions, conclusions?

i. Can I find the source again?
- Record the full reference details, including page numbers or a web address.
- For a website, also note the date you looked at it.

1. Record the source details fully
2. Make notes from the source
3. Write up your work from your notes.

▶ **Figure 4.13:** Evaluating a source for reliability and validity and for relevance to your own research

Recommendations

An important outcome of any piece of research into health and social care is that the researchers make recommendations, which should relate to the original purpose of the research, taking into account any limitations associated with your research methodology, such as what criteria you selected to narrow your search at the start. When making recommendations, you should always state clearly the extent to which they apply to a specific context – to, for example, 16–18 year olds – or can be generalised more widely – to, for example, all children and young people.

In a small scale project, such as your literature search, you would make perhaps no more than four or five recommendations. In more substantial formal research projects, there may be many more recommendations. An extreme example is the Francis Report (2013), which made 290 recommendations because there was so much amiss at the Mid Staffordshire Foundation Hospital Trust. Its recommendations led to the Care Act 2014, thus effecting significant social policy change, underpinned by law. In turn, this has affected working practices for managers and carers in services provided in hospitals, residential care and in the community. The impact of these changes will no doubt be monitored in research reports over the coming years. However, the steps taken as a consequence of the Francis recommendations will greatly reduce or eliminate a repeat of the poor standards of care associated with the Mid Staffordshire Foundation Hospital Trust.

Potential for further development of a research area

You should be able to state two or three recommendations to develop your literature search further. Possibilities that you might consider could include:

▶ exploring one of your lines of enquiry in more depth

▶ increasing the breadth of your lines of enquiry, for example to compare different service user groups or areas of provision

▶ carrying out a piece of primary research, perhaps suggesting a small action research project to 'test' a hypothesis that you have developed as a conclusion from your literature search.

Useful perspectives to consider with regards to developing your own research are the extent to which your literature search enables you to generalise your conclusions from the specific; or conversely, the extent to which your conclusions might be narrowed down and applicable to a more specific aspect of health and social care.

Potential for development of working practice and provision of services

This is your opportunity to relate your research to health and social care specifically rather than to the methods you have used. You should have completed the scrutiny of at least two articles and discussed, analysed and evaluated the data they contain thoroughly, so that you have a clear understanding of them. You should also have developed two to three lines of enquiry that enable you to link the different sources you have used, and to draw your own conclusions that are unique to your literature search. Your new conclusions should lead to a different understanding, one that you did not know before you started your literature search. The combination of conclusions you draw should also be different from the separate conclusions already published in the sources you have used.

You should also have thought about how your literature search could lead to improvements in health and social care, remembering the themes regarding the purpose of research in this unit are:

▶ improving outcomes for people using services

▶ informing policy and practice

▶ extending knowledge and understanding

▶ identifying gaps in provision.

You should be able to assess the extent to which the data might suggest possible developments that could be made into working practices and the provision of services. Possible developments relating to working practices are suggested in Figure 4.14.

> **Research**
>
> Investigate the recommendations made by the Francis Report and select examples that relate to each of the purposes of research identified in this unit.

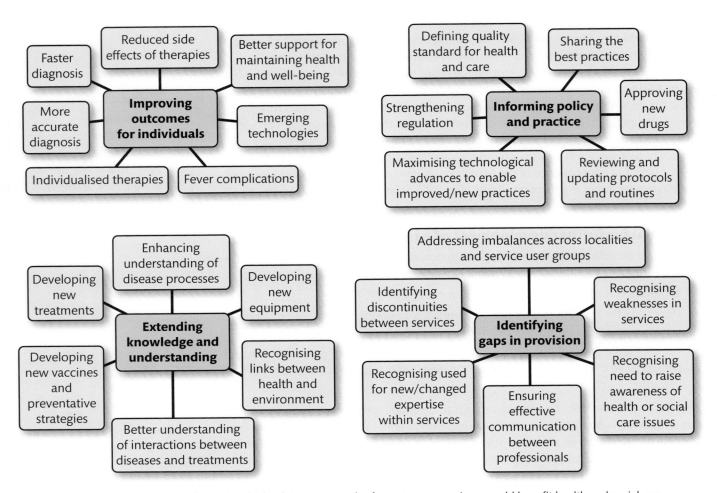

▶ **Figure 4.14:** Some of the potential ways in which a literature search of a contemporary issue could benefit health and social care

When commenting on the potential for further development of your research, you might refer back to the mind map you developed earlier and consider the lines of enquiry that you chose not to develop, due to lack of time. However, whatever you use to help you with this aspect of your literature search, you should ensure that you:

▶ provide at least two suggestions for each of working practices and provision, even if they are remote from the immediate focus of your literature search
▶ justify your suggestions, giving reasons for each
▶ briefly indicate what methodology might be appropriate
▶ outline the benefit to individuals using health and social care services.

The potential development you indicate might be a very direct consequence of your conclusions, or may be more removed – so you would need to be able to explain the links. For example, you may suggest that more research is carried out on the most effective means of improving support for children and young people affected by mental health issues, without necessarily specifying exactly what form this support should take.

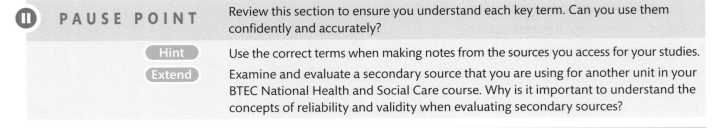

PAUSE POINT   Review this section to ensure you understand each key term. Can you use them confidently and accurately?

Hint   Use the correct terms when making notes from the sources you access for your studies.

Extend   Examine and evaluate a secondary source that you are using for another unit in your BTEC National Health and Social Care course. Why is it important to understand the concepts of reliability and validity when evaluating secondary sources?

Wider applications of research

Making recommendations for potential future areas of research

The outcomes, or conclusions, drawn from one research study may lead to even more possible lines of enquiry to investigate regarding an issue. Most reports of research in health and social care will include recommendations for future areas of research, which might include:

▶ investigating a local perspective to compare with a national one, or vice versa

▶ researching the impact of the issue on a different service user group from the one already studied

▶ comparing practices in one type of provision compared with another type of provision

▶ investigating the impact of a change in policy or procedure on a different group of health or social care workers

▶ measuring the impact of a change in health and social care over a longer timescale.

Recommendations of this sort, and others, should be evident in at least some of the secondary sources you use in your literature search. As indicated, you should be able to make recommendations of how your research might be taken forward by others wishing to extend your study. Your recommendations could involve primary or secondary research methodologies or a combination of both.

Implications of research for health and social care practice

Research that is relevant to health and social care practice will relate to practical aspects of what individual health and social care workers are actually doing in their day-to-day work. Possible implications might relate to the following considerations.

▶ What is the practice activity that the research is providing data about, for example techniques for healing leg ulcers? Could this aspect of wound healing be applied to other types of wound?

▶ What equipment and so on is required? How will its cost be met?

▶ Who carries out a particular care, or care-related activity, for example is this a nurse, a care worker or an informal carer?

▶ Where does a local health or social care activity take place, is it in the patient's home, in a health centre or in a district general hospital?

▶ Which is the best way to carry out a process, is it perhaps Method 1 or Method 2?

▶ When is the best timing of the process for maximum benefit, for example after a meal or before eating?

▶ Why is a process carried out, is the process still necessary in the context of new technologies, for example?

▶ How is the process carried out, what are the stages and sequencing of the process?

In a small literature search, such as that required for this unit, you will not be able to address answers to so many questions. However, you should consider the extent to which your conclusions might lead to changes in health and social care practices.

Implications of research for health and social care service provision

As explained earlier, the planning and organisation of health and social care provision is an important factor influencing an individual's access to the service/services they need. Professional researchers working for government, local planners, medical experts and others commission research from other organisations, or establish a dedicated research team, to research future needs for health and social care services. You should ensure that you include some sources in your literature search that discuss provision of services, and which make recommendations for change or improvements to services.

Assessment practice 4.3

In 2016, the Stroke Association reported that 1.2 million people in the UK were living as stroke survivors. Over a third of those surviving stroke in England, Wales and Northern Ireland require help with daily living activities after discharge from hospital. Furthermore, although strokes are the fourth most common cause of death in the UK, the incidence of strokes decreased by 19 per cent between 1990 and 2010. Those over 55 are most likely to have a stroke. However, a quarter of all strokes occur in people of working age. There are differences in incidence in different regions, and across different ethnicities. Certain lifestyle factors increase the risk of stroke.

Selected data, from a 2014 report of a UK-wide online survey of health professionals providing community-based stroke rehabilitation, indicated that of the over 400 service providers who responded, 83 per cent of their service users received support in their own home; and 53 per cent of the services provided support for between 5 and 12 weeks, involving two to five sessions per week. Although the type of service varied, 82 per cent of the teams were multidisciplinary. The report stated that 85 per cent of all teams included a physiotherapist, 84 per cent an occupational therapist, 64 per cent a speech and language therapist and 70 per cent an assistant. Only 19 per cent of the teams included a doctor. Other professionals were also involved in some teams.

1 Present the data in the above scenario in a systematic format.

2 Describe **two** possible lines of enquiry that could be investigated in a literature search and justify your choice.

3 Locate and analyse **two** secondary sources related to one of these lines of enquiry and develop reasoned arguments regarding how community-based rehabilitation service provision can enable survivors of stroke to lead independent lives in their own home.

4 Evaluate the effectiveness of rehabilitation services for patients following a stroke. **(15 marks)**

Further reading and resources

Aveyard, H. (2014) *Doing A Literature Review In Health And Social Care: A Practical Guide*, New York, NY: Open University Press/McGraw-Hill Education.

Denscobe, M. (2014) *The Good Research Guide: For Small-Scale Social Research*, Oxford: Open University Press

Stretch, B. and Whitehouse, M. (2010) *BTEC Level 3 National Health and Social Care: Student Book 1*, Harlow: Pearson Education Limited.

Websites

Charities sponsoring health and social care research into specific diseases/disorders

www.cancerresearchuk.org
Cancer Research UK: Information about all types of cancer, symptoms, treatments and prevention.

www.dementiauk.org
Dementia UK: Information about dementia, symptoms, treatments and prevention.

www.diabetes.org.uk
Diabetes UK: Information about diabetes, symptoms, treatments and prevention.

www.mentalhealth.org.uk
Mental Health Foundation: Research and support for people with mental health problems.

Websites

Government agencies

www.ons.gov.uk
Office for National Statistics: Official UK statistics about people, populations and communities.

www.gov.uk/government/organisations/public-health-england
Public Health England: Government agency responsible for monitoring and improving public health.

www.hra.nhs.uk
Health Research Authority: regulates and protects the interests of the public in health research.

www.hscic.gov.uk
NHS Digital: Provides information, data and IT systems for health and social care.

www.cqc.org.uk
Care Quality Commission: Monitors, inspects and regulates health and social care in England.

www.england.nhs.uk
NHS England.

www.health-ni.gov.uk
Department of Health – Northern Ireland.

www.wales.nhs.uk
NHS Wales.

Charities specialising in research into health and social care issues

www.kingsfund.org.uk
The Kings Fund: Charity which aims to improve health and care in England.

www.nuffieldtrust.org.uk
Nuffield Trust: Charity which aims to improve health and care in the UK.

www.wellcome.ac.uk
Wellcome Trust: Charitable foundation supporting scientists and researchers.

www.jrct.org.uk
The Joseph Rowntree Charitable Trust: Makes funding available by application for investigation in root causes of conflict and injustice.

www.barnardos.org.uk
Barnado's: Charity supporting children and young people.

www.actionforchildren.org.uk
Action for Children: Charity working to support children and young people.

Professional organisations

www.nmc.org.uk
Nursing and Midwifery Council: Regulates nurses and midwives in the UK.

www.hcpc-uk.org
Health and Care Professions Council (HCPC): Regulates and keeps a register of health and care professionals.

www.adass.org.uk
Association of Directors of Adult Social Services.

www.adcs.org.uk
Association of Directors of Children's Services.

THINK ▶FUTURE

Lilja Jones

Healthcare Assistant (HCA)

I'm a healthcare assistant on a busy orthopaedic ward. I provide personal care for patients, about half of whom are elderly, recovering from broken bones after falls at home. They tend to stay in hospital a long time and can get depressed.

Sister Smith, the ward sister, is carrying out an action research project for her Master's degree, studying the role of HCAs in reducing depression in these patients. I'm one of four HCAs participating in her research. She is observing me regularly in my interactions with the older patients. The four HCAs also take part in a weekly focus group meeting with Sister Smith to discuss the progress of our patients.

My understanding of the principles of research helps me to make more systematic contributions to the action research project. I'm more aware now of how I interact with my patients, so my practice is becoming more consistent for all patients. I also feel more confident in finding out more information independently, so I can better understand depression as an illness.

Focusing your skills

Extending your knowledge and understanding of health conditions affecting individuals using health and social care services

Your ability to meet the needs of individuals using health and social care services will be enhanced if you have a good understanding of the health conditions giving rise to their health and/or care needs.

- Use your literature search skills to access further information about depression, and in particular, the impact of lengthy stays in hospital on the wellbeing of elderly patients.
- Practise your skills of observation to assess the impact of care interventions in a clinical setting on the patients you care for by developing a simple observation checklist to document the frequency with which each patient demonstrates a positive behaviour.
- Triangulate what you have learned about what improves the morale of elderly patients on an orthopaedic ward with the information you have retrieved from your

literature search, so that you can evaluate objectively the effectiveness of different care interventions.

Improving your practice skills

Developing self-awareness about the effectiveness of your own skills in delivering personal care should help you to strengthen your support for each patient. A good way of doing this is to maintain a reflective diary or log of specific situations and incidents as they occur in your working day.

- Make notes of those incidents which have been challenging for you in some way, or where you have gained a new insight into an aspect of your work. Record the date, key context details (what/who/when/where/why/how etc) and then make a note of your personal feelings and points of learning from the experience, so that you can refer back to it if a similar situation should arise.
- Develop your skills in asking reflective, open questions of your peer healthcare assistants, your supervisor and others who work with you regularly, to help you to enhance your practice skills.

Getting ready for assessment

This Assessment Outcome has been written to help you to do your best when you take the assessment test. Read through it carefully and ask your tutor if there is anything you are still not sure about.

About the test

Part A will be issued to you a set period of time before the date of the Part B written assessment. Part A will consist of:

- **article 1** relating to research into a current health issue
- **article 2** relating to research into a current social care issue.

In the supervised time you are allocated for Part A, you will need to choose which of the two articles you will use as the basis of your own literature search relating to the issue explored in the article you have chosen. Once you have chosen the article, all your efforts in Part A should relate only to this one article. You will need to carry out your literature search, and allocate time towards the end of Part A to prepare the notes you will be allowed to take into the assessment room where you will sit the Part B written assessment. You will also need to prepare a formal list of the sources you have used to submit in your taskbook. You will work independently throughout Part A and will receive no feedback from your tutor.

The **Part B** controlled written assessment has two sections, one relating to each of the two articles. The full text of each article is included in the Part B paper.

Each section has questions that are contextualised to the relevant article, so check to make sure you go to the correct section for the article you have chosen. Questions may have sub-questions identified as a), b), c) and so on. It is unlikely that a question will have more than three sub-questions. The questions will require you to demonstrate that you:

- have acquired a full understanding of the article you have chosen
- have carried out an effective literature search relevant to an issue triggered by the article

- can apply your learning from any aspect of the unit content and from your literature search by demonstrating analytical and evaluative skills to answer the questions.

All questions on your chosen article are compulsory, and you should provide an extended answer to each one. Marks are allocated using mark bands 0–4. To earn the marks awarded for the higher mark bands, you will need to demonstrate your ability to apply your knowledge and understanding of the current issue using analytical and evaluative skills in a way that is relevant to the question.

Other points relating to your activity during Part A include the following.

- Aim to ensure you can relate data from your own literature search, either directly or indirectly, through your lines of enquiry and arguments to the four purposes of health and social care detailed in Section A of the unit content. Also ensure you can link your search clearly to the Part A article.
- Make sure the sources you use are current – aim to select sources that have been published within the last five years.
- Prepare a formal reference list of your sources that you can print and bring to the Part B assessment room.
- Prepare the notes you will take in to the Part B assessment in good time, do not leave it to the last minute. The notes you take in to the Part B assessment are likely to be specially prepared and not the original notes you make about each source, though they may include key aspects of your original notes.
- The notes you take in should be presented systematically, in such a way that helps you recall details about the sources and your reasoning during Part A. Mind maps, flow charts, use of bold, highlighting and colour etc could help you navigate through your notes more quickly during the Part B assessment.
- As the guidelines for assessment can change, you should refer to the official assessment guidance on the Pearson Qualifications website for the latest definitive guidance.

Sitting the test

- Listen to, and read carefully, any instructions that you are given at the start of the Part B assessment.
- At the start of Part B, locate the section relating to your chosen article.
- Attach the list of sources you have used in your literature search in the space allocated in the taskbook.
- Allocate the first ten minutes of the assessment time to reading each of the questions for your article carefully and ensure you understand the different focus of each question. You could annotate the Part B paper at this stage if you wish.
- Re-read the question to ensure you understand fully what is required by the question.
- Take three to four minutes to plan your response to each question, using the Part A notes you have brought with you. Pay full attention to the command verbs and defining phrases in the question and ensure you consider all parts of the question while you are preparing notes that plan for your answer.
- Decide the order or sequence in which you are going to present the points you make in your answer before writing up your response.
- If you get 'stuck' on a question and are not sure what is expected, move on to the next question and come back to this question at a later stage. Sometimes, a 'block' on your thinking on one question can be released by a trigger in the answer you are writing for a different question.
- Make sure you refer to the impact of research on health and social care practice – on the individuals using services, the impact on informing policy and on developing knowledge and understanding.
- Scan your response to check that you have at least met the Band 2 requirements, and that your meaning is clear. Cross out your planning notes neatly.
- Move to the next question and repeat the planning, sequencing and writing up process, again always referring carefully to the question.
- Allow time at the end of Part B to check your responses to each question against the expectations defined by the mark bands, amending or adding to each response, if possible, to strengthen it so that it meets all aspects of the question fully.
- Remember, you will only be awarded marks from the mark scheme if the points you make are included in your response to the relevant question. The points should be made in a way that is relevant to the question. Marks cannot be transferred from one question to another, so you need to ensure that the points you make are included in your response to the question for which the marks about those points are allocated. It could be relevant to refer to a source or piece of data more than once across the different questions. However, to be relevant to the question it is likely that you will be using the data in a different way in each of the questions.
- Aim to refer to between three and five sources in the course of your responses, or to demonstrate that you have read and fully understood the content of each source. However, referring to a source just for the sake of it, without demonstrating understanding of its content, is unlikely to add significantly to your marks.
- You cannot lose marks for a wrong answer; but blank spaces earn no marks and very short answers are likely to earn only a few marks.

> Arrive in good time so you are calm and focused, making sure you have brought your pre-prepared notes with you.

Command word	Definition – what it is asking you to do
Describe	Provide a thorough account, drawing on data from the article and the sources you have researched as relevant to the question asked in the assessment.
Explain	Provide possible reasons for the aspect of the issue required by the question.
Discuss	Consider the issue in detail, e.g. different lines of enquiry you have investigated and different arguments presented in your sources.
Assess	Consider the importance or significance of the evidence you have researched in relation to the question asked, leading to a reasoned judgement on the evidence, e.g. its characteristics, quality, extent or other feature relevant to the question asked.
Analyse	Detailed, systematic and reasoned exploration of the aspect of the issue required by the question based on 2–3 lines of enquiry.
Evaluate	Make a judgement, based on all the relevant information or data and arguments you have explored in your answer to the question.
Justify	Provide logical reasons based on the evidence (data and arguments you have presented) to the examiner to demonstrate you understand the issue thoroughly.

Remember, responses that are mostly descriptive will only earn a few marks whereas responses that include discussion, analysis and evaluation, consider several lines of enquiry, and give the reasoning that you developed from the secondary sources you accessed, analysed and evaluated in your literature search are likely to earn more marks. Presenting well-structured answers and drawing conclusions will also benefit your marks.

Part A

- Start work on the assessment immediately, in the first supervised session on your timetable.

- Read all the instructions provided carefully and ensure you fully understand what is required of you for Part A. Annotate the document if you find this helpful (but be mindful that you will receive only one copy of Part A, so avoid making the original text unreadable).

- Read both articles carefully, making a few notes, if this will be helpful to you.

- You must carry out your research independently, using a minimum of two secondary sources, in addition to the chosen article.

- Keep full records of all the sources you use – you may find it helpful to use software available to do this, so that the full titles and universal reference links (URLs) are automatically recorded, along with the access dates and other details, for your reference list.

- You should choose the article you are going to research early so that you allow sufficient time for the work involved in carrying out the research and condensing the notes that you can take into the examination room for Part B. Your tutor will tell you how many pages of notes you can take into Part B and in what format.

- Allocate time for each of the activities required to carry out your literature search, such as finding relevant sources to analyse and evaluate and developing potential lines of reasoning that will assist you in answering the questions in Part B of the assessment.

Part B

- For Part B, you should plan your time carefully to write your response to each question, and allow another time to review your response and amend/add to it, before moving to the next question. With the 10 minutes already spent at the beginning reading and understanding the differences between the questions, you should have 10-20 minutes at the end to check all your responses and add any details that you may have overlooked.

- Start planning your response to each question by making brief notes in the taskbook under each question, as ideas/points occur to you when you read each question at the start. Add to these and organise the points you want to make before writing your actual response to each question. Make sure that you provide sufficient detail in your responses to demonstrate your ability to explain, analyse and evaluate. Providing just a description will limit your marks.

Remember you will not lose marks for incorrect or irrelevant points in your extended answers, but you should aim to provide a significant response to each of the questions, making several points for each and in such a way that they are relevant responses to the question. Notes alone will not be sufficient to earn many marks. With so many marks allocated to each of a small number of questions, failing to supply a response, or only providing a weak response to one of the questions will very seriously affect the total number of marks you will earn for this unit, even if you earn good marks on the other questions.

Sample answers

If you organised your time well, you will have had plenty of time to analyse and evaluate the Part A source that you selected before the Part B assessment. Although a minimum of two sources are specified for your literature search, you should aim to use between five and ten sources. The extra knowledge and understanding gained should better enable you to produce responses that earn marks from the higher mark bands. This number of sources should enable you to explore two to three lines of enquiry relating to the article you have chosen (**either** Article 1 **or** Article 2, not both). Your skill will be to use your learning from studying this unit, and the knowledge and understanding of the issue that you have acquired over the duration of Part A, to produce appropriate answers in the Part B assessment.

Look at the sample questions that follow and our tips on how to answer them well.

Answering extended answer questions

Example:

These examples are based on *Is mental health care improving?*, a research report published by The Health Foundation in March 2015. The report is available at www.health.org.uk/sites/default/files/IsMentalHealthCareImproving.pdf

Question 1: What research techniques have been used to collect and present the data in this report? In your answer you should consider the reliability of the results of the research and the validity of the conclusions drawn.

Answer: The article presents statistics about the quality of mental health care in England for adults affected by common mental health problems, adults with severe mental health problems and services for children and young people. All the data was obtained from secondary sources so the method used was a literature search. The article lists 79 references and includes lots of statistics about the number of people affected by mental illnesses. The article includes several line graphs which help to show how various factors associated with mental health problems have changed in recent years. The research results are presented as a report with lots of sub-headings which help to identify the different variables studied in the research. There were no ethical issues regarding the research because it was a literature search and did not involve participants.

> Weak answer.

In this answer, the overall research method has been described at a basic level and there is acknowledgement of the scale of the study from the number of references. The presentation of the data is described and some very limited evaluative comments are included. Overall, the answer is sufficient for Band 2 marks. Using more specialist language, such as differentiating between quantitative and qualitative data, and paying more attention to the full requirements of the question would have earned more marks. Commenting specifically on reliability of the data, for example that many of the statistics were published by government departments, so are likely to be reliable, which in turn adds validity to the conclusions, and mentioning that the research only relates to England, so the conclusions may not apply in Wales or Northern Ireland, could have earned some Band 3 marks.

Question 2: What are the implications of this research for individuals with mental health problems and for mental healthcare services? Refer to the article and to your secondary research in your answer

Answer: The article identifies that about a fifth of people in England have a mental health problem. The charity Mind states that mental health problems are 25 per cent higher in Northern Ireland and identifies regional differences in England. The Health and Safety Executive reported a 60 per cent increase between 2011/12 and 2014/15 in the number of employees experiencing common mental health problems for the first time and taking time off work.

> Better answer.

This means that mental health problems affect the economy and the article says that in 2009/10 mental health problems was estimated to cost £105 billion in a year. The article states that a higher proportion of prisoners are affected by mental health problems than in the general population. This could be because people develop mental health problems while in prison or that mental health problems are more likely to lead to behaviours that result in being sent to prison. Drug addiction is a major problem in prisons and is generally known to be linked to mental health problems. Mental health is therefore a serious problem for individuals and for the country.

The Mental Health Foundation claims that relationships people have with each other are important for their mental health and they say that anything which helps people to have a social life rather than live in isolation is good. Having a job helps because it means people have to interact with their workmates and the article says that more people with mental health problems are now getting jobs. The article reports that support for people with common mental health problems has improved since 2010 but that more people with mental health problems now need hospital residential care which usually means they have severe mental health problems. Recent news relating to Southern Health NHS Foundation Trust shows that service users may die because support is inadequate. However, the article says that one of the problems in assessing the quality of services for those with mental health problems is that there is insufficient information available about the services in some areas of the country. This is especially the case for services for children and young people and sometimes they are admitted to hospital a long distance from their homes which adds to their problems. Psychological therapies and antidepressants can be prescribed to help those with common mental health problems and the article says there are targets for 15 per cent to start such treatments each year. The target is for therapy to start within 28 days of being referred but this is not being achieved for everyone.

Overall, care services for people with mental health problems need to be both improved and expanded to cope with the increasing number of people needing the services and to ensure that the quality of the services improves. More information about services so the best practices could be identified to improve other provision would also help as would more data about the effectiveness of different treatments.

> This is a better answer, justifying Band 3 marks. The response addresses the question and includes more detailed information, with specific examples, and also attempts to make links between different lines of enquiry. A reasonably thorough understanding of the issues around mental health is demonstrated and several sources from the literature search are referred to appropriately, and link to the content of the article. Some unsubstantiated claims are made such as regarding drug addiction and mental health, but overall there is good evidence of an effective literature search. Some recommendations are made. Points might be presented more systematically, and analysis and evaluative comments could be more evident to achieve Band 4 marks.

Work Experience in Health and Social Care 6

Getting to know your unit

If you are thinking about a career in health and social care, work experience is a good way of seeing if it is right for you by making you aware of the tasks and activities you may be required to do. In this unit, you will reflect on and develop the personal attributes and skills you need to work in this sector, and learn about the expectations of different professional roles. You will also develop a plan to support your learning while on a work experience placement, and record and monitor your progress in a work experience log. This is a practical unit that will teach you the benefits of work experience and provide a placement opportunity in which you can develop, apply and reflect on knowledge and skills in a real-life situation.

How you will be assessed

This unit is assessed through a series of internally assessed tasks set by your tutor and based on evidence you will collect in your work experience log. Throughout this unit, you will find assessment practices that will help you prepare for your final assessment. These do not contribute towards your final grade but give you an opportunity to practise so it is important that you complete them to the best of your ability. Your tutor can then advise you on how to do even better in your final assessment.

The final assessment set by your tutor will consist of several tasks based on your work experience placement, designed to meet the criteria in the assessment criteria table.

The following are examples of the sort of activities you can expect.

▶ Writing a letter applying for a work experience placement, in which you analyse and justify how work experience supports the development of your skills, attributes, understanding and knowledge, as preparation for work in the health and social care sector.

▶ Producing an action plan for your work experience, accompanied by a commentary explaining and assessing how well the plan provides support for work experience and your own learning and development.

▶ Preparing a report on your responsibilities and how you demonstrated and selected different work-related skills while on work experience.

▶ Writing a review of your work experience in which you reflect on the skills you developed and how it has contributed to your personal and professional development.

Assessment criteria

This table shows what you must do in order to achieve a **Pass**, **Merit** or **Distinction** grade, and where you can find activities to help you.

Pass	**Merit**	**Distinction**
Learning aim Examine the benefits of work experience in health and social care for own learning and development		
A.P1 Explain how work experience can support the development of own professional skills and personal attributes for work in the health and social care sector. **Assessment practice 6.1**	**A.M1** Analyse how work experience can provide support in gaining a realistic understanding of the health and social care sector. **Assessment practice 6.1**	**AB.D1** Justify the benefits of preparation in supporting own understanding of the expectations of work experience. **Assessment practice 6.2**
A.P2 Discuss ways in which work experience can inform own career choices and help prepare for employment in the health and social care sector. **Assessment practice 6.1**		
Learning aim B Develop a work experience plan to support own learning and development		
B.P3 Explain own responsibilities and limitations on work experience placement. **Assessment practice 6.2**	**B.M2** Assess the importance of own work experience plan to support own learning and development. **Assessment practice 6.2**	
B.P4 Explain how to meet own specific personal and professional goals while on work placement. **Assessment practice 6.2**		
Learning aim C Carry out work experience tasks to meet set objectives		
C.P5 Demonstrate work-related skills to meet set objectives for work experience tasks. **Assessment practice 6.3**	**C.M3** Demonstrate work-related skills with confidence and proficiency to meet objectives in different situations. **Assessment practice 6.3**	**C.D2** Demonstrate work-related skills proficiently, taking the initiative to carry out activities according to own responsibilities and setting's procedures and selecting appropriate skills and techniques for different situations. **Assessment practice 6.3**
C.P6 Discuss ways in which work shadowing and observation can support development of own skills while on work placement. **Assessment practice 6.3**		
Learning aim D Reflect on how work experience influences own personal and professional development		
D.P7 Review own strengths and areas for development in response to feedback on work experience placement. **Assessment practice 6.4**	**D.M4** Assess how self-reflection can contribute to personal and professional development in work experience placement. **Assessment practice 6.4**	**D.D3** Justify how planning for and reflecting on skills developed during own work experience placement have informed own future plans for personal and professional development. **Assessment practice 6.4**
D.P8 Produce a personal and professional development plan which identifies improvements to own skills for future development. **Assessment practice 6.4**		

Getting started

Ask a partner to list your strengths and weaknesses. Do the same for them. Swap lists and see if you agree with them. Are there any that are a surprise to you? Why? Reflect on what you have learned about yourself and how this may help in the future. Keep the list for future reference.

 A

Examine the benefits of work experience in health and social care for own learning and development

Developing skills and attributes

The **skills** needed to provide health and social care include many that you cannot easily learn at college, such as the ability to undertake practical tasks. These are usually learned in the workplace. Work experience is, therefore, crucial not only in giving you a taste of the job so you can decide whether it would suit you but also in helping you start to develop the skills you will need. It also allows you to see whether you have the personal **attributes** you need to work in this sector.

Key terms

Skill – the ability or talent to do something well.

Attribute – a quality which contributes to who you are, helps form your personality.

Work experience evidence log

Part 1: You will be expected to collect evidence of the skills and attributes you demonstrate during your work experience placement, such as tutor observations, work placement supervisor witness statements, reflective accounts and diary entries, and to record where this evidence is located in your portfolio in Part 1 of your work experience log. This record is self-assessed and must be signed off by your work placement supervisor and/or your tutor.

Part 2: You will also need to record how you demonstrate technical skills, and some specific areas of skills such as communication, data handling, personal responsibility, teamwork and interpersonal skills in Part 2.

Part 3: This focuses specifically on the work skills of health and safety, and of communicating professionally.

Part 4: This part of the log asks for evidence of your reflective practice, based on your developing skills and attributes.

Part 5: This section is a tutor observational visit report, assessing the level of all your skills and attributes and suggesting areas for development.

Part 6: This section is similar to Part 5 but is completed by your work placement supervisor.

▶ **Table 6.1** Some of the skills and attributes needed to work in the health and social care sector

Skills	Attributes
Communication	Compassion
Interpersonal	Positivity
Organisational	Patience
Technical/practical	Professionalism
Teamwork	Empathy
Literacy	Reliability
Numeracy	Honesty
Digital literacy	Integrity
Problem-solving	Hard working
Decision-making	Supportive
Competency	Professional
Reflective	Confident
Employability	Responsible

Reflecting on own skills and attributes and areas for development

Important preparation for work experience is to **reflect** on your own skills and attributes, and areas for development. To do this successfully, you need reflective skills. Reflective practice involves consciously thinking about an event or incident in order to learn from it. If something has gone well, you can reflect on it to see what you did, why it was a success, and use what you have learned to repeat the success in the future. If something has not gone as well as you would have liked, you can think about why this was so that you can improve in future. Reflection also helps you to understand why things are done in a certain way. For example, if you are on work experience in a primary school you may see a learning mentor spend 10 minutes at the start of each day with a young child with behavioural difficulties. Why spend a short period of time every day with the child instead of a whole hour on one day each week? Why at the start of the day instead of later in the day? Such reflection would lead you to realise that this practice calms the child down at the start of each day, reminding them how to behave and why they should behave, and does not allow them to forget – as a meeting only once a week would. The child is also likely to be calmer and more receptive at the start rather than the end of the day.

> **Reflect**
>
> Think about working with either young children or older people. Look at the skills and attributes in Table 6.1 and add any more you can think of. Do you have those skills and attributes? Refer back to the list of your strengths and weaknesses you generated. Identify three areas where you feel you need to improve. These are called areas for development.

> **Key term**
>
> **Reflect** – look back on actions and events to learn from them.

Developing professionalism

To be professional means to comply with the standards set by the workplace and by regulatory bodies. This will include punctuality, dressing appropriately, finishing tasks to a high standard, finishing tasks on time, acting responsibly, being prepared for meetings, treating others with respect, regular attendance, doing what you say you will do to the best of your ability, listening carefully and following procedures and policies. You may have some of these skills already but will develop them further on work experience, learning from the example set by those you work with.

Communication and interpersonal skills

Communication skills include listening, speaking, non-verbal messages and writing, be it with a pen and paper or electronically. They allow you to exchange information with others.

Good communication skills are vital for working in health and social care as they help you to:

▸ develop positive relationships with the people using the services and with their families and friends, so you can understand and meet their needs

▸ develop positive relationships with work colleagues and other professionals

▸ share information with people using the services, by providing and receiving information

▸ report on the work you do with people.

▸ How can you tell that the service provider in this photo has good interpersonal skills?

Link

You can learn more about communication in *Unit 10: Sociological Perspectives, and in Unit 5: Meeting Individual Care and Support Needs, learning aim A*. Other skills and attributes are also covered in *Unit 5, learning aim A*.

Interpersonal skills are those you use to interact and communicate successfully with others, face to face. This includes not just what is said but also how it is said and the non-verbal messages you send. This might be through tone of voice or body language, including facial expressions, posture and gestures. Even the way you dress communicates a message to others in a room.

Case study

First day of work experience

Abby has just returned home from her first day on work experience at a residential home for older people. She is exhausted from rushing around all day, and has found some of the residents quite hard to cope with but she has enjoyed herself. She spent quite a long time with Mildred, who is 93 years old, partially-sighted and very forgetful, as she has dementia. Mildred remembers words but often says them in the wrong order so that sentences make no sense. Abby was asked to take her from her own room to the dining room, sit with her to make sure that she ate and then take her into the lounge and encourage her to join in with the armchair aerobics activity. Because of Mildred's dementia Abby had to find other ways to communicate with her.

Check your knowledge

1 What skills will Abby have had to use to help her meet Mildred's needs?

2 What attributes will Abby have needed when dealing with Mildred?

3 How might Abby have communicated with Mildred?

4 Why does it matter that Mildred joins in with activities even though, due to her dementia, she might not remember doing so afterwards?

Organisational skills

Time management

Good time management allows you to finish tasks and feel in control, rather than being stressed and worried. Good time management includes prioritising tasks and making sure you have breaks to relax, which will make you more effective. If your work experience involves administration in health and social care, you may receive emails. It is important, where possible, to deal with them as soon as you open them so that you do not miss something that needs dealing with urgently and so they do not build up.

It is also important to either do one thing at a time and see it through, or to look for tasks that can be combined. For example, you may need to speak to a particular person at your work experience placement about a number of different things. Make a list of everything you need to ask them so you do not have to keep going back to the same person. This is a waste of their time because they are being continually interrupted, and of your time in going to and fro multiple times.

Prioritising tasks

Prioritising tasks means completing those tasks which are most important first. You can deal with a task efficiently by completing it well but it may be that you could have used your time more effectively by identifying the tasks which needed completing first before tackling any task.

A simple way to do this is to write a list of tasks and divide them into categories, maybe using highlighter pens to colour code them based on traffic lights:

▶ green needs doing straight away, so high importance and top of your to-do list

▶ amber needs doing later today or tomorrow, so medium importance and in the middle of your to-do list

▶ red needs doing in the next few days, so low importance and bottom of your to-do list.

Another way is to divide tasks into four, as shown in Table 6.2. Although you are unlikely to use this approach on work experience it is a useful tool in day-to-day life and in your future working life.

> **Reflect**
>
> List what you did yesterday and reflect on your time management. For example, did you not do something you intended to? Why not? Do you complete tasks such as homework assignments the moment you get them? Do you have to be reminded or do them at the last minute? Do you tend to complete the easiest, hardest or most boring task first? What has this shown you about yourself? How could you better manage your time?

▶ **Table 6.2** Categorising priorities

	Urgent	Not
Important	**Important and urgent** **Do it now** • Medical emergencies • Important meetings • Project deadlines • Crises	**Important but not urgent** **Decide when to do it** • Relationship building • Health and exercise • Preparation/Planning/Prevention • Personal growth • Training
Not Important	**Urgent and not important** **Delegate it** • Interruptions • Unimportant emails, mail and phone calls • Some meetings • Minor problems	**Not important and not urgent** **Do not do it** • Time wasting • Trivia such as gossip • Tasks to make yourself look busy • Distractions

Can you explain why it is important to be able to reflect on your own skills and attributes? Do you find this easy to do?

Hint   Write a list of what you should do and ways in which you should behave to show professionalism.

Extend   Prioritisation – how can a task be important/not urgent? Give an example. What might happen if you do not do these tasks?

Technical skills

Data handling

Data means any item of information, in whatever form it is presented. To be of use information has to be gathered and recorded in a systematic manner. This is called data handling. Data needs to be put in its proper place in its proper format and must be accurate, so it is accessible to, and useful for, other service providers who need it. You should never, for example, make notes about a service user's needs and store them in your pocket.

Different service providers will have different systems for data handling. You will be told how your work experience setting does this during your induction. They will also have policies and procedures in place and codes of practice written by regulatory bodies, such as the Care Quality Commission, for you to read and adhere to. Data can be as simple as a name, date of birth and address but it can also include tables, graphs, and images, such as scans.

Using specialist equipment

Specialist equipment may be needed to meet the needs of service users, such as a hoist used to lift an older, less mobile person. You will see such equipment in use at your work experience placement but will not be allowed to use it, except to assist a service provider who is using it. You may be allowed to use other equipment, such as thermometers, but only under supervision. If there is specialist equipment that you are allowed to use, your supervisor should make sure that you are properly trained to do so, and it is vital that you then follow both verbal and written instructions when using it. In the workplace, service providers are expected to keep up to date with developments in specialist equipment.

▶ Which health and social care settings do you think would use hoists such as these?

Teamwork skills

Teamwork is crucial when working in health and social care to ensure that both service users and providers get the care and support they need. Service providers share resources and work together. It is important to develop good relationships on your work placement, by being friendly, respectful and helpful. **Team** members need to be able to trust each other, with each person having a clear role within the team and using effective communication techniques. This is as important for teams who work together every day in a setting such as a care home as it is for teams who may only see each other occasionally, such as in medical or community care.

Key term

Team – a group of people working towards the same goal.

Discussion

In a small group think of a team, either one you have all been part of or a successful team that you all know of, such as a Premier League football team. Discuss and list what makes the team successful. Write and practise a role play demonstrating the difference between good and poor teamwork. Conclude with a memorable way of remembering skills needed for successful teamwork.

Confidence and personal responsibility

▶ **Confidence** is not something that can be learned but is a positive state of mind. You can boost your confidence by thinking positively, having an 'I can' attitude, focusing on the things you know you do well and making sure you have a good network of people who will support you. If you prepare for, and start, your work experience properly by improving your knowledge, researching the placement and the work they do, and asking for help politely and respectfully when needed, the service providers and users will respond positively to you. This will increase your confidence. Sometimes you will, for example, have a problem to solve or be left with time on your hands if plans change. If you are confident and try to come up with an idea of what you could do to solve the problem or fill the time, and ask first, your supervisor will be impressed that you have used your **initiative**.

▶ You are **responsible** for your actions. You have a **personal responsibility** to complete the work experience to the best of your ability, in such a way that you do what is expected of you, help the service users and do not create problems or extra work for the other service providers. It is important to complete any task assigned to you. If you leave something incomplete, someone else will have to finish it for you. This will cause irritation and make you look unprofessional. It will also affect the service users, leaving them feeling unsupported. You could even cause harm to your colleagues or to service users, if, for example, you leave something on the floor after an activity and cause an accident. Part of your personal responsibility is to be professional. If, for example, your supervisor gives you supportive criticism, accept it in the way it was meant and learn from it. If you do not understand, politely ask for the reason.

Key terms

Confidence – how you feel about your ability to perform certain roles or tasks.

Initiative – doing something to solve a problem before others do.

Responsible – a duty you are required or expected to do because it is morally right or legally required.

Personal responsibility – by choosing their own actions a person is **accountable** for them.

Accountable – required to explain actions or decisions to someone.

▶ Does this learner look confident and professional?

Ability to link theory to practice

Your work experience will be your first chance to put what you have learned in the classroom into practice. This may be through:

▶ better understanding how to cope with a small child who is feeling insecure on their first day at nursery and wants their mum

▶ dealing with a young person who is angry and uncooperative, but was abused as a child

▶ interacting with an older person who is bad tempered and ungrateful, because they are frustrated with knowing that they are losing control over their own life and body.

Knowing the theory for a service user's behaviour will make it easier for you to stay calm and be patient.

Ⅱ PAUSE POINT Can you explain what the benefits of work experience in health and social care are for your own learning and development?

Hint   Draw a concept map about skills and attributes.

Extend   One attribute is confidence. What are the benefits of being confident? How may being over-confident lead to problems?

Clarifying expectations for employment in health and social care

Respecting diversity and equality

Diversity

To respect **diversity** is to value the differences between people, such as **cultures**, **beliefs**, age, gender and disability. If you respect the diversity of the other service providers and the service users at your work experience placement, you will be able to learn about them, or from them, understand them and help meet the needs of those you are caring for. It is a legal requirement for all health and social care providers to respect and value all individuals, irrespective of their religious or cultural beliefs, attitudes or other differences. A team of service providers who have different interests and skills is more likely to be able to handle the range of tasks required when helping an individual, and the team will enjoy working together. By valuing diversity you can be a useful member of that team.

Equality

In the health and social care sector, equality means everyone having equal access to the services they need and receiving a service of equal quality that meets their personal needs, no matter where they live or how they live their lives. This is not the same as everyone receiving the same service. For example, everyone has the right to register with a doctor but a seriously ill person will need more of that doctor's time. You will find that treating people as individuals, by taking into account their different beliefs and abilities, is crucial when caring for others. You should acknowledge an individual's personal beliefs, even if you do not share them. If a person's religious belief means they need to wear a particular item of clothing, then you must allow them to do so. By doing so you are showing respect and making them feel valued as an individual.

> **Key terms**
>
> **Diversity** – variety or range.
>
> **Culture** – the beliefs, language, styles of dress, ways of cooking, religion, ways of behaving etc, shared by a particular group of people.
>
> **Beliefs** – strongly held opinions stored in the subconscious mind.

Link

Unit 5: Meeting Individual Care and Support Needs, learning aim A, also looks at diversity and equality.

For more information about confidentiality, refer to *Unit 5: Meeting Individual Care and Support Needs* sections B1, D3 and D4 and *Unit 7: Principles of Safe Practice in Health and Social Care* section A2.

Respecting confidentiality and dignity

Workers in health and social care have a duty of confidentiality that protects the rights of individuals. This means keeping information **confidential** by not sharing information about individuals without their knowledge and agreement, even with service users' friends, family or other individuals. On your work placement you should never:

▶ discuss one individual with another

▶ discuss matters relating to service users outside the care setting, or in a public place where you might be overheard

▶ share written information without permission

▶ leave records, in any form, insecurely stored

▶ leave records that are in use unattended, where they may be read by unauthorised people.

Maintaining confidentiality also **safeguards** service users. If, for example, you put a photo on any form of social media of a child who has been taken away from their abusive parents and adopted, those parents may discover the child's whereabouts. This would not only cause a great deal of distress to the new parents and the child, but would also get you and your work placement managers into a great deal of trouble.

All health and social care settings have procedures in place with regard to breaching confidentiality that must be followed. You need to read these carefully and, if in any doubt, ask your supervisor for clarification and advice.

It is very important that you protect the **dignity** of those in your care. For example, if a child wets themself you should take them away quietly to help them get changed, without drawing attention to the situation, so the child is not made to feel embarrassed and ashamed in front of their friends. If an older person wants the independence of doing a task themselves, you can respect their dignity by recognising their ability to do this, even though they may take a long time to complete the task.

Understanding health, safety and security

On work experience, you have a legal responsibility to be aware of your own and others' safety. For example, if you are working in a nursery or a residential care home and leave the door open or unlocked, a child could wander out and come to harm, or cause harm to others. You need to be clear about the limits of what you are, and are not, allowed to do as you are not employed as a member of staff. You are there to learn. Your work placement supervisor will tell you what you can do. It is important that you do not do anything without your supervisor's permission, for example taking the bedside off an older person's bed, which has been put there to stop them falling out of bed.

Every service provider, or someone like you on work placement, has a legal responsibility to safeguard the service users in their care and to make sure that the service users are both physically and emotionally safe. Along with the other service providers, you will

Key terms

Confidential – information that is secret and should not be shared without permission.

Safeguard – protect from harm.

Dignity – worthy of respect, a pride in oneself.

be asked to sign in and out of your work placement. This is so that the manager knows who is on the premises in the event of an incident, such as a fire. It also means that any unauthorised person who has no business to be there can be turned away.

You have a responsibility to behave in such a way that service users do not feel threatened or intimidated by you, for example by speaking in a gentle voice with a non-aggressive tone. If you spot a hazard that could potentially cause an accident, such as a curled up rug or anything else that could trip someone up, or a wet floor, or if you see someone harming someone else, you should report it to a supervisor straight away. If you do not follow safeguarding procedures you will be breaking the law.

▶ **Figure 6.1** Can you think of any other aspects of safeguarding?

Understanding and applying care values

Care values are standards of behaviour used by health and social care service providers. They underpin the principles on which service providers base their work. The NHS care values are shown below and are used at all levels of care and work in the NHS. When you are at a work experience placement, you need to ask your supervisor to explain the care values used in that care setting.

▶ **Table 6.3** NHS core care values

NHS values	What will they do to apply that care value?
Working together for patients	Do everything in the interest of patients with a view to providing services to meet local need.
Respect and dignity	Value and respect different needs and aspirations when designing and delivering services and treat all, whether service user, carer or member of staff, with respect and dignity.
Commitment to quality of care	Provide the highest standards of high-quality, safe and effective care.
Compassion	Treat all with sensitivity and kindness.
Improving lives	Improve both short- and long-term health and wellbeing of service users through excellent care.
Everyone counts	Treat everyone with equal respect and as being of equal importance, and use resources fairly for those most in need.

Research

Undertake research to find out the care values used in three other health and social care settings, including at least one social care setting. Compare them with the NHS care values by creating a table that shows the values for each setting. How similar are they? Which are on all the lists?

Preparation for employment in the sector

Work experience is invaluable preparation for working in the health and social care sector because it gives you the opportunity to:

▶ experience care work and gain some understanding of what is involved in caring for others

▶ practise the skills you have learned at college with real service providers and users

▶ learn new skills

▶ assess your own skills and attributes, and areas for development

▶ explore different areas of work in this sector to help you decide which areas you would or would not like to work in

▶ gain skills, knowledge and confidence to help you apply, and interview, for a job in the sector.

You can further prepare by researching different jobs online, or gain extra work experience by volunteering to help or getting a weekend or holiday job in a local heath or social care setting.

❚❚ PAUSE POINT   What are your expectations for employment in health and social care?

> Hint   Draw a spider diagram to show the different expectations for employment in health and social care.

> Extend   Why is it important to safeguard your own health and safety when caring for others?

Exploring career options

When selecting your work experience placement you need to consider factors such as your future career aspirations, where you can realistically travel to from where you live or who you could stay with if it is too far to travel, which area of health and social care you are most interested in, whether you prefer working in groups or alone, and whether you want to interact with service users or work in administration. You also need to decide what type of setting you prefer to work in and which age group and group of service users you would like to work with.

Working in different settings

Residential care

Residential care homes for older people are for service users who either can no longer live at home because they need support with personal care, such as washing, dressing, preparing meals, getting in and out of bed and staying safe, and management of any medicine, or for those who choose to live somewhere with more company and support, maybe after the death of their partner. Residential care homes are staffed 24 hours a day and different activities are offered to keep the residents active, both physically and intellectually. If you decide to do your work experience in a residential care home, you will need to like working with older people, have patience and a good sense of humour and be happy to chat with the residents.

There are also residential care homes for children whose families cannot look after them, maybe due to disability, complex health needs, severe learning difficulties or behavioural, emotional and social difficulties.

Hospital

There are many more jobs in a hospital than those of doctors and nurses. In fact there at least 350 different roles such as healthcare assistants, clerical staff, engineers and cooks. Working in a hospital means that you will need to be prepared for some upsetting experiences.

If you apply to do your work experience in a hospital, you could apply for a clinical placement. In this type of placement you will be taught to do practical tasks, such as taking measurements of blood pressure and temperature, and washing patients. This will always be under the supervision of an experienced member of staff.

Hospitals are open 24 hours a day but not all departments are open all of that time. For example, you could apply for a non-clinical placement to develop your office and administrative skills, and work in a team that supports clinical services.

Working with different age groups and service users

Children with special needs

Most children with special educational needs and disabilities (SEND) are taught in mainstream schools with extra support from teaching assistants. Those with more severe needs are taught in special schools, which are better equipped and where the teaching staff have been specially trained to deal with these difficulties. If you want to work with children with learning disabilities, it is important to be patient and to interact with the child rather than ignoring them and speaking to others about them. You will need to be observant, consistent, positive and use the child's preferred method of communication. You will also need to be firm and prepared to help with the child's personal needs.

Older people with dementia

Dementia is the word for a group of symptoms caused by brain cells no longer working properly. Alzheimer's disease is the most common cause of dementia. Dementia is **progressive** with, as yet, no cure. It affects a person's mental function and its early signs are difficulty in remembering words, disorientation, problems with everyday tasks, like forgetting how to make a cup of tea, and personality changes. Symptoms develop gradually, so ways can be found to cope with them, but eventually a person with dementia will present with some or all of the problems shown in Figure 6.2. People with dementia are cared for either in hospitals and care homes or in their own homes. In 2014, the Alzheimer's Society predicted that there would be 850,000 people with dementia in the UK by 2015, and estimated that this would rise to one million by 2025.

When caring for a person with dementia, it is important that you treat them with respect and consult them about their own care. They should not be excluded from any services because of their condition and should be kept as physically and mentally fit as possible, eating a healthy and balanced diet. If they feel better, they will enjoy life more. If you are helping them to dress, it is important to let them keep their own style to help preserve their identity. You will need to be patient, sensitive and tactful when helping them.

> **Key term**
>
> **Progressive** – symptoms will gradually get worse.

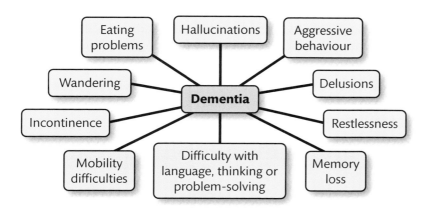

▶ **Figure 6.2** Do you know anyone with dementia? Do you recognise any of these symptoms?

Discussion

Print out the key dementia statistics from the Alzheimer's Society website (**www.alzheimers.org.uk**). In a small group of two or three, discuss the implications of these statistics for the UK. How does your group feel this situation could be dealt with? Produce a leaflet to share your ideas with the rest of your class.

Sources of information about careers in health and social care

Useful sources of information about careers in health and social care include:

▶ Online sources. There are many websites containing information about careers in health and social care. For example, The National Careers Service website. This site covers a wide range of careers, including information such as job profiles, work activities, working hours and conditions, and much more. Using a search engine, such as Google, to look at careers in health and social care generates many pages of websites, with the most widely used being at the top of the list.

▶ On the high street you can visit organisations such as recruitment agencies, Career Connect and Connexions, which offer careers information, advice, support and guidance for young people. For a list of these centres in your local area, use a search engine and go to websites such as Yell, where you can search for careers advice in your town. Wigan, for example, has a Skills Shop that offers careers advice in Wigan, and Wigan Council offers appointments through schools and colleges to discuss careers advice.

Research

Think of a career in health and social care that you may be interested in pursuing when you leave college. Research that career and produce a presentation based on your findings.

Using work experience to inform career choices, confirm ideas or consider alternative options

Your work experience should give you the opportunity to work with a health and social care service provider in an area that you may be interested in for your future career. You will complete your placement in one or more settings. By observing service providers at work you will gain an understanding of their roles and responsibilities. You will also be taught how to complete certain tasks and will be allowed to tackle some of them under supervision, as well as practise using, and developing, your skills in a real-life situation.

This experience will either confirm that this is the career choice you want to make or lead you to feel that it is not right for you, and that you need to consider alternative options, maybe in a different area of health or social care.

Assessment practice 6.1   A.P1   A.P2   A.M1

Write a letter of application to a health and social care setting that you are considering for your work experience placement. This might be a care home, day care centre, nursing home, hospital, GP surgery, children's centre or school for children with learning disabilities.

In the letter, explain how you hope the work experience will support the development of your professional skills and personal attributes, inform your career choices and help prepare you for employment in the health and social care sector. Make sure you analyse how you hope the work experience will provide you with the opportunity to gain a realistic understanding of the health and social care sector. Explain that if you are successful in securing a placement with them, you will be bringing your work experience log with you. You also need to explain the importance of the log book in providing evidence of your skills and attributes.

Plan

- What am I being asked to do?
- How will I approach the task?

Do

- I know how to structure a letter.
- I can explain why I have decided to approach the task in a particular way.

Review

- I can explain what I have learned.
- I can identify how this learning experience relates to future experiences in the workplace.

B   Develop a work experience plan to support own learning and development

It is important to plan and prepare carefully for your work placement. You'll need a work experience plan to do this properly. This learning aim covers the things you need to consider when drawing up your plan, such as planning your first day.

Preparation for work experience

Make sure you check your travel arrangements, where and who you are to report to, and read any introductory information you have been given, before your first day. Set off in plenty of time, to allow for rush-hour traffic, public transport delays or parking problems, and for finding the place and person you are to report to. If you have the opportunity, you could try a practice run. Do not be late. Remember that first impressions are important.

Reflect

Think back to a time when a new learner joined your class at school or college. What did you think about them when you first saw them? What gave you this impression? Once you got to know them better did you change your impression? Why?

Expectations for learners on work experience

Dress

It takes less than 30 seconds for someone to make a judgement about you based on your appearance, body language and how you are dressed. You should find out beforehand what is considered appropriate dress. Keep make-up and jewellery to a minimum, wear clothes that are neat, respectable, smart, clean and suitable for the role, with clean shoes or boots in which you can walk comfortably. Your hair should also be clean and tidy, and in some settings you may be asked to keep it tied back. Head coverings are acceptable if they are part of your culture or religion. If you know you look the part, you will feel more at ease and confident.

Behaviour

It is important that you behave appropriately on work experience. Be polite and respectful, speak clearly, be prepared to listen carefully and ask for help when needed. If you are asked to do something that you consider trivial, such as making a cup of tea for your supervisor, do it willingly and with a smile, remembering that everyone has to start somewhere. Show that you are interested and try to develop a rapport with both the service providers and users. Take positive criticism as being given to help you improve, and listen and act on the advice offered. Complete all tasks set and, if you find yourself with nothing to do, use your initiative. Maybe tidy up or talk to a service user, rather than sit in a corner and wait to be told what to do. Be professional, cheerful, approachable and a good team worker. Remember, you are there to learn and the other service providers have a lot to teach you.

Do not:

▶ do anything you have not been told to do, such as touch equipment or medication

▶ act as though you think you know everything

▶ gossip about colleagues or service users

▶ make a fuss if you feel you are being asked to do something inappropriate by your supervisor. If it is something you are being asked to do immediately, politely say you'd rather not to your supervisor. If your supervisor repeatedly asks you to do things you should not be doing, contact your tutor at the first opportunity.

Practical considerations

Find out what you need to take with you and whether you need to have any security checks done.

Disclosure and Barring Service (DBS) checks

The Disclosure and Barring Service check is the new name for the Criminal Records Bureau (CRB) check. If someone is applying for a job, whether it is paid or voluntary, which involves, for example, health care or working with children or vulnerable adults, or applying to foster or adopt a child, it is a legal requirement that they apply for a DBS check. The employer will ask for one to be carried out on your behalf if it is deemed to be necessary. The process involves completing an application form at the request of your employer, who will sign it and ask to see certain original documents such as your birth certificate or passport. The form is sent to the DBS. If the form has been correctly and accurately completed, and the facts do not raise any alarms, the DBS sends a certificate to the person who has applied for it. This certificate is shown to the employer to prove that the person has passed their DBS check.

If you are over 16 and there is any chance that you will have unsupervised access to children or vulnerable adults at your work experience placement, you may be expected to apply for a DBS check. Similarly, if a work placement supervisor is to have day-to-day responsibility for you, the school may ask for a DBS check on the supervisor. However, in almost all work placements this will not happen because the supervisor will not have regular unsupervised contact with you.

▶ Think about people you come across in your day-to-day life. Who do you think will have been DBS checked?

Responsibilities and limitations for learners on work experience

Your responsibilities will include behaving and dressing professionally, as already mentioned. You should also arrive on time and, if for any reason you are unable to attend one day, it is your responsibility to alert your supervisor and tutor as early in the day as possible, certainly no later than the start of the working day. Other responsibilities include following the policies and procedures of your placement setting, following instructions given and completing all tasks set by your supervisor to the best of your ability, seeking help if needed. You need to remember to complete your work experience log as regularly as possible, making sure you collect the supporting evidence required as you go along, rather than trying to do it all at the end of your placement. Very importantly, you must be aware of safety issues, for both yourself and others. Make sure you have read and understood all the health and safety policies and that you know key facts, such as the location of the fire exits. Report all incidents and accidents and, if something is your fault, admit it and apologise straight away.

You will also be made aware of the limitations of your role. You are not there as a paid member of staff or to fill a vacancy, you are there to learn. Your supervisor will explain to you exactly what you are and are not allowed to do, and it is very important that you work within these limitations. You would never, for example, be allowed to give anyone their medication, or let an older person with dementia wander out of a residential care home. Most organisations have a work experience policy, which can usually be found online, and can provide you with information about your responsibilities and limitations.

Providing intimate personal care

If you are on work placement at, for example a hospital or residential care home you might be shown how to give someone a bed bath or provide other forms of intimate care by a supervisor, if the patient gives their permission for you to be there. However, you would not be allowed or expected to attend to any intimate personal care tasks.

Handling confidential information

You will have a responsibility to respect the confidentiality of information you may have access to during your work placement. Many organisations have work experience confidentiality agreement forms and you may be asked to sign one before you start your placement. Remember that you must not refer to the names of individual service users in your work experience log and any photographs you include should be of objects such as wall displays, or the backs of groups of service users doing activities, so that their faces are not seen and they cannot be identified.

> **Link**
>
> This has been covered in learning aim A of this unit in the section on Clarifying expectations for employment in health and social care.

> **Research**
>
> Find some examples of confidentiality agreements on the internet. Then write a set of guidelines for a learner on a work experience placement on what they can and cannot do when handling confidential information, to keep themselves and the service user safe.

Researching specific work experience placements

Organisations

Your tutor will have a list of the appropriate settings for your work experience. Once you have decided which settings you would like to work in, you should research online to find out about specific organisations in your local area. Most settings have their own website but it is important to remember that this has been set up to attract service users to use their setting so it may not contain all the information you need. It is a good idea to look for inspection reports, for example, the Care Quality Commission monitors and inspects health and social care services, including hospitals, care homes, clinics and GP practices. You will find links to these reports on their website. These reports are in the public domain so anyone can read them. Other sources of information include local papers or the library.

Job roles

Information about specific job roles can be found on the internet or in offices on the high street, as mentioned earlier. Once you know what the role involves generally, you can research that role in the context of the setting and organisation in which you are interested. You could also talk to people, such as family and friends, who may work in the job role you are interested in to find out more.

> **Research**
>
> Pick a possible setting for part of your work experience placement and research the organisation and specific job role you are interested in within that setting. Make a one page information sheet to put in a class file for others to refer to.

Role of placement supervisors/mentors

The role of the work experience **supervisor** is an important one, because the lessons learned from a good supervisor will last a long time and may influence your career choices.

> **Key terms**
>
> **Supervisor** – a person who directs and oversees the work of a learner.

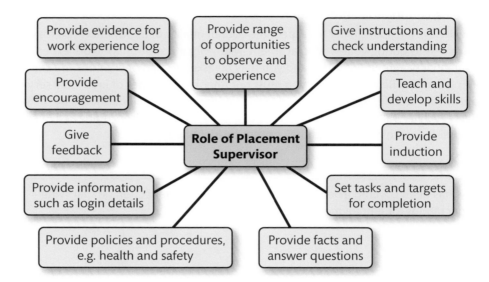

Role of Placement Supervisor

- Provide evidence for work experience log
- Provide range of opportunities to observe and experience
- Give instructions and check understanding
- Provide encouragement
- Teach and develop skills
- Give feedback
- Provide induction
- Provide information, such as login details
- Set tasks and targets for completion
- Provide policies and procedures, e.g. health and safety
- Provide facts and answer questions

▶ **Figure 6.3** Do you understand the difference between a supervisor and a mentor?

A **mentor** is someone who is not in a line management relationship with you but who can provide specific advice, guidance and training related to your work. A buddy may

Case study

First impressions

Peter and Maria are both going to the same place for work experience, a large rehabilitation centre for people who have some form of physical or brain injury.

Peter's parents work very hard but are not paid very much, so there is little spare money for clothes and bus fares. He decides to wear his only pair of trousers with a shirt and his school blazer, from which he has removed the school badge. His clothes are all clean and well pressed, even though they have been worn many times before, and he will be able to take the blazer off if he gets too warm. He is going to walk to his placement and has already had a trial run so he knows what time he needs to set off to arrive in plenty of time, and he knows which door he has to use to get in. When he arrives he waits patiently for someone to come to the door and then explains politely who he is and who he has been told to report to.

Maria's family are wealthy so money is no object. She decides to wear a designer jumper, because it is quite cool outside when she gets up, with a short skirt and high-heeled boots, because they go well with her outfit. She takes too long deciding what to wear and ends up taking a taxi to get there, arriving just on time. She rings the bell impatiently because she is anxious as she has only just arrived on time, and rushes inside saying, 'Hi. I'm Maria. I'm on work experience but I don't know who I need to report to.'

The centre is very warm because the service users are in bed some of the time and tend to feel the cold and there are several staircases but only two lifts, which they are asked not to use unless accompanying a service user.

Check your knowledge

1 What do you think the first impression of Peter and Maria on the service provider who answers the door will be?

2 What do you think the first impression of their joint work experience supervisor will be?

3 What is likely to happen when Peter and Maria start work around the centre, carrying cups of tea to residents and answering their buzzers?

4 What might the first impression of the residents be?

be allocated to look after you, for example at lunchtimes, and is someone you can ask questions of in a more informal way. They can give you informal support and advice when you need it.

⏸ **P A U S E   P O I N T**   Do you understand the expectations for work experience? What preparations will you need to make for your placement?

⬤ Hint   Write down all the points you can remember about how you need to prepare for work experience.

⬤ Extend   Why is it important to know the limitations of what you are allowed to do when on work experience?

Setting goals and learning objectives

An objective is more structured and specific than a goal. An objective is something that can be attained by taking certain steps. It is how you intend to go about achieving your goal. A **goal** is something you want to achieve. In order to get the most out of your work experience, it is important that you have a goal *and* **learning objectives**, which will give you the skills and knowledge that will help you achieve that goal. Your goal may be to choose a rewarding career in health and social care. Your objectives might be to gain a better understanding of various careers and roles, complete and review your work experience and complete this qualification, in order to make that decision and reach your goal.

> **Key terms**
>
> **Goal** – an aim or desired result.
> **Learning objective** – a statement of the steps to be taken to gain the knowledge and skills needed to accomplish a goal.

Reflecting on current knowledge and skills

In order to set yourself a learning objective relating to your own knowledge and skills, you need to reflect on your current knowledge and skills, identify what they are and any areas for development. There are two types of skills:

▸ transferable skills: these are general skills that you need in any job role, such as interpersonal, team working and time management skills

▸ career specific skills: these are skills you need to work in a specific sector of work, for example certain practical skills, such as how to take someone's temperature.

> **Reflect**
>
> Reflect on the skills and knowledge you will need for work experience. You will have found out what they are when you researched your work placement/s. List the skills, both transferable and career specific, and what you will need to know about to work in that setting. Compare this list with your current knowledge and skills. What areas do you need to improve?

Identifying own strengths and areas for development

In order to set goals and learning objectives for your work experience, you first need to identify your own strengths and weaknesses. One way of doing this is to use a technique called a SWOT (**S**trengths, **W**eaknesses, **O**pportunities, **T**hreats) analysis. You would need to write your strengths and weaknesses in the top two boxes of a table such as Table 6.4, and then decide how your strengths can create opportunities for you and how your weaknesses may hinder you. Although it is excellent to focus on your strengths, it is also good to face up to your weaknesses and see the potential for personal growth.

Using Table 6.4, do a SWOT analysis to identify your strengths and weaknesses in terms of your skills, attributes and knowledge. Swap your SWOT analysis with a friend. Study the analysis your friend has done of themselves and discuss both analyses, adding notes to your own, so you have a more thorough analysis. Use this to identify your five main strengths and five main areas for development.

Be totally honest with yourself. Do not claim something is a strength because you would like it to be true and think others would admire it in you. There is no point claiming to be confident if you are really shy. Similarly, do not put yourself down. If you are bubbly and outgoing then say that.

▶ **Table 6.4** Framework for a SWOT analysis

Strengths	Weaknesses
What do you do well?	What could you improve?
What do others see as your strengths?	What are others likely to see as a weakness?
Opportunities	Threats
How can you use your strengths to create opportunities?	What might happen if you do not overcome your weaknesses?
	How might your weaknesses allow others to gain an advantage over you?

Another aid to identifying your skills, attributes and knowledge is to take a psychological test or skills assessment online, such as the personality test on **www.123test.com**. Some of these tests are free and quick and give you a score on a number of important personality traits.

Work experience evidence log

Now you have practised reflecting on your current skills and knowledge and are about to start your work experience placement, you are ready to complete Part 1 of form HSC 5, which is for you to reflect on your skills at the start of the work placement, the attitudes you have developed and the experiences you have had, and how these have improved your performance.

Once you are on your work placement, you will be expected to self-assess your work skills by collecting evidence to prove that you have each skill. In your log form HSC T 3, Parts 1 and 2, identify the skills you need to consider. Each is linked to the National Occupational Standards (NOS) and/or Care Certificate Standards.

Identifying established standards and values required for health and social care professionals

The NHS Constitution

When the NHS was created in 1948 it was to make good health care available to all and was based on three core principles, namely that it:

▶ meets the needs of all

▶ is free at the point of delivery

▶ is based on clinical need, not ability to pay.

These principles have been central to the development of the NHS ever since. In 2011, the Department of Health published the NHS Constitution, which sets out the standards and values that guide the NHS in all aspects of their work. This was last reviewed in 2015, and full details can be found in the NHS Handbook. You have already learned about the six core care values (see Understanding and applying care values in learning aim A).

▶ **Table 6.5** The NHS Constitution (Source: These principles are taken from **www.nhs.uk**)

Key principles	Principle	What does it mean for service users?
1	The NHS provides a comprehensive service available to all.	• Designed to diagnose, treat and improve both physical and mental health. • Duty to all individuals and must respect their human rights. • Duty to promote equality through its services.
2	Access to NHS Services is based on clinical need, not an individual's ability to pay.	• Free of charge except areas such as travel costs, wigs, prescriptions, eye care and dental care unless for those with low income who qualify for help with charges.
3	The NHS aspires to the highest standards of excellence and professionalism.	• In high-quality care, staff they employ, train and develop, leadership and management, and innovation. • All service users and providers to be treated with respect, dignity, compassion and care.
4	The NHS aspires to put patients at the heart of everything it does.	• Support service users to promote and manage their own health. • Services reflect needs and preferences of patients and their families and carers. • Actively encourage feedback to inform improvement of services.
5	The NHS works across organisational boundaries and in partnership with other organisations in the interest of patients, local communities and the wider population.	• Integrated systems of organisations and services. • Bound together by common principles and values. • Work jointly with other local services to deliver improvements in health and wellbeing.
6	The NHS is committed to providing best value for taxpayers' money and the most effective, fair and sustainable use of finite resources.	• Public funds for health care used for benefit of all service users.
7	The NHS is accountable to the public, communities and patients that it serves.	• Funded through national taxation. • Local NHS and patients with their clinicians make most decisions. • NHS accountable to government who are accountable to Parliament.

Research

Research the principles on which social care in the UK is based. How similar are they to those for health care? Find a way to present your comparison as clearly as possible.

When you are doing research tasks online make sure you use:
• the most up-to-date websites by including the current year as part of your search
• UK websites.

Identifying SMART targets for own work experience

An important part of your work experience plan is to set targets. Targets are the small, very specific steps that you take to reach your goal. You have already learned that objectives are the larger steps you are planning to take towards achieving your goal. An objective might be to develop your ability to work with different groups of service users or to learn and develop a new range of skills. A goal is what you are aiming for, what you want to achieve. It is more general and either achieved or not achieved. Your goal might be to identify whether working in a particular health or social care setting is right for you.

A target should be SMART. An example of a SMART target is: It is Monday today. I will find out by this Friday which bus I need to catch to get to my work experience placement by 8.30 am each day.

▶ **S**pecific – the target is clearly stated, says exactly what you mean, and cannot be misunderstood.

▶ **M**easurable – it includes what you intend to find out and by when, so you can prove that you have met the target.

▶ **A**chievable – you must feel it is possible to achieve the target set otherwise you may be put off trying. Making a phone call or looking at a timetable by Friday is reasonable, so achievable.

▶ **R**ealistic – the target set must be realistic, you must be able to do it. It is realistic for you to be able to find out this information either online or via a phone call in the time you have allowed yourself.

▶ **T**ime-related – there is a deadline set by which to find out the information so progress can be assessed.

Work experience evidence log

Think about your work placement. Write five SMART targets for your work experience plan.

 PAUSE POINT Can you explain how to set goals and learning objectives?

> **Hint** Write down what you need to know before you can set goals and learning objectives for your work experience placement.

> **Extend** What is the difference between a target, a goal and a learning objective?

Setting personal development goals

To set a **personal development goal** you first need to reflect on your current skills and attributes to identify weaknesses, which you can then aim to improve. Reaching a personal development goal will help you in all aspects of your life. Reflective practice is thinking about what you do or know, and learning from it, to improve the way you work. By learning to do this you will increase in confidence and become a more **proactive** service provider.

You can use reflective skills to think about something you have done, such as an interview or a presentation, what you need to do better and how to make improvements next time you do something similar. Things you need to do better become your personal development goals.

> **Link**
>
> You started to learn about reflective skills at the start of this unit, in learning aim A.

Developing communication skills

Communication skills are considered to be one of the most important skill sets in every employment sector.

A personal development goal of developing your communications skills is quite general. It is better to first identify which aspect of your communication skills needs developing.

> **Key terms**
>
> **Personal development goal** – a goal that you aim for to improve some aspect of your skills and attributes to develop you as a person.
>
> **Proactive** – making something happen rather than responding to a situation after it has happened, e.g. having a 'flu jab rather than getting 'flu and having to take 'flu remedies.

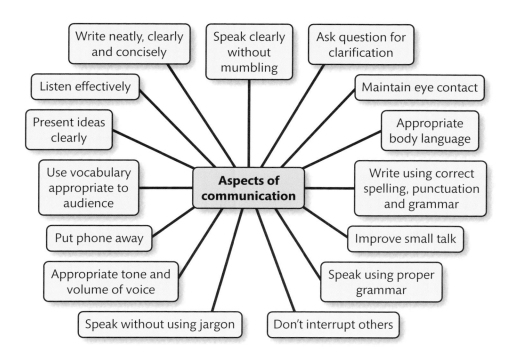

Aspects of communication:
- Write neatly, clearly and concisely
- Speak clearly without mumbling
- Ask question for clarification
- Listen effectively
- Maintain eye contact
- Present ideas clearly
- Appropriate body language
- Use vocabulary appropriate to audience
- Write using correct spelling, punctuation and grammar
- Put phone away
- Improve small talk
- Appropriate tone and volume of voice
- Speak using proper grammar
- Speak without using jargon
- Don't interrupt others

▶ **Figure 6.4** Can you think of any other aspects of communication that someone may need to improve?

Theory into practice

Reflect on a recent presentation you did to see how you could improve your communication skills. Repeat this process firstly with a conversation you have had recently with someone you did not really listen to properly, and secondly with a report or a piece of persuasive writing you have recently completed.

Create an action plan for the personal development goals you identified for developing your communication skills. In your action plan include a column for learning objectives, each of which would be to improve a specific aspect of your communication skills, such as 'listen more effectively'. Next, include a column, subdivided into several rows, for your learning opportunities to improve this aspect. For example 'I will listen carefully in my work placement induction meeting'. Complete your table with columns such as 'Progress made'. Then carry out your plan.

Discussion

In a small group, discuss situations or occasions when you have made a mistake or been criticised. How did it make you feel? Did you worry about it for a long time? Did you do anything to make sure it did not happen again? How could you have dealt with it better?

Work experience evidence log

Form HSC T Part 3 has a section that requires you to organise and plan a range of activities to implement in a health and social care setting, during which you will need to demonstrate your communication skills. This task would support a personal development goal of improving your communication skills.

Improving confidence

A lack of confidence can be caused by a variety of factors, such as criticism, being unhappy about personal appearance, being over-protected as a child, fear of the unknown, being unprepared, lack of skills or knowledge and previous failures. This can lead to being hesitant and withdrawn, using fillers such as 'um' and 'ah', a tendency to not try anything new and shying away from attention.

If one of your personal development goals is to improve your confidence these are some of the ways to do it.

▶ Plan and prepare for an activity, such as your first day of work experience or an interview, to reduce your fear of the unknown. This gives you a feeling of having more control over a situation.

▶ Think positively by feeling good about your strengths and seeing your weaknesses as something you can work on and develop to make you even stronger.

▶ Adopt a positive outlook towards others, try not to complain or criticise but be pleased for their successes.

▶ Accept compliments rather than trying to shrug them off or putting yourself down.

▶ Accept that everyone makes mistakes and/or is criticised, so see these as learning opportunities and as a way to improve, rather than feeling upset, embarrassed or offended.

▶ Avoid conversation fillers such as 'um', 'like' and 'ah'. Do not fiddle nervously with your hair or sleeves and take your hands out of your pockets.

▶ Take opportunities to improve your knowledge, skills and attributes so you feel less nervous and better prepared for new situations.

▶ Learn to be **assertive**. This means being able to stand up for yourself, or something you feel is right without being **aggressive** or upsetting yourself or others, staying calm, positive and firm, and repeating your point of view without apologising for anything you say. It does not mean being aggressive, arrogant or acting in a superior manner.

> **Research**
>
> Research assertive behaviour techniques. With a partner, work on a role play to show a situation where one of you is first **passive**, then aggressive, then assertive, to show others what is meant by being assertive and how to do it.

If you have a high level of self-confidence you will try most things and are more likely to be successful.

> **Reflect**
>
> Add a personal development goal of becoming more confident to your practice action plan. For example, 'I will increase my confidence in meetings so that I can make a positive contribution'. Complete the other columns of the plan.

Setting professional development goals

A **professional development goal** is something you should aim for in your working life in order to improve some aspect of your skills and attributes. You might reach this goal by going on a course, being trained by a colleague while at work or by practising a skill.

Developing competence

An important way to develop **competence** is on the job. Your work experience placement will be invaluable in developing your competence. For example, you will learn what is involved in various job roles and be trained to develop the ability to do at least part of that role successfully. Opportunities may arise for you to take part in

> **Key terms**
>
> **Assertive** – being confident and assured.
>
> **Aggressive** – behaving in a forceful way, ready to attack or confront.
>
> **Passive** – accepting or allowing what happens, without offering any resistance or response.

> **Key terms**
>
> **Professional development goal** – the aim to improve some aspect of your skills and attributes as part of your **professional** development.
>
> **Professional** – belonging to an occupation that needs special training or education.
>
> **Competence** – the ability to do something successfully or efficiently.

a training session with your colleagues at your work placement setting, or to attend a training course outside the setting. Reading and studying aspects of role requirements, such as policies and procedures, on your own will also help develop your competence.

You will learn about legislation that applies to your work setting, so will know the reasons why, and how to apply health and safety measures, for example. An important competence to develop is the ability to carry out risk assessments.

The National Occupational Standards (NOS), referred to in your work experience log, describe the minimum standard to which you are expected to work, and the skills, knowledge and understanding you need to undertake a task to a nationally recognised level of competence.

Work experience evidence log

You can prepare for learning about health and safety and security measures by completing the 'legislation and policies' pro forma in Appendix 2 of your work experience log. This requires you to research into some key pieces of legislation so you can see which of your setting's policies reflect different parts of the legislation.

Form HSC T Part 3 has a section that requires you to plan an activity with a service user and carry out a risk assessment. This would support a professional development goal of improving your competence in carrying out risk assessments.

Developing technical ability

Your work experience will also be invaluable in giving you opportunities to develop your technical skills. Some of the technical skills identified by the WorldSkills organisation for health and social care include the safe storage of materials, secure storage of medication, safe disposal of waste material, data handling, using specialist equipment, moving service users safely and monitoring health parameters such as blood pressure and temperature. You will know which technical skills you will need at your work placement and can set yourself a professional development goal based on these, for example to learn how to prevent and control infection.

▶ Do you always use the facilities provided in hospitals and other settings to help prevent infection?

Discussion

In a small group, discuss the technical skills you expect to come across on your work placements. Discuss which you think you will be allowed to try to use and develop yourself, and which you will only be allowed to watch others use. What is the difference between the two groups of answers?

Work experience evidence log

Form HSC T Part 3 has a section that requires you to select, follow and carry out the procedures to prevent and control infection. This would support a professional development goal of improving your competence in infection prevention and control techniques.

You are now ready to complete your personal and development plan, which is form HSC T 4 Part 3, and your work experience placement and action plans, which can be found in Appendix 2 of your work experience log.

Assessment practice 6.2   `B.P3` `B.P4` `B.M2` `AB.D1`

Write an action plan for your work experience. Write a commentary to accompany the plan in which you explain:

- your responsibilities and limitations
- how you plan to meet your personal and professional development goals
- the importance of your plan in supporting your learning and development while on work experience placement
- how you have prepared for your work experience, justifying the benefits of preparation in supporting your understanding of the expectations of work experience.

Plan

- Is there a form in my work experience log that will help me structure the first part of this activity?
- Do I need clarification around anything asked for in the commentary?

Do

- I can make connections between what I have learned and the task.
- I can seek support when I am unsure of how much detail to provide.

Review

- I can identify how this activity relates to the workplace.
- I can use this experience on my work placement to monitor my progress.

 C

Carry out work experience tasks to meet set objectives

Work experience tasks

You should now be ready to carry out your work experience placement.

Assisting and participating in clinical tasks (providing direct care for service users as appropriate)

Clinical tasks are tasks carried out on a service user, such as taking their temperature, rather than tasks based on theories or laboratory results. Carrying out a clinical task makes you a **direct carer** because you are providing care for a service user, as opposed to **indirect care**, when someone provides a service to help you, as a direct carer, look after a service user.

Interacting with service users

An important part of your work experience will be interacting with service users. To do this you will need to use your communication and interpersonal skills, covered at the start of this unit, to develop a rapport with service users so that they trust you and feel comfortable with you helping with their care. You will need to be flexible, patient, approachable and empathetic, while making sure you manage your time and get your tasks done.

For example, if you are working in a residential care home you will find that some of the residents are lonely, maybe having few visitors, if any, as their partners and friends of a similar age may have died. Spending time talking to them is an important part of the role. They will be happy to feel that someone is listening to them and making them feel as though they still have something worth saying. Asking them about their families by commenting on family photos, or asking what they used to do for work, will show that you are interested in them as a person. You will be asked to do tasks, such as collecting them from their room to go to the dining room, maybe taking them in a wheelchair or walking with them if they use a walking frame, or accompanying them on trips out, maybe to a local garden centre for coffee. You may also be asked to help run activities that keep the residents entertained and mentally alert. If you find yourself with free time, you could organise a sing-song or do puzzles with residents.

If you are working in a hospital, for example, service users may be worried or maybe even frightened, because they are ill or about to have an operation. Some will be feeling lonely and missing their families between visiting times, while some will receive no visitors at all. They will need reassuring and their minds taking off their situation so being kind and caring and chatting to them will be a comfort. You will also be doing tasks such as bed making, observing drug rounds and applying simple dressings, or maybe taking patients' blood pressure and temperature, under supervision. Or you may be asked to take service users for a walk up and down the ward as they start to feel better.

> **Key terms**
>
> **Clinical** – the observation and treatment of a person rather than looking at theories or laboratory research.
>
> **Direct carer** – someone who provides care for a service user, such as a doctor or social worker.
>
> **Indirect care** – providing a service that helps direct carers look after a person, provided by people such as GP receptionists or hospital chefs.

> **Discussion**
>
> Imagine that you are ill in hospital. With a partner, discuss how you might feel if no one came to visit you. How might this affect your recovery? The nurses are often too busy to stand and talk to patients for any length of time. What could a work experience learner do to help?

Wherever you are working, do not forget that you must know your limitations, and be mindful of them. You should not give advice to service users, for example, or promise them that they will get better, or take them for a walk outside without permission. You will not be involved in any activities where specialist training is involved, such as manual handling, or contact with clinical waste products.

Case study

Not the best of days

Josie is in her third week of work experience placement in a hospital. She is really enjoying the work and is beginning to feel relaxed and more confident. The role she is currently studying and supporting is that of a healthcare assistant.

Josie has helped to tidy up the ward and get the patients ready for afternoon visiting time and has finished the tasks she has been allocated. Her supervisor is on a break. Nirpal, who is 6 years old, has knocked a dressing off a wound on his arm and it has started to bleed. Josie decides to use her initiative and puts a wad of lint on it to stop the bleeding, securing it with sticking plaster as she does not know where the original dressings are kept.

She thinks this will do as a temporary measure. She has just finished, so has not had time to ask her supervisor to check she has done it correctly, when his parents arrive at visiting time. They express concern because Nirpal is allergic to sticking plaster. His parents are annoyed and Nirpal gets upset because he likes Josie and does not want her to get into trouble. Josie panics and takes the plaster off and the wound starts to bleed again.

Check your knowledge

1 What mistakes has Josie made?

2 What could have been the possible consequences for Nirpal in this situation?

3 What should Josie have done as soon as she realised she had made a mistake?

4 What lessons do you think Josie will learn from this incident?

Assisting with meals

If you complete your work experience in a setting where service users stay for at least the day, you may be asked to assist with meals. This could be helping staff tidy up tables and offering hand wipes before a meal, distributing meals and serving drinks, or maybe helping some service users by cutting up food or even feeding them. While you are doing this, you will be interacting with the service users. You will need to use your communication skills, as well as attributes such as patience and understanding. You might also be expected to complete a food record chart if you are in a hospital setting, for example.

It is very important that you take care to give the right meal to the right person, as keeping a patient properly fed aids their recovery. On a hospital ward, for example, patients will have chosen from the menu according to their likes and dislikes. Meals and visiting times are important events when you are in hospital. A service user may have been looking forward all morning to their meal. If they receive something they do not like it may not only be disappointing but they may not be able to eat it. More importantly, however, some will have chosen meals due to cultural or religious preferences, or due to allergies or other diet restrictions. Some services users may be waiting for investigations, or an operation and will have 'Nil by mouth' written above their beds and in their notes. If you give them a meal and they eat it, they may not then be able to have the operation or investigation, causing them and their families delay and distress. This will also waste hospital resources as their bed will be tied up for a day longer and the surgical staff will have allocated a theatre slot for that patient which they now cannot use.

It is important that you observe the correct procedures in regards to health and safety and hygiene, so if you are told to wear a disposable hair net and use hand gel, that is what you must do.

Assisting and participating in non-clinical tasks (not directly relating to the provision of care for service users)

Attending meetings

You may be invited to attend meetings, for example team meetings. This will be as an observer so it is important that you sit still and quietly and do not disturb other participants. You must listen carefully as you will learn about how meetings are run, both well and less well from the experience. You may also be asked for your opinion if, for example, they are talking about a service user you have spent quite a lot of time with.

General office tasks

You will be asked to do activities following clear guidelines, such as helping with errands, photocopying, filing and answering the telephone. You will be told by your supervisor that you should not have any inappropriate or unsupervised access to computers and service users' or staff members' medical records. It is important that you are mindful of the legislation regarding confidentiality and the confidentiality agreement you may have signed.

▸ Is your work experience clinical or non-clinical? Try to get experience of both before setting career goals.

Promoting person-centred approaches

A person-centred approach, or personalisation, means that the service user is at the centre of the care and support they are receiving and it is is matched to their needs. The quality of care you can provide will be improved if you know all about the person, not just what their capabilities and condition are currently. This allows for the fact that we are all individuals. If, for example, two people have the same illness it does not mean that their care and support needs are the same. A care plan sets out in detail the support and care that has been agreed for a service user. Representatives of the services the person needs meet and work together to make sure the service user receives the most appropriate and effective care. More importantly, the service user and their family are consulted on what they want to happen now, and in the future. You will be expected to treat a service user as the most important person when meeting their care and support needs by continually listening to them and their families, making accurate records and regularly referring to their care plan, as the care plan will continually change and evolve as care needs change. Again, this will require good communication skills.

Importance of supervision in work experience

Supervision is very important because a good supervisor makes sure that you understand the policies, procedures and legislation, such as health and safety, you must abide by. This will:

▸ stop you from causing harm to yourself, other service providers and service users

▸ protect you and the service provider from blame, by ensuring you do not make mistakes.

Link

Learning aim A of this unit covers confidentiality, as does Unit 5, learning aim D.

Unit 5: Meeting Individual Care and Support Needs, learning aim C gives more detail about promoting personalisation.

Learning aim B of this unit covers the roles of placement supervisors/mentors.

Key term

Supervision – directing and overseeing someone's (a learner's) work.

Without supervision, you would not be allowed to try certain tasks. Supervision also allows you access to someone with time to answer your questions, explain things to you and give you advice and support. Your supervisor introduces you to the setting and to the profession, laying the foundations for your future career.

Using work experience placement reflective journals to link theory with practice, reflecting on how work experience influences your own professional development

Completing your work experience log, which includes recording a reflective journal, is an essential part of your work experience placement.

▶ It is a crucial part of your assessment for this unit.

▶ It allows you to record evidence of the skills you have developed and demonstrated.

▶ It provides evidence of you having successfully completed the placement.

▶ It gives you the opportunity to reflect on your achievements, strengths and weaknesses.

▶ It provides evidence of you developing and improving your skills, attributes, knowledge and health and social care practice when you apply for a job in this sector.

▶ It allows you to see or apply what you have learned before the work experience in practice, so linking theory to practice.

By reflecting on your work experience reflective journal, you will be able to see how far you have developed professionally, decide whether this particular type of service setting is one in which you would or would not like to work in future, and work out what you now need to do to develop your skills, attributes and knowledge further, so identifying your professional development needs.

> **Discussion**
>
> In a small group, discuss your ideas on how your work experience log helps you link theory to practice, and how work experience is influencing your professional development.

Work experience evidence log

Form HSC T 4, Section 4, Part 2 encourages you to reflect on the skills and attributes you have developed on work placement, and how this has improved your performance.

 **PAUSE POINT**   Do you understand the tasks you may be expected to do during your work experience? Do any elements need clarification?

Hint   Draw a mind map of the key points.

Extend   Why is a person-centred approach so important in providing the best care and support for service users?

Work shadowing and observations

Work shadowing different professionals, as appropriate

You may be given the opportunity to **work shadow** one or more people for a day or two each. Work shadowing is where you observe someone in their day-to-day job, rather than having hands-on experience, to provide you with an insight into that job role. This allows you to:

▸ see how other staff and teams work

▸ gain insight into the roles and responsibilities of those you work shadow

▸ get a better idea of how different people work together in the same setting, so getting a better overview of the setting

▸ learn by observing and asking questions

▸ spend time reflecting on their role when talking to them about their job

▸ observe them doing tasks that you are not allowed to do.

You will observe the person you are shadowing taking part in a range of activities, such as watching them interact with service users, taking clinical measurements, using specialised equipment, attending meetings and interacting with other service providers, both from within and outside the setting.

Observing specific procedures, as appropriate

When you observe a service provider carry out a specific procedure, such as taking a service user's temperature, you need to be attentive, showing respect to the person carrying out the procedure. You must also respect the patient's privacy and that they may be feeling unwell, so ask questions after you have left their bedside. Remember that the focus must always be on the service user, so as well as observing the procedure, make sure you notice how the person carrying it out interacts with the service user, building **rapport** and implementing the care values. You should make notes and reflect on the experience as soon as possible afterwards, so you do not forget anything.

> **Key term**
>
> **Work shadowing** – observing a person doing their job to learn about their role.

> **Key term**
>
> **Rapport** – an understanding relationship between two people that allows communication between them.

▸ How does this healthcare professional show that she has a rapport with the baby whose temperature she is taking?

Working relationships and agreed ways of working in health and social care

There are many different working relationships in your work setting. These are all based on professionalism, values and principles of care. Everyone is expected to show respect to, and support the rights of, everyone they work with. Working relationships may be between colleagues, between managers and those whom they manage, or with service users. Some will be formal, for example with your work supervisor and those in more senior positions, or with professionals from outside your setting. Others will be more informal, such as with the people you work with every day and with other work experience learners. As you develop a working relationship with a service user it may become more informal. Talking about holiday plans and families helps you to get to know them better and helps them trust and like you, but it is inappropriate to become too close or involved.

Ways of working are agreed in every work setting. Policies and procedure will be in place to make sure that requirements, standards and expectations laid down by regulatory bodies and through legislation are met. There will be boundaries set by professional codes of conduct, and by an agreed code of conduct within your workplace setting. You will be expected to follow these ways of working to promote and maintain the health, safety and wellbeing of everyone who works there.

Reflecting on work practice and procedures used within the setting

Reflecting on work practice and procedures will help you to gain a better understanding of them and will also give you the opportunity to look for areas that can be improved. If you work in a residential care home, for example, you may think that the way laundry is managed in the care home is not very efficient, with residents regularly being given the wrong items of clothing. You might have a good idea to improve this process. You should suggest this to your supervisor tactfully. If your suggestion is implemented, it will benefit service users and reduce the time wasted by service providers in sorting out mistakes. It will give you a useful insight to record in your work experience log. Additionally, you will have the satisfaction of knowing that your idea and knowledge improved a working practice, which may be useful if you eventually pursue a career in this area.

> **Reflect**
>
> Reflect on your work experience setting. Can you think of any work practice which you have observed that seems inefficient? How could it be improved? In a small group, swap your ideas to see if others in the group think your idea would be an improvement.

Assessment practice 6.3   C.P5   C.P6   C.M3   C.D2

Reflect on tasks you have completed on your work experience, or, if you have not yet started your placement, during a holiday or weekend job or on your level 2 work experience. Write a report in which you:

- describe how you demonstrated work-related skills to complete three set tasks and for each one how you know you did this proficiently and confidently
- describe how work shadowing and observation can support the development of your skills while on work placement
- describe examples where you took the initiative to carry out activities within your limitations and those of the settings, selecting appropriate skills and techniques for at least two different situations.

Plan
- Which appropriate tasks have I completed?
- How will I structure this report?

Do
- I can ask my tutor or supervisor for clarification.
- I am recording any problems I experience and am looking for ways to solve these.

Review
- I know where I have learning gaps.
- I have a better appreciation of the importance of reflecting on practice.

Reflect on how work experience influences own personal and professional development

At the end of your work experience placement it is important that you reflect on the experience as a whole in order to work out what you need to do next.

Reviewing personal and professional development

Reflective practice is an ongoing activity

It is important to understand that reflective practice is an ongoing activity, which you should use throughout your working life. Service users will look to you to provide a high quality of care and support, so you will need to continually reflect on your working practice in order to keep improving it. Reflective practice enables you to be honest about your professional practice and challenges you to take a step back to look at your own experiences to get a better understanding of good practice, as well as the changes needed to improve what is working less well.

Theories and frameworks for reflective practice

Kolb developed a reflective learning cycle (1984) for learning through experience based on four stages.

▶ Experience – doing it.

▶ Observations and reflections – reviewing and reflecting on the experience.

▶ Conceptualise (development of ideas) – learning from the experience.

▶ Testing ideas in practice – planning, trying out what you have learned.

Gibbs developed this into his six-stage reflective cycle (1988), a model that encourages learning through repetition, by repeating an improved activity after carrying out the reflective cycle, as shown in Step by step: Reflective practice.

Step by step: Reflective practice   `6 Steps`

1 Description of the actual experience: What happened? What did you do and how did you do it?

▼

2 Feelings: What were you thinking and feeling? How did you react?

▼

3 Evaluation: What was good and bad about the experience?

▼

4 Analysis: What sense can you make of the situation? What have you learned from the experience?

▼

5 Conclusion: What else could you have done? What have you learned from reflecting on this experience?

▼

6 Action plan: If this situation arose again what would you do? What do you need to do differently next time?

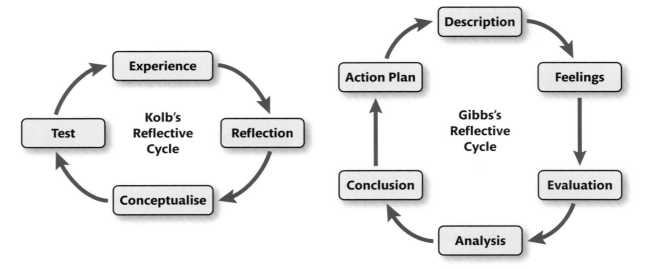

▶ **Figure 6.5** Compare the two models. Which do you feel is most useful and why?

Another, simpler method is to ask four key questions:

▶ What worked well and why?
▶ What did not work well and why not?
▶ What will I do the same next time?
▶ What will I do differently next time?

This is a similar approach to a SWOT analysis, which you learned about earlier in this unit (see learning aim B).

Research

There have been many theories and frameworks developed for reflective practice. Research five of them and put them in the order in which they were developed (chronological order). Produce a summary that is attractive and clear, in a style and form of your choosing, and be prepared to discuss which one you like best and why.

Reflect

Think about a task you have recently completed on your work experience. Use Gibbs's learning cycle to reflect on how you carried out the task and how you could do it better in the future. Then reflect on your overall personal and professional development during your work experience, using the Step by step: Reflective practice.

Reviewing work experience reflective journal

During your work experience you should have revisited and reviewed your work experience reflective journal regularly. It is good practice to set a time each week when you will check through it to see what you should be completing at that point, and to record the skills you have used that week. Now you have completed your work placement, you need to go through the whole of your log to see if there is anything missing.

Evaluating own performance

The practice of reviewing your work experience reflective journal at least once a week will ensure that you keep your log up to date, track your progress towards meeting

▶ Are you regularly completing and reviewing your work experience log?

your targets and development goals and encourage you to take action if progress is not as you wanted.

To evaluate your own performance you need to:

▶ ask yourself if you have met your targets

▶ try to be specific – do not make vague statements such as 'I think my communication skills are great overall', use expressions such as 'I have demonstrated good communication skills, especially in listening and writing. I still need to be more confident when speaking in a meeting or to a group of people, as shown when ...'

▶ not belittle your achievements – if your work placement supervisor praised the aspect of your work you are evaluating, say so. If you have shown, for example, your willingness to work hard by staying late to help a colleague finish a task, or have helped by volunteering to do something extra or something others did not want to do, say so

▶ be honest – if you made a mistake say so, but also say what you did to put the situation right

▶ not be defensive – if your tutor or supervisor says you have not shown a particular skill and you think you have, do not take it personally, ask for clarification and listen closely to what is said, so you can learn from what they are saying

▶ identify weaknesses and suggest what you need to do to put them right.

Discussion

With a partner, discuss any mistakes you made on your work experience and how you dealt with them. Looking back, do you think you could have dealt with your mistakes better? How? What have your mistakes taught you?

Reflecting on own personal and professional development

You need to use reflective practice to decide whether you have met your personal and professional development goals. Look back at the goals you set yourself and reflect on how far you have moved towards meeting those goals.

Work experience evidence log

You need to use reflective practice to complete the final part of your personal and professional development plan in your work experience log, which asks how reviewing your progress towards your goals over a period of time has helped your own professional development.

Form HSC T 3 will remind you about which skills for work in health and social care settings you managed to use and collect evidence of, so you can reflect on what you need to do to fill any gaps in those skills. You can also use form HSC T 5, the tutor observational visit report, and form HSC T 6, the work placement supervisor report, to reflect on those skills identified by your tutor and work supervisor as needing improving and developing.

 **PAUSE POINT**   Explain how you reviewed your personal and professional development. How did you use your work experience log to do it?

Hint   Write a step by step process for reflective practice.

Extend   Why do you think it is important to be specific when reflecting on and evaluating your own performance?

Using feedback and action planning

The importance of Continuing Professional Development (CPD)

Continuing professional development (CPD) keeps professionals updated with relevant information, skills, training and knowledge throughout their working life. Along with **experiential learning** it ensures that you remain competent in your chosen profession, so that you will be able to provide better quality care and support. If you are prepared to take opportunities offered for CPD, you are likely to move up the career ladder more quickly. Evidence of CPD on your CV shows prospective employers that you have a certain level of competence and that you are serious about succeeding in your career. If you have been lucky enough to have taken part in at least one training course while on work placement, you will be able to include the date, the title of the course and the training provider on your CV, as well as details about your work placement/s. This will stand you in good stead when you have an interview for your chosen job.

CPD is not only important for the individual and the setting they work in, but also helps to improve the work sector as a whole. Professional service providers go through a process called performance management, usually once a year, where **feedback** is given on strengths and weaknesses and targets are set for training to improve the weaknesses, whether these are in knowledge or skills. It is an ongoing process throughout a professional's working life.

> **Key terms**
>
> **Continuing Professional Development (CPD)** – the process of taking part in a range of learning activities to update, increase and improve your knowledge and skills throughout your working life.
>
> **Experiential learning** – information or skills acquired through experience and observation, while working.
>
> **Feedback** – reaction from other people about your performance, which can be used to inform improvement.

Identifying areas of positive and constructive feedback

When you have looked back through your work experience log, you will notice that there are places where your tutor or work experience supervisor has said some of your skills are good or excellent and you have received praise. This is called positive feedback. There may also be skills which have been identified as needing improving and developing, and maybe some comments to say what you need to do to improve. This is constructive feedback, which draws your attention to an area where you can improve. Such feedback is useful and is different from criticism which is given in a negative way and can upset and discourage you. A good supervisor will give you constructive feedback rather than criticism. You need to find the areas of positive and constructive feedback so that you know what you have done well and what you still need to strive to improve.

Work experience evidence log

Create a table with two columns. In the first column put the heading 'areas of positive feedback', in the second column put the heading 'constructive feedback'. Complete the table with examples from your work experience log.

Stay calm and carry on

Louise has recently finished her work placement at a GP's surgery in a health centre attached to a hospital. She really enjoyed her time there and felt she had become part of the team.

One of her most memorable experiences was when a 53-year-old man had a heart attack in the waiting area, where she was helping the receptionist behind the desk. The receptionist, who was her work experience supervisor, told Louise to run to get a doctor. Louise used her initiative and knocked on the nurses' door and shouted what had happened on her way down the corridor to find a doctor. She was mindful that all the

GPs had patients with them, so she stood in the corridor outside their closed doors and said calmly but loudly 'Is there a doctor available to help a man who has collapsed with chest pains in the waiting area, now please?' Several came running out and one of them went and gave the man CPR, while waiting for the paramedics to arrive.

Louise's work experience supervisor later gave her some glowing positive feedback in her work experience log, but also said that she had caused alarm among some patients when she had shouted outside the doors.

Check your knowledge

1   What positive feedback do you think Louise's work experience supervisor gave her about her skills and attributes in this situation?

2   How did Louise support the receptionist and help the patient?

3   Why did Louise not open a door and speak quietly to a GP?

4   What could Louise's work experience supervisor have said to make the feedback about shouting in the corridor more constructive?

Highlighting areas for improvement

Now you have evaluated your own performance and identified areas of constructive feedback, you know which skills and knowledge need improving. You need to highlight those which you feel are most important and which will help you most in the future, such as improving a specific area of your communication skills, trying to be more empathetic and learning more about a particular job role.

Work experience evidence log

There is a pro forma action plan that you can use to reflect on your skills and activities throughout your work placement. You can use one of the reflective practice methods described earlier to identify which skills and activities you need to develop further and to help you complete the final row of the form.

Creating an action plan for personal and professional development

Creating an action plan will help you focus your ideas and decide what steps you need to take to achieve your goals. Your plan should have a series of targets that you aim to meet to achieve each of your goals. An example for just one personal development goal is shown below. Other examples may have a different time scale for each step and several people identified to give support. A target in an action plan to meet a professional development goal might be to seek other work experiences or training.

Worked Example

Goal	Benefits	Steps needed	Timescale	Support
To improve my listening skills.	• More information shared. • Happier service users, colleagues, family and friends. • Fewer mistakes or misunderstandings. • Increased confidence. • Calmer atmosphere. • Better relationships.	Instead of thinking what to say next while the other person is speaking, focus on what is being said.	Friday	A tutor, family member or friend to have a conversation with me.
		Ask questions for clarification, to check you have understood what the speaker has said.		
		Reflect on what has been said by summarising and restating it to the speaker.		
		Listen to the words being said, but also be aware of how they are being said and of any non-verbal messages, such as body language.		
		Do not be distracted, for example by a mobile phone. Put it away, or turn it off, during a conversation.		
		Listen to feedback from the speaker.		
		Repeat the steps above until you receive positive feedback.	The following Friday	

Work experience evidence log

An action plan pro forma can be found in Appendix 2 of your work experience log.

> **Reflect**
>
> Reflect on your work experience. Pick one of your personal development goals and make a plan, using the same headings as in the Worked Example.

▶ **Figure 6.6** Do you know what all these terms mean? If not, look them up in a dictionary.

Identifying career goals

Now you have completed your work experience, you will have decided that a particular type of work and setting either is or is not right for you. To identify your career goals, you first need to decide on the area of health and social care in which you are most interested in working. You could reflect on your work experience placement to help you decide. You then need to decide what type of job in that area is best suited to your skills and attributes. Start by setting aside some time to think about this properly. Ask yourself questions such as those in Figure 6.7.

▶ **Figure 6.7** Can you think of any other questions that are important when setting your career goals?

If you need more advice, speak to people such as a tutor, a careers adviser or someone you know who works in the area you are considering, and use online research to gain further information. You could write an action plan to set out on the journey towards achieving your career goals.

You may decide to:

▶ go to college or university to gain qualifications, get the job you want and aim to get regular promotions until you are in a management position

▶ get a job and attend college on day release, or in the evening, and aim for promotion

▶ get a job and learn on the job, and either provide direct care and support to service users or aim for promotion.

Then set yourself a short-term goal (about one year), a medium-term goal (about five years) and a long-term goal (about 20 years), a vision of where you eventually hope to be in your career. Good luck.

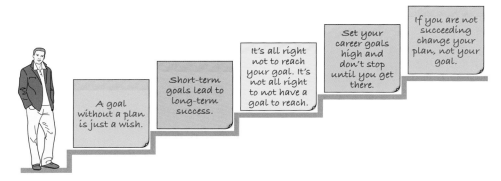

▶ **Figure 6.8** What are your aspirations? What are your career goals?

Assessment practice 6.4

Use and improve the work you have completed during learning aim D to write the following.

- A review of your own strengths and areas for development, in response to feedback on your work experience placement.

- A personal and professional development plan that includes your personal and professional development goals, based on the completion of your work experience placement.

- A report that assesses and justifies how planning and self-reflection on skills developed during your work experience has contributed to your personal and professional development, both during your work experience placement and in your plans for your future personal and professional development.

Plan

- What tasks have I already completed that will help me with this activity?
- Is there any part of this activity about which I need clarification?

Do

- I am spending some time planning out my approach to this activity.
- I understand when I need to be reflective and when I need to carry out commands, such as assess and justify.

Review

- I can explain what the task is and what skills I've used during its completion.
- I can make informed assessments of my development goals based on reflection.

Further reading and resources

General careers advice: **https://nationalcareersservice.direct.gov.uk, www.yell.com, www.careerconnect.org.uk**

Skills: **www.wikihow.com, www.skillsyouneed.com**

Employers' requirements for work placement: HSE – **www.hse.gov.uk**

Careers advice: Job roles in adult social care – **www.skillsforcare.org.uk**

NHS principles and care values: **www.nhs.uk/NHSEngland**

Dementia: **www.scie.org.uk/publications, www.alzheimers.org.uk**

Safeguarding young people on work experience: **www.education.gov.uk**

Research organisations: **www.cqc.org.uk**

National Occupational Standards: **www.skillsforhealth.org.uk**

WorldSkills standards in health and social care: **www.worldskills.org**

Careers and work experience placements: **www.healthcareers.nhs.uk**

Person-centred approaches: **www.citrustrainingsolutions.co.uk**

Job shadowing: **www.mmu.ac.uk**

THINK ▶FUTURE

Michael O'Hare

Work experience manager

I work in a large hospital and it's my job to organise our centralised work experience placement programme. I'm involved in communicating with tutors who are looking for work experience opportunities for their learners. I also have to complete paperwork that needs to be done prior to learners being placed here, and I act as supervisor while the learners are with us. When learners first arrive here, I give them an induction, which involves general information about the hospital and its work. The induction also details issues such as the rules and regulations that must be followed, including health and safety, the confidentiality agreement they need to sign, and what they will actually be doing on the placement. I organise any special clothing, equipment, security passes, ID badges and login details they may need and show them round. After this, I hand them over to their allocated mentor, who they will be working with, or work shadowing, in the department or on the ward in which they will be working. I'm on hand to provide help and advice if they have problems, do observations, give feedback and help them collect evidence for their work experience logs.

I'm in charge of the whole work experience programme, including mock interviews, in which the learners are given an experience of a job interview. This role is very rewarding, as I feel I'm helping young people towards their chosen career, and helping the mentors to develop different skills. I need to be approachable, empathetic, assertive, well organised and knowledgeable about the whole organisation and its work. I also need good skills in all aspects of communication.

Focusing your skills

Interpersonal skills

An important part of your work experience will be interacting with patients.

- Remember that you are a work experience learner, so tell the patient that and do not try to give any medical advice.
- Check that they want to chat, and if they do not, leave them alone as they may be in pain or tired.
- Ask the patient's permission if you want to ask about why they are in hospital, but you do not have to talk to them about their illness. They may prefer to talk about something else to take their mind off their problems.
- Some will be lonely as not all are lucky enough to have visitors, so you will lift their spirits if you spend some time talking with them.

Writing skills

You may be involved in adding information to a patient's records. If you are asked to do this, you should:

- listen very carefully and write the information down accurately
- ask for the information to be repeated if you did not hear properly
- write neatly and legibly, so others can read what you have written
- remember not to talk about any information you have been given.

Getting ready for assessment

Cosmina is working towards a BTEC National in Health and Social Care. She was given an assignment for learning aim B with the following title: 'Develop a work experience plan to support your own learning and development, and explain why it is important to do this'. The plan had to:

▶ include at least five goals, and the targets to be taken towards each of the goals, deadlines, benefits and support needed

▶ be clearly and attractively presented, and reflect her own responsibilities and limitations on her placement.

Cosmina shares her experience below.

How I got started

First I collected all my notes on this topic and put them into a folder. The textbook referred to pro formas in the work experience log, so I decided to read through the log to see what was included that would help me structure my plan. I also made contact with my work experience placement supervisor and asked if I could go along to ask him why he thought an action plan was a good idea. I talked to learners who had already been on a work placement to collect their opinions.

How I brought it all together

I decided to use a variety of fonts, colours and pictures to make the work look attractive.

▶ I wrote a short introduction to explain my responsibilities and limitations on work experience placement.

▶ I created my own version of a work experience action plan pro forma, which included my personal and professional development goals.

▶ I wrote a follow-up piece explaining why it is important to have a plan to support my learning and development.

▶ I wrote a conclusion that explained the benefits of planning and preparation in supporting my expectations of work experience.

I also included some quotes from my work experience supervisor.

What I learned from the experience

After looking at the action plan in the work experience log, I decided to create my own version. I spent quite a long time making it look attractive, and filled in a lot of the columns. Then I showed it to my tutor who advised me to use the headings from the one in the work experience log. She also pointed out that there was a worked example in learning aim D of the textbook that might help me. I wish I had shown it to my tutor before I'd spent a whole evening drawing up a template with the wrong headings. It was an easy job to change the headings, but I still felt I'd wasted some of the time. I also realised after I'd done quite a lot of work that I had confused the terms goals and targets. Although it didn't take long to put right, I was annoyed with myself that I hadn't checked my understanding.

I was glad that I asked my work placement supervisor for his opinion. I had only just met him as I'm about to start work experience, so it was good to get to know him a bit better before I started. I was apprehensive about approaching him, but was glad I made myself do it and feel that I have grown a little in confidence as a result.

Think about it

▶ Have you written a plan, with timings, so you can complete your assignment by the agreed submission date?

▶ Do you have notes on the key terms so that you know the difference between goals, targets and objectives?

▶ Is your information written in your own words, and referenced clearly where you have used quotations or information from a book, journal or website?

Promoting Public Health 8

Getting to know your unit

Assessment

You will be assessed by a series of assignments set by your tutor.

This unit will aim to help you understand the topic of how public health is promoted throughout the world, but especially in the UK. There will be research topics given to you by your tutor to help you with this unit and to assess your learning. Assignments will be set for each learning aim, with a pass, merit or distinction grade given. To obtain a distinction you must evaluate how far health strategies meet the aims of health factors in Britain, or another area of your choice, which must be approved by your tutor, and how successful a recent health strategy has been.

How you will be assessed

You will be assessed by a set of assignments set by your tutor, to ensure that you fully understand the topic of how public health is promoted in the UK and worldwide. There will also be role plays given to you by your tutor to help you with this unit and to assess your learning.

Assignments will be set for each learning aim, with a pass, merit or distinction grade given.

It is important to check that you have met all the Pass grading criteria as you work your way through the assignments. To achieve a Merit or Distinction, you need to present your work in such a way that you meet the criteria for those grades. To achieve Merit, you need to analyse and assess the impact of a recent health campaign; and for Distinction you need to evaluate and justify recent health campaigns.

Assessment criteria

This table shows what you must do in order to achieve a **Pass**, **Merit** or **Distinction** grade, and where you can find activities to help you.

Pass	Merit	Distinction
Learning aim A Examine strategies for developing public health policy to improve the health of individuals and the population		
A.P1 Explain the strategies used to develop public health policy in order for it to meet its aims. **Assessment practice 8.1**	**A.M1** Analyse how public health policy is influenced by strategies and patterns of health and ill health. **Assessment practice 8.1**	**A.D1** Evaluate how far the use of strategies and monitoring the health status of the population helps public health policy to meet its aims in reducing the factors that influence public health, with reference to a specific demographic area. **Assessment practice 8.1**
A.P2 Explain how monitoring information to determine patterns of health and ill health is used by government to inform the creation of public health policy. **Assessment practice 8.1**		

Pass	**Merit**	**Distinction**

Learning aim Examine the factors affecting health and the impact of addressing these factors to improve public health

B.P3 Explain factors affecting current patterns of health and ill health in a specific demographic area. **Assessment practice 8.1**	**B.M2** Assess the extent to which factors affect current patterns of health and ill health with reference to a specific demographic area. **Assessment practice 8.1**	
B.P4 Explain the impact of public health policy in minimising these factors in relation to a specific demographic area. **Assessment practice 8.1**	**B.M3** Assess how minimising the factors affecting health can contribute to improving the health of the population in relation to the area. **Assessment practice 8.1**	

Learning aim C Investigate how health is promoted to improve the health of the population

C.P5 Explain how approaches to health promotion and protection have been applied in a selected health promotion campaign. **Assessment practice 8.2**	**C.M4** Assess the success of approaches used to promote and protect health and prevent disease in a selected health promotion campaign. **Assessment practice 8.2**	**C.D2** Justify the approaches used to promote and protect health and prevent disease in a selected health promotion campaign. **Assessment practice 8.2**
C.P6 Explain how approaches to prevention and control have been applied in a selected campaign. **Assessment practice 8.2**		

Learning aim D Investigate how health promotion encourages individuals to change their behaviour in relation to their own health

D.P7 Explain how models or theories that justify behaviour change can be used to overcome barriers in relation to a selected health promotion campaign. **Assessment practice 8.2**	**D.M5** Analyse how theories or models and approaches have been used in a selected health promotion campaign to overcome barriers and increase public awareness. **Assessment practice 8.2**	**D.D3** Evaluate the success of a specific public health campaign in encouraging behaviour change in relation to health. **Assessment practice 8.2**
D.P8 Explain the features of a selected health promotion campaign and the approaches used to increase public awareness. **Assessment practice 8.2**		**D.D4** Evaluate how far a recent health promotion campaign met the aims of public health policy through the strategies and approaches used to improve the health of a demographic area. **Assessment practice 8.2**

A good place to start is discussing, in groups, health campaigns being promoted on the television, radio or posters on health that you have seen or read. After the discussion you can note what you believe the campaign is about and how effective it is.

A | Examine strategies for developing public health policy to improve the health of individuals and the population

The origins and aims of public health policy

On 5 July 1948 the National Health Service came into being, to ensure that people in the UK would receive free healthcare at the point of delivery, no matter what their income. It was the first health service of its kind in the world.

During and after the Second World War, the government and the major political parties became more aware and concerned about people's health. Additionally, there were considerations about recovery from serious injuries, some of which had never been seen before, due to the bombing raids in the UK and from those incurred by the people returning from fighting. Up until this time, people who could afford it had private health insurance to help towards their medical bills. Those who could not afford to pay for a doctor and for medicine went without proper medical help.

The government commissioned Sir William Beveridge to investigate ways in which the country could recover from the Second World War. Beveridge had much experience in political affairs and was an expert on the problem of unemployment. In 1942, the Beveridge Report (1942) was published. The report stated that the post-war period was a time for radical change and one recommendation was that the government should find ways to fight disease.

The public welcomed the Beveridge report. In 1940 measles became a **notifiable disease** in England and Wales. There had been an epidemic of measles in 1940, which was a very serious illness at that time, with approximately 400,000 cases reported. Approximately one in twenty babies died before their first birthday, and every year people died of infectious diseases such as pneumonia, meningitis, tuberculosis and polio. There was overwhelming evidence for the need for health care for all.

> **Key term**
>
> **Notifiable disease** – a medical condition required, by law, to be reported to government authorities.

> **Research**
>
> There was another measles epidemic in 1961 in the UK, with 763,531 cases reported to Public Health England. Look at the statistics provided on: **www.gov. uk/government/publications/measles-deaths-by-age-group-from-1980-to-2013-ons-data/measles-notifications-and-deaths-in-england-and-wales-1940-to-2013** to find out what the major difference was between the epidemics in 1940 and 1961. Why do you think this occurred?

Between the First and Second World Wars, from 1919 to 1939, there had been numerous reports on improving healthcare but nothing had been implemented. In 1945, the new Labour government took on the recommendations of the report and the National Health Service Act was passed in 1946, and came into force in 1948. The National Health Service (NHS) would be completely financed by tax, would benefit every person in the country and be available from the cradle to the grave. For the first time, people could receive diagnosis and treatment of any illness, either at their home or in hospital, including dental and ophthalmic care, regardless of their ability to pay. The implementation of a National Health Service has had a significant impact on the nation's health, improving the health of millions.

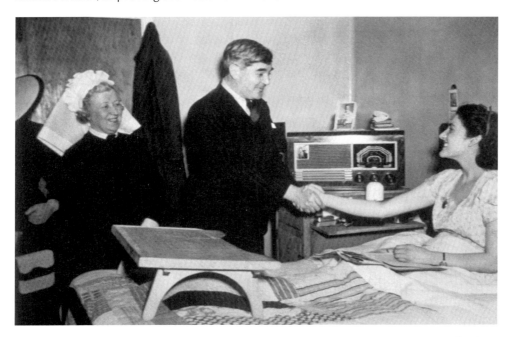

▶ Aneurin Bevan, the Minister for Health, visiting the first patients of the new NHS at Trafford General Hospital in July 1948

Aims of public health policy

Planning national provision of health care and promoting the health of the population

The government has an overriding moral aim to make sure that the health of its citizens is paramount, and this became even more prevalent due to the health of people during and after the Second World War. The NHS started to provide a more accessible health service to meet the aim of public health policy by ensuring fair and impartial health services across the whole of the UK, so that an acceptable standard of good health would be experienced by the whole population regardless of social standing and geographical location.

To meet the needs of a changing demographic, public health policy needs to be responsive. To plan for future needs and to provide care in acute situations such as the swine flu epidemic in 2009, the government needs to gather statistical data and commission reports into current trends in health within the nation as well as attempting to predict future developments in the health status of the nation.

Information on the factors that influence health such as lifestyle choices, unemployment, education, housing, prevalence of disease and poverty help to shape the planning process for health provision. Public expectations of health provision and the protection that it provides for their welfare have increased with technological advances in medicine and equipment. Health trends have changed over the years, as more medical conditions become treatable and life expectancy has increased.

Currently, public health policy has to address a range of issues such as dementia, mental health issues and rising rates of resistance to antimicrobial treatments as well as raising awareness of the importance of healthy eating, exercising, moderation in alcohol consumption and stopping smoking.

Case study

Debbie Does Her Best

When Debbie's marriage to Tahir broke up and she lost her job at the biscuit factory she had to leave her comfortable life behind and start again with two young children. Accomodation was very expensive in the city she lived in and in order to move out of emergency accommodation provided by social services, Debbie borrowed money for the first month's rent and a bond on a flat from her family.

Debbie's flat was damp, black mould covered the walls and condensation ran down the windows. The flat was expensive to heat and the children often slept with clothes on top of their pyjamas in the winter. Debbie developed depression because of the break up of her marriage and the state of her housing. She found it impossible to find employment and she was upset that she couldn't give the children a varied diet.

Check your knowledge

1 What health problems could the children develop by living in this environment?

2 How can unemployment have an impact on the short term and long term health of families?'

3 Why is nutrition important to health?

4 How can depression and unemployment affect health?

Identifying and monitoring needs

It was noted by health officials that due to food rationing during the war and the ten years after it, that people's health improved. This was also investigated. Local authorities at this time introduced Children's and Mental Health Departments to help support illness and conditions brought on by war, or poverty, and this became known as the 'social citizenship' agenda, in which the government became the provider for the welfare of all, for the first time. The World Health Organization (WHO) in 1946, identified health as a separate issue in which governments must be involved, to the benefit of people's physical, mental and social wellbeing, and not just for treating diseases. An active role in raising public awareness continued through the 1970s and 1980s with public information films on topics as varied as the safe handling of fireworks and crossing the road safely, through to sexual health.

The government's role in understanding and predicting social change is pivotal in the treatment and control of disease. As social influences such as the media and peer pressure become more prevalent, health policy needs to become more responsive. Examples of this include campaigns to raise awareness of the dangers of illegal drug use and the impact on the community of driving while under the influence of alcohol or drugs. The government response to medical evidence of the link between smoking and various types of cancer, including lung cancer and throat cancer, have led to a range of interventions controlling not just the advertising of cigarettes but also restictions on where individuals may smoke. Smoking in the workplace was banned in England on 1 July 2007.

Research

Investigate the government's response to the link between childhood obesity and type 2 diabetes in children. What initiatives has the government tried to persuade parents, carers and children to improve nutritional standards?

Identifying and reducing inequalities

It was not until 1974 that the NHS was responsible for the majority of public health. Prior to this, the NHS was being established, spreading across the nation and reclaiming responsibility for the health of all citizens. However, with the population's health needs differing enormously between rural and industrial areas, for example, establishing local authorities was found to have more of an impact on the provision of appropriate health services.

Protecting society from health threats

From the 1970s onwards, factors such as crime rates, housing conditions, pollution, economic regeneration and education were observed as affecting the health and wellbeing of people. There are worldwide and national guidelines about monitoring these issues and suggesting improvements to protect the population from these hazards. For example, there is legislation about the disposal of toxic waste and standards governing air quality in cities with regard to vehicle emissions.

A new local authority role, Director of Health, required local authorities to be directly responsible for the health of their residents. All communicable illnesses are reported through a GP, or local hospital, to a regional health team who monitor the overall incidence. If several cases of an infectious disease are reported, then an outbreak management team investigates, monitoring its spread throughout the local area, and putting in place medical resources to prevent further spread.

Wherever possible, preventative measures are used against infections that are likely to occur on a seasonal basis. For example, flu vaccination is offered to vulnerable people, including the elderly, or those with a specific health condition such as diabetes, to prevent the illness in these groups. The immunisation of babies and infants to prevent the spread of communicable diseases such as mumps, measles and rubella, is another example of a preventative measure.

Controlling an outbreak of an infectious disease would include a case definition report. This includes information about the time, place, the person and the illness, so that a picture can be established to understand where the outbreak started. The local health authorities use this information to report to the national health body, which allows monitoring of whether the outbreak is spreading or decreasing, and appropriate resources to be implemented to prevent further spread.

Addressing national health problems

National health problems are issues that can affect any sector of society, although they may be more prevalent in some sectors than others, or some regions may find themselves at higher risk than others. Air pollution, for example, affects everybody but some areas have higher pollution than others. An example of this would be traffic pollution being higher in the cities. Further to this, some sectors of the community may be more affected by a problem than others. Someone with Chronic Obstructive Pulmonary Disease (COPD) will suffer more breathing difficulties than the average person when air pollution levels are high.

Poor diet and the build-up of fatty deposits in the arteries which break free and block vessels in the brain is one cause of stroke.

Developing screening programmes

Screening is a way of identifying people who may be at a high risk of contracting a disease or condition, for example bowel or cervical cancer or glaucoma. If the individual is found to have a health problem after the screening test, further investigation will be recommended. A screening programme has to be cost effective for the health service. There are more than 100 screening programmes in the UK.

Screening programmes in the UK are targeted to sections of society that have already been identified as at a higher risk. A family history of breast cancer for example may put a woman at higher risk of developing the disease.

Certain age groups also have a higher prevalence of disorders. Cholestererol testing and blood pressure checks are routinely offered to people over 40 as the conditions that can come with having elevated levels of cholesterol or having high blood pressure, such as stroke, can strike without warning.

 PAUSE POINT   Why did the NHS come into being?

> **Hint**   Think about how people afford and pay for health care.

> **Extend**   What was the immediate impact of the National Health Service Act 1946 on people's health at that time?

Strategies for developing public health policy

Strategies

The Department of Health (DH) is the government department responsible for identifying the nation's health needs in England, and for developing programmes to reduce risk and screen for early signs of disease. The DH works with other agencies to gain a full understanding of the issues around the nation's health to create national policies and legislation. The agencies include:

▶ the Care Quality Commission (CQC)

▶ the Health and Social Care Information Centre

▶ NHS England

▶ Health Education England.

Present policies from the DH include:

▶ cancer research and treatment

▶ children's health

▶ dementia

▶ drug misuse and dependency

▶ health and social care integration

▶ obesity and healthy eating.

Each of these policy issues is broken down into further areas of concern. For example, 'School Food' looks at caterers introducing healthier foods into school menus, and includes research undertaken by Public Health England, Government Buying Standards and the Children's Food Trust.

The Scottish Health and Social Care Directorate reports to the Secretary of Health on the health and wellbeing of its citizens in 14 regional health authorities. The health services work with partners and the public to provide safe, effective and person-centred healthcare. A recent strategy, part of the Quality Strategy, was 'Better Health, Better Care', which proposed that NHS staff, patients, and carers should better understand their rights and responsibilities. This strategy aims to ensure compassionate staff, good and clear communications, a safe environment and clinical excellence.

In Northern Ireland, the Public Health Agency (PHA) works to increase wellbeing and to decrease inequalities in the health of its population. The PHA reports to the Department of Health (Northern Ireland). A recent strategy, 'Making Life Better', was created to help individuals have greater control of their own health, and to be supported by the health services in helping them achieve this.

The NHS Wales strategy, 'Together for Health', aims to improve health services for the benefit of the Welsh people. Another NHS Wales strategy, 'Working differently – working together', sets out how to improve health information for the future.

Planning and evaluating

The DH undertakes research into all areas of the nation's health. By using a range of different agencies throughout the UK, the DH obtains the right information for what to plan and put into place to help and support people with their health. The same agencies can also feed back to the DH on any improvements needed in health care for their area.

According to the NHS Health Check Implementation Review and Action Plan 2013, the seven most preventable causes of death were alcohol consumption, high blood pressure, smoking, obesity, cholesterol, poor diet and lack of physical activity. By challenging the public's acceptance of the inevitability of disease as being unrelated to lifestyle choices, the government can formulate strategies that help the public to help themselves.

Obesity is another health issue that is affecting more people in England than in many other developed countries. Public Health England reports that one in five children entering primary school is already overweight or obese. 'Obesity and healthy living' is the government's policy that aims to create a downward trend in the levels of excess weight in adults and children by 2020. This will be achieved through a series of a public awareness drives by the government that encourage people to eat a healthy diet and exercise more.

Obesity is a particular issue in deprived areas. If the current trend continues, it is predicted that 70 per cent of adults will be overweight or obese by the 2030s. The financial costs to society associated with obesity-related diseases are increasing, such as type 2 diabetes and coronary artery disease. Action to tackle obesity is one of PHE's seven priorities. National mapping of weight management services (2015) was research undertaken by PHE working with other, more local, agencies in an area of northern England to gather data on obesity.

Minimising harm from the environment

The Department for Environment, Food & Rural Affairs (Defra) has responsibility for minimising harm to the population from environmental conditions that could cause disease.

Pollution

A current concern is poor air quality, which is estimated to shorten life expectancy by about seven or eight months. Pollution from the density of road traffic in some London streets surpasses the annual European air pollution targets within days.

Defra works with Environmental Protection UK to implement The Air Quality Strategy for England, Scotland, Wales and Northern Ireland. The strategy aims to minimise levels of harmful industrial pollutants in the air such as lead, sulfur dioxide and nitrogen oxide; levels for their output are set and checked nationally, as are emissions from industry and sea pollution.

Recycling and waste management

For issues around recycling and waste management, the government works closely with the Environment Agency, who in turn works with local agencies concerned with waste and recycling. This is to ensure that waste management companies are regulated and monitored by local authorities issuing permits to companies applying to recycle and dispose of waste. The waste is categorised (for example hazardous chemicals, metal, medicines, batteries or paper) with regulations for all types of waste. One such regulation is the Waste Electrical and Electronic Equipment (WEEE) guidance for approved authorised treatment facilities and approved exporters, which was updated in January 2016. The guidelines set targets for the recycling of items such as small and large household appliances, IT and telecommunications equipment, lighting equipment, electrical and electronic tools, toys, leisure and sports equipment, medical devices (except implanted/infected products), display screens and photovoltaic panels.

Case study

A Little Won't Matter

When Kristof was young he had a transistor radio and it used up batteries quickly and batteries were expensive so he didn't use the radio very often. When the batteries wore out he threw them in the bin.

Forty years later, Kristof has, among other things: a mobile phone, an electric toothbrush, a torch, an electric car key, an electric cigarette, a cordless door bell, a smoke detector, a laptop and a small clock in every room to help him organise his life.

Kristof likes new things so he updates his appliances as often as he can afford to. The things that Kristof doesn't need and can't sell he throws away. Kristof has never seen the point of going to the council tip as the dustbin men come every week and empty his bin. He never uses the council recycling services.

Check your knowledge

1 What problems could the batteries cause to the environment if not disposed of safely?

2 How can Kristof reduce the amount of damage that he causes to the environment by using his electrical equipment?'

3 Why is it important for public health that people are aware of environmental issues such as the safe disposal of toxic materials?

There are many other everyday items that can cause ill health if they are not disposed of correctly. All drugs including prescription medications, over-the-counter medications and illegal drugs have the potential to cause harm to public health if they are not disposed of appropriately. Medication should be returned to the pharmacist for safe disposal, not flushed down the toilet where it can enter the water course and cause contamination.

Many other products such as engine oil, paint, baby wipes and even the fat from cooking have the potential to contaminate the water course or damage the sewage system. Blocked waste pipes or sewage pipes can force sewage to back up into people's homes, flooding them with faecal matter which, if ingested, exposes the residents to a potential range of bacterial illnesses of the digestive system.

Food safety

The Food Standards Agency (FSA) is a non-ministerial government department responsible for food safety and hygiene throughout the UK. The FSA works with seven other agencies and local authorities to enforce food safety regulations. The Welsh government is responsible for nutrition policy in Wales.

The Advisory Committee on Novel Foods and Processes advises the FSA about **genetically modified** foods and irradiation of foods. Genetically modified crops and irradiation of foodstuffs are considered by scientists working in the field not to be riskier to human health than conventional food. However, the general public has frequently expressed concerns about their safety and regulation, including labelling and environmental impacts.

Key term

Genetically modified – altering the DNA of an organism (food or plant) to create something that does not occur through natural reproduction.

Research

Investigate the government's current health campaign: Sugar Smart 2016. Create information for a display board for staff and other learners at your school or college. What do you think this campaign hopes to achieve?

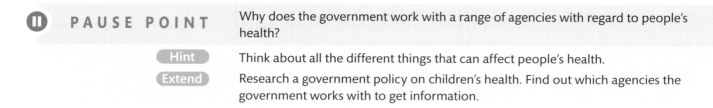

PAUSE POINT   Why does the government work with a range of agencies with regard to people's health?

Hint   Think about all the different things that can affect people's health.

Extend   Research a government policy on children's health. Find out which agencies the government works with to get information.

Monitoring the health status of the population

Health monitoring is an important way of maintaining the nation's health. By closely monitoring outbreaks of diseases, or the increase of the incidence of illnesses seriously dangerous to health, local, regional and governmental departments are able to put in place the necessary resources.

Sources of information for determining patterns of health and ill health

Sources are wide and varied. The DH website reflects the many agencies that report to government about health-related issues.

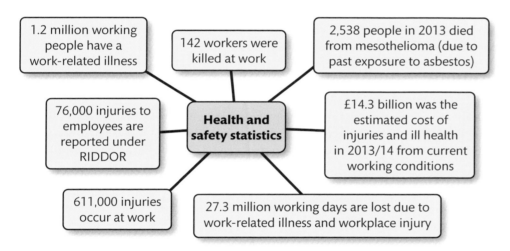

▶ **Figure 8.1:** Key health and safety statistics, Great Britain (2014/15) (source: www.hse.gov.uk/ statistics)

Where do you think the information in Figure 8.1, as reported to the Health and Safety Executive (HSE) comes from? There are several data sources for injury and ill health statistics in Britain, some of which were mentioned in relation to the work of the DH (see the section on Strategies for developing public health policy). The HSE is a government agency, reporting directly to the government, which is used to report injuries, illnesses and diseases related to work. It obtains its data from the agencies with which it works. It is a legal requirement to report incidents and ill health at work to enable the HSE, and other agencies, to gather data about how and why risks arise, and to investigate serious incidents with a view to their prevention.

RIDDOR

Reporting of Injuries, Diseases and Dangerous Occurrences Regulations (RIDDOR), covers the reporting by employers of any diseases or illnesses affecting their workers that are potentially caused by the work environment. This is useful in determining the healthcare needs that occur in certain occupations. The data can also be used to see whether any further precautions are required for certain tasks. Employers may think any incidents are isolated, whereas by reporting it to the HSE, it may be shown to occur frequently in certain occupations. The information can be used to support workers' health and to put safe working practices in place.

The Labour Force Survey (LFS)

The LFS surveys more than 40,000 households in Britain to determine whether occupants have work-related illnesses. Again, this information is fed back to the HSE for further investigation. Various government departments use LFS results when checking the effect of existing policies, to inform future policy changes and when deciding on the best uses of public resources. Additionally, the European Union uses LFS results to determine UK funding for improvement of employment prospects, facilities and opportunities in local areas.

The Health and Occupational Reporting network (THOR)

THOR is a group run by the University of Manchester to produce statistical information from specialists seeing patients for work-related respiratory disorders and skin diseases. More than a thousand specialist doctors voluntarily provide information, with an estimated 25,000 plus cases of occupational disease and work-related ill health. The data is used to inform the national agenda and to provide a resource for participating doctors, applied occupational health epidemiology, and other research. Since 2005, THOR has also collected information about, and conducted research on, the costs of work-related sickness absence.

Statistics

The World Health Organization (WHO)

The UK government gathers information and statistics from scientific research, including from the WHO and each country within the UK, to ensure local, regional and national health is monitored so that resources can be planned based on specific needs.

The WHO is an agency of the United Nations concerned with international public health. The organisation is responsible for the World Health Report and its current priorities include driving the development of international reporting, publications and networking.

As a global organisation, the WHO gathers information from its 194 members (and two associate members) around the world about health problems. This information is disseminated globally so that appropriate resources and advice can be given to help with specific health issues.

The WHO has recently been involved in the study of maternal, newborn, child and adolescent health on a global, regional and national level. The UK and other member states have provided national statistics. The WHO uses this data to inform all countries about inequalities in health care and which wealthier countries can help poorer countries financially or by supporting healthcare initiatives. The WHO also works with countries to try to deal with health problems in the best way possible.

Government, regional and local

The DH relies on local and regional health authorities to monitor and report on the health of the population in the area for which they have responsibility.

GPs, pharmacists, hospitals, health centres run by specialist groups, for example sexual health clinics, have to report all diseases and illnesses causing a serious threat to health to local health authorities. This includes meningitis, norovirus and measles, so that the local health authority can provide relevant resources and guidance to the medical profession. In turn, the local authority has to report these diseases or illnesses to the regional health authority, which provides more guidance or resources, if needed. The regional health authority monitors the local situation to see whether the disease spreads or is controlled.

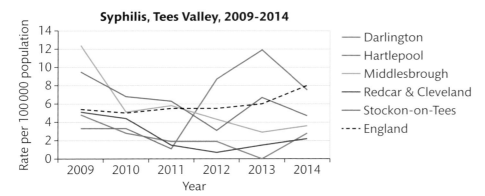

▶ **Figure 8.2:** Can you suggests some reasons why the levels of syphilis vary between years in these five locations in comparison to the rest of England and how this could impact health promotion campaigns in these areas? Source: Public Health England

The regional health authority reports health issues to the DH, which monitors the situation and provides extra resources, if necessary. They report to the European Union, which then reports to the WHO, so that an overall picture of the population is monitored and helped when necessary. The Zika virus is being closely monitored in this way and guidelines are being set and resources are being created to keep people informed of the risks and to try to control infection rates.

Health studies

Sometimes the government commissions reports on specific health matters, such as the Black Report on the inequalities of health provision or the Acheson Report (the Beveridge Report 1942 is also an example of a commissioned health report).

The Black Report 1980

In 1980, the Department of Health and Social Security published a report that focused on health inequalities in the UK. The report highlighted that ill health and death rates were higher in poorer areas of Britain. In more affluent areas, the rate was lower. Despite the establishment of the NHS in 1948, the gap appeared to be widening. The report reflected that in different parts of the country, life expectancy differed by ten years. It also reflected that professional people had a healthier lifestyle than unskilled workers. This was reported as due to the professional people's awareness about healthy diet, looking after themselves and seeing doctors when needed. It was also shown that women tended to have more illnesses. However, it was suggested that men were less likely to see a doctor when they were ill, meaning that women tended to lead healthier lives as their health problems were dealt with. The Black Report suggested policies that the government should implement to combat these inequalities, although these were not implemented at the time. However, the report led to an assessment by the Office for Economic Co-Operation and Development (OECD) and the WHO of health inequalities in 13 countries.

The Acheson Report 1998

In 1998, the Acheson Report was still showing inequalities in health care according to an individual's economic status. The report called for more funding for nutritional education in schools through the curriculum, and for teaching children, especially those in deprived areas, to budget and cook healthy meals. It also suggested that schools deciding to sell their playing fields and receiving less funding for free school meals had led to a worsening of health for children living in poverty.

The report contained policy suggestions to lessen these health disparities, which influenced the government green paper Our Healthier Nation: A Contract for Health (1998) and the white paper Saving Lives: Our Healthier Nation (1999).

How data is used by public health practitioners to monitor and respond to public health issues

The DH publishes statistics gained from data to:

▶ inform debate on health issues

▶ inform decision making in health care

▶ commission research into a specific illness or diseases causing concern.

Data is important to the delivery of appropriate health care. Up-to-date information is crucial to prevent the spread of diseases and to support patients with the necessary medicines. Knowing about a health concern in a local area gives people control of their lives and helps to increase their wellbeing. If patients are aware of certain diseases that may affect them they can decide what action to take to minimise risk to their health, for example the uptake of the annual flu vaccine by vulnerable people.

Health practitioners use data to help people decide on sensible health precautions to take when travelling. For example, charts are available for GP practices that show travel destinations with the appropriate vaccines required when travelling to that part of the world.

If an outbreak of a disease affects a community, health practitioners can obtain data to see whether their area will be affected, enabling them to order supplies of the appropriate drugs to ensure patients are treated quickly. For example, cases of avian flu (bird flu) can be monitored around the world and if British people are travelling to affected areas, vaccines and medical care can be put into place to support them.

PAUSE POINT How is data used by the DH in understanding the spread of an epidemic?

Hint Epidemics affect large amounts of the population.

Extend How does the DH track the spread of infection to keep British people informed?

Groups that influence public health policy

Government and government agencies

Every country has a department of health with the responsibility of overseeing the wellbeing of its citizens and advising the government about the best quality of care. This is achieved by using current data, obtained from local, regional or global agencies.

In England, the DH is the main government body that oversees reports and gathers evidence of illness and disease. It advises the government about shaping and funding health care. In Scotland, the Health and Social Care Directorate performs this role.

Pressure groups

In Britain, pressure groups use the data they collect to persuade the government to change policies or to fund particular causes. Such groups include Age UK, the British Heart Foundation and ASH (Action on Smoking and Health).

Age UK

In 2009, Age Concern and Help the Aged merged to form a new charity, Age UK. Its aim is to help people enjoy later life, with the ethos that 'ageing is not an illness, but it can be challenging'. Age UK is the largest charity working for the benefit of the over sixties and provides services and support for older people at a national and local level. It regularly conducts research into the health of the over sixties, and tries to persuade the government about health and care improvements that could be made for this age group. This may include issues about human rights, age discrimination and the effects of ageing in a rural society. It commissions reports when needed and analyses findings to support its policies when trying to influence national or European government decision-makers. Age UK also supports local concerns and individual cases.

British Heart Foundation (BHF)

The BHF is the largest independent funder of **cardiovascular** research. Its vision is that nobody should die prematurely or suffer from heart disease. It researches into the causes of heart disease, its diagnosis, treatment and prevention. BHF research has helped the NHS to develop new techniques, such as **angioplasty**.

Action on Smoking and Health (ASH)

ASH was established by the Royal College of Physicians as a charity to eliminate the effects of smoking. Their policies aim to bring awareness of the effects of smoking to the public, as well as to try to change government policy to try to reduce addiction.

> **Research**
>
> Visit the websites of Age UK, the British Heart Foundation and ASH to find out more about the types of research they undertake and how they put pressure on the UK government as a result of their findings.

> **Key terms**
>
> **Cardiovascular** – the heart and blood vessels.
>
> **Angioplasty** – a procedure that uses a balloon to widen blocked or narrow coronary arteries. Angioplasty is now a common and routine operation in heart surgery.

International groups

World Health Organization (WHO)

The WHO was formed in April 1948. Its headquarters are based in Geneva, Switzerland, and it has offices all around the world. The purpose of the organisation is the physical, mental and social wellbeing of all peoples in the world. The WHO works with more than 150 countries around the world. Its purpose is to lead on world health, within the United Nations system, in countries where action is needed. The WHO works with a country's policymakers to ensure that the country receives appropriate health support and guidance. It also works with universities and other educational institutions around the world, the private medical sector and national governments to resolve critical health issues. Some examples of the health problems that the WHO has recently been involved with are:

▶ HIV

▶ Zika virus

▶ malaria

▶ tuberculosis (TB).

The WHO sets the standards for research and ensures that the findings are translated and known throughout the world. This enables all governments to be aware of current research to ensure that their population receives the most up-to-date medical assistance. The WHO also tries to regulate the prices of medical help, by supplying medicines or equipment and by leading in the financial assistance of poorer countries.

> **Research**
>
> In groups, investigate the WHO and its centres around the world. Each group should select a different region of the world, and find out about its major health problems. Each group should share its findings with the other groups.

▶ A WHO worker training nurses in Sierra Leone to use protective clothing in the Ebola outbreak of 2014

United Nations (UN)

The UN was founded in 1945, after the Second World War, to take action on the main issues affecting the world, including health, human rights and internal peace and security. Its main headquarters are in New York, where governments meet to negotiate ways to improve problems.

Some of the issues facing the UN around the world in regard to health are:

▶ sustainable food sources in poorer countries, to try to eradicate hunger

▶ stopping the practice of female genital mutilation (FGM) by 2030

▶ monitoring international human rights treaties.

National groups

National groups operate in specialist areas of health to support the UK population to maintain and improve its health. These groups carry out research in their specialist area. For example, based on research evidence, Cancer Research UK informs the government about breakthroughs that may require government influence or legislation to be implemented for the benefit of all people with cancer.

National Institute for Health and Care Excellence (NICE)

NICE is an organisational body that puts in place improvements in health and social care. It monitors systems and organisations involved in health issues in Britain. NICE reviews evidence-based guidance and sets standards to ensure the most up-to-date and best practice in any health problem is followed by all health authorities, charities and private practices, to ensure the safety of service users. Some of the evidence-based guidelines from NICE include:

▶ cancer service guidelines

▶ clinical guidelines

▶ medicines practice guidelines

▶ public health guidelines

▶ safe staffing guidelines

▶ social care guidelines.

Research

Go to the NICE website: **www.nice.org.uk** and search for NICE guidance on health protection. What recent guidelines have been published concerning public health? Explore one guideline and make notes about its recommendations.

Cancer Research UK

The aim of Cancer Research UK is to use research findings to eliminate cancer. It is a charity and receives no government funding. Cancer Research UK reports that the ten-year survival rate for all types of cancer has doubled in the past 40 years and that it wants to continue to improve this figure. Cancer Research UK works in four main areas of cancer research:

▶ helping to prevent cancer

▶ earlier diagnosis

▶ developing new treatments

▶ personalising treatments to meet individual health needs and to make treatment more effective.

Current research includes:

▶ lung cancer research – as the second most common cancer in the UK, Cancer Research UK is campaigning hard to stop smoking, the main cause of this cancer

▶ pancreatic cancer research – survival rates are almost non-existent as it is difficult to diagnose pancreatic cancer early enough, Cancer Research UK is researching early detection methods

▶ oesophageal cancer research – survival rates for this type of cancer are still low

▶ brain tumour research – there are over 100 different types of brain tumour, and Cancer Research UK is working to find causes and cures.

For further reading, please visit: http://www.cancerresearchuk.org/about-cancer/causes-of-cancer/can-cancer-be-prevented (accessed September 2016)

Examine the factors affecting health and the impact of addressing these factors to improve public health

Factors affecting health

Socio-economic factors

It has long been recognised that social and economic background affects an individual's health, wellbeing and overall life expectancy.

The WHO states that the conditions in which people are born, grow, live, work and age will determine their health and wellbeing. Additionally, health and wellbeing are affected by social and economic factors, such as access to money, power and resources. These factors (called social determinants) cause health inequities within and between countries.

In 2011, the British Medical Association (BMA) published *Social Determinants of Health – What Can Doctors Do*. The report reflects that inequalities in health and social care are determined by a person's age, income, education, occupation, gender, ethnicity and where a person lives within Britain. The report aims to help doctors identify and take actions, which are neither necessarily medical nor requiring medical knowledge, to make a positive difference. For example, doctors can use their position and their expertise to advocate for change in areas outside traditional medical areas, and promote research into prevention measures.

Evidence from the Office for National Statistics (ONS) shows how a person's position on the neighbourhood income deprivation calculator affects their life expectancy.

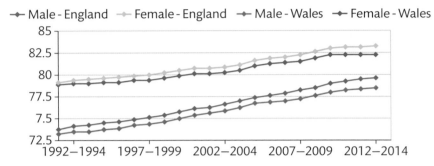

▸ **Figure 8.3:** Life expectancy, England and Wales, 1992–2014 (source: Office for National Statistics)

Cities such as Glasgow, Liverpool and Manchester, with high levels of poverty, have higher levels of death in young men. Drug use, alcohol abuse and high suicide rates are more prominent factors in poorer communities. Understanding and acting on this information can improve how health needs are met and lives can be made better.

> **Research**
>
> Search the ONS website for its bulletin: *Life Expectancy at Birth and at Age 65 by Local Areas in England and Wales: 2012 to 2014.* What conclusions can be drawn from the main points at the start of this bulletin?

Education is also a factor that can affect people's health, especially during the early development of physical and emotional health. What children are taught before they go to school has a great impact, which can affect their health and wellbeing, and even their future parenting skills. Although information about healthy eating and lifestyles is taught in school, in poorer communities the theory is not always practised outside school. There are several reasons for this, including lack of parental interest, lack of money to purchase healthier food options, playing with computer games instead of playing outside, plus concern about letting children play outdoors. In cities, places to play may be restricted or vandalised where they do exist, plus air pollution is now seen as a major health concern.

Environmental factors

The environment in which a person grows and lives has a major influence on their health and wellbeing.

Poor housing and homelessness

Poor housing can cause many illnesses. Damp walls or floors, especially with mould growing on them, may causing respiratory problems. People often become depressed and anxious about their poor living conditions and may become mentally ill. Dark lanes, poor lighting, having no safe places for children to play or people to walk outside, rubbish on the streets and lack of green spaces, all contribute to ill health.

Homeless healthcare teams operate in many areas around the UK. They are multi-disciplinary teams that provide care and support in their local area for homeless individuals or families. These teams have contacts with many other agencies supporting homeless people.

People may become homeless through a range of issues, for example they may be refugees or travellers, they may have mental health issues, their relationship may have broken down or they may have financial problems. People sleeping rough may not have identification papers or evidence of an address, so may not be able to claim the benefits that could help them with shelter and food. Organisations such as local authority homeless healthcare teams and social services departments may be able to help homeless people to access medical help, food and temporary accommodation.

Access to exercise facilities

One of the main drives by the government is to reduce obesity and improve the health of the population. Exercise helps individuals to achieve and maintain a healthy weight.

Gyms and fitness centres are good places to exercise. However, people may not be able to afford to join a gym or a fitness centre, or pay for exercise classes. Some gyms and fitness centres offer monthly membership and some local authorities allow discounts at fitness centres for people claiming certain benefits.

Many local authorities also supply fitness machines in local parks for anyone to use free of charge. However, people who work during the daytime may have safety concerns about using this equipment to exercise in the evenings when they are free to do so. People who like to run or jog may be concerned about poor lighting, uneven pavements, busy traffic and many other issues that may make exercising in their local area unsafe.

Playing outside and participating in organised and unorganised sporting activities helps children's wellbeing and health. Concerns about their safety, including from violent attacks, involvement in minor crime and exploitation by drug dealers or paedophiles has led to many parents not allowing unsupervised outdoor play. Additionally, many children prefer to stay indoors and play computer games and lack the enthusiasm to participate in sports or exercise. This has contributed to many health issues such as obesity and a re-emergence of rickets (a condition that causes bone deformities in children through softening and weakening of their bones). NHS Choices has reported a slight but significant increase in cases in recent years. Many of these children have low levels of vitamin D in their blood (which may be caused by low exposure to sunlight).

Air pollution

Air quality monitoring sites, which are situated in several hundred locations throughout the country, record all the different types of pollutants in the air for that area. People living in cities are more prone to health concerns than those living in smaller towns or villages. Vehicle fumes affect air quality; the closer to a main road the higher the pollution is, whereas just 30 metres away the pollution drops quite significantly. Valleys hold pollution whereas areas of land higher up are less polluted. Winds can blow pollution to places nearby that normally have a lower pollution rate.

Genetic factors

Children resemble their parents because they inherit genetic information passed on to them by their parents. Children usually look a little like their father, and a little like their mother, but they will not be identical to either of their parents. This is because they inherit half of their features from each parent. All human cells normally contain 23 pairs of chromosomes, one chromosome from each pair is inherited from the mother and one from the father through sexual reproduction. Chromosomes contain genes and there may be different forms of the same gene, caused by mutation in the genetic code, for example for inheriting eye colour. Some features vary due to environmental

> **Research**
>
> In pairs, research air pollution in your area by going to the government website: **https://uk-air.defra.gov.uk** and choosing a location or postcode area. Check for your nearest monitoring site. What information does it give you?

causes. For example, the weight of identical twins is likely to vary if one twin is fed more than the other.

Some health problems and medical conditions can also be inherited when there is a faulty version of a gene. Whether a medical condition arises depends on:

▶ what genes are inherited

▶ whether the gene for that condition is dominant or recessive

▶ environmental factors, including preventative treatment.

Most health conditions are caused by a combination of genetic and environmental factors such as diet and exercise. It is likely that in the future, research will identify the specific combination of genes and environmental factors that will enable individuals to know which medical conditions they are most likely to develop, thus significantly reducing the possibility of developing them.

Genetic mutations can be caused by exposure to specific chemicals, such as those in cigarette smoke, or radiation. They can also occur when DNA is not copied correctly during cell division.

Sickle cell anaemia

Sickle cell anaemia is a genetically inherited condition affecting the formation of red blood cells. These cells are normally small in size, round in shape and flexible. They contain haemoglobin, a protein that combines with oxygen. Red blood cells carry oxygen around the body to supply cells with oxygen, which is used to break down sugar and release energy.

In sickle cell anaemia, a mutated form of haemoglobin causes the red blood cells to become crescent shaped when oxygen levels are low. The distorted, or sickled, red cells cannot pass through the smaller arteries and arterioles and can block these blood vessels. This is a sickle cell crisis and causes severe pain, and tissue and organ damage. The sickled cells have a shorter lifespan than normal red cells, and they are not replaced as quickly, which leads to anaemia.

In Britain, sickle cell anaemia is more commonly found in people of African or Caribbean descent. However, it is also found in people from the Middle East, Eastern Mediterranean and Asia. The mutant gene has to be inherited from both parents for the child to get sickle cell anaemia. However, sickle cell trait occurs when the gene is inherited from one parent only. A person with sickle cell trait is said to be a carrier of the disease and their blood will contain some sickle cells. However, they will be able to produce normal haemoglobin and it is unusual for them to experience any other symptoms. Carriers may pass the abnormal gene to their children.

If someone in a family has a sickle cell disorder then all the family are checked for it. Pregnant women are tested within ten weeks of a pregnancy starting. If a woman is found to be a carrier, then the father is checked too, as the condition is only passed on when both parents are carriers.

Lifestyle factors

A person's lifestyle has an effect on their health and wellbeing. If a person has a poor diet and misuses drugs and alcohol, then the person's health will be detrimentally affected. The Black Report showed that economic and social lifestyle has either a positive or negative impact on a person's health. The health of people living in poorer communities is less good than the health of those living in more affluent areas, and they also have a lower life expectancy.

Diet

To eat a healthy diet the balance of nutrients taken in needs to be right. To do this, it requires eating the right amounts of a range of foodstuffs. Poor diet is when a person is not eating the nutrients they need to be healthy, and it can refer to either malnutrition or obesity. Obesity is currently of concern to the health services, particularly obesity in young children. NHS Direct reports that it is estimated that one in every four adults in Britain, and one in five children aged between 10 and 11 years old are obese, which places the UK at the top of Europe's 'obesity league'.

Obesity can be defined as when a person is more than a third over the normal weight for their age, height and body type. This can be due to a diet that has more calories than the body needs, which is then stored as fat. It may also be due to lack of exercise. The Body Mass Index (BMI) can be used as a baseline guide for whether someone is overweight or underweight. The BMI assesses the relationship between a person's height and weight. However, this measure should be used with caution as using it could mean that a very muscular person would be considered obese. It is, therefore, now more usual to also look at the relationship of the individual's waist measurement to their height.

Obesity can lead to serious health problems, such as:

▶ type 2 diabetes

▶ coronary heart disease

▶ breast cancer

▶ bowel cancer

▶ stroke.

It can also lead to psychological problems such as depression, low confidence and low self-esteem, and feelings of isolation. These conditions can affect relationships with partners, family and friends.

 PAUSE POINT Reflect on the area in which you live and the main factor that affects your health.

 Hint Think about genetic, lifestyle, environment and socio-economic factors.

Extend Research your area. How might one factor influence the health of the public more than the others?

Substance misuse

Substance misuse includes taking illegal drugs such as cocaine, heroin or cannabis and can cause severe health problems.

Apart from making a person chilled or relaxed, using cannabis can cause problems such as feeling sick, feeling sleepy, making things harder to remember and paranoia or panic attacks.

Taking heroin and cocaine is addictive. It can cause very serious physical and psychological damage, as well as incurring debt through financing the habit, leading some users into crime.

The NHS and many charities, such as **FRANK**, support people trying to stop taking illegal drugs.

Public Health England's *Alcohol and drugs prevention, treatment and recovery: why invest?* (2013) reported that:

> **Key term**
>
> **FRANK** – national drug education service set up in 2003 by the DH and Home Office to provide education to reduce the use of both legal and illegal drugs, through its website and media campaigns.

- almost 3 million adults use illegal drugs
- there are almost 300,000 heroin or crack users
- 40 per cent of prisoners have used heroin
- more than a million families have had drug-related problems
- a typical heroin addict spends over £1400 a month on drugs; hence it is a big cause of crime
- communities feel safer in areas where there are drug treatment centres (as crime tends to be lower in these areas).

The annual cost to society of drug addiction is just over £15 bn. The NHS spends about £500 m a year on treating drug misusers. It costs about £40 m a year when children have to be taken into care because of their parents' drug misuse.

Alcohol

Alcohol misuse over a long period of time can lead to:

- heart disease
- stroke
- liver disease
- liver cancer
- mouth cancer
- pancreatic cancer.

Alcohol misuse also causes social problems, such as unemployment or divorce, and sometimes homelessness. There are a number of charities that work to reduce the harm caused by alcohol-related problems, including Alcohol Concern (in England and Wales) and Alcoholics Anonymous (Great Britain) Ltd.

In *Alcohol and drugs prevention, treatment and recovery: why invest?* (2003), Public Health England reported that almost 10 million adults are at risk of ill health from high levels of alcohol consumption, with 1.5 million adults having alcohol addiction. In 2012, alcohol-related causes were linked to:

- approximately 20,000 deaths, including a quarter of all deaths among young males aged 16–25 years and nearly 15 per cent of road deaths
- high reporting of domestic violence
- marriage breakdown
- physical and emotional problems in children living with parents with alcohol problems
- almost 50 per cent of violent assaults.

This has cost the NHS £3.5 bn, and lost productivity has cost the nation £7 bn. The total cost to society is estimated at about £20 bn.

It is estimated that the result of interventions in young person's drug and alcohol problems could lead to savings of £4 m in health care, and £100 m in crime. Interventions can also help young people re-enter education, employment or training, which will help them economically, with an estimated saving to government spending of £160 m.

The European Code Against Cancer recommends that men should not drink more than two standard measurements of alcohol a day, whereas women should only drink one standard measurement of alcohol a day. (A standard measurement is considered to be 10–12 grams of pure alcohol, and this equates to, for example, about half a pint of beer (330 ml), a small glass of wine (175 ml), or a standard measure (25 ml) of spirits.)

However, new UK government guidelines state that the alcohol limit for men and women should be the same and that neither group should regularly drink more than 14 units per week spread evenly across a few days. It also recommends that people should have at least two alcohol-free days a week.

Links between disease and other factors

The NHS, government agencies and charities promote a healthy lifestyle with positive life choices to ensure people lead healthier lives. Poor lifestyle choices can cause higher crime levels, severe health problems and premature deaths. There is currently concern about the increasing numbers for obesity, alcohol and drug misuse, which are costly for society to deal with. It makes financial sense for the government to invest in public health campaigns and help centres as these numbers are predicted to increase even further over the next fifteen years. Should this happen, then the budget for the NHS will also need to increase.

Obesity

In 2015, Public Health England recorded the annual cost to the NHS for treating people with obesity as being £5.1 bn. The wider cost to the economy was estimated at £27 bn, which includes the cost of medication (£13.3 bn) and sickness absences.

Obesity was estimated to account for sickness absences totalling £16 m and social care costs of £352 m. If the current trend continues, by 2034 it may mean that two in three adults will be overweight or obese.

There are financial and health costs. It is reported that obese children experience bullying and stigmatisation, suffer low self-esteem and ill health. If a child is overweight they are at an increased risk of being overweight in adulthood, leading to high blood pressure, bone and joint problems, breathing difficulties and premature death.

Social factors play an important role in obesity, such as:

▸ increasing number of fast food outlets, which sell products high in saturated fat and salt

▸ many people feeling they do not have the time to cook using raw ingredients

▸ lack of cooking skills, with many not knowing how to cook healthy meals

▸ the perceived cost of buying healthy foods, particularly for those with low incomes

▸ working long hours

▸ lack of exercise, with lifestyle changes meaning that many people spend long hours using a computer at work, increases in using social media and spending time playing games online.

Cancer

It is unclear what causes cancers but lifestyle choices are seen as a factor. Research has proved that smoking is a lifestyle choice that can increase the risk of developing lung cancer, respiratory disorders and many other health problems.

In the UK, approximately 29 per cent of cancer deaths are caused by smoking. Smoking can also increase the risk of developing mouth, throat, lung, bladder, kidney and pancreatic cancers. **Passive smoking** also increases the chances of developing cancer.

Cancer Research UK states that changes in lifestyle could prevent about 40 per cent of all cancers. These changes include:

▸ not smoking

▸ maintaining a healthy bodyweight

- reducing alcohol intake – from January 2016, UK government guidelines recommend that the limits for men and women should be the same, and that it is safest to avoid drinking alcohol or limit intake to less than 14 **units of alcohol** per week
- eating a healthy, balanced diet
- exercising and being active
- avoiding infections such as **human papilloma virus** (HPV), for example by practising **safe sex**
- taking precautions when exposed to the sun, for example by using high protection factor sunscreen or sunblock, covering exposed areas of skin, wearing a hat and keeping out of the sun during the hottest periods of the day
- avoiding cancer risks in the workplace.

Research

In pairs, research a national health risk (provided by your tutor), for example cancer (breast, lung, pancreatic, prostate), obesity, or drug and alcohol abuse. Find out what government initiatives are presently in place. Share your findings with the other pairs.

The socio-economic impact of improving the health of individuals and of the population

The Black Report highlighted the impact of social and economic circumstances on an individual's health, particularly on ill health. Healthy people spend more, making the economy richer. Businesses prosper when workers are healthy, as reported by the WHO.

The government is extremely concerned about the expense of health and social care. The NHS has reported that caring for individuals with type 2 diabetes, for example, costs the country almost £9 bn a year. The government has driven public health campaigns for healthy living, including Sport For All and media campaigns about healthy eating, such as Change4Life.

Reducing health and social inequalities

If social inequalities were reduced, then the population would become healthier. A healthier population works better, has less time off sick, and has increased productivity, which leads to a wealthier nation.

Improvements in more disadvantaged communities

Improving health outcomes for more disadvantaged communities depends on the resources and facilities available. Help may be provided by local or national funding or from the National Lottery funding a specific programme. Usually the services are offered by voluntary groups who may arrange and/or organise and run classes, for example nutrition advice classes or exercise classes such as Zumba or yoga.

Local community groups can influence and empower their local community to set up and maintain facilities, such as safe play areas for children. They can also represent the local community at local authority level in issues such as improving availability and condition of local authority housing.

Life expectancy and quality of life

According to the ONS, life expectancy has increased significantly in the last 30 years in Britain. For example, in England, a boy's life expectancy at birth increased by 5.9 years and a girl's by 4.1 years.

The NHS has contributed to people surviving major illnesses and improved the quality of life for people living with illness. A person's quality of life depends on their physical, psychological, emotional, social and occupational wellbeing. Disorder or disruption of any of these factors can lead to ill health.

Reduced demand for or pressure on health and social care services

People are living longer. Older people may become frailer, sicker and require more health and social care than younger people. The need for residential and nursing care for the elderly has increased, especially with the change to traditional family patterns (including moving away from local areas, divorce, separations and non-nuclear family types), which means that family may not exist or be able to care for elderly family members. Lifestyle choices by younger people may also have an impact on the future demands placed on the healthcare system. According to diabetes charities there were 533 cases of type 2 diabetes in under 19s in 2016. Type 2 diabetes is usually only seen in people over the age of 40 and poor diet and nutrition choices are often blamed for this rise. Supporting young people to make healthier lifestyle choices in all aspects of their lives including alcohol consumption, sexual activity, diet and exercise and illegal drugs will help to reduce the pressure on health and welfare services.

Looking at the way services are provided will also have an impact on the pressure on health and social care services. More treatment in the community could reduce the number of expensive hospital admissions, larger specialist services could create centres of expertise and improve the quality of care.

The health and social care services are going through big changes, to ensure that they can provide economically efficient services now, and also in the future. Private sector care is also growing to meet demand.

❚❚ PAUSE POINT   How do you think your lifestyle influences your health and quality of life?

> Hint   Reflect on lifestyle choices, from diet and physical activity to drinking, smoking and social choices.

> Extend   List your lifestyle choices in columns – good choices against poorer choices. Should you change any aspects of your lifestyle? Add another column and state the changes you would make against each lifestyle choice you want to change.

Carry out research on each of the four factors (socio-economic, environment, genetic or lifestyle) that affect health in your local community. Then research how public health policy helps in reducing the problems of health in your area.

1 Using an example from each health factor, explain why monitoring this data on health and ill health can affect the promotion of health in your area.

2 Analyse the way in which patterns of health and ill health have helped to form public health policy, giving examples.

3 Assess the impact of minimising the factors that affect health on improving health in your area.

4 Evaluate how far strategies and monitoring health status to form health policy has affected health in your area compared to different parts of the country.

Plan
- What is the task? What is it I have been asked to do?
- How confident do I feel in answering this?
- What areas will I struggle with?

Do
- Do I know what I am doing?
- Can I identify where I need to improve?

Review
- Can I evaluate what I have done and how I approached the task?
- Have I learnt from this and can I make changes to my work to make it better next time?

C Investigate how health is promoted to improve the health of the population

The role of health promoters

Aims

The aim of health promoters is to improve the health of individuals and populations. Health promoters include global organisations such as the WHO, and national governments, local health authorities, local government and specialist departments researching specific aspects of health. The aim of all governments is to promote the health of their own population and to narrow the divide between health inequalities.

Global health promoters

World Health Organization (WHO)

The WHO's main purpose is to coordinate international health within the United Nations framework. It directs health systems and leads on the promotion of healthy living throughout the world, working with global policymakers and health partners to assist countries in the development of healthcare systems. The WHO gathers information from countries experiencing health problems, such as the recent outbreaks of Ebola and Zika virus, to gain a better understanding about controlling the disease locally and globally, as well as assisting the affected areas with managing and treating the disease.

Child Family Health International (CFHI)

The CFHI is a non-government organisation that specialises in global health education programmes, educating families in low and middle-income countries around the world. It provides support for local communities in ten countries in South America, Asia and Africa. Working alongside local health professionals, CFHI volunteers provide programmes that include health and safety, paediatrics, nursing and care in community clinics and cover many more local and national issues.

Save the Children

Save the Children is a charity. It operates with the sole purpose of supporting the health of children worldwide. By participating in local communities, it aims to develop improved, healthy living conditions for children; ensuring that every child survives into adulthood by being protected from harm and by being educated about healthy living.

Médecins Sans Frontières (MSF)/Doctors Without Borders

MSF is an organisation that provides medical help and emergency medical aid in areas of armed conflict, to populations or communities in distress, where there are epidemics and natural or human-created disasters, or to communities excluded from other sources of health care.

The International Union of Health Promotion and Education (IUHPE)

IUHPE is an independent, professional association of individuals and organisations working worldwide to improve health and wellbeing through education, community action and the development of healthy public policy. It publishes a quarterly, multilingual journal *Global Health Promotion*, of authoritative peer-reviewed articles about health promotion initiatives.

National, regional and local health promoters

England

The Department of Health (DH) is responsible for health and wellbeing in England and Wales. It leads on health policies for short- and long-term challenges to the health of the population. It is responsible for funding and delivery of health services, and is accountable to parliament for the health of the nation. The DH works with 28 agencies and public bodies, including Public Health England, Health and Social Care Information Centre and Health Education England. These agencies and public bodies report directly to the DH, supplying specialist research data when requested. In 2013, NHS England took on the responsibility of planning and delivery of health services and is directly accountable to the DH. NHS England leads the NHS in England, setting priorities to improve health and care. It commissions healthcare services in England, sharing out more than £100 bn in funds for GPs' contracts, pharmacists, and dentists. It supports Clinical Commissioning Groups (CCGs), which plan and pay for local services such as hospitals and ambulance services.

Wales

NHS Wales provides health care to about 3 million people and is responsible for services, policy and funding for current and future care in Wales. It was formed in 2009 when the Welsh Assembly decided that NHS services should provide care at a more local level. NHS Wales is accountable to the Welsh government, it has seven Local Health Boards, each responsible for its own area and three national NHS Trusts (whose responsibilities include the operation of Public Health Wales).

Northern Ireland

Health and Social Care Northern Ireland (HSC) is responsible for public health and, unlike England and Wales, it is also responsible for social care. Hospital care is provided by the five regional trusts responsible for health and social care in their local area.

The Public Health Agency (PHA) was established in April 2009 as part of the HSC reforms. Its role is the regional organisation of health protection, and health and social wellbeing improvement. The PHA operates in three areas: Public Health, Nursing and Allied Health Professionals, and Operations.

Regional and local health trusts

Foundation Trusts are independent trusts accountable to their local community. Local people can be on the board of governors. Trust governors have the responsibility to approve or amend changes to suit the local community needs in which the trust operates. All decisions about planning future changes to the trust have to be presented to the board of governors.

The Health and Social Care Act 2012 set out the statutory requirements of a local authority with regards to the health and social care of its local population. Within this area are NHS Foundation Trusts, which through NHS Improvement monitor hospital performance, and how funding is spent, and developed so that services improve.

Link

To learn more about the new structure visit **https://improvement.nhs.uk/**

Local hospitals and community services

Clinical Commissioning Groups (CCGs) have a major role in the health of their local areas. CCGs are led by local groups that include all GP groups in their area, which gives GPs and other clinicians influence over commissioning decisions.

The CCGs report to NHS England and are responsible for:

▶ hospital care

▶ rehabilitative care

▶ urgent, emergency and out of hours care

▶ most community health services

▶ mental health and learning disability services.

Research

In pairs, research how the local health authority in your area is arranged. Produce a poster detailing the procedure for reporting health problems such as heart attacks, lung disease caused by asbestos, obesity, strokes, different types of cancer, sexually transmitted disease, kidney disease, bladder problems or arthritis.

❙❙ PAUSE POINT   Think about a time that you, or a person you know, wanted information about a certain health topic. How easy was it to obtain it and who provided the information?

Hint   Did you find out through a leaflet from your GP practice, or your local pharmacist, or did you use a website? List places from which you found the information.

Extend   Obtain a range of health promotion materials and find out who provided the information for them.

Approaches to promoting public health and wellbeing

Monitoring the health status of the community

Using information and data gathered from around the country, Public Health England produces meaningful health intelligence reports about trends, specific diseases and disorders, how health inequalities are being dealt with and the impact of interventions on health care. These reports enable healthcare practitioners, policymakers and commissioners on health matters to make informed decisions about implementing care.

Identifying those most at risk

Children

A group of professionals and representatives from across the children's sector, the Children and Young People's Health Outcomes Forum (CYPHOF), advises on improving children and young people's health outcomes. Health prevention services are targeted at children as they are seen as being young enough to develop good health and lifestyle behaviours and to avoid damaging behaviours in the future. The CYPHOF reported that although statistics for young people smoking and drinking and teenage pregnancies have fallen in recent years, 20 per cent of children are now obese. Evidence drawn from health data about children, such as *Fair Society, Healthy Lives* (Marmot Review, 2015), notes that what affects children, from conception onwards, has lifelong effects on their health. This includes issues of attachment, obesity, heart disease, mental health, educational achievement and economic status. Health education issues are taught in schools, including information about healthy eating, awareness of the effects of long-term smoking, taking illegal drugs, and sexual health.

Unemployed

Data provided by the ONS shows clear and defining information about the relationship between poor health, the devastating symptoms of mental ill health and unemployment. A person who is unemployed has more chance of feeling less valued, maybe becoming depressed and developing an unhealthy lifestyle. Due to their mental health and lack of wealth they may not exercise or eat healthily, and hence could become obese, leading to a premature death. Other ONS statistics indicate that unemployed people are more likely to experience:

▶ long-standing (chronic) illness

▶ poorer mental health

▶ higher levels of psychological distress

▶ higher hospital admissions.

Older people

According to the Office for National Statistics in 2011 there were 9.2 million people in England and Wales aged 65 and over. This represents an increase of 900 000 since the previous census in 2001. Of those aged over 65, only 50 per cent stated that they felt that their health was 'very good' or 'good'. Within the general population excluding those over 65, almost 90 per cent rate their health as 'good or 'very good'

With the numbers of older people in Britain increasing significantly, it is important for health services to understand the health needs of the elderly. Many older people remain active, which helps maintain good health and quality of life, whereas some who are less physically active, which may be due to economic circumstances or physical impairments, develop health needs.

Promoting health and welfare is different in different regions; it is often funded by charities or the local council and not all elderly people can access resources such as:

▶ leisure centres having free membership for the over 60s

▶ fitness clubs in community centres offering free activities such as yoga and Pilates

▶ drives to encourage walking and cycling for people who find running difficult.

Minority ethnic groups

A minority ethnic group is defined as a group within a community which has a different race or culture to the majority of the group. Minority groups can come from anywhere and in the shifting demographics of some city populations, the minority groups can change as the population moves and changes, to the point where some former minority groups become the majority. Discrimination against minority ethnic groups can lead to individuals within the group becoming depressed and anxious. The advertising campaign, 'Time to change' included people from minority ethnic groups in the hope that people would start the conversations about mental health. Many earlier campaigns only depicted white people, which may have lessened their impact on minority ethnic groups. It has been recognised that more campaigns are needed to work with ethnic groups on a national scale and not local areas, which has limited impact. Diabetes UK ran a campaign including minority ethnic groups in which there are a large number of people, who possibly due to their diet, have coronary disease, or strokes which are brought on by diabetes.

Health surveillance programmes

The Health and Safety Executive (HSE) monitors illness at work. It requires health checks in the workplace, for example on noise levels or the use of solvents and other biological agents that can be hazardous to health. Many of these health checks are required by law. This type of health surveillance is important to detect ill health caused by occupational environments early, so that employers can take improvement measures to prevent further adverse effects on their employees' health. Data gathered by the HSE is made available to other employers, so that they can also take action to make their workplaces safer. The HSE also provides information to help design training programmes to improve work conditions.

Targeted education, health awareness and health promotion programmes

The government sponsors campaigns to reduce smoking, to improve sexual health and to encourage healthy eating to avoid obesity. Educational programmes have been introduced to help children understand the consequences of living an unhealthy lifestyle and the benefits of improving their eating habits. Parenting skills are being run in schools and for young mothers to show how the benefits of a caring relationship with their baby can help them and their baby develop.

There are also initiatives to improve the health of people who are unemployed, which include:

▶ reduced entry fees to leisure centres
▶ Mind, the mental health charity, gives grants to run gardening and DIY projects, to help support wellbeing and to improve skills for future employment
▶ the Prince's Trust supports many projects for young unemployed people
▶ volunteering opportunities, to help people gain new skills and re-engage with their local community.

PAUSE POINT

Can you recall any health education you received in primary school? If so, how did it impact on you?

Hint

Think about school activities around cooking and physical exercise. Did some have hidden health promotion benefits, such as sports day?

Extend

What is happening now in regard to promotion of health? Is this different from when you were in primary school?

Socio-economic support to reduce health inequality between individuals and communities

Winter fuel payments

People over 60 years of age are automatically paid winter fuel allowance (qualifying ages are published annually on the government website), if they receive a state pension or another social security benefit (other than Housing Benefit, Council Tax Reduction, Child Benefit or Universal Credit). Other people who qualify but do not get paid automatically have to make a claim. This allowance helps to pay heating bills and avoid older people dying of hypothermia in extremely cold conditions. In extremely cold conditions, an extra payment may be claimed for each seven-day period of very cold weather in certain months, which is paid into the same account as other benefits being paid.

Winter fuel payments do not affect the amount paid when claiming other benefits.

Free school meals

The government is driving the promotion of healthy eating habits. The Children and Families Act 2014 requires all government-funded schools to offer free school meals to every pupil in reception class, year 1 and year 2. This includes providing packed lunches for children when they are on a school outing. Families who are claiming certain benefits may also be able to claim free school meals for children attending nursery or for their older children.

Housing support

People who may need support to live independently include those with learning difficulties, those with mental health issues, young single parents, those at risk of becoming homeless and individuals recently discharged from prison. A team of social workers will assess individual cases to see whether they qualify for support. Support is usually provided by local councils or landlords, by offering help with:

▶ budgeting and paying bills

▶ planning meals and shopping

▶ emotional support

▶ social or leisure activities.

Improving access to health and care services

The National Institute for Health Care and Excellence (NICE) recommends measures to improve health and social care services to health boards around Britain, which local authorities and their partners must implement to ensure fair access for all, especially for vulnerable people. Some vulnerable people do not visit health and social care services, which increases their risks of poor health. Local authorities are best placed to know the communities in their geographical area and how to improve health and care services for the more disadvantaged people living in poorer areas. Local authorities also implement strategies to increase healthy life expectancy for all groups of people living in their area.

Co-ordinating national and local services

Inquiries into the poor care standards at the Stafford Hospital and Winterbourne View Care Home, highlighted that it is vital that there is a coordinated, national, integrated care programme for every person in Britain. It is inefficient for organisations and authorities to work in isolation, which can result in local authorities and government agencies being unaware of services that provide poor quality care. It is essential that there are seamless and coordinated services between physical and mental health, primary and secondary care, and health and social care. Government departments work with the organisations commissioning care, such as the NHS Confederation, the Care Quality Commission and the Care Provider Alliance, among others, to ensure this happens.

Disease registration to inform of health trends and for strategic health planning

In Britain, local health authorities report any outbreak of a disease in the area for which they are responsible. This information is generated from GP reports, health charities (such as Cancer Research UK) and private health agencies. In turn, the information is passed to the DH, to form a picture of the health of the nation at any given time. If a serious outbreak of a disease is detected, this is reported to the WHO. The WHO tracks the data, to see whether medical assistance and resources are needed to prevent a serious epidemic of a disease, which could become worldwide. The recent outbreak of infection by the Zika virus has recently been tracked by the WHO. Visitors to affected areas, especially to Brazil (the hosts of the 2016 Olympic Games), will be monitored closely to ensure they do not carry the virus back to their country. This will be achieved through publishing health information about the virus, including campaigns to educate people about how to prevent infection, and continuous monitoring of outbreaks.

Statutory duty to notify certain communicable diseases

All registered medical practitioners have a statutory obligation to report certain infectious diseases to the local authority health protection team. Written notification must be sent within three days of diagnosis, or it can be provided verbally in the case of an emergency. Two of the infectious diseases that must be reported in this way are measles and tuberculosis.

Measles

Measles is extremely contagious. It is spread through droplets when an infected person coughs or sneezes. In the last serious measles outbreak in 1961, there were more than 700,000 cases reported. Since vaccination was introduced in 1967, the incidence has significantly decreased.

However, in 2000, the MMR vaccine (which was being routinely used against measles, mumps and rubella) was incorrectly linked to autism, and many parents stopped having their children vaccinated. As a result, in 2006 one child in the UK who had not been vaccinated died of measles. In 2013, in the region of 2000 cases were reported, 257 people were admitted to hospital with serious complications, and in Wales a young man died.

Tuberculosis (TB)

TB is a bacterial infection spread by droplets when an infected person coughs or sneezes. It is the single highest cause of death by any disease worldwide. The WHO reported that, in 2014, 9.6 million people worldwide fell ill with TB, and 1.5 million died from the disease.

About a third of the world's population has latent TB. These individuals have been infected with TB bacteria but have not yet become ill. They cannot transmit TB but there is a small risk that they will develop TB at some stage in their lifetime. However, people whose immune systems are compromised are at a much higher risk of becoming ill; for example, those living with HIV, people who are malnourished, people who have diabetes and smokers.

Active TB is extremely contagious. It infects the body and particularly affects the respiratory system although it can affect any body system, including the lymph glands, bones and nervous system. Early symptoms include cough, fever, night sweats and weight loss, which can be mild and, therefore, ignored for some time – causing delays in seeking treatment.

TB is a treatable and curable disease.

⏸ PAUSE POINT How does supporting health education needs bring about changes in people's attitudes about looking after themselves?

> Hint Think about provision of extra support for those in need.

> Extend Using data from the NICE publication 'Preventing excess winter deaths and illness associated with cold homes' (2016), explain how the government's 'winter fuel payments' help to improve people's health.

Approaches to protecting public health and wellbeing

Protecting public health

Public health protection teams (HPTs) provide specialist public health advice and support to the NHS, local authorities and other agencies throughout the country by providing support with:

▸ local **health surveillance**

▸ alert systems

▸ investigating and managing health protection incidents.

Local health professionals report outbreaks of infections, incidences of chemical and radiation hazards, and major health emergencies to their local HPT. If healthcare professionals are unsure of what action to take in an outbreak of disease or a major health concern, they can seek help and advice from the local or national public health teams. If necessary, the HPT will pass this information to Public Health Europe and the WHO.

National and local action plans for infectious diseases

Wales has Public Health Wales in place and their stated aim is a Healthier, Happier and Fairer Wales. They have a range of policies concerning health and work, and you can find information on people's rights in work and health on their website. The general public can contact Public Health Wales to find out information on health services and concerns. Health professionals inform them of an outbreak of a disease or can get support if they need it.

Environmental surveillance and intelligence gathering

Surveillance is important in public health work to ensure the spread of diseases is reduced both nationally and within a local area. Data received from public health surveillance informs public health actions about the treatment of disease and minimisation of spread of infectious diseases, programme planning and evaluation. Surveillance is a continuous cycle of data gathering, so that historical data can be consulted when there are outbreaks of disease, and the treatments in those outbreaks can be evaluated and used as a guide about how to proceed in the current outbreak. Data is gathered through local and national sources that register health conditions.

> **Key term**
>
> **Health surveillance** – a system of checks, which may be required by law, to detect ill effects and hazards to health, provide data, and monitor control systems (and check for lapses) to provide protection against hazards to health and wellbeing.

Some examples of some of the surveillance topics include:

▶ mortality data – all deaths must be registered regardless of where or why they occur, rates of deaths in hospitals, rest homes, at home and those caused through car accidents, injuries at work etc can be analysed for patterns

▶ infectious disease data – all outbreaks and control measures used in cases of infectious diseases such as measles and TB, must be reported so that they can be monitored

▶ environmental hazards data – statistics about environmental concerns, for example from a gas storage unit are compiled and monitored by the Environment Agency

▶ cancer data – the National Cancer Registration Service provides data to the ONS about new cases of cancer and cancer survival, monitors new cases of cancer in the population and looks at trends and geographical patterns to detect risk factors and cancer clusters

▶ acute and chronic disease registers – the General Lifestyle Survey provides data about, for example asthma, cardiovascular disease, diabetes, mental health and dental health.

The surveillance data allows for strategic planning and allocation of resources at a local, national and global level. The use of strategic information and intelligence also allows for review of whether treatments are successful or not, what is required to improve public health and health care and the actions taken in disease outbreaks (which may inform future actions).

Environmental controls

Waste disposal and treatment

There are regulations governing the safe disposal of clinical waste and many other products. Table 8.1 shows some of the main methods of disposal of waste from healthcare sources.

▶ **Table 8.1:** Main methods used for clinical waste disposal

Method	Used for	Comments
Incineration	Most items of clinical waste	• Guidelines provided by Department for Environment, Food and Rural Affairs (Defra) for compliance with the European Community (EC) Directive 2000/76/EC on the incineration of waste. • Seen as the best method for healthcare waste. • Guidelines cover hazardous or toxic waste, to ensure that fumes from incineration are controlled, and that ashes are placed in an area that cannot infect animals or people. • Pressurised containers and batteries should not be incinerated as these may explode and cause damage to equipment and personnel. • Also inadvisable to incinerate products made of heavy metal, as toxic metal fumes could be released into the atmosphere.
Chemical disinfection	Potentially infectious liquid waste such as blood, urine, faeces and hospital sewage Sharps disposal	• Uses antimicrobial chemicals. • Sharps are usually shredded before the chemical process starts. • Chemicals used for disinfection are themselves hazardous, so the people involved in the waste process must be properly trained and use appropriate personal protection equipment.
Inertisation	Pharmaceuticals Incineration waste	• A process of mixing waste with cement, which holds the toxins within it. • This mixture is then poured into a specially measure pit to set or used to create cement pellets. • The pit/pellets are then buried under strict control methods and in special sites.

Waste disposal includes the disposal of carcasses. Defra provides guidelines, *Fallen stock and safe disposal of dead animals* for the disposal of farm animals, which must not be burned or buried on farm land. There is separate guidance for the disposal of diseased or potentially infected carcasses, for example animals suspected of being infected with TSE (transmissible spongiform encephalopathy – a cause of variant Creutzfeldt-Jakob (so-called mad cow) disease in humans).

PAUSE POINT   How easy is it for you and your family to recycle waste in your area? What type of disposal method is used?

Hint   You could look at your local authority environment website.

Extend   Research the data given by the environment website about how much recycling costs, the benefits to the community of recycling and what the recycling is used for.

Water supply

The Drinking Water Inspectorate oversees the quality of drinking water by ensuring that water companies operating in England and Wales supply safe drinking water to consumers such as homes, hospitals, businesses and anywhere where drinking water is available from a mains tap. It ensures that the quality of the water meets legal requirements set out in The Water Supply (Water Quality) Regulations 2000.

In Wales the quality of water is ensured by the National Public Health Service for Wales.

In Scotland, water regulations are overseen by the Scottish Environment Protection Agency (SEPA), to ensure safe clean water meets the health requirements.

In Northern Ireland, the Drinking Water Inspectorate has the responsibility of ensuring that water is safe.

Food production, preparation, storage and sales

The FSA regulates food production in Britain and is led by the European Union legislation on food standards. The FSA represents England, Wales and Northern Ireland in the European Union, and is involved in setting the nutrition and health agenda at European level. The FSA has a statutory requirement to protect people's nutritional health in Britain. Its responsibilities cover food production, preparation, storage and sales. The Food Standards Act requires businesses involved with food products to ensure that:

▸ foodstuffs are kept free from harmful substances that may cause health concerns to consumers

▸ food products are correctly stored

▸ food products that are sold are of the nature, substance and quality that consumers expect

▸ food products are not falsely labelled, advertised or presented to mislead consumers.

The FSA defines food as 'any substance or product, whether processed, partially processed or unprocessed, intended to be, or reasonably expected to be ingested (eaten) by humans'.

The courts decide penalties but abide by the guidelines set out by the FSA. In England and Wales, the Magistrates' court can imprison offenders for up to two years and fine them a limitless amount. In Scotland the Sheriff court can fine an offender £20,000, and impose a maximum of one year in prison.

Regulations, control and monitoring of public areas and work environments

Defra has authority over all aspects of the environment, including air pollution, traffic noise, litter and mess on the streets, graffiti and antisocial behaviour such as noisy neighbours. The department sets guidelines for local authorities to follow and has systems in place for the reporting and investigation of issues.

The department works closely with European and other international bodies to ensure that standards are followed. One of the standards covers air quality. Britain is experiencing many problems in trying to reduce the levels of nitrogen dioxide, which is a dangerous gas produced by car fumes. Some streets in London surpass the annual levels for emissions of this gas within days.

Noise nuisance is another area of environmental concern, especially in regards to occupational, aviation, road and rail noise. Defra sets policies and legislation for local authorities to manage noise, helping improve people's quality of life. Research led by the London School of Hygiene & Tropical Medicine, and published in the *European Heart Journal* in 2015, suggests that long-term exposure to traffic noise is linked to deaths and an increased risk of strokes, particularly in elderly people.

The role of microbiology services to identify and control outbreaks of food-, water- or airborne disease

The role of local and national microbiological services is to identify, isolate, treat and prevent human infections caused by pathogenic (disease causing) organisms.

When an individual has an infection, depending on the signs and symptoms, a sample may be taken for analysis, for example urine, faeces, skin, blood or saliva. The sample is sent to a local pathology laboratory for analysis; this may be a department within a large hospital. The results usually take several days, depending on the tests required. (Some results may be available in hours and others may take longer than the three days.)

Microbiology services are broken into different departments:

▶ bacteriology and mycology – to detect infections caused by bacteria and fungi

▶ virology – to detect infections caused by viruses

▶ serology – to detect infections in blood samples

▶ infection control – to control infections in hospitals, in particular those due to methicillin resistant staphylococcus aureus (MRSA).

Identifying and controlling diseases spread in food

Public Health Laboratories (PHLs) are based within large NHS trusts and they can test samples and provide specialist support in situations where there is an outbreak or incident of disease caused by contaminated food. Information is then shared with other departments such as Environmental Health.

Premises may be checked by Environmental Health Officers. The EHO can visit premises where there have been reports of illness which may be due to food purchased from those premises, or where there are reports of vermin infestations. They have the power to enforce immediate closure of premises that they consider pose a risk to public health and will not lift the closure order until they are satisfied that the conditions that they impose for the safe handling of food are met.

Identifying and controlling diseases spread by water

The PHL can identify and isolate the pathogens that cause outbreaks, such as Legionnaires Disease caused by the legionella bacteria which can be spread either in water or in water vapour (shower heads or cooling towers, for example, may be sources of infection), and it is the responsibility of the employer to ensure that the guidance of the Health and Safety Executive is followed in the workplace to ensure the safety of staff, visitors and the wider public. The regulations for ensuring safety are covered both by the Health and Safety at Work Act (1974) and Control of Substances Hazardous to Health Regulations (2002) COSHH.

Research

Research an environmental issue in your local area such as, graffiti, noise, nitrogen dioxide emissions or antisocial behaviour. Find out what your local authority is doing to reduce the effects of these issues. Also find out what health effects, if any, there have been on the local population due to the issue you are researching.

The consequenses of an outbreak can be very serious. For example, an outbreak of Legionnaires Disease in 2002 in Barrow-in-Furness resulted in seven people dying and 180 being infected with the disease. After the first two cases were linked to Barrow-in-Furness, an Outbreak Control Team (OCT) was established to identify the source of the outbreak, which turned out to be an arts and leisure facility in the city. It then became the role of the OCT to manage the consequences of the outbreak.

Identifying and controlling airborne diseases

Airborne diseases are spread by respiratory droplets or dust from one person contaminating someone else. The pathogens involved may be viruses, bacteria or fungi. The PHL can formulate an emergency response to naturally occurring pathogens such as SARS or H5N1 influenza as well as providing specialist support in the event of a bioterrorist threat.

The role of field epidemiology in controlling communicable disease

People working in field epidemiology around the world track and report outbreaks of infectious diseases to local, national, regional and world health authorities. This enables resources to be appropriately allocated to the area of outbreak. It also enables global authorities to put in place controls to prevent the spread of the infection. The Ebola outbreak in Uganda in 2007 was reported through field epidemiology experts. A WHO task force coordinated the response to this outbreak and although it lasted several weeks, it was contained in a local area.

Preparedness and response

Field workers and trained personnel were quickly sent to help isolate the outbreak in that area and report any further cases. All outbreaks of Ebola in neighbouring countries were reported. Teams of nurses and doctors were trained in treatment methods, and national and world military personnel were trained in how to set up treatment camps. The WHO mobilised collaborating laboratories in France and West Africa to diagnose cases. Médecins Sans Frontières set up isolation facilities. With multidisciplinary teams working effectively together the Ebola outbreak was brought under control before it became a world health problem causing thousands of deaths.

Research
Access the WHO website and read the report about key events in the WHO response to the Ebola outbreak. Suggest ways in which this could have been controlled.

Specific programmes for health protection

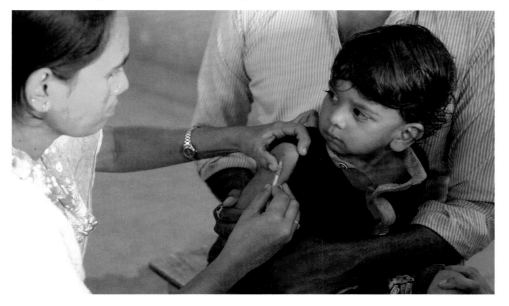

▶ Child receiving immunisation

Immunisation

Immunisation protects the population from preventable infections such as tetanus, diphtheria, measles, mumps, polio and influenza.

Older and vulnerable people are offered flu jabs every winter. People over 65 years of age, and vulnerable people, are offered immunisation against pneumococcal polysaccharide (PPV) influenza and shingles, which are all serious infections.

In the UK, childhood vaccination programmes are designed to protect young children from dangerous infections. These programmes include:

▶ at two to four months old – diphtheria, pertussis, polio

▶ at 12 to 13 months old – measles, mumps and rubella (MMR)

▶ between two and 17 years old – influenza

▶ for girls aged between 12 and 14 years – human papillomavirus (HPV).

Health screening

Screening is an effective way of checking a person's health status to identify individuals at higher risk of a disease or condition, allowing them to choose to have treatment should the disease or condition be found. Screening may be offered to all individuals in a population or only to people at risk of developing specific conditions such as cancer, diabetes or sickle cell anaemia. Screening programmes should be of benefit both to the individual and to society as a whole, and not impose too high a cost on the NHS.

The UK National Screening Committee (UK NSC) advises the NHS on which screening programmes to offer. Table 8.2 shows some examples of the current population screening programmes available through the NHS.

▶ **Table 8.2:** Examples of UK population screening programmes

Condition/disorder	Available to
Abdominal aortic aneurysm	All men in England aged 65 years and over.
Bowel cancer	All men and women in the UK aged 60 to 74 years (offered every two years).
Breast cancer	All women in the UK aged 50 to 70 years (in some areas and cases it may be offered to younger women).
Cervical screening	All women in England aged 25 to 64 years (offered every three years to women aged 25 to 49 years, and every five years to women aged 50 to 64 years).
Diabetic eye screening	All people with type 1 and type 2 diabetes aged 12 years or over.
Foetal anomaly screening (including for Down's syndrome)	Pregnant women, between 10 and 14 weeks of pregnancy.
Infectious diseases in pregnancy screening	All pregnant women are screened for HIV, hepatitis B and syphilis.
Newborn and infant physical examination screening	All newborn babies are screened within 72 hours of birth, and then again between six to eight weeks old for conditions that may affect the heart, hips, eyes and (in boys) testes.
Newborn blood spot screening (the 'heel-prick')	All newborn babies are screened for sickle cell disease (SCD), cystic fibrosis (CF), congenital hypothyroidism (CHT) and inherited metabolic diseases such as phenylketonuria (PKU).
Newborn hearing screening	All babies born or resident in England within four to five weeks of birth, but not after three months of age. Babies with a known risk of hearing impairment or deafness from another condition are not eligible.
Sickle cell and thalassaemia screening	All pregnant women. Fathers-to-be, where the mother is a genetic carrier. All newborn babies (part of the newborn blood spot screening programme).

Screening is not 100 per cent accurate. However, if a condition or disease is found it can be investigated and medical treatment given. Screening may lead to difficult decisions, for example a pregnant woman may have to decide whether or not to carry on with a pregnancy if a particular health condition is detected in the baby.

Genetic screening

Genetic screening is offered to people susceptible to developing a specific inherited disease or condition. These screening programmes are offered for newborns, older children, couples or individuals before and during pregnancy. Genetic screening includes sickle cell disease, which if detected early can reduce childhood deaths or severe health problems. Women with a history of premenopausal breast cancer in their family can be screened for the abnormal genes: BRCA1 and BRCA2 genes. Abnormal BRCA1 and BRCA2 genes account for about 1 in 10 of all breast cancers, but their presence does not mean an individual will get breast cancer.

Case study

Angelina Jolie

Angelina Jolie's grandmother, mother and aunt all died of breast or ovarian cancer. She was screened and found to have BRCA1 gene mutation. She was told she had an 87 per cent chance of developing breast cancer and a 50 per cent chance of developing ovarian cancer. In 2013, Angelina Jolie had a double mastectomy to reduce her risks of developing these cancers, and she now has regular screening tests. (She later underwent surgery to remove her ovaries and fallopian tubes after a blood test indicated early signs of cancer.)

Check your knowledge

1 What effect do you think Angelina Jolie's decision to make her health concerns public has had on women in the UK? See if you can find any information about the 'Angelina effect'.

2 Do you think this generally had a positive or negative impact on women's attitude towards breast screening?

 PAUSE POINT How are vulnerable people around the world protected from disease and illness?

 Hint Think about monitoring and control, and the organisations that provide this support.

Extend How is the Zika virus being monitored and controlled?

Disease prevention and control methods

Prevention and control of communicable diseases

The prevention and control of communicable diseases in the UK is the responsibility of the DH. Communicable diseases can be controlled by immunisation, good environmental health and leading a healthy lifestyle. People can be educated through television and radio adverts, information in GP surgeries and health information campaigns.

Good hygiene

Diseases, such as ordinary coughs and colds, which are spread through airborne droplets from an infected person coughing or sneezing, can largely be prevented by practising good hygiene. Individuals should be educated to cover their mouths with a tissue when they cough or sneeze. Afterwards, they should safely dispose of the tissue in a covered bin and wash their hands. Washing hands after using the toilet can prevent the spread of illnesses, such as those caused by *E. coli*. In hospitals, medical centres, schools and colleges a biological hand wash is available for people to use to avoid cross contamination.

Vaccination against TB

An individual can be protected against tuberculosis (TB) through vaccination with the Bacillus Calmette-Guerin (BCG) vaccine, which is not part of the NHS vaccination schedule. BCG vaccination is only offered to babies and children considered to be at risk, for example those living in an area with a high rate of TB, or those whose parents or grandparents have lived in countries with a high rate of TB.

BCG vaccination may also be offered to older children at risk who did not have the vaccine as a baby. Some adults (between the ages of 16 and 35 years) whose work exposes them to the risk of contracting TB, for example those working in laboratories, veterinary staff, care home staff, people who work with refugees and healthcare workers, may also be offered the vaccine.

The bacteria in the BCG vaccine are weak. The vaccine works by triggering the immune system against the disease, without causing it, thus providing immunity. It is about 70 to 80 per cent effective against severe forms of TB, including TB meningitis in children. However, it is less effective in preventing the more common form of TB in adults, respiratory TB – hence vaccination is not offered to people over 35 years of age.

Preventing the spread of bacterial meningitis

Antibiotics are a proven medicine against bacterial infections and are prescribed by GPs and hospital doctors if required. A course of antibiotics are given which must be completed by the patient to ensure a full recovery from an infection. Many people do not complete the full course as when they start to feel better they stop taking the antibiotics. As healthcare workers, be aware that people in your care must be encouraged to finish the complete course. In the case of bacterial meningitis, antibiotics may also be prescribed as a precautionary measure for people with prolonged contact with an infected person. This can include anyone living in the same house, halls of residence or a boyfriend or girlfriend of the infected person. These people may not show symptoms but the antibiotic course must be completed to ensure that the infection is not spread. People with only brief contact will not be offered a course of antibiotics as over-prescription of unnecessary treatments leads to antibiotic resistance and is an unneccesary expense. Antibiotics will not be prescribed for viral meningitis as antibiotics are ineffective in the treatment of viruses and this condition usually gets better on its own.

Prevention and control of non-communicable diseases

Non-communicable diseases (NCDs) are all diseases that are not infectious or contagious. This includes cancers, chronic respiratory (lung) disease, cardiovascular (heart) disease and diabetes, which are the commonest causes of death worldwide. Mental illness is also included as an NCD as data from the DH suggests that mental health illness shortens life expectancy, which may be because people with mental illnesses do not look after their physical health. In the UK in 2014, NCDs accounted for 557,000 deaths. The UK government has declared their intention to prevent and control NCDs to the WHO.

The main causes of NCDs are cardiovascular disease (31 per cent) and cancers (29 per cent). Contributory factors are poor mental health, smoking, poor diet, lack of physical activity, substance abuse, alcohol abuse and obesity. Early detection and management of NCDs can help delay more complicated health problems, and reduce the cost to the NHS. It was estimated that in 2013 the cost of cardiovascular disease to the NHS was £6.8 bn, including treatments, surgery and medicines. Diabetes and its complications is estimated to cost £9 bn a year. Many NCDs can be prevented by individuals adopting healthier lifestyles, which can be achieved through education and support with mental health issues.

A United Nations meeting in 2011 concluded that governments around the world must do more about the prevention of the NCD epidemic. Governments need to do more to deal with poverty, which is a big factor affecting people's health.

Raising awareness of causes

There is a government drive to reduce the NCD risk factors, with campaigns to reduce salt and trans fats (trans fatty acids) in food and to promote breastfeeding which is a healthier choice for babies than formulated milk feeds.

Contributory lifestyle factors

A person's lifestyle may be a contributory factor to their wellbeing. A person with a healthy lifestyle is likely to be healthy. However, a person who does not take care of their health and wellbeing may experience poor health and, potentially, premature death.

Skin cancer

Skin cancers are categorised as melanomas and non-melanomas. Melanomas originate from melanocytes, and usually start as moles; non-melanoma skin cancers that arise from other skin cells are more common (except in young people). However, both types of skin cancers can be caused by exposure to the sun, and also from overuse of ultraviolet sunbeds. People with fairer colouring are more prone to the harmful effects of the sun.

Largely under reported until recent years, the incidence of skin cancers has risen more than six-fold since the 1970s; the British Skin Foundation reports that more than 100,000 cases are reported each year, making skin cancer one of the most significant causes of cancer in the UK. Skin cancer is often diagnosed early as it can be readily seen, meaning treatment is usually more successful.

There have been recent health promotion campaigns to raise awareness about the causes of skin cancers and to encourage people to apply high protection factor sunscreen, especially to areas of skin most exposed to the sun.

Coronary heart disease

Eating too much fat or salt, and not exercising, raises the risk of an individual developing coronary heart disease later in life. Healthy foods and the importance of exercise are now promoted in primary schools, so that children grow up with a better understanding of how to live a healthy lifestyle.

There have been many public health campaigns to raise awareness of the lifestyle factors that contribute to good or poor cardiac health. Currently, the government has campaigns specifically targeting measures to improve coronary health such as Sugar Smart, Start 4 Life and Change4Life, and stopping smoking.

Socio-economic support and protection benefits

It is important to help people with low incomes to achieve healthier lifestyles, decreasing their dependence on health and social services, improving their quality of life and enabling them to live longer and healthier lives.

> **Research**
>
> What is the government currently doing to promote the prevention and control of NCDs? Use your findings to create a display board for your school/college.

In some areas of the UK, people over 60 may be entitled to use leisure centres free of charge, to help maintain a healthy and active lifestyle. Transport services have discounts for many people, including seniors, enabling older people to travel more and to visit friends and relations. In many areas of the UK, people over 60 years old can use public transport free of charge.

Pensions

The basic state pension is a regular payment from the government. A person with sufficient national insurance contributions, receives a pension from the state when they reach state pension age. The pension age is set by the government and can be changed in a financial budget. The amount a pensioner receives is fixed by the government, but is increased each year according to rises in earnings, the cost of living or inflation rates. There are different rates for a single person's pension and a married couple's pension.

People may also receive a private pension; either one that they have made independent savings for, or one received from contributions they made to a pension fund through their employment.

An individual can continue to work and still be paid their state pension and/or a private pension.

Free school meals

Free school meals help children receive a healthy meal once a day while at school. Under the school food standards, schools must provide high-quality meals consisting of meat, poultry or oily fish, fruit and vegetables, bread, cereals and potatoes. There should not be any drinks with added sugar, crisps, chocolate or sweets, and no more than two portions of deep fried food per week.

The government's Universal Infant Free School Meals policy allows for infants from Reception class through to Year 2 to receive free school meals. Families claiming certain benefits can also claim free school meals for their older children or younger children in nursery.

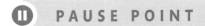

PAUSE POINT   Describe three ways in which vulnerable people and children are supported in improving their health.

 Hint   Think about the benefits for adults and health promotion programmes in schools.

Extend   Use official data to analyse the affect that the three ways of support you identified have improved the health of the vulnerable people or children concerned.

D Investigate how health promotion encourages individuals to change their behaviour in relation to their own health

Features of health promotion campaigns

Health promotion campaigns can either be charity-led, for example Cancer Research UK campaigns, or nationally organised as with campaigns such as Change4Life, which is run by the NHS. These campaigns are run to inform people about how to improve their personal health, so that they become aware of the positive changes they can make and the impact it will have on their overall wellbeing.

Relation to health policy

Government agencies responsible for setting health policy use current trends about health problems to improve health policies. In this way, health policy works towards creating a healthier population.

This is achieved by testing policies already in place, analysing what is working and what needs to change, and retaining only those policies that work. The knowledge gained is used to enable health professionals to educate the population through health campaigns to improve health, or aspects of health. For example, current UK health concerns, and consequently targeted campaigns, include obesity, alcohol, drug activity and smoking.

Objectives

The objectives of health campaigns are to improve the health of the population, to educate the public how to improve and maintain their health, and how to live life to its full potential.

Target audience

The key step in any health communication and in social marketing is to identify the section of the population that might benefit from a particular campaign. The more that is known about this section, the better the campaigns will be in targeting this group of people and in getting the right message across to ensure that the right policies are put into place.

Researching the target audience can be done by health professionals passing data to medical research companies, who use various sources, such as the internet and social media, to build a profile of the target group. From this, campaigns can be created and tested on a sample group to see whether the campaign would influence them to make a specific change. Issues such as language use, using appropriate actors and relevant situations are taken into account, to ensure that the right message is being delivered and that the relevant people can relate to the campaign.

> **Research**
>
> Look at the health campaign about mental health issues – 'It's time to talk, it's time to change'. What do you think were the reasons behind its launch in 2007? You could also access the Mind website to research the effect the campaign has had on attitudes about the stigma of mental health.

Reasons for approach – media resources

Approaches to campaigns have to take into account how people communicate. Currently social media is a big part of most people's lives, including for people aged over 65 years old. Part of the research before launching a campaign is to find out from participants how they communicate, and which media platform would make the best impact, for example:

▶ television – will probably reach the largest audience, but careful research is required to ensure the times and programmes the target audience watches

▶ radio – again, reaches a large audience, but research will need to look at **demographics** and specific stations

▶ social media/websites – research required to see which types the target audience most uses, for example whether they use Snapchat as opposed to Twitter, Facebook or Instagram

▶ magazines – for different age groups and interests.

> **Key term**
>
> **Demographics** – statistics about the population and particular groups within it, for example age, income and education.

All media sources can be used effectively, as long as the right media resource is used. Much research is needed to find the right approach for a campaign and to ensure its maximum impact. People will quickly disengage with a health promotion message if they feel that they are being made to feel like they are not good enough, not trying hard enough or the information is aimed at someone else. Getting the balance right between making an individual feel bad about an unhealthy activity that they want to do and educating them about a healthy option without stigmatising or criticising them can be very difficult, especially if the activity is not something that they openly discuss or which is bound in social taboos. An example of this would be using a condom with a new sexual partner. Many females feel awkward carrying condoms and some men may find using them changes the sexual experience.

It is also important that the information is current and, where appropriate, complies with legislation, policies and procedures. An example of this would be manual handing legislation in the workplace. All places of work are subject to the Health and Safety at Work Act (1974) and the rules apply to staff, volunteers and visitors. Safe practices such as how to handle and load, for example a crate of milk, a box of paper or a person, must be handled in accordance with the current advice and the methods have changed over the years. It is important that everyone has up-to-date training.

Ethical considerations

Ethics is the discipline involved in moral reasoning, especially applied to behaviour. Before campaigns are undertaken there are ethical questions that must be considered about the implications for the target population. The two main ethical questions being as follows.

What is considered a healthy society?

Although this question pertains to everyone in society, it can sometimes be seen to relate only to people living in poor communities or people living unhealthy lifestyles. In a healthy society, everyone should not only look after their own health but ensure that other people's health and wellbeing is catered for. In a healthy society, there would be little or no illness or poverty, people would have access to nutritious food, clean water, fresh air and healthy, outdoor exercise.

What should health campaigns contribute to a healthy society?

Health promotion campaigns should educate everyone about what contributes to a healthy lifestyle as well as the consequences of making poor lifestyle choices. This needs to be done in a way that avoids stigmatising people with a particular health problem, making them feel guilty about their condition or implying that it is 'their own fault' that they are unhealthy. A good campaign should be informative and enable people to make their own judgements about their lifestyle.

Considerations about the ethical implications of health promotion vary widely. However, the following points should be considered when planning campaigns.

Does the health promotion campaign:

▸ limit or increase the freedom of individuals – care must be taken not to criticise or ridicule an individual's lifestyle, or to make them feel self-conscious, if a person feels threatened by a health campaign, it is likely to prevent them from taking part in activities that could help improve their wellbeing

▸ benefit all – for example, it cannot be only for those who can afford a gym membership or to buy organic food

▸ blame or stigmatise – someone who has a disability, who is sick or at higher risk of developing a disease or condition should not be made to feel like a 'victim'

▸ distribute benefits fairly – the campaign benefits should help all of the population.

<aside>
Key term

Ethics – the discipline involved in moral reasoning about what should be done.
</aside>

Analysis of data about health promotion campaigns

Data obtained during and after promotion is used to evaluate campaign outcomes against original objectives. This is essential to judge whether a campaign has been successful or not. It also enables lessons to be learned to either maintain a successful campaign for the future, or to make changes to unsuccessful campaigns to help ensure future success.

Influence of campaign focus

Target audience

In 2010 the DH started raising awareness about poor lung cancer survival rates. In 2011, a campaign focusing on earlier diagnosis of lung cancer, 'Be clear on Cancer' was developed. Data had shown that people were presenting at GP surgeries with late-stage disease, and that only 5 per cent of people survived for five years or longer following a diagnosis of lung cancer.

▶ Example of a poster from the Be Clear on Lung Cancer campaign (source: Evaluation of the Be Clear on Cancer lung cancer awareness campaign regional pilot, East and West Midlands (2015), Department of Health and Public Health England)

Ethical considerations on chosen model

Three main questions were raised at a meeting before the campaign was released.

▶ Would the campaign work?

▶ Would it cause panic, with anxious people queuing outside GP surgeries for further information?

▶ Was it ethical to run, or would it make existing lung cancer patients more aware that their condition was terminal?

Before running the campaign nationally, research was undertaken to see whether these questions could be answered. It was decided to run pilots in the east and west Midlands area. Two 30-second television adverts were targeted at working men and women in the 50+ age group. There was one advert featuring a man and one featuring a woman, both characters had persistent coughs and eventually went to see their GP to talk about it.

After the advert was run, evidence was gathered from GPs and hospitals in the area and analysed to see what effects the campaign had produced. From the evidence, it was seen that more cancers had been identified at an earlier stage than previously, and not just lung cancer. The Midlands pilot campaign had been successful and so from 2012 it was run nationally. 'Be Clear on Cancer' is still run by Cancer Research UK and due to its success now includes other types of cancer such as breast, bowel and bladder.

PAUSE POINT In two minutes, write down all the media campaigns that you can remember seeing or hearing about.

Hint Think about all the media you use such as television, Facebook, radio, posters at bus stops or train stations, magazines etc.

Extend Look for health campaigns currently being advertised. How many can you identify? Have you added to your initial list? Explain the difference between those you identified initially and those you later identified.

Barriers to participation and challenging indifference

Cost

Lifestyles depend on the financial situation of individuals or families. If a person or a family has a moderate to high income, they are more likely to live a healthier lifestyle. They will be able to afford gym membership, to buy nutritious food, are likely to be better educated and to be more interested in living healthily. By contrast, people living on lower incomes or in poverty are more likely to eat a poor diet, be unable to afford to go to a gym or leisure centre and generally have a poorer lifestyle. Sporting activities can be expensive, which may prevent some children and adults from playing team games to keep fit. For example, joining a football team may entail having to buy kit, pay fees, pay for travel to away fixtures and pay to join in social activities. Poorer individuals and families may struggle to pay for nutritious foods on a regular basis and so buy cheaper food that contains more fats and salts. This affects their immediate health as well as their life expectancy.

Individual resistance/indifference

Some people are not interested in making the effort to eat well or to exercise, or they have an 'it won't happen to me' attitude. For example, it can be difficult to persuade a small child or teenager to eat well as they might not be able to envisage the effects on their health in several years' time. This may be due to apathy or to mental health issues.

Some people feel threatened by specific healthy activities, such as taking part in sport. They may recall negative experiences of school, of being forced to join in a sporting activity, or they may think that participating in sport will not be of benefit to them. Negative attitudes may be caused by lack of self-esteem, not being encouraged by family or friends when they were younger, or parents or carers passing on negative health behaviours.

Additionally, there is a thinking strategy, the 'tomorrow syndrome', where exercise and healthy eating will start tomorrow – and, of course, tomorrow never comes!

Accessibility of resources

Accessibility is important, and everyone should have access to sporting activities, leisure centres and travel, enabling them to participate in activities and improve their lifestyle. If facilities are inaccessible, due to their location or the difficulty experienced in travelling to them, this will prevent people taking part in exercise or social activities. Local authorities have an obligation to ensure that everyone living in their area has access to health and leisure facilities. Additionally, local authorities often reduce costs, or offer free admission for people receiving benefits or for elderly people. There are usually concessionary rates for other groups such as children. Travel costs are also often reduced or free for children, people receiving benefits and older people.

Every organisation is covered by the Equality Act 2010, to ensure that facilities are accessible for all, regardless of health or disability, and that people can use the facilities safely.

Lifestyle factors

An individual's lifestyle may affect their participation in activities. Poor diet causes lack of energy, obesity and weight gain, which may make individuals unwilling to take part in sporting or leisure activities. Obese and overweight people may feel embarrassed about taking part, or they may not be encouraged to take part.

Smoking may make a person breathless, making it a struggle to join in leisure activities effectively.

The media

The media plays an important role in encouraging participation in leisure activities. However, in the past, reports have tended to focus on extremely fit and attractive people enjoying sport. This can have a negative impact on, for example an overweight person with a negative body image who wants to take part in sport. Inaccurate reporting about the 'perfect body' is often reflected in magazine articles, on television, in social media, websites and advertising. There are many articles that disguise a person's true statistics and in which their images have been air-brushed to achieve an 'ideal look'. Striving to achieve this ideal can have a negative effect on a person's attitude and desire to take part in activities where their body may be on show to others. Women in particular may feel that they are bombarded with images of the 'perfect body'.

However, there has been a recent move towards change and the image of sport is being portrayed more inclusively, for example coverage of the Paralympics and Invictus Games, advertising people with disabilities taking part in sport and other physical activities and adverts featuring people of all shapes and sizes taking part in sports. Media coverage such as this encourages people to participate, regardless of skin colour, health and body shape.

Some people may feel uninterested about participation because they have heard the message so many times that they have simply stopped listening. If an individual lacks both the will, determination and drive to engage in physical activity and they also don't personally identify with people that are physically active, then they can be very difficult to engage in healthy activities.

Salad is a Garnish not a Food

Butch drove a lorry, a large HGV, up and down the country and all over the Continent. Butch was away from home for days at a time and he often ate his meals at motorway service stations or roadside cafes. Butch neither loaded nor unloaded his truck as there were forklift drivers for that. Butch turned his steering wheel and the pages of his daily newspaper which he read on his allotted rest periods.

Butch knew the names and relationship statuses of the rich and famous but thought their lives mainly irrelevant to the kind of graft that he did, day in day out.

Butch suffered with obesity, constipation and piles. He could only just walk 300 metres before he was out of breath but that didn't matter to him, his partner loved him the way he was.

Check your knowledge

1 Why did Butch think that he did not need to exercise?

2 How did the people around Butch contribute to his lack of exercise?

3 What could Butch have done to increase his levels of activity?

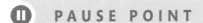

PAUSE POINT   What makes people resist improving their health?

> Hint   Think about mental and physical behaviours.

> Extend   Ask people in your class about eating habits and changes they could make to improve their diet. Are there any reasons why they would not make the changes?

Models and theories that justify health behaviour change

Health belief model

The health belief model was developed by social psychologists in the 1950s. The model studied people's attitudes and beliefs, to determine their health behaviours. The model proposed that people would change their attitudes towards their own health if they were faced by threat of a disease that they considered would cause serious health problems for them, and that they would take action to find out about the symptoms and the best way to treat it. However, if people do not feel they are at serious risk, they will continue their unhealthy lifestyle in the false belief that ill health will not happen to them.

▸ **Table 8.3:** The health belief model

Concept	Definition
Susceptibility	An individual's assessment of the risk of getting a disease. For example, if a young person believes a certain disease only affects older people, they are less likely to take actions to prevent getting it.
Severity	The individual's view about the disease's impact on their health. Impacts range from the worst scenario of death, to disablement, severe pain and how long illness will last.
Benefits	The individual's view of how much a medicine or treatment would help.
Barriers	Difficulties an individual perceives about taking medicines or receiving treatments, including cost, physical and psychological side effects.
Action	Prompts the individual may use to take the prescribed action, for example using their mobile to remind them to take the medicine, using a wall or email calendar etc.
Self-efficacy	The belief an individual has about taking the prescribed medicine or treatment. They may not take it even if they know the medicine is good for them. Family and friends can encourage the individual to take it.

Theory of reasoned action

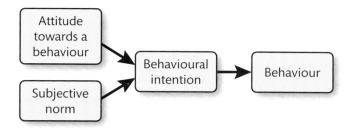

▶ **Figure 8.4:** The theory of reasoned action (source: Usability news, *'E-Commerce, the Consumer Decision Process, and the Theory of Reasoned Action', by Fred Volk*)

The theory of reasoned action was first developed in mid-1970s. It is mainly concerned with behaviour, but recognises that situations have an effect on it. For example, a teenager's attitude towards the behaviour of smoking may be either favourable or unfavourable. Much will depend on their pre-existing attitudes to smoking, learned through from their parents or through education. The **subjective norm** is peer pressure about smoking, whether there is pressure to smoke or not. The teenager's behaviour about smoking or not smoking is formed from their attitude towards the behaviour, the subjective norm and their own reasoned intentions.

There are two parts to a reasoned action; the 'attitudes' and the 'norms' that predict behavioural intent. Attitudes lead a person to want to do something, but the relevant norms persuade the person to do something else. Attitudes and norms can be further divided, meaning that if another person wants to persuade someone to do something they may have many options.

▶ Attitudes can be broken down into evaluation and strength, so a person evaluates a situation and the strength of their attitude decides how much they want to do it.

▶ Norms can also be divided into normative beliefs – where a person thinks what others would expect them to do, and motivation to comply – where a person thinks how important is it to do what others expect of them.

If an attitude is stronger in a person than the norm, then the attitude part will win, and vice versa.

For example, if a doctor is trying to persuade a patient to take medicine and the patient has a positive attitude towards taking it, 'I've heard the medicine is really good', then it will be easy to persuade them to take the medicine. However, if the patient has a negative attitude, for example, the last time they took that medicine it made them feel nauseous, the doctor must try to reduce that attitude and persuade them to take the medicine, maybe by emphasising how the medicine will improve their current condition. Another way of persuading a patient to take the medicine is through normative beliefs. For example, the doctor could either emphasise that the person's family would like them to take it, or that other people with the condition are taking it and it is having positive effects on their health.

Theory of planned behaviour

This theory evolved in the 1980s and is based on reasoned action theory. It has been used successfully to predict a person's health behaviour and intention including drinking, smoking, breastfeeding, substance misuse and many other things. The theory believes that behavioural intentions depend on motivation and the ability to control their behaviour.

Key term

Subjective norm – a perceived social pressure that arises from an individual's perception of what other people would think or do in similar circumstances.

▶ Table 8.4: The six components of planned behaviours

Component	Description
Attitude	The individual's positive or negative evaluation of something.
Behavioural intention	The individual's motivational strength to do something.
Subjective norms	Whether other people approve or disapprove.
Social norms	The cultural influences that impact on an individual's decision.
Perceived power	What the individual believes will help or impede their decision.
Perceived behavioural control	The individual's perception of the difficulties that may influence their intentions.

When working with a patient, a healthcare professional will need to know what influences there are on that patient, and work out strategies to overcome any negative influences to ensure the health of the patient improves.

Stages of change model

In the 1990s, researchers working in the field of alcoholism developed a six-stage change model to help alcoholics overcome their addiction. It was thought that if a person understands their readiness to change they could use the six-stage model to choose the right course of action for them. From this research it was seen that the stages of change model can be used in all areas of health care. The six stages identified are: precontemplation, contemplation, determination, action, maintenance and termination.

Precontemplation

This falls into four groups.

▶ Reluctant – where the individual does not see the problem, which could be due to their reluctance, lack of knowledge, willingness or drive to consider change, or they may not be fully aware of their health condition.

▶ Rebellious – the individual wants to make their own decisions, they are resistant to being told what to do.

▶ Resigned – the individual has given up hope of changing, they may be overwhelmed or have tried before and failed.

▶ Rationalising – the individual has answers as to why their health issue is not a problem, or that the proposed change may be for others but not for them.

Contemplation

In this stage, the individual may be willing to change but has not yet decided to start on the process of change. They realise there is a problem, they may think of previous attempts that have failed. They are weighing up the pros and cons.

Determination

This is the crucial stage when the individual will definitely try to change. However, without proper plans and support from professionals, change will often fail. It is vitally important that the right support is in place.

Action

This is the stage where the individual puts their plans to change into action. It is a good idea for them to inform others of their intentions, so they know they are being watched and monitored. If a good plan has been put into action, the individual will start to see the result of the change and experience a positive feeling about it, which will motivate them further.

Maintenance

The action stage usually takes between three and six months to complete. After this time, the real test is to maintain the change. It is easy for an individual to fail to cope with the long-term effects of change, to stop taking their medication, to go back to unhealthy eating habits, or go back to smoking or drinking or taking drugs. The individual must learn coping strategies for the future.

Termination

This is the stage where the change is complete and the individual is living confidently with the changes they have made.

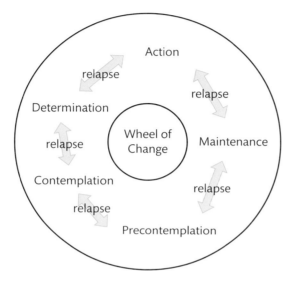

▶ **Figure 8.5:** The wheel of change

Social learning theory

Social learning theory was developed in the 1970s by Albert Bandura. It is based on theories about conditioning and linked to cognitive learning. Bandura observed that children learned by observing and copying the behaviours (modelling) of people around them. There are many influential models in a child's life such as parents, family, TV and other media characters, friends and teachers. Models may provide positive or negative behaviours to imitate. Children will imitate behaviour regardless of whether the behaviour is 'appropriate' or not. This process continues into adulthood. Social learning theory explains the continuous development of behaviours throughout life. This can have an impact on health if, for example, a school teacher tells children not to smoke because it increases the risk of developing cancer but the teacher has been witnessed having a cigarette. In this theory the behaviour will make a greater impression than the words.

Approaches to increasing public awareness of health promotion

The government sponsors many health awareness campaigns and activities to improve people's health, leading to reducing the future cost of health care, and helping people to achieve their full potential, have a good quality of life and reach full life expectancy. Celebrity chefs are actively seeking to promote healthy eating education and to create healthy eating plans for school meals. For example, Jamie Oliver was active in lobbying the government to make changes to school meals and is currently involved in launching Food Revolution Day, to raise awareness of global health issues around food.

Health education activities

Eat well   Move more   Live longer

▶ **Figure 8.6:** Change4Life campaign logo

One of the main campaigns the government sponsors to improve and maintain a positive healthy lifestyle is Change4Life. Other campaigns include Eat Well and Get Going.

Change4Life

Change4Life is a campaign in England and Wales, sponsored and run by the NHS, to make people more aware about healthy eating and the food they eat. The campaign also includes information about exercise.

The Change4Life campaign includes the following.

▶ Sugar Smart – which aims to educate people about how much sugar they are eating, including the health consequences.

▶ Eatwell – which provides guidance about the quantities of food a child or adult should eat, including the eatwell plate. This is part of the school curriculum to educate children in healthy eating.

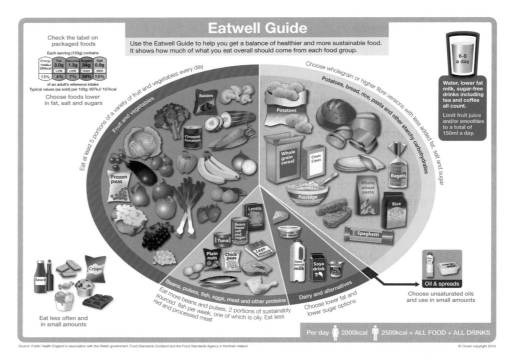

▶ **Figure 8.7:** The eatwell plate

▶ Get Going – which encourages exercise and activities, providing information about how to get involved with local leisure centres and what daily exercises can be done.

There is also information on the Change4Life webpage about eating less salt, drinking less alcohol and how to find out about local activities.

In Scotland there is the 'Eat better, Feel better' campaign, the first community health project in Scotland to support people to eat more healthily through providing information about cooking skills, budgeting and meal planning.

The Public Health Agency in Northern Ireland runs the 'Get a Life, Get Active' campaign, to encourage people to be more physically active.

Government standards for school lunches

The government's *School meals – healthy eating standards* (2015) sets out the quality and range of food that must be served in all schools including state-maintained, academies and free schools. The standards also apply to all food sold by schools throughout the school day, from breakfast, snacks, tuck shops, lunches and after school clubs. It advises on how much a child should have from each food group, and suggests the type of food to eat. The suggested foods are nutritionally sound and adhere to current nutrient-based standards. The standards also make recommendations that the food should be interesting and creatively presented, to make eating a positive experience for schoolchildren. The aim is to encourage children to develop and maintain a healthier approach to the food they eat.

Social marketing approach

Social marketing was established in the 1970s to sell ideas, attitudes and behaviours rather than just products. The concept behind the model was to change social behaviours for the benefit of society. It has been used effectively in international health programmes on contraception, drug abuse, heart disease and organ donation.

Marketing mix

The design of social marketing is that it should offer the consumer something rather than trying to sell them an idea. Social marketing, like commercial marketing, uses the marketing mix to achieve this. The limitation of the marketing mix is that companies can decide what the consumer wants/needs, and use research data to confirm that the consumer needs their product to meet that want/need. The marketing mix helps the process of social marketing to ensure that health programmes are run, that people are aware of them, that they are accessible and available to all. It also ensures that they are used effectively to improve the health of populations around the world.

Product

The product in social marketing may not be a physical/tangible object such as a medicine, but could be a service such as a promotional campaign about eating healthily or breastfeeding. Health promoters will need to research to discover what people see as their problem, and what could help them, which then forms the product. Further research is then needed to find out what they feel about the product and whether it would help them, and how important they feel about taking action to improve their health problem by using the product.

Price

The 'price' refers to what the individual must do to improve the problem, either in terms of a monetary transaction or in terms of time, effort, risk of embarrassment or disapproval. For example, for some women having a mammogram or having their breasts checked may be too embarrassing, and for some men having their testicles or prostate checked may also be too embarrassing. If the 'price' is too high when set against the benefits then the service or 'product' will not sell. To ascertain the right 'price', there must be research to ensure the right cost is set for people to use the service/product.

> **Research**
>
> Find out what health promotion campaigns are running in your area. Create a poster for learners in your school or college that shows information about how they can get involved in the campaign and the health benefits of joining in.

Place

Place describes how the individual finds the 'product' or how it is brought to them. For a physical item, this includes distribution networks, transport services, shops, warehouses, and places where the 'product' is given to consumers free of charge. Researching the shopping habits of a population and area provides information about where they shop and determines where the 'product' is sold or given. The places in which this happens must be accessible for all to enable consumers to get the 'product'. In small rural areas, or where people have transport or mobility problems, their needs must be catered for or they will not be able to use the product. For example, mobile medical centres may be used in rural areas to bring the service to the user, or a free volunteer-run taxi service may be used to help transport people needing assistance to get to the required service.

Promotion

Promotion is concerned with advertising. How the health messages are transmitted into people's homes, working lives, schools, universities, colleges, shopping and leisure activities is important. This is mainly done through integrated media promotion, for example simultaneous advertising on multimedia networks such as television, radio and magazines. Research is crucial to ensure effective awareness and promotion of the health and wellbeing benefits of the product, so that there is sufficient demand.

Some other marketing mix considerations

'Publics' are the people involved in the production and distribution of the product or service, and those who buy or use them. External publics include consumers and also policymakers, funders, and people who monitor the programme. Internal publics includes everyone involved in the production and approval of the product or service, such as the scientists involved in the research and government departments who approve and set standards for the product or service.

'Policy' is necessary to motivate consumers using the product or service by informing them about the necessity for their health of buying the product or using the service.

'Purse-Strings' are based on government or foundation funding, or public donation to ensure health programmes are funded, and made available for the public (consumers). 'Partnerships' help fund certain projects, for example Public Health UK work in partnership with Cancer Research UK, which relies on public donations.

 PAUSE POINT	Look for a social marketing campaign locally, e.g. posters or displays about cancer, obesity, or benefits of regular exercise.
Hint	Look for posters at train stations or bus stops. There might be something in a magazine or on a school/college noticeboard.
Extend	Choose one of these campaigns and discuss a) what improvement the government hopes to make and b) how effective this campaign has been/might be in improving the health of the population.

Role of mass media

Mass media is a powerful tool in promoting health. Mass media include television and radio broadcasts, magazine and newspaper adverts and articles, billboard posters, the internet and social media, and the distribution of information leaflets. It is used as part of the social marketing mix and, if done correctly, can have a huge impact on the success of a health campaign. The storylines in soaps on television and radio play a significant part in bringing health and social care issues to the public attention; themes have included alcoholism, paedophilia, dementia, cancer, sudden infant death syndrome, learning difficulties, physical disabilities and voluntary euthanasia.

Newspapers have alliances with political parties, which can affect what statistics and information they report, and people should be made aware of this when reading information about certain campaigns. Television broadcasts should be neutral and the broadcasting standards authority ensures that all adverts on television are accurate, reliable and do not deceive the public.

Community development approach

Health campaigns that are set in a community are extremely successful for the needs of the people in that particular area. Health centres, as well as volunteer groups offer information on health matters that are relevant to the local area, which may differ from the needs of other parts of the country. This approach can use local data to pinpoint accurately the health needs of the community. This could depend on the main local employment and health concerns around that; for example, the health needs of a community where a nuclear power plant is the main employer will be different from those where farming is the main occupation. Health campaigns will differ in urban and rural areas, and the average age of a community will also inform health campaigns.

Holistic approach, participation and empowerment

By knowing the local community a holistic approach can be used, whereby the overall health of a person can be looked at with regards to their local environment. This approach empowers the local population to participate in health campaigns as they can be seen to deal with local concerns.

Benefits and limitations

If a health campaign is run by a local community, it may have more of an impact than a national campaign, as the local population has a relationship with local healthcare professionals or volunteers running the campaign. However, there are limitations. Local people may not want to be involved with campaigns and community health programmes run by other local people. They may feel that they do not want those people knowing about their particular and personal health problems and concerns.

Two-way communication

Health campaigns can be promoted in many forms and settings. This includes in schools, health and social care settings, in the theatre and through drama (where drama companies act out health situations or perform plays about health awareness). Using drama to open discussions with children about bullying, for example, can be a very effective way of allowing children to try to empathise or explore feelings in a controlled environment. Soap operas on British television often list helpline numbers after the shows for people to support people who may have been affected by a particular storyline.

For people in crisis with mental health issues, organisations like the Samaritans provide support over the phone. Similarly, charitable organisations such as NSPCC, offer phone services to children to provide counselling and guidance to children who are or have been subject to abuse. Being creative about health awareness promotion may be a better approach for some people who might not otherwise connect with a health promotion campaign. Mark Haddon's play and book *The Curious Incident of the Dog in the Night-Time* looks at the effects of autism on a young person. Plays about mental health issues and their effects can make many people aware about mental health concerns.

Technology including apps, websites and social media, allow the use of interactive learning programmes in health promotion campaigns. People can manage changes in their own health and lifestyle through the use of apps, for example to lose weight, stop smoking and count their steps each day. Devices can be linked, such as wristbands to smart phones, the technology becomes motivational. However, for some it is still too expensive, complicated or they don't want to use it.

The important thing to remember is that everyone is an individual and people respond to different methods of promoting health. It may be necessary to try a number of different methods to get the message through.

National campaigns

The government and charities work in partnership to sponsor national health promotion campaigns that bring attention to specific health issues and work towards changing people's negative lifestyle choices. Some of the government campaigns are delivered by the NHS, for example Change4Life, and others are delivered by organisations such as the BBC, for example the Get Inspired campaign.

Campaign to encourage physical activity

Get Inspired is the legacy of the 2012 London Olympic Games, to help promote activity in people's lives. It is run by the BBC, which organises different activities for sport through volunteer sporting organisations throughout the country. The purpose of the campaign is to inspire people to become interested in sport and also to take part in sporting activities, so that they have fun, develop fitness and improve their health. The many activities offered include adventure sports, badminton, cycling and hockey. Information about the campaign can be found on the BBC website.

Campaign to encourage health eating

Change4Life is a campaign run by the NHS to promote healthy eating and lifestyle choices. Change4Life works with national partners, including commercial brands, government departments and NGOs, to get its message to as many people as possible, to help influence people's behaviour.

Campaign to encourage stopping smoking

The smoking ban, which includes any covered or indoor areas, was a campaign started in 2007, as a consequence of the Health Act of 2006. In 2016, an article by the health editor in the *Daily Telegraph* reported that since the ban started, heart attacks have fallen by 40 per cent.

Campaign to encourage stopping drinking

DrinkWise Australia is a social change organisation that encourages a safer drinking culture. It has run campaigns such as Kids Absorb Your Drinking, Kids and Alcohol Don't Mix and a campaign aimed at 18 to 24 year olds, Drinking – Do it Properly.

Drink Wise Age Well is a campaign in Wales that looks at responsible drinking, to help people take better control of their alcohol consumption. Drink Wise Age Well is funded through the Big Lottery scheme. Joint research by universities in England, Scotland, Wales and Northern Ireland showed that the over fifties age group had a high consumption of alcohol, and consequently had alcohol related health problems. The research highlighted that different geographical areas had different concerns, but all were related to alcohol consumption. Drinking may have increased in this age group for a number of reasons including loneliness, retirement, changes in financial circumstances, loss of a sense of purpose and bereavement.

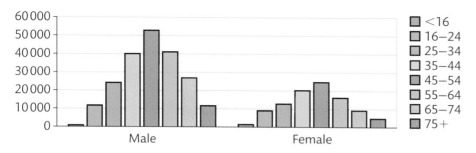

▶ **Figure 8.8:** Number of alcohol-related hospital admissions in 2013–14, in England

Campaign to reduce teenage pregnancies

According to Brook, an agency that works with young people on issues of sexual health and pregnancies, there are 38,000 teenage pregnancies each year in the UK. Almost three quarters of this number are unplanned, and about half will be aborted. The government drive is to include extensive sex education in schools and colleges to reduce this number. This will be included in the curriculum as part of the personal, social, health and citizenship education (PSHCE) programme. The reasons for teenage pregnancies relate to lack of knowledge, peer pressure to have sex, poor access to advice and support and low self-esteem and aspirations. The consequences of teenage parents are seen as poorer health outcomes for the baby, poor emotional health and wellbeing for the teenage mother and the chances of both baby and mother living in poverty.

Assessment practice 8.2   C.P5   C.P6   D.P7   D.P8   C.M4   D.M5   C.D2   D.D3   D.D4

Research a current health campaign looking at its features and explain how it increases public awareness about the health problem. Look at two approaches used to promote this campaign to the public. Explain how effective these approaches have been. How does this protect the public from the health problem? Follow up by researching how these two approaches prevent and control the increase in the specific health problem.

Now looking at the models of behaviour, assess how effective this campaign has been in increasing public awareness of the health problem and whether it has resulted in significant changes to improve health.

Still using this campaign, explain and then analyse how the theories of behaviour were used to persuade people to use the product.

Finally, explain the features of the campaign and the approaches used to make the public aware of it. Evaluate the data collected and analyse how the campaign changed/did not change public behaviour with regards to health.

Plan

- What is the task? What is it I have been asked to do?
- How confident do I feel in answering this?
- What areas will I struggle with?

Do

- Do I know what I am doing?
- Can I identify where I need to improve?

Review

- Can I evaluate what I have done and how I approached the task?
- Have I learnt from this and can I make changes to my work to make it better next time?

Further reading and resources

British Medical Association (2011) *Social Determinants of Health – What Doctors Can Do*, **www.bma.org.uk**

The Marmot Review (2010) *Fair Society, Healthy Lives*, **www.ucl.ac.uk/marmotreview**

The Food Safety Act 1990 (2009 edition) *A guide for food businesses*, **www.food.gov.uk**

Non-communicable diseases in the UK, A briefing paper prepared for the UK Parliament (House of Lords) (2011), **www.c3health.org**

DWI (2009), *Drinking Water Safety – Guidance to health and water professionals*, **www.dwi.gov.uk**

Websites

General information

www.gov.uk
UK government: General information about public health legislation.

www.hse.gov.uk
Health and Safety Executive: Information about risk assessment, COSHH and RIDDOR, shaping and reviewing regulations, producing research and statistics and enforcing legislation.

www.nice.org.uk
National Institute for Health and Care Excellence: Non-departmental Public Body (NDPB) accountable to the Department of Health, providing health and social care information.

www.ons.gov.uk
Office for National Statistics: Official UK statistics about people, populations and communities.

www.citizensadvice.org.uk
Citizens Advice: Information about rights and responsibilities (provide free, confidential and impartial advice).

Specific information

www.ash.org.uk
Action on Smoking and Health (ASH): Public health charity campaigning to eliminate harm caused by tobacco.

www.ageuk.org.uk
Age UK: Information to inspire, enable and support older people.

www.bhf.org.uk
British Heart Foundation: Information about all aspects of heart disease.

www.brook.org.uk
Brook: Information about sexual health and wellbeing for young people.

www.cancerresearchuk.org
Cancer Research UK: Information about all types of cancer, symptoms, treatments and prevention.

www.macmillan.org.uk
Macmillan Cancer Support: Provides cancer services, campaigns and fundraising events.

www.ovg.ox.ac.uk
Oxford Vaccine Group: Registered clinical trials unit providing information about all aspects of vaccines and infectious diseases in the UK.

www.sicklecellsociety.org
Sickle Cell Society: Information about sickle cell disease.

www.who.org
World Health Organization: Information about international health, health systems, health promotion, communicable diseases and non-communicable diseases, corporate services, preparedness, surveillance and response.

www.un.org
United Nations: Information about sustainable development and humanitarian assistance, international law and maintenance of peace and security, protection of human rights, climate change.

THINK ▶FUTURE

Brandon Myres

Social Worker, specialising in fostering

I've been a social worker for ten years. I decided to specialise in fostering as my mother fostered several children when I was young. Although I didn't like the intrusion of other children in my home in my life as a teenager, I now appreciate the positive impact it had on the children my mum fostered. In our local authority, we're always short of foster carers. We run many campaigns in local newspapers, on radio stations, as posters near to bus stops and train stations, and on the side of buses, in the hope of increasing the number of foster carers in the community. Sometimes we're successful after a campaign and get to train some new foster carers, other times we're not. We meet with the marketing team to discuss campaigns, and we work alongside them in creating new promotional ideas about fostering.

After studying a level 3 BTEC in Health and Social Care, I obtained a social science degree as I knew I wanted to become a social worker. While studying, I volunteered for a charity working with families who were finding it difficult to cope with money, health and social issues. I found this work very rewarding and it increased my desire to become a social worker. I also helped to run a playgroup for children from refugee families in transition. This was great fun, but also made me extremely sad when I heard their stories. But, I hope I helped them a bit in adapting to their new lives in this country. My work experiences helped me to gain knowledge and experience about working with people who need help, which has definitely helped me in my career.

Focusing your skills

Health assessment

- When I meet a family or an individual for the first time, I need to know about their lifestyle choices. For example, how they make decisions about diet, their medical needs and general wellbeing, including their mental health. This gives me a good understanding of what they do and don't know.
- I then have to work with them over a period of time, helping them understand how they can improve their lifestyles and choices. This can take a long time as sometimes they are very reluctant to change as they may be confused, wary or unwilling to make changes.
- To do this effectively, I need to know the different ways of providing support and the current information available to educate them about new ideas, including looking after their health, claiming the benefits they are entitled to, what support networks are available to them etc.
- I work with a range of agencies that guide me and supply me with current health information.

- I follow confidentiality rules by making sure all my notes are kept in a secure place, and I only pass information on to members of the team on a need-to-know basis, and with the family or individual's consent.
- I attend regular training, to ensure I'm up to date with current information and local authority procedures, including reporting safeguarding incidents, which I occasionally have to do.
- Once I've completed my assessment of the family's needs, I need to know when and what the next stage of referral is.

Knowledge of current health issues

One of my responsibilities is to keep up to date with current health information and what is available for people who need support. Training is a good way to do this and I take up as many training courses as I can. I also look at current health trends on government websites and ways that health can be improved.

Getting ready for assessment

Bailey is working towards a BTEC National in Health and Social Care. For learning aims A and B, he was given an assignment with the following title 'What health campaigns have there been recently in the local area? What impact have these campaigns had on the health of the local population?' He had to write an article for a local health magazine explaining what the campaign was about and why it was relevant to the local community. The article had to explain:

▸ the campaign and its aim

▸ why the campaign was necessary

▸ how the results would be analysed.

How I got started

First I collected all my notes on this topic and put them into a folder. I decided to divide my work into three parts, one about the campaign, one on the health of the local community and finally an analysis of my research. I needed to make sure I included enough work in each section to achieve all the criteria.

I divided my notes into the three parts, a general part, which explained the campaign and its aim. I made sure I had the information I needed by visiting relevant government and health-related websites. I then researched local data on the health needs of the local community that were relevant to the campaign. From this information, I designed a survey-type questionnaire, which I used to interview a number of residents about their knowledge of the campaign and how it had impacted on their lives.

From this, I could see whether the aims of the campaign were met in my local area, and I could then analyse the results to finish my article for the magazine.

How I brought it all together

I decided to use a variety of fonts, colours, pictures, statistical graphs and data to make the work look interesting. I didn't use names from the survey to protect individual's confidentiality.

For case studies and examples, I took some from our lessons and my research. Finally, I wrote a short summary as a conclusion to the article.

What I learned from the experience

I used examples from lessons and from visits. I wished I'd made clearer notes during my research as I realised afterwards that I didn't have all the information I needed. It was really good to speak to people as it brought the campaign to life. However, as this was the first time I'd done anything like this, I was also a bit taken back by people's honesty about their health.

I wasted too much time arranging the survey, thinking that I would have enough time to bring it all together and analyse it. Next time I would get the survey organised quicker as by the end everything was a rush.

Think about it

• Have you written a plan with timings, so that you can complete your assignment by the agreed submission date?

• Do you have notes on the campaign and its aims?

• Is your information written in your own words, and referenced clearly where you have used quotations or information from a book, journal or website?

Supporting Individuals with Additional Needs

12

Getting to know your unit

While working in health and social care, you may care for a full range of individuals who have additional needs. Individuals with these additional needs have a right to receive the best quality care and support. This unit aims to give you specialist knowledge that can be crucial to ensuring that those with additional needs meet their full potential.

How you will be assessed

You will be assessed by a set of assignments set by your tutor to ensure you fully understand the topic of how individuals with additional needs are supported. There will also be role plays given to you by your tutor to help you with this unit and to assess your learning. Assignments will be set for each learning aim, with a pass, merit or distinction grade given. To obtain a distinction you must evaluate the support given to two individuals, one being a child the other an adult, and the effectiveness of their support and the effect the support has on their lives.

Assessment criteria

This table shows what you must do in order to achieve a **Pass**, **Merit** or **Distinction** grade, and where you can find activities to help you.

Pass	**Merit**	**Distinction**

Learning aim Examine reasons why individuals may experience additional needs

A.P1 Explain diagnostic procedures to determine additional needs for one child and one adult with different additional needs. Assessment practice 12.1	**A.M1** Assess the requirements of one child and one adult with different additional needs. Assessment practice 12.1	**A.D1** Evaluate the significance to the individuals, their families and society of a diagnosis of additional needs. Assessment practice 12.1

Learning aim **B** Examine how to overcome the challenges to daily living faced by people with additional needs

B.P2 Explain how disability can be viewed as a social construct. Assessment practice 12.2	**B.M2** Assess the impact of challenges to daily living that may be experienced by one child and one adult with different additional needs, and how effectively these challenges are overcome. Assessment practice 12.2	
B.P3 Describe how health or social care workers can help one child and one adult with different additional needs overcome challenges to daily living. Assessment practice 12.2		

Learning aim Investigate current practice with respect to provision for individuals with additional needs

C.P4 Explain the benefits of adaptations and support provided to one child and one adult with different additional needs. Assessment practice 12.3	**C.M3** Analyse how the provision and support provided for one child and one adult with different additional needs have benefited them. Assessment practice 12.3	**BC.D2** Justify the support and adaptations provided for two individuals with different additional needs to help them overcome challenges to daily living, with reference to statutory provision. Assessment practice 12.3
C.P5 Explain the impact of statutory provision on the support provided for one child and one adult with different additional needs. Assessment practice 12.3	**C.M4** Analyse how statutory provision has impacted on current practice in caring for one child and one adult with different additional needs. Assessment practice 12.3	**BC.D3** Evaluate the impact of providing support for two individuals diagnosed with different additional needs in improving their wellbeing and life chances. Assessment practice 12.3

Getting started

Work in groups and list of what you think the term 'additional needs' means to a wheelchair user, a blind person, a person with a terminal illness, or to a deaf person. Each group could choose a different individual with additional needs and think about their needs when travelling, working, and in other daily situations. When studying this unit, see whether you were right or whether you need to make any amendments to your lists.

A Examine reasons why individuals may experience additional needs

▶ A person with additional needs playing cricket

Diagnosing or determining additional needs

Definitions of mild, moderate, severe and profound learning disabilities

Learning disabilities can be described as mild, moderate, severe or profound. However, these are terms to help understand the level of support an individual may need. They do not tell you anything about who the person really is, so be careful about using generic terms when describing an individual.

▶ Mild learning disabilities are considered to be when an individual is able to talk but maybe not understand or be able to explain new information easily. They may, for example, need more time to fully understand complex ideas.

▶ Moderate learning disabilities are considered to be when an individual finds daily living activities, such as dressing themselves, more complicated and they may have only basic language skills to explain how they are feeling or what they want.

▶ Severe and profound learning disabilities are considered to be when an individual may have only very basic language skills and will perhaps communicate through gestures rather than words. These individuals will need a high level of support and will usually have more than one disability that requires support.

Definitions of the range of learning disabilities can change, so it is always best to check them using a trustworthy source.

Key terms

Diagnose – identify the nature of an illness or other medical condition by examination of the **symptoms**.

Symptoms – physical or mental features of a medical condition, which can be seen or felt by the patient, for example a headache or redness of the skin. They are often subjective and may not be visible to other people.

Research

There are a number of sources where you can find out more about learning disabilities. You could access websites such as the British Institute of Learning Disabilities (BILD) and NHS Choices. Health centres, hospitals and social services departments provide leaflets and further information can be found in various government white papers, such as *Valuing People: A New Strategy for Learning Disability for the 21st Century* (2001).

Diagnostic procedures, tools and standards used to diagnose a disability

Now that you have a basic understanding of the different range of learning disabilities, you need to look at how individuals are **diagnosed**, the procedures taken by professionals, the tools they use and the standards they follow.

Diagnostic procedures used to diagnose a disability

Diagnostic procedures to determine what type of disability an individual has will be different for each condition, so it is important to research various websites linked to a specific disability.

In the following case studies a young person and an adult explain what it has meant to them to live with dyslexia, which can be mild, moderate or severe.

> **Key term**
>
> **Diagnostic procedures** – techniques used to identify a specific illness or medical condition.

Case study

Justyna, a young person with dyslexia

Justyna was assessed as having dyslexia when she was eight years old. She is now 14 years old and has received support since her diagnosis. Justyna describes her experience.

'When I was assessed and found out I had dyslexia it felt like something made up, because no one had told me about it before.

It makes me sad sometimes and I cry when I think how I couldn't learn. I thought I was stupid or something, because my friends understood what was being taught in school and I didn't. I couldn't read, and I'd forget things, which made people laugh and tease me. It was just so frustrating because I knew I could do it. Most of the time I understood what was being said but couldn't write it down or understand the words I was expected to read. I'm up there with the best now! And I don't forget stuff for school as it is all colour coded for each day, like everything with a purple stripe is for Tuesday. My advice to people is that if you feel like you're not coping with reading or don't understand stuff, then tell someone and find out what is wrong and get the right support. Try to be confident; there is nothing to be ashamed of.'

Check your knowledge

1 How would you feel if you were Justyna before getting support?

2 How did getting support help Justyna with her emotions and day-to-day living?

Case study

Joe, a van driver living and working with dyslexia

Joe was recently diagnosed with dyslexia through a work initiative. He describes his experience.

'I've been a delivery driver for most of my life. People are startled to think I couldn't read or write and say, "how'd you get about?", but once I'd learned as a young kid to ask for directions to places, I remembered how to get there. Most deliveries were to the same places, so it was all right. I had new places to deliver to, but I got there by asking people for directions. I left school with no qualifications and teachers used to call me thick, I couldn't wait to leave. I was 17 when I passed my driving test. I liked driving my uncle's car, and back then the driving test only needed me to identify pictures of road signs, which was easy as my brother and uncle had helped me. Soon after, I got a job driving a delivery van.

Recently a work initiative, run by a proper trained person, diagnosed me with dyslexia. She couldn't believe I could do my job, but luckily for me my company kept me on as I'd been with them for nearly 40 years. The company supported me in being mentored by a specialist. I sometimes have embarrassing situations when I'm not driving and asking for info, say, if I am on my own at a station, but in a way I've gotten used to it. I sometimes think, what I could've done if I'd the right support at school. But then I tell myself, "Joe, there's no use thinking back!"'

Check your knowledge

1 How do you think Joe has coped in his life?

2 How would you describe Joe's disability – mild, moderate or severe and profound? Explain your answer.

As you have seen, dyslexia affects an individual's reading, writing, ability to organise and time management. It does not affect their overall intelligence in social situations, or their ability to understand real-life situations. They are able, for example, to go to the cinema or cook a meal.

❚❚ PAUSE POINT   What are the different types of learning disabilities?

Hint   There are three levels.

Extend   Write an explanation about each one.

Diagnostic assessment is used in health and social care settings to provide detailed information about an individual's need for support. Assessment may include:

▶ finding out about the individual's concerns
▶ establishing their experiences of home life, their education and whether they receive any social care
▶ looking at their medical history
▶ finding out whether they have had any specific assessment by a medical professional or team
▶ a physical examination.

Once an individual's profile has been created, the professionals can determine specific support needs.

Diagnostic tools used to diagnose a disability

▶ Dyslexia. Diagnostic assessments for individuals with dyslexia are completed in different ways. If a child or young person needs an assessment in school, college or university, this is usually carried out by a qualified specialist teacher who has an Assessment Practising Certificate. If the individual has left education or is working, the assessment is usually carried out by a chartered psychologist, registered with the Health and Care Professions Council, who specialises in specific learning difficulties.

The assessment for dyslexia normally covers literacy and numeracy, as well as memory and processing skills. Another sign of dyslexia is poor organisational skills, such as forgetting school work or not knowing what to take to school or college. Further tests may be needed, as dyslexia has a wide range of effects on a person and it can be difficult to determine the level of support that an individual may need. Using information from the specialists' assessments, strategies can be put into place to help people such as Justyna and Joe to live with dyslexia.

▶ ADHD. This is usually first noticed by parents or teachers. A Child Behaviour Checklist (CBCL/6-18) is used to confirm diagnosis. For diagnosing children between 6 and 18 years of age, parents and/or teachers are asked to use a marking scheme, with a rating scale for questions about the child's behaviour. The information from the allotted scores contributes to further assessment and diagnosis by specialist doctors and psychologists.

▶ Dyspraxia. This is a condition in which the individual has issues with coordination. This may first be observed by parents and/or teachers. Diagnosis is usually made by a multidisciplinary team consisting of a paediatrician, a paediatric neurologist, a physiotherapist, an occupational therapist and a speech and language therapist. In the UK, the assessment method most likely to be used is 'Motor ABC'. This tests a child's gross and fine motor skills. The child will be asked to perform simple movements to test gross motor skills such as moving around, jumping and balancing; and drawing and placing small pegs in holes to test fine motor skills. The child's ability to perform these skills is rated and compared with the normal range for children in their age group. There will also be an assessment of their mental ability and a full medical history, to exclude other possible causes.

Standards used to diagnose a disability

Standards of practice are given in the Children and Families Act (2014) as well as in the new SEND Code of Practice, which came into effect on 1 September 2014.

> **Key term**
>
> **Standards of practice** – conditions set by central government, local government and local health authorities that care providers must follow.

Several organisations supply important information about specific disabilities, including case studies, diagnostic tools to assess specific needs, the qualifications needed by the assessor, and the standards by which they have to abide.

For example, the following organisations support people with specific learning disabilities, as well as generally providing support and guidance to people with a learning disability, their families and carers.

▶ The Foundation for People with Learning Disabilities

▶ The National Autistic Society

▶ The Stroke Association

▶ The Royal Mencap Society

▶ The Epilepsy Society

▶ The British Dyslexia Association

Professional background, qualifications and experience of those undertaking the diagnosis and assessment

Specialists who work in social services, medicine or nursing, or teaching have to be qualified at degree level. To diagnose and assess people with a learning disability in a specific area, they then have to undertake further study and specialise in that area of care. For example, dyslexia assessments can be carried out by an appropriately qualified specialist teacher who has both a postgraduate Diploma in Specific Learning Difficulties and an Assessment Practising Certificate. The Professional Association of Teachers of Students with Specific Learning Difficulties (Patoss) provides a list of qualifications that teaching professionals need before they can diagnose and assess students. An educational psychologist needs a degree in psychology, accredited by the British Psychological Society (BPS), before completing a BPS accredited doctorate programme.

Parameters used to describe the diagnosed condition

> **Key terms**
>
> **Specialists** – people trained to a very high standard in a specialist subject, who have studied a curriculum set and recognised by a university or other accredited institution, and passed the relevant exams so that they can work in that specialism.
>
> **Prognosis** – a practitioner's opinion or judgement about how an individual will recover from an illness or injury.
>
> **Impairment** – mental or physical weakness. For example, a visual impairment means that an individual is unable to see clearly.

▶ **Table 12.1** Examples of conditions, their causes and **prognosis**

Type of condition	Cause	Severity	Stability over time	Prognosis
Stroke	A blood clot or a bleed that interrupts the blood supply to the brain. Can result from lifestyle choices such as smoking, high blood pressure, obesity, high cholesterol levels, diabetes and excessive alcohol intake. Increasing age and a family history of strokes increase a person's risk of having a stroke.	Life threatening when it happens, with muscle paralysis and speech impediment.	In the short term, there may be: • paralysis of one side of the body, depending which side of the brain is affected • loss of mobility • loss of speech • memory loss • depression, anxiety, frustration and anger. Depending on severity of stroke and extent of damage, recovery and rehabilitation may be prolonged over several months or even years.	There may be long-term disability, including mobility and speech problems. Some individuals may never recover former abilities, affecting their ability to work or participate in daily living activities. They may have anxiety, panic attacks, inability to express emotions and apathy. Communication **impairments** may cause social isolation. Some individuals may develop seizures. Some individuals may develop dementia.
Coronary artery disease	Usually caused by a build-up of fatty deposits in the coronary arteries, making the arteries narrower and reducing the blood flow to the heart muscle. Increased risk of coronary artery disease is caused by: • smoking • high blood pressure • high blood cholesterol • lack of regular exercise • diabetes • obesity, or being overweight • family history of coronary artery disease.	May cause angina (pain in the chest), especially during physical exertion. Life threatening if the arteries become completely blocked, causing a heart attack.	Can be managed with medication to relieve angina, and lifestyle changes to prevent further damage to the coronary arteries. For more serious cases, interventions may include: • angioplasty and insertion of stents • insertion of a pacemaker • coronary artery bypass surgery.	Early detection greatly increases the individual's chances of surviving and living with coronary heart disease. Changing lifestyle to improve diet, maintaining a healthy weight for height, stopping smoking and taking regular exercise will also improve the individual's chances of survival.
Alzheimer's disease (AD)	Caused by parts of the brain shrinking, with structure and function of brain areas affected. Abnormal deposits of protein (amyloid plaques) and tangles of nerve fibres containing tau, along with imbalances of acetylcholine have been found in the brains of people with AD. Risks of developing AD are increased by: • age – doubles every five years after age 65, although about 5% will be under 65 • family history – in a few families, may be caused by the inheritance of a single gene • Down's syndrome • head injuries.	Increasing loss of memory, confusion and change of personality. Ultimately life threatening.	There is currently no cure for this progressive condition. Treatments are available to slow progression but there is no evidence that dietary supplements can reverse the condition. However, research shows that risks of developing the condition can be reduced by eating a healthy diet, taking regular exercise and avoiding high blood pressure and blood cholesterol. Treatment does not prevent progression but may improve quality of life.	Individuals with AD have a life expectancy of about eight to ten years after their symptoms begin. This varies depending on their age at diagnosis and many other factors.

▶ **Table 12.1** – *continued*

Hearing impairment	Types and causes may vary: • congenital, genetic or caused by maternal infection with rubella • following an illness or ear infection • tumour on acoustic nerve • age-related (presbycusis) – starts at about 40 years of age and increases until by the age of 80, most people have some hearing impairment • occupational damage – repeated exposure to loud noises over time damages the sensitive hair cells inside the cochlea, risk is increased when working with noisy equipment, working in environments with loud music and regularly listening to music at a high volume through headphones • following sudden accidental exposure to very loud noise, such as an explosion that damages the acoustic nerve • temporary – due to build-up of earwax or an infection.	Hearing loss may be total or partial and may be in one or both ears. The loss may be progressive, as with illness or infection, or sudden, as in an injury. If the individual previously had full hearing, they may become shocked, angry, frustrated and depressed about their hearing loss. They may have difficulty in adapting to changed or changing hearing status. They may feel isolated, especially in social situations.	Depending on the cause, hearing impairment may be temporary or permanent. Temporary losses usually completely resolve once the underlying cause has been removed, for example removing earwax or treating an infection. Depending on the cause and severity of hearing loss, permanent loss can be improved with: • hearing aids • cochlear implants • lip reading.	Continually improving with new technological advances.
Visual impairment	There are many causes, including: • inherited conditions – such as retinitis pigmentosa • infections – including maternal infection with rubella • injury – particularly injuries to the cornea • amblyopia – impaired vision in one eye due to lack of use in early childhood • cataracts – the leading cause of blindness in the world • diabetic retinopathy • glaucoma – raised pressure within the eyes, which damages the optic nerve • ageing process – people lose ability to focus on close objects or to see small print clearly	Vision may be missing or lost in one or both eyes. An individual may be born with visual impairment. The loss may be progressive, as with illness or infection, or sudden, as in an injury. If previously sighted, they may become shocked, angry, frustrated and depressed about their sight loss. They may have difficulty in adapting to changed or changing visual status. They may feel isolated.	Depending on cause, visual impairment may be temporary or permanent. Loss may be temporary, for example, following a head injury or eye injury, or when an individual has cataracts removed and a replacement lens implanted. Depending on cause and severity, treatment can be with: • corrective lenses (spectacles or contact lenses) • corrective surgery such as laser treatment • removal of cataracts and replacement with implanted lenses or spectacles.	Continually improving with new technological advances. For example, cortical implants are small devices that can be implanted to partially restore vision by direct stimulation of the visual cortex.

▶ **Table 12.1** Examples of conditions, their causes and prognosis – *continued*

Type of condition	Cause	Severity	Stability over time	Prognosis
	• age-related macular degeneration causing progressive loss of the visual sharpness and inability to focus • cancer, such as retinoblastoma.		For conditions that are progressive or cannot be treated, support may be in the form of communication aids such as: • providing large print text for individuals with some vision • use of Braille to read by touch • software to convert computer text to audio • using a guide dog to aid mobility and alert user to dangers in their surroundings.	
Type 1 diabetes	Pancreas stops producing or does not produce insulin, which is most likely an autoimmune disorder. May be a family history of diabetes.	Life threatening if not properly controlled. Complications may include serious health problems, such as: • visual impairment and eventual blindness • skin infections, particularly feet • persistent ulcerating sores, combined with poor blood supply to lower limbs, which may require foot or leg amputation • difficulty controlling blood pressure and cholesterol levels, which may lead to heart attack or stroke • nerve damage, causing pain, itching, tingling, and numbness • erectile dysfunction • kidney damage and eventually kidney failure.	Lifelong – chronic disease, currently no cure. Can be stabilised by injection of insulin combined with controlled dietary intake of carbohydrate and sugars.	Maintaining strict control and balance of blood sugar levels provides a good quality of health and prevents or delays complications. Advances include the use of an insulin pump to avoid repeated injections. The pump is a battery-operated device that provides your body with regular insulin throughout the day. Insulin pens may make injection easier and equipment more portable, especially for adolescents. Research is investigating using stem cells to create insulin-producing cells.
Type 2 diabetes	Pancreas does not produce sufficient insulin for the body's needs. Associated with obesity and tends to be diagnosed in older people. More common than type 1 diabetes. Of the 3.9 million people living with diabetes in the UK, 90% have type 2 diabetes.	Life threatening, if not properly controlled. Complications are similar to those for type 1 diabetes. However, loss of sight is a particularly common problem.	Can be stabilised with proper dietary control. May require medication, such as metformin, to reduce the amount of glucose the liver releases into the bloodstream and to make cells more responsive to insulin. If medication is not effective, insulin injections may be required.	Reducing weight, taking more exercise and maintaining strict control and balance of blood sugar levels provides a good quality of health. Regular eye tests and taking care of feet are also important to avoid long-term complications.

Research

Your tutor will give you a range of diagnosed conditions to research for: a baby, a small child, a person with dementia and a person with a brain injury. (You could extend Table 12.1 to include the conditions that you have researched.)

In small groups, discuss your findings and what you feel about them. Remember all points are valid, and all views are to be respected and remain confidential in the classroom.

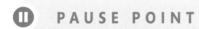   **PAUSE POINT**   What are the different types of diagnostic investigations carried out on babies both before and after they are born?

Hint   Concentrate on investigations for brain or spinal cord damage.

Extend   List the reasons why these investigations may be carried out.

Cognitive and learning needs

Learning difficulties

Dyspraxia

Dyspraxia is a motor skills disorder that affects an individual's ability to do practical things such as riding a bike, playing games and, later on in life, will affect their ability to drive a car and to perform certain skills at work. Dyspraxia can also affect an individual's memory and processing, so it is sometimes referred to as Developmental Coordination Disorder (DCD). It is unclear what causes dyspraxia, but it is known that the condition interrupts signals from the brain to the body.

The first **signs** that a child has dyspraxia are often seen by their GP, or the special educational needs coordinator (SENCO) at school. The child will be referred to a specialist paediatrician for assessment and/or a paediatric occupational therapist for further checks and a diagnosis. If needed, other specialists may become involved; for example, a neurodevelopmental paediatrician, who specialises in the central nervous system.

Key term

Cognitive – mental processes of the brain, that help you understand and comprehend; your memory and your reasoning.

Signs – observable physical features of a medical condition, which can be seen or felt by a medical practitioner or healthcare worker, for example a lump or a bruise; as opposed to symptoms, such as a headache, which are subjective and reported by an individual, and may or may not be observable.

Parents of children with dyspraxia can contact the Dyspraxia Foundation and the special educational needs (SEN) department at their child's school for support. The child needs to visit the school and become familiar with their surroundings. For example, like any child, they need to know where to find their classroom and the toilets. They will have two timetables, one to keep in their school bag and one for their bedroom wall, so that they can organise themselves for the day ahead at school. The parents need to communicate closely with the educational support team at school, college or university, so that everyone is communicating about the individual's needs. As the child grows older, they will want to be involved in decisions about their care and education, so they should attend any meetings where this is discussed.

Each child is unique and should never be compared to another child. The aim is for the child to learn strategies to cope with daily life and work so that these strategies become routine. For example, stickers can be used to help organise items and timetables, clothing needs to be easy to put on and cups should not be overfilled to help avoid spills. Teachers need to use different methods of presenting material as children with dyspraxia usually find it difficult, for example, to learn from material displayed on the classroom board. Children with dyspraxia should be taught in an environment with very few distractions and with carefully planned lessons. Care is needed when planning physical education schedules to ensure that children do not become confused and upset, as children with dyspraxia will find it difficult to catch a ball, for example.

Dyslexia

As the case studies about Justyna and Joe (see Diagnostic procedures used to diagnose a disability) show, dyslexia is a specific learning difficulty that causes problems with reading, writing, spelling and organisation. Individuals with dyslexia are unable to process graphic images correctly. The individual is no less intelligent – they can still understand complex information delivered in other formats, such as orally. However, a person with dyslexia may find it difficult to cope, as in many cases they struggle to organise their lives. The individual may find it very difficult to cope with written work, either in their education or at work. This can lead to frustration as the world is full of written information, and the ability to organise oneself is vital to daily living. This can lead to low self-esteem, so it is important that there is early diagnosis and the individual is taught coping strategies.

Attention deficit hyperactivity disorder (ADHD)

ADHD symptoms are usually diagnosed between the ages of three and six years old. Children with ADHD tend to have disorganised and chaotic behaviour, they are more temperamental and have high energy levels.

There is no simple diagnostic test for ADHD and a number of specialists, such as a psychiatrist, a paediatrician and a learning disability specialist may be involved. Assessment may include:

▶ physical examination, to exclude other causes for the symptoms
▶ a series of interviews with parents and/or the child
▶ interviews or reports from other significant people, such as teachers.

There are strict criteria for formally diagnosing ADHD and a child must have six or more symptoms of inattentiveness or hyperactivity and impulsiveness. They must also have these symptoms before they are 12 years old, the symptoms must have lasted for more than six months and must have been noticed in more than one setting, for example at home and at school. This is to make sure that the symptoms are not just a reaction to a particular individual in a setting. Symptoms should also make the child's life difficult on a social or academic level and not be part of a developmental disorder, a difficult phase or any another condition.

There is still no real understanding of the causes of ADHD, although many scientific studies indicate that a combination of circumstances such as poor nutrition from a very early age, brain injury or a hectic social environment may have significant implications. Genetics may also play a part. ADHD continues throughout a child's development into teenage life, which is often a hectic and disorganised phase and having ADHD may intensify the experience.

ADHD is treated by trying to reduce the symptoms. This may be with medication, psychological treatment or a combination of both; each child is unique and so each case needs to be treated differently to ensure the child receives appropriate support.

For example, a specialist community paediatrician may prescribe medication to support the child's anxiety, alongside other interventions, such as treatment for psychological and behavioural needs and educational support.

Children and young people with ADHD can find life in school or college difficult. However, if the school or college has support systems in place, their condition should not lead to poor or challenging behaviour. Teachers and support workers involved with children with ADHD have to be specially trained to ensure that these children enjoy rather than struggle with their educational experience.

Positive nurturing is considered to be a way to help support a child's intellectual development. Positive relationships between family, peers, teachers and support workers usually lead to happy children who find it easier to learn. In turn, this helps children to develop resilience into adulthood.

Parents will need to know about support groups in their local area, as well as national organisations such as UKAP (the UK ADHD Partnership). Once diagnosed and after the right treatment has been established, most children's ADHD symptoms will improve.

Autism-spectrum disorders (ASD)

ASD is a condition that affects social interaction, communication, interests and behaviour. It includes Asperger syndrome and childhood autism. Signs of ASD start when a child is very young and, although there is no cure, much is now known about ASD. There are support programmes in schools and from specific organisations that work with children with ASD. There is no single specific treatment that meets all the support needs of a child with ASD. Each child is unique and must be treated differently. Treatment, or intervention, aims to support a child's communication, social and cognitive (thinking) skills, and academic skills. Treatment will always involve a range of specialists, known as a multidisciplinary team, working together with a child and their family. This team may include:

▶ a paediatrician

▶ a psychologist

▶ a psychiatrist

▶ a speech and language therapist

▶ an occupational therapist.

After a detailed assessment, an individual personalised support plan will be created, which will usually be coordinated by the child's **key worker**.

Key term

Key worker – a healthcare professional who is the main contact person for a team, an individual being cared for and their family.

The NHS Choices website pages about ASD contain a number of real-life stories from people with ASD. Eugen Bleuer first described the condition in 1908, but the term was not used until 1943, when Leo Kanner, a child psychiatrist, undertook a study of 11 children with autism.

There are adults with ASD who have not been diagnosed, but when a diagnosis is made, it often comes as a relief as it gives people an explanation for their different perceptions of the world. Diagnosis and support can help an individual to make adjustments in their life and enable them to lead a full and independent life.

Asperger syndrome

Asperger syndrome is a form of autism. It is a lifelong condition that affects how a person relates to, and makes sense of, the world. For example, when you meet people you interpret and respond to their facial expressions, tone of voice and body language. Mostly, you can tell what that person's mood is – whether they are happy, angry or sad. An individual with Asperger syndrome will usually find it harder to understand these signals and will find it more difficult to communicate and interact with other people, causing them to feel anxious and confused. Some individuals with Asperger syndrome take literal meaning from metaphors so, for example, sayings such as 'I wear my heart on my sleeve' can be very confusing. Although individuals with Asperger syndrome are often of average or above average intelligence, they experience three main difficulties, which are usually called the 'the triad of impairments':

▶ social communication

▶ social interaction

▶ social imagination.

Knowing the individual with Asperger syndrome is important to help develop a more personal approach to their individual needs, and how they can best be supported. For example, what they are good at, what they like to do, their special interests, their friends and family, things that cause them anxiety, how they prefer to relax if they become stressed, the type of friends they like, what they like about themselves, what important routines they have, either daily or weekly, or any other times. Understanding how they learn, what makes them relax and what colours and sounds they like can also be useful when helping them to be calm and relaxed.

Pervasive developmental disorder not otherwise specified (PDD-NOS)

This is a group of disorders that affect the development of communication and social skills. The symptoms are similar to autism and Asperger syndrome, but do not meet these exactly. Sometimes children show other symptoms that are not associated with the specifics of having autism or Asperger syndrome, and hence a spectrum of symptoms is associated with the child. Symptoms of PDD-NOS may include:

▶ problems with using and understanding language

▶ difficulty relating to people, objects and events

▶ playing in an unusual way with toys and objects, such as ordering, reordering or categorising toys instead of playing with them or just carrying toys around without playing with them

▶ difficulty with changes in routine or familiar surroundings

▶ repetitive body movements.

The relatively new diagnosis of PDD-NOS is used when the development of a child's verbal and non-verbal communication skills is pervasively and severely impaired to the point that it affects their reciprocal social interaction.

Studies on PDD-NOS suggest that people with this condition can be placed into one of three groups. These are:

▶ a high functioning group (about 25 per cent) where symptoms overlap with Asperger syndrome

▶ a second group (about 25 per cent) where there is closer resemblance to autistic symptoms

▶ a third group (about 50 per cent) that meets all diagnostic requirements of autistic disorder but where symptoms are mild.

Childhood disintegrative disorder

Childhood disintegrative disorder is a regressive condition, similar to autism, which affects a child's language, social and motor skills development. The effects may be very obvious or may be less noticeable. It is usually diagnosed at around three or four years old when a child will suddenly regress in their development. For example, words that the child knew will suddenly become unknown, and they fall behind in their vocabulary development. Where a child has been socialising easily with other children, they suddenly find it difficult to join in. Regressing motor skills make holding items, playing physical games or using the computer difficult.

⏸ PAUSE POINT   What is ASD?

> Hint   Difficulty with communication may be a symptom.
>
> Extend   What information would you need about a person with ASD before putting a support plan into place?

Inherited conditions

Inherited conditions are disorders caused by faulty genes and so are passed from parent to child. Each cell in the body contains 23 pairs of chromosomes, which a child inherits from their parents. Characteristics such as eye or hair colour, a person's height and build are passed on in this way. However, if the parent has a faulty gene this can also be passed on to their child. Inherited disorders include type 1 diabetes, sickle cell anaemia and cystic fibrosis.

> **Research**
>
> Undertake internet research to find out which medical conditions can be genetically inherited. Which conditions are inherited when only one parent passes on a faulty gene? Which conditions are inherited only when both parents pass on the same faulty gene?

Down's syndrome

Down's syndrome is a genetic condition. The nucleus of each cell within the body contains 46 pairs of chromosomes, 23 from the mother and 23 from the father. An individual with Down's syndrome has an extra chromosome – chromosome 21 – making a total of 47 chromosomes. It is not fully understood how the extra chromosome happens and, in most cases, Down's syndrome is not inherited; it is simply an isolated genetic mistake occurring at conception. However, in some cases, a genetic mistake is passed from a parent to a child because of **translocation** of chromosome 21, even though the parent does not have Down's syndrome themselves. Down's syndrome occurs in all ethnic groups, in every country and across all social classes. The chance of having a baby with Down's syndrome is higher for mothers who are older, although more babies with Down's syndrome are born to younger women.

> **Key term**
>
> **Translocation** – a chromosome abnormality caused by rearrangement of parts between chromosomes. In Down's syndrome, an extra piece of chromosome 21 attaches itself to another chromosome.

▶ People with Down's syndrome usually have distinctive features

Each child is unique and they will inherit individual characteristics, such as eye and hair colour, from their family. However, all children with Down's syndrome will have some degree of learning disability and the distinct facial characteristics of the condition.

The Down's Syndrome Association states that:

▶ around 1 in 1000 babies are born with Down's syndrome

▶ there are 40,000 people in the UK with this condition

▶ Down's syndrome is not a disease

▶ the average life expectancy of a person with Down's syndrome is between 50 and 60 years, with a small number living into their seventies.

Children and young people with Down's syndrome can achieve their full potential with effective health care and good parental support including activities with their family and at school, encouragement in sport and vocational work. About 10 per cent of children with Down's syndrome have additional needs, such as ASD or ADHD, and additional medical complications, and again good support from their family and healthcare professionals is essential.

Huntington's disease (HD)

HD, which used to be called Huntingdon's chorea, is an inherited disorder of the central nervous system. The first sign of HD is normally when a person is between 30 and 50 years old, with changes in the individual's behaviour, thinking and emotions. There are a wide range of symptoms and every person with HD, including those in the same family, will show different signs of the disease. The early symptoms include: slight, uncontrollable muscular movements, stumbling and clumsiness, lack of concentration, short-term memory lapses, depression and changes of mood – sometimes including aggressive or antisocial behaviour. HD is an inherited condition and if someone else in the family has the condition, the diagnosis may be made early, and the correct support for the individual's medical needs can be arranged.

An individual with HD may become dependent on a carer such as their partner, a close family member or a friend, which may put the relationship at risk. A local specialist HD adviser should be able to help support the individual and their family. Social workers can also advise on what local support is available. Sometimes an individual with HD will require residential care. The Huntington's Disease Association is a source of information and support.

Dementia and Alzheimer's disease

Dementia is a term that describes persistent disorder of mental processes, including memory loss, personality changes and difficulties with thinking, problem solving and language. This is mainly caused by Alzheimer's disease or problems with the blood supply to the brain, for instance caused by a series of mini strokes, generally described as vascular dementia.

There are many types of dementia, as the term describes the way the brain is affected by certain diseases, which include Alzheimer's disease, vascular dementia, dementia with Lewy bodies (DLB), frontotemporal dementia, Creutzfeldt-Jakob disease, Korsakoff's syndrome, HIV-related cognitive impairment and mild cognitive impairment. Each type of dementia has specific symptoms, depending on how they affect the brain. An individual may have more than one type of dementia, which is known as 'mixed dementia'. Having dementia in the family does not necessarily mean it will be inherited, but the chances are slightly higher. The biggest risk for dementia is age. The Alzheimer's Society gives the risk of developing dementia for people aged between 65 and 70 years as 2 per cent, increasing to 20 per cent for those over 80 years of age.

Alzheimer's disease is the most commonly known form of dementia. The Alzheimer's Society reports that there are currently more than 520,000 people in the UK with it. Symptoms can be mild at the beginning and worsen as the brain deteriorates and the condition starts to interfere with daily life. Memory loss is the most obvious symptom, where the individual forgets recent events or is unable to learn new information. This is caused by damage to the hippocampus, the part of the brain responsible for memory.

Memory loss affects individuals in various ways, for example:

▶ losing items around the house

▶ struggling in a conversation to find the right word

▶ forgetting recent events

▶ forgetting a familiar person's name

▶ getting lost in familiar places

▶ forgetting events such as appointments or anniversaries.

▶ Alarms can remind people with early symptoms of dementia to take pills

A partner or close family member or friend can help an individual with early symptoms to use coping mechanisms, such as notes and alarms to remind people to take pills or send birthday cards, for example. However, when the disease progresses and the symptoms become more severe, the individual's behaviour may change, they may become quickly agitated and react aggressively, constantly repeat the same question and have disturbed sleep patterns. This can be a burden on their carer and close family and additional support may be required. In the later stages of Alzheimer's disease, the individual may forget to eat or walk, become frail and require help with personal hygiene and other daily needs. Depending on their age at diagnosis, people with Alzheimer's disease may live from eight to ten years following the onset of the disease.

Early onset Alzheimer's disease, where people develop symptoms as early as in their thirties or forties, tends to happen in families, sometimes with several generations affected. Early onset Alzheimer's is caused by genetic mutations.

Needs of older people

Memory loss and slower cognitive speed

Cognitive abilities usually deteriorate with age. Some mental capabilities decline from middle age, including memory, processing speed, reasoning, and multi-tasking. Slower cognitive speed produces much of the age-related decline. While slowing of the ability to process ideas is a normal part of ageing, some people experience a severe deterioration in cognitive skills, leading to dementia.

Some older people need 24-hour care; for example, if they need to take regular medication and will not be able to remember to take it, or if they wander off and are in danger of becoming lost or injured, or they may need help with preparing food and eating.

If an elderly person is in the early stages of dementia, a carer may be able to cope with the level of support required. However, as the individual ages and/or their condition worsens the carer may not have the skills or physical strength to continue the support.

For example, if an individual becomes aggressive or requires help with mobility, the carer may not have the physical strength or skills to cope. Specialised care from health professionals will be needed. If a higher level of care or supervision is required, the individual may need residential or nursing care.

Life-long learning

Some older people may want to learn and 'silver surfers' is a term now widely used for people over 50 years old who use the internet on a frequent basis for research, learning opportunities (such as FutureLearn and U3A), shopping and social networking. Some sources report that older people use the internet an average of four hours more per month than 18 to 24 year olds. Far from being isolating, it is considered that for older age groups, particularly for those with mobility issues, the internet has allowed them to stay in contact with friends and relatives, and has opened up learning opportunities.

It is vital for older people to be included in community activities to maintain their health and wellbeing. When older people do not have these opportunities, they are at greater risk of becoming isolated and depressed. Local libraries provide a good meeting place, along with support and courses. Voluntary transport services can assist individuals with mobility issues, or learning disabilities, which prevent them travelling independently. The health and social care system plays a vital part in making sure communication between care provision services is effective and works for an individual.

According to BILD, people with learning disabilities are living longer. Life-long learning can have a huge impact on their self-esteem and self-confidence, and support should be put in place to help support them with this. Older people with a learning disability are a diverse group and may face the 'double jeopardy' of age and disability discrimination.

Physical and health needs

Needs of older people

As people get older their health needs may change, depending on their previous and current lifestyle, their mental health and where they live. An older person is usually considered to be someone over 65 years of age. These individuals have seen many changes in their lives, including many advances in health care, which include people living longer than ever before, resulting in more people with health needs due to ageing. Older people tend to experience loneliness, especially if they have reduced mobility and a reduced income. Older people tend to have more healthcare needs than younger people. In turn, this requires more healthcare professionals, and more health and social care services and resources.

Arthritis

Arthritis, inflammation of the joints, is a term for more than a hundred different conditions that cause joint pain or joint disease. Inflammation is the body's response to injury, infection or disease. Extreme inflammation in the joints causes pain, stiffness and swelling.

The commonest type of arthritis is osteoarthritis, often called 'wear and tear' or degenerative arthritis. It mainly affects older people. Another common type of arthritis is inflammatory arthritis, including rheumatoid arthritis, where the immune system attacks the joints, and gout, caused by uric acid crystals forming in the joints. There are many other types of inflammatory arthritis such as psoriatic arthritis and **ankylosing spondylitis**.

> **Key term**
>
> **Ankylosing spondylitis** – a form of spinal arthritis, seen mostly in young males, causing immobility and fusion of the vertebral and sacroiliac joints.

A joint, for example the knee or elbow, is where two bones are connected by ligaments. The joint muscles and tendons surrounding the joint allow movement to take place. Synovial fluid inside the joint lubricates it and assists movement, while cartilage inside the joint provides shock absorption. In osteoarthritis the characteristic pain, swelling and disability is caused by thinning of the cartilage and bony outgrowths from the sides of the joint; along with increased amounts of fluid and worn cartilage inside the joint.

The pain and sometimes deformities caused to a joint, particularly the weight-bearing joints such as the hip and knee, not only cause pain but can restrict an individual's mobility. Initially, support for the individual may include provision of aids for daily living activities; however, eventually, surgical intervention, such as joint replacement, may be required.

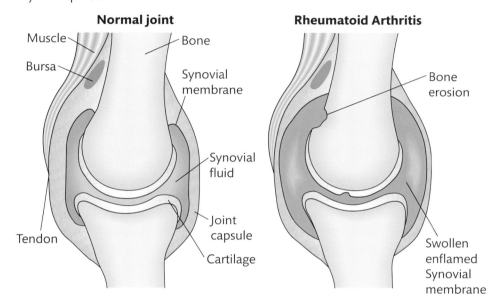

▶ **Figure 12.1** Rheumatoid arthritis in knee joint

Other conditions affecting the musculoskeletal system include soft tissue pain (including **fibromyalgia**), back pain and connective tissue diseases (CTD). These may cause a range of symptoms and disabilities as well as painful, swollen joints.

Back pain is very common and has a number of causes, such as a slipped disc. The areas of the back most affected are muscles, discs, bones, joints or ligaments. The spine is a complicated structure so GPs and specialists may find it difficult to pinpoint the exact cause of pain.

CTD affects ligaments, tendons and cartilage. This type of tissue connects parts of the body, such as joints, but is also found in the lungs, kidneys and skin. Therefore, as with back pain, it can be difficult to find the exact cause of the problem and may require several visits to specialists to pinpoint it. The treatment and support required for individuals with back pain or CTD will depend on their symptoms.

Diabetes

There are two main types of diabetes. Type 1 is where the pancreas does not produce any insulin or insufficient insulin for the body's needs, or where insulin does not work properly, known as insulin resistance. Type 1 diabetes usually occurs in people under forty years old, and is the main type of diabetes in children. Individuals with type 1 diabetes require frequent blood glucose monitoring and insulin injections for the rest of their lives. Some people with type 1 diabetes experience hypos (hypoglycaemia), a

Key term

Fybromyalgia – a condition in which there is widespread pain as a joint, part of the body or the entire body becomes extra sensitive to pain. There is no cure and treatment aims to ease some of the symptoms.

potentially life-threatening condition where the individual's blood sugar levels are too low for their body's needs, either through not eating after insulin injection, or caused by the onset of an illness, such as flu. Common symptoms include sweating, hunger, tiredness, blurred vision, lack of concentration, headaches, tearfulness, irritability and occasionally, if severe, collapse and unconsciousness. If the person is awake, taking glucose, such as a sugary drink, should quickly raise blood glucose levels. If the person is unconscious, it is vital to get medical help as soon as possible.

Type 2 diabetes is more common in older people, usually over forty years of age. Insulin is necessary for the body to absorb food and use it for energy. The early symptoms of this type of diabetes include tiredness and inability to focus or concentrate. Later symptoms, which can lead to irreparable damage, include:

▶ personality change

▶ unsteadiness

▶ losing consciousness, which could lead to cognitive damage

▶ stroke

▶ recurrent infections, particularly of the feet and lower limbs, sometimes leading to gangrene requiring surgical amputation of the affected limb(s)

▶ blindness.

Type 2 diabetes may be picked up through a urine test, done as part of a routine health check or prior to medical treatment. Diagnosis will require blood glucose levels to be measured, which is usually done at a GP surgery. If the blood glucose level is above a certain range further checks will be made, normally a fasting blood test. Most hospitals now have diabetic clinics with specialist care including a nutritionist. Once diagnosed, the individual will usually be prescribed medication, or in severe cases insulin. In less severe and borderline cases, a nutritionist works with the person to see if the glucose levels can be controlled by dietary changes alone. Type 2 diabetes is increasingly diagnosed in older people due to unhealthy lifestyles and diet.

Diabetes is a life-long condition. People with diabetes will either have to inject insulin (type 1 and some type 2) or take medication for the rest of their life. Everyone who has diabetes should also monitor their diet as the consequences of too much glucose in the blood can lead to complications and irreparable damage.

Older people with diabetes should be taught to care for their feet properly to avoid damage that could lead to infections. If an individual cannot do this, due to other conditions such as poor eyesight, immobility or dementia, then they will need early referral to a chiropodist.

Cardiovascular disease (CVD)

CVD includes all the diseases of the heart and circulation such as coronary heart disease, angina, heart attack, congenital heart disease and stroke.

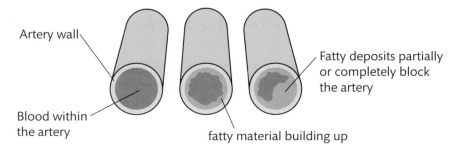

▶ **Figure 12.2** Fatty deposits (atheroma) building up in an artery

Palpitations may be the first sign of CVD, although in most cases they are harmless. However, when palpitations are followed by dizziness or tightness of the chest, they can be a sign of a heart attack.

CVD is caused by a build-up of fatty substances in the arteries. Eating an unhealthy fatty diet and lack of exercise can contribute to this condition. If an individual is overweight, or has diabetes, they are more likely to develop CVD. If the GP suspects that an individual has CVD they will refer them to a specialist and further tests may be carried out, which may include:

▸ electrocardiogram

▸ X-rays

▸ echocardiogram

▸ coronary angiography

▸ magnetic resonance imaging (MRI).

Key term

Palpitations – rapid, strong, or irregular heartbeat that may be caused by agitation, exertion, or illness, usually only lasting for a few seconds.

Research

Research the above tests. You should gain an understanding of them and how they can help diagnose the problem. You should also be able to describe what will happen to help prepare someone having these tests.

Once a diagnosis has been made the specialist will prescribe the appropriate treatment. This may involve medication, dietary advice and advice from a physiotherapist about an exercise plan. The individual's GP will monitor their progress. To remain well, they will need to follow a healthy diet and take regular exercise. If they are a smoker, they will be advised to stop and given appropriate support to do so.

⏸ **PAUSE POINT**   What are the different types of diabetes? What causes diabetes and how is it treated?

Hint   Think about the individual's age and lifestyle.

Extend   What might be the consequences of not treating type 2 diabetes? Describe the complications, how they can be avoided and what support an individual may need if they develop complications.

Health needs

Physical needs

An individual's physical needs and requirements for support will depend on their disability, injury or illness. For example, someone with a broken leg will need short-term support with mobility. However, if an individual has been paralysed through illness or injury they are likely to need long-term support with mobility, such as using a wheelchair, being supplied with aids and taught how to use them, to help with their daily living activities. Their home may have to be adapted to enable them to live independently, for example, fitting a downstairs shower room and toilet, or installing ramps in place of stairs.

Cystic fibrosis

Cystic fibrosis (CF) is an **inherited** condition where the lungs and digestive system become clogged up with a thick, sticky mucus. This can cause many problems for the individual, from coughing constantly to frequent chest and lung infections as well as difficulty in putting on weight. Currently there is no cure for CF so the treatment is to make life as easy as possible for the person. Symptoms usually start when a person is young, so they have the rest of their lives with it. Physiotherapy and medication are used to support a person with cystic fibrosis.

Key term

Inherited – people inherit things from their parents through genes as the baby is growing in the womb. Eye and hair colour, height and build are a few examples of things a person inherits.

In the 1960s, children with CF were lucky to survive beyond five years old. There are more effective treatments and, for some individuals, there is the option of a lung and heart transplant. Individuals can now expect to live at least until middle age, or even longer. This means that there are now more adults with CF than children. However, they are encountering new challenges and issues associated with living with CF and partners or family members may have to take on more caring roles.

Some of the issues related to living longer with CF include:

▶ Nutrition. Some people with CF may need extra nutrition, either via a tube through the nose, or directly into the stomach as there seems to be a link between having a higher bodyweight and good lung function.

▶ Medication and treatment. Individuals may need to take more and/or different medication. Physiotherapy may need to change if, for example, osteoporosis develops. Chest and upper body percussion may not be suitable where bones are less dense and prone to fracture.

▶ Finance and pensions. The condition may cause prolonged illness and absence from work. People with CF may have expected to die young, and so pensions are becoming more of a concern for many as they survive longer.

> **Research**
>
> The singer Bianca Nicholas has CF. Access the NHS Choices page for CF to find out how Bianca copes with living with the disease.

Sickle cell disorders

Sickle cell disorders are inherited conditions that mainly affect people with an African ethnic background. This disorder affects the person's red blood cells, making them die off earlier than they should, which causes anaemia and in turn makes the person feel fatigued. The treatment for this is for the person to not get dehydrated, to rest when needed, and to get medical treatment in an emergency when they are feeling extreme pain, and having breathing problems among other symptoms.

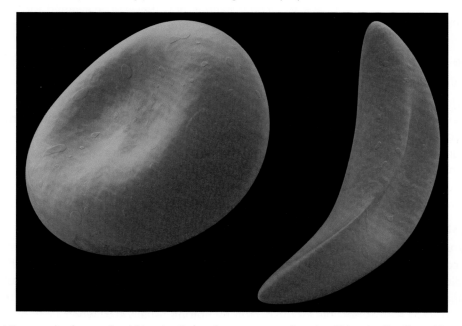

▶ Micrograph of normal red blood cells (erythrocytes, round) and red blood cells affected by sickle cell anaemia (crescent-shaped)

Stroke

When a person has a stroke and/or **transient ischaemic attack (TIA)** they may be paralysed or their speech may be impaired, which may make understanding their needs difficult. The effects on the individual will depend on which part of the brain is affected. Strokes are caused either by a clot blocking an artery supplying blood to the brain, or a blood vessel bleeding into the brain. You may hear a stroke referred to as a cerebrovascular accident.

TIAs and minor strokes may cause temporary or little, if any, disability. However, major strokes can leave the individual paralysed on one side of their body, with visual and speech impairments. When caring for people following a stroke you will need to be aware, particularly when offering food and drinks, that they may not be able to see them if they are not in the range of vision of their unaffected eye, and that they may not be able to reach them if you place them on their paralysed side.

A range of care professionals may be involved in the care of someone who has had a stroke, including:

▶ medical and nursing professionals, who will oversee the care of the individual and prescribe the necessary medication and treatments

▶ physiotherapists and occupational therapists, who will assist the individual with mobility and rehabilitation of daily living needs, such as eating and drinking independently, dressing and other basic tasks

▶ speech therapists, who will assist the individual to regain speech, or find alternative ways of communicating.

Mental illnesses

Mental illness or mental health problems cover a vast range of conditions, including anxiety, depression and bipolar disorder. The Health and Social Care Information Centre estimate that around a quarter (23 per cent) of people in Britain will have a mental illness at some point in their lives, impacting their ability to carry out daily activities and routines. Most of us can recognise the symptoms of mental illness in ourselves, such as feelings of unease, worry or fear – especially if associated with a specific event, such as taking an exam. However, mental illness is when these feelings are severe, long lasting and completely take over an individual's thoughts.

Due to the vast range of mental health problems and their causes, it can be difficult for a person to find the right support; GPs can arrange for further specialist help.

> **Key term**
>
> **Transient ischaemic attack (TIA)** – sometimes called a mini stroke, and is caused by a temporary disruption to the blood supply to part of the brain. Symptoms are similar to those of a stroke, but a TIA only lasts for a few minutes or hours, and is usually over within 24 hours.

> **Research**
>
> Access the Mind website to find out about different types of mental health problems. What additional needs do you think people with mental health problems have? How do you think carers and healthcare professionals can best support individuals with these conditions?

NHS Choices reports that about half of people returning to work following a long-term absence have been absent due to mental health issues including depression, anxiety and bipolar disorder. Although the majority of people with a mental illness can still carry out normal daily activities such as working, shopping and cooking, they often find these activities harder to do. When suffering from severe depression, a person may feel suicidal and it is important that carers, family, friends and healthcare professionals are aware of the support that organisations such as the Samaritans can provide.

Mental illness can affect a person's physical health; for example, people with depression often have cardiovascular diseases or diabetes. This may be because their mental illness means that they neglect their health and personal care.

It may be much harder for people with mental illnesses to get care and support for their physical disorders. It is, therefore, important that carers, family and health professionals look out for signs of physical disorders and help the individual to get the care that they need.

Sensory disabilities

A sensory disability is a disability of sight, hearing, smell, touch or taste. Your sight and hearing provide most of your sense of the world around you. Impairment or loss of one of these senses will have a great impact on lifestyle and how an individual functions. As people age, their senses tend to become less sharp and loss or impairment of hearing or sight can lead to isolation.

Glasses and hearing aids, and some lifestyle changes, can improve an individual's ability to hear and see.

Deafness and hearing impairment

Some people are born deaf or become deaf due to an illness or an accident. Some people have a hearing impairment where they can only hear a certain amount of sound.

Individuals with tinnitus hear a persistent noise from inside their body. It is often described as a ringing, buzzing, humming or whistling noise. While for some people this may only be intermittent and a minor irritation, for others it can be continuous and can have serious effects on their everyday life. In severe cases it can affect concentration, and cause problems with sleeping and depression. Sometimes a cause can be found and treated, but in other cases the individual can be taught ways of coping with it.

Communication can be improved with hearing aids for those with hearing impairment, and by teaching sign language and lip reading to those who have little or no hearing. Additionally, for some people there is the possibility of an electronic implant (cochlear implant) that works by providing sound signals to the brain, replacing the damaged part. Hearing loss can be very isolating and may lead to mental health problems, so it is essential to ensure that the correct support is in place.

Visual impairment

Some people are born without sight or lose their sight due to an illness or an accident. Some people have a visual impairment where they only have limited vision, or can only see shadows or shapes. Although they may have no other physical disability, this can have a severe impact on their lifestyle. For example, while mobility may not be an issue, navigating around obstacles and avoiding danger may be difficult. Many people with visual impairments move around with confidence using aids such as a guide dog or a white stick. Reading is made possible by using Braille, using the accessibility option on a computer, using video magnifiers or speaking software.

Currently, research is being undertaken into retinal implants, which stimulate retinal cells to provide the individual with light perception and object recognition. A retinal implant may partially restore sight for people who have degenerative disorders, such as retinitis pigmentosa or macular degeneration. As soon as someone is diagnosed with a visual impairment, they will be referred to a specialist, who will assess their individual needs, so that they can access the correct support for their daily living activities.

▶ Does this person have a mental illness? It is hard to tell.

Accidents

Accidents can change a person's life, or end it. In 2014/15, according to a work related survey, there were 611,000 accidents at work; and of these accidents, 142 people were killed. People can sustain minor injuries at work, during sport or from domestic activities, that can be dealt with in an accident and emergency/urgent care department. However, more serious accidents may cause loss of a limb, brain damage from a head injury or paralysis from a spinal cord injury, and the individual may need care for the rest of their lives.

Paraplegia

While paralysis can be temporary or even momentary, injuries that sever the spinal cord cause irreparable damage. Paraplegia is caused by damage to the spinal cord at or below chest level, affecting the person's ability to use their legs (paraplegia). If the damage is above chest level, it will affect their ability to use their arms and legs (quadriplegia/tetraplegia). When an individual sustains an injury causing paraplegia or tetraplegia, it will be devastating for them, their family and their friends, and providing the right support and information will be vital. They will need emotional as well as practical support to help them cope with the changes. They may require financial support and will need a rehabilitation programme specific to their needs. Communication between the various support services will be important, especially in the early days, to ensure that longer-term as well as short-term needs are considered.

Loss of a limb

People with diabetes are at particular risk of lower limb infections, particularly of the toes and feet, which may become gangrenous and require surgical amputation. Amputation of a limb or part of a limb, either accidental or through surgical removal will result in many physical and emotional needs, both during recovery and when the individual resumes their usual life activities. Adjusting to life after loss of a limb will involve emotional readjustment, rehabilitation, physiotherapy and occupational therapy. Losing a limb, or part of a limb, will not only affect a person's **body image**, but will also cause altered **proprioception**. It will take much time and energy from the person to use their body without the limb, and they may have to learn to use a **prosthesis**. Initially, loss of a lower limb, or part of it, may require the individual to learn to walk with crutches until their **stump** heals sufficiently for them to use a prosthesis. For many very elderly people, this may not be possible and they will have to adapt to using a wheelchair for mobility for the rest of their lives.

Infectious diseases

Most infectious diseases, especially common childhood complaints such as measles or chickenpox, have no lasting effects. When the individual has the infection, they will require care to control a high temperature and soothing lotion to be applied to any rashes. However, individuals may have additional needs following a severe infection, such as meningitis, poliomyelitis or necrotising fasciitis (galloping gangrene).

Currently, all babies born or moving into the UK are eligible for a schedule of vaccinations against the more common infections that occur in childhood, such as polio and meningitis. These can leave a child with lifelong disabilities such as hearing loss, visual disturbances, muscle shrinking, limb deformities and breathing disorders. Although polio has largely been controlled in the UK since the early 1980s, some older people will have long-term disabilities caused by outbreaks in the early 1950s and may have mobility issues and poor health associated with this.

> **Key terms**
>
> **Body image** – how a person sees their physical self, including their thoughts and feelings about their body.
>
> **Proprioception** – unconscious awareness of movement and spatial orientation that comes from within the body, which informs the individual, for example, whether they are upright or prone.
>
> **Prosthesis** – an artificial part that is used to replace a missing or diseased body part – could be external (e.g. replacing a missing limb) or internal (e.g. a pacemaker, used to stimulate heart beat).
>
> **Stump (residual limb)** – the part of a limb that is left beyond a healthy joint following amputation.

Pregnancy and birth

Women can experience problems during pregnancy and birth, which can lead to them having specific additional needs. Pregnancy and birth puts a huge amount of physical and emotional strain on the mother's body, and she may need additional support during the pregnancy, birth and afterwards.

Some examples of complications for the mother during pregnancy and birth are:

▶ backache

▶ vaginal bleeding, sometimes leading to severe haemorrhage and miscarriage

▶ constipation

▶ deep vein thrombosis (DVT)

▶ high blood pressure and pre-eclampsia

▶ pregnancy induced diabetes

▶ prolapse of uterus during childbirth, or shortly after

▶ damage to the bladder and/or bowel, which may be caused by instruments (such as forceps) used during delivery and can lead to incontinence later in life.

Some examples of complications for the baby during pregnancy and birth are:

▶ various defects caused by the mother's lifestyle, such as smoking and drinking alcohol during pregnancy

▶ brain damage due to lack of oxygen during a difficult birth, sometimes caused by the umbilical cord wrapping around the baby's neck or a breech birth (where the baby presents bottom or legs first)

▶ damage from forceps used to assist in a difficult delivery, which may cause palsy and facial injuries, bruising and swelling on the head, skull fractures, seizures and brain damage.

The mother and baby will need to be treated according to their specific needs. Obstetricians and midwives will be involved in the mother's care and some specialists, for example paediatricians, nutritionists, physiotherapists and mental health experts may also be involved. Additionally, the mother may have an existing health problem such as asthma, diabetes, a mental health problem or a heart defect, meaning she will have a wider range of support needs during pregnancy and birth, and following the birth.

Social and emotional needs

Needs generated by family circumstances

Specific needs of looked-after children

The NSPCC defines 'looked-after children' as children cared for by the local authority for more than a 24-hour period. Children may become looked-after for a variety of reasons including if their family situation becomes abusive, or their parents cannot cope with looking after them due to mental health disorders or addictions, or their parents simply cannot care for them. The decision to remove a child may have devastating effects on the child and the rest of the family. Even where a child is being abused, they may still love their parent(s) and feel a sense of loss at the separation. The child will need sensitive care from the people around them.

It may be possible for social services to place the child with a close family member, when there is confidence that the child will be safe and well cared for. This will be a high priority as the child may feel more secure in an environment with close relatives caring for them. This placement will be monitored.

However, sometimes fostering may be a short- or a long-term solution. This involves placing the child with foster parents who are trained to look after the needs of children removed from their own parent(s). Foster parents will provide a stable and nurturing environment until the child is able to return to living with their parent(s). However, in some circumstances this may not be the right decision or the parent(s) may have died. In this case a permanent solution will be for the child to be adopted.

It is important to determine the child's individual needs in order to provide a stable and nurturing environment, and to maintain and develop the child's sense of identity with their birth culture. Meeting the child's educational needs and trying to maintain a sense of stability and continuity is also important, and where possible the child will remain at the same school they have been attending. Depending on the situation that required the child to be taken into care, they may keep contact with their family or family members. Sometimes this will be through supervised meetings with a parent or parents. Looked-after children may be bullied about being in care, or they may not be able to focus on their education and so not achieve their full potential. Social services and other individuals involved in the child's care will monitor the situation to ensure a child's emotional security and wellbeing is at the heart of the care provided.

A few children are so emotionally damaged by their abuse that they may not be able to live with a family; in these cases, social services will place them in a hostel or, if they are old enough, in their own flat. These children will be closely monitored and supported by a paediatric psychologist.

Once a child is 18, they are seen as an adult and considered to be independent. Even if living with a foster family, they will be moved and placed in a shared house or flat. They will receive less monitoring and support from social services, although these are available if needed. A looked-after child who has a learning difficulty may not be considered able to live independently until they are 25, although this depends on the specific needs of the person, who may require lifelong care.

Bereavement

The death of someone close to you is always a traumatic experience. The older a person becomes the more likely they are to experience close family and friends dying. Most people will need emotional support during and after a bereavement, often just someone listening to them or doing something small, such as helping with shopping or cooking.

For some people, however, the experience is so intense that they will need support from an experienced bereavement counsellor. Losing a child, or a child losing a parent, can be especially traumatic and properly trained staff may need to offer support. There are bereavement counselling services such as 'Cruse' who provide individual or group support from trained counsellors. Healthcare professionals will be aware of these services and contact details are usually available at most GP surgeries and health centres.

School refuser and bullying

A child might refuse to go to school because they are being bullied, or there may be other causes. School refusal is different from truancy, as a school refuser experiences anxiety or fear about attending school and a sense of isolation. Schools and social services can provide emotional support, advice and counselling for children experiencing these feelings. Where a school is unable to provide this level of support, the child might be referred to a mental health child counsellor. If a child becomes school phobic, an educational psychologist may become involved. The child will require understanding and sympathy, and support with school attendance during this difficult time.

In 2013, ChildLine reported that around 45,000 children talked to them about bullying, and other organisations suggest that nearly half of children and young people have been bullied at school at some point in their lives.

Bullying can range from teasing and spreading rumours, to physical harm. It includes name-calling, taking (and sometimes spoiling) people's belongings, excluding people from groups and threatening them. Children and young people may be bullied about their appearance, sexual orientation, having a disability, their race or religion or because of their social circumstances. Sometimes there does not appear to be any reason why a child is picked on.

Bullying is a serious situation. It can cause long-term damage to an individual and will need to be properly managed. It can be difficult for schools to do this, but with careful support by properly trained health or teaching professionals it can be resolved. Parents and carers may also require support for their experiences, which may include a sense of isolation, worry, anger and anxiety.

▶ An upset child being comforted by a teacher

Needs generated by being elderly

When working in health and social care, it is important to recognise and manage service users' social and emotional care. Health and social care professionals should be aware of the range of support networks and specialists available to support an older person's care needs, and how these services can be accessed.

Loss of loved ones

Elderly people are more likely to experience the death of friends or family, which can be very traumatic for them. A healthcare worker will need to be sensitive about how a service user is feeling, and support them where necessary. Listening will usually help, and may give you a sense of the support they need, if any. Sometimes just talking about the person who has died will be enough for the person to deal with their grief. However, a volunteer or a bereavement counsellor may need to provide longer-term support.

Fear of dying

When someone close to them dies, this may make an individual start to fear their own death, particularly an older person. This is a natural reaction. The older a person becomes, the more the thought of their own death is likely to be in their mind. This may make the individual feel depressed or anxious. Listening to a service user's concerns is part of a carer's work, particularly when looking after elderly people, and training in listening skills will help.

Family far away

Sometimes a person's close family lives far away and visits to or from them are infrequent or rare. This is especially so where people have migrated to Britain and left family in their own country. For older people, this may mean that they have little or no support from their family when they are no longer fully able to care for themselves. Health and social care professionals will need to manage this situation carefully to ensure that the person is supported emotionally, physically and financially.

Isolation

Being away from family, or not seeing or having regular contact with another person on a daily basis, can bring on a sense of isolation. Not having anyone to talk to can have a devastating effect on a person's mental health. Some elderly people enjoy their own company, but if several days go by without any contact with family or friends, neighbours or carers, they may feel lonely and depressed. It is difficult for home help carers to spend much time with people as they will have many people to see in a day. However, their visit may be highly valued by the service user, especially if a good relationship exists between them. Talking and listening may help alleviate negative feelings about being lonely. Showing an interest in the service user's life, their family and friends, can have positive effects on their mental health. The internet can be used to communicate with family and friends around the world. If an older person is unsure or not confident about using the internet, there may be local instructors who will offer free computer courses. Local charities or religious centres usually offer many types of support, including with transport and providing day centres where older people can meet and enjoy a meal.

▶ Older people may feel isolated from family and friends

Lack of money

If an elderly person only has a state pension to live on, they may not be able to afford the lifestyle they used to have. However, they will still have to pay for heating, lighting, cooking and food, and may still be paying rent or a mortgage, which may not leave much money for social activities. One of the biggest concerns for many older people and their families is having to pay for care, particularly residential care.

The government, and many charities, offer free financial advice for elderly people. Some charities will help with outings and clubs for elderly people with a limited income.

Needs affected by the learning environment

A learning environment is the physical location, context and culture in which learning takes place. This may, or may not, be in a school or training centre. Individuals are always learning and learning can take place in many different situations. A person's ability to learn can be affected by several factors. For example, if learning is taking place in a building, it has to be fully accessible and designed to be inclusive. People with a disability, older people with mobility problems, families with children under five years old, and carers and friends accompanying them should all be able to access the building. Planning must consider adequate lighting, air quality and ability to use communication aids, such as hearing loops. A useful document to read is on the government website titled *Building Regulations 2010 Approved document M – Access to and use of buildings, Vol.2, Buildings other than dwellings.*

PAUSE POINT Why is it important to know about a person's family circumstances when treating them?

> Hint   Development and relationships.

> Extend   Why would looked-after children have different needs to children in a nuclear family?

Assessment practice 12.1

`A.P1` `A.M1` `A.D1`

Scenario 1

Marion is aged 79 and lives with her husband, Sean, in a 4-bedroom house where they run a small lodgings. The house has three levels and they both have to clean rooms every day which keeps them fit but it is tiring. Marion has fallen down a few times and while she has not suffered any serious injury, Sean is very worried about her. Unknown to him, Marion knows she is losing her sight but doesn't want to worry Sean, or her family, as the small business helps with their holidays and money for their children and grandchildren. Sean speaks to his oldest son for help.

Scenario 2

Bronwyn is at primary school when, during the lunch period while playing with friends on the school's artificial turf, she has an epileptic fit. This is the first time she has experienced it and when she recovers, is confused and upset as her head hurts where she banged it on the ground during the seizure. A trained member of staff looks after her while they wait for an ambulance and for her mum to arrive. Bronwyn does not have another seizure during this time.

Using your research and notes to help you, explain the diagnostic procedures involved in assessing the additional needs of Marion and Bronwyn. From this, assess the support requirements of these two people.

Now evaluate the significance of the diagnosis for the individuals, their families and for society.

Plan
- What is the task? What is it I have been asked to do?
- How confident do I feel in answering this?
- What areas will I struggle with?

Do
- I know what I am doing.
- I can identify where I need to improve.

Review
- I can evaluate what I have done and how I approached the task.
- I have learnt from this and can make changes to my work to make it better next time.

B   Examine how to overcome the challenges to daily living faced by people with additional needs

Definitions of disability

Medical and social models of disability

There are two models of disability:

▶ the medical model, which looks at a person's impairment and tries to treat it with medication and other specialist interventions, such as surgery

▶ the social model which was devised by disabled people for disabled people and views disability as being caused by the way society is organised. It aims to find ways of removing barriers that restrict life choices for disabled people so that they can live independently. For example, this may mean installing a lift that meets accessibility standards so everyone can access a building without having to ask for assistance.

Research

Visit the Scope website and read the real-life examples of the social and medical disability models in action. Using this website, undertake some research to review these examples and reflect on which is the best model for someone with a disability.

Understanding of disability and dependency as social constructs

In the past, people with a specific impairment or additional needs have been treated as disabled and expected to be **dependent** on others to fulfil their daily living activities and social needs. However, in recent years this has come to be seen as a **social construct**. The social model of disability, which was devised by people with disabilities, proposes that society should not view individuals as disabled but that there should be mechanisms in place for people with specific needs to feel equal to people who do not have those needs and able to live their lives independently, without relying on family, friends or carers to assist them with daily living tasks. The Equality Act 2010 (revised and updated in 2015) is a legal framework to protect the rights of all individuals and advance equality of opportunity for all.

Definitions of disability, disablement, discrimination and impairment

Disability

A disability is any physical or mental condition that limits the movements, or restricts the senses or activities of an individual. The Equality Act 2010 states that 'you are disabled if you have a physical or mental impairment that has a "substantial" and "long-term" negative effect on your ability to do normal daily activities'.

The important phrases are 'substantial' and 'long-term', which mean the condition is more than minor or trivial. 'Long-term' means the condition affects the person for more than 12 months.

Disablement

Disablement is the noun associated with the verb disable. In health and social care, this is any condition that makes an individual unable to perform daily activities without assistance, which may arise from a physical or mental impairment, such as inability to see or hear, lack of mobility or a learning disability.

Discrimination

Discrimination is when an individual is treated less fairly than other people because of the way they look, their nationality or ethnicity, their gender or sexual orientation, their age or for any other reason. It is important that health and social care professionals treat all service users equally and provide the same opportunities for everyone they care for. People must not be discriminated against because of their disability.

Impairment

Impairment is when a person loses a function of any part of their body, whether physical or mental. For example, a person who has a problem with their sight has a visual impairment, if a person was born without a limb or has had a limb removed, they have a physical impairment.

Discuss

In a small group, think about situations in which a service user may be discriminated against. How do you think they would feel? What can health and care professionals do to avoid this happening?

Key terms

Dependency – relying on another person, object or routine in order to cope with daily living activities.

Social construct – an idea or notion of any given society that may not represent reality but appears to be natural and obvious to the people who accept it.

Minimising environmental and social challenges

Access and barriers

Public buildings

Planning practice guidance, accessible from the government website, sets out conditions of good practice for making buildings accessible for everyone regardless of their age, gender or disability. The document explains the purpose in making areas of movement inclusive, enabling everyone to move throughout a building without any barriers. Consideration is given to older people's needs, to families with children in pushchairs, carers, and friends and relatives of people with disabilities. The guidance includes details about steps, the width of toilets and making lifts wide enough for people using a wheelchair. Access ramps should be at the main entrance. Design considerations are given to issues such as the height of hand basins, to make them accessible for children. Baby changing facilities are positioned in areas accessible to both men and women.

Public transport

In 2004, the Department for Transport (DfT) introduced a policy to help promote social inclusion by tackling accessibility problems, including the provision of guidance to and support for local transport. The Centre for Research in Social Policy produced a report in 2012, 'Accessibility Planning Policy: Evaluation and Future Directions', about the concerns of transport organisations in trying to provide full physical accessibility and availability. The report identified some important barriers to access, which could have a serious impact on an individual's lifestyle in terms of educational and employment opportunities. These barriers included the availability and physical accessibility of transport, its cost, where services operated (especially in terms of inaccessible places) and concerns about safety and security when travelling. Additionally, for some there is an unwillingness, or lack of confidence, about travelling, which could lead to social isolation. Local transport planners are responsible for provision and cuts to budgets have had a significant impact on transport funding.

▶ Blind person getting support from a station assistant

> **Research**
>
> In two groups, research the accessibility of local transport services and buildings. One group should research access to buildings, and the other should research the accessibility of transport services.
>
> Each group should present their findings to the other group, so that everyone in the class has an understanding of local accessibility issues, and whether there are any challenges for people with additional needs.

Ⅱ PAUSE POINT At your educational establishment, what would be the physical and social challenges for a person who is blind?

Hint Think about stigma, barriers and buildings.

Extend Investigate a local leisure centre or a local railway station for accessibility issues.

Minimising barriers

Ramps

Part M of the Building Regulations 2010 sets out the legal requirements for accessibility to buildings for people who use a wheelchair. The regulations inform all businesses, regardless of size, about how to make reasonable adjustments in accordance with the Equality Act 2010, to help all people, whether employees or visitors, access and use their buildings. The regulations also cover access to toilets (sanitary provision) for people in wheelchairs, and access to lifts.

Translation

The UK is a multi-ethnic society and English may be a second language for some people. Many organisations, including local authority organisations, offer information in a language other than English. Social services employ interpreters, and private interpreters may be used by law firms, doctors and schools to ensure everyone can access the information and advice they need.

Information in large print and Braille

People with a visual impairment can request information printed in larger size, or in Braille. This may not be readily available, but will usually be provided if requested beforehand. For example, an individual with a visual impairment could ask their bank to send statements in large print or Braille.

Employment

Adaptations to work environment

A person cannot be dismissed or asked to retire if they become disabled. Employers must adapt the working environment to meet the needs of current or future employees who may have a disability. For example, ramps will need to be installed if access is only by steps. A personal evacuation plan must be prepared for employees and other individuals who access the building who may have impaired mobility. Special equipment must be provided in case there is a fire and the lifts cannot be used. However, the Health and Safety at Work Act 1974 (HASAWA) accepts that it may not be 'reasonable or practicable to make certain adjustments, such as installing a lift in a very old building that lacks space for this type of equipment'.

Employment law

HASAWA protects employers and employees against any form of discrimination. Employers are protected if an employee makes a complaint of discrimination but the employer can prove that certain criteria had been met to ensure equal treatment. For example, an employee has a back problem and needs a specially designed chair. The employer provides the chair but the employee does not use it. The employee's condition worsens, they take time off sick and make a formal complaint against their employer. In this case, the employer has provided the equipment and so can claim protection under employment law. However, if the employer did not supply the required chair and the employee is unable to work because their condition worsens, then the employee has a case for discrimination against their employer.

Employment law also covers areas such as:

▶ Job application forms, which must be inclusive, or alternatives such as in Braille, large print, or in a different language, must be available. If the form is online, the individual must be able to read it using **assistive technology**, such as reading software.

▶ Special arrangements for an interview. For example, ensuring a suitable time is available to interview an individual with type 1 diabetes so that they can balance their insulin injection and carbohydrate intake appropriately (to avoid a hypoglycaemic episode (sugar low)).

▶ Terms of employment, which includes pay, promotion and training opportunities, dismissal, redundancy, discipline and grievances. If an employee feels they have been discriminated against by a work colleague, line manager or their employer concerning any of these points they should complain, in the first instance, directly to the person or organisation. The employee can ask someone else to help ('mediation' or 'alternative dispute resolution') or, if all else fails they can make a claim in a court or tribunal. The Equality Advisory Support Service (EASS) can provide further information and support.

Key term

Assistive technology – devices for people with disabilities that help them to maintain or improve their ability to perform daily living activities.

Research

Go to **www.gov.uk** and search for information about employing people with a disability. What other employment laws protect people's rights at work?

Communication aids

A person returning to work who has become unable to communicate for any reason, such as following a stroke or accident, may require adjustments in their workplace to facilitate communication. Different tools or techniques can be used, such as adaptive keyboards, specialist switches, pointing or scanning devices. Training must be offered on how to use the new equipment and how it works.

Inclusion

Leisure activities

It is important for a person's wellbeing and development to feel they are an integral part of society. Leisure activities are a way of meeting other people, relaxing and keeping fit. The Equality Act 2010 requires centres offering leisure facilities to ensure they are built or adapted so that everyone can use them. For example, a leisure centre must have access for individuals using a wheelchair, including access into the swimming pool (if it has one) by a slope or a hoisting mechanism, accessible changing rooms, shower facilities and toilets. Additionally, parking for disabled drivers must be provided close to the centre, the main entrance doors must be double width and open automatically. All staff working in the centre must have received disability awareness and equal opportunities training.

Internet and social networking

The 2003 World Summit on the Information Society (WSIS) declared that the internet's guiding principle should be that it is for everyone to use. The World Bank estimates that one billion people, or 15 per cent of the world's population, experience some form of disability. Access to and use of the internet can assist people with disabilities to live independently, to communicate their needs to those around them and to maintain relationships, or find new friendships. Therefore, all computer programs need to be designed to be inclusive so that everyone can use them. For a person with a disability this might include using assistive technologies (software programs). For example, a visually impaired or blind person might use assistive technology that converts information on a website from text and images to speech, so they can hear it rather than read it. Removing barriers to using technology enables people with disabilities to use and contribute to the rich culture of the internet. Other barriers may include affordability of a computer and assistive technologies, and the availability of the internet.

> **Discussion**
>
> Discuss the types of support that may be required when using the internet for someone with:
> - dyslexia
> - visual impairment
> - repetitive strain injury (RSI)
> - hearing impairment
> - weakness following a stroke
> - no upper limbs.

> **Research**
>
> Find out about the services and provision made by educational establishments to support learners with additional needs. You could start with:
> - Special Educational Needs (SEN) in schools
> - Additional Learning Support (ALS) in colleges
> - University Disability Advisory Service in universities.
>
> Note: Each university may have a different name for this service, so search generically for '[name of university] disability support'.

PAUSE POINT   Describe access arrangements.

> **Hint**   Access should be for all.
>
> **Extend**   What do you think a person using a wheelchair would do if they could not access a building to meet someone? What laws and regulations cover this situation?

Daily living activities

Shopping

Most people with a disability get help and support with shopping, and other daily living activities, from their family and friends. However, if they need extra support or do not have friends or family who can help, social services may provide assistance. Help with shopping may be particularly required, for example, if a person with agoraphobia (fear of open spaces, especially public spaces) is finding it difficult or impossible to leave their house. People with limited or no mobility will also require help.

If the person has access to the internet and the ability to use it, online shopping may be a suitable way of maintaining choice and independence.

> **Discussion**
>
> How could this person be helped to overcome agoraphobia? What specialist help is needed, and if you were a friend supporting someone with this condition what would you do to help?

Home and personal care services

When someone loses the ability to care for their surroundings and their personal hygiene it can affect their self-esteem, confidence and sense of identity. Having to accept help can feel like a regression to childhood.

Personal care is a particularly difficult area of care for people to accept help with, as it is something you learn to do from an early age, and usually do in privacy. When assisting an individual with their personal/intimate hygiene needs, the carer must be respectful of the individual's privacy and dignity. The carer should be sensitive to their service user's moods and feelings.

Mobility aids

Mobility aids may be needed if a person has a physical disability or a person's age means they may not be as agile as they once were. These aids help with independence, which in turn helps with self-esteem and inclusion. For example, equipment such as a rollator, a three-wheel walker, which can support someone to walk inside their home or outside.

Minimising personal challenges

Physical

Dressing, washing, feeding

Health and social care workers have a responsibility to provide care for their service users, including support and assistance with daily living tasks that their service user can no longer perform unaided. However, whenever possible, you should encourage your service user to do as much as they possibly can for themselves.

Care may involve assistance with a wide range of needs, including personal care such as washing, dressing and feeding. Carers need to pay attention to their service user's privacy, dignity and general comfort while attending to personal care. You should avoid jokes or casual conversations as you may inadvertently embarrass them. However, if they want to talk to you, it could be a good time to find out more about them as a person; their life story, family and friends and their experiences. If your service user is confused and does not understand what is happening to them, you will need to reassure them using a gentle voice, or gentle singing. Everyone is different and you will need to find what helps your service user to cope.

If your service user is unable to feed themselves, make sure you do not rush them. This is especially important if your service user has swallowing difficulties. You should try not to let hot food become cold or, for example, ice-cream to melt. You should prepare food according to your service user's culture and religious needs.

Link

See *Unit 19: Nutritional health.*

Indoor/outdoor activity

Several television documentaries have highlighted concerns about lack of care and activities to stimulate people in residential care. Remaining active and socially involved is important, especially in the earlier stage of dementia where the individual needs to have as near a normal lifestyle as possible. Individuals will enjoy doing different things, which may depend on their mood and mobility. It is important to find out what activities your service user enjoys. This could range from shopping, to watching television, to talking to friends or to going to the theatre. Your service user may enjoy playing games, singing, going for a walk in a nearby park, swimming and many other activities. Each day is different and you may find that your service user's preference will change each day. However, you should offer them the opportunity to take part and have as much fun as possible. There are many video clips online that show how providing stimulating activities for individuals in residential care is beneficial to an individual's self-esteem and confidence, and helps to avoid depression.

▶ A person with Down's syndrome working in a garden centre

Intellectual

▶ Education. Mental stimulation encourages the brain to keep working and has been linked to improving mood. People with additional needs should be supported in accessing the courses and programmes available. However, buildings and equipment may sometimes be a barrier to attending and help may be needed from the local authority. You should also be aware of the many online courses available (often free, for example FutureLearn) and support your service user, if necessary, to access and use them.

▶ Media. Newspapers, magazines, the television and radio may all present challenges for an individual with additional needs. If your service user has a visual impairment, you could help them to choose suitable audio books, or an assistive program on their computer that will convert text to speech. If they have a hearing impairment, many television programmes have audio, subtitle and signing options.

▶ Internet. There are assistive technologies to help people with physical impairments to use computers. Software is available such as a speaking programme that can read text from a website. Text can be enlarged so that someone who has some vision can read from the screen. Local training courses are open for elderly people to attend and learn how to use the internet. Some programs can be built specifically for the needs of your service user, especially if they require help to speak.

▶ Telecommunications. Hearing loops can be installed in buildings for people with hearing impairments. Telephones are available that provide a visual rather than auditory signal for incoming calls. Mobile phones also have accessibility options, such as larger screens, or larger buttons on older types of phones, and options for the phone to vibrate or flash rather than ring for incoming calls and texts.

Emotional

▶ Isolation. The local authority may provide trips and activities for your service user and their families. As a carer you can talk to your service user, and maybe their family, to find out the different activities that may be suitable and which they might enjoy. Keeping active and joining in with social activities helps to stimulate your service user and stop them feeling isolated. Specific charities organise outings for people with additional needs where they can enjoy mixing with other people with additional needs and their families. Socialising with people in similar circumstances can provide a good help and support network.

▶ Depression. Depression is a horrible illness that may be caused when an individual is unable to accept that they have additional needs, or because they feel that they are never given a chance to be themselves. Carers, parents and family members directly involved in the care of an individual with additional needs may also become depressed. Having to provide constant care may damage their relationships with their spouse, other children, family and friends. Children may have learning difficulties, which can be mild or severe. If the disability is severe, they may never become self-sufficient, which can be stressful for the people caring for them. People who have had an accident resulting in life-changing impairments may have particular difficulties in accepting their altered lifestyle.
Your counselling and listening skills will be very important when working with individuals with additional needs and their families. You may be able to suggest ways of coping and involving specialist support at an early stage.

▶ Dependency. Individuals with additional needs may depend or rely on people for care and support. Carers may be family, friends or health professionals. Support can range from simple tasks like buying their favourite magazines, to accompanying them to a leisure centre, to personal care and high-level health support. Social services or other healthcare professionals will assess an individual's needs and arrange for appropriate support to enable them to lead as fulfilling and independent a life as possible. However, carers should not always do everything for the individual as they need to be encouraged to do as much for themselves as possible. This will give them a sense of independence and increase their self-esteem.

▶ Friendships, personal relationships. Family, carers and health professionals should encourage individuals with additional needs to enjoy a social life and to form personal friendships. Enjoying a varied social life and a range of friendships helps to avoid frustration, boredom and depression.

Attitudes of others

Awareness of attitudes and need to support people with additional needs

Working in health and social care, it is likely that you will come up against various forms of **discrimination**. Individuals with additional needs may be the target of personal remarks and strange looks. They may have difficulty accessing buildings, be unable to read signs, people trying to be helpful may make decisions for them, or ask you questions that should be directed at your service user. They may be denied empowerment in meetings as well as during social activities. It is important that your service user is not excluded from decisions concerning them. Your role as a carer will be to ensure that they are empowered and included at all times. You should report any concerns that your service user, or their independence, is being abused to your line manager.

Discrimination usually arises from ignorance about the person discriminated against. Often people who discriminate are unaware of the harm they can cause.

Stereotyping and judgemental assumptions

Stereotyping can cause suffering and unhappiness. For example, just because an individual has a mental health problem, a limb missing, or because they follow a different belief does not mean that they are like everyone else with a mental health problem, a missing limb or of that belief. It is a judgement or assumption about someone. Assuming that an older person would not go to a rave or someone who has lost a leg cannot carry heavy shopping, is making an assumption without knowing what the individual wants or can do. A health and social care worker must be aware of stereotyping and not make assumptions about what their service user can or cannot do, or what they do or do not want and how they are feeling.

Marginalisation

Marginalisation is when a person or a group of people are made to feel excluded, isolated and unimportant. For a person with additional needs this can be a traumatic experience. Many individuals with additional needs may feel excluded from activities, employment and a social life, due to stereotyping and ideas about what the limitations of their disability are, or what people think they should or should not be allowed to do. Lack of accessibility can be marginalising.

Discrimination

Not doing something to help others who have additional needs achieve something they want to do is discriminatory. For example, a person who is paralysed following a stroke who would like to go swimming finding that there is no lifting device to help them into the water. Organisations, especially public organisations, have to make reasonable adjustments to ensure people are not discriminated against, and providing a hoist would be considered a reasonable adjustment.

Disempowerment

An individual with additional needs must be included in any decision-making about their care and medication. This is so that they are empowered in their support and care. It must be decided whether a child is **Gillick competent**; that is, whether they have enough understanding and intelligence to make decisions about their own health and treatment. Empowering individuals, by giving them choices, means that they are more likely to be involved in and comply with a treatment or care plan.

Labelling

Labelling is applying a description to an individual or group of individuals, usually based on their external appearance. Labelling can be positive, such as that a person is good at sport, or it can be negative if it is offensive or derogatory, such as calling someone 'ginger nut' because they have auburn hair.

Key term

Gillick competence – a term used to decide whether a child (aged 16 or under) is considered able to consent to their own medical treatment without the need for parental permission or knowledge. The term originates from a legal case about contraception.

Case study

But words can't hurt

There had been a lot of name calling at break time, but especially aimed at Jorji. Jorji had her right leg amputated following a car accident. She's just getting used to a new prosthesis, but it is making her limp. The other kids had been calling her 'peg-leg' and 'Long John Silver' or asking her if she had lost her parrot or eye patch. She was feeling really low and miserable when she got into her health and social care class.

Mr Adusi, their tutor, was surprised to see some of this behaviour when he was in the college cafeteria. He had thought about it and came up with a new activity for the health and social care group to try. Mr Adusi gave everybody a piece of scrap paper and told them to scrunch it up. He then said they should very quietly tell the paper that it was ugly, horrible, worthless, a waste of space, it should be torn up and burned, and any

other nasty thing they could think of. Mr Adusi then told everyone to open up their piece of paper and apologise to it for saying such nasty things. After the class had done this, Mr Adusi said, 'Although you have apologised to your paper, all the wrinkles you can see are the scars of your abusive language, which will remain for a long time – if not forever'.

Check your understanding

1 Do you think this was a good way to deal with what had happened to Jorji at break time?

2 How do you think the name calling affected Jorji's self-image, confidence and self-esteem?

3 Do you think the people calling Jorji names realised the harm they were causing?

Assessment practice 12.2   B.P2 B.P3 B.M2

Explain how the term disability comes about and how it can be viewed as a social construct.

Using the two scenarios from assessment practice 12.1, describe the help Marion and Bronwyn might receive from health or social care services to overcome the daily challenges that they might face.

Assess the extent to which these challenges impact on the lives of Marion and Bronwyn and how effectively the support from health or social care services can help them overcome their various challenges.

Plan
- What is the task? What is it I have been asked to do?
- How confident do I feel in answering this?
- What areas will I struggle with?

Do
- I know what I am doing.
- I can identify where I need to improve.

Review
- I can evaluate what I have done and how I approached the task.
- I have learnt from this and can make changes to my work to make it better next time.

Investigate current practice with respect to provision for individuals with additional needs

Professionals involved in supporting individuals with additional needs

Many professional services are involved in supporting people with additional needs. Each profession has entry qualification requirements and training standards that must be met by people working within the support system.

Community learning disability nurse

The role of the community learning disability nurse is specifically about supporting people with a learning disability to meet their full potential. The role involves helping a person to be physically and mentally healthy, working with them in their home, at their educational setting, in their workplace or in a community or residential home. The nurse also supports people with a learning disability to access healthcare services and acts as their advocate; the nurse explains what is happening if they are confused, and helps other healthcare professionals to understand the individual's support needs.

Occupational therapist

Occupational therapists (OTs) support individuals in carrying out everyday activities. Individuals may require support with daily living activities if they were born with a disability, such as cerebral palsy, or acquire a disability, such as weakness or paralysis following a stroke or they are recovering from an illness or injury. OTs advise people how to carry out tasks, which may involve using supportive equipment or assistive technology, or helping them to adapt to a new way of doing a task. OTs may work in a hospital, in a person's home, at a GP practice, at a person's workplace or in an educational setting.

Physiotherapist

Physiotherapists work with people who have a physical difficulty as a result of illness, ageing, being injured at work or playing sport, or following a stroke. Physiotherapists devise treatment programmes of manual therapy, therapeutic exercise or ultrasound, to improve movement and functioning, as well as general health and wellbeing. They may use other techniques, such as exercises carried out in water (hydrotherapy or aquatic therapy) or acupuncture.

Physiotherapists mainly work in a hospital or specialist rehabilitation setting, but may visit people in their homes.

Psychiatrist

Psychiatrists are medical doctors who have undergone additional training to specialise in the diagnosis and treatment of mental and emotional disorders. They support people with conditions such as depression, bipolar affective disorder, learning difficulties, anxiety, eating disorders, schizophrenia, dementia, and drug and alcohol abuse. A psychiatrist may further specialise in adult or child care, to work with adolescents, old people, people with a learning disability, or in forensic, medical and liaison psychiatry. A psychiatrist may work in a medical setting in a general or an acute specialist hospital, or they may visit people in their homes.

Psychologist

A clinical psychologist will have gained a degree in psychology and further studied for a doctorate in clinical psychology. Clinical psychologists support people with a wide range of mental health problems including depression, eating disorders, harmful thought

▶ A physiotherapist working with a client

patterns and addiction, children with behavioural and emotional difficulties and young offenders. They are interested in their patients' psychological rather than physiological condition, and use therapies such as **cognitive behavioural therapy (CBT)**. Psychologists normally work in NHS settings in hospitals and health centres as part of a mental health team. They may also work in social services, in educational settings and in prisons.

The difference between a psychiatrist and a psychologist

Psychiatrists and psychologists have different approaches to solving mental health problems. They are both trained in psychotherapy – talking with individuals about their problems. However, psychiatrists are medical doctors whereas psychologists have a doctoral degree in an area of psychology, and they are not medical doctors.

As they are medically trained doctors, psychiatrists can prescribe medication to treat their patients. They will investigate whether there is an underlying biological or neurochemical problem causing their patients' symptoms, such as a vitamin deficiency or thyroid dysfunction. Psychologists study their patients' behaviour, their sleep patterns, eating patterns and negative thoughts and work with the patient to change or modify these behaviours.

Social worker

Social work involves a wide area of work and many specialisms. A social worker supports people and their families through difficult situations, and in improving their current lifestyle. They work with vulnerable people, helping to protect them from abuse or harm. They support people to live independently. Their client groups can include elderly individuals, children and adults with physical and learning disabilities, young offenders, people with mental health problems, people with addiction problems, refugees and asylum seekers, foster carers, adopters and families who are potentially breaking up. Social workers may work in a hospital, a local authority setting, young offenders units, special clinics and prisons. They also visit people in their homes. Social workers are usually part of a multidisciplinary team working with a variety of other professionals, such as doctors, nurses and police officers, to support their clients.

Speech and language therapist

Speech and language therapists support people who have difficulties in speaking and communicating, eating, drinking and swallowing. They work with people with a range of speech and language difficulties including language delay, voice disorders, stammering, language impairment and selective mutism (an anxiety disorder that prevents an individual, usually a child, from speaking in certain social situations). These conditions may be caused by a stroke, a head injury, Parkinson's disease, dementia, throat cancer, learning difficulties, mental health issues, hearing impairment or other physical disabilities. Speech and language therapists mainly work in hospitals, educational settings and community health centres; they may visit a person in their home.

> **Key term**
>
> **Cognitive behavioural therapy (CBT)** – a practical talking therapy used to improve an individual's state of mind, helping them to manage problems by changing the way they think or behave. CBT focuses on current problems or issues, rather than on what happened to an individual in the past.

▶ A teacher interacting with child with learning disabilities

243

Special needs teachers

Special educational needs teachers (SENs) specialise in working with children who have specific needs such as physical difficulties, sensory impairments, speech and language difficulties, learning difficulties or a variety of other physical, social or emotional needs. The person coordinating learning support is known as a SENCO. In an educational setting, SENs and SENCOs are assisted by teaching assistants who look after children's physical needs and provide additional support for learners, for example helping them understand instructions, and providing comfort and reassurance when children are frustrated or upset.

Some children with learning disabilities may have more than one disability such as auditory and visual impairment, which makes communicating difficult. Children with multiple learning difficulties need specific learning strategies to support their educational needs and the SEN's key role is to identify and support their individual needs. SENs create safe, stimulating and supportive learning environments in which they deliver individualised teaching programmes to develop the children in their care to their full potential.

Support and adaptations for individuals with additional needs

Equipment and adaptations

Special equipment and communication aids are important to enable people with additional needs to carry out daily tasks, live independently and feel included in society.

Mobility aids

Mobility aids help an individual with a physical disability to walk. This, in turn, enables them to perform a range of tasks such as preparing and cooking food, and dressing and going to the toilet. They also help them to go to work, have hobbies and take part in activities. Examples of mobility aids include motorised scooters, wheelchairs, walking frames, stairlifts, adjustable beds and chair raisers.

Daily living adaptations

There is a vast range of equipment available to assist people with everyday tasks, such as making a cup of tea. Occupational therapists will assess individual needs and supply appropriate equipment based on that assessment. Adaptive equipment for everyday use is available for all areas of the home and workplace and includes items such as perching stools, food trolleys, kettle tippers, support and grab rails, raised toilet seats, commodes, shower chairs, fall monitors and flashing doorbells.

Paraplegia is paralysis (complete loss of functioning) of both lower limbs, usually caused by a spinal cord injury below the level of the first thoracic verterbra, or in some rare cases by an illness. Individuals may also experience a range of other changes such as incontinence of urine and faeces, issues with body temperature control and chronic pain. Following the accident or illness that caused paraplegia, an individual will initially be cared for in a hospital setting. However, in the longer term, people with paraplegia are usually cared for in their own home. A variety of assistive equipment is available to support their care, including pressure relieving mattresses and pads, hoists and other transfer aids to assist moving position, powered or manually operated wheelchairs, ramps, incontinence pads, reachers (to help pick up small items) grab rails and aids to help with dressing.

Communication aids

Communication aids may be used by people with a speech, visual or hearing impairment to help them interact and exchange ideas and information with other

Research

Using the internet, research aids to daily living and make a list of items that are available to support people with additional needs, including those for individuals with paraplegia.

people. Aids range from simple communication boards to sophisticated electronic equipment.

▶ Communication boards can assist with verbalisation or replace speech if for any reason an individual cannot communicate verbally. They usually contain letters, common words or phrases and images of everyday items. The individual can simply point to the letters, words or images to communicate their needs. They are also known as symbol boards, word boards or letter boards and include Bliss boards.

▶ Information may be provided in large print or Braille for individuals with visual impairments.

▶ Assistive technologies are available such as software to convert text to speech, or to enable operation by eye gaze or voice recognition, and computer switches for easier internet access.

▶ Sign language communicates by using gestures, facial expressions and body language. It is used mainly by people with hearing impairments. British Sign Language (BSL) is the preferred language in the UK for people with hearing impairments.

▶ Makaton is a language programme designed for individuals who experience frustration because they cannot communicate properly. It helps people to communicate by using signs and symbols, which are used in spoken word order, alongside speech. This provides extra clues about what someone is saying.

▶ Some people with hearing impairments learn to lip read. Some people are really good at this skill, which is made much easier if the person talking speaks clearly. Clear speech involves making sure that words are pronounced properly and slightly louder, and that speech is slightly slower – with pauses between key phrases.
People with hearing impairments can also use technical aids such as hearing aids and cochlear implants to augment hearing. Hearing aids may lessen the impact of hearing loss. Some people do not want to wear a hearing aid as they think it will be unsightly or make them look old. However, digital hearing aids are small and work better than older analogue aids. Cochlear implants are electronic devices that are surgically implanted to replace the function of a damaged inner ear. They do not amplify sounds but act like the cochlea and provide sound signals directly to the brain.

▶ People using BSL

Therapies

Occupational therapy

Occupational therapy involves assessing an individual's needs and creating an individual treatment plan to support those needs. The plan will identify goals, which have been agreed with the service user, to maintain, regain, or improve independence. Various techniques may be used including changes to an individual's home or work environment, and using specialised equipment. After identifying the difficulties a person has with everyday tasks, occupational therapists can help by working with the individual to teach them how to do a task or use specialised equipment, and by helping them practise until they feel confident to do the task or use equipment alone.

People with depression may lack the drive or energy to carry out everyday activities such as getting up in the morning, washing and dressing or socialising. Their lack of energy can affect their ability to work, or to keep a job. Occupational therapy can also help to motivate them, help them to develop coping strategies and to balance their energy levels with work requirements.

Case study

Sasha – clinical depression

Sasha was diagnosed with clinical depression ten years ago, when she was sixteen. She has feelings of guilt, disturbed sleep, self-harms and has been suicidal. Sasha has been in and out of work since she was 19. She tends to leave jobs when she feels unable to cope, or is too ill to leave home.

Sasha has been in her current job for six months. She works in a large, open-plan office with twelve other people. Recently, Sasha appears withdrawn, she has unexplained and prolonged crying spells, is often late for work and forgetful. Colleagues find her odd and are not sure how to approach her. Sasha has received a letter from her line manager asking her to attend a meeting and telling her that someone from HR will also be there. The letter also tells Sasha that she can bring a friend with her for support, if she wishes to do so. Sasha is very upset by what this meeting may mean and asks her occupational health worker, Dana, for help. She has also asked Dana to come to the meeting with her.

Check your knowledge

1   How might the occupational health worker support Sasha in the meeting?

2   What information would the occupational health-worker be able to give regarding Sasha's condition?

3   What do you think might be the right way forward for both Sasha and her employer?

Art therapy

Art therapy is a form of psychotherapy. Art therapists work with people of all ages, who may have a wide range of difficulties or disabilities such as mental health problems, learning disabilities, physical illnesses or impairments or behavioural issues. Various art media such as painting, sculpting and pottery are used to help individuals express themselves. Therapy may be delivered to an individual or to a group.

Music therapy

Music therapy is an established way of helping people to cope with injury, illness or disability. Music affects people at an emotional level and, depending on the context and the music, can make an individual feel happy or sad. It can evoke memories and people often associate specific pieces of music with significant life events. Most people respond to music, and music therapists build on this to enable individuals to maximise their emotional wellbeing. A wide range of musical interventions can be used, including different styles of music and using different instruments (including voice). Recent research has found that singing in a choir has more positive effects on mental wellbeing than playing team sports.

Speech therapy

Speech and language therapy provides support and care for children and adults with communication, eating, drinking and swallowing difficulties. Therapy will start with an assessment of the individual's specific speech. Where there is a physical disorder, such as tongue tie (tightness between the underside of the tongue and floor of the mouth) making it difficult for a baby to feed, the therapist will work with other health professionals to resolve the problem. If an individual has problems with articulation or fluency, the speech therapist will show them how to make the proper sounds, this involves the individual practising the sounds until they are confident in making the right sound. Sometimes, the therapist will ask the individual to look in a mirror to help them see that they are making the right shapes with their mouth. When dealing with young children, this will often be presented as a fun activity.

Physiotherapy

Physiotherapy helps to bring back movement and functions of joints and muscles when someone has been injured, had an illness or been immobile, has had an operation or has a disability. It may also be used to train individuals, particularly people with back injuries or following sporting injuries, to avoid future damage. Physiotherapists look at the health and wellbeing of the individual rather than simply concentrating on their specific injury or illness.

Short and long-term support

Some individuals with additional needs only require short-term support; for example, when it is following an accident, or an operation, and therapy will usually be in a hospital setting. However, some individuals will need longer term therapy which may be delivered in a specialist centre or in their own home. Individuals with conditions such as cystic fibrosis will need chest percussion all their lives, so this technique may be taught to family members or close friends. Long-term support will usually involve a multidisciplinary team and require frequent review to ensure that an individual's needs are met as they get older or their condition changes.

❚❚ PAUSE POINT   List a range of communication aids available for someone who cannot verbalise.

Hint   Think visually.

Extend   Investigate a communication system that helps a person relate to the world about them.

Financial support for individuals with additional needs

Individuals who are absent from work for a long time due to injury, illness or disability may require financial support, which will usually be in the form of state benefits. Specific information about the exact amounts that an individual may claim can be found on the government's website. Even if the individual thinks they know what they can claim for, it is essential to check the website as benefits change. People working in the health and social care sector should also keep up to date with information about financial support that the people they are supporting may be entitled to.

Welfare rights

Welfare rights mean that an individual has the right to know what benefits they are entitled to and to receive their entitlement of state benefits. It is also an individual's right to be treated fairly by the system.

State Pension

In the UK, people who have reached their pension age can claim a state retirement pension (SRP) if they have made sufficient contribution, through National Insurance payments. In some cases where full contributions have not been paid, an individual may be entitled to a reduced pension payment.

Pension Credit

Pension Credit is an income-related benefit made up of two parts, a guarantee credit and a savings credit. A guarantee credit tops up a person's weekly income if it falls below a certain amount. A savings credit is an extra payment for people who have saved money towards their retirement.

Housing Benefit

If an individual's income is below a certain threshold, Housing Benefit will be paid towards costs such as rent. The amount an individual receives depends on their income and personal circumstances. It cannot be used to pay for heating, hot water, energy or food.

Council Tax Benefit

Each council runs their own scheme. It will depend where a person lives as to how much they will receive in benefit. It will also depend on personal circumstances; for example, residency status, if there are a number of children living in the property and whether any other benefits are being claimed.

Health benefits

Individuals whose income is below a certain level can get help with some healthcare costs, or exemptions from charges; for example, they may be eligible for free dentistry, free prescriptions and free eye tests.

Support for people at work

Disability Employment Advisors (DEA)

People with conditions or disabilities that affect their ability to work can get support and assistance from a work coach. Work coaches can be accessed via Jobcentre Plus. They are trained to help you to find work and, if necessary, retrain to gain new skills. They can also help with advocacy, interview training and preparing an individual to re-enter the workforce.

Work Choice Programme

Work Choice is a government supported disability employment programme providing support to people with complex disabilities who cannot be supported through mainstream employment programmes. The programme helps people with disabilities to become work ready, find work and stay in employment. The programme is run by many charitable organisations.

Transport

Blue Badge scheme

The Blue Badge scheme operates through local authorities for people who are registered disabled. It may be used by the person who is registered or they can nominate two drivers to help with transport needs. Displaying their Blue Badge entitles the individual to park in disabled parking bays, usually near to main entrances of shops, workplaces, health and leisure centres and other buildings. The local authority can be asked to put a parking bay outside the home of a person registered as having mobility impairment.

Shopmobility

Shopmobility is a scheme to allow access to shopping areas for people with additional needs, especially mobility needs. It is mainly a free service, although there may be a small charge in some areas. Shopmobility provides manual or electric wheelchairs, scooters, rollators and portable hearing loops. Several supermarkets operate their own assistance for people needing mobility support.

▶ Ramp being used on a bus by a person in a wheelchair

Accessible buses and taxis

The Public Service Vehicles Accessibility Regulations 2000 (PSVAR) cover issues of access to public transport. With the exception of a few older buses, all buses now have access ramps for people who use wheelchairs or pushchairs, and space has been made available on the bus for the wheelchair or pushchair. At busy times, precedence is given to people using wheelchairs over those with pushchairs. Bus companies are also required to provide information systems on every bus, such as an auditory information system for people with visual impairments, and a visual display system for people with hearing impairments or who are deaf. The companies must also ensure that priority seats for elderly people, people with a mobility problem and women who are pregnant are near to the entry and exit doors.

Most taxi companies provide a taxi with an accessibility ramp. A person requiring this type of assistance will be given priority when booking the taxi. The majority of licensed black cabs have fitted ramps. A person using a guide dog is permitted to take their dog in a taxi, unless the driver has an exemption certificate to show that they are severely allergic to dogs.

Support for carers

Carers have a high level of responsibility and need to be cared for too. The Care Act 2014 recognises this, and also the health and financial problems that can affect carers. The Act mainly deals with carers over the age of 18. Clause 10 of the Care Act requires that carers receive an assessment to consider how the provision of support would enable a carer to achieve their desired day-to-day outcomes. The assessment must also consider whether the carer is willing, and able, to continue to care. It will also consider the resources and support the carer can access from the wider community.

Carers Allowance

Caring can be challenging in many ways. It may mean that the carer is unable to work and that the household's income is low, causing financial hardship. Carers allowance is a benefit available for a carer of an individual claiming disability allowance, an attendance allowance or the daily living component of the Personal Independence Payment (PIP). The carer must provide care for at least 35 hours a week. Rules change regularly so it is advisable to check the current rules and regulations for claiming this allowance.

Statutory provision for children with additional needs

Legislation applicable to England, Wales or Northern Ireland periodically changes. It is always worth checking what legislation currently applies to the area you live in.

Common Assessment Framework (CAF)

The CAF is a system for gathering information concerning a child's needs and assessing how these needs can be met by the relevant support services. This may include occupational health, physiotherapy and counselling, support with travel, education and support for any other needs. The CAF was introduced under the agenda of Every Child Matters and is a voluntary process requiring informed consent from the child and their parents/carers.

The CAF is for children in need of support in one or more of three areas:

▸ growth and development
▸ additional educational requirements
▸ family and environment issues and any specific needs of the parent/carer.

Special Educational Needs and the Local Offer

The Local Offer is a regulation ensuring that children with special educational needs receive all the support they need from local health services and schools in the local area.

Every local authority has to write a Local Offer that is available on the internet. The local authority must also make sure that people without access to the internet can see it. Under this regulation, the local authority must provide the child and their family or carers with information about all healthcare and educational support networks available to them. The child and their family or carers are consulted to see which local offer best meets the needs of that child to ensure their health and wellbeing, and best prepares the child for adulthood and independent living.

To do this accurately, local authorities have to consult with various agencies. This includes all local education providers, from early years up to and including university, and their governors, or proprietors, or advisory boards. It also includes youth offending teams, and anybody involved in preparing children and young people for adulthood and independent living.

The local authority will also have to consult the National Service Commissioning boards, Clinical Commissioning groups, the local NHS trust or NHS foundation in the area, the local health board, and the local health and wellbeing board about issues relating to health.

The Local Offer should also provide information about the transport services available to children and young people with special educational needs or disabilities, and whether there is help available to pay for these services.

Education, Health and Care plans (EHCs)

Local health and education services have to produce an EHC plan for children, and young people up to the age of 25, with special educational needs and disabilities. The EHC identifies and plans the support required, and sets out what has to be in place to support the specific child or young person. This plan follows the child/young person through their education and is reviewed regularly by health and educational personnel involved in providing the support.

 **PAUSE POINT**   Name two statutory provisions for children with additional needs.

        Hint   Statutory means a requirement set in law.

        Extend   Explain the Special Education Needs (Local Offer) and see how this is in place in your educational setting.

Codes of practice for children with special educational needs

The Special Educational Needs and Disability (SEND) code of practice provides statutory guidance for health services, local authorities, educational settings and youth offending teams, to ensure that all services provide the best support for a child and young person with additional needs.

Statutory provision for adults with additional needs

Codes of practice, legislation and policies

Health and social care workers caring for adults or children with additional needs must be aware of and follow current legislation, codes of practice and policies. These require that the person with additional needs should be properly supported; and further require that the individual is not discriminated against in employment, in an educational setting, or when supported at home. These codes of practice and policies are based on guidance and recommendations set out in the Human Rights Act 1998, the Equality Act 2010, and the Northern Ireland Act 1998, Part VII.

Care and support statutory guidance under the Care Act 2014

The Care Act 2014 covers the requirements for support for people over 18 years old who need additional support. The Act requires local councils to provide care services for people with additional needs, to prevent problems before they arise. Local councils are responsible for giving the right advice and guidance to individuals and their families. Information includes the correct support for their needs, information about voluntary support groups and other health organisations or charities. The local authority must ensure that the individual and their carers understand the law and receive the care they are entitled to. If an individual's additional needs are not met, they have the right to ask the courts to decide whether the local authority abided by the Care Act or not. The care and support provided for covers a wide range of individual needs, such as assistance with:

- getting out of or into bed
- washing (body)
- eating or cooking
- socialising with family and friends.

It also covers the needs of the carer, to ensure they are looked after as much as possible. It enables individuals requiring additional care to ask a friend, a family member or someone else of their choice to provide that care, rather than someone provided by the local authority. The government pays towards the service, which is means-tested to see how much funding a person is entitled to.

Guidelines for caring for adults with mental illness

The National Service Framework for Mental Health

This framework sets out the national quality standards for mental health services, making services easier to access and creating a provision that can prevent crises for individuals with mental health problems. These quality standards help the service user and their carers by:

- involving them in the planning and receiving of care
- delivering quality care and treatment
- being non-discriminatory
- being accessible to people who need it
- promoting independence
- being accountable.

It also supports children under the age of 18 who have a mental disorder, or who are living with someone who is mentally ill.

Mental Health Act 2007

The Mental Health Act 2007 is legislation in England and Wales that sets out the processes for admitting people with mental health disorders to hospital, detaining them and treating them without their consent. It also states the safeguarding requirements to follow if a person is seen as a threat to themselves or to others. The term sectioning may be used when people are admitted and treated compulsorily; this refers to the various sections of the Act that apply to the circumstances of their admission.

The Act recognises civil partners and long-term unmarried partners in its list of nearest relatives. The nearest relative has certain rights, including that they must be informed about decisions to detain their relative for treatment, unless it is not practicable to do so or it would result in an unreasonable delay to treatment. They can also apply to have their relative admitted to hospital compulsorily for assessment and treatment, although this power is rarely used. They can also ask for their relative to be discharged, unless a judge or magistrate has ordered the detention.

If an individual with a mental health problem thinks the person legally named as their nearest relative is unsuitable to make decisions about their care, they can apply to the County Court to change the named person.

If an individual with a mental health disorder needs an advocate, the Act requires the local authority to ensure that an independent mental health advocate is provided. If an individual with a mental health disorder is under 18 years of age, the hospital is required to provide appropriate accommodation that is suitable for someone of their age.

Mental Capacity Act 2005

The Mental Capacity Act 2005 is legislation applying to carers or families looking after individuals with profound and multiple learning disabilities (PMLD) or with Alzheimer's disease who do not have the mental capacity to look after themselves in a safe way or make decisions about their own welfare. The Act requires that a person who lacks mental capacity has legal representation by act of attorney to involve their families and carers in making decisions about personal welfare, property and affairs in the best interest for the person lacking mental capacity.

Personal health budget

A personal health budget is an agreed amount of money to be used for an individual's identified health and wellbeing needs. The local NHS teams work with an individual needing a support plan and agree the budget with the individual.

The NHS introduced personal health budgets to help people needing care to manage it in the way that they want. The main aim is to allow individuals with long-term health conditions or disabilities to be in control of and have choice about their health care and support. A care plan is organised with the NHS team that sets the outcomes the person wants to achieve, and a budget is applied to this. The individual can allocate money to the care they want; for example, they could use it for therapies, equipment and assistive technology, and personal care.

Requirements for charities providing essential care and support

The Charity Commission is the regulatory body that covers the legal requirements for all charities. All documents relating to running particular charities and their statutory regulations can be found on the UK government website. Under the law, charities working with people and children who need care and support have a duty of care to make sure their service users are safe and protected from harm. To do this, charities have to carry out enhanced criminal record checks before staff start to work with vulnerable people. The charities must also have a safeguarding policy in place to make staff and users aware of abuse, what it is and how to spot and report it, and how to respond to abuse rapidly and with confidentiality. If a charity works with children, a Child Protection Policy must also be in place.

The government acknowledges that support should be person-centred and that people should be able to choose their support, and that an integrated system of support can work for some people. In the integrated support system, charities are involved in providing a seamless service between other agencies providing care and support for a person. Charities can offer a cost effective way of providing care. Although they receive commissions from the NHS, they can also self-finance through donations. The NHS is responsible for the quality of service provided and charities work closely with them to ensure that all care guidelines are met. Charities are accountable for the services they provide. They must also agree to co-operate with other services involved in an individual's care by ensuring that all data relating to a person's risk factors, identified needs, care plans and status are shared in the best interest of that person.

Health and wellbeing boards were established by the Health and Social Care Act 2012. They provide a network for key health and care personnel to work together to improve the health and wellbeing, and reduce the health inequalities, of a local population. Charities form part of this network.

Rudy has complex needs

Rudy is fifteen years old and has dyslexia and a visual impairment. He has recently been diagnosed as having attention deficit hyperactivity disorder, ADHD. Rudy attends a school where he sees a special educational needs teacher for support with his visual impairment and a specialist for support with his dyslexia. He also meets with a specialist at the local hospital for support with his visual impairment. He has an Education and Health Care plan for supporting his needs related to dyslexia and visual impairment. Local services, his family and the school are now looking at how they can support his needs relating to ADHD.

Check your knowledge

1 What should the school and local health authority do now?

2 How might Rudy be involved?

3 How might Rudy feel about a) not being involved or b) being involved with his support?

Person-centred care for all individuals with special needs

Involving patients in their own care

Throughout this unit, it has been stressed that it is essential to involve individuals in decisions about their care. It is important to ensure that individuals requiring care are shown compassion, dignity and respect. Even if a person is not able to communicate, they need to be informed about what is happening to them, how they are being cared for, by whom and why.

Involving patients as equal partners in decision-making

People who have disabilities or care needs due to illness or injury should be involved in decisions about their care and have a choice about how they are cared for. Each health organisation has an advisory committee team, which should include a service user in any decision-making about service provision. Patients should be treated as equal partners in their care and support, and this will mean including them in decisions about:

▶ self-managed support

▶ access to personal health records

▶ personal health budgets

▶ care planning and treatment decisions.

In 2010, the government presented *Equity and Excellence: Liberating the NHS*. The maxim of this report is that there should be 'no decision about me without me'. The report sets out to make the NHS accountable to patients, to increase shared decision making and allow patients to access all their records, so that they can make informed decisions about their treatment. It also proposes increased funding to achieve these aims.

Involving communities in decisions about the design and delivery of services

Equity and Excellence: Liberating the NHS looks at supporting local communities to lead decisions about their delivery of health services. The report recognises that local health authorities are best placed to meet the care of their communities. Depending on their facilities, local health authorities can also offer competition for services, so that costs can be reduced for services. This offers cross-relationships between health authorities providing services, depending on expertise and contracts, and may offer better quality and value. The report suggests that involving communities in decisions puts patients at the heart of health care, so that they can choose the services they want and where they want them from.

A major concern of all health authorities is the increasing care needs of elderly people. There are currently more than 10 million people over 65 years old in the UK and projections are that this will rise to 19 million by 2050. This poses significant issues for local health authorities trying to design local health services for the future.

Assessment practice 12.3   C.P4   C.P5   C.M3   C.M4   BC.D2   BC.D3

Scenario 1

Adrian has autism spectrum disorder (ASD) and receives support through the SEN department of his secondary school. He was assessed in primary school and given an Education and Health Care plan (EHC). This involved input from his doctor, nursery school, family and a child psychologist. The plan gives advice on how Adrian works and what he finds difficult, as well as strategies to help him overcome difficulties which frustrate him. The school regularly meets with an ASD specialist who also visits Adrian to discuss with him and his family any changes to his support plan. Adrian can let the specialist know how he is getting on with the support he is receiving.

Scenario 2

Anna-Regina lives alone and has been diagnosed with early stage dementia. She has started to forget the names of her distant family and grandchildren. Some days she forgets to eat but she does not want to go into a rest home. Her daughters have contacted social services and her GP. It has been agreed that a health visitor will visit regularly to assess Anna-Regina. The health visitor ensures Anna-Regina takes her medicine and eats a hot meal that her daughters have prepared for her and left in the freezer.

- Explain and analyse the benefits that the various support measures should have on Adrian and Anna-Regina's lives.
- Explain what statutory provision they both receive and the impact it should have on their lives.
- Analyse the extent to which statutory provision affects current practice in caring for individuals with additional needs.
- Evaluate the impact of the support they are both receiving in terms of their improved wellbeing and life chances.
- Justify the support these two people receive to help them overcome daily challenges in connection to statutory provision.

Plan
- What is the task? What is it I have been asked to do?
- How confident do I feel in answering this?
- What areas will I struggle with?

Do
- I know what I am doing.
- I can identify where I need to improve.

Review
- I can evaluate what I have done and how I approached the task.
- I have learned from this and can make changes to my work to make it better next time.

Further reading and resources

Mental Health Act 2007, Ch.12. Available from: **www.legislation.gov.uk**

Mental Capacity Act 2005. Available from: **www.legislation.gov.uk**

Care Act 2014. Available from: **www.legislation.gov.uk**

Part M of the Building Regulations 2010. Available from: **webarchive. nationalarchives.gov.uk**

Department for Health (May 2013). *Integrated Care and Support: Our Shared Commitment.*

Department for Health (2010). *Equity and Excellence: Liberating the NHS.*

Centre for Research in Social Policy (2012). *Accessibility Planning Policy: Evaluation and Future Directions.*

Communities and Local Government (2005). *Planning and access for disabled people: a good practice guide.*

Kirby, A. (2002). *Dyspraxia: The Hidden Handicap.* London: Souvenir Publishers Ltd.

Colley, M. (2006). *Living with Dyspraxia: A Guide for Adults with Developmental Dyspraxia.* London: Jessica Kingsley Publishers Ltd.

Websites

Learning disabilities

General: **www.bild.org.uk, www.nhs.uk**

ADHD: **www.adhdfoundation.org.uk, www.ukadhd.com, nimh.nih.gov**

Autism spectrum disorders: **www.autismspeaks.org**

Dyspraxia: dyspraxiafoundation.org.uk **www.nhs.uk**

Down's syndrome: **www.downs-syndrome.org.uk**

Other conditions

Alzheimer's disease: **www.alzheimers.org.uk**

Diabetes: **www.diabetes.org.uk**

Disability: **www.scope.org.uk**

Heart disease: **www.bhf.org.uk**

HIV/Aids: **www.healthtalk.org**

Huntington's disease: **http://hda.org.uk**

Sensory impairment: **www.sense.org.uk, www.hearingdogs.org.uk, www.rnib. org.uk, www.guidedogs.org.uk**

Stroke: **http://pathways.nice.org.uk/pathways/stroke**

Mental health

General: **www.anxietyuk.org.uk, www.mind.org.uk**

The Samaritans: **www.samaritans.org**

General

Health and Safety Executive: **www.hse.gov.uk**

Citizens Advice: **www.citizensadvice.org.uk**

THINK ▶▶FUTURE

Angela Douglas-Hills

Disability advisor

I've been arranging support for learners who have a learning difficulty and/or disability, for eleven years. Part of my job involves me assessing their support needs and arranging the appropriate support in order for them to access the college and all the college's facilities. Support includes assisting learners with mobility or visual impairments to move around college, note taking (for learners who have dyslexia, ADHD or any other learning difficulty that makes it difficult for them to concentrate, or have a physical disability that affects their motor skills) and arranging assistive technology for learners who find the regular college equipment difficult to use. I discuss the individual learner's needs with the relevant staff, and the support that will be put in place for them. Everyone involved with the learners know that they should inform me if there are problems. Additionally, I have regular review meetings with all staff and the learners we're supporting to ensure that everything is going to plan.

I obtained a social science degree. Afterwards, I worked mainly in playgroups and day centres with children with disabilities, I also gained experience working with women and children fleeing domestic violence. I went to Italy for three years to teach English to young children and adults, mainly to have a break from my work. After returning to the UK, I spent two years working in a day centre supporting clients with a range of disabilities, before starting work at this college. This range of experience helped me to gain a better understanding of supporting learners with additional needs.

Focusing your skills

Risk assessment

- When I meet a learner for the first time, I need to know if they have an Educational Health Care (EHC) plan that tells me what their specific needs are and what support they had at their previous school or college.
- I work with the learner to assess their current support needs and the specific support they will need while at college.
- To do this effectively, I need to know the details of the Equality Act 2010 and the college's legal responsibility to provide support for learners with learning difficulties and/or disabilities, including learners with mental health problems.
- I follow confidentiality rules by making sure all my notes are kept in a secure place, and I only pass on to members of staff on a need-to-know basis and with the learner's consent.
- I attend regular safeguarding training to ensure I'm up to date with current practice. I'm also up to date with college procedures about reporting safeguarding incidents, which I occasionally have to do.
- In some cases, I undertake additional risk assessment to ensure learners stay safe within college, including personal evacuation plans (PEPs) for learners who would need assistance to evacuate the building during an emergency.
- I sometimes liaise with other agencies to obtain more information about a specific learner's additional needs or to provide feedback on their progression at college. These agencies may include a learner's mental health support team, their social services care worker, the local education authority and their occupational therapist.

Getting ready for assessment

Faith is working towards a BTEC National in Health and Social Care. For learning aim B, Faith was given an assignment titled 'How to support one child who is blind and one adult with a mental health problem to overcome challenges to daily living'. She had to write a feature for a college magazine being published in December explaining a day in the life of those people, and how they overcome the challenges they face during the day and evening. The article had to:

- explain their disability
- assess the impact of the challenges they face during that day
- justify the support they receive to help them throughout the day, referencing statutory provision.

Faith shares her experience below.

How I got started

First I collected all my notes on this topic and put them into a folder. I divided my notes into the three parts, a general part, which explained what a disability is, then a specific part for the additional needs of the child and a part for the adult. I needed to make sure I included enough work in each section to meet all the criteria. I made sure I had information on what is meant by having a disability, the research I did to assess the impact of the challenges the child faced during a day, and the research I did on the adult and their challenges.

I arranged to meet a child with a mobility problem who used a wheelchair and was willing to be part of my project and their parents to ensure they knew what I was going to do and write. I then went to the secondary school which the child attended to ask if I could observe how staff supported the child, and to see what challenges the child had in that day at school. I designed a survey-type questionnaire for the child to complete from the time they woke up until the time I arrived, so I had their experience of washing, dressing and having breakfast. I then went with them to school and watched what happened, and wrote notes on challenges they faced in lessons, eating lunch and using the school's facilities. After school I asked them to carry on the questionnaire for the evening. Once the child had completed the questionnaire I picked it up and put the research in my folder. I also arranged to do the same with an adult; my friend's grandmother, who has dementia, and lives with them. I observed what I could during a Saturday when we went shopping with her grandmother and had lunch together. I kept notes and made sure everyone knew that my notes were confidential and that real names wouldn't be mentioned.

How I brought it all together

I decided to use a variety of fonts, colours and pictures to make the work look interesting. (I was careful to avoid pictures of the individuals I was working with to protect their confidentiality.) To start, I wrote a short introduction to the article. For each person, I:

- wrote a 'case study' to show their daily routines

- assessed the challenges they had during the day
- wrote in detail justifying the support they needed to ensure they were able to live their lives, and then looked at their statutory rights in the care needs and the duty of care for children and the elderly.

For case studies and examples, I took some from my lessons and my visit to the school and with the elderly person. Finally, I wrote a short summary as a conclusion to the article.

What I learned from the experience

I wished I'd made clearer notes during my visits as I realised afterwards that I didn't have all the information I needed. It was really good to observe the two case studies during a day, but I wished I'd stayed with the child in the evening when she went to the cinema. I had the notes she'd made, but I think if I'd observed her in the evening I would've had a better idea. I wasn't really ready for the visit to my friend's grandmother. I think I should've observed her for a short time at first, then I would've felt more confident in doing a real observation. I was a bit taken aback by it all.

Next time I would get organised quicker and look at all the things I needed before I started my observations, so I would look at the statutory rights as I was doing it so I could ask questions of the people concerned rather than writing what I thought about it afterwards and having to call them back to ask questions, which made me look as if I hadn't planned it well enough, which I hadn't. At the end it was a rush!

Think about it

- Have you written a plan with timings so you can complete your assignment by the agreed submission date?
- Do you have notes on statutory rights for each age group that will help you when explaining why the support is needed and how it is used?
- Is your information written in your own words and referenced clearly where you have used quotations or information from a book, journal or website?

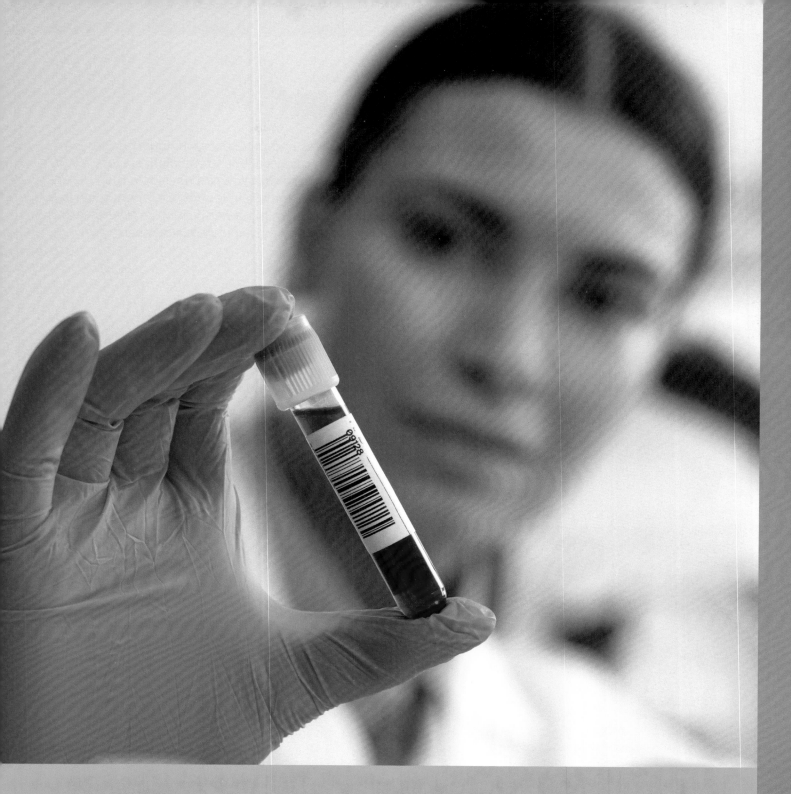

Scientific Techniques
for Health Science   13

Getting to know your unit

Knowledge of laboratory processes and procedures is important for anyone looking to work in health science. This unit includes a lot of laboratory-based practical work, so that you can develop a full understanding of investigative and analytical laboratory techniques. It will support your progress to further or higher education in health care, and is directly related to microbiology, physiology, biochemistry and biomedical science.

How you will be assessed

This unit will be assessed by a series of assignments set by your tutor. Throughout this unit you will find assessment activities that may help you work towards your assessment. Completing these activities will not mean you have achieved a particular grade but the research you carry out for them will be relevant and useful when you come to carry out your final assessment.

It is important to check that you have met all the Pass grading criteria as you work your way through the assignments. To achieve a Merit or Distinction, you need to present your work in such a way that you meet the criteria for those grades. To achieve Merit, you need to analyse and discuss relevant issues; and for Distinction you need to assess and evaluate.

The assignments set by your tutors will consist of a number of tasks designed to meet the criteria in the table below. Some tasks will be written and some will be lab-based practical exercises. Tasks may also involve reviewing and analysing case studies.

This table shows what you must do in order to achieve a **Pass**, **Merit** or **Distinction** grade, and where you can find activities to help you.

Pass	Merit	Distinction

Learning aim **A** Understand how a health-related laboratory deals with samples sent for analysis

Pass	Merit	Distinction
A.P1 Explain the procedures for a sample sent to a health-related laboratory. Assessment practice 13.1	**A.M1** Assess whether the health and safety requirements of a chosen health-related laboratory are adequate to deal with a pathogen sample. Assessment practice 13.1	**A.D1** Justify the procedures used in a health-related laboratory for sample analysis. Assessment practice 13.1
A.P2 Explain how in vitro and in vivo diagnostic tools are used safely in a health-related laboratory. Assessment practice 13.1		

Learning aim **B** Carry out investigations using techniques similar to those in a health-related laboratory

Pass	Merit	Distinction
B.P3 Perform and report on an aseptic technique involving accurate measurement of micro-organisms. Assessment practice 13.2	**B.M2** Analyse the outcomes of practical investigations and relate them to work done in a health-related laboratory. Assessment practice 13.2	**BC.D2** Justify the laboratory techniques used for practical investigations in meeting desired outcomes. Assessment practice 13.2
B.P4 Perform and report on an experiment involving the correct preparation of standard solutions. Assessment practice 13.2		**BC.D3** Evaluate the usefulness of the procedures and techniques used in health-related laboratories in providing a diagnosis for health professionals to work with. Assessment practice 13.2
B.P5 Perform and report on food analysis techniques to accurately measure lipid and acid content. Assessment practice 13.2		
B.P6 Perform and report on a practical investigation to accurately measure the effect of antiseptic/disinfectant. Assessment practice 13.2		

Learning aim **C** Carry out investigations using light microscopes similar to those in a health-related laboratory

Pass	Merit	Distinction
C.P7 Perform a practical investigation involving the staining of cells and their temporarily fixing on a microscope slide. Assessment practice 13.3	**C.M3** Analyse the advantages of using photomicrographs compared to slides fixed using a temporary fixing method. Assessment practice 13.3	
C.P8 Record observations of a prepared slide of cells seen under two different magnifications of a microscope. Assessment practice 13.3		

Getting started

Have you used a microscope before? Have you prepared microscope slides and made drawings of those specimens, following the conventions? Have you carried out any microbiological practical using aseptic technique? Have you ever used chromatography? Do you know what pathologists do? Do you understand the role of public health laboratories? Record what you know now and then see how many more laboratory practical protocols you are familiar with when you have completed this unit.

A   Understand how a health-related laboratory deals with samples sent for analysis

The diagnostic tests and analyses carried out in health-related laboratories underpin all areas of health care and public health, including food safety and environmental health.

Health-related laboratories

There are different types of health-related laboratories, including public health laboratories, hospital pathology laboratories and research laboratories.

Public health laboratories

Many public health laboratories are specialised clinical departments that are based within large NHS Trusts, they may be within or attached to hospitals. These laboratories carry out general clinical tests, as well as specialised microbiology tests. They may offer specialist medical microbiology support and investigate outbreaks and incidents of infectious diseases. Public Health England's (PHE) public health laboratories are at the forefront of research and development in medical microbiology, including the identification of antibiotic resistance.

Hospital pathology laboratories

Many people assume that pathologists only study dead bodies to ascertain the cause of death. Although some pathologists carry out **autopsies**, many others investigate the causes and progression of diseases in living people. More than 70 per cent of diagnoses in the NHS involve **pathology**; this is, therefore, a central part of health care. Pathologists analyse samples of blood, urine, faeces and tissue to look for abnormalities, or to confirm that everything is normal. Pathology is important in the preventative screening of the population that helps with early detection, early intervention and better **prognosis** for potentially fatal conditions.

Pathologists work in hospitals, as well as in GP practices within interdisciplinary teams made up of other doctors, scientists, nurses and healthcare professionals to diagnose, treat and prevent diseases and illnesses.

Pathology bridges theoretical science and the practice of medicine. It underpins all aspects of patient care – from diagnostic testing and treatment to genetic technologies and preventative measures to reduce the incidence of disease.

Millions of pathology tests are carried out each year. Many of these tests contribute towards advances in cancer treatment, safe blood transfusions and organ transplants, developing vaccines and treating inherited conditions.

PHE is an executive agency sponsored by the Department of Health. It aims to protect and improve the nation's health and wellbeing and to reduce health inequalities. It does this by:

> ### Key terms
>
> **Autopsy** – post mortem examination of a body to find the cause(s) of death.
>
> **Pathology** – the science of the causes and effects of disease.
>
> **Prognosis** – the likely outcome of a medical condition.

▶ researching, collecting and analysing data to improve understanding of health

▶ helping local authorities and the NHS to develop the public health system

▶ advising the government and NHS, and encouraging discussion to make the public healthier.

PHE, based at Porton Down in Wiltshire, carries out research into dangerous viruses, such as the Ebola virus, and helps develop protective clothing for front-line workers dealing with such an outbreak. It is also concerned with making sure that innovative science and technology contributes to defence and security in the UK by preparing for dealing with bioterrorist attacks and chemical warfare. It develops protective clothing and military respirators for the Armed Forces and researches into health problems such as Gulf War syndrome and the Zika virus.

Research laboratories

Pathologists, biomedical scientists and clinical biochemists in research laboratories, carry out research to:

▶ find treatments for cancer

▶ develop vaccines against infectious diseases

▶ ensure blood transfusions are safe.

Research laboratories also develop more effective and faster tests for aiding the diagnostic process. They may also develop improved equipment for monitoring or treating patients.

Research findings have led to:

▶ a change in surgical techniques, such as those used for bowel cancer – where the survival rate at five years has increased from 40 per cent to 70 per cent

▶ development of point-of-care testing (POCT), which involves non-laboratory healthcare professionals performing laboratory tests or analyses in the clinical setting – making medical care delivery to critically ill patients faster

▶ effective treatments for babies in the uterus for conditions such as haemolytic disease of the newborn

▶ identification of the bacterium *Helicobacter pylori* as the cause of stomach ulcers, leading to a simple and effective treatment, namely antibiotics.

Case study

Bowel cancer screening

Margaret was one of the first people to receive a bowel cancer screening test kit through the post at age 60. At first she was not keen on completing the test, which involves dipping a small stick into your faeces and smearing it onto the card provided, on three separate occasions, and then returning the card by post . One of her friends did not carry out the test because he felt he did not want to hear bad news, and another friend just forgot to do it. However, Margaret did the test and received a letter saying the result was indeterminate and that she needed to do it again. She did this and was then invited to attend for a colonoscopy, which showed very early stage bowel cancer.

Margaret was operated on very soon afterwards. Because the cancer had been diagnosed early, she did not need chemotherapy. Neither was a sufficiently large area of her colon removed for her to need a colostomy. Ten years on, she is still fit and well and enjoying life. Margaret helps to raise awareness of the importance of people taking up the offer of the screening test. She has also campaigned to extend the age range of those to whom screening is offered.

Check your knowledge

1 Why do you think only about half the people receiving a bowel cancer test kit actually carry out the test?

2 Why does early diagnosis of cancer lead to a better prognosis (outcome)?

3 Why do you think it is important to extend the age range of those screened?

Types of work carried out by health-related laboratories

Table 13.1 shows some examples of the different areas of work carried out by pathology laboratories.

▶ **Table 13.1:** Different areas of work carried out by pathology laboratories

Area of work	Description and some examples of the work
Forensic pathology	Ascertaining the cause of death, including cases where there are suspicious circumstances.
Haematology	The study of disorders of the blood such as anaemia, leukaemia, haemophilia and haemolytic disease of the newborn. Development of blood typing tests.
Histopathology	The study of diseases of human tissue. **Biopsies**, for example, are examination of lumps removed from the breast to see if the tumour is cancerous, **differentially stained** tissue samples are examined under a microscope to identify different tissue components and cancers.
Cytology	Screening of cells under a microscope to look for abnormalities, for example examining cervical smears to look for signs of cancer.
Chemical pathology	The study of chemicals in blood and other body fluids such as urine and cerebrospinal fluid (CSF).
Medical microbiology	The study of causes, treatment and prevention of infectious diseases; identification of causative agents and testing bacteria for antibiotic resistance.
Toxicology	Investigating suspected poisonings; analysing and testing substances for toxicity such as food (including dairy products and shellfish), cosmetics, household products, pharmaceuticals, pesticides, medical devices, plants, metals and industrial chemicals.
Immunology	The study of immunity, allergies, autoimmune diseases such as multiple sclerosis and rheumatoid arthritis, histocompatability (tissue typing and matching) for organ and bone marrow transplants, developing the use of stem cells for treatment.
Genetics and genomic medicine	Pinpointing the genetic causes of certain diseases. **Genomic** testing of newborn babies for cystic fibrosis, testing babies with diabetes to find if they need to be treated with insulin or with tablets to stimulate the pancreas, testing women for BRCA1 and BRCA2 mutations, which indicate a high risk of developing breast cancer, testing DNA from tumours to find which drugs will be effective in treating specific cancers, the 100,000 **genomes** project, which sequences the genomes of NHS patients with rare diseases and with cancers to better understand these conditions. Genomic medicine uses **bioinformatics**.
Reproductive medicine	Development of infertility treatments such as IVF (*in vitro* fertilisation), PGD (pre-implantation genetic testing and diagnosis) and ICSI (intracytoplasmic sperm injection – where a sperm is injected into the cytoplasm of an egg to aid fertilisation).

> **Key terms**
>
> **Biopsy** – pathology examination of body tissues taken from a living patient, to find the cause of a disease/illness.
>
> **Differential staining** – process using more than one chemical to stain tissues, cells or structures, showing differences between them.
>
> **Genomics** – a science discipline that sequences and analyses the functions of genomes.
>
> **Genome** – all the genetic material in a cell/organism.
>
> **Bioinformatics** – interdisciplinary field of science (includes maths, statistics, computer science and engineering) that develops methods and software for understanding biological data.

Each area of pathology specialism has its own training and exams and those graduating from the courses may work in laboratories, clinics and on hospital wards.

Public health laboratory services offer specialist medical microbiology support by carrying out diagnostic tests to identify bacteria, viruses and fungi suspected of causing diseases during an outbreak. Samples are collected under strictly controlled conditions, clearly labelled and sent swiftly by courier to the laboratories for testing. On receipt, careful records are kept of the origins of each sample. Such record keeping is part of quality control measures, as most laboratories receive many samples each day for testing, the tests must be carried out within a short time frame and the results must be sent back to the correct source so that they reach the correct patient.

Link

For more about quality control procedures in laboratories see the section on Quality assurance.

Diseases the laboratories test for include hepatitis C (a liver infection caused by a virus), HIV, viral infections of the respiratory tract, and sexually transmitted infections (STIs). These laboratories may use molecular diagnostic tests including the PCR (polymerase chain reaction) to increase the amount of DNA or RNA from the causative organism so that it can be investigated and the organism identified. Public health laboratories also play an important part in the surveillance of community and healthcare associated infections (HCAI), including outbreaks of serious infections such as SARS (severe acute respiratory syndrome) and the H5N1 strain of influenza, as well as **antimicrobial** resistance.

Key terms

Antimicrobial – substance that kills or prevents the growth of micro-organisms.

Parasite – an organism that lives in or on another organism (the host), from which it obtains nourishment; the host is harmed in the process.

Discussion

IVF is a technique pioneered almost 40 years ago, when it was referred to as 'test tube babies'. In 1978, Louise Brown was the first baby born using this technique. Some people were opposed to it as being 'unnatural'. Today there are more than five million babies worldwide who have been born following IVF treatment. Couples who have been unable to conceive may be entitled to receive one cycle of fertility treatment at NHS expense. However, this is not always successful and many will need to pay for further cycles of treatment.

Discuss whether IVF is any more 'unnatural' than any other medical intervention. Does 'unnatural' mean 'unacceptable' and if something is 'natural' is it always 'good for us'?

Table 13.2 shows some of the clinical and laboratory tests carried out by public health laboratories. Eighty per cent of all test results are now available within three days.

▶ **Table 13.2:** Some of the clinical and laboratory tests carried out by public health laboratories

Type of test	Examples
Serological tests	Tests for antibodies in blood serum (blood fluid without blood cells) to confirm infections such as measles, mumps, CMV (cytomegalovirus), hepatitis D, *Treponema pallidum* (causative agent of syphilis).
Faecal antigen detection	Tests for *H. pylori* (causative agent of stomach ulcers) and some viruses.
Molecular detection	Tests for HIV (human immunodeficiency virus), CMV (cytomegalovirus), HPV (human papilloma virus – causes genital warts and cervical cancer), *Clostridium difficile* (causes diarrhoea), Influenza A and B, *Bortadella pertussis* (causes whooping cough).
Mycobacterium tuberculosis complex	Direct detection of *M. tuberculosis*, together with tests to identify the strain and whether it is susceptible or resistant to antibiotics.
Mycology tests	Tests on pathogenic fungi to see if they are susceptible or resistant to fungicides.
Parasitology tests	Microscopic examination to identify medically important **parasites**.
Bacteriology tests	Microscopy, cultures and susceptibility testing for bacteria that may infect the gastrointestinal (GI) tract, the upper respiratory tract, ears, noses, eyes, blood, CSF, wounds, tissue, genital tract, urine, pus, sputum, also tests for bacteria in organs during post mortem examinations, and screens for MRSA (methicillin resistant *Staphylococcus aureus*).
Food, water and environmental tests	Hygiene screens of food samples and food preparation surfaces for the presence of pathogens such as *Salmonella* and *Campylobacter*, *Vibrio listeria* and *E.coli* O157. Tests food for spoilage organisms such as yeasts and mould fungi, shelf-life testing of food, water quality testing in swimming pools, testing for *Legionella* bacteria in water samples.

Case study

Tattoos and piercings

Kim runs a tattoo and piercing parlour. She has undergone special training about viruses, such as HIV and hepatitis C, as well as bacterial infections, which can be passed from one customer to another if equipment is not properly sterilised. Kim knows that she must wash her hands and wear disposable gloves before tattooing

anyone. She always uses single-use, disposable needles and dye tubs.

Check your knowledge

1 What sort of infection control measures should someone check for if they wanted to get a tattoo or piercing?

 PAUSE POINT   What is the difference between mycology tests and bacteriological tests?

Hint   Think about which types of organisms are being tested for.

Extend   What is the difference between diagnosis and prognosis?

Diagnostic tools

Key terms

In vitro – in glass, for example in a test tube.

In vivo – in living cells/tissues.

LDL – low density lipoproteins, these protein and lipid complexes carry cholesterol in the blood and 'dump' cholesterol into the artery walls, causing fatty plaques that increase the risk of artery disease; also called 'bad cholesterol'.

HDL – high density lipoproteins, these protein and lipid complexes carry cholesterol in the blood and sweep some cholesterol off the artery walls; also called 'good cholesterol'.

Some tests are carried out in test tubes and are described as ***in vitro*** (in glass). These tests are carried out on samples of body fluids such as blood, urine and cerebrospinal fluid (CSF), which have been collected and sent for analysis.

Tests carried out on/in people's bodies are described as ***in vivo*** (in living bodies) diagnostics. These tests include X-rays, CT scans, MRI scans and immunodiagnostics.

In vitro diagnostic tests

In vitro diagnostic tests are a type of medical procedure that tests body fluids to detect, diagnose or monitor diseases or conditions, such as pregnancy, to detect susceptibility to disease, and to determine a course of treatment.

Blood tests

Blood sampling is the most commonly used medical test. It is easy to obtain a blood sample, which can then be tested for a wide range of substances. A blood sample may be used to test for an individual's general health, to determine whether they have an infection, to look for certain disorders and conditions and to see how well an individual's body is functioning. Some examples include testing for:

▶ cholesterol (**LDL** and **HDL**) levels

▶ triglyceride levels

▶ blood glucose levels

▶ insulin levels

▶ electrolyte levels (for example potassium, sodium and calcium ions)

▶ metabolites and enzymes that indicate heart, liver and kidney function

▶ hormone levels, such as thyroid stimulating hormone or growth hormone

▶ blood cell count for the type and number of cells in a sample, such as haematocrit (the percentage of red cells in blood), white cell count or a full blood count

▶ infection markers, erythrocyte (red blood cell) sedimentation rate

▶ cross-matching for blood and organ transplants

▶ DNA, which can be obtained from the white blood cells, for genetic testing

▶ alcohol and drugs levels

▶ blood culture tests, to detect harmful bacteria or fungi that release toxins and cause sepsis (the body's reaction to widespread infection, which may result in organ failure and death).

Urine tests

Urine tests are also easy to perform and fairly commonly used. Many tests can be performed in the clinic or GP surgery and provide an immediate result. Urine test strips or dipsticks are used to analyse a sample. These are cardboard sticks containing chemical pads, which are dipped into the service user's urine. The chemical pads react (by changing colour) when removed from the urine sample. For example, test strips can be used to detect:

▶ levels of glucose in urine, which may indicate diabetes

▶ certain proteins in urine, which may indicate heart disease, high blood pressure or kidney infection

▶ the hormone hCG (human chorionic gonadotrophin), which indicates pregnancy in women and testicular cancer in males.

Other urine analysis tests need to be performed in a pathology laboratory including, for example, those that detect:

▶ high levels of **bilirubin** in the urine (which may cause the urine to be brown or black in colour and indicate the presence of gall stones or liver infections), **Addison's disease** and **Cushing's syndrome**

▶ high levels of **creatinine**, which may indicate kidney failure

▶ alcohol and drug levels.

Key terms

Bilirubin – waste product made from breakdown of bile salts.

Addison's disease – a rare disorder of the adrenal glands that causes low blood pressure, generalised weakness, progressive anaemia and bronzed skin.

Cushing's syndrome – a rare disorder, which is commoner in women, involving overproduction of corticosteroid hormones ('stress' hormones) by the adrenal cortex causing weight gain and obesity, high blood pressure, high blood glucose levels, tiredness and generalised weakness.

Creatinine – breakdown product of creatine phosphate found in muscles, removed via kidneys; elevated levels in blood indicate renal failure/kidney disease.

Stool tests

Stool testing is testing of faeces for occult (hidden) blood, parasite infestations and infections. Testing for faecal occult blood (FOB) is a commonly used test, traces of blood in the faeces that cannot necessarily be seen may indicate bleeding somewhere in the gastrointestinal tract. A home test kit is offered as part of routine screening to all 60–74 year olds in England. (People over 75 years of age can also request this test.) This test is important in the early detection of colorectal (bowel) and stomach cancers. If routine screening shows any level of occult blood in the faeces, the person may be invited to have an **endoscopy** (**colonoscopy**) to investigate the cause, which could be tumours in the bowel.

Tests on faeces can also indicate infection by parasites such as threadworm, hookworm and tapeworm. Some viruses can be found in faeces, and the toxins from *Clostridium difficile* can confirm infection with this bacterium.

Key terms

Endoscopy – examination of the inside of the body using a specialised tube (an endoscope).

Colonoscopy – an endoscopy specifically used to look at the inner lining of the large intestine (rectum and colon), using a thin, flexible tube (a colonoscope).

A faecal fat test may be carried out to investigate the cause of long-term diarrhoea, especially with bulky, offensive smelling stools. A high fat content in the stools may indicate conditions such as Coeliac disease.

Sputum

Sputum is a mixture of saliva and mucus. It is coughed up from the respiratory tract. Large amounts of sputum, especially if discoloured or very thick and sticky, may be caused by infections and other diseases of the respiratory tract, for example influenza, tuberculosis (TB), pneumonia and fungal infections of the lungs, such as **aspergillosis**. Blood in the sputum may indicate lung cancer. Excessive amounts of sputum may indicate chronic obstructive pulmonary disease.

Cerebrospinal fluid (CSF)

CSF is the fluid that surrounds the brain and spinal cord. A sample can be taken by a lumbar puncture (spinal tap) to help confirm diagnosis of meningitis and multiple sclerosis. It can also be tested for levels of the neurotransmitter serotonin, which helps regulate mood, appetite, sleep, memory and learning. It has been reported that low levels of serotonin may be associated with abuse or depression.

> **Key term**
>
> **Aspergillosis** – disease caused by a mould fungus, *Aspergillus spp*, which usually affects the respiratory system.

Case study

Phlebotomy

Phlebotomists are trained to take blood samples from patients. The composition of a person's blood indicates their general health status, and the composition may be affected by many medical conditions. For these reasons, blood tests are the most commonly used medical tests.

Phlebotomists usually take blood samples from easily accessible veins, such as those running over the inside of the elbow joint. However, when someone is very ill it may sometimes be necessary to take a sample from an artery, for example for blood gas analysis – measuring levels of oxygen and carbon dioxide to check pulmonary (lung) function and to measure blood pH (acidity or alkalinity).

The speed, efficiency and accuracy of blood tests have improved greatly. One sample of blood can be used to test for many substances, and the results are sometimes available within minutes. This is a great help to doctors examining patients in the accident and emergency department, for example. Some research laboratories have produced microchip blood tests where a few drops of blood can be tested for many substances. This will make blood tests even easier as all health professionals can obtain a drop or two of blood from a finger-prick test. This already happens in the blood transfusion service, where it is routine to use a finger-prick sample to test for the iron content of a potential donor's blood.

Midwives and health visitors use a heel-prick to take a sample of blood from all newborn babies to test for PKU (phenylketonuria) – a genetic disease that affects only a few people but which causes irreparable brain damage if not diagnosed and treated very early.

Check your knowledge

1 Why are blood tests the most commonly used medical tests?

2 What substances, when present in the blood in abnormal levels, can affect your health and how do they affect it?

3 Why do you think blood is usually taken from a vein rather than from an artery?

4 Why do you think a potential blood donor's blood is tested for iron content? What else would a donor's blood be tested for?

In vivo diagnostics

Medical personnel sometimes need to see what is going on inside a living patient's body. Equipment such as X-ray machines and CT, MRI and ultrasound scanners enable such examinations and reduce the need for invasive explorative surgery.

X-rays

X-rays are a form of electromagnetic radiation. They are part of the electromagnetic spectrum and have short wavelengths (0.01 – 10 **nm**) – shorter than the wavelength of ultraviolet light. High-energy X-rays are used for medical imaging of bones and lungs. Patients are exposed to a short burst of X-rays. A thin metal filter is placed over the window of the X-ray tube to absorb low energy X-rays, leaving high-energy rays to bombard the body.

Bones, which contain high amounts of calcium, absorb many of the X-rays, reducing the amount of X-rays reaching nearby soft tissue, which makes bones show up as an X-ray image (radiograph).

Lungs contain trapped air, which has a lower rate of absorbing X-rays than that of the ribs, so chest X-rays can help to confirm the diagnosis of lung cancer, pneumonia or pulmonary oedema (fluid retention). X-rays can also detect gall stones, kidney stones and dental problems. X-rays are less useful for imaging soft tissues.

Angiograms

Angiograms are X-ray images of arteries and veins, which cannot be seen clearly on ordinary X-rays, after the injection of a radio-opaque substance (usually an iodine compound). A radiologist looks at the images produced to see whether there are any obstructions to blood flow or any blocked blood vessels.

> **Key term**
>
> **Nanometre (nm)** – unit of linear measurement; 10^{-9} metre (or one billionth of a metre).

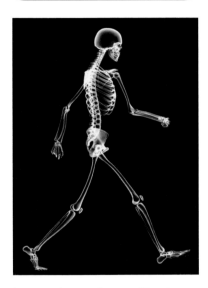

▶ X-ray showing bones of head, neck, rib cage and hands

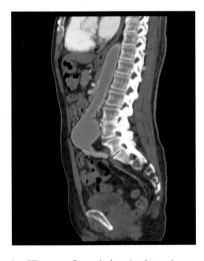

▶ CT scan of an abdominal aortic aneurysm – the area highlighted in pink shows the bulging aorta and the blue areas show fatty plaques deposited in the artery walls

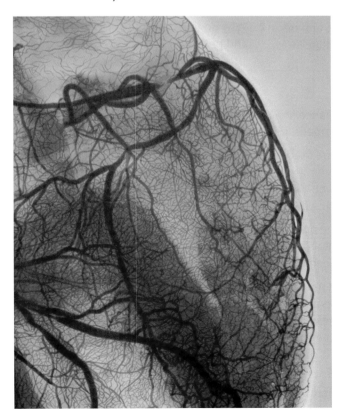

▶ Colour-enhanced angiogram of the heart showing obstruction in a major coronary artery – the obstructed section can be seen as a break in the dark red vessel at the top centre

CT scans

Computerised tomography (CT) images are of specific areas (slices) of the body, which are obtained from a huge series of two-dimensional X-ray images taken in different directions. These cross-sectional images are combined to give a three-dimensional image of the inside of the body, which particularly gives a better picture of tumours.

Case study

Aahan Patel – radiographer

After obtaining a Diploma in Health and Social Care and seven GCSEs, including maths and physics (at grade C or above), Aahan went on to obtain a degree in diagnostic radiography. Radiography is a strictly regulated profession and radiographers are required to meet certain standards in order to practise safely, lawfully and effectively. All radiographers in the UK must be registered with the Health and Care Professions Council. They must also meet the standards of the Society of Radiographers' Code of Professional Conduct. This code sets out the values and behaviour expected of radiographers in their dealings with patients and colleagues, including respect, empowerment, empathy, trustworthiness, integrity and justice. Aahan must enjoy working in a team, be caring and supportive and able to put patients at ease, be calm under pressure, such as when dealing with medical emergencies, be good at communicating, and be confident with working with leading edge technology as well as being adaptable and able to learn new skills.

Aahan is a diagnostic radiographer and uses CT scans, X-rays and MRI scans to diagnose illnesses and injuries in patients. He plans to do further part-time specialist postgraduate training in ultrasonography, while continuing to work in his current post.

His friend is a therapeutic radiographer who treats people with cancer. Both types of radiographers are important members of a large medical team in the hospital. They work alongside oncologists, physicists and other healthcare professionals. Radiographers also work alongside surgeons, such as cardiologists, as they can help the cardiologist place the pacemaker wires correctly.

Check your knowledge

1 How do you think radiographers aid cardiologists to correctly position a pacemaker and its leads?

2 Why do you think you need an interest in biology and physics to study radiography?

MRI scans

Magnetic resonance imaging (MRI) is a way of creating detailed images of the soft-tissue internal organs, for example the heart, muscle or brain.

MRI scans can be used to diagnose multiple sclerosis, brain tumours, torn ligaments, tendonitis, cancer, strokes, injuries and abnormalities of joints and the spine, liver disease, endometriosis (inflammation of the lining of the uterus) and abnormalities of the uterus causing infertility.

An MRI machine does not use radiation. It has strong magnets, contained in liquid helium to maintain a very low temperature, which create a magnetic field that causes protons (hydrogen ions) to vibrate.

Tissues contain much water (H_2O), and, therefore, many protons. Normally these water molecules are randomly aligned in the body but in the magnetic field of the MRI scanner the water molecules align. A second magnetic field is turned on and off in a series of quick pulses, causing each hydrogen atom to alter its alignment and then revert to its original state. These changes are computed to give a detailed cross-sectional image of the individual's internal organs.

The individual has to lie very still, for up to an hour, on a bed that is moved into a tunnel shaped scanner, which is open at both ends. Babies, young children and people who are claustrophobic may be given a general anaesthetic to relax them and prevent them from moving.

Patients with pacemakers or other metal implants cannot have an MRI scan as the magnetic field can affect the working of the pacemaker or make implants move.

(a)

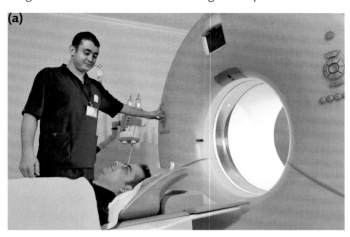

(b)

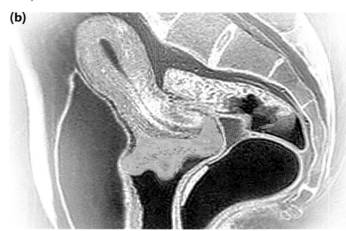

▶ (a) An MRI scanner (b) Colour enhanced MRI scan showing cervical cancer (shown as yellow)

Not all hospitals have MRI machines and many service users have to travel to another hospital if they need an MRI scan.

Ⅱ   **PAUSE POINT**   In what ways are MRI scans less risky to patients than X-rays and CT scans?

Hint   Think about what X-rays can do to living cells.

Extend   Why do patients having an MRI scan have to remove all jewellery?

Ultrasound scans

Ultrasound scans (sometimes called sonograms) use high frequency sound waves, which cannot be heard by humans, to create an image of part of the inside of the body. A lubricating gel is put on the skin surface above the area to be investigated. This allows the probe to move smoothly and to transmit the sound waves into the body. If the service user is allergic to latex, a latex-free cover is used on the probe.

The sound waves bounce off different internal parts of the body creating echoes, which are picked up by the probe and turned into a moving image that is displayed on a screen.

Ultrasound scans can be used externally or internally. There are no known risks of using external ultrasound scans.

Externally, ultrasound scanning can be used to monitor the growth and development of foetuses or for guiding a surgeon during certain procedures (such as inserting pacemaker leads). Internally, ultrasound scans involve the use of an **endoscope** with a light and an ultrasound probe. This may be inserted into the oesophagus to examine the inside of the gut. From the oesophagus the probe can also collect images of the heart (this procedure is called a transoesophageal echo (TOE)). Endoscopes may be used to examine the colon (colonoscopy) for tumours, following a positive result for a faecal occult blood test.

There is a small risk of internal damage and bleeding with internal scans. In order to mitigate this risk the colon is puffed up with air before the endoscope is inserted. For a TOE the patient is sedated as swallowing the endoscope is very uncomfortable and stimulates the gag reflex and a mouthguard is used to prevent them biting the endoscope.

Key term

Endoscope – a narrow, tubular (often flexible) instrument used to examine inside the body; may have an instrument attached to enable a biopsy to be taken or for surgery to be performed.

Immunodiagnostics

Immunodiagnostics uses an **antigen–antibody** reaction. It can be used to detect very small amounts of biochemical substances. Antibodies specific to (having a variable region that fits) the antigen molecule to be detected are tagged. This means they are joined to a chemical that **fluoresces** or to an enzyme that causes a colour change when placed in a reagent or dye. Antibodies specific to antigens on particular tissues or cells can be joined with a dye and then used to stain histology specimens on microscope slides.

ELISA (Enzyme Linked Immuno Sorbent Assay) tests are sensitive and inexpensive. The pregnancy test kit uses an ELISA test, which was developed to detect low levels of the hormone hCG in urine. Very soon after conception the hormone hCG is secreted and, as its concentration in the blood increases, it is excreted in the urine. The sampler stick in the pregnancy test kit contains antibody molecules specific only to molecules of hCG. The results of the test depend on whether the antibodies react with hCG. A positive result, the formation of a blue line, indicates a pregnancy. A negative result, when the antibodies are not combined with hCG, is indicated by a coloured line.

Antibodies and tumours

Monoclonal antibodies can be used *in vivo* to identify cancerous tumours in organs and also to monitor whether the tumour is shrinking during treatment.

When cells become cancerous they express different antigens on their cell surface membranes. Monoclonal antibodies specific to those abnormal antigens can be made and tagged with radioactive isotopes. The antibodies are then injected into the patient's blood. As they travel around the body the antibodies will join to cancer cells and a scan shows the position of the **radioactive isotopes** and hence the tumour(s).

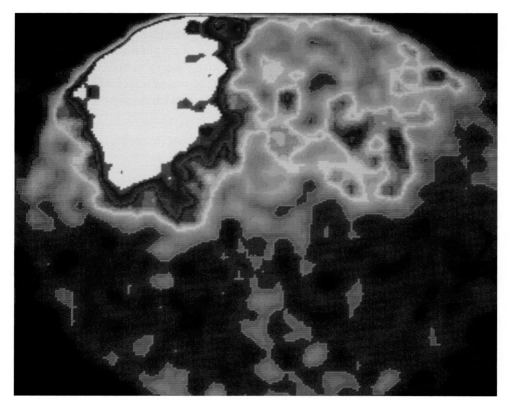

▶ Coloured immunoscintigram of a malignant tumour (cancer) of the colon, shown as white in the scan

A new screening test is being trialled where antibodies to haemoglobin detect small traces of blood in faeces, which is a better test for bowel cancer.

Procedures for samples

There are some risks associated with collecting samples from patients, for example introducing an infection while taking blood because micro-organisms on the patient's skin, or the phlebotomist's hands, may be transferred to the puncture wound accessing the vein. If micro-organisms are introduced to the sample, this could give false results and lead to inappropriate treatment. To mitigate these risks the phlebotomist:

▶ cleans their hands with soap and hot water, or with alcohol rub

▶ wears a new pair of sterile gloves for each procedure

▶ cleans the patient's skin with isopropyl alcohol

▶ uses a new sterile needle and syringe to take the sample(s)

▶ disposes of the used gloves and needles in appropriately labelled bins, for safe disposal.

Sterilisation

Sterilisation refers to the procedure to make an object free of live micro-organisms. Objects can be sterilised by heat or by certain chemicals, such as alcohol, bleach, **disinfectants** and **antiseptics**.

Plastic objects such a syringes, catheter tubes and Petri dishes can be sterilised by exposure to gamma rays. Glassware and operating instruments are sterilised in an autoclave. An autoclave is an instrument that works like a pressure cooker, raising the pressure and, therefore, raising the boiling point of water. Heating at high temperature kills most micro-organisms.

▶ An autoclave

Nutrient media are made up and then autoclaved before being poured into Petri dishes for use in culturing micro-organisms for identification or carrying out antibiotic sensitivity tests.

> **Key terms**
>
> **Disinfectant** – substance that can be applied to surfaces to kill micro-organisms, or to inhibit their growth.
>
> **Antiseptic** – substance that can be applied to skin or other living tissues, such as teeth, to kill micro-organisms, or to inhibit their growth.

Investigative procedures

Weighing

Some samples, such as tissues, may need to be weighed. For this, precision balances are used. Medical waste also has to be weighed, and records kept for traceability. Precision balances, accurate to two decimal places, are used to weigh out ingredients for making up culture media, test reagents and solutions of specific concentrations.

Patients and service users are sometimes weighed so that their BMI (body mass index) can be worked out. In many cases surgeons will not operate on patients whose BMI exceeds 40. A BMI of over 30 indicates obesity, which poses risks when undergoing a general anaesthetic and surgery.

$$BMI = \frac{\text{mass in } \textbf{kilograms (kg)}}{(\text{height in metres})^2}$$

Measuring liquids

Graduated syringes, with a scale to indicate volume, can be used to collect specific volumes of body fluids. As substances tested for are expressed in concentrations such as **mmol**/L, the analyst needs to know the volume of fluid collected and tested. A doctor then compares the test result to known normal, low and high values to know how to treat the individual.

The volumes of liquids used in making solutions of specific concentrations for staining specimens to be examined under a microscope or for reagents to test for specific chemicals need to be accurately measured. Volumes are measured in syringes, measuring cylinders, graduated pipettes, micropipettes or volumetric flasks. The apparatus is calibrated to a high degree of precision and accuracy. The units used for measurement are litres (L), **millilitres** (10^{-3}L) or **microlitres** (10^{-6}L).

Determining pH

The pH is a measure of the acidity or alkalinity of an aqueous (watery) solution. This is a numeric scale that indicates the concentration of hydrogen ions. The scale is the logarithm to base 10 of the reciprocal of the hydrogen ion concentration.

pH = log 1/[H^+] where [H^+] is the concentration of hydrogen ions in moles per litre (mol L^{-1})

The pH scale is set using a set of standard solutions established by international agreement. Primary pH standard values are confirmed by measuring the potential difference (voltage) between a hydrogen electrode and a standard electrode, such as one made of silver chloride. The pH of unknown solutions can be measured using universal indicator paper, universal indicator solution or with a pH meter.

Acids have a pH of between 0 and 6.9; bases have pH values of between 7.1 and 14; pH 7 is neutral.

It is important to measure the pH of different body fluids, organs and cellular compartments, which are normally regulated as part of the acid-base homeostasis process, as this process can be disrupted by disease processes. The pH of blood is 7.365 and there is not much room for deviation from this value.

Analysis – qualitative and quantitative

Some tests merely show that something is either present or absent. Data generated by such tests is described as qualitative. If the test shows how much of a substance is present, therefore generating numbers, the data is described as quantitative. Semi-quantitative data gives data limited to a few different values. Quantitative data can be compared to a known range of normal values and can also be analysed by statistical tests.

Kilograms (kg) or grams (g) – units for measuring mass.

Mole (mol) – the amount of a chemical substance that contains as many atoms/molecules as there are atoms in 12 g carbon, which is 6×10^{23}. It is equivalent to the gram molecular mass, for example a mole of glucose, molecular mass 180, is 180 g.

Millimole (mmol) – 10^{-3} mole; 1 mmol glucose is 0.18 g.

Litre (L) – unit of volume; equal to 1 cubic decimetre (1 dm³), which is a cube of 10 cm × 10 cm × 10 cm; equal to 1000 cm³.

Millilitre (mL) – unit of volume; 1 cm³; 10^{-3} L.

Microlitre (µL) – unit of volume; 10^{-3} mL; 10^{-6} L.

If many people within a population are tested for the level of a certain substance, for example potassium ion concentrations in blood, the mean value can be found by adding all the values and dividing by the number in the sample. The larger the sample the more accurate (the nearer to the true value) the mean value is likely to be. Once the mean value has been found the standard deviation can be worked out so that clinicians can compare results to see whether they fall within an acceptable range of the normal values.

$$SD = \frac{\sqrt{\Sigma(x_n - \bar{x})^2}}{(n-1)}$$ where $\Sigma(x_n - \bar{x})^2$ = the sum of the squares of the difference between individual values in the data set and the mean value of the data set

n = the number of samples in the data set

The standard deviation indicates how spread out about the mean the data are, it shows how varied the data within the sample are. If the data show a normal distribution then 68 per cent of the readings will fall within one standard deviation, 95.5 per cent will fall within two standard deviations, and 99.7 per cent of the sample will fall within three standard deviations.

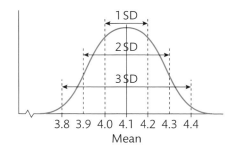

▶ **Figure 13.1:** Normal distribution – if the mean value is 4.1 and 1 SD is 0.1 then 1 SD is 4.0 – 4.2, 2 SD is 3.9 – 4.3 and 3 SD is 3.8 – 4.4

❚❚ **PAUSE POINT**   What are the units for measuring (a) mass (b) volume? What does a pH of 4.5 indicate about a solution?

Hint   Look at the sections on measuring mass and volume, and determining pH.

Extend   How would you make up a litre of 2 M glucose solution?

Data recording and manipulation

In a laboratory there may be several hundred samples being tested at any one time, so good organisation and accurate record keeping are paramount. Paper records and computer records need to be easily located. Therefore, data may be manipulated to organise the information, making it easier to read or find. Data may be recorded and archived in alphabetical order, or according to the service user's name, NHS number or national insurance number.

The data generated when samples are tested must be carefully and accurately recorded. The samples sent to the laboratory should be clearly labelled with the individual's name, date of birth, address, NHS number and the date the sample was obtained. Accurate records are needed so that each individual receives the correct results, which will inform the clinician about the best and most appropriate course of treatment. The data will be compared to sets of figures that give accepted ranges to see whether the individual's values are within the normal range, lower than normal or higher than normal.

In IVF clinics and laboratories accurate record keeping is particularly important to ensure that eggs, sperm and embryos are all traceable.

Case study

The Douglas Babies

In 1946, in England, Wales and Scotland, a survey of all mothers (and subsequently of their children) who gave birth during a specific week in March began. The purpose of the survey was to learn about the social and economic factors affecting the long-term health of the babies as they grew up, and also to assess how effective the midwife and obstetric services were at preventing infant death and in promoting health. In 2016, more than 3000 of the original 5362 babies born during that week reached age 70. The survey, started by Dr James Douglas, has shown that babies born to mothers in poor economic circumstances are four times more likely to die in infancy than babies born to more affluent mothers.

This cohort of people has been followed at intervals throughout their lives. In the 1980s, Professor Michael Wadsworth directed the study. The cohort has been monitored for their mental and physical health, and their life circumstances. The study is now investigating aspects of ageing and chronic diseases.

The study has shown that:
- low birth mass (weight) babies tend to have a higher blood pressure later in life than those who were normal birth mass

- people whose fathers were more affluent and had skilled occupations have fewer health problems and better cognitive ability later in life than those whose fathers were less well educated
- breastfeeding improved long-term health and cognitive abilities.

Other studies have also used large data sets and found that maternal nutrition during pregnancy can influence the long-term health of the children, and of those children's children.

Between 2006 and 2010, the UK Biobank was established, and recruited 500,000 people from across the UK, aged between 45 and 69, to take part in a study. Many physiological measurements were taken from these participants and they answered questionnaires about their diet and lifestyle, and undertook cognitive tests. The data are available to scientists to help them discover why some people develop particular diseases and others do not.

Check your knowledge

1 Why do you think people in the study had their blood pressure measured?

2 Why do you think long-term studies such as the 'Douglas Babies' study and UK Biobank are useful?

Research

Go to **www.qcnet. com/portals/50/pdfs/ qcworkbook2008_jun08. pdf** to find out more about laboratory quality assurance.

Quality assurance

At any one time, a laboratory may have between 700 and 1000 samples for different types of tests. These tests are closely monitored and quality controlled. The purpose of laboratory quality control (QC) is to detect, reduce and correct any deficiencies in a laboratory's analytical process. QC also gives a measure of reliability – how well the system reproduces the same result over time and over different conditions.

QC procedures are run:
▶ at the beginning and end of each shift
▶ after an instrument is serviced
▶ when reagent lots are changed
▶ after an instrument has been calibrated
▶ if test results seem wrong or inappropriate.

Quality assurance oversees documentation, clinical labelling, packaging, storage and distribution of samples.

Health and safety requirements

Around 250,000 people work in biomedical laboratories in the UK, with about 13,000 scientists working in NHS laboratories. The nature of this work means that these people are routinely exposed to the risk of infection and therefore, these workplaces must have procedures in place to minimise those risks.

Legislation

The Health and Safety at Work Act 1974 is legislation which embodies regulations that apply to all laboratories where biological agents are handled, including work with patients and in human healthcare settings. There is also guidance for personnel who have responsibility for assessing and managing risks from exposure to **biological agents**, for example a Grade 3 biomedical scientist (BMS3), a clinical director or nurse manager. All organisations must have arrangements in place to manage all aspects of health and safety.

COSHH regulations

Control of Substances that are Hazardous to Health (COSSH) is legislation covering work with any substance that could pose a hazard to human health, including chemicals, fumes, dusts, vapours, mists, gases and biological agents (germs). Employers are provided with information on how to do this, along with safety data sheets and international symbols with which to label reagents and specimens. This is particularly pertinent when working with pathogenic microbes and the potential risk of infection. The control measures used in laboratories will depend on the biological agent that may be present.

There is also guidance from ACDP (Advisory Committee on Dangerous Pathogens) about managing risks in laboratories and healthcare premises, including how to protect against blood-borne infections such as HIV and hepatitis.

UK and European legislation covers the carriage of dangerous goods, including how they are classified, packaged and labelled before being transported by road, rail or air. Clear labelling ensures that the lab receiving the samples can contain them appropriately and deal with them safely.

RIDDOR

Reporting of Injuries, Diseases and Dangerous Occurrences Regulations 2013 (RIDDOR) is specific health and safety legislation requiring any deaths, diseases, injuries and dangerous occurrences, including near misses, in the workplace to be officially reported.

Hazards and risk assessment

A hazard is something that has the potential to cause harm.

A risk is the hazard multiplied by the exposure to the hazard.

A risk assessment is a means of determining the risk associated with a particular hazard.

The person responsible for health and safety in the specific workplace must:

▸ identify the hazard

▸ decide who is at risk, and how harm could be caused

▸ assess the likelihood of harm arising, and whether the existing precautions that are in place are adequate to prevent such harm

▸ record findings and selected control measures, and identify the necessary actions to reduce risk of exposure

▸ review and revise assessments as necessary, especially if the nature of the work changes or an incident indicates that the present measures are not adequate.

▸ Every organisation must have a written policy detailing the procedures that are in place to reduce and control risks and manage all aspects of health and safety. The policy must be available to all employees who must be made aware that

> **Key terms**
>
> **Biological agent** – a **micro-organism**, cell culture or human endoparasite (a parasite living inside its host) that may cause infection, allergy, toxicity or create another hazard to human health.
>
> **Micro-organism** – a microbiological entity, which may be single-celled or multicellular that is capable of replication or of transferring genetic material; for example, fungi, viruses, bacteria and some protoctists.

they have to adhere to the policy. Organisations also appoint a health and safety officer/advisor who must be competent and able to advise both employees and management. Procedures include the use of personal protective equipment, reporting of accidents and incidents, emergency exit procedures and the correct disposal of wastes. Areas within the workplace must also be marked – for example, laboratories that contain pathogens and other biological agents and patient isolation rooms within a hospital are marked with a biohazard sign. All containers holding chemicals or biological agents are also clearly labelled and marked with the appropriate hazard symbol.

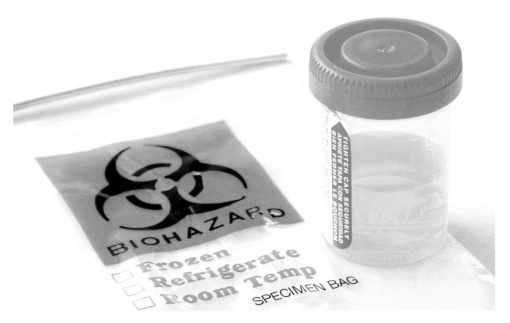

▶ A urine sample in a specimen bag and displaying a biohazards symbol

Personal protective equipment and procedures

Protective clothing and spare clean uniforms must be made available to laboratory and healthcare personnel. Laboratory personnel wear lab coats. In some cases, they may also be required to wear face masks, hair coverings, disposable aprons, gloves and special footwear.

All personnel should observe the policy in place for minimising infection risks, such as:

▶ regular hand washing and using alcohol hand rub gels
▶ using disposable gloves, needle safety devices and aseptic procedures for disinfection and decontamination
▶ isolating patients who carry MRSA (methicillin-resistant staphylococcus aureus)
▶ overseeing domestic cleaning and waste disposal.

Using a laminar flow cabinet

Laboratory personnel may work with live cultures in a laminar flow cabinet, which is an enclosed space made of stainless steel and with no gaps or joints where micro-organisms could collect. These cabinets operate at negative air pressure, so that a smooth flow of air is constantly drawn into the cabinet. The air from the cabinet is then filtered so that no microbes can escape into the environment. When the cabinet is not in use, an ultraviolet lamp is left switched on to kill any micro-organisms. If laminar flow cabinets are not used, then good aseptic technique is practised (see the section on Aseptic techniques used in health-related laboratories).

Accident procedures

The health and safety officer within an organisation must ensure that all personnel know how to respond to an accident or dangerous incident. There must be procedures in place to follow in the case of spillages or injuries. Information about dealing with emergencies should be in clear view of employees, who should know how to contact the emergency services, if and when necessary. Incidents and accidents should be reported and the data kept for a long time, in some cases for many years. This is because some incidents may lead to later problems; for example, exposure to some biohazards can cause cancer many years later (often after the person is no longer working in that environment).

Emergency exit procedures

All employees should be familiar with the procedure for evacuating the building of all personnel during emergencies, such as fire or floods, or after a major biohazard spillage. The procedures to be followed should be placed where they are clearly visible, in each work area, and regular evacuation practices should be held.

Disposal of waste materials

Within laboratories, hospital wards and GP surgeries there are clearly marked receptacles for biological waste, such as sharps (needles), syringes, tweezers and dressings. These are all potential sources of infection as they may contain body fluids such as blood, urine and faeces, and micro-organisms. Biohazardous waste has to be treated, for example by heat, to sterilise it before disposal.

> **Research**
>
> Go to **www.hse.gov.uk/ biosafety/biologagents. pdf** to find out more about the health and safety requirements and procedures when working with biological agents.

Assessment practice 13.1   `A.P1` `A.P2` `A.M1` `A.D1`

1   You are the health and safety officer within a GP surgery. Prepare a leaflet that can be displayed to inform all nurses in the practice about the procedures for samples to be sent to a medical laboratory for testing.

2   Produce a poster to show how *in vitro* and *in vivo* diagnostic tools are used safely in a health-related setting.

3   Choose one type of health-related laboratory and research to find out about its health and safety requirements. Write a report to assess whether its health and safety requirements are adequate to deal with pathogen samples.

4   Justify the procedures you have described for this health-related laboratory for sample analysis.

Plan
- Do I know what I am being asked to do?
- Do I have enough information or should I extend my research?

Do
- Do I know what I want to achieve?
- Can I check my work to see where I have gone off task and can make changes to put this right?

Review
- Can I instruct someone else on how to complete the task more efficiently?
- Do I know what I would do differently next time and the approach I would take with the parts that I found difficult this time?

B Carry out investigations using techniques similar to those in a health-related laboratory

You may be able to carry out some practical protocols very similar to some of those used in health-related laboratories. These include aseptic technique, analyses and some investigative microbiological techniques.

Aseptic techniques used in health-related laboratories

It is important that samples are not contaminated by any other micro-organisms, so that the micro-organisms found within the samples can be correctly identified as the causative agents for an individual's infection.

Sterile collection of swabs

Clinicians (nurses, doctors and other health professionals) are responsible for the collection and safe transportation of samples to laboratories for testing. The validity of the test results depends on good practice in the pre-test stage, which includes swabs from certain areas, such as the individual's skin, throat and nose. If the samples are contaminated, this may produce misleading results, wrong diagnoses and inappropriate antibiotic treatment. The following guidelines are used by clinicians who collect samples.

▶ The procedure is explained to the patient, who has a right to refuse.

▶ All specimens should be treated as potentially infectious. However, when there is a strong suspicion that a patient is highly infectious then they should be isolated – even before the test results are found.

▶ If it is suspected that the patient has a viral haemorrhagic fever, such as Ebola virus, the infection control team must be consulted before any specimens are taken.

▶ Before collecting the sample, hands must be washed and gloves worn; in some circumstances other protective equipment should also be worn.

▶ Sterile swabs are used to sweep the body surface, which are then placed in a sterile container with a close-fitting lid.

▶ Specimens must be clearly labelled, at the point of taking the swab, to identify their source. Laboratory request forms are printed from the Patient Information Management System (PIMS), which include labels that can be printed and used to label the specimens. These labels are bar-coded to provide an audit trail. The laboratory request form should include the patient's name, date of birth and NHS number, the type of specimen and the site from which it was collected, the date and time of collection, the patient's diagnostic history and question(s) to be answered by the test(s), details of any antimicrobial drugs given, and the consultant's name.

▶ All specimens are transported, along with their laboratory request forms, in a double-sided self-sealing polythene bag.

▶ Sterile cotton swab used to take samples of cells for testing

---

Discussion

Ideally swabs should be taken and tested for micro-organisms before treatment begins. Why do you think this is? Why do you think treatments for suspected sepsis should begin before the test results are available?

Principles and preparation of culture media

Culture media are nutrient solutions or gels used in laboratories to grow bacteria and fungi. These micro-organisms can only grow if they have a favourable environment that includes water, the nutrients they need and a suitable temperature. The growth medium, whether solid, semi-solid or liquid, is prepared according to instructions (recipes) and then heated in an autoclave to sterilise it. Liquid media, in closed tubes, can then be cooled and refrigerated before being used. The solid media, in flasks stoppered with cotton wool and foil covers, is cooled to about 50°C, kept at that temperature in water baths, and then poured into sterile Petri dishes. As it cools further it sets and the Petri dishes (also called agar plates) can be stored in stacks, upside down, in the fridge, prior to use. They are stored upside down so that any condensation runs onto the lids and not onto the solid nutrient media.

Nutrient media contain:

▶ a source of carbon, such as glucose, which can be respired to release energy and carbon, so micro-organisms can synthesise organic molecules, for example proteins, fats and carbohydrates
▶ a source of nitrogen, such as peptones (partially digested proteins), which enables the micro-organisms to make amino acids and hence proteins, nucleic acids and other chemicals such as ATP
▶ distilled water, which is a solvent for the other components
▶ growth factors such as specific amino acids
▶ inorganic nutrients and trace elements
▶ buffers (chemicals that resist changes in pH when acid or alkali are added) to maintain the pH.

Liquid media

Liquid media, such as nutrient broth, are usually used in tubes or flasks to study the growth of micro-organisms. The liquid medium becomes cloudy (turbid) as the micro-organisms grow and the increasing optical density can be read with a spectrophotometer or colorimeter to show turbidity and, therefore, the extent of the growth. The growth of specific micro-organisms under different conditions (for example, temperature or pH) can be investigated using liquid media.

Semi-solid media

Semi-solid media are used for studying how micro-organisms move. They are also useful for growing anaerobic micro-organisms (those requiring the absence of oxygen to grow). In addition to the components of nutrient media, they contain a solidifying agent, such as agar (a gel obtained from seaweed). Solid media contain more agar than do semi-solid media.

Solid media

Solid media are used in Petri dishes to grow micro-organisms and to:
▶ observe the morphology of their colonies
▶ isolate specific types from a mixture of different bacteria
▶ count the number of bacteria in 1 mL of a diluted or undiluted sample
▶ investigate the antibiotic sensitivity of specific bacteria
▶ detect specific biochemical (metabolic) reactions of micro-organisms, indicating which enzymes and, therefore, which genes are present, to aid identification of the micro-organisms.

Slants of solid media in tubes can be inoculated with stock cultures of micro-organisms and kept refrigerated.

Deep agar tubes can be used to investigate the oxygen requirements of bacteria.

Composition	Chemically defined media: composed of only pure chemicals in known quantities, also known as synthetic media.
	Complex media: composed of complex material such as yeast or beef extracts, chemical composition is poorly defined (it is not known exactly what is in them) but they are rich in vitamins and minerals.
Function	All-purpose media: contain all ingredients of nutrient media listed above so can support the growth of most types of bacteria, they do not contain any special additives.
	Selective media: nutrient media, but with added special substances that inhibit the growth of some types of micro-organism and enhance the growth of other types.
	Differential media: allow identification of micro-organisms as they contain substances that only certain types of bacteria can metabolise, producing a visible reaction such as a colour change. Many differential media are also selective.
	Enrichment media: contain specific growth factors that allow the growth of metabolically fastidious organisms (organisms that require specific nutrients for growth).

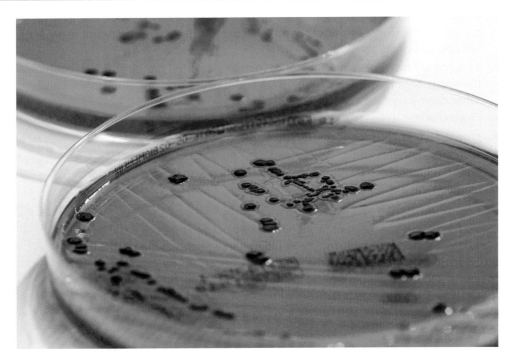

▶ *Salmonella enteric* bacteria growing on a selective culture medium, XLD-Agar, used to isolate Salmonella species, which cause gastroenteritis

Inoculation, incubation and microbiological transfer

The culture media to be used are sterile as they have been prepared aseptically. This ensures that only the micro-organisms deliberately added (**inoculated**) are present to grow for identification and/or investigations.

Before transferring micro-organisms from a liquid stock culture always swirl the stock culture as micro-organisms may be settled on the bottom of the flask or tube. The stock culture should have been made up about a day before you use it, so that the micro-organisms are in their log or exponential growth phase (undergoing cell division and growing well).

Aseptic technique is very important for every stage of transferring and growing micro-organisms, in order to avoid contamination of the stock culture media, to avoid adding unwanted micro-organisms to the cultures and to avoid contaminating personnel.

Key terms

Inoculation – the introduction of micro-organisms, such as bacteria, into/onto the liquid or solid media.

Aseptic technique – practices and procedures performed under carefully controlled conditions to minimise contamination by micro-organisms.

Personal care

You should not carry out practical procedures if you have a heavy cold or upset stomach.

▸ Cover cuts and grazes on exposed areas with a clean waterproof dressing.

▸ Avoid hand-to-mouth operations, such as chewing pen tops. Never eat or drink in the laboratory.

▸ Always wear a clean disposable apron to protect your clothes and to reduce the risk of contaminating the cultures you are inoculating. At the end of the session place the apron in the bag provided for potentially contaminated materials.

▸ Before you start the procedure, wash your hands with warm water and antiseptic soap, then dry them thoroughly with a paper towel, which you then place in the appropriate bag for disposal.

Surfaces and equipment

Benches should have smooth surfaces so that micro-organisms cannot collect in crevices.

▸ Swab the bench with disinfectant and leave for 10–15 minutes. Wipe the bench dry with a paper towel and place this in the appropriate disposal bag.

▸ Before you inoculate plates or tubes, label them with your name, the date and the bacterial culture. Always label Petri dishes on the base, not on the lid, using a marker pen (this avoids licking a label to stick on).

▸ Work near a lit Bunsen burner. Keep the flame on yellow when not in use, this is a cooler and safer flame and more easily seen.

Sterilising instruments

Sterilise your instruments before use.

▸ Adjust the Bunsen flame so it is hot and blue, hold wire loops or metal forceps at a 45° angle in the hottest part of the flame until they are red hot.

▸ Allow the instruments to cool in the air and then dip into a pot of 70 per cent methanol, and hold in the flame again briefly to burn off the methanol. Keep the methanol away from the Bunsen flame.

▸ Sterilise glass instruments, such as spreaders, by dipping them in methanol and flaming them lightly.

▸ Plastic instruments that have already been sterilised should only be used once and then discarded in the appropriate container.

▸ Pass the necks of the culture tubes or flasks through a hot Bunsen flame before and after using a pipette or loop to take out a sample. Never place bungs or caps from flasks or tubes on the bench, hold on to them.

▸ While inoculating Petri dishes, use one hand to lift the lid and keep it over the base while you spread the bacteria, using the loop or a glass spreader in your other hand. Do not put the lids down on the bench.

▸ Once you have inoculated Petri dishes, replace the lids and secure them with two pieces of tape. Do not place tape all around the lid as this excludes air and may encourage the growth of anaerobic micro-organisms.

▸ Report any spillages immediately.

▸ Place all instruments into a pot of disinfectant after use or dispose of them appropriately.

(a)

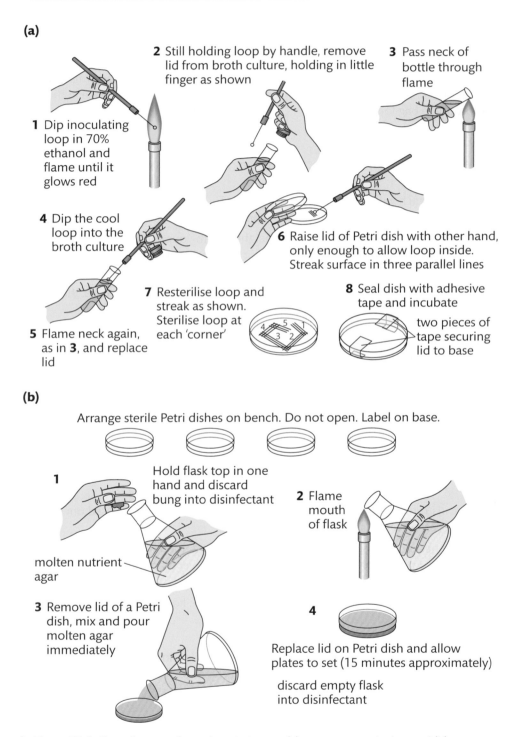

1 Dip inoculating loop in 70% ethanol and flame until it glows red

2 Still holding loop by handle, remove lid from broth culture, holding in little finger as shown

3 Pass neck of bottle through flame

4 Dip the cool loop into the broth culture

5 Flame neck again, as in **3**, and replace lid

6 Raise lid of Petri dish with other hand, only enough to allow loop inside. Streak surface in three parallel lines

7 Resterilise loop and streak as shown. Sterilise loop at each 'corner'

8 Seal dish with adhesive tape and incubate

two pieces of tape securing lid to base

(b)

Arrange sterile Petri dishes on bench. Do not open. Label on base.

1 Hold flask top in one hand and discard bung into disinfectant

molten nutrient agar

2 Flame mouth of flask

3 Remove lid of a Petri dish, mix and pour molten agar immediately

4 Replace lid on Petri dish and allow plates to set (15 minutes approximately)

discard empty flask into disinfectant

▶ **Figure 13.2:** Flow diagram of aseptic technique to (a) prepare a streak plate and (b) pour an agar plate

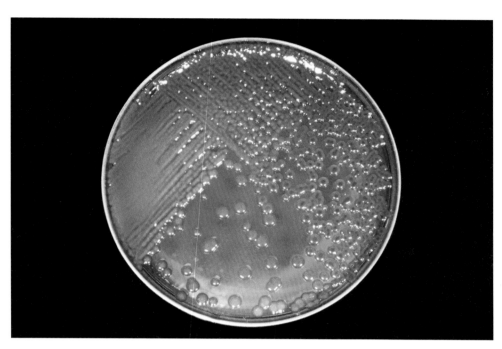

▶ Streak plate showing colonies of the bacteria *Klebsiella pneumoniae*, Gram negative rod-shaped bacteria that are normally found in human mouths, skin and intestines

Step by step: Incubating inoculated plates and tubes

You can incubate your plates and tubes at temperatures up to and including 30°C. The temperature you choose will depend on the investigations you are carrying out. It will also depend on whether or not you have access to a thermostatically controlled incubator.

- Incubate plates upside down so that any condensation runs onto the lid and not onto the colonies of bacteria or fungi growing on the plates. You can stack several plates on top of each other.
- When examining or counting the colonies, do not open the lids.
- If you wish to use some of the bacteria for staining and microscopic examination (see section on Gram stain tests, and section on Preparation of slides) your laboratory technician will place some filter paper soaked in a bactericidal agent in the lid of the Petri dish 24 hours before you examine the plates. You can then open the lid and use a sterile loop to transfer bacteria from a colony (or fungi from a mycelium) onto a microscope slide.

Discussion

You will only ever use harmless micro-organisms for your practical investigations. Why do you think you should still follow aseptic technique?

Counting techniques

It is often necessary to determine the number of micro-organisms in a particular sample. For example the number of micro-organisms present in some foods can indicate whether the food is safe to eat. Micro-organisms can be counted directly or indirectly.

Direct counting

Direct counts are slow and laborious. Direct counting can be done under a microscope using a counting chamber, electronic particle counter or fluorescent dyes.

Step by step: Using a haemocytometer

A haemocytometer is a counting chamber that was originally used to count the number of blood cells in a small volume of blood. Yeast cells are large enough to be seen with a light microscope at × 400 magnification. The haemocytometer slide (see Figure 13.3 (a)) has a grid etched onto the middle section that is slightly lower than the rest of the slide. When a special coverslip is placed firmly on the slide it forms a chamber of known depth, 0.1 mm, so you can calculate the volume of liquid over each etched square.

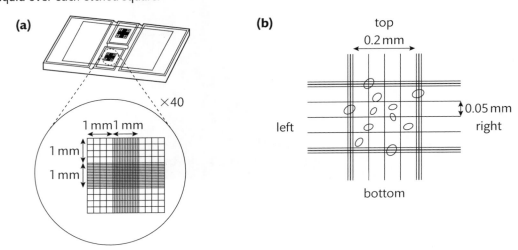

▶ **Figure 13.3:** (a) A haemocytometer slide (b) Using a haemocytometer slide to make a total cell count

- Breathe onto the haemocytometer slide and then, using your thumbs, press the coverslip firmly into place so that you can see the iridescence of Newton's rings (the interference pattern created by reflection of light between two surfaces).
- Shake the tube of liquid medium in which the yeast cells have been growing.
- Use a graduated pipette and take 1 mL of this liquid and add it to 9 mL of sterile water in a test tube. This dilutes the yeast sample by × 10. The dilution factor is 10^{-1}.
- Mix the diluted yeast sample well by rolling the tube between your palms and use a pipette to introduce a small amount to the slide, allowing some to trickle into the grooves under the haemocytometer coverslip. Blot any surplus liquid from outside the coverslip.
- Observe the haemocytometer grid under the microscope, on low power.
- Focus on the central grid area, where there are 25 squares, each of which is sub-divided into 16 smaller squares.
- Count the yeast cells in five of the 25 squares (80 small squares in total). To avoid bias, count the central square and the four corner squares. The volume of liquid over the 80 small squares is 0.02 mm³ (0.02 μL).
- Do not count any cells on the top or left side boundaries, so that the same cells are not counted twice.
- Now you know how many yeast cells there are in 0.02 μL of diluted liquid you can calculate the number of yeast cells in 1 mL of undiluted sample. There are 1000 μL in 1 mL (1 cm³).

    If there are N yeast cells in 0.02 μL of diluted solution

    Then in 1 mL undiluted solution there are $N/0.02 \times 1000 \times 10$ yeast cells.

This method, as well as being a direct counting method, is also a total count as it counts dead and living yeast cells.

Direct counting using fluorescent dyes

The cells are stained and, when subjected to ultraviolet light, the stained living cells fluoresce. The micro-organisms in a known volume of sample may be stained with acridine orange and then the sample is passed through a 0.22 μm filter. The micro-organisms are trapped on the filter, which can be viewed under a microscope.

Another fluorescent dye, cyanoditolyl tetrazolium chloride (CTC), binds to respiration proteins in the cells and can demonstrate living cells. Auramine and rhodamine bind to the cell walls of *Mycobacteria* and emit bright yellow or orange colours under a fluorescent microscope.

Indirect counting

These methods include using a spectrophotometer or colorimeter to measure the turbidity (cloudiness) of a liquid sample. Greater turbidity indicates high growth of micro-organisms. A colorimeter or spectrophotometer shines a beam of light of known wavelength (colour) through a sample placed in a special plastic container called a cuvette. A photoelectric cell picks up the light that has passed through the sample and the scale tells you how much light has been absorbed. Bacterial cells in the liquid scatter the light from the beam, so less light reaches the detector.

Step by step: Using a colorimeter

When using a colorimeter, the device is zeroed between each reading by placing an appropriate 'blank' sample to reset the 100 per cent transmission/0 per cent absorbance. In Figure 13.4, the blank would be uninoculated sterile liquid medium. Colour filters produce light of specific wavelengths. For this type of investigation a green filter is often used, producing light of wavelength 550 nm.

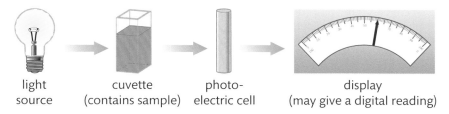

| light source | cuvette (contains sample) | photo-electric cell | display (may give a digital reading) |

▶ **Figure 13.4:** Using a colorimeter

- Fill a cuvette with uninoculated liquid culture medium and place it in the special chamber in the colorimeter. Use a green or blue filter. As the light shines through the sample, set the absorbance reading to 0, as this sample is clear and so there is no absorbance.

- Now fill another cuvette with some cloudy medium that has had micro-organism cells growing in it. Remove the blank cuvette and place this one in the colorimeter. Use the same filter as before and measure the absorbance.

The colorimeter cannot distinguish between dead and living cells but this method is quick and easy.

Colony counts

Another indirect counting method is to plate out a known volume of sample, diluted or undiluted, onto nutrient agar plates, incubate for a specified time at a certain temperature and then count the number of colonies on each plate. Each colony has arisen from a single bacterium that landed on the plate and divided, by binary fission, many times, forming a clone. This gives a *viable* count as only living cells divide and form colonies. However it is time consuming and uses a lot of equipment.

Step by step: Colony counts

Using aseptic technique:

- Take 1 mL of an inoculated liquid broth sample of *E. coli* bacteria and add it to 9 mL of sterile water in a test tube. This gives a × 10 dilution (dilution factor 10^{-1}).
- Roll the tube between your palms to mix the contents. Transfer 1 mL from this tube to another tube containing 9 mL sterile water. This gives a dilution of × 100 (10^{-2}).
- Repeat the first step over and over so that you make dilutions of × 1000 (10^{-3}), × 10,000 (10^{-4}), × 100,000 (10^{-5}), × 1,000,000 (10^{-6}) and × 10,000,000 (10^{-7}). (See Figure 13.5)
- Use a sterile pipette to transfer 1 mL of the × 100 diluted sample to a sterile nutrient agar plate, suitably labelled on the base. Use a sterile bent glass rod to create a lawn of bacteria on the nutrient agar. Replace the lid and tape in two places.
- Repeat the step above for all other diluted samples.
- Incubate the six inoculated plates, upside down, at 30°C for 24 hours.
- Count the colonies on the plates that produce between 20 and 200 colonies. You can divide the plate into sections by drawing on the base or lid, using a marker pen, and use a colony counter to click each time you use the pen to place a dot over a colony.
- Multiply the number of colonies counted by the dilution to estimate the number of bacteria in 1 mL of undiluted sample.

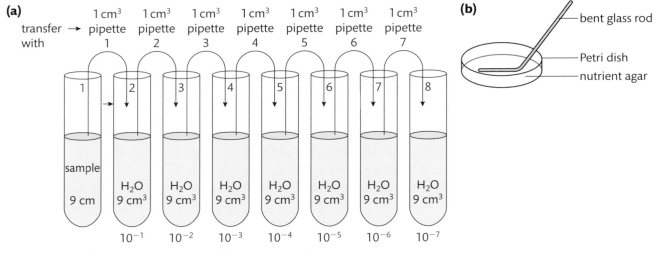

▶ **Figure 13.5:** (a) Making a serial dilution (b) Using a spreader

Most probable number (MPN) method

This method dates back to the early days of microbiology but is still used to estimate numbers of coliform bacteria in water, milk and some foods. Coliform bacteria are found in mammalian intestines and are passed out with faeces. They are Gram negative rod-shaped bacteria that can ferment the sugar, lactose. The resulting acid they produce can change the colour of an indicator added to the sample, and the gas the bacteria produce collects in a special inverted tube in the incubated sample. Samples are serially diluted and added to a growth medium with an indicator and gas collection tube. The numbers of samples that give a positive result (acid and gas) at each dilution are compared to statistical tables and a most probable number per mL can be found.

Measurement of microbial biomass

Microbial biomass increase can be used to assess the growth rate of some micro-organisms, for example fungi. If a liquid nutrient culture medium is inoculated with a fungus, the mycelium (mycelial mat) can be weighed at intervals and its mass determined. The mass of bacteria can be found and an estimate of cell numbers calculated from a calibration curve.

Growth rates and antibiotic sensitivity of micro-organisms

When a sample of bacteria is introduced into a fresh culture medium, the bacterial cells do not at first divide. There is a lag phase when the bacteria are 'getting used to' the new medium. The genes coding for the enzymes they require to digest the nutrients in the medium are being switched on and will soon be expressed. Once this happens and the cells can obtain nutrients and make ATP, they start to divide. The population grows exponentially, doubling at every cell division. This growth phase is called the log phase. As the cell numbers increase exponentially soon there are hundreds of millions of cells present. This leads to competition for space, nutrients and, if the bacteria are aerobic, oxygen. This state, plus the accumulation of their toxic metabolic by-products, leads to the stationary phase, where the numbers of cells dying equals the numbers of new cells arising. Eventually more cells die than are produced and the population enters the decline phase. The phases of the growth curve are shown in Figure 13.6.

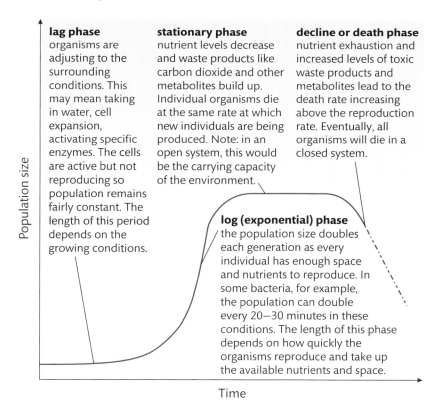

lag phase
organisms are adjusting to the surrounding conditions. This may mean taking in water, cell expansion, activating specific enzymes. The cells are active but not reproducing so population remains fairly constant. The length of this period depends on the growing conditions.

stationary phase
nutrient levels decrease and waste products like carbon dioxide and other metabolites build up. Individual organisms die at the same rate at which new individuals are being produced. Note: in an open system, this would be the carrying capacity of the environment.

decline or death phase
nutrient exhaustion and increased levels of toxic waste products and metabolites lead to the death rate increasing above the reproduction rate. Eventually, all organisms will die in a closed system.

log (exponential) phase
the population size doubles each generation as every individual has enough space and nutrients to reproduce. In some bacteria, for example, the population can double every 20–30 minutes in these conditions. The length of this phase depends on how quickly the organisms reproduce and take up the available nutrients and space.

Population size

Time

▶ **Figure 13.6:** Growth curve for a population of bacteria

The growth rate of a sample of bacteria can be estimated by measuring the turbidity of a sample in a suitable culture medium, incubated at a suitable temperature and pH, every half hour and plotting a graph. If the turbidity is proportional to cell numbers, it can be estimated how long it takes for the cell numbers to double. This is called the generation time. Some bacteria have a generation time of 30 minutes, whereas *Mycobacterium tuberculosis*, which causes TB, is slow-growing and has a generation time of about 22 hours.

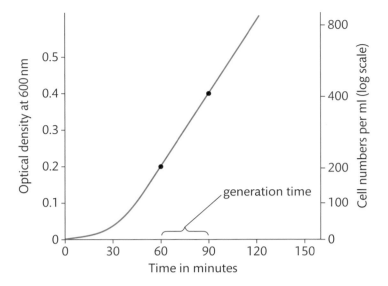

▶ **Figure 13.7:** Indirect method for determining generation time

Antibiotics often affect growing bacteria, slow-growing types are less easily dealt with by antibiotics and a longer course of antibiotics may be needed. Doctors often prescribe broad spectrum antibiotics for an infection when tests are not carried out to identify the pathogen. If these antibiotics do not work, then tests are carried out to identify the bacterium and to find which antibiotics will be most effective against it.

▶ The bacteria are spread onto agar plates and discs impregnated with various antibiotics are added to the agar plates.

▶ If the bacteria do not grow in an area surrounding the disc, where the antibiotic has diffused from the disc into the agar, then the antibiotic is killing the bacteria or preventing their growth.

▶ The wider the zone of inhibition (visible area of no growth) the more effective that antibiotic is against that type of bacterium.

▶ Clinicians will try to select an antibiotic that is effective at stopping the growth of the bacterium and that avoids or minimises unpleasant or dangerous side effects.

Some bacteria have evolved resistance to antibiotics and a few types of antibiotics are used only for treating bacteria resistant to the more usually used antibiotics.

Gram stain tests

One of the first investigative tests carried out to identify the bacteria in a sample is the Gram stain, developed in 1884 by the Danish microbiologist Hans Christian Gram. This stain can distinguish between Gram positive and Gram negative bacteria. It is still an important diagnostic technique, as Gram positive bacteria have different cell wall structures from those of Gram negative bacteria and respond differently to antibiotics. Penicillin prevents cell wall synthesis in growing Gram positive bacteria but is ineffective against Gram negative bacteria.

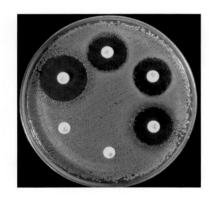

▶ Antibiotic resistance in *E. coli* bacteria – these bacteria are sensitive to four of the antibiotics, as shown by the clear zones of inhibition around the discs, but are resistant to two antibiotics as shown by the bacteria growing close to the discs

Step by step: The Gram stain test

- Use a pipette to place a drop of sterile water on a clean microscope slide.
- Use a sterilised microbiological wire loop to transfer some bacteria from a colony, or from a liquid culture, into the water on the slide. Move the loop in a circular motion to spread the bacteria on the slide, making a smear.
- Allow the slide to dry, either in the air, over a beaker of hot water, or by passing it quickly to and fro in a hot Bunsen flame. This heat fixes the smear onto the slide.
- Add one drop of crystal violet stain to the smear and leave for one minute. This stains the bacterial cell walls.
- Wash off the excess crystal violet, using tap water.
- Flood the smear with Gram's iodine solution. This is a mordant (a substance that combines with a dye or stain and fixes it in a material) – it intensifies the violet colour of the stain.
- Wash off the Gram's iodine with tap water.
- Add 95 per cent ethanol, drop by drop, until no more violet colour washes from the smear.
- Counter-stain the smear with pink safranin for 45 seconds.
- Wash off the safranin with tap water.
- Gently dry the slide in a blue Bunsen flame.
- Place a drop of cedar oil on the slide and examine the bacteria, using the oil immersion objective on a light microscope (see the section on Use of light microscope).
- If the bacteria are Gram positive, they will have retained the purple stain.
- Gram negative bacteria have a thinner wall and two lipid membranes on either side of the wall. This allows the ethanol to wash out the crystal violet and these bacteria stain pink from the safranin they have taken up.

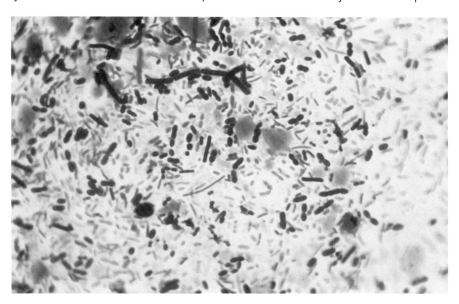

▶ Gram-stained light micrograph of bacteria sampled from a normal healthy human intestine, the dark-stained bacteria are Gram positive and those stained pale pink are Gram negative

Safety tips

Avoid skin contact with the chemicals: crystal violet, Gram's iodine, ethanol and safranin.

When bacteria are viewed under a microscope their shape and size can also be seen. Rod-shaped bacteria are described as bacillus (plural: bacilli). Round bacteria are described as coccus (plural: cocci). Using the Gram stain, bacteria can be described as Gram positive bacilli, Gram positive cocci, Gram negative bacilli or Gram negative cocci. Some bacteria, such as *Vibrio cholerae*, *Mycobacterium tuberculosis*, *Mycobacterium leprae* and *Mycobacterium bovis* are neither Gram positive nor Gram negative and they can be identified with a special acid-fast stain. Table 13.4 shows some important Gram positive and Gram negative bacteria.

▶ **Table 13.4:** Some important Gram positive and Gram negative bacteria

Gram positive cocci	Staphylococcal (in clusters) – can produce the enzyme catalase, which breaks down hydrogen peroxide. *Staphylococcus aureus* may cause hospital acquired infections.
	Streptococci (in strings) – cannot make catalase. *Streptococcus pneumoniae* causes meningococcal meningitis. Other streptococci cause sore throats, tooth decay and endocarditis.
Gram positive bacilli	*Bacillus cereus* causes food poisoning, *Clostridium tetani* causes tetanus, *Clostridium botulinum* causes botulism, and *Clostridium difficile* causes severe diarrhoea and colonitis.
Gram negative cocci	*Neisseria gonorrhoea* causes gonorrhoea – these bacteria occur in pairs (diplococcus).
Gram negative bacilli	*Escherichia coli* occurs normally in the gut but some strains (e.g. 0157) can be harmful. *Salmonella enteriditis* causes food poisoning, *S. typhi* causes typhoid fever, *Yersinia pestis* causes bubonic plague, and *Bortadella pertissus* causes whooping cough.
Gram negative curved rod	*Vibrio cholera* causes cholera.
Gram negative helical shaped	*Treponema pallidum* causes syphilis, *Borrelia* causes Lyme disease, *Helicobacter pylori* causes stomach ulcers, and *Campylobacter jenuni* causes food poisoning.

PAUSE POINT

Why is the Gram stain the first step in identifying the type of bacteria causing an infection?

Hint How does the Gram stain distinguish between different types of bacteria?

Extend What type of stain is used for Mycobacteria?

Analysis techniques in health-related laboratories

Many of the techniques used for analysis in laboratories are similar to those practised in schools and colleges during science lessons.

Calculations of concentrations of solutions

One of the basic chemistry skills is calculating the concentration of a chemical solution.

Concentration refers to the amount of solute (usually a solid, such as table salt) that is dissolved in a solvent (usually a liquid, such as water).

Concentration may be expressed in many ways, for example per cent by mass, per cent by volume or molarity.

$$\text{Per cent composition by mass} = \frac{\text{mass of solute} \times 100}{\text{mass of solution}}$$

$$\text{Per cent composition by volume} = \frac{\text{volume of solute} \times 100}{\text{volume of solution}}$$

Molarity is the most commonly used unit of concentration.

A mole is the molecular mass of a substance in grams. For example, one mole of sucrose is 342 g. The molecular formula for sucrose is $C_{12}H_{22}O_{11}$. This means that each molecule of sucrose contains six atoms of carbon, 12 of hydrogen and 11 of oxygen.

Key term

Molarity – the number of moles of solute per litre of solution.

The relative atomic mass of:

▸ carbon is 12

▸ hydrogen is 1

▸ oxygen is 16.

Thus the molecular mass of sucrose is $(12 \times 12) + (22 \times 1) + (11 \times 16) = 144 + 22 + 176$
$$= 342$$

Preparing solutions of known concentrations

Step by step: Solution preparation

To make 1 litre of 1 M sucrose solution

• Weigh out 342 g sucrose and place it in a volumetric flask.

• Add distilled water and shake the flask to dissolve the sucrose.

• Now carefully add more distilled water until the level of liquid in the flask reaches the 1 L mark.

> **Key term**
>
> **Stock solution** – a concentrated solution that can be diluted to lower concentrations for actual use.

▸ Volumetric flasks

From a **stock** 1M (I molar) **solution** you can make solutions of different molarities, as shown in Table 13.5.

▸ **Table 13.5:** Making different concentrations of sucrose solution from a stock solution

Volume of 1 M stock solution sucrose (mL)	10.0	9.0	8.0	7.0	6.0	5.0	4.0	3.0	2.0	1.0
Volume of water (mL)	0.0	1.0	2.0	3.0	4.0	5.0	6.0	7.0	8.0	9.0
Concentration of resulting sucrose solution (M)	1.0	0.9	0.8	0.7	0.6	0.5	0.4	0.3	0.2	0.1

⏸ **PAUSE POINT**   How would you make a 1 M solution of fructose?

（Hint）   Fructose, like glucose, is a monosaccharide. What is its molecular mass?

（Extend）   How would you make up a 0.25 M solution of fructose?

Dilution factors

Earlier in this section you will have seen that serial dilutions are often used when estimating the numbers of micro-organisms in a sample. When a sample is diluted by adding 1 mL of the sample to 9 mL of sterile water, giving a total of 10 parts:

▸ The 1 mL sample is now 1/10 of the final solution. The dilution factor is 1:10 or 1/10 or 0.1. Another way of writing 0.1 is 10^{-1}.

▸ If 1 mL of this diluted sample is added to 9 mL of sterile water, the dilution is now 1/100 or 10^{-2}. This resulting solution is 100 times more dilute than the original. See Figure 13.5 (a).

Radionuclide techniques

Nuclear medicine imaging is used to diagnose some conditions. The patient is injected with or swallows a solution containing radioactive pharmaceuticals, such as iodine-123 or thallium 201, which emit gamma rays. These radiopharmaceuticals (also called tracers) have a short half-life and quickly decay away, so that the radioactivity disappears soon after the test has been carried out. A scan of the body, or part of it, shows where the radionuclide has accumulated and which may indicate damage or abnormalities. The radiation dose is kept as low as possible and these techniques are only used where the benefits outweigh the risks.

▸ Iodine-123 is used to investigate the thyroid gland.

▸ Thallium 201 is used to study the heart.

Nuclear medicine tests are unlike other scans in that they tell clinicians something about the workings (physiology) and/or blood flow of the structure being investigated, and not just what it looks like.

In some cases, the nuclear medicine scans can be superimposed on CT scans to give detailed diagnostic information about the anatomy and physiology of body structures.

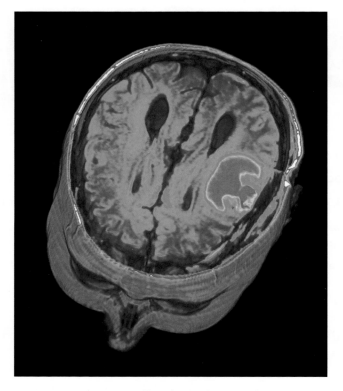

▸ Functional magnetic resonance imaging (fMRI) scan showing a brain tumour

Chromatography

Chromatography is a laboratory technique to separate the components of a mixture. It was first used to separate the mixture of pigments in chlorophyll extracted from plants.

Step by step: Chromatography of chlorophyll

You can carry out an exercise in thin layer chromatography of chlorophyll.

- Place a leaf on a microscope slide and use another microscope slide to scrape the juice out of the leaf.
- Use a pipette to add six drops of propanone to the green mush that is now on the slide.
- Transfer the dark green liquid to a watch glass.
- Use a hairdryer to remove all the water from the extract. Add three drops of propanone to the dried extract and mix with a fine paint brush.
- Cut a thin strip from a thin layer chromatography (TLC) plate. The strip needs to be thin enough to fit into the chromatography tube. Draw a pencil line about 1 cm up from the base of the TLC piece. Do not touch the TLC plate surface with your fingers.
- Use a paint brush to transfer a drop of leaf extract to the middle of the pencil line you have drawn. Allow this spot to dry. Repeat this process until the spot is very dark green.
- Slot the TLC strip into a groove in the cork stopper of the chromatography tube. Place the solvent in the bottom of the tube, so that it is no more than 0.5 cm depth.
- Insert the stopper and TLC strip into the tube.
- As the solvent travels up the TLC plate, each pigment in the chlorophyll travels at a different rate and the coloured pigments spread out.
- Calculate how far each pigment spot travels compared to the distance travelled by the solvent. This is the R_f value for each pigment.

$$R_f = \frac{\text{distance travelled by pigment}}{\text{distance travelled by solvent}}$$

Research

Go to **www.saps.org.uk/secondary/teaching-resources/181-student-sheet-10-thin-layer-chromatography-for-photosynthetic-pigments** to find out more about thin layer chromatography.

Besides paper chromatography, which is similar to thin layer chromatography but uses paper, and thin layer chromatography, there are also liquid and gas (sometimes called gas-liquid) chromatography techniques.

All forms of chromatography work on the same principles.

▸ They all have a stationary phase, either solid or a liquid supported on a solid.
▸ They all have a mobile phase, called the **eluate**, which is the sample to be analysed.
▸ The mixture to be separated is dissolved in a solvent, called the eluent. This is the mobile phase.
▸ The mobile phase carries the mixture through the stationary phase.
▸ The various components (**analytes**) of the mixture travel through the stationary phase at different speeds and, therefore, spread out and separate from each other.

Key terms

Eluate – a solution obtained by elution – the process of extracting one material from another by washing with a solvent.

Analyte – a substance whose chemical constituents are being identified and measured.

The practical example given in the step-by-step chromotagraphy of chlorophyll uses planar chromatography; the stationary phase is in a plane. It will work with paper but TLC uses an **adsorbent** layer, such as silica gel coated onto an inert substance. TLC is faster than paper chromatography.

Phases in chromatography

▶ In column chromatography – the stationary phase is within a tube, either packed in to the whole space in the tube or fixed to the sides of the tube.

▶ In liquid chromatography – the mobile phase is liquid. This can be carried out with planar or column for the stationary phase.

▶ In gas (gas-liquid) chromatography – the mobile phase is a gas. This could be vapour produced from a liquid. The gas travels through the stationary phase, which is in a column.

> **Link**
>
> See *Unit 23: Biomedical Science*, section on Blood components for more about blood.

Chromatography is used in blood purification and processing so that donated blood can be safely used therapeutically. Platelets may be obtained from blood for treating patients with severe blood disorders, including leukaemia.

> **Key terms**
>
> **Adsorbent** – able to hold on to (adsorb) substances.

Electrophoresis is used in laboratories to separate large molecules such as proteins and nucleic acids based on their size. The molecules move through a gel that is covered with a buffer solution. Because the molecules have an overall negative charge, they are attracted to a positive anode. In a set time, the smaller molecules move further through the gel than do the bigger molecules.

Changes in levels of metabolites in body fluids and cells can indicate that a cell is over- or under-producing particular proteins, and other chemicals produced during reactions catalysed by enzymes (proteins). Such changes indicate that particular cells are malfunctioning, which may be due to a genetic defect, cancer, infection or degeneration. Chromatography and electrophoresis can also be used to detect abnormal levels of metabolites, to help diagnose genetic diseases such as phenylketonuria (PKU), sickle cell anaemia and alkaptonuria.

To give a more accurate diagnosis, chromatography can be used in association with mass spectroscopy.

▶ A set of high performance liquid chromatography (HPLC) columns used to separate mixtures of biological molecules

Spectroscopy

Mass spectroscopy is a type of analysis that determines what molecules are present in a sample, based on the spectrum produced by the ions of those molecules.

The sample to be analysed is vaporised and then bombarded with a beam of high-energy electrons to ionise (create charged particles by displacing electrons from molecules) molecules within the sample. Losing an electron weakens bonds within the molecule; collisions by electrons give the molecules more kinetic energy. As a result, when the molecules travel through the spectrometer tube they break into fragments.

Charged plates in the spectrometer's ionisation chamber cause ions to accelerate into an analyser tube, which is surrounded by a magnetic field that deflects the ions. The subsequent flight path of the deflected ions depends on its molecular mass and charge, and on the strength of the magnetic field. At each specific magnetic field strength, only ions of a certain molecular mass will collide with the detector and be recorded.

The strength of the magnetic field is increased bit by bit to produce a mass spectrum. This can be interpreted and the relative abundance of the various ions in the sample can be seen.

▶ A mass spectrometer – the sample is ionised and deflected when in a strong magnetic field and the different components separate due to differences in their charge and mass, which cause differences in their deflection

Clinical diagnostic mass spectrometers are valuable diagnostic tools. They can analyse very small samples rapidly and at the same time detect many different types of molecules in the sample, even when those molecules are present in very low concentrations. Because small samples can be used, this technique is especially good for diagnosing illnesses in children, who may not be able to produce a large sample.

Analytes and **biomarkers** in blood serum or urine can be assessed using mass spectroscopy. The presence of drugs, toxins and hormones in body fluids, such as urine, can also be found using this technique. Techniques are being developed to use mass spectroscopy to detect:

▶ neonatal brain injury

▶ infection by a pathogen

▶ cardiac health status

▶ all types of cancer

▶ allergies

▶ mental health and psychiatric disorders

▶ abnormalities during pregnancy.

Mass spectrometry is superseding the use of chromatography for analysing clinical samples.

Key term

Biomarkers – certain proteins that are produced in abnormal amounts by cells and, under certain pathological circumstances, can be used to diagnose specific conditions.

Biomarkers for Alzheimer's disease

Mass spectroscopy-based analysis at Uppsala University has looked at proteins in the cerebrospinal fluid (CSF) of ten people with Alzheimer's disease (AD) and ten controls. They found that eight proteins were expressed differently in the two groups. Four of these proteins are for cell adhesion, migration and morphology. The other four may be important for synapse development. Changes in the amounts of proteins in the CSF indicate changes in the brain and nervous system. The proteins extracted from the CSF were digested with the enzyme trypsin and then liquid chromatography and mass spectroscopy were used to find out which proteins were present.

The research team found 894 different proteins in the CSF, of which 162 were altered in patients with AD, and 32 of those to be statistically significantly altered. The team published their findings so that other research groups could replicate the investigations and verify the findings. Eight of the altered proteins seem to be useful as biomarkers and may lead to better diagnostic techniques for identifying patients who will develop AD.

Check your knowledge

1 Why do you think it will be useful to diagnose AD much earlier, before severe symptoms appear?

2 What sort of people do you think were in the control group?

3 Why is it important that scientists publish their research?

Growth counting

You have already read about some indirect and direct methods for counting growing bacteria (see the section on Counting techniques). Table 13.6 summarises some growth counting methods and their applications, and evaluates the usefulness of each one. The simplest methods are most commonly used and deemed to be accurate enough.

▶ **Table 13.6:** Some growth counting methods

Method	Application	Comments
Direct microscopic count, using a haemocytometer, a Petroff-Hausser counting chamber or an electronic device – a Coulter counter.	To find the number of bacteria in food samples, such as milk, or in vaccines against bacterial diseases.	This method cannot distinguish between living and dead cells. Clumps of cells within the counting squares may make it difficult to accurately count cells.
Colony counts (plate counts) to give a viable cell count. A viable cell is one that can divide and increase cell numbers. The sample may be spread, with a glass spreader, over an agar plate or added to the warm molten agar before it is poured into a Petri dish.	To find numbers of bacteria in milk, soil, water, laboratory cultures.	Very sensitive but time consuming, and uses a lot of apparatus. Makes the assumption that each colony arises from one single bacterium, but bacterial cells in sample may be clumped together, so each colony has arisen from one colony-forming unit.
Turbidity (optical density) measurement using a spectrophotometer (colorimeter).	Estimation of large numbers of bacteria in clear liquid samples, such as broths. No good for milk.	Quick and easy and liquid samples can be taken from the stock at intervals to estimate growth rates. Needs calibration to convert optical density readings to cell numbers. Cannot detect cell densities of less than 10^7 per mL.

▶ **Table 13.6:** *continued*

Method	Application	Comments
Measurement of total nitrogen content or total protein content.	Can be used for very dense cultures, where cell numbers cannot be estimated using direct counts or colony counts.	Assumes that as cells divide and grow the DNA (which contains nitrogen) content doubles and protein content increases. Only used in research laboratories.
Measurement of biochemical activity such as rate of oxygen uptake, rate of carbon dioxide production, rate of ATP production.	Microbiological assays.	Needs a fixed standard for calibration so that biochemical activity can be related to cell numbers.
Measurement of dry mass or wet mass of cells or of volume of cells after centrifugation (spinning at high speed so that cells go to the bottom of the suspension and can be extracted).	Measurement of total cell yield in cultures.	Sensitive but needs calibration. Cell sizes of different micro-organisms vary. Dry mass of about 10^6 cells of *E. coli* is 150 mg. Dry mass is about 10–20% of wet mass.

Decay counting

You have learned that radionuclides are used in some methods of diagnoses (see section on Radionuclide techniques). Radionuclides are radioactive isotopes of elements. About 70 occur on Earth. Each type of radionuclide has a specific half-life. The half-life of a particular radionuclide is the time taken for half of its radioactive atoms to decay. This means that after that time, half of its radioactivity has been lost. After another period of the same time, half of the remaining half of radioactivity has been lost. This exponential pattern of loss of radioactivity is called radioactive decay, and is due to particles (and energy) being emitted from the unstable nuclei of the elements. Some radioactive isotopes lose alpha particles (helium nuclei of two protons and two neutrons), some lose beta particles (electrons are lost from protons, which then become neutrons) and some emit gamma rays (not particles but a form of energy).

For medical diagnosis using nuclear medicine imaging, the radionuclides are taken internally and external detectors (gamma cameras) outside the body capture the radiation emitted from within the body and form images. This differs from X-ray imaging where external radiation is passed through the body to form an image. Widespread clinical use of nuclear medicine began in the 1950s and by the 1980s radiopharmaceuticals had been designed for use in diagnosing heart disease. At that time, single photon (light particle) emission computed tomography (SPECT) was developed, which allowed clinicians to see a 3D image of a patient's heart. This also established the medical field of nuclear cardiology.

Many medical radionuclides are produced in a nuclear reactor but some are made in a cyclotron (a type of particle accelerator). An important medical radionuclide is molybdenum-99 (Mo-99), one of the fission products of uranium. Mo-99 decays by emitting beta radiation and has a half-life of 66 hours. It then becomes technetium-99 (Tc-99), the most widely used medical radionuclide, which decays inside the patient's body emitting gamma rays that are captured by a gamma camera outside the body. It decays fairly quickly to a relatively non-radioactive isotope, so the patient is exposed to ionising radiation for a very short period of time.

Most diagnostic radionuclides use gamma ray emitters, which have a very small risk of causing cancer or damaging the patient's body. Therapeutic radionuclides use beta emitters, which damage cells and can, therefore, destroy cancer cells.

Research

Go to www.youtube.com/watch?v=4grQSLmWXQk to watch bacteria dividing and increasing their numbers, as seen under a microscope.

Research

Read about nuclear medicine online to find out more about use of radionuclides.

Food analysis techniques

The food industry is very competitive and food manufacturers continually try to increase their share of sales. In order to do this, they need to ensure their products are of higher quality, less expensive and more desirable than those of their competitors while at the same time being nutritious and safe. There are government regulations and recommendations concerned with maintaining the quality of food to ensure that the food industry provides consumers with food that is nutritious and safe. There are specified food standards to be met. Food manufacturers also have a duty to inform consumers about the nutritional value of food.

You have already read about techniques and tests that can be done to ensure the food is not contaminated with unwanted micro-organisms. Food manufacturers also need analytical techniques to analyse food materials before, during and after the manufacturing process to ensure that the final product meets the desired standards. The food products need to have consistence in appearance, taste, texture and shelf-life. Sometimes the ingredients vary, but if food manufacturers understand the roles of each different food ingredient they can adjust the manufacturing process to produce consistent products. Raw materials, as well as finished products, have to be analysed. During processing, samples are withdrawn and analysed in a quality assurance laboratory, so that if problems are detected then the manufacturing process can be adjusted accordingly. This can be slow and involves the loss of some of each batch, so more rapid, precise and non-destructive analytical techniques are favoured.

Here you will consider some ways of assaying the lipid, ascorbic acid and amino acid content of food.

Case study

Potatoes

Food companies need to react to changing tastes and consumer demands so that the sales of their products remain high.

Angharad Jones is a scientist in a large food company. Angharad carries out basic research to gain a better understanding of the roles of various ingredients of products, and how each is affected by environmental changes, for example storage temperatures.

Potatoes are well known as starchy vegetables but they also contain reducing sugar. The more sugar the potatoes contain then the browner the chips made from them will be. The brown colour is due to chemicals called acrylamides, made by a reaction between reducing sugar and amino acids at temperatures above 100°C (as in frying).

Angharad reads relevant journals to keep informed about research in the food industry and she has read that acrylamides have been linked to cancer.

Lower sugar varieties of potatoes produce less acrylamide. She uses a quick, precise, easy and non-destructive method to test different varieties of potatoes for their reducing sugar content. The method involves dipping a reagent stick into potato tissue and watching for a colour change and then comparing it to a range of standards to find the percentage of reducing sugar.

Using low reducing sugar varieties is safer but gives paler chips. However, the frying methods can be adjusted to keep the same brown colour that consumers like.

Other research laboratories are developing genetically modified (GM) varieties of potatoes with a lower reducing sugar content.

Check your knowledge

1 Suggest why boiled potatoes do not go brown.

2 Explain why Angharad is using low sugar varieties of potatoes to make frozen chips.

3 Why are GM low sugar potatoes being developed?

Lipid content

Lipids or fats give food texture, taste, some necessary nutrients (essential fatty acids and cholesterol) and a lot of energy. Food research has placed great emphasis on manipulation of lipid content to change food texture, fatty acid and cholesterol composition, to decrease the total fat content and make the fats more biologically stable. Food scientists need to be able to assay (find out) the total lipid content, saturated fatty acid content and cholesterol content of food products. Such information has to be displayed on the nutrition labels.

> **Link**
>
> For more information about lipids or fats, see *Unit 24: Biochemistry for Health*, learning aim A.

▸ Fat content can be determined by using an organic solvent, such as alcohol or chloroform, to extract the lipids from a food sample.

▸ Fatty acid content can be found by gas chromatography. The triglycerides are first hydrolysed (broken down) to glycerol and fatty acids.

▸ Cholesterol content can be ascertained by gas chromatography, high performance liquid chromatography and by enzyme techniques. For enzymic determination, cholesterol is separated from fatty acids. An enzyme, cholesterol oxidase, is added to the free cholesterol and this initiates a series of chemical reactions leading to a yellow dye, the quantity of which can be determined by spectrophotometry.

▸ Fatty acid content. Lipase enzymes can be used to digest the fats in a food. This releases fatty acids, which lower the pH. A pH probe can read the pH, the lower it is the more fatty acids have been released. A set of standards of lipids of known concentrations can be made and digested with lipase enzymes, and their pH read, for comparison against the unknown food samples.

▸ Oxidation of lipids in foods is a major cause of food spoilage, which leads to loss of nutrients as well as unacceptable flavours and texture.

Ascorbic acid content

▸ Ascorbic acid is vitamin C. Some foods contain ascorbic acid that has been added as a preservative, because it is an antioxidant – it delays oxidation of other constituents in the food and delays spoilage. Humans cannot synthesise ascorbic acid but it is an essential nutrient needed for making collagen, which is found in blood vessel walls, bones and connective tissue. Humans obtain ascorbic acid from their diet.

▸ There are various chemicals that react with ascorbic acid and quantitative tests, involving **titration**, can show the concentration of ascorbic acid in foods.

> **Key term**
>
> **Titration** – a technique where a solution of known concentration is used to determine the concentration of another solution with which it reacts.

> **Research**
>
> Go to **www.outreach.canterbury.ac.nz/chemistry/documents/vitaminc_iodine.pdf** to find out how to measure the ascorbic acid of foods using titration with iodine solution and starch solution as an indicator.
>
> Go to **www.saps.org.uk/secondary/teaching-resources/191-measuring-changes-in-ascorbic-acid-vitamin-c-concentration-in-ripening-fruit-and-vegetables** to find out how to measure the ascorbic acid content of foods using a chemical called DCPIP.

Amino acid content

Humans need to eat about 50 g of good quality protein every day. Humans cannot store dietary protein, which is why you need to eat it every day. It is of no advantage to eat more than you need as the excess is broken down to urea and excreted in urine. Animal protein (eggs, meat, milk and cheese) contains a higher proportion of the ten essential amino acids that humans need to obtain from their diet in order to make proteins than vegetable proteins, apart from soya, do.

All amino acids contain nitrogen and one method of finding amino acid content is to test for nitrogen content in foods. However, other chemicals, such as DNA, RNA, ATP, some vitamins and the coenzyme NAD, also contain nitrogen. The Kjeldahl procedure for measuring the nitrogen content of food can be used for comparing protein content, as it is assumed that each type of cell contains similar amounts of non-protein nitrogen.

Most food analyses test for total nitrogen content and use a formula to estimate the protein content of food.

To analyse and find which amino acids are in foods, proteins are first hydrolysed to break them down to amino acids. The relative amounts of specific amino acids can be found in a food sample by using high-performance liquid chromatography. The column uses silica gel and hydrocarbons as the stationary phase. The amino acids in the eluents are detected using a fluorescence detector (see the section on Chromatography). Gas-liquid chromatography and thin-layer chromatography may also be used.

Food processing techniques may alter the amino acid content of foods, so laboratories have to compare the protein and amino acid content of foods after processing. In some cases, microbial assay can be used. Micro-organisms with known amino acid requirements are grown in the processed food and their growth rates measured and compared with those grown in non-processed foods.

Using a practical microbiology skill

You can carry out practicals in your school or college laboratory and become familiar with many of the techniques used in health-related laboratories. Using aseptic technique, you can pour agar plates, inoculate them by using a spreader or by streak plating, and inoculate liquid media. You can then practise counting colonies and measuring growth in liquid media by using a colorimeter/spectrophotometer (see the section on Principles and preparation of culture media).

You can also practise making solutions of known concentration; for example, you could follow a recipe and make up some liquid or solid media. You can practise making serial dilutions (see the section on Colony counts), for example of milk, and plating out from some of the dilutions to estimate the numbers of bacteria per mL.

> **Research**
>
> Go to **www.nuffieldfoundation.org/practical-biology/making-nutrient-agars** for information and recipes to make up agars.
>
> Go to **www.rpgroup.caltech.edu/courses/aph162/2007/Protocols/Size-rate%20 protocols.pdf** or to **www.microbiologyonline.org.uk/teachers/preparation-of-media-and-cultures** for information about making up liquid culture media.

You can also practise using a haemocytometer and you may count yeast cells (see Step by step: Using a haemocytometer) and estimate how many are present in 1 mL of stock solution.

Effectiveness of different antiseptics or disinfectants

Antiseptics and disinfectants are chemical substances used to prevent contamination and infection by micro-organisms.

Antiseptics are antimicrobial substances that can be applied to living tissue, such as skin, to reduce the possibility of infection or sepsis. Examples include alcohols used in hand gels, thymol used in mouthwashes, tinctures of iodine used for cleaning skin and wounds, chlorine compounds used for wound irrigation, soaps and detergents, silver used in wound dressings, honey used in wound dressings.

Disinfectants are antimicrobial substances that are applied to non-living surfaces to destroy micro-organisms on those surfaces. Examples include bleach, Virkon®, and phenolic compounds such as Lysol®.

Once you have mastered using aseptic technique, and practised all the techniques mentioned earlier, you can plan and carry out a practical investigation to find the effectiveness of different antiseptics or disinfectants.

There are various methods that you could use.

1 You can inoculate solid nutrient agar plates with bacteria, such as *E. coli, S. albus* or *B. subtilis*, taken from liquid stock cultures and then, using a narrow diameter cork borer, make a well in the centre of the plate and add a known volume of the antiseptic or disinfectant, at a known concentration. These plates can be taped and labelled but must be incubated the right way up. After incubation at 30°C for 24 hours the clear zones of inhibition around the wells can be measured and compared. Do not take the lids off the agar plates to do this.

2 Another method is to soak paper discs (made from filter paper using a hole-puncher) in different solutions of antiseptic/disinfectant, for a specified time. Then, using sterile forceps, you can place the soaked discs onto inoculated agar plates, incubate and compare the zones of inhibition.

3 A third method is to inoculate liquid media with a sample of bacteria and then add a known volume of known concentration of the antibacterial substance, incubate and measure the turbidity using a spectrophotometer. You will need a control liquid media that is not inoculated to use as the blank.

4 A fourth method is to add a known volume of a specific concentration of the antibacterial chemical solution to a liquid culture of the chosen bacterium for a specified time. Then, using aseptic technique, take one loopful of the bacterial culture and either plate it out, incubate for 24 hours at 30°C and count the colonies, or inoculate a tube of sterile liquid culture, incubate at 30°C for 24 hours and measure the turbidity.

You can compare the effectiveness of:

▶ two or more different antiseptics
▶ two or more different disinfectants
▶ other substances known to have antibacterial properties, such as garlic extract, lemon juice or tea tree oil.

Before you carry out your investigation you will need to write a detailed plan and have it checked by your tutor.

Your plan should include:

▶ a clearly stated and testable hypothesis (prediction)
▶ the background biology that indicates the rationale behind the investigation and explains your prediction; you can do some research using the internet and textbooks to find out more about the effect of antiseptics and disinfectants on bacterial growth

▸ clearly stated independent and dependent variables

▸ the control variables, why they need to be controlled and how you will control them

▸ a list of apparatus and reagents needed; include here the species of bacteria and the type of antibacterial substance you will use

▸ a risk assessment

▸ a step-by-step method

▸ how you will analyse and present your data.

You need to draw up a suitable table, decide whether you will produce a graph from the data, and investigate suitable statistical tests to be used.

Once you have had your plan checked and approved, you can carry out your investigation. Write up the report of your investigation. In your report, discuss the sources of errors and limitations of the practical protocol you used. Suggest possible improvements and further investigations that could be carried out. If different members of your class investigate different antibacterial substances, you can share your findings with others in your class. Make sure that you correctly reference all sources of information you have used.

Lowest effective concentration of antiseptics or disinfectants

You can choose one antiseptic, disinfectant or other antibacterial substance. Plan and carry out an investigation to find the lowest concentration of your chosen substance that prevents the growth of the bacterium you are using.

▸ The independent variable (IV) is the concentration of the antibacterial substance.

▸ The dependent variable (DV) is the growth of the bacteria. This can be measured by the diameter of the zone of inhibition or by using turbidity.

▸ Control variables include: species of bacteria, volume of antibacterial solution, depth of nutrient agar in Petri dish or volume of liquid culture used, nutrient content of the growth medium, pH of growth medium, incubation temperature and length of time for incubation.

▸ You also need to set up a control, such as an uninoculated plate or liquid culture tube.

Growth requirements of particular bacteria

You can investigate the growth requirements of one type of bacterium. Bacteria need certain basic nutrients and physical factors, such as temperature and pH, to sustain life.

You can investigate, using turbidity, how well your chosen bacterium grows in yeast broth, nutrient broth, glucose broth and inorganic synthetic broth. You should keep species of bacteria, volume of broth, size of initial inoculum (one bacteriological loopful), pH, incubation temperature and incubation duration constant.

▸ IV is the type of medium.

▸ DV is the turbidity that indicates growth rate.

Another investigation is to use a growth medium suitable to promote the growth of your chosen bacterium and vary:

▸ the incubation temperature

▸ the pH.

Write a plan, have it checked and approved and then carry out your investigation. Write a report and share your findings with others in your class.

Effect of exposure to UV light

Ultraviolet (UV) light has short wavelength and damages DNA and RNA of living organisms, including bacteria. It, therefore, causes mutation and can interfere with replication and protein synthesis. UVB and UVC have the shortest wavelengths. These are filtered out by the Earth's atmosphere but a UVC wand may be used to rid surfaces, equipment and water of growing bacteria. UV light with a wavelength of 265 nm seems to have the most effective antibacterial properties.

> **Research**
>
> Go to **www.youtube.com/watch?v=z1Pm38YzLqc** to find out more about the effect of UVC light on bacteria.

If you have access to a UV wand or lamp, you can shine it onto a culture of bacteria for a specified length of time and then take a sample of the treated bacteria, inoculate it into a new sterile liquid or solid medium, incubate and examine for growth of bacteria.

Different groups could investigate different types of bacteria, or different lengths of exposure, and findings could be shared with others in your class.

> **Safety tip**
>
> You will need to carry out a risk assessment and wear protective goggles.

⏸ PAUSE POINT   What are the growth requirements of bacteria?

> **Hint**   Think about what different types of bacteria need to grow.
>
> **Extend**   What is the difference between antiseptics and disinfectants?

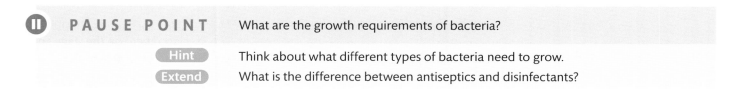

Assessment practice 13.2   `B.P3` `B.P4` `B.P5` `B.P6` `B.M2` `BC.D2` `BC.D3`

1 Perform an investigation, and write a report, on an aseptic technique involving accurate measurement of micro-oganisms, such as counting yeast cells using a haemocytometer and estimating the cell count per mL, or serial dilution and colony counts to estimate the number of bacteria in 1 mL of stock culture.

2 Perform and write a report on an investigation involving the correct preparation of standard solutions, such as a liquid bacterial culture medium.

3 Perform an investigation and report on food analysis techniques to accurately measure lipid and ascorbic acid contents.

4 Perform and report on an investigation to accurately measure the quantitative effect of an antiseptic or a disinfectant on the growth of a type of bacterium.

5 For each practical investigation you have carried out and reported on, analyse the outcomes and relate them to work done in a health-related laboratory.

6 In each case, justify the laboratory techniques used for the practical investigations.

7 Evaluate the usefulness of the procedures and techniques used in health-related laboratories for providing a diagnosis for health professionals to work with.

Plan
- Do I know what I am being asked to do?
- Do I have enough information or should I extend my research?

Do
- Do I know what I want to achieve?
- Can I check my work to see where I have gone off task and can make changes to put this right?

Review
- Can I instruct someone else on how to complete the task more efficiently?
- Do I know what I would do differently next time and the approach I would take with the parts that I found difficult this time?

C Carrying out investigations using light microscopes similar to those in a health-related laboratory

Use of light microscope

One of the most useful tools for a microbiologist is the light (optical) microscope. It is the first way in which micro-organisms, which are invisible to the naked eye, can be seen. You will have light field optical microscopes in your school or college and, if they have oil immersion objectives, you will be able to see bacteria and yeast cells magnified 1000 times. Optical microscopes are also used in hospitals and research laboratories. They are relatively cheap, easy to use and portable.

Optical microscopes use a part of the electromagnetic spectrum called visible light, which has a wavelength of between 400 and 700 nm. This wavelength range means that structures closer together than 200 nm (0.2 µm) will appear as one object. Hence, optical microscopes have a low resolution and although they can be used to view whole bacteria they cannot show details of their internal structures. For this, the more expensive, and more difficult to use, electron microscopes are needed. Electron microscopes use a beam of fast-moving electrons, which have a very short wavelength, giving higher resolution and much higher magnification.

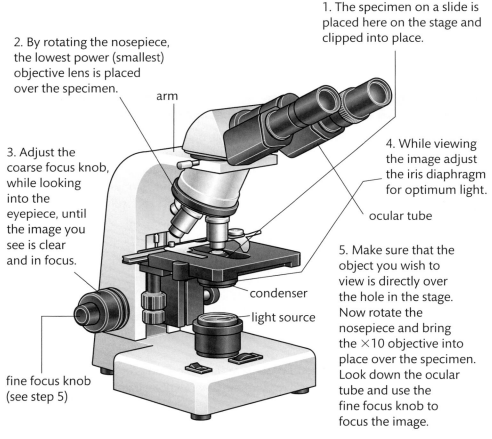

2. By rotating the nosepiece, the lowest power (smallest) objective lens is placed over the specimen.

arm

1. The specimen on a slide is placed here on the stage and clipped into place.

3. Adjust the coarse focus knob, while looking into the eyepiece, until the image you see is clear and in focus.

4. While viewing the image adjust the iris diaphragm for optimum light.

ocular tube

5. Make sure that the object you wish to view is directly over the hole in the stage. Now rotate the nosepiece and bring the ×10 objective into place over the specimen. Look down the ocular tube and use the fine focus knob to focus the image.

condenser

light source

fine focus knob (see step 5)

6. Repeat step 5 using the ×40 objective lens.

▶ **Figure 13.8:** Annotated diagram showing how to use a light microscope – note that when you carry a microscope you should hold it by its arm in one hand while having your other hand under the base

Types of light microscopes

As well as the bright field optical microscope there are other types of optical microscopes, including the following.

▶ Phase contrast microscopes, which have special lenses that give enough contrast for the user to see unstained micro-organisms. They can, therefore, be used to see living micro-organisms clearly.

▶ Dark ground microscopes that show the illuminated micro-organisms against a dark background.

▶ Fluorescent microscopes that use an ultraviolet light source to illuminate a specially stained specimen, causing it to fluoresce.

▶ Laser scanning microscopes, also called confocal microscopes, use laser light to scan an object. The resulting pixel information is assembled by computer to give a high resolution image. These are used in medicine to view, for example, fungal filaments within the cornea of the eye of a patient with a fungal corneal infection, allowing swifter diagnosis leading to earlier, more effective treatment.

Advantages of using light microscopes

Light microscopes are:

▶ relatively inexpensive

▶ easy to use, with a small amount of training

▶ portable, and can be used outside of the laboratory if necessary.

Light microscopes can magnify objects up to 1500 to 2000 times, allowing users to detect abnormalities in some types of cells or tissues. This allows microbiologists to observe some bacteria, protists and fungi. They can also be used to examine living specimens, such as micro-organisms.

Limitations of light microscopes

Light microscopes use rays of visible light, with wavelengths between 400 nm and 700 nm. Consequently their resolution is low, because the wavelength of light is too large for the light rays to get in between some of the small structures inside cells. This means that at magnifications above × 2000 the magnified image is not clear.

Using higher magnifications

Scientists sometimes need to examine cells and micro-organisms at higher magnifications than can be produced by light microscopes. For this, they need to use electron microscopes, which use a fast beam of electrons instead of light rays. The electrons have a much smaller wavelength and produce very highly magnified and very clear (high resolution) images. Electron microscopes have enabled scientists to see fine details of the structures of bacteria and viruses, as well as of human cells and organelles. However, these microscopes are very expensive and it requires a great deal of training and skill to use them. They cannot be used to examine living specimens as the specimens must be placed in a vacuum.

Preparation of slides

Certain procedures and techniques are common to all cytological (cell) studies. For tissues taken from human patients, which consist of many adjacent cells, a problem to overcome is how to make a thin enough section of about 5–10 μm, ideally one cell thickness, so that light can pass through the slide and individual cells can be seen clearly. An instrument called a microtome is used to make thin sections or a swab can be taken, for example of the cervix, making a smear of a few cells. The tissues are fixed onto a slide using special chemicals called fixatives.

When observing micro-organisms, there is no need for sectioning and you only need to perform a smear preparation.

Step by step: Making a smear and simple staining

You can make a smear of bacteria from a liquid culture or from a colony taken from an agar plate.

- Use aseptic technique.
- Use a sterile loop to take one loopful of liquid culture. Spread this drop onto a clean microscope slide, or take a small amount of one colony of bacteria from an agar plate and rub the loop into a drop of sterile water on a clean microscope slide.
- Flame the loop and cool before placing it onto a mat on the bench.
- Dry the slide over a beaker of hot water, on a warming plate or by passing swiftly back and forth in a hot Bunsen flame.
- Once the smear is dried and fixed onto the slide, add one drop of dye, such as methylene blue, and leave for one minute.
- Use a pipette to wash off the dye and hold the slide over a large beaker to catch the washing off water.
- Dry the slide in air or over hot water/a hot plate.

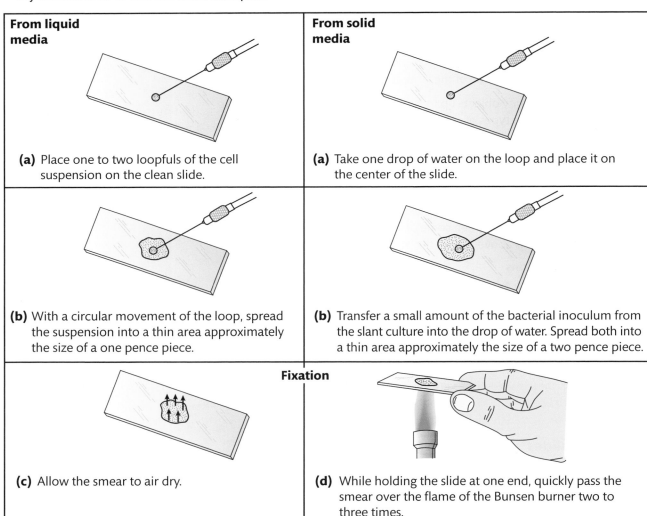

From liquid media	From solid media
(a) Place one to two loopfuls of the cell suspension on the clean slide.	**(a)** Take one drop of water on the loop and place it on the center of the slide.
(b) With a circular movement of the loop, spread the suspension into a thin area approximately the size of a one pence piece.	**(b)** Transfer a small amount of the bacterial inoculum from the slant culture into the drop of water. Spread both into a thin area approximately the size of a two pence piece.

Fixation

(c) Allow the smear to air dry.	**(d)** While holding the slide at one end, quickly pass the smear over the flame of the Bunsen burner two to three times.

▶ **Figure 13.9:** Preparation of a microscope slide

You can now view the slide under a microscope (see the section: Examination of prepared slides).

Step by step: Gram stain

Make a heat-fixed smear of the bacteria you wish to examine. Ideally make two slides, one of *E. coli* (a Gram negative rod-shaped bacterium) and one of *S. albus* (a Gram positive coccus). Make sure the slides are clearly labelled.

- Add one drop of crystal violet to each fixed smear for one minute.
- Wash off the stain with water.
- Apply a drop of Gram's iodine for one minute. This is a mordant and intensifies the colour of the stain.
- Wash off the Gram's iodine with water.
- Add 95 per cent ethanol, drop by drop, with the slide held over a beaker to catch the alcohol running off the slide, until no more colour leaves the smear and the alcohol runs clear.
- Counterstain with safranin for 45 seconds.
- Wash off the safranin with tap water and dry the slide.

You can now view the slide under a microscope.

Step by step: Negative staining

Negative staining uses a stain such as nigrosin or Indian ink, which has negatively charged chromogen, which will not penetrate the bacterial cells, because bacteria have negative charges on their surface. The unstained cells are clearly seen against a dark background. This stain is good for showing the shape of bacteria and because no heat is involved, the shape will not be distorted.

- Use a pipette to place a drop of Indian ink at one end of a microscope slide.
- Place a loopful of bacteria from a liquid culture, or some bacteria on a loop taken from a colony, into the drop of ink.
- Use another slide to spread the drop out across the slide, making a thin smear.
- Do *not* heat-fix the smear. The slide is now ready for examination under a microscope.

Step by step: Examination of prepared slides

- Place one drop of immersion oil onto the stained, fixed smear. This oil has a refractive index (light-bending power) similar to that of the objective lens of the microscope. It allows the objective lens to be placed very close to the specimen.
- Place the slide on the microscope stage and adjust the nosepiece so that the oil immersion (× 100) objective lens is directly above the smear.
- Switch on the sub-stage illumination and make sure the sub-stage condenser is fully up, so that maximum light passes through the specimen on the slide.
- Carefully adjust the coarse-focus knob and bring the stage up, so that the oil immersion objective lens is in the immersion oil on the slide.
- Look down the eyepiece and slowly adjust the fine-focus knob, to move the objective lens away from the slide, until the bacteria come into focus.

You can make drawings of the bacteria you see and annotate them to show their names, shape and whether Gram positive or Gram negative.

When you have finished, and before putting the microscope away, place your slide in a pot of disinfectant and use lens tissues to clean the objective lens and the microscope stage.

Step by step: Use of different magnifications

For examining bacteria, you may use the oil objective lens straight away. However, for examining human tissue preparations you will need to use low power first and then higher power objective lenses.

You can use prepared slides of human tissue, such as epithelial cells lining the respiratory tract.

- Place the slide on the microscope stage, with the specimen over the hole in the stage.
- Rotate the nosepiece so that the lowest power objective ($\times$ 4) lens is above the specimen. The objective lens magnifies the object forming an image.
- The eyepiece lens magnifies the image so if the eyepiece objective has a magnification of $\times$10 and the objective lens has a magnification of $\times$ 4 then the total magnification is ($\times$ 4 $\times$ 10) = $\times$ 40.
- This is linear magnification, which means that you see an image 40 times longer and 40 times wider than the real object on the slide.
- Switch on the sub-stage illumination and adjust the sub-stage condenser, so that it is about halfway between up and down.
- Turn the coarse-focus knob, so that the objective lens moves down towards the slide as far as it will go.
- Now look down the eyepiece and slowly turn the coarse-focus knob so that the objective lens moves away from the slide, slowly, until the specimen comes into view.
- Adjust the condenser, if necessary; if the specimen is very pale, you will need less light but if it is dark you will need more light.
- Adjust the fine-focus knob to bring the object into sharp focus, giving a clear image.
- Make sure that the part of the specimen you wish to view under higher power is in the centre of your field of vision under low power magnification.
- Carefully rotate the nosepiece until the next higher power objective lens clicks into position above the specimen.
- Look down the eyepiece and carefully move the fine-focus knob so that the new objective lens moves slowly away from the slide until you see a sharp image. Note the objective lens magnification and the eyepiece lens magnification and calculate the total magnification.
- Repeat the previous step but using higher power objective lens.
- Make labelled and annotated drawings of the specimen. You can make a low power plan, which does not show any individual cells, and then a high power drawing of part of the specimen.
- Remove the slide from the microscope stage and place it back in the slide cabinet.
- Use lens tissues to clean the objective lens and the microscope stage, before putting the microscope away.

Interpretation of slides and photomicrographs

A micrograph is a photograph or digital image taken through a microscope and showing a magnified image of a specimen. An electron micrograph is prepared using an electron microscope. A photomicrograph is prepared using an optical microscope.

Scientists trained in microscopy can interpret these photographs and, knowing the magnification, can work out actual sizes of the structures visible in the micrograph. They may be able to identify the type of bacteria and determine whether there are abnormalities, such as cancer or infecting pathogens, in human cells or tissues.

Some microscopes have a **graticule** in the eyepiece. A stage micrometer is used to calibrate the graticule at different magnifications and then the measurements of a specimen can be obtained.

> **Key term**
>
> **Graticule** – measuring device used in the eyepiece of a microscope. Once calibrated, it can be used to measure dimensions of objects viewed with the microscope.

Photomicrographs provide a permanent record of specimens and are very useful for teaching purposes, as well as for patient records, or for comparing a patient's progress over time and during treatment.

If a bar indicating the image of a line of specified length, such as 5 µm, is superimposed on the photomicrograph, then the magnification factor and the real size of the specimen can be calculated.

(a) <u>L.P. Plan</u> × 100 scale × 1

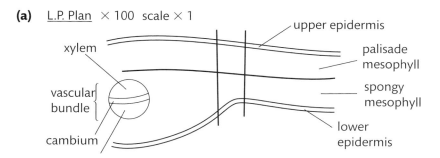

- upper epidermis
- xylem
- palisade mesophyll
- vascular bundle
- spongy mesophyll
- cambium
- lower epidermis

(b) <u>H.P. Drawing</u> × 100 scale × 2

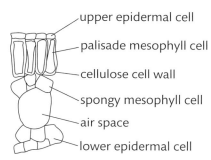

- upper epidermal cell
- palisade mesophyll cell
- cellulose cell wall
- spongy mesophyll cell
- air space
- lower epidermal cell

▶ **Figure 13.10:** (a) Low power plan and (b) High power drawing of a specimen

Ⅱ PAUSE POINT What are the advantages and disadvantages of using light microscopes, compared to electron microscopes, to view micro-organisms?

Hint Think about how easy the two types of microscopes are to use, and the costs associated with them.

Extend If you are using a light microscope with an eyepiece lens of × 10 and an objective lens of × 100, what is the total magnification of the image of the specimen you can see?

Assessment practice 13.3

1 Perform a practical investigation involving the staining of cells and their temporary fixing on a slide. You can use bacteria or yeast cells, or use a clean cotton bud to take a swab from the inside of your mouth (cheek lining).

2 Record observations of a prepared slide of cells seen under two different magnifications of a microscope.

3 Analyse the advantages of using photomicrographs compared to slides fixed using a temporary fixing method.

Plan
- Do I know what I am being asked to do?
- Do I have enough information or should I extend my research?

Do
- Do I know what I want to achieve?
- Can I check my work to see where I have gone off task and can make changes to put this right?

Review
- Can I instruct someone else on how to complete the task more efficiently?
- Do I know what I would do differently next time and the approach I would take with the parts that I found difficult this time?

Further reading and resources

Books

Cappuccino, J.G. and Welsh, C.T. (2016) *Microbiology – A Laboratory Manual*, 11th edition, San Francisco, Ca: Benjamin Cummings.

Bradshaw, L.J. (1992) *Laboratory Microbiology*, 4th edition, Oxford: Harcourt College Publishing.

Nielsen, S. (ed.) (2014) *Food Analysis (Food science Text series)*, New York, NY: Springer.

Websites

http://people.umass.edu/~mcclemen/581Introduction.html
University of Massachusetts: Information about food analysis.

www.nhs.uk/NHSEngland/AboutNHSservices/pathology/Pages/pathology-services-explained.aspx
NHS Choices: Information about pathology services.

THINK ▶FUTURE

Andrea Bray

Biomedical Scientist

I obtained vocational A-levels and started working in an NHS laboratory in a large hospital. I studied for a degree in biomedical sciences while working. Once I'd obtained my degree and having worked in a laboratory and produced a suitable portfolio of evidence, I obtained a Certificate of Competence, awarded by the Institute of Biomedical Science (IBMS). I also obtained a specialist diploma in medical microbiology and am registered with the Health and Care Professionals Council (HCPC).

At present I'm Band 2 and carry out a range of routine healthcare science activities, including sample preparation and storage. I organise and take responsibility for my own work, maintaining and keeping clinical records, completing incident forms (where needed), assisting in the audit process and suggesting improvements (where appropriate). I receive samples and enter data on the computer system. Sometimes I identify mislabelled specimens and also help the quality control system in the lab by identifying unsuitable samples or process failures. I'm responsible for day-to-day management of stock control and usage; for example, checking stock levels of blood transfusion units. I help maintain a clean and safe working environment and process samples for research and development, clinical trials and equipment testing.

Once I've worked at this level for a year or two, during which time I'll continue my professional development by attending short courses on research and development, quality control and health and safety procedures, I'm hoping to enrol onto the NHS scientist training programme. This is a three-year, work-based training while being paid, and leading to a higher specialist diploma from the IBMS. This could lead to a senior scientist position.

Once I've achieved my goal, I may continue working in a hospital lab or look for work in a related field, such as veterinary services, pharmaceutical labs, the Food Standards Agency, the Medical Research Council, or the Health and Safety Executive.

My boss is currently working on a thesis and hopes to achieve fellowship status, and then chartered scientist status, which is an international recognition of his high professionalism and competence. I also hope to gain chartered scientist status one day.

Focusing your skills

General skills required for laboratory work

- Good practical laboratory skills.
- Awareness of health and safety issues and the need to carry out risk assessments when working with body fluids such as blood, pus, urine, faeces and sputum, and also with various hazardous chemicals.
- High degree of manual dexterity.
- IT skills, to use the laboratory information systems, email, internet and intranet, plus automated operating systems and various software packages.
- Ability to work accurately and efficiently, prioritise tasks and meet deadlines.

Personal qualities required for laboratory work

- Patience.
- Willingness to accept responsibility.
- Ability to work flexibly, and with a range of equipment and techniques.
- Communication and teamworking skills.
- Ability to maintain client confidentiality.
- Ability to work under pressure while maintaining standards.
- Willingness to work alone or under instruction.
- Ability to be responsible for own training and continuing professional development.
- Willingness to support other staff and take part in the appraisal process.

Getting ready for assessment

Massoud Barzani is studying for a BTEC National in Health and Social Care. He has been given an assignment to carry out a practical task of investigating the effectiveness of an antibiotic against two types of bacteria. Massoud shares some aspects of his experience below.

How I got started

I asked my tutor if the college had antibiotic discs, cultures of bacteria, microbiology practical equipment and an autoclave. I found that we had all of these things as well as an incubator.

Think about it

I read about antibiotics and how they work on bacteria. I found out that some antibiotics are only effective against Gram positive bacteria and some are effective against Gram negative bacteria. I then found out that we have cultures of both Gram positive and Gram negative bacteria. The bacteria we can use are harmless but I still had to observe all the health and safety guidance and carry out a risk assessment. I also researched about statistical tests and decided to do a Mann Whitney U test to compare the effectiveness of penicillin against *E. coli* and *S. albus*, and to compare the effectiveness of tetracycline against *E. coli* and *S. albus*.

How I brought it all together

I drew up a plan, had it checked and then ordered the equipment and chemicals I needed. I made sure that I had enough time to carry out the protocol and to come back into the lab to take the agar plates out of the incubator at the required time. I placed them in the fridge until next lesson when I could measure the zones of inhibition.

What I learned from the experience

I learned a lot about how different antibiotics work and about the differences between Gram negative bacteria such as *E. coli* and Gram positive bacteria such as *S. albus*. I also developed my skills at using aseptic technique, using a sterilised spreader to make bacterial lawns, accurately measuring the zones of inhibition, how many replicates to have in order to generate enough quantitative data for the statistical tests, and how to safely dispose of the plates at the end of the practical.

Think about it

▶ Have you written a plan with timings so you can complete your assignment by the agreed submission date?

▶ Do you have notes on the principles behind and uses of antibiotics?

▶ Do you fully understand how to carry out the protocol and what is happening at each stage?

▶ Can you present your findings to others in your class, and explain what you did and what you found?

▶ Is your information written in your own words, and referenced clearly where you have used quotations or information from a book, journal or website?

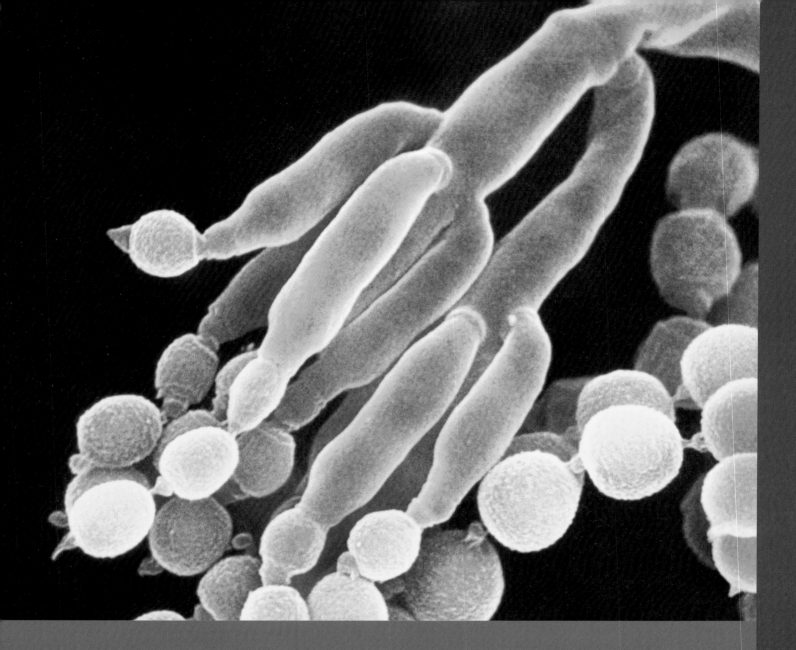

Microbiology for Health Science 15

Getting to know your unit

A good knowledge of the characteristics of micro-organisms, the conditions they need to grow, their transmission routes and how to control their spread, as well as the consequences of disease outbreaks, is essential for anyone wishing to enter a career in health. It is also essential for anyone working in communities where diseases could spread, such as nurseries, schools, canteens and restaurants, hospitals, the workplace and the home.

How you will be assessed

This unit will be assessed by a series of internally assessed tasks set by your tutor. Throughout this unit you will find assessment practices that may help you to work towards your assessment. Completing these practices will not mean you have achieved a particular grade but the research you carry out for them will be relevant and useful when you come to carry out your final assessment.

It is important to check that you have met all the Pass grading criteria as you work your way through the assignments. To achieve a Merit or Distinction you need to present your work in such a way that you meet the criteria for those grades. To achieve Merit you need to analyse and discuss relevant issues and for Distinction you need to assess and evaluate.

The assignments set by your tutors will consist of a number of tasks designed to meet the criteria in the table on the next page. Some tasks will be written and some will be laboratory-based practical exercises. Tasks may also involve reviewing and analysing case studies.

Assessment criteria

This table shows what you must do in order to achieve a **Pass**, **Merit** or **Distinction** grade, and where you can find activities to help you.

Pass	Merit	Distinction

Learning aim **A**   Understand the concepts of microbiology relevant to health science

Pass	Merit	Distinction
A.P1 Explain the requirements that selected micro-organisms need to thrive and how these requirements can be controlled. **Assessment practice 15.1**	**A.M1** Analyse the structure of selected micro-organisms and their reproductive methods, and how their transmission can be controlled. **Assessment practice 15.1**	**A.D1** Justify the methods used to control two different micro-organisms. **Assessment practice 15.1**

Learning aim **B**   Examine the role of micro-organisms in human health and disease

Pass	Merit	Distinction
B.P2 Compare the transmission routes of microbes involved in human diseases and relate them to specific infections. **Assessment practice 15.2** **B.P3** Explain how the immune system is involved in protecting the human body from harmful micro-organisms. **Assessment practice 15.2**	**B.M2** Analyse the terms used in epidemiology to show how they apply to the transmission of infectious diseases and human immunity. **Assessment practice 15.2**	**BC.D2** Evaluate the reasons for and consequences of the spread of diseases becoming more global. **Assessment practice 15.2**

Learning aim **C**   Investigate the impact of diseases and their treatment in a global context

Pass	Merit	Distinction
C.P4 Discuss the factors that might be involved in the control of separate outbreaks of two different diseases. **Assessment practice 15.2** **C.P5** Explain the consequences of an outbreak, citing examples in each case. **Assessment practice 15.2**	**C.M3** Assess the effectiveness of the factors involved in controlling diseases globally. **Assessment practice 15.2**	

Learning aim **D**   Investigate the health benefits of micro-organisms

Pass	Merit	Distinction
D.P6 Outline how micro-organisms are used by two different commercial enterprises. **Assessment practice 15.3**	**D.M4** Analyse the social benefits to humans of three micro-organisms. **Assessment practice 15.3**	**D.D3** Evaluate the positive and negative effects of the interrelationship between humans and micro-organisms. **Assessment practice 15.3**

Getting started

What types of micro-organisms can you name? Are all micro-organisms harmful? Are some useful – if so, in what ways? What do the terms endemic, epidemic and pandemic mean? What are the main transmission routes for disease-causing micro-organisms? Do you know what gut flora (microbiota) is? Have you heard of the human microbiome? Do you know what 'aseptic technique' is? See how well you can answer these questions when you have completed this unit.

A The concepts of microbiology relevant to health science

Until the late nineteenth century, people believed that disease was caused by miasmas – evil smells in the air. We now know that disease is caused by micro-organisms. People also didn't understand what made food rot, and there were no antibiotics to cure infections, or vaccines to control their spread.

Scientists now understand that micro-organisms are found just about everywhere, even in hostile environments, such as hot sulfur springs and thermal oceanic vents.

In this section, you will learn about types of micro-organisms, what they need in order to grow, their structure, how they reproduce and methods for controlling them.

Micro-organisms

The words, *microbe*, **micro-organism** and *germ* usually make people think about diseases or decay, such as food spoilage. Many people have heard of bacteria and viruses, although most are not clear about their differences.

There are four main groups of micro-organisms – **viruses**, bacteria, fungi and protocista (protocists). In the 1980s, an infecting agent that is not a micro-organism was identified and named a prion (prion protein).

Viruses

Viruses occur in all types of ecosystem and can infect all types of living organisms – bacteria, protoctists, fungi, plants and animals. They have probably been around for as long as the first life forms. Viruses have aided the process of evolution as they transfer genes between species. In fact, between 8 and 10 per cent of our **genome** is viral in origin.

Viruses are the most abundant entities on Earth. They are far smaller but even more numerous than bacteria.

▸ It is estimated that there are several hundred thousand species of viruses. Viruses can infect all other types of organisms on Earth. Among the diseases they cause in humans are HIV/AIDS, hepatitis (A, B and C), measles, mumps, influenza, colds, polio, glandular fever, herpes, viral meningitis, chickenpox and Ebola. Some viruses cause cancers, such as leukaemia and cervical cancer, which is caused by the human papilloma virus (HPV). Smallpox was a viral disease that was eradicated by 1980, but samples of the virus are kept in high security laboratories for research purposes.

▶ Transmission electron micrograph (TEM) with colour added of (human papilloma virus, HPV), diameter of this virus is about 50 nm

Bacteria

Bacteria are single-celled (unicellular) **prokaryotic** organisms. They range in size from 0.2 to 2 μm in diameter and from 1 to 8 μm in length. Bacteria evolved about 3.5 billion years ago and some live in extreme environments, such as in thermal oceanic vents, hot sulfur springs, and in the Earth's crust. Many types inhabit the intestines of animals, including humans. This relationship is symbiotic and these bacteria are essential to us. Distinct communities of up to 30,000 different species of bacteria also live in the roots, on leaves and inside the flowers of plants. These bacteria help plants obtain nutrients and resist diseases.

However, some types of bacteria are **pathogenic**. Bacterial diseases include bubonic plague, anthrax, meningococcal meningitis, cholera, syphilis, tuberculosis (TB), leprosy, bacterial pneumonia and whooping cough.

Many bacteria are useful and some are used in making foods such as sourdough bread, yoghurt and cheese.

Key terms
Prokaryotic – cells that have cell surface membranes, cytoplasm and a cell wall but do not have a proper nucleus containing DNA. Their DNA floats free in the cell's cytoplasm.
Pathogenic – capable of causing disease.

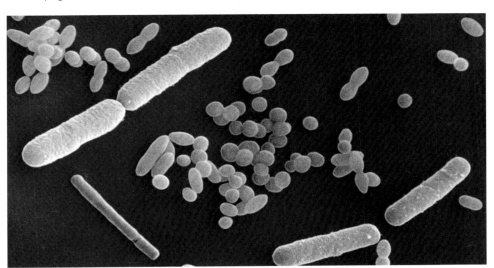

▶ Scanning electron micrograph (SEM) with colour added of a variety of bacteria from the human intestine, × 8000

Fungi

Fungi are **eukaryotic** organisms. Some, such as yeasts, are single-celled and some, such as mushrooms, are multicellular. Fungi are abundant in all parts of the world and are the main decomposers, meaning they feed on and break down dead matter in ecosystems, helping to recycle the nutrients. Some fungi are parasites and can infect other organisms. Among those that infect humans are types of yeast, which cause:

▶ candidiasis (thrush)

▶ ringworm and athlete's foot (tinea)

▶ farmer's lung (aspergillosis).

Some fungi produce antibiotics, and certain types produce substances that inhibit viruses or cancer cells.

Multicellular fungi, such as mushrooms, can be a source of food. Yeasts are used for making bread, beer and wine. Mould fungi may cause food spoilage.

▶ SEM with colour added of the surface of a human tongue infected with *Candida* fungus, × 1000

> **Key term**
>
> **Eukaryotic** – cells that contain a nucleus and membrane-bound organelles; organism made of eukaryotic cells.

Protocista

The kingdom protoctist contains species that do not fit into the other four kingdoms (prokaryotes, fungi, animals and plants). All members of the protoctist kingdom are eukaryotic. Some of the organisms in this kingdom are micro-organisms such as:

▶ unicellular green algae (plant-like).

▶ protozoa (animal-like). Protozoan infecting agents cause malaria, sleeping sickness and amoebic dysentery.

▶ slime moulds and water moulds (fungus-like). Water moulds (oomycetes) have a cell wall that contains cellulose.

▶ SEM with colour added of two human red blood cells and malaria parasites at the merozoite stage of their life cycle, × 4000

Prions

During the 1960s, research scientists thought that forms of transmissible spongiform encephalopathies, such as scrapie in sheep, and kuru (laughing disease) and new variant Creutzfeldt-Jakob disease (vCJD) in humans, were caused by infectious proteins.

Prions (pronounced *pree-ons*) is a term first used in 1982 and means proteinaceous (made of protein) infectious particle. It is derived from the words **pr**otein and infec**tion**.

Prions are not living organisms, but misfolded proteins (proteins that are incorrectly folded and consequently misshapen). These misfolded proteins are stable and not **denatured** by heat or digested by protease enzymes. When they are transmitted to another organism, prions can cause some of the organism's proteins to misfold and form aggregates (clumps) that accumulate in the infected tissue (brain and nerve tissue) causing tissue damage and cell death. The spongiform diseases caused by prions are not treatable, and are usually fatal.

> **Key term**
>
> **Denatured** – having the molecular shape permanently changed, leading to the molecules not being able to function.

▶ TEM with colour added of prion proteins taken from the brain of an infected hamster, × 49,720

Variant CJD

Over the last 20 years, there have been around 200 cases of vCJD in the UK. Before this new variant form was identified, Creutzfeldt-Jakob disease (CJD) was known, but rare. Most cases were described as sporadic, between 5 and 10 per cent of cases were due to a mutation in the patient's genes, and less than 5 per cent were iatrogenic (caused by accidental infection from surgical instruments or blood transfusions). CJD normally affected people in their late sixties, but in 1994 a case appeared in a younger person. This new form of CJD is a type of transmissible spongiform encephalopathy, and is a progressive neurodegenerative disease. Symptoms include depression, anxiety, apathy, unsteadiness, involuntary movements and finally immobility and muteness.

After other cases appeared during the 1990s, scientists worked out that this new variant (vCJD) is caused by a prion. This prion has been in sheep for a long time but they are usually slaughtered before showing symptoms. The remains of sheep carcasses have been rendered and made into a protein-rich feed supplement given to cattle. However, in 1980 the ways in which the carcasses were rendered changed, and this allowed the prions to transmit from sheep to cattle. Brain and spinal cord tissue from cattle were used in processed foods, which was the most likely route of infection to humans.

In the UK, five million cattle suspected of having BSE (bovine spongiform encephalopathy, caused by prions) were slaughtered to prevent further spread of BSE and vCJD. The WHO set up and runs training courses for surveillance systems in many countries to prevent another such outbreak. Cattle over the age of 30 months must not be used for consumption unless they test negative for BSE.

Not all countries have such stringent rules and people need to be wary of eating processed meat products while travelling in such places, for example some countries in Africa.

Check your knowledge

1 What do the terms neurodegenerative disease and iatrogenic mean?

2 What was the most likely route of infection for prions that caused vCJD to be transmitted from infected sheep to humans?

3 How was the spread of BSE and vCJD brought under control?

PAUSE POINT Compare, by means of annotated diagrams, the structures of prions, viruses, bacteria, fungi and protoctists.

Hint State whether the entity is living or non-living, eukaryotic, prokaryotic or akaryotic. Explain these terms.

Extend Discuss whether viruses are living or non-living entities. Which features seem to indicate they are living or are not living?

Requirements of micro-organisms for growth

Growth is an increase in cell numbers, and all single-celled micro-organisms grow by replicating. They need optimum conditions for such growth, which include:

▶ a source of energy

▶ nutrients – a source of the building blocks of life, which may also be a source of energy

▶ suitable temperature

▶ **host** organisms

▶ water

▶ suitable oxygen concentrations.

Scientists need to know and understand the growth requirements of micro-organisms so that they can culture (grow) and study them in laboratories, or to grow them on a large scale to produce useful products.

Energy

Some types of bacteria can carry out **photosynthesis**, using light as their energy source. They synthesise the organic molecules, such as amino acids, nucleic acids, fats and carbohydrates, from which living matter is built. They are described as *photoautotrophic*. Some obtain their energy from chemical reactions. These are described as *chemoautotrophic*.

Many bacteria obtain their energy, via respiration, from food they have digested and absorbed. Such bacteria are described as *heterotrophic*. Fungi and many protoctist micro-organisms are also heterotrophic.

Nutrients

All life forms on Earth are carbon-based, hence they need a source of carbon. Fats and carbohydrates contain carbon, hydrogen and oxygen. Amino acids, proteins and nucleic acids, as well as many other important compounds such as ATP (adenosine triphosphate, the universal energy currency used in all cells) and vitamins also contain nitrogen.

Heterotrophic bacteria, fungi and protoctists need to obtain these nutrients. They live on their substrates (source of nutrients) and secrete enzymes to digest (break down to smaller molecules) the food. The products of digestion are then absorbed into their cells.

When growing bacteria and fungi in laboratories, scientists use special media. Solid media consists of agar jelly with nutrients added to feed the microbes. Liquid media is broth with added nutrients.

Viruses do not feed. They can only reproduce when inside a living cell of another organism (the host).

> **Key terms**
>
> **Host** – organism in or on which a parasite lives and from which the parasite obtains its nutrients and shelter; an organism infected by an infecting agent or pathogen.
>
> **Photosynthesis** – process by which plants, algae and some bacteria use sunlight as a source of energy to synthesise organic molecules from carbon dioxide and water; chlorophyll traps the light energy and enables the process to be carried out.

▶ Cultures colonies of *Staphylococcus aureus* bacteria growing on a special (selective) agar medium that promotes the growth of this type of bacterium and inhibits the growth of other types. *S. aureus* can cause boils, abscesses, pneumonia and food poisoning.

▶ *Penicillium* fungus growing on nutrient agar in a Petri dish

Temperature

All living organisms require a suitable temperature to live in. Their optimum growth temperature is the one at which they grow and reproduce at the fastest rate. This optimum temperature allows their enzymes, which catalyse (speed up) all metabolic reactions, to work at their optimum rate. Metabolic reactions are the chemical reactions that take place inside living cells to sustain life. Anabolic metabolic reactions involve making larger molecules from smaller ones, using energy. Catabolic metabolic reactions involve splitting large molecules into smaller ones, and usually release energy.

Pathogenic bacteria are adapted to live at the temperature of their host organisms. Many free-living bacteria also live at temperatures between 20 and 45°C. These bacteria are described as mesophiles.

Psycrophiles are bacteria that grow best within a temperature range of –5 to 20°C.

Thermophiles are bacteria that grow at temperatures above 45°C. Some bacteria can grow in hot springs or thermal oceanic vents at temperatures of 100°C or even higher. Very high temperatures may denature proteins in living cells. Consequently many life forms do not exist at high temperatures.

▶ Geothermal pool in New Zealand. The water is coloured due to minerals in it and the temperature is around 75°C. Some algae and bacteria live in these waters.

Viruses can only reproduce in host cells and some are destroyed by heat. Blood and blood products are heat treated to destroy any viruses, such as HIV.

Protoctists grow best within a temperature range of between 10 and 45°C.

Host organisms

Pathogenic fungi, bacteria and protoctists, as well as viruses, can only infect suitable hosts. Smallpox was a viral infection that only affected humans. The Ebola virus exists in fruit bats (where it does not appear to make them ill) and some primates such as monkeys, but can transmit to humans. Bats, monkeys and humans are all hosts for the Ebola virus.

Water

All living organisms need water. About 80 per cent of all living cells consist of water. Water is the ideal medium for living organisms as it resists fast temperature changes and provides a liquid medium for all metabolic reactions, which take place in solution.

Oxygen

Some bacteria and fungi can respire **anaerobically** and do not need oxygen. Micro-organisms that need oxygen for their respiration are described as **aerobic**. Some pathogenic micro-organisms may live in areas of very low oxygen concentration, such as in the gut. These are described as microaerophilic.

> **Key terms**
>
> **Aerobic** – requiring oxygen.
>
> **Anaerobic** – not requiring oxygen.

> **Link**
>
> See *Unit 13: Scientific Techniques for Health Sciences*, sections A3, B1, B3 and C1 for some practical activities involving microbiology, such as investigating the optimum conditions for fungal and bacterial growth and for information about aseptic technique.

❚❚ PAUSE POINT   What do micro-organisms need to grow?

      Hint   Think about and explain *why* the micro-organisms need each of the conditions you describe.

      Extend   Suggest how scientists may grow viruses in a laboratory. Find out if your ideas are correct.

Structure and reproduction of micro-organisms

Viruses

Viruses are described as **akaryotic** because:

▶ they are not made of cells but consist of a capsid (protein coat) made of smaller units called capsomeres surrounding some nucleic acid, either DNA or RNA, but not both at the same stage of the life cycle; the nucleic acid contains **genes**

▶ some have a **lipid** envelope around the protein coat

▶ they do not have **cytoplasm**, membranes or **organelles**

▶ they can only reproduce when inside a host cell

▶ they can be crystallised and kept for long periods of time

▶ when they are not inside a host cell they exist as independent particles called virions.

> **Key terms**
>
> **Akaryotic** – having no cell structure, no cytoplasm and no organelles. Consists of nucleic acid and a protein coat.
>
> **Gene** – length of DNA that codes for one or more proteins, or that codes for a regulatory length of RNA.
>
> **Lipid** – fats or their derivatives, including fatty acids, oils, waxes and steroids. Insoluble in water but soluble in organic solvents, such as ethanol.
>
> **Cytoplasm** – gel-like substance enclosed by the cell surface membrane, about 80 per cent water; medium in which many metabolic reactions take place. Organelles are suspended in the cytoplasm.
>
> **Organelle** – organised and specialised structure within a cell. Some, e.g. mitochondria, are membrane-bound and are found only in eukaryotic cells. Ribosomes are not bound by a membrane and occur in prokaryotic and eukaryotic cells.

There are many different types of virus, so they display a wide variety of shapes and sizes. Most are much smaller than bacteria, with diameters of between 20 and 300 nm. (One nanometre is one millionth of a mm.) Some filoviruses, such as Ebola virus, are much longer, up to 1300 nm (1.3 μm), with a width of 80 nm.

Because viruses are not cellular, they cannot reproduce by cell division. The replication of viruses takes place inside a host cell. They use the host cell organelles to build new virus particles that then rupture and kill the host cell as they burst out of it. Each new virus particle can then infect another host cell. Figure 15.1 shows the structure of an influenza virus.

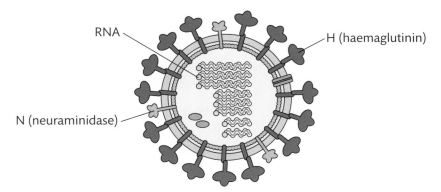

▶ **Figure 15.1** Structure of an influenza virus. The protein spikes on the surface are H (haemaglutinin) and N (neuraminidase). Inside the virus is its RNA.

Bacteriophages

Bacteriophages are viruses that infect bacteria. They attach to the bacterial cell surface and inject their nucleic acid into the bacterium. The genes on the viral nucleic acid can then be expressed. The viral nucleic acid is replicated and the structures inside the bacterial cell, such as ribosomes, are 'hijacked' and used to assemble many new viral protein coats. When several hundred new virus particles have been made inside the bacterium, the cell ruptures, releasing the new viruses (see Figure 15.2).

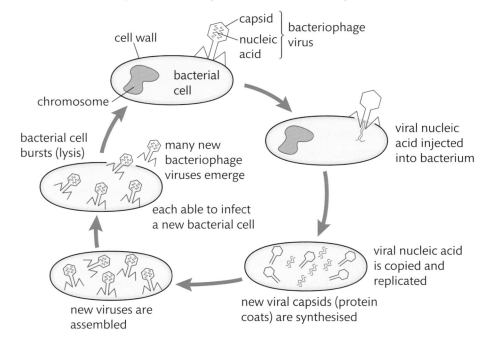

▶ **Figure 15.2** Replication cycle of a bacteriophage virus

Retroviruses

Retroviruses have RNA genomes and they contain the enzyme reverse transcriptase. During their replication cycle inside a host cell, they use this to produce copy DNA, using RNA as the template. This is the opposite of transcription. The DNA may then be incorporated into the host genome (host DNA in the cell nucleus) and this may remain inactive for several years. The double-stranded copy DNA is then used as a template to make single-stranded RNA, which is packaged into the new virus particles that can burst out of the infected cell.

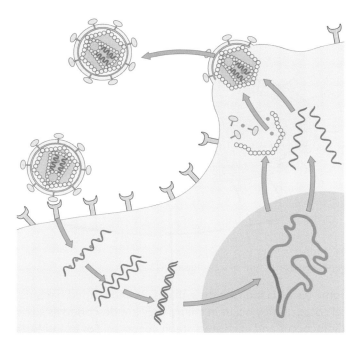

▶ **Figure 15.3** Replication of a retrovirus such as HIV

In the above replication of a retrovirus, the glycoprotein spikes on a virus envelope attach to the antigens on the surface of a T-lymphocyte white blood cell. The RNA viral genome (red) and reverse transcriptase enzyme (blue dots) are injected into the cell. Reverse transcriptase catalyses the transcripiton of RNA to DNA which then integrates into the host genome and may remain dormant there for several years. When activated the virus genes direct the synthesis of new virus particles that bud off from the cell, taking part of the host cell surface membrane to form its envelope.

Most retroviruses infect vertebrates. Because they incorporate their gene into the host genome, they may cause some types of cancer, as this insertion of viral genes can disrupt the action of host genes that control normal cell division. Human T-cell leukaemia is caused by a retrovirus. HIV is a retrovirus. Not all RNA viruses are retroviruses. The influenza virus contains RNA but it is not a retrovirus.

Bacteria

Bacterial cells are prokaryotic. They have:

▶ a cell surface membrane

▶ cytoplasm

▶ a cell wall made of peptidoglycan

▶ no membrane-bound organelles

▶ no proper nucleus – their DNA floats free in the cytoplasm

- smaller rings of DNA, called plasmids, as well as the large circular loop of DNA
- smaller ribosomes than those of eukaryotic cells.

Some bacteria also have:

- an outer capsule
- hair like structures called pili, for adhering to surfaces or to host cells
- one or more flagellae – whip-like structures to propel them.

Figure 15.4 shows the generalised structure of a bacterial cell.

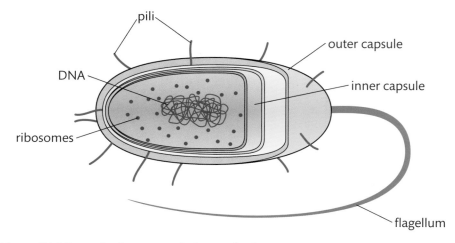

▶ **Figure 15.4** Generalised structure of a bacterial cell

The names of some bacteria indicate their shape. Round shaped bacteria are described as coccus (plural cocci). If they occur in chains they are described as streptococci, in pairs they are diplococcus and in clusters staphylococcus. For example, the name *Staphylococcus aureus*, a bacterium which lives harmlessly on the skin but can cause infections if they enter a deep wound, tells us that this bacterium is round and occurs in clusters. *Streptococcus mutans* lives in human mouths and can cause tooth decay – its name tells us that it is round and occurs in chains.

- Rod-shaped bacteria are described as bacillus (plural bacilli). *Bacillus cereus* in rice causes food poisoning. *Lactobacillus bulgarica* is used when making yoghurt.
- Some bacteria are spiral (corkscrew-shaped). Examples are *Spirillum minus* that causes rat-bite fever and spirochetes such as *Helicobacter pylori* that causes peptic ulcers, *Borrelia sp.* that causes Lyme disease and *Treponema pallidum* that causes syphilis.
- Curved rods (comma-shaped) are described as vibrio. An example is *Vibrio cholera* that causes cholera.

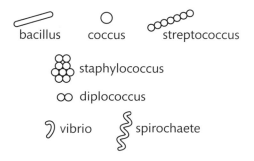

▶ **Figure 15.5** Bacterial shapes

Bacteria reproduce asexually by *binary fission*.

1 Their DNA uncoils and replicates.

2 Their plasmid DNA also replicates.

3 The DNA molecules are pulled to opposite ends of the cell and then a wall forms between them.

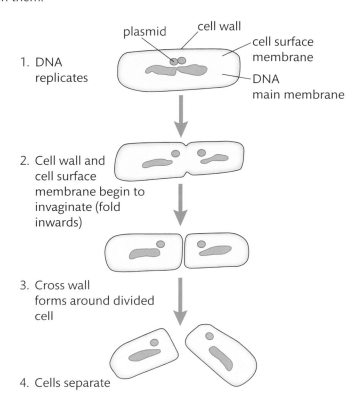

1. DNA replicates

plasmid   cell wall   cell surface membrane   DNA   main membrane

2. Cell wall and cell surface membrane begin to invaginate (fold inwards)

3. Cross wall forms around divided cell

4. Cells separate

▶ **Figure 15.6** Binary fission in bacteria

Fungi

Fungi are eukaryotic. Their DNA is in the form of linear chromosomes that are housed inside a nucleus. Each cell contains a nucleus, bound by a double membrane, which houses the DNA. They also contain membrane-bound organelles such as mitochondria.

Some fungi, such as yeasts, are unicellular. Fungi cell walls contain chitin and their cells grow as long, tubular, thread-like filaments called hyphae, which grow at their tips.

Fungi are more closely related to animals than to plants.

Yeasts

Yeast cells reproduce by budding. The parent cell forms a protuberance or bud, and as the bud elongates the DNA in the cell nucleus replicates, the cell nucleus divides into two and one nucleus migrates into the bud. A wall forms between the bud and parent cell and the bud breaks away.

Moulds

Moulds reproduce by forming spores, which may be sexual or asexual. Asexual spores form in sporangia at the tips of aerial hyphae, from one organism. Sexual spores form when cells of two organisms fuse.

Sexual spores are not produced as often as asexual spores. Sexual spores often have to survive adverse conditions before they germinate.

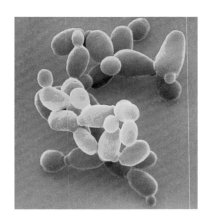

▶ Colour enhanced SEM of yeast cells, *Saccharomyces cerevisiae*, budding × 23,000

▶ Light micrograph of the fungus *Aspergillus niger*, with sporangia that house spores at the end of the aerial thread-like hyphae, × 13

Protozoa

Protozoan protoctists are unicellular eukaryotic cells. Some reproduce asexually by fission, budding or schizogony (multiple fission).

Some protozoans can reproduce sexually.

▶ Two fertilised cells are produced when haploid nuclei (nuclei with half the normal number of chromosomes) from different cells fuse. Each fertilised cell contains DNA from another individual.

▶ When these fertilised cells divide, their daughter cells will not be genetically identical to the original parent cell.

Some protozoa are parasites and cause diseases such as amoebic dysentery, giardiasis and toxoplasmosis. The protozoa causing these infections are transmitted via faeces or faecal contamination of food or water.

Some protozoan parasites are spread by insects, which transmit the protozoa when they bite humans. The insects are the **vectors** (but not the cause) of the diseases. For example:

▶ female *Anopheles* mosquitoes are vectors for *Plasmodium* and spread malaria

▶ sand flies are vectors for *Leishmania* and spread leishmaniasis

▶ tsetse flies are vectors for *trypanosomes* and spread African sleeping sickness.

Plasmodium

Plasmodium causes malaria. When a female *Anopheles* mosquito bites an infected human, she sucks up some plasmodium parasites – males and females. Inside the mosquito, the plasmodium parasites reproduce sexually forming zygotes. These zygotes bore into the mosquito's gut wall and reproduce again to form thousands of **sporozoites**.

Key terms

Vector – an organism that transmits a pathogen from one organism to another.

Sporozoites – a motile, spore-like stage in the life cycle of some parasites/pathogens, such as *Plasmodium sp*. that causes malaria.

These sporozoites invade her salivary glands and when she bites another person, they pass into their blood. The sporozoites enter the human's liver cells and divide asexually to make thousands of invasive **merozoites**. Merozoites leave ruptured liver cells and enter red blood cells where they feed and reproduce asexually to release many more merozoites. Some of these form male and female cells that can reproduce sexually, if they are taken up by another female mosquito. Figure 15.7 shows how the *Plasmodium* parasite reproduces.

> **Key term**
>
> **Merozoites** – a stage in the life cycle of plasmodium that can start a new cycle of development.

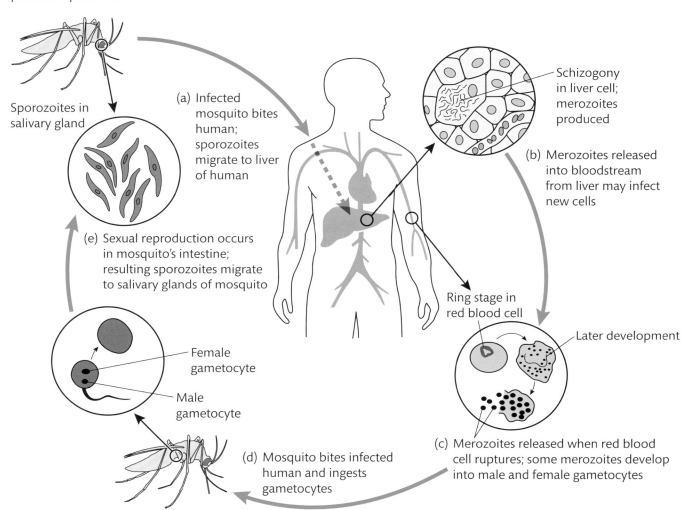

▶ **Figure 15.7** How the plasmodium parasite reproduces

Labels in figure:

Sporozoites in salivary gland

(a) Infected mosquito bites human; sporozoites migrate to liver of human

Schizogony in liver cell; merozoites produced

(b) Merozoites released into bloodstream from liver may infect new cells

(e) Sexual reproduction occurs in mosquito's intestine; resulting sporozoites migrate to salivary glands of mosquito

Female gametocyte

Male gametocyte

(d) Mosquito bites infected human and ingests gametocytes

Ring stage in red blood cell

Later development

(c) Merozoites released when red blood cell ruptures; some merozoites develop into male and female gametocytes

Trypanosomes

These protozoa have flagellae for movement. They spend some of their life cycle (about three weeks) in an insect, the tsetse fly, where they reproduce in the insect's gut and salivary glands by binary fission. When the tsetse fly bites a human, trypanosomes are passed into their blood, and may also pass to lymph and spinal fluids, where they reproduce further by binary fission. Trypanasomes cause sleeping sickness. One type of trypanosome causes Chagas disease in humans and can be spread via faeces.

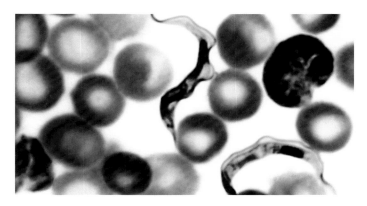

▶ Light micrograph of *Trypanosoma lewisis,* a protozoa parasite that infects rodents and lives in their blood, × 3000

PAUSE POINT

Are the folowing akaryotic, prokaryotic or eukaryotic: plasmodium, yeast, mushroom, potato blight (a water mould), human immunodeficiency virus (HIV), *Staphylococcus aureus,* human papilloma virus (HPV)?

Hint   Think about the kingdom that each organism in the list above belongs to.

Extend   Explain the difference between a vector and a parasite.

Methods of controlling micro-organisms

It is important to control and prevent the spread of micro-organisms to minimise the risk of infection. This is particularly important in hospitals where there are many sick people whose immune systems are weak or compromised, as well as people with wounds that may provide an entry route for pathogens.

Control techniques

▶ **Table 15.1** The main features of various control techniques

Control technique	Features
Disinfectants	Antimicrobial agents that can be applied to non-living objects such as surfaces and instruments to kill micro-organisms on those surfaces. Examples include phenol, Dettol, bleach, alcohol, formaldehyde, hydrogen peroxide, iodine solution, ozone gas and copper.
Antiseptics	Antimicrobial agents that can be applied to skin to reduce the risk of infection and sepsis. Antibacterials may be *bacteriostatic,* and prevent bacteria from multiplying, or *bactericidal,* and kill bacteria. Examples include TCP, hydrogen peroxide, ethanol, boric acid, tincture of iodine, phenol and salt water.
Antibiotics	Chemicals produced by micro-organisms that can kill or inhibit the growth of other micro-organisms, mainly bacteria but also some fungi and protozoans. Examples include penicillin, tetracycline, amphotericin, voriconazole, bacitracin.
Antivirals	Chemicals that prevent virus entry into host cells. Examples include Tamiflu, antibodies, chemicals that prevent the virus from uncoating such as amantadine, or chemicals that can inhibit the replication of viruses inside host cells, such as interferon, acyclovir, azidothymidine (AZT), zidovudine.
Viricides	Chemicals that can kill viruses on surfaces such as door handles and hospital surfaces. Examples include copper, virkon, bleach, Lysol.
Autoclaves	These are like pressure cookers. At increased pressure steam generated by heating water reaches temperatures of 115–120°C and can kill viruses and bacteria. Used, for example, to sterilise instruments used in operating theatres.
Radiation	Gamma rays can irradiate equipment such as Petri dishes to kill any bacteria and viruses. UV light may also kill bacteria.
Drying	Removal of water prevents micro-organisms from reproducing. This is one method of food preservation.
Refrigeration	At low temperatures (4°C) most bacteria (except psychrophiles) reproduce slowly, so this method prolongs the storage time of foods.
Freezing	Very low temperatures, for example -19°C slow microbial reproduction, enabling food to be stored for up to two to three years.
Antimicrobial soaps	Solid and liquid soaps reduce surface tension and damage the cell surface membranes of micro-organisms.

Case study

Antiseptic copper

Ancient Egyptians used copper to treat chest wounds. Ancient Greeks, Romans and Aztecs used copper compounds to treat burns. Today this ancient remedy is being used to tackle infectious microbes in hospitals.

Many hospitals are now considering using an extremely thin coating of copper on high-touch surfaces such as taps, toilet flush levers, drawer handles and stair rails, because copper kills bacteria and inactivates viruses. Copper ions disrupt the normal charge distribution on the surface of the microbes and eventually lead to them bursting. Micro-organisms can remain alive on stainless steel surfaces.

Hospitals are considering using this approach because hand washing alone is not enough.

Check your knowledge

1   Why do you think high-touch surfaces need to be treated?

2   Why do you think hand washing alone has not solved the problem of pathogen transmission in hospitals between staff, patients and visitors?

Vector control

You have already learned (see Protozoa) that some pathogenic micro-organisms are spread by vectors. The female *Anopheles* mosquito is the vector for *Plasmodium*.

Some ways of preventing the spread of *Plasmodium*, in areas where there is malaria, include:

▶   using insecticides to kill the mosquitoes

▶   sleeping under nets to prevent mosquitoes biting

▶   avoiding marshy areas when outdoors, as that is where mosquitoes breed

▶   wearing long sleeves and trousers in the evening, as this is when mosquitoes bite

▶   taking systemic antimalarial prophylactic drugs, so that the medication is in your blood and will kill any *Plasmodium* injected by an insect bite. These drugs have to be taken every day, before, during and after your visit to the area. Some are taken less frequently but it is important to take antimalarial prophylactic medication exactly as prescribed by your doctor or as directed by your pharmacist.

There are no vaccines or prophylactic (preventative) drugs for trypanosomes, but people can try to avoid being bitten by wearing long sleeves and trousers, using insect repellent, avoiding bushes as tsetse flies rest in bushes, and inspecting vehicles for tsetse flies before entering.

Policies and procedures for infection control in Great Britain

The increased incidence of MRSA (methicillin-resistant *Staphylococcus aureus*) and other antimicrobial resistant micro-organisms means that care providers and health-care professionals should follow National Institute for Clinical Excellence (NICE) guidelines to prevent such infections. The Care Quality Commission (CQC) sets standards that it monitors and updates, and inspects establishments to ensure these procedures are followed and standards are met.

There are also policies to prevent the spread of infections such as Ebola, norovirus and *Clostridium difficile*.

Michael's infected pacemaker – managing biofilms

Michael had a new pacemaker inserted a year ago. Soon after the operation the pacemaker moved, and examination of tissue showed an infection. He was given a course of oral antibiotics. The infection appeared to have been combated but a few months later the flesh near the pacemaker was red and inflamed and a hole had appeared.

A transoesophageal echocardiogram (TOE) showed that the pacemaker leads were infected and coated with a **biofilm** of bacteria. The infected pacemaker and leads were removed and Michael was treated with strong intravenous antibiotics for six weeks, to prevent bacteria in his blood settling on his heart valves and causing endocarditis.

Biofilms form when groups of micro-organisms stick together and coat a surface. They produce a matrix of slime, making them difficult to kill using antimicrobials such as antibiotics.

Certain bacteria can form biofilms on non-living surfaces such as rocks, showers, counters, inside water and sewage pipes, drains and filters. They can also form on living surfaces such as teeth (plaque is a biofilm), pacemaker leads and artificial joint implants. Biofilms on teeth can cause gum disease, infected pacemaker leads can cause endocarditis and sepsis, and bacterial growth on joint prostheses can lead to bone infections.

Check your knowledge

1 What do you think was the source of infection of Michael's infected pacemaker?

Key term

Biofilms – thin layers of mucilage (slime) adhering to a surface and containing bacteria, which make the slime. Biofilms may alter bacterial metabolism and make it harder for antibacterial medicines to work.

Protective clothing

Establishments, such as hospitals and research laboratories, should provide protective clothing for their employees. Examples of protective clothing and their uses are outlined in the section below on barrier nursing.

Isolation

For patients that could infect other patients or medical personnel, as well as the standard precautions and basic hygiene practices, there are additional precautions involving isolating those patients to reduce the spread of infection, which include the following:

▶ Identifying potentially infectious patients – staff need to recognise which patients have diarrhoea, skin rashes, coughs, who use ostomy tubes or bags, or have seeping wounds such as pressure ulcers. The patients identified should be seen in a separate room away from other patients.

▶ Contact precautions – personnel treating potentially infectious patients should wash their hands and wear gloves and gowns before touching the patients or their belongings. After examination, medical personnel should wash their hands with soap and water (alcohol gels do not kill viruses or certain bacteria such as *C. difficile*) and the examination room should be disinfected. Patients with diarrhoea should use a separate bathroom.

▶ Droplet precautions – patients with respiratory tract infections that can spread via droplets should be cared for in a separate room. Medical personnel may also be asked to use a separate entrance to the room, and to wear a face mask before entering the room to examine the patient. The patient may also wear a face mask. Good hand hygiene should be practised and the examination room should be disinfected after use.

Barrier nursing

▶ Everyone involved in health care should be educated about infection and its control. This includes the use of hand decontamination, aseptic technique, safe use and disposal of sharps and use of protective clothing. Wherever carers deliver care they must have protective clothing, materials for cleaning hands, and boxes for disposing of sharps.

▶ Carers must decontaminate their hands before and after contact with each individual patient, immediately after any exposure to the patient's body fluids or where a patient has *C. difficile*. Carers should wet their hands with tepid water, apply soap solution and rub hands together vigorously for 15 seconds making sure soap reaches the fingertips and areas between the fingers, before rinsing and drying with paper towels. When dealing with patients, healthcare workers should be bare below the elbows, not wear wrist or hand jewellery, have short fingernails with no nail polish, and cover any cuts with waterproof dressings.

> **Research**
>
> There are several videos on video-sharing websites showing good hand washing techniques, for example, **www.youtube.com/watch?v=vYwypSLiaTU**.

▶ Latex gloves (or alternatives – but not polythene – if the patient or carer is allergic to latex) must be worn for invasive procedures such as giving injections and for dressing wounds or contact with mucous membranes, such as in the mouth. The wearer should put on the gloves *immediately before* attending to the patient. Afterwards the gloves should be removed (without touching the outside) and discarded. New gloves should be used for the next patient, or before carrying out a different treatment on the same patient.

▶ Single-use gowns and/or disposable aprons should be worn if there is a risk of exposing clothing to blood or other body fluids. The exposed side should not be touched when removing the gown or apron.

▶ Face-masks and eye protection may also be used. Again, the exposed side should not be touched after use.

▶ Healthcare workers dispose of waste in the appropriate colour-coded bins or bags, so that it can be disposed of according to legislation and policies.

▶ Patients and carers should be educated and trained about the correct, hygienic use of catheters, drips and feeding tubes.

> **Discussion**
>
> In small groups, discuss why nurses should put on a fresh pair of gloves *immediately before* attending to each patient, rather than in the corridor before entering the ward.
>
> Share your ideas with others in your class.

Antimicrobial action of soaps

Liquid and solid soaps may kill bacteria, as they lower surface tension and interfere with the integrity and function of the bacterial cell surface membrane. They should be used for routine hygiene, such as hand washing after urination and defecation, and before preparing or eating food, as well as before putting on gloves to treat a patient and for fingertip to elbow washing prior to putting on gloves and carrying out surgery.

Some soaps are more effective than others and recent research shows that prolonged use of a particular type of soap can lead to the evolution of resistance in bacteria.

> **Research**
>
> Go to **http://pubs.sciepub.com/ajmr/2/6/3/** for more information about the antibacterial action of soaps.

Case study

Imelda, a care home worker

Imelda Santos has worked in care homes for many years. During the last few years she has seen an increase in infections that are difficult to treat. Many elderly people have weakened immune systems and are, therefore, more susceptible to infection. In addition, many of the bacteria they are exposed to are resistant to antibiotics. Infection control is extremely important. People working in this sector should keep up to date with and be able to implement the correct infection control procedures and policies.

Imelda is responsible for coordinating infection control and making sure that staff have regular training, so they can implement good practice. She and her team carry out risk assessments within the care home setting, create and use a reporting system to report all relevant incidents, and constantly review the existing policies and practices to make sure they are up to date.

Imelda makes sure that all care workers attend courses, verified by the CQC, where they learn about how people can become infected, different types of pathogens, infections particularly associated with care homes, how to wash hands effectively, personal protective equipment, the chain of infection, how to prevent infection and the importance of policies and legislation about infection control.

Imelda also makes sure that the latest and most up-to-date information booklets published by the Department of Health and Public Health England (PHE) are available for staff to access.

If there is an outbreak of an infectious disease within the home, Imelda has to report it to PHE. Health protection nurses at PHE are then responsible for monitoring the outbreak and giving advice on how to control it.

Check your knowledge

1 What sort of infections do you think are most likely to spread easily within a care home?

⏸ PAUSE POINT   What are the main features of barrier nursing?

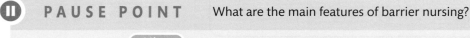

Hint   Barrier nursing involves protocols to reduce the risk of nurses being infected by patients.

Extend   Why do hospitals have isolation wards?

Assessment practice 15.1   A.P1   A.M1   A.D1

An infection control nurse in your local hospital has asked you to produce a leaflet that can be made available for the nursing staff. She also wants a poster to inform patients and their visitors about the importance of infection control.

In the leaflet and poster, you should cover the following:

1 Explain what the pathogenic bacteria and viruses likely to be found in a hospital need to survive. Explain why hospitals are good breeding grounds for pathogens. Explain how the requirements for growth of these micro-organisms can be controlled, in order to help contain the spread of infectious organisms.

2 Explain the structure of bacteria and viruses and how they reproduce, and indicate how this knowledge can be used to help stop the spread of these micro-organisms.

3 Describe and explain the methods used to control two different, named micro-organisms. Indicate why the methods you have chosen are effective and not harmful to humans.

Plan
- Do I know what I am being asked to do?
- Do I have enough information or should I extend my research?
- How confident am I about my abilities to complete the task?
- Are there areas I may struggle with?

Do
- I know what I am doing and what I want to achieve.
- I can check my work to see where I have gone off task and can make changes to put this right.

Review
- I can explain what the task was and how I approached it.
- I can explain what I would do differently next time and the approach I would take with the parts that I found difficult this time.

B   Examine the role of micro-organisms in human health and disease

Many diseases are caused by **infecting agents** such as viruses, bacteria, protoctists, fungi or larger **parasites**, such as worms and insects (lice and fleas). Infecting agents live in or on the body, and if they cause disease they are described as pathogens.

Infectious diseases are also called communicable diseases as they can spread from person to person, or from animals to people. Some communicable diseases, such as:

▸ athlete's foot, influenza, colds, measles, mumps and chickenpox are spread via normal social contact

▸ typhoid, salmonella, campylobacter, hepatitis A and cholera are spread via contaminated food or water

▸ HIV/AIDS, syphilis, hepatitis B and the human papilloma virus (HPV) (which causes cancer of the cervix) are spread via body fluids – for example, blood to blood or via sexual intercourse

▸ malaria, dengue fever and sleeping sickness are carried by insects.

> **Key terms**
>
> **Infecting agent** – an organism that infiltrates another living organism (the host), and causes an infectious disease. Infecting agents may be a virus, bacterium, fungus or parasite.
>
> **Parasite** – an organism that lives in or on another living organism (the host), obtaining its nourishment and shelter from the host, and causes harm to the host. The host receives no benefit from the parasite.

Epidemiology

Epidemiology is the study of the distribution and determinants of diseases (and other health problems), and the factors that affect their spread in defined populations (groups of people in a city, county or country). Epidemiologists gather information about the distribution of specific diseases throughout the population and, from the evidence, they identify the risk factors for the disease. This evidence helps shape public health policies to try to reduce or prevent the occurrence of that disease. Such information can also help scientists to identify the cause of the disease and, in the case of an infectious disease, how it is transmitted. For any specific disease, epidemiologists gather information on how many people are ill (morbidity) and how many have died (mortality). They adjust these figures to *rates* (numbers per 100,000 people in the population) so they can make comparisons year on year, or area to area. Epidemiologists also look at the incidence (number of new cases in the population per week/month/year) and prevalence (the number of people with the disease in a population in any given week/month or year).

Such epidemiological data indicates the nation's health and can predict the preventive and treatment regimes that will need to be implemented by the health services.

Case study

Snow's pump

Dr John Snow is regarded as one of the founders of modern epidemiology. London suffered a series of cholera epidemics during the nineteenth century and, in 1854, during one of them, he proposed that the disease was spread via drinking water. He came to this conclusion by mapping where cases of cholera were concentrated. He noticed that many cases were in the vicinity of a pump in Broad Street, where people obtained their drinking water. It was later realised that sewage from a nearby cesspit was contaminating the water in this well. Despite scepticism from local authorities, the parish council removed the handle from the Broad Street pump at Snow's request, and the cholera epidemic quickly subsided.

Check your knowledge

1 What is the organism that causes cholera?

2 Under what circumstances today, do cholera epidemics occur?

3 What is the treatment for cholera?

Endemic

If an infectious disease is always present in a particular area or population it is described as endemic. Tuberculosis (TB) is endemic in most parts of the world. Many people have the bacteria that cause it in their lungs, but if the immune system is efficient the bacteria are kept dormant.

Epidemic

A sudden outbreak of an infectious disease, such as influenza or measles, affecting many people in an area or population is called an epidemic.

Pandemic

If the epidemic spreads across a large area, such as a continent or the whole world, it is called a pandemic. Every few years there is an influenza pandemic, the most recent started in 2009.

Transmission routes

Pathogens can enter their host in a variety of ways. These ways are called transmission routes, as shown in Table 15.2.

Case study

Catching polio from changing a baby's nappy

Marek caught polio when he changed his baby's nappy. The baby had been vaccinated at three months old against polio, which is caused by a virus. The polio vaccine can be passed into the baby's nappy for up to six weeks after the baby has been vaccinated. A parent or carer who has not been vaccinated should take great care to always wash their hands thoroughly, with hot water and soap, after changing a nappy of a recently immunised baby. Alcohol hand rubs are not effective against viruses.

Check your knowledge

1 Discuss the pros and cons of having alcohol hand rubs in hospital wards.

▶ **Table 15.2** Transmission routes of various pathogens

Method of transmission	Examples
Direct contact – **fomites** are objects or substances that can carry infecting agents and transfer them from one person to another. They include computer keyboards, door knobs, operating tables, stethoscopes, clothing, blood-pressure cuffs, IV drip tubes, catheters, food preparation surfaces and utensils, towels, bedding, bed frames, skin cells, hair and money.	Many hospital-acquired infections, such as MRSA and norovirus, are transmitted by items of hospital equipment or health personnel clothing. Viral infections, such as colds and flu, can be spread by hand-shaking. Foodborne infections can be spread via preparation surfaces and utensils.
Body fluids – liquids originating from inside the body, e.g. blood, semen, vaginal secretions, saliva, sputum, breast milk, faeces, sebum, pus, mucus, tears, urine, vomit.	HIV/AIDS, Ebola, hepatitis B, CMV (cytomegalovirus).
Airborne – the infecting agent/pathogen can be breathed out in **droplets** by an infected person and breathed in by another person.	Measles, colds, influenza, anthrax, smallpox (eradicated but samples of the virus still exist), TB.
Foodborne – the pathogen or a toxin made by it are transmitted in food that is unhygienically handled, stored or prepared. Some foods, such as fungi, contain mycotoxins. Decaying food may contain poisonous alkaloids (ptomaines). Salad vegetables grown using human sewage as fertiliser and not properly washed, may be a source of infection.	*Bacillus cereus* in rice, *Salmonella*, *Campylobacter* and *E. coli* food poisoning, *Listeria*, typhoid fever, cholera (shellfish), Creutzfeldt-Jakob disease, norovirus, hepatitis A, ergotism. Undercooked infected meat may contain worm parasites or protoctists such as *Entamoeba histolytica* that causes amoebic dysentery. Cholera can also be spread via infected food.
Waterborne – pathogens may enter water sources if sewage contaminates drinking water. This may happen in countries where sanitation is inadequate, in refugee camps, or after a catastrophe such as an earthquake.	Travellers' diarrhoea, cryptosporidium, dysentery, cholera, typhoid fever, hepatitis A. Parasitic infections such as schistosomiasis (bilharzia) can be acquired by swimming in infected water.
Vector borne – transmitted via bites of insects and ticks.	Malaria (protozoan spread via female *Anopheles* mosquitoes), dengue fever (virus spread via female *Aedes aegypti* mosquito), Lyme disease (bacteria spread via ticks), leishmaniasis (parasite spread by female sand flies), yellow fever (virus spread by *Aedes* mosquitoes), Chagas disease (protozoan spread by *Triatomine* bugs), bubonic plague (bacteria spread by fleas), typhus fever (bacteria spread by lice), sleeping sickness (protozoan spread by tsetse flies).
Transplacental – vertical transmission from mother to foetus across the placenta.	CMV, HIV, syphilis, gonorrhoea, *Chlamydia*, herpes simplex, human papilloma virus, rubella, toxoplasmosis, hepatitis C, parvovirus.

▶ Mosquito

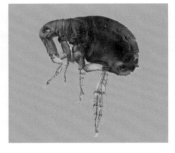

▶ Flea

▶ Tick

▶ Louse

Case study

Educating about cytomegalovirus (CMV)

Agnes is a nursery teacher. She has recently attended a course about CMV, which is a common virus belonging to the herpes family of viruses. It is spread via body fluids such as the urine, saliva, blood, tears, stools, cervical secretions and semen of infected individuals. It can also be passed from children to adults, for example when adults wipe children's eyes or noses, dress their wounds or when they change their nappies. Most cases do not produce any symptoms, and if they do then the symptoms are similar to those of flu, with a high temperature and sore throat. Once someone has been infected with CMV the virus stays inactive in their body, not causing problems unless the infected person is immunocompromised (their immune system is weakened), for example by being HIV+ or receiving immunosuppressant drugs after an organ transplant.

If a pregnant woman receives an active CMV infection from young children, the virus can be passed across the placenta to their foetus, or to the baby during birth or in breast milk. A few babies infected in this way may suffer problems such as learning difficulties, seizures, blindness and hearing loss.

Between 10 and 80 per cent of children in childcare centres excrete CMV in their urine. Agnes is now going to inform her colleagues about CMV. Together, they will develop a strategy to make sure that everyone knows how to practise good hygiene when changing nappies, helping the children to use the toilet, or wiping their eyes and noses. This is important for everyone but particularly important for any nursery teachers and assistants who may be pregnant, planning to become pregnant, or whose partner is pregnant.

Check your knowledge

1   What sort of practices would need to be implemented to reduce the risk of nursery teachers and assistants becoming infected with CMV?

2   Why is it particularly important for nursery teachers of childbearing age to avoid becoming infected with CMV?

3   Why is it important for any male members of staff to avoid becoming infected with CMV?

❚❚ **PAUSE POINT**   Without copying from Table 15.2, list how pathogenic micro-organisms can be transmitted from person to person. For each method name at least one example of a micro-organism spread in this way.

> **Hint**   Think about direct, person-to-person contact, as well as indirect means, such as via faeces contaminating drinking water or food. Remember how vectors can transmit diseases.

> **Extend**   Find out about the risks to pregnant women from contracting toxoplasmosis from cat litter trays.

The role of normal flora and the human body

When bacteria were first identified they were classified as plants because they had cell walls and, at the time, all living organisms were classed as either plants or animals. The term *flora* referred to plants in an area, so the bacteria living in and on the body were called the *human body flora*. Scientists have since found out much more about living organisms and they use a five kingdom classification system: bacteria, protoctists and fungi, animals and plants; plus viruses, which are not truly living and so do not fit into any of these five kingdoms. The micro-organisms (bacteria, viruses, fungi and protoctists) in and on people's bodies are now called the **microbiota**.

Symbiotic relationship

The several thousand species of micro-organisms that normally colonise (live in) the gastrointestinal (GI) tract (gut), saliva, mouth lining, throat, upper and lower respiratory tract, conjunctiva of the eye, vagina and on the skin surface have a **symbiotic** (both micro-organism and host benefit) relationship with people. They obtain shelter and nutrients from people (the hosts) and supply them with some nutrients (for example vitamin K), hormones (some help regulate appetite) and many other products of their genes (the **microbiome**). They also help reduce infections from other invading micro-organisms by competing with them for space and food, or by secreting chemicals that kill them.

Key terms

Microbiota – all the micro-organisms in a particular habitat, such as in the human body.

Symbiotic – interdependent relationship between organisms of different species.

Microbiome – all the genes of the microbiota, the products of many of which are essential for a person's wellbeing.

The organisms of the gut microbiota are essential for people's wellbeing. Newborn babies' GI tracts are colonised from bacteria obtained from the mother's anus and vagina during birth, and from the mother's skin after birth. Each human harbours between 10 and 100 trillion micro-organism cells – far more than the number of cells in our bodies, weighing between 1.5 and 3.0 kg in total. Imbalances in microbiota, caused by prolonged exposure to antibiotics or eating a diet lacking fruit and vegetables, in the range of species present in people's bodies can contribute to health problems, such as obesity.

Treatment of hospital acquired Clostridium difficile

When John was in hospital being treated with intravenous antibiotics for several weeks to treat endocarditis, he contracted an infection of *Clostridium difficile*. Everyone has these bacteria inside their digestive tract but the other bacteria usually keep them in check so that they do no harm to their host. However, if you are treated with a long course of antibiotics, some of your gut bacteria can be killed and the *Clostridium difficile*, known as *C. diff,* can multiply and release toxins that cause swelling and irritation of the colon. This is known as colitis and the symptoms are diarrhoea, fever and abdominal cramps.

This infection can be difficult to treat and John had been given various antibiotics (vancomycin and fidaxomicin) with no positive result. He suffered from recurring bouts of *C. diff*, which was very debilitating and could eventually prove fatal. He had read about the gut microbiota and discussed them with his GP who recommended that he have a faecal transplant. This involved a doctor or nurse placing a sample of faeces, taken from a healthy donor and that had been screened, into his colon, using a catheter. It worked (as it does in over 90 per cent of cases) and he is now well again. His GP has advised him to maintain a healthy diet to encourage the growth of the good bacteria in his colon. This diet involves plenty of fruit and vegetables, especially leeks and onions.

Check your knowledge

1 Why do you think the donor of the faeces has to be healthy?

2 Which diseases do you think are being looked for when the donated faeces is screened?

Infection sources

Different pathogens have different routes into the body or infective sites. Respiratory pathogens are usually airborne, whereas intestinal pathogens are usually food- or waterborne, or spread by the faecal–oral route (faeces to hands to food via preparation or eating). Table 15.2 outlines various infective sites and routes of transmission.

Everyone is exposed to micro-organisms every day and needs this exposure for their immune systems to function efficiently. There are various barriers to each potential route of infection, such as skin, sebum, tears, mucus in the respiratory tract, and stomach acid. If the number of invading micro-organisms is too great for the normal barrier defences to prevent entry, then an infection results. The number of pathogenic organisms necessary to cause an infection is called the **infective dose**.

Reservoirs of infection

Certain areas of the body, such as the large bowel, nose, skin and wounds, act as **reservoirs of infection**, harbouring a range of microbiota. These areas are technically all outside the body proper, and in the right place, some of the micro-organisms, such as those in the gut, are essential for people's wellbeing. As long as micro-organisms from these reservoirs don't breach the barrier between the body and the outside, they do not cause any harm. However, if any of these bacteria enter the body's tissues, for instance through a wound or a breach in the bowel wall, they can cause disease.

Normal skin bacteria, such as *Staphylococcus aureus,* and normal nose or gut bacteria can cause problems if they enter an open wound. MRSA is a skin-dwelling bacterium that is resistant to many antibiotics, including methicillin, and when it enters a wound from the skin of a patient or a member of the healthcare team, it may cause skin infections, sepsis, endocarditis, pneumonia, and joint or bone infections.

Micro-organisms living in or on any particular person may not do that person any harm or cause any symptoms. However, if they spread to a person who is **immunocompromised**, or if they spread to an open wound on or another person, they may cause sepsis (blood poisoning) or tissue necrosis (tissue death).

Key terms

Infective dose – amount of pathogen needed to cause an infection in the host.

Reservoir of infection – principal habitat where an infectious agent lives and proliferates, includes humans, animals, plants, soil or other substances such as biofilms.

Immunocompromised – having a weakened/less efficient immune system, for example due to being HIV+, taking immunosuppressant drugs following transplant surgery, treatment with chemotherapy for cancer, following another infection or having neutropenia (lack of certain white blood cells).

Opportunist infections

These are also referred to as opportunistic infections. They are caused by micro-organisms that are normally held in check by the host's immune system but can proliferate when the host is immunocompromised or has an altered microbiota. TB is an opportunist infection. Most people harbour the bacterium *Mycobacterium tuberculosis* within macrophages (types of phagocytic white blood cells) inside their lungs. As people age, become ill or malnourished or immunocompromised, for example by being HIV+, the bacteria can cause TB. Other examples of opportunist infections are:

▶ thrush caused by the fungus *Candida albicans*

▶ diarrhoea caused by *Clostridium difficile*

▶ Kaposi's sarcoma caused by *Human herpesvirus 8* in people who are HIV+.

Carriers of infectious micro-organisms

Human beings

Some people can carry certain micro-organisms while not succumbing to infection. However, they can pass the infecting agent to others, who suffer from a disease as a result. Mary Mallon (1869–1938) was the first person identified as a symptomless carrier of the bacterium *Salmonella typhimurium* – the cause of typhoid fever. During her career as a cook 'Typhoid Mary' (as she became known) infected about 50 people, three of whom died.

Ⅱ PAUSE POINT   What are opportunist infections?

> **Hint**   These organisms thrive when they get an opportunity – a 'lucky break'.
>
> **Extend**   Why do you think people may suffer from candidiasis when they have been taking antibiotics?

Case study

Galloping gangrene

Ainsley went into hospital for a routine operation and contracted a type of gangrene called necrotising fasciitis. This is sometimes known as 'galloping gangrene' because it spreads throughout the body so quickly. It is caused by a streptococcus bacterium that may live in the throats of some people, doing them no harm. However, if it enters a deep wound it may be fatal. The

hospital found that one member of the operating team was a carrier of this bacterium, *Streptococcus pyogenes*.

Check your knowledge

1 Explain why medical staff should be screened to see if they carry this bacterium.

2 What do you think should be done about staff found to be carriers of *S. pyogenes*?

Animals

Animals can carry and pass infecting agents to humans. Diseases spread in this way are termed zoonoses (see Table 15.3).

▶ **Table 15.3** Some examples of zoonoses

Carrier	Example of zoonosis
Pigs, domestic and wild birds – ducks and chickens, seals, whales	Influenza virus, transmitted through the air in droplets.
Many mammals including bats, dogs, monkeys, racoons, foxes, cats, cattle	Rabies – in countries where rabies is endemic – not in the UK. Virus is passed in saliva when the animal bites or licks the broken skin of a human.
Fruit bats, forest antelopes, chimpanzees, monkeys	Haemorrhagic fever – Ebola, the virus passes through body fluids and organs.
Ticks	Lyme disease – the bacteria are transferred from deer to humans via tick bites.

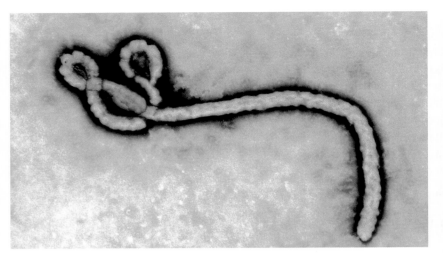

▶ TEM of an Ebola virus. Ebola haemorrhagic fever is a severe and often fatal disease, first identified in 1976 near the Ebola river, after which it is named, in the Democratic Republic of the Congo. Ebola is a large virus with a diameter of 70 nm. It may be transmitted to humans from fruit bats.

▶ Fruit bat feeding on nectar from a banana flower

Research

Med-Vet-Net is a European network for public health, food and veterinary researchers who work on diseases that can spread from animals to humans (zoonoses).

An example is *Campylobacter* bacteria, which is carried by many chickens. When the chicken is cooked these bacteria are killed but people need to be educated *not* to wash out the body cavity of the raw chicken before cooking it. This is because the water in the cavity creates aerosols (droplets) that can rise in the air and rain down onto food preparation surfaces, or fruit and salads that will not be cooked. As the droplets contain *Campylobacter* bacteria, when they are ingested they can cause severe food poisoning.

In some countries chicken carcasses destined for human consumption are rinsed in dilute bleach to kill *Campylobacter*. This is not allowed in the UK. Find out more about this practice. In small groups, discuss the advantages and disadvantages of this practice. Do you think this practice should be allowed in the UK?

Types of infections

We have already seen some examples of diseases caused by various types of micro-organism in learning aim A of this unit. Table 15.4 lists further examples.

▶ **Table 15.4** Types of infections

Infecting agent	Examples
Viruses	Colds, influenza, measles, mumps, poliomyelitis, rubella, chickenpox, HIV/AIDS, hepatitis (A, B and C), herpes, Ebola haemorrhagic fever, avian flu in humans, Zika virus.
Bacteria	Tuberculosis (TB), salmonella food poisoning, staphylococcal food poisoning, streptococcal sore throat, whooping cough (pertussis), meningococcal meningitis, bacterial dysentery, cholera, diphtheria, scarlet fever, bubonic plague, syphilis.
Fungi	Candidaisis (thrush), tinea (athlete's foot, ringworm).
Protozoa	Malaria, sleeping sickness, trichomoniasis.
Prions	Bovine spongiform encephalopathy (BSE), Creutzfeldt-Jakob disease (CJD).

⏸ **PAUSE POINT** Explain, with examples, the terms: gut microbiota, symptomless carriers of infections, zoonoses and opportunist infections.

Hint Give full explanations, and only refer to one or two examples in each case.

Extend Why do you think carriers of zoonoses are not described as vectors?

The role of the immune system

All living organisms, including plants and bacteria, have defences against invading pathogens. Taken together, these defences form part of the organism's immune system.

Primary defences are part of the *innate* immune system and are mechanisms to prevent the entry of pathogens. In humans these include the following:

▶ Tears – contain the enzyme lysozyme, which breaks down bacterial cell walls, and antibodies.

▶ Ear wax – lines the ear canals and traps pathogens.

▶ A mucus plug in the cervix of the uterus – protects the uterus and its contents.

▶ The vagina has fairly acidic secretions – this inhibits the growth of many micro-organisms.

▶ Skin – a large organ that covers the body, protecting the inner structures. There are two layers: an inner layer, the dermis, which contains hair follicles and blood vessels; and an outer layer, the epidermis. A layer between them divides to make new skin cells that migrate upwards, becoming flattened and hardened (keratinised) with keratin protein. By the time (30 days) these cells reach the surface of the skin they are dead and form a mechanical barrier against pathogen entry.

▶ Mucous membranes – the airways, lungs and digestive system are at risk of being infected when air is breathed in or food is being digested. They are protected by mucous membranes containing goblet cells that secrete mucus. This mucus can trap pathogens. Some cells lining the respiratory tract also have cilia (hair-like projections) that can move and waft the pathogens trapped in the mucus back up to the throat where it can be swallowed or coughed out.

▶ Stomach acid – kills ingested pathogens when coughing, sneezing and vomiting – reflex actions that eject potential pathogens from the body.

Secondary defences are responses activated when a pathogen has entered the body.

▶ **Mast cells** detect pathogens in body tissues and release **histamine**, a signalling molecule that affects other cells and tissues. Histamine release causes:

  ▶ more blood to flow into the skin capillaries

  ▶ the walls of the skin capillaries to become more porous, enabling phagocytic white blood cells, such as neutrophils, to squeeze out from capillaries into the tissue and ingest the invading micro-organisms

  ▶ many neutrophils to be made in the bone marrow in response to an infection. These engulf and digest pathogens – eating themselves to death; the dead neutrophils collect at the infected area, forming pus

  ▶ **tissue fluid** to leak out into the surrounding tissues, causing swelling (oedema).

▶ These events are known as the *inflammatory reaction* and are part of the *non-specific immune response*. The response is the same each time. The extra blood flow and swelling also cause the area to look red and swollen and feel hot.

▶ The excess tissue fluid drains into the lymph vessels and any micro-organisms within the tissue fluid then come into contact with lymphocytes, which initiates a specific immune response.

Key terms

Mast cells – type of white blood cell, found in connective tissue, that releases histamine during inflammatory reactions.

Histamine – chemical released by some cells of the immune system in response to injury or infection.

Tissue fluid – extracellular fluid that bathes cells. It comes from the fluid part of blood that has been forced out of blood capillaries and later goes back into the blood capillaries or the lymph system.

Neutrophil binds to the opsonin attached to the antigen of the pathogen

The pathogen is engulfed by endocytosis forming a phagosome

Lysosomes fuse to the phagosome and release lytic enzymes into it

After digestion, the harmless products can be absorbed into the cell

▶ **Figure 15.8** Phagocytosis

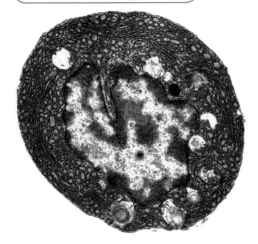

▶ Colour enhanced TEM of a plasma cell. Plasma cells contain a lot of rough endoplasmic reticulum with ribosomes, the sites of synthesis of the many antibodies they secrete.

The specific immune response

All cells have either proteins or **glycoproteins** embedded within their cell surface membranes called **antigens**. Each organism's antigens are specific and only found on the cells of that organism (or in the case of viruses, on their outer coat).

Macrophages are a type of **phagocytic leucocyte** made in the bone marrow. They travel in the blood as monocytes and then pass out of capillaries into tissues where they mature into macrophages.

When a phagocytic macrophage ingests an invading pathogen:

▶ It partly digests (breaks down) the pathogen and displays the pathogen's antigens on its cell surface membrane. In this way it becomes an **antigen-presenting cell (APC).**

▶ The APC displays the pathogen antigens to other types of leucocytes – T-lymphocytes and B-lymphocytes. In your body, there may be just one B-cell and one T-cell with a receptor on their cell surface membranes that fit the particular antigens being presented. Antigen presentation increases the chance of the correct B-cell and T-cell being found.

▶ Once the correct B-cell and T-cell have been selected in this way, they both proliferate by dividing many times by mitosis.

▶ The B cells produced by these divisions develop into two types of cell:

  ▶ Plasma cells, which circulate in the blood and produce many molecules of special proteins called antibodies. Each B-cell in your body carries a slightly different DNA code. Once a specific B-cell has been selected by antigen presentation, all the plasma cells **cloned** from it make identical antibodies.

  ▶ Memory cells, which remain in the body for many years, forming an immunological memory. The T-cells derived by mitosis differentiate into four types of T-cell:

   • T helper (T_h) cells, which release cytokines (chemicals) which stimulate B-cells to develop T killer or T cytotoxic (T_c) cells, which attack and kill infected body cells (and cancerous cells)

   • T memory (T_m) cells, which remain in the body giving long-term immunity

   • T suppressor (T_s) cells, which dampen down the reaction and help to prevent autoimmunity.

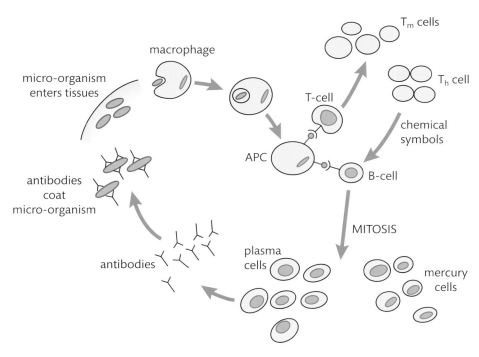

▶ **Figure 15.9** Summary of the specific immune response

Antibodies/immunoglobulins

Antibodies are Y-shaped glycoproteins, also called immunoglobulins. Each is made of a constant region that is the same for all antibodies, consisting of four polypeptide chains – two light and two heavy – with hinge regions made of **disulfide bonds**, giving some flexibility.

> **Key term**
>
> **Disulfide bond** – a chemical bond between two sulfur atoms within a molecule. These bonds are very strong and not broken by heat.

Each also has two variable regions where a specific sequence of amino acids gives a particular tertiary structure (3D shape) complementary to the shape of the antigen to which the antibody is specific. Antibodies may attach to antigens on the surface of pathogens.

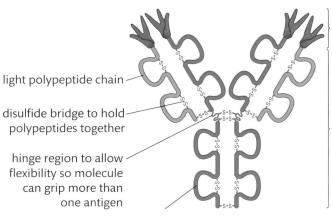

light polypeptide chain

disulfide bridge to hold polypeptides together

hinge region to allow flexibility so molecule can grip more than one antigen

variable region which has a shape specific to the shape of the antigen

constant region which is the same in all antibodies – it may have a site for the easy binding of phagocytic cells

▶ **Figure 15.10** An antibody

There are three main types of antibody.

▶ Opsonins – which bind to antigens on the pathogen, covering its surface and displaying their constant regions that phagocytic leucocytes recognise, enabling the phagocytes to ingest the pathogens. Such coating of antigens also prevents the pathogen from entering a host cell.

▶ Agglutinins – which can bind one variable region to an antigen on one pathogen, and the other to an antigen on another pathogen of the same type. In this way, they can cause virus particles to clump together, making it impossible for the viruses to enter host cells.

▶ Anti-toxins – which bind to molecules of toxin made by the bacterial pathogens, making the toxin harmless.

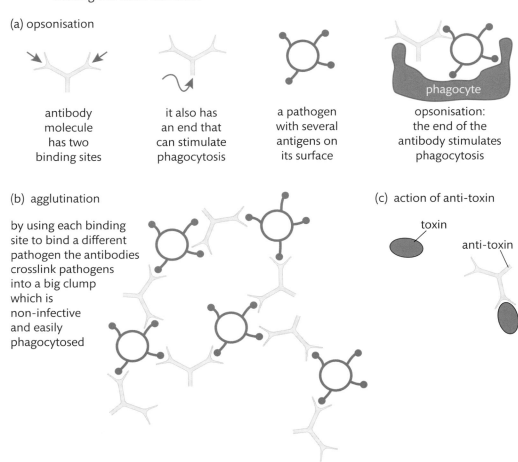

(a) opsonisation

| antibody molecule has two binding sites | it also has an end that can stimulate phagocytosis | a pathogen with several antigens on its surface | opsonisation: the end of the antibody stimulates phagocytosis |

(b) agglutination

by using each binding site to bind a different pathogen the antibodies crosslink pathogens into a big clump which is non-infective and easily phagocytosed

(c) action of anti-toxin

toxin

anti-toxin

▶ **Figure 15.11** The actions of different types of antibodies

Key terms

Lymphocytes – a type of white blood cell. They are small (about the same size as red blood cells) and each contains a large nucleus. There are two types – B-lymphocytes and T-lymphocytes.

Plasma cell – a cell derived from a B-lymphocyte cell, which is stimulated by antigen presentation to divide. Plasma cells secrete many antibodies.

Memory cell – B- or T-cells that remain in the body for a long time giving an immunological memory and enabling a faster immune response when next infected by the same pathogen.

Primary and secondary responses

When a specific pathogen first invades your body a primary specific immune response is initiated. However, it is quite slow and takes time to produce enough **antibodies** to combat the infection. Hence you suffer the symptoms of the disease while this response is happening.

Once you have recovered, levels of these antibodies in your blood fall rapidly. However, memory B-cells and memory T-cells remain in your body. If that same type of pathogen invades your body again, these memory cells recognise its antigens and react very swiftly, making lots of antibodies – more quickly and in greater numbers than during the primary response. This swifter response is the secondary specific immune response. The concentration of antibodies rapidly reaches a high level and combats infection before you suffer any symptoms.

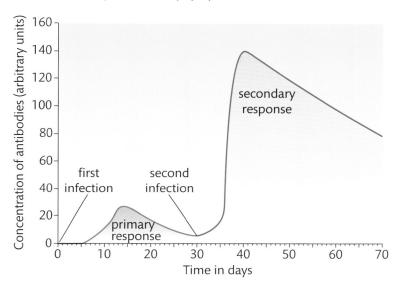

▶ **Figure 15.12** Primary and secondary response to infection

Vaccination

Vaccination is the deliberate exposure of a person to a specific type of pathogen that has been killed or treated to make it harmless, or to its antigens, to stimulate an immune response. As a result their body makes memory cells that remain, giving long-term **immunity**. Toxoids (toxins, such as tetanus toxin, treated to make them harmless) can also be injected, to stimulate the production of antitoxins and the corresponding memory cells. Vaccination involves active immunity where your immune system is activated and makes its own antibodies.

▶ Active immunity is the body's immune response in which it makes antibodies to a specific antigen. It may be natural, as in having the disease, or artificial, following vaccination.

▶ Passive immunity is where you are given ready-made antibodies. This happens naturally when antibodies pass from mother to foetus before birth or to the baby after birth in the first breast milk (colostrum). It may be artificial when antibodies are injected into a person, for example, an anti-tetanus injection.

> **Key terms**
>
> **Antibodies** – Y-shaped immunoglobulin proteins made by plasma cells derived from B-lymphocytes. Each type of antibody is specific to a particular type of antigen.
>
> **Immunity** – the ability of an organism to resist an infecting agent, due to presence of memory cells.

As a child in the mid-1700s, Dr Edward Jenner had been variolated against smallpox. (Variolation was the practice of inoculating some pus from a blister on someone suffering from smallpox under the skin, which we know now contains the variola virus that causes smallpox.) As an adult, Jenner noticed that milkmaids (who milked cows by hand) who had contracted cowpox (a mild disease called vaccinia, causing blisters on their hands) did not catch smallpox. Jenner took fluid from a cowpox blister on a cow udder and inoculated it under the skin of a boy. Later, Jenner deliberately inoculated the same boy with smallpox pus; the boy did not get smallpox. The practice of cowpox inoculation was safer than variolation.

In 1798, Jenner introduced the practice of vaccination. He envisaged that one day there would be no smallpox. By 1858 vaccination of infants was compulsory in the UK.

However, by the end of the 1960s, smallpox (*Variola*) was still endemic in Africa and Asia. The WHO began a programme to eradicate it. When a case was reported, ring vaccination was used – all the contacts of the sufferer were vaccinated to break the chain of infection. The last case of smallpox was in 1978, and by 1980 it was declared eradicated.

Samples of the smallpox virus are still kept in high security laboratories, so that if the disease should re-emerge vaccines could be made.

Discuss the pros and cons of keeping samples of the smallpox virus. Do you think all samples should be destroyed? Give reasons for your answer.

PAUSE POINT
Why do you think active immunity lasts a long time but passive immunity is fairly short-lived?

Hint
Think about what happens during an immune response, and what remains in the body to make someone immune.

Extend
Explain how the structure of antibodies makes each type specific for a particular antigen.

Community immunity

Thanks to ring vaccination, smallpox was eradicated.

Because vaccination is now so successful, children in developed countries rarely suffer from potentially serious diseases such as polio, measles, diphtheria, meningococcal meningitis and scarlet fever. However, these diseases still cause many children in the developing world to die or become disabled.

Children in developed countries are protected from infectious diseases because nearly everyone is vaccinated. This provides **herd immunity**; once enough people are immune the pathogen cannot spread as there are not enough susceptible hosts to infect. Scientists have estimated that at least 95 per cent of the population must be vaccinated against measles to prevent an epidemic.

Key term

Herd immunity – protection of a population from infectious disease that occurs following a very large percentage of the population being made immune to the infection.

In the UK there is a vaccination schedule, so that:

▶ children are offered vaccinations at appropriate ages against diseases such as pneumonia, meningitis C, diphtheria, tetanus, polio, whooping cough, mumps, measles and rubella; additionally, young teenage girls are offered an HPV (human papilloma virus) vaccination to protect them against cervical cancer

▶ professional health workers and people aged 65 and over are offered vaccinations against influenza (flu) and pneumonia, however, because the flu virus has a high mutation rate, this vaccine is offered every year using three types of attenuated (weakened) flu virus strains, which are predicted to be likely to infect people in that specific winter period

▶ those over 70 are offered vaccination against shingles.

In addition to this schedule, people with specific health problems can ask for vaccines against hepatitis B, TB and chickenpox.

> **Discussion**
>
> A vaccine for meningitis B is offered to children in the UK in their first year of life. Older children are not offered this vaccine although their parents can pay for it if they wish. However, following the death of a two-year-old girl, the demand for the private vaccine has outstripped supplies.
>
> Discuss the pros and cons of extending the vaccine for meningitis B to older children.

People intending to travel abroad can request, and pay for, vaccinations against diseases such as hepatitis A, typhoid, cholera and yellow fever. As yet, there is no effective vaccination against malaria but prophylactic tablets may be taken before, during and after travel to areas of high risk.

> **Discussion**
>
> In small groups, discuss the impact on a community if several parents decide not to have their children vaccinated.
>
> Discuss the impact on communities of the flawed report linking the measles vaccine with autism.

Investigate the impact of diseases and their treatment in a global context

Factors in controlling diseases globally

Some infectious diseases may only be endemic in certain parts of the world, due to climatic factors that allow the insect vector to survive. However, many infectious diseases do not recognise territorial boundaries and can spread across the world, aided by the increased speed of international travel, whereby people incubating an infection but showing no symptoms can travel vast distances, in the company of others, before becoming ill.

Many factors affect people's health, genetics and lifestyle are two of them. However, environmental and social factors are also very important and can impact on the incidence and prevalence of infectious diseases. Climate change, political unrest, conflicts, lack of sanitation, undernutrition, demographic changes, such as an increasing and ageing population, poor education and poverty all increase the chances of people becoming infected. Low income countries may not be able to afford well organised health services, or provide adequate health care.

Personnel with knowledge and experience

There is a world shortage of trained medical and support personnel with appropriate levels of relevant knowledge and experience. More nurses, doctors and birth attendants are needed in many countries, including the UK. There are international organisations, such as MSF (Médecins Sans Frontières/Doctors Without Borders) and the International Red Cross and Red Crescent Movement.

Research

Using the internet, you can find out more about international medical and humanitarian aid organisations:

www.icrc.org

www.redcross.org.uk/About-us/Who-we-are/The-international-Movement/The-Movement

www.msf.org.uk

www.who.int/en

Discussion

In small groups, discuss the ethics of developed countries 'poaching' medical personnel from less economically developed countries. Bear in mind that those poorer countries have paid for the training of those medical personnel.

Global health

Global health focuses on people across the whole planet. It involves collaborative and transnational research and action to promote health for all.

It builds on national public health programmes developed during the twentieth century. Whereas medical science focuses on individuals – diagnosis, treatment and medical care – public health focuses on communities and populations, how to prevent diseases and promote physical and mental health. It does this by organised and community efforts such as improved sanitation, vaccination programmes and education of individuals about hygiene and nutrition. It also involves:

▸ disease surveillance systems

▸ public health laboratories

▸ the organisation of medical and nursing services, enabling early diagnosis and efficient treatment of diseases

▸ child immunisation programmes

▸ health screening programmes

▸ ensuring that every individual in the community has a standard of living adequate to maintaining health.

Epidemiologists

Global health organisations use **epidemiologists** to gather data about patterns of disease in specific populations. This can help establish the cause of the disease and inform policy makers about how to contain its spread and treat it. They can also find out about the risk factors for specific diseases. Poor countries have a greater disease burden than rich countries.

> **Key term**
>
> **Epidemiologist** – scientist who studies patterns of diseases within populations by analysing data to find out what causes disease outbreaks (epidemics).

> **Discussion**
>
> Why do you think poorer countries have a greater disease burden than rich countries? Share your ideas with others in your class.

The World Health Organization (WHO)

In 1945, just after the Second World War, the United Nations (UN) and World Bank organisations were established. In 1948, member states of the UN created a specialised agency – the WHO. WHO headquarters are in Geneva, Switzerland.

The core functions of WHO are:

▶ promoting and maintaining global health security

▶ providing assistance to countries to help them improve their community health.

Its objective is to attain the highest possible level of health for all people.

As well as medical and organisational personnel, WHO needs economic advice to carry out cost effectiveness research and cost benefit analyses, to find the best approach to allocate health resources for optimal health outcomes. It is also informed by social science research findings to understand the determinants of health and the reasons for social inequalities worldwide.

WHO's severity and danger levels

WHO should be able to assess severity and danger levels when there is a new disease outbreak. This involves assessing how severe the outbreak is and what level of danger it poses to the country or to the rest of the world. Having assessed the danger and severity level, it is better able to put into place measures to treat affected individuals and to reduce the spread of the disease.

Since its creation, WHO has played a leading role in eradicating smallpox and is working towards eliminating polio. Current priorities include HIV/AIDs, malaria, TB and Ebola, as well as non-communicable diseases, sexual and reproductive health, nutrition and food security, ageing, occupational health and substance abuse.

Water Aid

WaterAid is an international not-for-profit organisation. It was set up in 1981 in response to the United Nations initiative to provide clean water for all. WaterAid has offices in 37 countries and aims to transform lives by improving access to safe water, sanitation and hygiene. In 2015 it launched its global strategy with the target of reaching everyone everywhere by 2030. In 2006, the founder of the Glastonbury Festival, Michael Eavis, and his daughter visited WaterAid's work in Mozambique.

In 2007, 130 volunteers from WaterAid helped at the Glastonbury Festival. This practice has continued and the number of volunteers has increased to 450. WaterAid volunteers aim to get festival goers waiting to use the loos to sign a petition urging world leaders to prioritise safe water, sanitation and hygiene. WaterAid also organises many fundraising events such as running, cycling and sporting challenges.

Check your knowledge

1   Which diseases will be reduced by the introduction of clean treated water and improved sanitation?
2   Visit **www.wateraid.org/uk** to find out more about this organisation and its work.

Controlling a global disease outbreak

Being prepared for a pandemic mitigates (reduces) its impact.

Resources required for pandemics

Countries and organisations need to ensure they have the resources required for dealing with a pandemic. Resources include medical and support personnel, vaccines, medicines, mobile field hospitals, body bags, antimicrobial chemicals, cleaning materials and disinfectants. They also need transport and may need protection when working in areas where there is a threat of terrorist attack or in a war zone.

Factors to consider

Countries and organisations have to consider factors such as the cost and availability of health personnel, the availability of drugs and vaccines, the terrain and geography of the area, for example – can medical personnel get to areas where people are sick? They need to know the local customs to make sure their interventions do not offend, or to find out if any customs may be increasing the spread of the disease and how they can best inform people of this. These organisations may also need permission from the country's government to enter an area, and may need to negotiate with local government officials to agree how much care they can give and how much intervention they can carry out.

Roles of authorities

Various authorities, such as governments, health authorities and non-government organisations, will be involved in responding to a pandemic and need to be coordinated. For example, Médicins Sans Frontières (MSF)/Doctors Without Borders played a key role during the Ebola outbreak. Public Health England also played an important part by helping to confirm the presence of Ebola viruses in infected tissues and giving advice to medical personnel.

Health services should be able to predict the need for and prepare for extra hospital beds that may be required, as well as extra personnel to deal with the influx of patients. Less vulnerable patients may be treated at home, following guidelines about reducing the spread of infection. As a pandemic can temporarily overwhelm the health services, some other interventions may have to be postponed, such as operations for non-life-threatening conditions.

Health personnel and carers should be offered a vaccine, if available, as they will come into contact with many infected people. Where appropriate, they should be trained in barrier nursing and provided with specialised protective clothing.

There may be an increase in the death rate, and appropriate services need to be ready to deal with the safe disposal of the bodies.

Other public services may need to make contingency plans as high rates of absenteeism due to illness will disrupt public transport, police services, communications and most business and production centres.

The role of the international community

Governments need to have sufficient money available to deal with the economic costs of a pandemic. They may also direct the use of armed forces to assist with transport of medical and other emergency supplies to an affected area.

WHO uses disease surveillance and epidemiological data to assess the severity of a pandemic to ensure the areas involved:

▸ reduce high risk behaviours of people, which can spread the disease, by supplying information

▸ improve the detection, investigation and reporting of cases so the early warning system is strengthened

▸ contain an emerging pandemic virus by isolating sick people, and preventing their travel

▸ increase preparedness for the pandemic among communities – for example, by making sure that enough vaccines and antiviral or antimicrobial drugs can be made in time, and can be sent to all relevant countries

▸ make sure that scientists understand the virus and the disease it causes.

Response and intervention must be rapid and occur at the start of an outbreak.

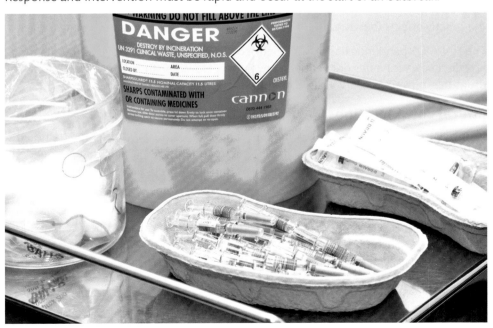

▸ Equipment, such as pre-filled syringes, aids the rapid administration of vaccines to an area to prevent further spread of the disease

Effects of an outbreak

When there is a widespread outbreak of an infectious disease many people are affected, not only those suffering from the infection. It will affect:

- members of the family of those infected
- their communities
- the wider society/country.

On an individual basis, if you know that, for example, there may be a flu pandemic caused by the H5N1 virus, you can make sure you have:

- enough of your usual medication in your home
- plenty of non-prescription health remedies, such as painkillers and cough medicines
- a food store within your home
- resources to adequately heat your home
- spoken to family members about what will be needed to care for them, or for you if you become ill.

During a pandemic:

- practise good hygiene – particularly hand washing
- live a healthy lifestyle in respect of diet, exercise, sleep and low alcohol use
- avoid close contact with people who are sick
- cover your mouth and nose when sneezing or coughing, and avoid touching your nose, eyes or mouth.

Consequences to society of a disease outbreak

If many individuals within a community comply, then the risk to the community and to the wider society is reduced. If many in the community are affected, it will have adverse effects such as loss of productivity at work, overstretching of the health services and greater welfare needs. In less economically developed countries, these adverse effects are usually far greater than in developed countries. For example, where HIV/AIDS has claimed many lives, a large number of children have been orphaned and this greatly affects their future life chances in terms of education and earning capacity.

The HIV/AIDS pandemic has been difficult to deal with because the virus mutates and an effective vaccine has not yet been developed. However, there are effective antiviral drugs that prevent the HIV virus from replicating.

Ethical considerations

In any disease outbreak, those dealing with it have to consider whether the treatments pose any ethical problems. In some cases, the treatments, behaviour changes needed to prevent the spread of the disease, or the disposal of bodies may offend local customs. These issues have to be evaluated and weighed against the possibility of the outbreak spreading worldwide if the local customs are given precedence.

Health workers and volunteers need to be protected against catching the disease and, in some cases, their options may include being offered drugs or vaccines that have been tested on animals but have not been fully tested by clinical trials. This poses an ethical problem. However, the alternative of not being vaccinated or given the drugs may be certain death; in such circumstances, there are arguments for using those drugs.

Dealing with a large outbreak diverts resources away from other health areas, leaving clinics unable to deal effectively with routine health problems such as maternity care. It may also expose weaknesses in a society's infrastructure such as water supply, sanitation, roads and education.

Problems associated with using treatment regimes and ideas not familiar to a society

In some areas of the world, the local customs may aid the spread of the disease. This was the case with Ebola in West Africa, where family members usually wash the bodies of their deceased relatives, and mourners may touch the body of the deceased. These are dangerous practices as the Ebola virus is spread in body fluids and via surfaces touched by the individual with Ebola, such as bedding, towels and clothing. However, it took some time to persuade people not to carry out this ritual custom.

During the Ebola outbreak, from March 2014 to November 2015, health workers had to be trained in extreme barrier nursing. Additionally support workers, such as cleaners and those dealing with dead bodies, needed special training and protective clothing. Ensuring that burials are carried out quickly, safely and with dignity is crucial to safeguarding communities from further spread of the Ebola virus. People had to be educated about the risks and provided with washing kits, washing stations and protective clothing.

Case study

Médicins Sans Frontières (MSF) and the Ebola epidemic of 2014 to 2015

During the period March 2014, when the outbreak was made official, until November 2015, MSF established 15 Ebola Management Centres and Transit Centres and dealt with one third of all confirmed cases in this outbreak. It provided 530,000 protective suits and many equipment kits.

Dealing with patients and trying to prevent the spread of the virus was made difficult due to many factors. The disease is not easy to diagnose as the early symptoms are not specific to Ebola. Later symptoms include vomiting, diarrhoea, rash, impaired liver and kidney function and finally internal and possibly external bleeding. The symptoms may take between two and 21 days to appear.

Many people do not understand what causes the disease and there is stigma attached to it. This often leads people who think they have it to hide and not visit a clinic for diagnosis and treatment. Infected people need to be isolated, and all medical staff and visitors need to wear protective suits. Local personnel had to be trained in barrier nursing, and about the correct way to safely dispose of all medical waste and bodies.

MSF also had to gain the trust of people, as it is the lack of trust and fear about the disease that helps it spread. Because people had not had access to reliable information and were afraid to take their loved-ones to a clinic or hospital, infected people were often not isolated. Shared bedding and towels helped to spread the disease and local burial customs, where family members wash the body and mourners touch the body, also exacerbated the problem.

During this time, 28 MSF staff members contracted Ebola, of whom 14 died and 14 survived.

Although the outbreak has been officially declared over, there are still cases occurring in Guinea and lives are being lost; mainly due to a weak surveillance system that is fragmented across the region, so we cannot be complacent.

Check your knowledge

1 Which local customs made it hard for MSF to stem the spread of Ebola?

In the affected countries, there are misconceptions and stigma associated with many infectious diseases, including Ebola and HIV/AIDS. Such stigma may lead to people failing to seek treatment and, with undiagnosed infectious people in the community, the disease spreads. Additionally, both Ebola and HIV/AIDS have non-specific early symptoms (such as headaches and fever) similar to those of less serious infections. This makes diagnosis difficult and Ebola can only be confirmed after laboratory tests, which in themselves constitute a biohazard.

Trained medical personnel had to overcome a certain amount of hostility in the local community and negotiate with religious leaders to help them gain the trust of those infected, their families and others in the community who were at risk of infection. In some areas, geographic factors such as the vast distances and rough terrain make the logistics of the exercise very difficult. For example, outbreak prevention kits containing protective clothing, bleach and cleaning materials had to be distributed and medical waste had to be safely and properly disposed of.

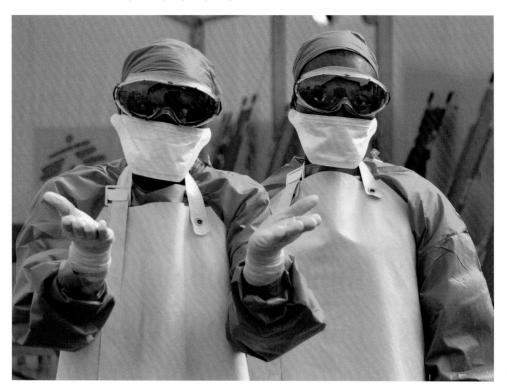

▶ Doctors wearing protective suits outside an Ebola treatment centre in Nigeria during the 2014–15 Ebola outbreak

Misuse and abuse of medicines and antibiotics

Antibiotics have been used since the 1940s and have saved many millions of lives and contributed to the extension of life expectancy. However, they are not always correctly used and when incorrectly used (abuse) can cause problems.

GPs, and some hospital doctors, usually prescribe a broad spectrum antibiotic (one that is effective against many types of bacteria) for an infection that they think is caused by a bacterium. However, if the individual does not improve then a sample is taken and sent to a laboratory to identify the causative bacterium. This will establish which types of antibiotics the infecting organism is sensitive to, or resistant to. The most appropriate type of antibiotic can then be prescribed.

In the past, doctors in the UK may have prescribed antibiotics when they were not actually needed as people often ask for antibiotics when they have a cold or flu, not understanding that antibiotics *cannot* deal with viruses. In the UK you cannot buy antibiotics over the counter; they have to be obtained on prescription. However, in some countries people can buy antibiotics in pharmacies and may use them inappropriately.

For several years some antibiotics have been used **prophylactically** in animal feed.

Many bacteria have, therefore, been exposed to antibiotics and some populations of bacteria have **evolved** resistance to antibiotics by **natural selection**.

Bacteria can pass some of their DNA to other bacteria. Because of this, genes for antibiotic resistance can spread from one bacterial population to another. Many bacteria are now resistant to several types of antibiotics, including the powerful antibiotics used in hospitals for the worst types of bacterial infection. As this is such a potential threat Nesta, an innovation charity, is offering a £10 million prize to scientists who can solve the problem by finding new and effective antimicrobial medicines.

> **Key terms**
>
> **Prophylactic** – preventive measure.
>
> **Evolution** –appearance of new species as the result of a gradual change, over many generations, in the genetic make-up of existing species.
>
> **Natural selection** – a mechanism for evolution. All species overproduce young and there is a struggle for existence as they compete for resources. Individuals differ from each other (genetic variation) and those individuals best adapted survive longer, producing more young, many of whom inherit the favourable characteristics. The frequency of the favourable characteristic within the population gradually changes.

Case study

Finding a suitable alternative to antibiotics

Microbiologists are investigating some old remedies for treating wounds. Some time ago, someone cleaning out their pond cut themselves and developed a very nasty skin infection that did not respond to antibiotic treatment. In desperation he tried treating it with manuka honey and the infection cleared up. This example is 'anecdotal evidence' but it is often the starting point for further research.

Research with manuka honey and *staphylococci* bacteria has shown that it arrests their cell development – this can be seen using an electron microscope. Wound dressings containing manuka honey are available to treat skin conditions such as infected leg ulcers.

Honey is a complex substance, and it is not yet know exactly which component(s) inhibit bacterial growth.

Ⅱ PAUSE POINT   Make a list of all the behaviour changes people had to make after the early 1980s to reduce the risk of HIV infection.

(Hint)   Think of the transmission routes of this virus and what can be done to stop transmission along those routes.

(Extend)   Hepatitis C is a virus spread via contaminated blood and needles. Explain why tattoo parlours and ear-piercing establishments need to be well informed about hepatitis C.

1   A nurse in your local GP practice wants posters to inform patients about the importance of vaccinations, and the vaccination schedule for children. You have offered to make these posters.

   • On your poster, you need to show the ways in which diseases can spread from person to person, giving specific examples.

   • Explain, with annotated diagrams, how the immune system protects the body from harmful micro-organisms.

   • Use the terms that are used in epidemiology and indicate how they can apply to the transmission of human diseases.

   • Write a short article for a health magazine to evaluate why some named diseases can quickly spread across the world, the consequences of this and why travellers should be vaccinated against certain diseases.

2   Write an article for a local newspaper or magazine discussing all the factors involved in controlling outbreaks of two named diseases, for example influenza (flu), measles or Ebola.

   • Explain the consequences of the outbreaks you have discussed.

   • Assess the effectiveness of all the factors you have discussed.

   • Discuss why some diseases spread globally and evaluate the reasons and consequences of this.

Plan

   • Do I know what the task I am being asked to do is?

   • Do I have enough information or should I extend my research?

   • How confident do I feel in my own abilities to complete the task? Are there any areas I think I will struggle with?

Do

   • I know what it is I am doing and what I want to achieve.

   • I can check my work to see where I have gone off task and can make changes to put this right and get back on track.

Review

   • I can explain to someone else what the task was and how I approached it.

   • I know how I could approach this task more efficiently next time.

   • I know what I would do differently next time and the approach I would take with the parts that I found difficult this time.

D   Investigate the health benefits of micro-organisms

Bacteria evolved when Earth cooled, about 3.5 billion years ago. For about 3300 billion years they were the only life form. While many other life forms evolved, bacteria remained and have survived all the mass extinction events. In this unit, the focus has been on infections caused by bacteria (and other micro-organisms) but many bacteria are beneficial. For example:

▶ they help recycle nitrogen and other minerals needed for healthy growth of plants and animals

▶ some live in root nodules of leguminous plants (peas and beans) helping them grow and produce food for humans and livestock

▶ they help break down sewage and aid decomposition of dead matter

▶ some break down toxins

▶ some are a source of antimicrobial chemicals, such as *streptomycin*

▶ certain types can be used to make silage for animal feed.

The bacteria and other micro-organisms, microbiota, that live in or on people help keep invading pathogens at bay. They help you to digest your food and to regulate your appetites. The products of the microbiome (all their genes) when expressed (used to direct the making of proteins) contribute greatly to people's good health and wellbeing.

Humans also make use of bacteria and other micro-organisms in food production, making vaccines and genetic engineering.

Using micro-organisms in food production

Types of food that can be produced

Humans have made bread, beer and wine for many thousands of years. Yeast cells live naturally on seeds and fruit surfaces so fermentation occurred naturally, although people did not then understand the biology behind the process as scientists do now.

▶ **Table 15.5** Examples of types of foods that are made using micro-organisms

Micro-organism	Food made
Fungus – yeast (*Saccharomyces cerevisiae*)	**Bread**. One of the oldest prepared foods. The single-celled fungus respires sugars in the dough and produces carbon dioxide that causes the dough to rise.
Fungus – yeast: *Saccharomyces cerevisiae*, for beer *Saccharomyces carlsbergensis*, for lager	**Beer.** Made from barley seeds soaked in water and incubated. The seeds germinate and produce enzymes to digest the starch in them releasing sugar. The seeds are then roasted and crushed, steeped in hot water to obtain the sugar, hops are added to give a bitter taste, and the resulting cooled wort is incubated with yeast. Yeast respires the sugars anaerobically and produces ethanol and carbon dioxide. The resulting beer or lager can be bottled, canned or stored in barrels. Spent yeast can be used to make Marmite or for additives to food products to give a meaty (umami) flavour.
Fungus – yeast (*Saccharomyces cerevisiae*)	**Wine.** Fermented grapes (and other fruits or grains such as rice) are fermented with extra sugars and yeast that respires the sugars anaerobically, producing ethanol and carbon dioxide. Other metabolites (chemicals) produced by the yeast cells and by the plants, depending on the area – geography, soil, climate and geology, plus the genetic characteristics of the plant, give wine its distinctive flavour.
Bacteria – *Acetobacter*	**Vinegar.** Made when acetic acid bacteria ferment alcohol in beer or wine, producing acetic acid.
Bacteria – *Lactobacillus bulgaricus* and *Streptococcus thermophilus*	**Yoghurt.** Cultures of bacteria are added to milk that has been heated to denature its proteins. The bacteria respire lactose sugar in milk and produce lactic acid that coagulates milk protein.
Bacteria and sometimes mould fungi	**Cheese.** Milk protein (casein) is coagulated by the action of bacteria and the enzyme rennet. The solids are separated and pressed into shape. Some cheeses have a rind consisting of white mould and some have blue mould fungus throughout. Cheeses are left to mature in cool dark places (e.g. caves) and last a long time – an early method of food preservation.
Bacteria – e.g. *Leuconostoc, Lactobacillus* and *Pedicoccus*	**Sauerkraut and kimchi.** Fermented shredded vegetables. Bacteria ferment sugars in the vegetables to lactic acid.
Fungus – *Aspergillus oryzae*	**Soy sauce.** Made from fermented paste of boiled soya beans.

Production of single-cell proteins as a food source

Micro-organisms can be grown on various substrates (material on which the micro-organisms can be grown and on which they feed) obtained from waste materials and then processed to provide food for humans or livestock. If the food produced is protein, it is called single-cell protein (SCP). Substrates include:

▶ whey – the liquid waste from milk used to make cheese

▶ molasses – from the sugar refining process

▶ sulfite liquor – obtained from the wood pulping industry

▶ agricultural waste, such as straw

▶ waste from brewing

▶ straight chain alkanes (hydrocarbons) from the oil refining industry.

▶ **Table 15.6** The advantages and disadvantages of SCP as a food source

Advantages	Disadvantages
Micro-organisms have a high growth rate and they can be grown in large vessels, called fermenters, housed anywhere in the world and under carefully controlled conditions, so this process is not climate-dependent. The fermenters do not take up much land space.	SCP may be contaminated with the substrate. They also need to be centrifuged and filtered to extract the protein and then dehydrated – these processes need expensive equipment.
The substrates they grow on would otherwise be wasted.	Prokaryotic micro-organisms (bacteria) have a high nucleic acid content, particularly RNA. High levels of RNA in the diet can cause health problems for humans, such as gout and kidney stones. SCP with high RNA content can be used for animal feed.
Scientists have carried out research and selected strains of micro-organisms that produce high yields.	The species of micro-organism used must be carefully chosen so no pathogens are present.
The protein content of the micro-organism cells is high – about 30–70% of the cells' dry mass.	Aseptic technique is used to prevent contamination by other micro-organisms. However, at some stage in the process the micro-organisms may be killed to reduce risk of infection.
These single cell proteins contain many essential amino acids so they are of high nutritional quality. The organisms may be genetically modified to produce specific essential amino acids.	Some types of SCP have unpleasant smells and tastes.
Producing protein in this way uses less water than producing food by traditional agriculture.	

Quorn is a food that looks like and has the texture of meat. It is made from mycoprotein derived from the fungus *Fusarium venenatum*. The fungus culture is dried and mixed with egg white to bind it. It is used for cooking and in many ready meals. Its carbon footprint is much less than that of beef.

▶ All of these food items that look like meat are made from Quorn, a mycoprotein produced by the fungus, *Fusarium venenatum*

Spirulina is a filamentous blue-green bacterium that has been grown for many years as a food source. It is photosynthetic and can be grown in ponds, harvested and then dried. It has a high nutrient value.

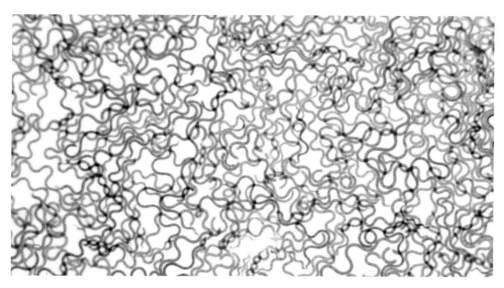

▶ Light micrograph of the cyanobacterium *Spirulina platensis* × 100. Each filament is a colony of bacterial cells. These organisms can photosynthesise and live in water

Ⅱ PAUSE POINT   In what ways are bacteria essential to other types of living organisms?

> **Hint**   Think of what the bacteria inside living organisms do, and what bacteria in the soil/ water of ecosystems do.

> **Extend**   In what ways are fungi (a) useful and (b) potentially harmful to humans?

Further uses of micro-organisms

Antibiotics

Antibiotics are chemicals made by micro-organisms to kill or inhibit the growth of other micro-organisms. Bear in mind that many micro-organisms live in soil and are competing with other species of micro-organisms for nutrients, space and water, so a chemical that can reduce the growth of its competitors gives these micro-organisms an advantage.

The first antibiotic identified and used was penicillin, from the mould fungus *Penicillium rubens*. Prior to the 1920s, some scientists had discovered that certain moulds reduced the growth of some bacteria. Penicillin was discovered in the 1920s and first used medicinally in the 1940s. This antibiotic prevents growing Gram-positive bacteria from making their cell walls. Consequently, the bacteria take up water by osmosis, swell and burst. Penicillin has saved many lives. However, it does not work against Gram-negative bacteria or the tuberculosis bacterium and some people are allergic to it. (Gram-positive bacteria and gram-negative bacteria are different types of bacteria.)

Other antibiotics are available. Some combat Gram-negative bacteria, some combat fungi and some are used to treat protoctist parasites.

However, antibiotics do *not* work against viruses. This is because antibiotics interfere with some aspect of the pathogen's cellular structure or metabolism and viruses do not have any cell structure or metabolism.

Some antibiotics are *bactericidal* – they kill bacteria, others are *bacteristatic* – they prevent the growth of bacteria.

Antibiotic	Source	Used to treat	Mode of action in pathogen
Penicillins: Penicillin Amoxicillin Methicillin	Mould fungus *Penicillium spp.* Some are semi-synthetic, derived from penicillin	Streptococcal infections, syphilis, Lyme disease	Interferes with cell wall synthesis
B-lactams e.g. cephalosporins	Semi-synthetic, derived from mould fungus *Cephalosporum*	Wide range of bacterial infections	
Bacitracin	Bacterium, *Bacillus subtilis*	Eye and ear infections Usually administered in ointment	
Teicoplanin	Bacterium	MRSA, endocarditis	
Vancomycin	Soil bacterium, *Amycolatopsis orientalis*	MRSA, colitis, *C. difficile*, pneumonia, skin infections, endocarditis Usually given intravenously	
Colistin	Bacterium, *Paenbacillus polymixa*	Eye, ear and bladder infections	Interferes with cell membrane structure and function
Ciproflaxin	A fluoroquinolone	Urinary tract infections, bacterial diarrhoea, gonorrhoea, joint infections	Inhibits replication of DNA so prevents cell division
Norfloxacin	Synthetic fluoroquinolone		
Rifampicin	Soil bacterium, *Amycolatopsis rifamycinica*	Meningococcal meningitis, typhus fever, cholera, MRSA, TB, leprosy, legionella, bubonic plague	Inhibits the first stage (transcription) of protein synthesis
Chloramphenicol	Filamentous bacterium, *Streptomyces venezuelae*		
Oxytetracycline Tetracycline Doxycycline	Filamentous soil bacteria, *Streptomyces rimosus* *Streptomyces aureofaciens* *Streptomyces sp.*	Syphilis, chlamydia, Lyme disease, malaria, acne, pneumonia, chronic bronchitis, campylobacter, anthrax, bubonic plague	Inhibits the translation stage of protein synthesis at ribosomes
Clarythromycin	Semi-synthetic, made from erythromycin	Streptococcal infections, stomach ulcers, Lyme disease, syphilis	
Erythromycin	Bacterium, *Saccharopolyspora erythraea*		

Vaccines

Weakened or killed viruses and bacteria are used to make vaccines. Because the microbes are inactive they cannot make the vaccinated person ill. However, the antigens on their surfaces can still provoke an immune response in the person. The memory cells created in the individual's body will be the same as if they had been infected with a live pathogen of the same type. If the vaccinated person is infected by a live pathogen then they can quickly make the necessary antibodies to combat the infection. For some vaccines, just the antigens of the pathogen are injected to stimulate an immune response; DNA plasmids of bacteria are used. Such DNA vaccines are termed third generation vaccines.

Vaccination is an extremely cost effective way of preventing infection.

Insulin

Insulin, a small protein hormone, used to be obtained from frozen pig pancreases. However, this could not provide enough insulin to treat all individuals with diabetes.

Insulin helps regulate blood glucose levels. It causes excess glucose, absorbed from the gut into the blood, to leave the blood and enter the liver, muscle and other cells for conversion to glycogen for storage, or for respiration.

By the 1970s, scientists had discovered that insulin is a small protein, made of 51 amino acids.

Recombinant DNA technology (genetic engineering) is now used to make insulin using genetically modified bacteria, usually *E. coli*.

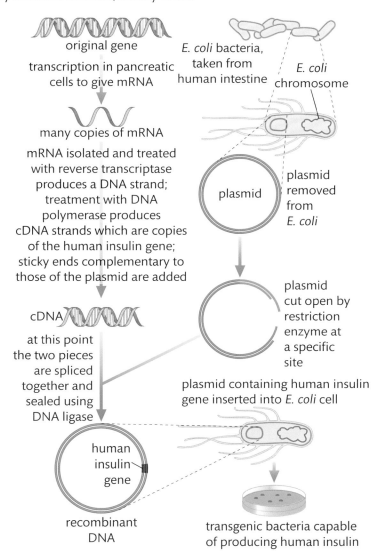

▶ **Figure 15.13** Production of bacteria containing the human insulin gene

Genetic engineering

Humans have altered the genomes of many species used in agriculture and horticulture for thousands of years using **artificial selection** (selective breeding). However, this has always been a rather 'hit or miss' affair. Since the 1970s, scientists have been able to manipulate the genomes of these organisms by genetic engineering, which is much more specific.

Genetic engineering, also called genetic modification, is where new DNA is added to an organism's genome. This manipulation of the organism's genome involves biotechnology and uses many enzymes obtained from micro-organisms and sometimes uses bacterial plasmids as the vector to carry the new DNA into the modified organism.

Key term

Artificial selection – selective breeding; where humans select plants or animals for their desired characteristics and breed only from those chosen specimens.

- When a foreign gene has been introduced into a cell the cell is described as *transformed*.

- The bacterium *Agrobacterium tumifaciens*, which infects plants causing crown gall, inserts genes into its host and this may be genetically modified and used as a vector to introduce new genes into crop plants.

- Viruses are one of nature's own genetic engineers as they insert genes into their hosts (8–10 per cent of our genes are viral in origin). Scientists can modify viruses by inactivating the viral genes so the virus is harmless, and inserting a desired gene and then using the modified virus as a vector.

- Gene editing is a fairly recent addition to the range of genetic engineering techniques and this uses enzymes and other proteins (CRISPR/Cas9) obtained from bacteria. It offers a way of removing faulty **alleles** of genes that have a dominant inheritance pattern and replacing them with normal functioning alleles. In the future, this could mean that scientists may be able to cure Huntington's disease.

- The production of human insulin is an example of genetic engineering, in which the key enzymes used for production are obtained from micro-organisms.

- Micro-organisms are used in genetic modification and are the source of some key enzymes used in the process. Reverse transcriptase enzymes are obtained from retroviruses. Restriction endonucleases are obtained from bacteria, which have these enzymes to protect themselves from attack by phage viruses (viruses that infect bacteria).

> **Key terms**

Allele – alternative forms of a gene, found at the same place on a chromosome, arising from mutation.

▶ Golden rice is a genetically modified form of rice

▶ **Table 15.8** Some uses of genetic engineering

Type of genetic engineering	Examples
Genetically modified crops A gene for a desired characteristic is obtained from one species and inserted into another species.	**Golden Rice**™ is modified to contain a gene, obtained from daffodils, that causes rice plants to express a gene for making vitamin A in their seeds (rice grains). This staple food can be made available at no greater cost to consumers than standard rice and could prevent blindness and death in many countries, e.g. India, due to vitamin A deficiency. **Potatoes**, an important staple crop, can be modified to be resistant to late blight and nematodes, reducing the need for pesticides. Low sugar potatoes can also be produced reducing the generation of the carcinogen acrylamide when potatoes are heated to 120°C, e.g. when fried.
Diagnostic tests Clinical geneticists use diagnostic tests to make accurate diagnoses so they can tailor treatments to an individual's specific genetic make-up.	Diagnostic genetic tests are available to detect carriers of recessive disorders such as Tay-Sachs and cystic fibrosis; X-linked disorders such as haemophilia and fragile X syndrome; late onset disorders such as Huntington's disease; prenatal diagnosis, e.g. Down's syndrome, newborn screening, e.g. for phenylketonuria (PKU); pharmacogenomic testing – e.g. testing a patient's cytochrome 450 enzyme system to see how they will metabolise a specific drug, such as warfarin.
Gene therapy Involves inserting functioning alleles of genes into a patient's cells to treat or prevent a genetic disease. Vectors such as liposomes (small aggregates of lipids with a gene inside) or modified harmless viruses are used to introduce the functioning alleles into living cells.	Some forms of blindness (e.g. retinitis pigmentosa – a form of retinal degeneration), SCID (severe combined immunodeficiency); Parkinson's disease, cystic fibrosis and haemophilia, may be able to be treated with gene therapy.
Genome editing The **CRISPR/Cas9** system is a prokaryotic immune system that protects bacteria and archaea from attack by phage viruses. Scientists have isolated it and can use it as a gene editing tool.	The Cas9 protein and guide RNA molecules can target a particular DNA sequence, snip out (using an endonuclease enzyme) a faulty allele and insert a functioning allele in its place. This has great potential for treating genetic disorders caused by a *dominant* allele. It may be able to be used in xenotransplantation to edit out pig viral genes associated with pig organs.
Pharming Genes for human pharmaceutical proteins that are too large to be made in bacterial cells, are inserted into sheep or goats, near to a promoter for a beta-lactoglobulin gene. These genes are only expressed in mammary tissue, so the protein can be harvested from the animal's milk.	**Alpha-antitrypsin** can be used to prevent hereditary emphysema. The gene for the protein alpha-antitrypsin, which inhibits antitrypsin action in lungs that causes breakdown of elastin in alveoli walls, is inserted into sheep embryos and the pharmaceutical is obtained from the sheep's milk. **Spider silk** fibres have tensile strength five times greater than steel of the same diameter. Spiders are impossible to farm but genes for spider silk have been inserted into goats. These GM goats produce spider silk in their milk. Silk can be used for cables, sutures, artificial ligaments and bullet proof vests.
Genetic testing This involves medical tests to identify changes in chromosomes, genes or proteins, which can rule out or confirm a suspected genetic condition, or determine a person's chance of developing or passing on a genetic disorder to offspring. Some tests are available via the NHS to specific groups of people and some are only available privately, hence this is testing and not screening.	**Pre-implantation genetic testing** for chromosome abnormalities such as Down's syndrome (trisomy 21), Edwards' syndrome (trisomy 18), Angelman syndrome or Prader-Willi syndrome. Testing to establish the possible cause of cancer within a family. **Predictive testing**, such as for the presence of *BRCA1* or *BRCA2* genes for breast cancer. Tests for bowel, prostate and ovarian cancer genes are also available on request, privately.
Xenotransplantation As techniques for organ transplantation have improved there is a shortage of organs for such operations. In the future, it may be possible to modify the organs of other animals.	It may be possible to genetically modify organs of animals, such as pigs that have a very similar physiology to that of humans, so that the surface antigens on the organs are identical to those of humans. This would mean that these organs would not be rejected. However, scientists now know that all animals have viral genes in their genomes; our viral genes do not harm us and pig viral genes do not harm pigs but if pig viral genes were transplanted, along with the organs, into humans, these genes could pose problems.

Discussion

Discuss the pros and cons of genetically modified food crops.

Assessment practice 15.3 D.P6 D.M4 D.D3

Your local primary school is teaching its Year 6 learners about micro-organisms. For their stimulus material, they have asked the learners to bring in examples of useful things made for humans by micro-organisms. The learners have brought in empty wine and beer bottles, yoghurt, cheese, soy sauce, bread, and empty medicine bottles that contained amoxicillin. One, whose mother has diabetes, has brought in an empty insulin container.

The primary school teacher has asked you to help with some details of how some of these products are made commercially.

- Choose two commercially made products that use micro-organisms in their production. Produce an illustrated and annotated flow chart that outlines how these micro-organisms are used in the processes you have chosen.
- Write a short account that analyses the social benefits to humans of three named micro-organisms.

Although some micro-organisms make us ill, humans rely on micro-organisms for recycling nutrients in ecosystems, as a source of antibiotics and we also rely on our intestinal bacteria. The study of microbiology has given scientists some useful tools for DNA technology, for example genetic profiling (DNA fingerprinting) relies on the use of restriction endonuclease enzymes obtained from bacteria.

- Produce a poster evaluating the positive and negative effects of the interrelationship between humans and micro-organisms.

Plan
- Do I know what the task is and what I am being asked to do?
- Do I have enough information or should I extend my research?
- How confident am I in my abilities to tackle this task?

Do
- I know what it is I am doing and what I want to achieve.
- I can check my work to see where I have gone off task and can adjust my approach to make changes to put this right.

Review
- I can explain to someone else what the task was and how I approached it.
- I understand now how I could approach this and complete the task more efficiently next time.
- I know what I would do differently next time and the approach I would take with the parts that I found difficult this time.

Further reading and resources

de Kruif, P. (2002) *Microbe Hunters*, New York: Harcourt Publishing.

Johnson, S. (2006) *The Ghost Map: the story of London's most terrifying epidemic and how it changed science, cities and the modern world*, London: Penguin.

Steams, J. and Surette, M. (2014) *Microbiology for Dummies*, Hoboken, NJ: John Wiley & Sons.

Walker, S. (2006) *Biotechnology Demystified*, New York: McGraw-Hill.

Websites

www.microbiologyonline.org.uk
Microbiology Society: Online resource to support microbiology tutors and learners.

www.healthcareers.nhs.uk
Health Careers: Information about careers in the NHS.

https://nationalcareersservice.direct.gov.uk
National Careers Service: Information about careers in microbiology.

THINK ▶FUTURE

Aedan Brennan
Infection control nurse

I trained as a nurse and worked in that capacity for five years. I then decided to train further as an infection control nurse.

As I already had a degree in nursing, I studied for a Masters degree for two years, while working in a hospital. Once I'd obtained this, I got a job as an infection control nurse and, after two years' experience, I sat an exam set by the Association for Professionals in Infection Control and Epidemiology (APIC) to obtain Certification in Infection Prevention and Control.

I'm responsible for educating medical personnel in the hospital about means of controlling the spread of infection. I monitor the use of hand gels and hand washing, and make sure all nurses know how to use gloves and protective clothing. If there is an outbreak of an infection, such as norovirus, I work to try and isolate the source of infection. I'm also involved in making policies for the hospital to ensure that incoming patients are tested for MRSA and, if necessary, isolated.

I have to keep up to date with information on antibiotic resistance and its evolution in bacterial populations.

Focusing your skills

Helping to reduce the spread of hospital acquired infections

It is important for infection control nurses to understand why infections can easily spread throughout hospitals so that they can take appropriate action to reduce it. Some areas, such as operating theatres, have to be very clean as surgical incisions provide an easy entry route for micro-organisms. Infection control nurses need to liaise with many departments in the hospital, particularly nurses on surgical wards and operating theatre staff and they need particular skills to do this.

The problems

Hospitals are full of people who are ill, who may be infected with micro-organisms and who may have weakened immune systems.

- What are the implications for infection control of staff and visitors moving about the hospital? How could you minimise risks?
- Why do areas such as operating theatres have to be kept very clean?

The skills

Infection control nurses need to liaise with many departments in the hospital, particularly nurses on surgical wards and operating theatre staff and will need to keep up to date with latest research and development in ways to control infection. They will also need more general skills, including:

- an enquiring an analytical mind
- good scientific methodology
- good oral and written communication skills
- the ability to lead and manage.

Getting ready for assessment

Fabian is studying for a BTEC National in Health and Social Care. He has been given an assignment for Learning aim D, where he was asked to demonstrate the principles of genetic engineering using 3D models. Fabian shares some aspects of his experience below.

How I got started

I read about how genetic modification is carried out in my textbook, and in some other biology texts I found in the library. I also researched online and found some video clips that showed the process using animated diagrams. I made sure I fully understood the process.

Think about it

I thought about how to make a simple model that would not cost a lot of money or take too much time. I made a list of the sort of material I would need, and tried to use everyday items.

How I brought it all together

I used a piece of fabric to make a model plasmid. I made it into a circular piece/loop and then cut it by a staggered cut, as the restriction endonuclease enzymes do, and added Velcro to the now exposed 'sticky ends'. I had another piece of fabric, of a different colour with sticky ends and Velcro so that this piece could slot in when the 'plasmid' was opened. I used a large empty plastic lemonade bottle to represent a bacterium and made some holes in the plastic so I could push the recombinant plasmid into it.

What I learned from the experience

I forgot to keep a note of where all my information came from, and I needed to do this as you should always acknowledge your sources of information. There are also conventions to follow when referencing a piece of work. I could have improved the model by having something to represent the restriction endonuclease enzymes and the DNA ligase enzymes, and I could have had a big box to represent ice, and one to represent a water bath set at 40°C.

Think about it

▶ Have you written a plan with timings so you can complete your assignment by the agreed submission date?

▶ Do you have notes on the principles and uses of genetic engineering?

▶ Do you fully understand the processes that you are trying to show with your models?

▶ Can you demonstrate your model to others in your class and answer any questions that they may ask?

▶ Is your information written in your own words and referenced clearly where you have used quotations or information from a book, journal or website?

Caring for Individuals with Dementia

17

Getting to know your unit

Assessment

You will be assessed by a series of assignments set by your tutor.

A diagnosis of dementia can be a challenging experience for individuals and their relatives. However, by the end of this unit you should appreciate the importance of maintaining independence and dignity. Your service user will go through a broad range of emotions, face new and unforeseen challenges and require differing amounts of support at different times. You will need to be versatile and resilient in order to support them effectively.

You will have a duty of care to your service user and you will need to employ a broad range of skills in order to deliver high quality, person-centred care.

How you will be assessed

This unit will be assessed by a series of internally assessed tasks set by your tutor. Throughout this unit you will discover assessment practices that will help you to work towards your assessment. Completing these practices will not mean that you have achieved a particular grade, but that you will have carried out useful research or preparation for your assessment tasks.

In order to succeed in the tasks of your assignments, it is important that you have met all of the Pass grading criteria. You can do this as you work your way through the assignment.

If you are hoping to achieve a Merit or Distinction, you should also ensure that you present the information in your assignment in the style that is required by the relevant assessment criterion. For example, Merit criteria require you to assess and analyse and Distinction criteria require you to evaluate and justify.

The assessment set by your tutor will consist of a number of tasks designed to meet the criteria in the table. This is likely to consist of a written assignment but may also include activities such as:

▶ creating a report identifying types of abuse and neglect, and the procedure for documenting and reporting safeguarding concerns

▶ analysing and reflecting on case studies of accidents and/or incidents in health and social care settings

▶ creating a file on policies, practices and protocols for promoting safe practice in health and social care settings.

Assessment criteria

This table shows what you must do in order to achieve a **Pass**, **Merit** or **Distinction** grade, and where you can find activities to help you.

Pass	Merit	Distinction

Learning aim **A** Examine types, causes and symptoms of dementia

Pass	Merit	Distinction
A.P1 Explain the causes of three different types of dementia. **Assessment practice 17.1**	**A.M1** Analyse how the different types of dementia might be identified by their symptoms. **Assessment practice 17.1**	**AB.D1** Evaluate the importance of understanding how different types of dementia can have a progressive effect on all aspects of a person's health and wellbeing. **Assessment practice 17.1**
A.P2 Explain symptoms of three different types of dementia. **Assessment practice 17.1**		

Learning aim B Examine effects of dementia on people who have the condition

Pass	Merit	Distinction
B.P3 Explain effects of three different types of dementia on the mental and physical health of individuals who have the condition. **Assessment practice 17.1**	**B.M2** Assess how the different types of dementia can have progressive effects on a person's mental and physical health and their quality of life and wellbeing. **Assessment practice 17.1**	
B.P4 Discuss effects of three different types of dementia on the quality of life and wellbeing of people who have the condition. **Assessment practice 17.1**		

Learning aim C Investigate the concept of person-centred care for people who have dementia to maintain quality of life and wellbeing

Pass	Merit	Distinction
C.P5 Explain how person-centred care is applied for one individual who has one type of dementia. **Assessment practice 17.2**	**C.M3** Assess why the principles of person-centred care are important to maintain the dignity, rights and entitlements of one individual who has dementia. **Assessment practice 17.2**	**C.D2** Justify the impact and benefits of holistic person-centred care on one individual who has dementia. **Assessment practice 17.2**
C.P6 Explain why a flexible approach is needed when planning care for one individual who has one type of dementia. **Assessment practice 17.2**		**C.D3** Evaluate how current practice in dementia care meets the needs of an individual with dementia, through managing its effects and maintaining health and wellbeing. **Assessment practice 17.2**

Getting started

Dementia is a progressive, degenerative disorder. One of the symptoms is memory loss. Discuss the social, emotional and safety implications of memory loss on the service user, and on their family and friends.

A Examine the types, causes and symptoms of dementia

To provide effective and compassionate care for individuals with dementia, it is important to realise that not only are there different types of dementia, but that there is also a range of symptoms that individuals with dementia may display. You may find yourself caring for people with dementia in their own homes, helping them to maintain their independence, or you may be caring for a larger number of people with dementia in a care home. While caring for your service users, you may find that on some days, or in some circumstances, their symptoms may be better or worse than at other times. This inconsistency in behaviour may make providing care challenging. It is important to remember that your service user is at the centre of their care and that their needs and safety should be your priority. Dementia is generally considered to progress in three stages – early, middle and late stage. However, individuals will experience dementia in their own unique way.

Types and causes of dementia

Alzheimer's disease

The most common cause of dementia is Alzheimer's disease. It is caused by a build-up of protein 'plaques' and 'tangles' in the brain, meaning that the nerve cells cannot pass on signals effectively. This condition causes an interruption in brain activity and the nerve tissue eventually dies.

Case study

Learning to cope

For Deborah, finding out that her father, Jim, had dementia was devastating. She had relied on her dad for years, helping with odd jobs around the house, mending broken fences, fixing her car and keeping the peace when there were family arguments. Jim is only 62, a strong man with a mild temperament. Deborah has just had her second child. She has been relying on Jim helping her and her husband Mike to raise their children; especially as Mike works away a lot, leaving Deborah to cope on her own. Deborah feels like the future she had planned has been stolen from her.

Deborah had noticed that Jim was forgetting things like people's names, attending appointments, paying bills, and he would sometimes get lost when driving.

The family thought it was just old age creeping up on him. However, Deborah came back from a quick trip to the local shop one day and realised that her father had turned the gas cooker on but forgotten to light the flame. She turned the cooker off, opened the windows wide and let the gas escape. Jim was really upset that he could have caused a disaster – but he did not remember going into the kitchen and turning on the gas.

Check your knowledge

1 How is dementia going to affect the lives of Jim, Deborah and Mike?
2 Why is Deborah going to need to rely on her father less for practical help?
3 Why might Jim need emotional support from health professionals?

Alzheimer's disease appears to be the slowest form of dementia to develop. However, many factors can affect the speed of progression. An individual with early onset Alzheimer's, (dementia that develops before the age of 65) may experience the most rapid deterioration, as might individuals with additional health conditions such as diabetes, heart disorders, those who have had repeated strokes or a tendency to infections. Research also indicates that an individual's genetic make-up may be a contributory factor.

Vascular dementia

Vascular dementia is the second most common type of dementia, and the commonest type of vascular dementia is subcortical dementia. Vascular dementia is caused by a reduction in the supply of blood to the brain. To maintain proper function, the brain needs a constant supply of blood. The blood travels in blood vessels as part of the **cardiovascular system**. If the blood vessels leak blood or become blocked this can damage the brain cells and eventually they will die.

The blood vessels in the brain may be damaged by a number of lifestyle choices, such as smoking or an unhealthy diet. Cerebral **atherosclerosis** occurs when the vessels in the brain become blocked by the build-up of calcium, fatty substances, cellular waste and cholesterol. If the vessels are blocked then blood cannot get through to the brain tissue.

Vascular dementia can cause the brain cells to die, causing problems with cognition. Cognition includes judgement, attention, problem-solving and memory. Vascular dementia can impact the activities of daily living significantly, such as the ability to maintain hygiene, sleeping, working and engaging in leisure activities. There are several different types of vascular dementia and these types progress differently.

Vascular dementia may be stroke or post-stroke related. A stroke caused by a clot forming in the heart and travelling to the brain, or forming in the brain itself, can block the blood supply to the brain tissue. Different arteries branch off the carotid arteries and blockages in these various branching arteries can have different effects on individuals, depending on where the blockage occurs.

> ### Research
>
> Research which parts of the body are affected when clots occur variously in the anterior cerebral artery, the middle cerebral artery and the posterior cerebral artery.

The extent of the damage to the brain of the individual depends on the length of time that there was oxygen deprivation, and where in the brain the blockage occurred. According to Alzheimer's Society, approximately 20 per cent of strokes lead to the development of dementia, and the risk may increase with repeated strokes.

If a large or medium-sized vessel is blocked, the individual may not even realise that they have had a stroke, or the symptoms may be temporary and last less than 24 hours. The blockage clears itself and the individual does not realise that they have had a **transient ischaemic attack**. If the blood supply to the brain is interrupted, even for a short time, a small area of brain tissue will die. This is called an **infarct**. If the infarct occurs in an important part of the brain, then this can lead to a condition known as single infarct dementia. It is more common for these infarcts to occur over a number of weeks and in different parts of the brain. When this damages significant areas, it is known as multi-infarct dementia.

> ### Key terms
>
> **Cardiovascular system** – body system consisting of veins, venules, capillaries, arteries, arterioles, the heart and blood, which facilitates gas exchange and the transport of nutrients to and waste from cells.
>
> **Atherosclerosis** – a disease of the arteries in which fatty material deposits build up on their inner walls, damaging them by causing narrowing and hardening of the affected arteries.
>
> **Transient ischaemic attack** – a brain clot, often temporarily causing the same symptoms as stroke, but may also include confusion, dizziness and lack of coordination and blurred vision.
>
> **Infarct** – obstruction of the blood supply to an organ or an area of tissue causing tissue death (necrosis), usually caused by a thrombus (blood clot) or an embolus (a thrombus that has moved).

Disease of the small vessels, lying deep within the brain, is known as subcortical dementia. In this condition, the tiny vessels within the brain lose their flexibility and become thick-walled and twisted. The reduction in blood flow causes damage to the nerve fibres, which are responsible for transmitting electrical impulses in the brain. The bundles of nerve fibres are called 'white matter' and small vessel disease can have a large impact on the function of this tissue.

As the small vessels are deep within the brain, the symptoms are different from stroke-related dementia.

Mixed dementia is a condition where the changes in the brain are from more than one type of dementia. At least 10 per cent of people diagnosed with dementia are said to have mixed dementia. This means that they have symptoms similar to Alzheimer's disease and vascular dementia.

PAUSE POINT   Can you explain the causes of Alzheimer's disease and vascular dementia?

Hint   They both involve changes within the brain.

Extend   Why does dementia progress at different speeds for different individuals?

Dementia with Lewy bodies (DLB)

DLB is often misdiagnosed as the symptoms are similar to **Parkinson's disease** and Alzheimer's disease. This type of dementia is caused by abnormal protein deposits – Lewy bodies – in the nerve cells of the brain.

More research is needed to establish why Lewy bodies appear in the brain but their appearance is linked to low levels of dopamine and acetylcholine, and the progressive loss of connections between nerve cells, death of nerve cells and eventual death of brain tissue.

The location in the brain of the Lewy bodies will affect the symptoms that the individual experiences with this condition. If the Lewy bodies are in the outer layers of the brain, then cognitive function will be impaired, but if the Lewy bodies are in the base of the brain then, as with Parkinson's, this will affect fine and gross motor skills.

According to Alzheimer's Society, approximately one third of individuals diagnosed with Parkinson's disease go on to develop dementia.

> **Discussion**
>
> Is it important for care workers to understand the type of dementia that their service user is diagnosed with?

Frontotemporal dementia (FTD)

One of the less common causes of dementia is FTD, also known as Pick's disease or frontal lobe dementia. Frontotemporal refers to the lobes of the brain affected by this disease. Located just behind the forehead, the right frontal lobe is responsible for behaviour and emotions, and the left is responsible for language.

In this type of dementia the nerve connections are lost, as are some of the chemical messengers, and the pathways for transmitting impulses change. Eventually, the brain tissue in the frontal lobes shrinks.

Key term

Parkinson's disease – a disorder characterised by slow movements, rigidity and tremors, caused by an insufficient amount of dopamine in the brain due to the death of brain cells.

FTD is caused by a build-up of proteins in the lobes of the brain. One cause is genetic, where the genetic coding that forms the genetic identity of an individual has a malformation that results in the build-up of proteins. Current research suggests that early onset FTD (before the age of 65) may have a genetic link. Apolipoprotein E (APOE) appears to increase the risk; with variant e4 appearing to be the greatest risk.

Other, rarer, forms of FTD can be caused by **Creutzfeldt-Jakob disease** (CJD) and human immunodeficiency virus (HIV). Approximately half of people diagnosed with HIV have neurocognitive disorders, which can affect memory and thinking. The introduction of antiretroviral drugs has reduced the prevalence of this type of dementia among individuals with advanced HIV from 30 per cent to around 2 per cent.

> **Key term**
>
> **Creutzfeldt-Jakob disease** – condition caused by an abnormally shaped protein, called a prion, infecting the brain. New variant CJD is believed to be caused by consuming meat from cattle infected with bovine spongiform encephalopathy (BSE).

Research suggests that individuals with Down's syndrome are genetically more prone to develop the protein plaques in the brain that cause the symptoms of Alzheimer's disease. Changes in the brain may occur as they reach their forties and fifties and individuals with Down's syndrome can suffer increased aphasia, difficulties with processing language.

Consuming large quantities of alcohol can raise blood pressure, raise cholesterol and damage blood vessels, all of which can increase the risk of stroke and impaired cognition. Drinking more than the recommended daily limits for alcohol is a risk factor in the development of dementia, as is **binge drinking**. Alcohol-related brain damage (ARBD) shares many symptoms with dementia, including language impairment, but in contrast to dementia, with the right support and by remaining alcohol free, there may be partial recovery of the faculties.

> **Key term**
>
> **Binge drinking** – drinking heavily in one session leading to symptoms such as speech slurring, loss of balance, slowing of mental processes or behavioural changes, e.g. violence or aggression.

> **Research**
>
> What are the government's recommendations on the safe limits for alcohol consumption?

Head injuries can also damage the brain, causing problems ranging from epilepsy to behavioural changes similar to the symptoms of dementia. Individuals who consume more than the recommended levels of alcohol are more prone to falls or getting into fights, which can lead to brain injury.

❚❚ PAUSE POINT   Why is it difficult to help someone overcome their addiction to alcohol, even if they know that it is damaging their brain?

    Hint   Typically, middle-aged people are affected by ARBD. Why might people with ARBD be hard to reach for health campaigns?

    Extend   Why might ARBD be misdiagnosed, or go undiagnosed?

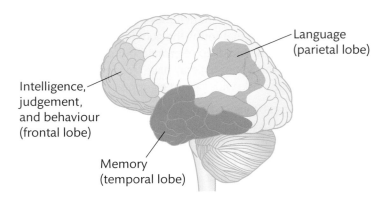

Intelligence, judgement, and behaviour (frontal lobe)

Language (parietal lobe)

Memory (temporal lobe)

▶ **Figure 17.1** Different parts of the brain can be affected by different types of dementia, meaning that the signs and symptoms of disorders can vary or be similar

Symptoms of dementia

It is essential that you are observant and considerate in your care for individuals with dementia. As a carer, you need to develop an understanding of the range of symptoms that your service users may display and not only meet their day-to-day needs, but also plan for their future care needs as their disease progresses and their needs increase. The levels of support required will vary depending on whether they are in the early, middle or late stage of the disease, but it is vital that you remember that your care should not only be needs-led but also patient-centred.

Alzheimer's disease

Alzheimer's disease is a progressive degenerative disease, the symptoms may initially be very mild and worsen as time goes by. The symptoms may start to interfere with a service user's daily life. You may find that as you work with different services users, all with the diagnosis of Alzheimer's disease, that they experience the condition in slightly different ways.

One of the most common symptoms of the disease is memory loss and usually short-term memory is most affected. You may find that your service user has a very clear recollection of significant events in their childhood but cannot remember what they had for breakfast. This can be quite scary for the service user and they may feel frustrated, particularly if their short-term recall used to be good.

You may also find that individuals with Alzheimer's disease get lost, even if they are in an environment that they are especially familiar with, such as a trip to their local corner shop. This can be very distressing, both for the individual and for their family and friends. A feeling of being lost in an area that you feel that you should know can be alarming for someone in the early stages of Alzheimer's disease. It is a reminder that their independence and sense of competence are being eroded. For family and friends, there may be worries about personal safety, especially that the individual may wander into an unsafe situation such as onto a canal tow path or motorway, simply because they are lost.

Individuals with Alzheimer's disease may be prone to mood swings, and can also become paranoid and angry with the people closest to them. They may forget things constantly and need things repeated many times. This can be challenging for the people providing their care.

You should try to keep in mind the emotional support that friends and family may need. The person that they knew is slipping away from them. Your service user may display a range of behaviours that were never previously part of their character, such as being uninterested in the world around them, and being snappy or distrustful. This can be frustrating and exhausting for friends and family, and you should acknowledge the pressure they may be under and try to be supportive.

Case study

What's his name again?

Margaret used to be a guide in a museum. At 82 she is still physically active and has always been involved in the local community. As a young woman, Margaret fought hard to get a university education and has worked hard all of her life. She studied entomology and had articles published in scientific journals.

When Margaret was 77, she realised that something was wrong when she started having trouble remembering things that she should know, such as forgetting her neighbour's six-month-old grandson's name. Margaret and her neighbour have known each other for many years and Margaret can recall many shared memories from their past of funny events that had occurred years before, but she could not recall the baby's name.

Things got worse when Margaret realised that she could not find the words that she needed to finish her sentences. She would get so far; then nothing. She would stare blankly and a puzzled look would creep across the face of the person she was talking to. There were other things too, such as when her houseplants died because she either watered them three times a day or did not water them at all for a month. Sometimes she

would stand in the supermarket staring at the shelves unable to remember what she was shopping for, or even why she was in the shop at all.

The realisation that she could not find her way back home after a trip to the local park was a particularly painful experience for Margaret. She'd suddenly felt vulnerable and alone. Every direction she'd turned in seemed unfamiliar and she'd had a rushing sensation of panic filling her head, drowning out the sounds around her. It had been almost overwhelming. Luckily Margaret had spotted the postman, whom she'd known for years, and he had kindly seen her home. However, this situation had knocked her confidence and shaved a layer off her sense of independence.

Check your knowledge

1 Why might Margaret feel awkward around new people?

2 What practical steps could Margaret take to help her with her short-term memory loss?

3 What impact could short-term memory loss have on Margaret's personal safety?

4 What support needs could Margaret have at this stage of her disease?

As the disease progresses, the symptoms will become worse. There may be restlessness, agitation, sleeplessness and episodes of aggression. Your service user may need assistance with eating, drinking (they may have swallowing difficulties that cause them to choke on food or drinks) and personal hygiene.

It can be hard to maintain a person's continence when they have lost the ability to recognise the urge to go to the toilet, and it is common for people to become incontinent of urine, or of both urine and faeces. This can be a particularly sensitive issue to deal with as people tend to see their toilet needs as a very private issue, and their incontinence may cause them embarrassment. You should always try to maintain the dignity and privacy of the people that you are caring for, but also remember that they will quickly become sore or develop skin infections if you do not help them to keep their skin clean and dry in the groin area, as both yeast and bacterial infections thrive in moist, warm conditions. Some people respond well to routine, especially if it is punctuated by something very familiar such as mealtimes. Therefore, they may wish to go to the toilet when they smell food, or you could routinely suggest they use the toilet before meals.

If continence cannot be maintained, incontinence pads come in a variety of sizes and absorbencies and it is important to use the right size for your service user. Some individuals in the later stages of dementia may remove their pad and leave it lying around. You must remember that this act is simply a reaction to their discomfort with the pad. Check that the size and fit are appropriate for the service user and that it is being changed frequently enough, as a soiled pad next to the skin will be uncomfortable.

▶ What is a soft diet? Why might someone with late stage dementia need their food prepared in this way?

Vascular dementia

The symptoms of vascular dementia vary greatly, depending on what has caused the disease. As with Alzheimer's disease, memory loss and general forgetfulness is common.

You may notice that tasks your service user may have performed all of their lives are becoming more difficult as they lose the ability to stay focused, for example counting change, shopping or paying bills.

There will often be problems with decision making, being or staying organised and following sequenced instructions. Processing information becomes slower than previously, and concentration will become poor with sudden, brief periods of confusion.

They may also have problems in perceiving objects in three dimensions. This could mean that not only will your service user have difficulty picking objects up, because they are struggling to judge the depth and breadth of objects, but they may also have problems judging the speed of traffic, making driving or crossing the road problematic and more dangerous than usual. You need to be aware of the added safety implications for your service users if they have **visuospatial** impairment, and the risk assessments and adjustments that you will need to make to keep them safe.

Key term

Visuospatial – perception of how far away objects are from each other, or how close together they are.

You may notice that your service users are subject to mood swings. They may become more irritable or tearful, or happier than usual, for no apparent reason. As with other forms of dementia such as Alzheimer's disease, depression is not uncommon. This may be because the individual is aware of the changes to their mental state and the impact that this degenerative disorder is having on their life, and on the lives of those around them.

⏸ PAUSE POINT   Why is it important to stay calm and reassure individuals with dementia, even when they are exhibiting signs of aggression?

Hint   Consider the impact of noise and confusion on a service user who is highly agitated.

Extend   Why might other services users unwittingly complicate volatile situations?

Depending on what has caused the vascular dementia, the symptoms can vary. If your service user has had a stroke then they may also need support with the physical effects of a stroke, such as weakened limbs or difficulty speaking or swallowing. The symptoms may stabilise for a while, but then go through periods of rapid decline, before stabilising for a while. This contrasts with Alzheimer's disease, where there is usually a steady and progressive degeneration of an individual's faculties.

Vascular dementia usually causes individuals to act 'out of character', with accompanying confusion and disorientation. Eventually, your service user will become less aware of what is happening around them, and will need support and care for all their physical needs. It is important that you remember to maintain the dignity and privacy of your service users, even when they have no self-awareness, or awareness of their surroundings or of others. At this point, your duty of care will extend to acting in the best interests of your service user.

Research

Research the progression of subcortical vascular dementia. What happens and why might the symptoms get worse gradually? Suggest ways in which this may affect the care needs of your service user.

▸ Why is it necessary to provide intellectual stimulation for service users with middle stage dementia?

Dementia with Lewy bodies (DLB)

It is not uncommon for someone with DLB to have problems maintaining attention and in staying alert. Attention span can fluctuate widely over the course of the day, or even over the course of an hour. There may also be issues around judging distances, and some visuospatial impairment.

Your service user may be suffering from delusions and hallucinations, such as believing that their partner is an imposter or is trying to kill them. You must be mindful of the support needs of their relatives, as these episodes can be very distressing for the service user, their family and friends.

An individual with DLB may have increasingly atypical sleep patterns, meaning any 24-hour carers may need additional support. Sleeping in the day and being restless at night can be exhausting for carers who have to get up in the night, especially if it is combined with fainting, difficulties with decision making and organisational tasks. Although it may seem easier to make decisions for your service user without consulting them, such as choosing their clothes or what they eat, it is important that they are given the chance to make a choice.

You may find that your service user is prone to falls and you will need to be aware of the hazards in their immediate environment. Do not try to rush a person with DLB if you are assisting them to walk. Their movements will be slower and less certain, trying to rush them because you are in a hurry will distress them, and may cause them to fall and sustain an injury.

> **Safety tip**
>
> Ensure that your manual handling training is up to date, and practice what you have learned on the training course. It is very easy to get it wrong when trying to deal with someone who is falling, and you could potentially injure both yourself and your service user.

In the later stages of the disease, your service user may have difficulty swallowing, which can increase the risk of choking and of contracting chest infections. You need to be aware of any dietary restriction that your service user may have, such as for pureed food only. Your service user may also require **aspiration**. If this is the case, you should make sure that you are trained and confident in the use of suction aids.

> **Key term**
>
> **Aspiration** – using suction to remove fluid from a body cavity.

Frontotemporal dementia (FTD)

The symptoms for FTD vary depending on where in the frontal or temporal lobes the damage has occurred. The initial symptoms may be easy to miss, but they will get more noticeable as the disease progresses.

For example, an individual with behavioural variant FTD may begin to lack inhibitions – they may act impulsively and make rash decisions, or they make inappropriate comments about others. They may lose sympathy, empathy or any interest in the wellbeing or welfare of those around them. They could come across as boorish or unfeeling, cold or distant.

Case study

Not the woman I married

Life had never been easy for Stefan, but it had never been this hard. He had tried to be a good husband, he had always worried that clever, beautiful Angelika was too good for him.

He had always been scared she would leave him, so he made allowances for lots of things such as her spending all her time with their children and excluding him from their games. She spent a lot of money on clothes and going out with friends. The change in her behaviour was so gradual that Stefan could not say when it had started.

First he noticed the excessive spending. Angelika would spend thousands of pounds on kitchen equipment and then never use it. She would become angry and hostile with him and the children if they said anything critical. Stefan tried not to think about the time his line manager had dropped around to the house with some paperwork. Angelika had made sexual advances to him in front of the children. He thought that Angelika was bored of being a housewife.

It had been so different when they met 13 years ago at the newspaper where they both worked. They were both 27 and from similar backgrounds. She had been vibrant, funny and caring. She had looked after him when he had chickenpox, and comforted him when his father died.

It was not until Angelika's mother, Marji, visited from Poland that Stefan was made to think about the dramatic changes in Angelika's behaviour. Marji took Angelika to the doctor and insisted on a referral to a specialist. At the age of 40, after a series of tests, Angelika was diagnosed with frontotemporal dementia. Stefan cried all night, partly for himself but mainly for Angelika.

Check your knowledge

1 Why do you think that Stefan had not suspected that Angelika had dementia?

2 Why is it important to consider the emotional impact of diagnosis on the family of people with dementia?

3 Why is it important for Stefan to maximise Angelika's independence, while trying to ensure her safety?

An individual with progressive **non-fluent aphasia** is likely to experience early problems with speech, and the individual may stumble over words or mispronounce high-usage words. They may understand single words but not complex sentences.

As the condition progresses, the symptoms become more aligned to the other forms of dementia and speech and behaviour will continue to deteriorate, independence becomes restricted and eventually all care needs must be met with assistance.

Your service user is an individual and so may have a range of symptoms, alongside the more common ones. It is your job to ensure that their care needs are met while still safely maximising their independence.

Key term

Non-fluent aphasia – condition in which damage to the left frontal area of the brain, associated with ability to use and understand language, causes the individual to struggle to speak, omit words and use very short sentences. Also called Broca aphasia.

Mrs Kazinska used to be so nice

Mrs Kazinska worked in a sweet shop for many years with her husband Kristoff. All of the local children knew them, as the shop was close to the junior school. Mrs Kazinska was a cheerful woman. She loved nothing more than chatting to the adults as the children squabbled over penny sweets and cola cubes.

However, Mr Kazinska noticed that his wife's behaviour was changing. She was becoming cold and distant. It seemed that every thought that came into her mind also came straight out of her mouth, no matter how hurtful or critical it was. People thought that Mrs Kazinska was being rude and they stopped coming into the shop. However, Mrs Kazinska was completely unaware of the effect that she was having on others.

To begin with, Kristoff got very angry with his wife. However, he soon realised that shouting at her about it was not helping, as she would just stare at him blankly, not understanding what he was going on about.

Check your knowledge

1 What might make a doctor think that Mrs Kazinska has FTD?

2 Why is it important for Mrs Kazinska to be properly diagnosised?

3 Why might Kristoff need support to manage his wife's symptoms in the early stages?

4 List the support needs Mrs Kazinska will have in the late stages of her disease.

Some people only experience some of the symptoms of a specific type of dementia. Sometimes they will get some of the later symptoms, such as being unable to swallow properly, earlier than usual for the progression of that disease.

Table 17.1 shows some of the early symptoms of the four main types of dementia. Often there are other health problems that may cause additional symptoms, such as sleeplessness or aggression. It is important that an early diagnosis is made by a specialist in order for individuals and their families to access the appropriate medical and social support available.

▶ **Table 17.1** Early signs and symptoms of dementia

Early symptoms	Type of dementia			
	Alzheimer's disease	Lewy body dementia	Frontotemporal dementia	Vascular dementia
Memory loss	✓			✓
Confusion	✓			
Mood swings	✓			✓
Lack of inhibitions			✓	
Hallucinations		✓		
Acting out of character			✓	✓
Slow movements		✓		
At risk of falling		✓		
Loss of interest	✓		✓	
Difficulty with verbal communication	✓	✓	✓	✓
Depression	✓			✓
Problems following sequenced instructions				✓
Poor concentration		✓		✓
Problems with visuospatial awareness		✓		✓

Other common symptoms

In the middle stages of dementia, your service users may need support with a range of issues. They may be confused or forgetful, which could impact on every aspect of their lives – such as forgetting to eat, forgetting that they have purchased something and buying it repeatedly, or allowing food to rot because they forget to throw it away.

You may find it difficult to care for your service user as they may try to hide their actions from you. They may become aggressive, resistant to help or unwilling to engage with a treatment plan. Your service user may be depressed, anxious or finding it very difficult to express themselves. They may have problems that they are embarrassed to seek help for, such as bladder or bowel incontinence.

Your service user may become frustrated when they are unable to communicate their needs. Or they may repeat things constantly, but forget to tell you something significant. They may forget who you are and worry that you are a stranger in their house, or they may repeatedly call you by the name of a long-dead relative.

In the later stages, your service user will need all of their care needs met as they become more and more detached from the world around them. It is important to remember that this progression can be very hard for friends and family to deal with, and that they may also need your support.

 ## B Examine the effects of dementia on people who have the condition

Effects of dementia on mental and physical health

As a care worker, it is important that you not only recognise the signs and symptoms of dementia in your service users, but that you also consider the impact on every aspect of their physical health and quality of life.

By taking a holistic approach to caring for your service users, you can take an active role in improving their wellbeing. It is important to remember that your service user is going through a transition process, which will gradually reduce their independence, reasoning, rationality and sense of self. During this process, they will still have physical, intellectual, emotional and social needs. It is vital that you understand the transition process and **advocate** effectively on their behalf.

> **Discussion**
>
> Do the early and middle stages of dementia progression have an impact on self-esteem and feelings of **validation** and achievement?

Everyone has a concept of self, a uniqueness that makes them an individual. To support your service users you must consider the aspects of self that will change.

> **Key terms**
>
> **Advocate** – a person speaking on behalf of someone else, who puts their case forward, especially where an individual is unable to speak for themself.
>
> **Validation** – recognising or affirming that something is based on truth or fact, or the worth of a person or their feelings and opinions, making the person feel valued or worthwhile.

▷ Why is it important to understand the principles of 'needs-led' care service provision for individuals with dementia?

▷ **Table 17.2** Examples of behavioural changes that may occur in individuals with dementia

Aspect of self	Change to previous behaviour	Potential impact on the individual	Opportunities for support and care
Reasoning	• becomes increasingly irrational • fails to perceive risks in situations • may change spending habits, spending excessively when they used to be frugal	• may spend more than they have and not be able to pay bills • may become more vulnerable to theft or exploitation	• build a professional and trust-based relationship with your service user and their family • do not just tell them what to do as this is disempowering • you may be able to prompt them to consider the risks that they are taking • document all concerns in the service user's notes • report concerns to your manager
Information processing	• slowing down of information processing as their condition progresses	• awareness of changes in their mental processes • becomes upset and frustrated at the loss of their faculties	• be patient, think before you speak • do not finish their sentences for them • maximise your service user's independence • meet their needs for validation and self-worth • avoid mocking or deriding your service user • report any concerns about disrespectful behaviour towards your service user to your manager
Communication	• struggles to find the right words • loses the thread of a sentence • asks the same question repeatedly and frequently, even though you have already answered it	• becomes frustrated or anxious at the deterioration in their ability to express themselves • may begin to feel lonely or isolated	• be patient, avoid being brusque or dismissive • always answer their questions calmly and respectfully • remember that communication is an opportunity to promote feelings of self-worth and validation
Sleeplessness and restlessness	• long bouts of sleeplessness • moves around a lot in the night • continually walks around from room to room	• becomes frustrated, aggressive or anxious	• do not try to prevent your service user from moving • ensure their environment is as safe as possible • try to find out why they are restless and moving about • request a medication review, they may benefit from a change of medication or from being prescribed a sedative
Movement	• develops jerky or uncoordinated movements • loses ability to perceive distance, speed or the space between small objects • develops a tendency to shuffle, stumble or fall	• may be unaware of the change in their movements • becomes frustrated, especially if they used to have very good fine motor skills, for example if they were an artist or an engineer	• carry out a risk assessment of your service user's environment and the activities they participate in • take extra care when crossing the road with them • do not try to stop them if they are falling, you might injure them or yourself • ensure that your manual handling training is up to date • liaise with the occupational health team • promote your service user's independence by encouraging them to use any available assistive or adaptive equipment

Case study

Don't ask

Sanjay looked around him, he knew there was something, there at the edge of his mind, but the thought was just out of reach.

Leslie was Sanjay's new care worker. Leslie had made the wrong career choice by going into care work. He found the work tiring and boring, and the service users got on his nerves. He was not like Sanjay's previous carer, Merrill. Merrill was relentlessly positive, endlessly patient, kind and genuinely interested in the welfare of the people he looked after. Merrill used to ask Sanjay about his favourite memory, or what it had been like when Sanjay was growing up. Sanjay would have chatted happily until something else caught his attention and he wandered off.

However, when Sanjay asked Leslie for the third time that morning, 'Is Kauser coming to see me?', Leslie looked up, sighed loudly and said, 'How many times have I got to tell you? Kauser is dead, so no she is not coming to see you.'

Sanjay started to cry. He remembered his wedding day so well, he remembered the love he felt for Kauser, his wife, the way his heart would race when he glanced up and saw her at the breakfast table, the warmth of her touch and his pride at the birth of his children.

He did not remember that this had happened forty years ago, that his wife had been dead for two years or that he now lived in a care home. Sanjay's grief and sadness was overwhelming. Ten minutes later, Sanjay looked up. Leslie was standing in front of him saying something about a cup of tea. 'Is Kauser coming to see me?' said Sanjay. Sanjay's tears dropped quietly into his teacup as he heard, for what he thought was the first time that his wife was dead.

Check your knowledge

1 How did Leslie feel about being asked the same question over and over again?

2 What was wrong with the way that Leslie dealt with the situation?

3 What could Leslie do to help Sanjay during this stage of his illness?

▶ Why is it important to promote social interaction for individuals with dementia?

⏸ **PAUSE POINT** Why should care workers try to investigate the causes of behaviours rather than just manage the behaviour?

     Hint Consider the longer-term care needs of the service users, not all behaviour changes are inevitable or unresolvable.

     Extend Why might the service user be reluctant to try new treatments or therapies?

▶ **Table 17.3** Behavioural changes, their impact and management

Aspect of self	Change to previous behaviour	Potential impact on the individual	Opportunities for support and care
Behaviour	• may think that they are in danger • may become bored and not interested in their surroundings	• may not be aware of the way that their behaviour is perceived by others • may be confused by the reactions of those around them • may be oblivious to the reactions of those around them • may be unaware if they are taking risks and putting themselves in danger	• try to find out why your service user behaves in certain ways – maybe there is a trigger for the behaviour • try to see things from their perspective; they may be removing their clothing because they are feeling hot or uncomfortable • report changes in behaviour to your manager, so that causes such as unsuitable medication or the need for more social interaction can be dealt with
Anxiety and fear	• panic attacks • feelings of impending doom • poor concentration • increasing tiredness, restlessness and irritability	• may hoard food or waste products • may be emotionally demanding, seeking constant reassurance and comfort • may follow carers around	• be aware of the different types of anxiety disorders in order to identify your service user's specific needs • reassure them, but remember that reassurance is not a long-term solution • establish a good working relationship with them, talk to them and make reasonable adjustments to their care • ensure that their underlying issues are addressed, and that they receive appropriate support • report your observations to your manager – a combined approach of talking therapy and medication may be required
Depression	• persistent sadness and morbid thoughts with no apparent external cause • may have feelings of despair that dominate their everyday life	• may be overwhelmed by their feelings • exacerbation of behavioural changes, such as poor appetite or aggression	• be patient and provide appropriate reassurance • maintain a regular routine • where possible, remove irritants, such as loud radios or flickering lights • encourage moderate exercise and participation in group activities • request a medication review, sometimes a change in medication or the short-term prescription of antidepressants may help

Effects of dementia on quality of life and wellbeing

The needs of people with dementia change as their condition progresses. Depending on the type of dementia that they have, they may need support with their personal safety, making sure that the gas cooker is turned off after use, for example, or making sure that they know where to catch the bus to get back home. Sometimes, they just need patience and understanding as they try to communicate, or they need a little extra help managing housework or their finances. It is important that the care that they receive is appropriate to their needs, and does not strip away their independence if there are still things that they can do for themselves.

When people with dementia are first diagnosed and they become aware of the prognosis of their condition, they often go through an emotional transition. Emotional welfare and wellbeing may fluctuate and change, so it is important that the people around an individual with dementia are supportive and responsive to changing needs.

Individuals with dementia will ultimately need all aspects of personal care provided for them. However, they are unlikely to be aware of what is being done for them, by whom or what standard of care is being provided. This makes them particularly vulnerable to abuse or neglect. As a care worker, you must strive to maintain the professional standards expected of all care professionals.

Loss of dignity and privacy

Working with an individual with dementia, particularly during the later stages of their illness, can be very challenging. You will be expected to meet all their care needs, such as washing and dressing, feeding and mobility. At the same time, you may also have to manage some challenging behaviours. For instance, the service user may make a frail or a determined attempt to scratch or slap you, or they may be shouting or making repetitive sounds. It is vital you remember that your service user may only be expressing their frustration and discomfort.

Always try to maintain the dignity and privacy of your service user. Remember to draw the curtains and talk to the service user with compassion and respect, even if you think that they cannot respond.

Case study

Pressures of care work

It was only when Precious became really confused that her daughter Shanice decided that the care home was the best place to provide her care. Shanice lives in the next town and has been worried about her mum ever since the night when the police called to say that Precious had been found in a street in her night attire. Precious was a long way from home. She was cold and tired and could not explain how she came to be out in her carpet slippers and dressing gown.

Precious has now been in the care home for a year. Her dementia is advancing quite rapidly. Samantha is Precious's key worker, and she is also the key worker for seven other residents, who all need to be helped to get up, wash and dress ready for breakfast every day. Samantha is very busy and she cuts corners where she can in order to get everything done.

One morning, Precious is irritable as she had not slept well, and as Samantha tugs and twists Precious's arm into her dress, Precious starts to cry out. Samantha shouts at her: 'Shut up!' At that moment, Shanice walks into the room for an early visit as she is due to catch a plane to go on holiday.

Check your knowledge

1   Why was Precious distressed?

2   Why was shouting at Precious the wrong thing for Samantha to do?

3   What does Samantha's manager need to do about the working conditions for her staff? Remember that she has a duty of care to them as well as to the service users.

Increasing difficulty in managing daily routine and personal care

Personal care is something that individuals with dementia find increasingly difficult to manage. But it is important to remember that how you look, your style of clothing and how you like to smell are all expressions of your identity. They are conscious decisions that people make. Even choosing not to wash is a decision, if it is deliberate. For individuals with dementia, it becomes increasingly difficult to make those choices. You should encourage your service user to make these choices for as long as they are able to. The support you give them with personal care and dressing should be done tactfully and with respect.

Research

What equipment and adaptations can be made to the homes of individuals with dementia to promote their independence and safety? How can these items help the service user to stay independent?

▶ How could having her hair styled be helping with some of the symptoms of this lady's dementia?

Increasing inability to manage own affairs

As a care worker, you may occasionally find that your service users will confide in you about their financial affairs. Individuals with early stage dementia often worry about what will happen when they can no longer manage their finances independently. There are things that can be done to help them to control their finances in both the short and the long term. Encourage them to talk to a social worker or check the government website, about their entitlement to benefits.

The Citizens Advice Bureau and the Money Advice Service are also good sources of information. Your service user may wish to investigate **power of attorney**. There are two types of power of attorney, ordinary (general) and lasting. Ordinary power of attorney is a temporary measure and is usually used to cover specific assets, for example to manage a bank account and pay bills for someone for a short period of time, for instance if the individual has to go into hospital. It is only valid when the individual still has mental capacity and is able to make their own decisions.

There are two types of lasting power of attorney (LPA), one for property and financial affairs and the other for health and welfare. These legal agreements should be drawn up when the person still has capacity. An LPA gives the chosen attorney or attorneys the legal power to make decisions on the person's behalf once they are no longer capable of making those decisions for themselves. Setting up an LPA is only possible when the person has the capacity to choose their attorneys (in this sense, the person/people who are authorised to act on their behalf). Care must be taken to ensure that an individual with early stage dementia is not being coerced into signing over their rights. Once put in place, the LPA can be activated when required (once the person has become incapable of making their own decisions) by registering it with the Office of the Public Guardian. The decision to activate the LPA should be validated by a professional, such as a doctor, solicitor or social worker.

Another option to help individuals with early stage dementia to manage their financial affairs is for them to open a joint account with a partner, relative or a trusted friend, in order to be prepared for when they can no longer make those decisions alone.

As the service user becomes more vulnerable, it can be easy for people to take advantage of them. It is important that you are vigilant for signs of financial abuse and report any concerns to your manager.

However, you should also be careful not to become open to allegations of financial abuse. You may think that you are performing an act of kindness by shopping for a service user. They may ask you to take the money out of their purse or wallet, or try to give you a bank card to use. Contactless payment is easy, but if the service user cannot remember asking you to shop for them, or they deny that they did, you will not have any witnesses to confirm your account of the situation. You could find yourself subject to a criminal investigation.

Increasing lack of social interactions

Individuals with dementia may find themselves socially isolated for a number of reasons. Some forms of dementia can make the individual withdraw from social interaction. For other individuals, the early stages of dementia can make them feel distanced, confused or unable to keep up with the social interactions around them.

For other people with dementia, it is the society that they used to be part of that withdraws from them. People stop visiting or cross the road to avoid them. This can exacerbate the person's feelings of isolation and exclusion.

Social interaction should be encouraged as it improves quality of life and can prolong the retention of independence and life skills. It can improve self-esteem and reduce anxiety and depression.

When working in care, it is important that, where possible, you promote integration for your service users. Research has shown the positive impact of appropriate social activities and integration. A television screen displaying films and images that are likely to have been stored in the long-term memory of a person with dementia is going to be more beneficial to their mental health and emotional wellbeing than more up-to-date images or news programmes. This is because the short-term memory has been lost, and they will find it easier to relate to the films and music they enjoyed when they were younger. This kind of stimulation can help rekindle memories and slow down deterioration of the long-term memory. If you find yourself working in a care home where the television and radio appear to be more appropriate for the staff than the residents, you may want to discuss this with the manager.

▶ Why might some games be more appropriate for individuals with dementia than others? List some games that would be appropriate and explain why they would help an individual with dementia.

PAUSE POINT   Why should care workers continue to promote social interaction, if a service user has refused to engage in a social activity?

Hint   Why might the service user be reluctant to engage in social activities?

Extend   Why should you be responsive to a services users mood fluctuations? How can this responsiveness enhance interactions?

Exclusion and loss of status

The way that a service user feels about their diagnosis initially may not be a true reflection of the way that people around them feel about the condition. However, what is important is how the individual with dementia perceives their changed health status. They may also fear a change in their social status. In some cultures, and within all societies, there are always people who do not want to associate with people who are experiencing mental deterioration. Whether it is ignorance and they believe that they will catch a disease like dementia or that they are intolerant or lack understanding of people with the disorder, sometimes some sections of society choose to exclude others.

People with dementia may lose friends once diagnosed, and may find it hard to make new friendships. They can become isolated because they no longer want to engage in social activities. Also, they may be side-lined because they can no longer do what they did before. For example, they may be asked to step down from a voluntary position, such as treasurer of a social club, because they can no longer do the job properly. If the individual withdraws because they fear social exclusion, then the situation becomes a self-fulfilling prophecy.

Joining a support group and seeking interaction will help rebuild the service user's self-esteem. However, you should not insist that your service user attends a group as you must always be mindful of their dignity and self-respect.

People with dementia often experience discrimination, even in healthcare situations, and may lack the mental capacity to challenge discrimination and poor care. The Equality Act 2010 aims to ensure that reasonable adjustments are made by employers and service providers to protect the rights of people with disabilities and ensure that they receive equal treatment. As their condition deteriorates, you may need to advocate more on your service's user's behalf.

Loss of skills

In the early stages of dementia, many individuals are acutely aware of their loss of skills, whether it is in memory and communication, or movement and dexterity. The knowledge that these abilities are lost and that the degeneration is progressive is very stressful and can be very depressing. As a care worker, you need to empathise with your service user. You should be sensitive and considerate, compassionate and understanding in the way you acknowledge their loss of skills.

An assessment by an occupational health practitioner may help maintain the independence of people in the early and middle stages of dementia. As an individual's short-term memory deteriorates, simple things such as using alerts on a smart phone (if your service user has one), or simply writing lists can help with day-to-day activities such as shopping and eating, looking after pets or paying bills. Non-slip jelly mats can make it easier to carry things on a tray for people with vascular dementia who may have poor spatial awareness. A person's needs are individual, and may fluctuate from day to day, so it is important for you to be responsive to the situation.

There will come a point when someone with dementia is no longer safe to drive. The loss of independence that this causes can have a big impact on emotional wellbeing, as well as a practical impact for the individual and their family, especially if they are the only driver. Finding suitable alternatives for transportation can be difficult and expensive and some people can be very reluctant to give up their driving licence. It is yet another social and emotional adjustment for people with dementia and the situation can be made harder, or more dangerous, if they forget that they are not supposed to drive. You may have to deal with these sensitive situations. You should remember that it can be frustrating for people with dementia to lose their independence, which is part of their identity.

▸ Different social events appeal to different people. Remember to promote both choice and inclusion in your care work.

Discussion

Is it acceptable to expose an individual with dementia to the risk of social rejection if there is a chance that attending an event might increase their social circle?

Assessment practice 17.1

| A.P1 | A.P2 | B.P3 | B.P4 | A.M1 | B.M2 | AB.D1 |

To assist a care worker as they begin a new job working with elderly dementia patients, you need to help them to understand the different types of dementia that the service users in their care may have, the progression of their illness and the impact that it will have on the intellectual, social and emotional welfare of their service users.

- Write a case study for three of the main types of dementia explored in this unit, explaining their impact on the service user.
- Identify the signs and symptoms, and causes of the different types of dementia. Compare and contrast the symptoms for each type.
- Identify the effects of three types of dementia on health and wellbeing, as well as on quality of life.
- Using the information you have gathered, evaluate why it might be important to understand how the different types of dementia can have a progressively degenerative impact on the health and wellbeing of the individual.

Plan
- Do I know what I am being asked to do?
- Can I imagine myself as a senior carer instructing a new starter, or should I try to interview a care worker about what they do?
- Have I read enough case studies to be confident in writing my own and including enough detail but not making it too long?

Do
- I know what I want to achieve.
- I can check my work to see where I have gone off task and can make changes to put this right.

Review
- I can instruct someone else on how to complete the task more efficiently.
- I know what I would do differently next time and the approach I would take with the parts that I found difficult this time.

C Investigate the concept of person-centred care for people who have dementia to maintain quality of life and wellbeing

Principles of person-centred care

Care should recognise the uniqueness and individuality of the person who has dementia. Person-centred care establishes a firm foundation for the delivery of support during the progress of the disease for the individual with dementia. By following the **nursing process** and establishing a needs-led care package, you can deliver efficient and appropriate care to your service user. It is important to regularly review the usefulness of the care you give, so that support can be increased in line with your service user's needs.

Dignity, privacy and respect

People with dementia can present care workers with challenging behaviours, because of their condition. Dignity, privacy and respect are fundamental to all care provision and you, as a care worker, should be sensitive to the needs of your service users. Individuals with dementia, particularly late stage dementia, are slightly different from most other service users in that they will not complain if the care they receive is below standard. This makes them very vulnerable to abuse and neglect. They may be susceptible to many different types of abuse and some forms are easier to identify than others. Bruises or broken bones, for example, are easier to see than emotional abuse.

Be observant of the practice in your workplace. Report your concerns to your manager and document any incidents, accidents or near misses, using the appropriate paperwork for your workplace.

Discussion

Do individuals with dementia deserve more protection from abuse or neglect under the law than other service users?

Independence, rights and empowerment

Promoting independence for your service users when they are confused or presenting you with challenging behaviours can seem a difficult proposition. However, promoting independence and empowering your service user is part of your job as their advocate, especially as their disease progresses and their capacity to exercise their rights without support diminishes. Try to take every opportunity to encourage your service user to make choices about what they want. Allow them to choose between activities that might interest them, such as a trip to a museum or watching an old film. This can make a person feel that they have control over some aspects of their life. Try not to rush the decision-making process or be dismissive of the simple choices that people make. For example, a service user may want to watch the epic film 'Mother India' for the third time in a week. This may be because although they cannot remember they've seen the film three times that week, they can remember the moving plot and dramatic visuals of the film. You need to respect their choice and maybe use it as an opportunity to discuss growing up, struggles and injustice and what the past was like for them.

Case study

I'm still here, somewhere

Mildred stares out of the window, silently. She was always silent. It was raining hard, just as it did that day when she was eleven years old and the bottom field flooded on her father's farm. She remembered quite clearly being woken in the night, pulling her waterproofs on over her nightclothes and going out to help her brothers and her father rescue the sheep.

When she first came to the care home, Mildred was happy to talk about the past; it seemed less confusing than the present. Now, some days, everything is confusing and Mildred is becoming more and more withdrawn.

In the lounge of the care home, Mildred's care worker, Sue, watches Mildred. Sue has heard Mildred's story many times in the past and she senses that Mildred

would like to go out. So, when the storm passes, she helps Mildred into her wellingtons and lets Mildred put on her coat. She takes Mildred outside and smiles as Mildred splashes happily in the puddles. They walk a while and talk a little. As they return to the care home a rainbow appears and Mildred says she is happy now that all the sheep are in.

Check your knowledge

1 Why is it important to learn the life story of your service users?

2 Why is it important for Sue to allow Mildred to do as much as she can for herself?

3 What should Sue have done if Mildred had refused to go out?

4 How do you think this event helped Mildred?

Recognition of cultural and religious differences and requirements

Some events on the cultural calendar are celebrated nationally. They are opportunities to get together, eat different food to usual and mark the passing of time. In the UK, Christmas is one such event, but it is important to be sensitive to the cultural events of all of your service users. Everyone should be given the opportunity to participate in all cultural events.

This is called **inclusion** and it promotes a sense of belonging. This is particularly important for individuals with early or middle stage dementia who are still aware of their cultural norms and who may experience feelings of detachment or exclusion from what is going on around them because of confusion or the loss of the ability to communicate effectively.

> **Key term**
>
> **Inclusion** – being part of an institution, event or culture.

It is important that you are sensitive to the cultural needs of your service users and that you are aware of any restrictions this may include. This is particularly important for individuals with dementia as when their dementia progresses they may forget some of the key principles that they have always lived by. For example, if your service user is a practising Rastafarian, they will never have eaten pork. As their memory deteriorates, they may forget what pork is and try to eat it. While the service user may be living from moment to moment, their family may be upset that their relative's cultural norms are not being observed. While it is still possible to negotiate with your service user, you should be calm and respectful in explaining why they are being given an alternative meal. If the problem is persistent or ongoing, then it is important that the family are made aware of the issue and the steps that you have taken in providing an alternative meal, but that your service user is choosing to eat something else. People with dementia may forget to eat or forget that they have eaten, they do not always respond to the stimulus of hunger, or they may find their taste buds have altered or need a soft diet. It is important that you try to balance your service user's diet so that they do not become undernourished or malnourished.

> **Research**
>
> Research the difference between 'undernourished' and 'malnourished'.

Entitlement to advocacy

You will often find yourself in the position of advocate for your service user, and this is a position of trust. If your service user has needs and entitlements, then they should be met. As their condition deteriorates, they may lose the ability to ask for what they need or what they deserve, and it will be up to you to see that they get it. This can include appropriate treatment, the correct diet and even the benefits to which they are entitled. If you are unsure, or feel that your requests will be ignored, then you should refer the issue to your manager and document your concerns.

PAUSE POINT   How can person-centred care improve the quality of life for your service user?

Hint   What are the potential consequences of denying a service user their rights?

Extend   How can disempowerment and neglect lead to abuse? Why are individuals with dementia more at risk of this type of abuse?

Safeguarding people who have dementia

Safeguarding in care is key to the quality of care delivered. Safeguarding policies and procedures are enforced by legislation and everyone has a responsibility to protect themselves, their colleagues and their service users from harm. The safety of your service user is not just the responsibility of your manager. You also have a responsibility under the law to protect and promote the rights and wellbeing of your service users.

It is not enough to just acknowledge that your service users are vulnerable; you need to be vigilant in promoting and upholding their rights to safety, dignity and independence as part of your advocacy duties as a care worker.

Protection versus independence and rights

Your training as a care worker should meet the needs and demands of the duties that you are expected to perform. Common training programmes include dementia care, manual handling, first aid, food hygiene and challenging-behaviour management. However, if your service user has additional needs, you have a right to expect training specifically targeted to the performance of this procedure to enable you to carry out your duties safely. For example, if your service user needs suction because they have swallowing difficulties you will need to be trained in how to manage and use the equipment safely, and causing the least discomfort possible to your service user.

It is important when caring for individuals with dementia that you are mindful of the impact your interventions have on their sense of personal identity. This is particularly important in early and middle stage dementia, when your service users may be feeling vulnerable, confused or disempowered. There are technological interventions that can alert you to potential dangers, while maintaining the dignity, privacy and independence of your service users. In a care home, for example, a mattress sensor can detect if someone has got out of bed.

Research

Find out what other assistive technology is available to alert staff that a person with dementia is in a dangerous or vulnerable situation. How do these devices enable maintenance of the service user's dignity and privacy?

Safe, enabling/empowering environments

The risk of falls is higher for individuals with dementia, for a number of reasons. If their dementia was preceded by a stroke, then it is not uncommon for them to experience physical impairment and lasting muscle weakness. Dementia can also affect balance and special perception, so it is important to consider the safety of your service user's living environment.

Check the floor surface is not lifting or damaged. Rugs can present additional and unnecessary trip hazards and spills must always be thoroughly cleaned up. Sufficient lighting and removing low objects, such as occasional tables and foot stools, and installing grab rails in appropriate places will also reduce the risks of falls. Gas detectors and medication dispensers can be very useful in avoiding accidental injuries such as gas poisoning or taking too much medication, not taking a complete dose of medication or failing to take it at all. Pendant alarms, fall detectors, smoke alarms, call buttons, removing hazards or replacing equipment, such as unsafe gas fires, can also help to maintain a safer environment for your service users.

Safety tip

If you are unsure about a particular surface that your service user may walk on, you should check it first. Surfaces, such as wet decking, may look safe but can be very slippery or uneven.

You can help your service user feel calm and comfortable in their environment by playing music that they remember. Their long-term memory will last longer than their short-term memory, so the music selected can be from decades before. Choosing the right music can reduce your service user's anxiety, irritability and restlessness.

Awareness of cultural and religious differences

Culture, belief and religion are three different concepts, and it is important to recognise the impact of this on the care you provide.

▶ A religion is an organised and recognised form of worship, with conventions that are observed by its followers, and shared beliefs. Religious practices are often observed in a building set aside for that purpose, for example a church, temple or mosque.

▶ A belief is a concept usually held as part of a formal religion, it involves accepting that something exists or is true, especially if there is no proof of its existence. Some people's beliefs may not involve religion, such as believing in luck or astrology.

▶ Culture encompasses the ideas, customs and social behaviours of a particular grouping of people, or of society. This may be on the basis of their shared race, social class, language or age. Individuals may identify with more than one culture.

In a multicultural society, it is important to recognise and respect all cultures, different traditions, religions and the festivals that are part of them. Your opinion of a particular race, religion, culture or belief system should have no impact on the quality of care that you deliver.

You need to be aware of the principles and restrictions that are part of different cultural and religious teachings, so that you can support your service users effectively.

▶ How can acts of collective worship benefit individuals with dementia and their families?

Awareness of representation and advocacy

Some individuals in the earlier stages of dementia may have done some 'advanced care planning'. This is where people make decisions about their future care, before their disease progresses and they become unable to make decisions about what they want or need. They may make decisions in advance about treatments that they do or do not want in the future.

As a care worker, you need to be aware of whether your service user has made any advanced decisions, and also if they have nominated someone to have an LPA (see learning aim B, Increasing inability to manage own affairs). Different countries within the UK have different legislative systems, for example the rules about power of attorney are different in Northern Ireland and laws on advanced decisions do not apply.

> **Research**
>
> Research what happens to people who lose mental capacity through dementia, but have not nominated anyone to have lasting power of attorney for them.

Ⅱ PAUSE POINT Why do carers need to be aware of their role in the duty of care that they have for their service users?

(**Hint**) What are the potential consequences of not safeguarding the welfare of your service users?

(**Extend**) Why are people with dementia more likely to have their personal choices made for them? How can this affect their welfare?

Assessment of needs, protection and safety

Once an individual has been diagnosed as having dementia, you will need to support them with the changes that they are going through. You will play a large part in their day-to-day care and it is important that you establish a rapport with your service user to maximise their quality of life.

As you get to know your service user and spend time with them, you will begin to develop an understanding, not only of the progression of their dementia, but also of their character, preferences and needs.

Social services will also assess and review your service user's needs, to identify their support needs and entitlement to social services funded care. Each country in the UK has a different set of criteria and different provision. It can be very distressing for relatives to find that access to the services they feel their relative requires is not available, and they may need support with this. You will need to check what is available in the area where you deliver care, as funding for this sector frequently changes and there are regional variations in the provision.

> **Research**
>
> Research 'needs assessment' and the Care Act 2015 to discover the process of accessing support in England.

Communication and behaviour needs

You will need to find strategies to manage behaviours such as restlessness or obsessive/repetitive behaviour, to keep people safe and to maintain their dignity.

Before you start to care for an individual, it is important that you know their needs, and whether or not they can be met. One model of practice that you could use is 'the nursing process', first described in 1958 by Ida Jean Orlando, an American nurse, as a four-stage process. It has been modified over the years and is now commonly described as a five-stage process: 'assess, analyse, plan, implement and evaluate'.

> **Research**
>
> Research 'the nursing process' and write a short report on the benefits of a structured approach to meeting complex care needs.

Case study

All words; no communication

It is Nicola's first day in charge of the dementia care wing of the nursing care home. It all appears noisy and chaotic. The curtains are half shut in the lounge and the lighting is dim. There is a man in a chair in the corner of the lounge shouting 'one, two, three' loudly at no one in particular. Another lady is wandering around, shuffling her feet in badly-fitting slippers, going up to the pictures on the walls, touching one and then moving on to the next. In a chair, in the corner is a woman sewing invisible outfits on an invisible sewing machine. Only the movement of her hands gives away her activity.

A television is blaring away in a corner of the lounge, with no one watching it, while a radio is booming out pop music from the other side of the room. Nicola bumps her leg on a coffee table; the sharp corner is certain to cause a bruise.

Away from the residents and clustered around a table, the staff are sitting drinking coffee and chatting to each other. Nicola goes over to them and is told that it is break time. It does not take all of Nicola's training for her to realise that this environment is not suitable for individuals with dementia. Nicola reads the notes of the residents. She thinks about the nursing process and how to set about changing the way things are done in the care home.

Check your knowledge

1 Why is it important to promote communication with individuals with dementia?

2 Why is it a safeguarding issue if all the staff take their break at the same time?

3 Can you identify at least five hazards in this case study?

4 What simple activities could you suggest that would benefit the residents and how will those activities help?

Aids and assistive technologies

It is important that you are aware of the different types of technologies available to care workers, how to use them and at which stage they will no longer be useful.

Think carefully about the tasks you are assisting with. For example, if you are assisting a service user to wash, is the floor dry? Do you need an anti-slip mat? Can they stand during the whole procedure or do you need a bath chair?

Research

To read more about assistive devices, go to Alzheimer's Society website, at **www. alzheimers.org.uk**, and search for 'Assistive technology - devices to help with everyday living'. Create a spidergram with the headings: communication, safety, and daily living. Then identify the situations in which a specific product might help to make an individual's life easier.

As your service user's condition deteriorates, you will need to evaluate the effectiveness of the equipment that you are using. For example, your service user may forget to use a safety alarm or a pager and you may have a false sense of security about their safety, if you think that they are using it. Your service user might use the alarm or pager frequently or for no reason, causing frustration for you and for your colleagues. This may also mean that in a real emergency there is the danger that the alarm will not be attended to promptly.

However, some devices are useful, particularly in the early stages of the disease. Locator devices for things that are frequently lost, such as keys, can help give your service user a sense of independence and security.

If you are caring for someone in their own home, then the earlier equipment is introduced, usually the more chance that your service user will use it safely and appropriately. Try not to introduce equipment that needs a number of sequenced steps in order to use it, as it likely to frustrate your service user when they cannot recall what to do. For example, a mobile phone with an automatic screen lock is less appropriate than a cordless phone pre-programmed to dial an emergency contact.

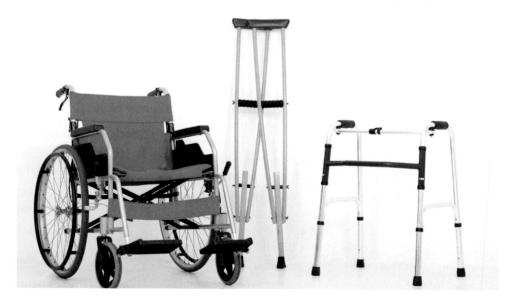

▶ Ensure that all safety equipment meets safety standards, is fit for purpose and is the right size for the service user

Diet and medication

You need to make sure that you empower your service users and give them the opportunity to make informed choices for as long as they are able to. Be aware of things such as what they like to eat and how they like to eat it. Someone may like cheese, for example, but only if it is melted on toast. By promoting choice, you are encouraging your service users to maintain their independence for longer and not allowing them to slip into institutionalised behaviours.

Medication cannot cure dementia, but medications can slow down some of the symptoms. You should encourage your service users to take their medication as prescribed. Using devices such as reminder alerts and individual dose containers can help to remind your service user when they need to take their medication, and may make it easier for you to check that they have done so. You should observe your service user for signs that their medication is doing what it should, or for any side effects or adverse reactions.

Make sure that you check the medication in the pill dispenser is correct for your service user and, if the tablets are a different shape or colour to the ones that the patient usually has, contact the pharmacist for guidance before you administer the pills.

Personal care routines

For most adults, personal care is a private experience and recognising that they can no longer take care of this without assistance can be a difficult adjustment. Encourage your service user to do as much as they can for themselves, to maintain a level of independence. You could, for example, mime washing your face as a memory prompt.

You can make the process of personal care a more tolerable experience if you are sensitive to the needs of your service user. If you are assisting them to bathe, be aware of the water temperature, check it before they get in and while they are bathing, body heat can be lost by evaporation. So remember that the bathroom should also be warm. You cannot judge whether your service user is feeling cold by your own temperature, you are fully dressed!

Remember that bath hoists can be uncomfortable after quite a short while. If you are helping your service user to shower, be cautious of trips, slips and falls. Close curtains and cubicle doors and avoid all personal or jocular comments about an individual's appearance, or any offensive smells.

Discussion

Is it acceptable to follow all instructions in the workplace without questioning why you are performing the tasks that you have been given?

Ensuring protection and limiting vulnerability

You will need to ensure that your service user is protected from the wide range of activities that can upset them, hurt them or exploit their vulnerability. Dementia can be a very isolating disease and your service user may behave in ways that make them very vulnerable. You will need to make sure that they are physically safe if, for example, they are restless and tend to wander. You will need to ensure that they can engage in recreational activities safely. You should document all financial transactions that you are expected to perform, such as paying the milkman. You must also report any financial irregularities to your manager.

Maintaining a safe, enabling environment

When caring for someone in their home, there are many steps that you can take to improve their safety and promote their independence. Individuals with dementia can forget to take the necessary steps needed to have a good quality of life. They may forget to throw food away, so that it rots. This may happen because they have a hoarding behaviour, a memory issue, confusion or depression. They may forget to pay bills, resulting in utilities such as electricity or gas supply being cut off. They may be unable to keep their house clean and tidy.

Your role as a care worker is to create and maintain an environment that maximises the independence and quality of life of your service user, and to take practical steps to ensure their welfare. Try to ensure that you are alert to hazards that could potentially harm your service user, especially if the hazard is a temporary one, such as Christmas trees or Diwali diva lights. Wires should not trail across the floor and naked flames, such as candles, should not be left unattended.

Try to make it as easy as possible for the individual with dementia to carry out their daily activities without feeling that they need to ask for help. For example, put labels on cupboards to indicate their contents.

▶ **Figure 17.2** Clear labels on foodstuffs or cupboards can promote independence for your service user

PAUSE POINT   Why is it important to encourage people with dementia to do what they can themselves when it is quicker to do it for them?

Hint   What is de-skilling, and why will it happen to individuals with dementia?

Extend   What activities can you think of to help individuals with dementia make the most of the skills that they still have?

Health and wellbeing

Holistic care takes account of every aspect of an individual's health and wellbeing, rather than just treating the cause or symptoms of their illness. It is about attempting to meet the physical, intellectual, emotional and social needs of the individual, which may involve using a variety of treatments, therapies and activities.

Safe handling and administration of medication

Individuals react differently to medications and you should observe your service user for reactions to medication, especially to new medications. If your service user is self-medicating, ensure that they are taking the correct dose, which will become especially important as their memory deteriorates. If your service user misses a dose, they should take it as soon as they remember (if it is the same day). If it is the next day, they should just take the dose for that day. The NICE guidelines advise against taking a double dose the next day. If your service user continually misses doses but wants to take their medication, it may be better for them to stop self-medicating and pass responsibility to their carer. Before taking on this task, you should make sure that you are trained in the safe handling and administration of medication.

▶ Boxes such as this are available from pharmacists and can help your service user remember to take their medication – remember to document all medication administered

Diet and nutrition

It is important that you encourage your service user to maintain a healthy diet. If they lose too much weight, they may be more vulnerable to infection. Dehydration or constipation are problems that can result from poor diet. You should monitor the amounts that your service user eats and drinks as they may forget to ask for food or fluids, or they may be unable to find the words to ask for what they want. Pain, tiredness and depression can also affect your service user's appetite. Equally, some individuals with dementia can forget that they have already eaten and be constantly looking for food. If your service user wants to eat immediately after eating, you could offer smaller portions rather than trying to withhold food, which could lead to aggressive confrontations.

You should provide a varied and healthy diet, and always be sensitive to any cultural requirements or preferences. As the service user reaches the later stages of dementia, swallowing may become a problem, and a high calorie soft or fluid diet and dietary supplements may be required.

Try to work around your service user, create a relaxed atmosphere and encourage them to eat and drink. If they get up in the night, try giving them healthy snacks. You could also offer them foods with stronger flavours, as an individual with dementia may experience changes in what they can taste. As their disease progresses, your service user may prefer sweeter foods. People with dementia are unlikely to respond to operant conditioning so do not try tactics like withholding dessert if they have not eaten their main course. Cognitive impairment may mean that they no longer recognise food.

Complementary therapies

You should not encourage your service users to use complementary therapies as an alternative to medical intervention, as there is no scientific evidence that they are effective in treating dementia. However, some non-invasive therapies, like massage and aromatherapy, can be useful for treating symptoms such as anxiety. It is important to remember that your service user is the one who decides whether or not to participate in this type of therapy. Many individuals with dementia enjoy these types of therapies and find them helpful in dealing with some of their symptoms. However, the individual should fully understand what the treatment involves and it may be better in the later stages of the disease, especially if there is severe cognitive impairment, to avoid these treatments.

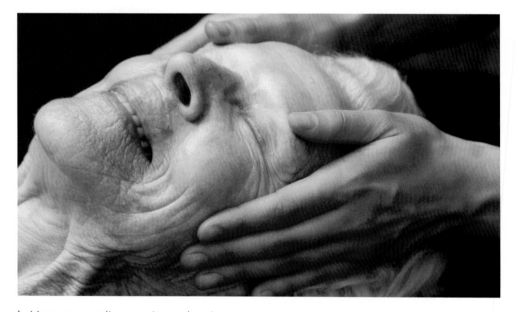

▶ Massage can relieve tension and anxiety

Activities and exercise

Physical activity can reduce the risk of falls by improving balance, improving mood and improving sleep patterns.

Research suggests that remaining active and exercising can slow the progression of some types of dementia in the early stages by improving memory. Before you embark on an exercise programme with your service user, you need to consider the stage of their illness, their age, whether they have other illnesses and their general levels of fitness. Always undertake a risk assessment of any activities that you participate in with your service users, and consult their families where appropriate. Sometimes exercise can only be undertaken after seeking medical advice. If your service user has dementia after having suffered a stroke, follow the advice of their physiotherapist.

Gardening, indoor bowls or skittles, walking and seated exercises are usually recommended. Swimming is excellent exercise, but not suitable for everyone and your service user should never be unsupervised.

Helping your service user to reminisce, by creating a memory book from old photographs, watching old films and listening to the music of their past, may help to stimulate their memory. This can raise self-esteem and re-empower your service users.

▶ Pictures and items from a bygone age can stimulate memories, conversation and social interaction; this could enhance the mood of your service user

Sensory stimulation

As an individual's dementia progresses and their speech, cognitive skills and interactions diminish, sensory stimulation becomes increasingly important to their quality of life and wellbeing.

Your service user is likely to still have some, if not all, of their senses and these can be stimulated in a number of ways.

▶ Touch – for example, you could massage your service user's hands, maybe offer them a manicure or hair-do, let them hold your hand if they need reassurance, provide materials that they like to feel and touch (such as velvet, satin, faux fur or hessian).

▶ Vision – for example, they may enjoy bubble light tubes, Diwali lights, going for a walk and looking at something different, such as autumn leaves. Within their home, ensure that there is appropriate lighting and views to the outside. Bright colours can be used in active areas and more restful colours in lounges and dining areas. Where appropriate, hang photographs or pictures that stimulate memories (avoiding abstracts).

▶ Hearing – for example, playing soothing music that was popular in the individual's younger years and providing musical experiences (such as dancing, singing and clapping), providing opportunities for both social and quieter conversation.

▶ Smell – smells can evoke specific memories; providing scented flowers or plants, or creating a sensory garden with herbs may be appreciated. You should also be aware that your service user may take pleasure in food smells such as coffee, or bacon or bread cooking.

▶ Taste – as your service user's sense of taste may alter as the disease progresses, you should find out their likes and dislikes so that you can provide interesting and varied meals.

However, it is important to get the balance right as too much sensory stimulation might overload your service user's senses and cause them to become restless and agitated.

 PAUSE POINT   Why is it important take a holistic approach to person-centred care?

Hint   Why is it important to respond to the reactions of your service user?

Extend   How can diminishing communication skills impact on the concept of self?

Responsive and flexible planning to maintain quality of life and wellbeing

Person-centred care is dependent on a process of planning, implementing and reviewing. It is important that you are not only aware of your performance in the workplace, but also that you reflect on ways that it can be improved to enhance the experience of care for your service user.

The care planning cycle

One of the models for promoting appropriate care is the care planning cycle. It will enable you to plan effectively for the fluctuating needs of individuals with all kinds of care needs, including dementia.

Care plans are designed to identify the care needs of the individual, the methods of meeting those needs and the people responsible for carrying out the tasks. This document is organic and needs to be reviewed as your service user's needs change.

Use of the care planning cycle

A care plan can be a very effective tool when used properly. It is important to note that the care plan forms part of the service user's notes. If there are questions about the care that a service user receives, institutions such as the CQC can ask to look at their care plans. Care plans should be reviewed regularly, especially in the case of vascular dementia patients, whose condition may suddenly deteriorate after a period of relative stability.

Involvement of person in own care planning

For care planning to be effective, your service user should be as involved as much as possible. During the early and middle stages of the disease, when communication is easier and there is less cognitive impairment, it is easier to achieve this. Take time to find ways for your service user to communicate their preferences. Be patient and creative in the way that you gather information. You may find picture boards helpful, especially if your service user cannot find the words to express themselves.

Be sensitive to your service user's body language. It is important that the care plan meets their needs, if they are tired, depressed or in pain when you are trying to make the plan with them, they may agree to things that they do not really want just so that they can be left alone.

Involvement of family and friends in care planning

Family and friends can be a useful source of information when care planning, especially if they are going to be involved in providing care. They may be more aware of your service user's needs and have some strategies for care that you may not have thought of. For example, your service user may prefer having a bath before they go to bed to having a shower in the morning.

Research

Imagine that you are caring for an individual with dementia. Write a brief account of their symptoms and then research the care planning cycle. Apply the different stages to the individual with dementia who you have described.

Current strengths and abilities

The objectives in a care plan should be achievable and must reflect your service user's current range of abilities. As their dementia progresses, you must be sensitive to the changes in these abilities. If your service user can no longer stand up to be showered but the care plan states that they can, then the care plan must be changed. Remember that the purpose of this document is that a carer who has never met your service user ought to be able to read it and know exactly how to meet their care needs. Out-of-date information, or misinformation can be harmful and may lead to accidents, injury or even death.

▶ Individuals with dementia are more prone to falls. Regularly review the support needs of your service users and ensure that care plans are up to date.

Individualised activities and exercise

It is important to remember that everyone is an individual and person-centred care should reflect this. Try to ensure that the care that you give celebrates diversity and inclusion, and at the same time recognises and supports the individual's uniqueness. However, if your service user is not happy to join in, they should not be forced to do so. You may be able to find an alternative that will better suit their personality and preferences.

> **Discussion**
>
> Is there anything wrong with ensuring that all service users comply with the same routine if the standard of practical care is adequate and safe?

Case study

Arthur battles on

The Second World War was very real for Arthur, more real than what he is looking at now. All around him is noise and confusion. People are smiling and laughing and there is a lot of food around that Arthur does not fancy eating. During the war, Arthur had flown planes and commanded men. He does not like the fuss and nonsense of social events and always tended to leave all of that 'socialising and maintaining relationships' business to his wife. He has fathered three children, who he sent off to boarding school because he believed in 'discipline and order'.

Ismail is Arthur's key care worker. He knows the signs – today is going to be challenging! Arthur has become more confused over the last couple of weeks. Arthur's care plan is quite clear on the most effective ways to meet his needs. Ismail's shift ends and during the handover he mentions that Arthur's mood is low. Dave is new and has never met Arthur before. He does not read any of the care plans and decides that he will organise a party for all of the residents, with party poppers, crackers and funny hats.

As the party poppers go off around him, Arthur starts to panic, he thinks they are shooting at him but he does not know who 'they' are.

Check your knowledge

1 How can a care plan help you to meet the needs of patients who are unfamiliar to you?

2 Why should a care plan be reviewed as the service user's needs change?

3 Whose needs is Dave meeting?

Assessment practice 17.2

C.P5   C.P6   C.M3   C.D2   C.D3

Person-centred care is fundamental to the needs-led provision approach of the caring professions. Individuals with dementia often need someone else to identify their needs, particularly as their dementia progresses.

- Explain how this approach can be applied to one type of dementia and why the flexibility involved is important.
- Write an account of the most common errors that can be made when trying to meet the needs of people with dementia, and consider the potential impact on the individual.
- Explain how using the person-centred approach can maintain the dignity and rights of the individual.
- Consider whether using holistic care principles is justified against the cost financially, and in manpower.
- Evaluate the approaches currently used to provide dementia care with regards to maintaining and managing health and wellbeing.

Plan

- Do I know what person-centred care is?
- Do I need to interview someone who works specifically in this area so that I can get an overview of the application of the process?

Do

- I know how I want my account to look.
- I can check my work to make sure it is relevant and there are no grammatical errors.

Review

- I can justify my conclusions.
- I know how to reflect on my performance objectively and how I could plan and use my time more efficiently next time.

Websites

www.citizensadvice.org.uk
Citizens Advice: Advice on power of attorney.

www.ageuk.org.uk
Age UK: Information and advice about the types of support available for carers, and facilities in the local area.

www.alzheimers.org.uk
Alzheimer's Society: Information, guidance and advice on all aspects of dementia.

www.alzheimersresearchuk.org
Alzheimer's Research UK: Information, facts and statistics relating to Alzheimer's disease.

www.dementiafriends.org.uk
Dementia Friends: Information about how to get involved in supporting people with dementia and raising awareness of the condition.

www.moneyadviceservice.org.uk
The Money Advice Service: Advice and guidance on financial issues.

www.dementiablog.org/terry-pratchett-on-dementia
Terry Pratchett's dementia blog: Personal insight into author Terry Pratchett's experiences of dementia, and the challenges he faced.

THINK ▶FUTURE

Hannah Matthews

Mental health nurse BSc (Hons)

I became interested in dementia care when I was doing my nurse training. I've always had an interest in the functioning of the mind and I realised that I was also very interested in what support could be given to people who were going to lose their mental capacity. I realised very quickly that dementia was an extraordinary illness. The progression of the deterioration and the inevitability of the prognosis were huge adjustments for the service users to make. It also struck me that the impact on the family of this life-changing disorder could be very profound too.

I knew that I wanted to have a positive impact on the lives of these people and on the lives of their family and friends. I wanted to support them to retain as much of their 'self' as they could for as long as possible. Planning, implementing and reviewing tailored care programmes gives me an immense feeling of satisfaction. I truly believe that I'm not only meeting needs but also enhancing the quality of life of my service users and that of their family and friends. Dementia cannot be cured and the end stage can be very difficult, especially if the individual has been a resident for a long time. I always see it as a privilege to ensure the dignity and respect that everyone deserves at the end of their lives is provided for my service users.

Focusing your skills

Promoting holistic care

People are more than the collection of their symptoms or the diagnosis of their disease.

- The wellbeing of your service user is as important as their health. Remember to consult your service user about their preferences.
- You should be adaptable and responsive to meet the communication needs of your service users. Be alert to their body language.
- Try to stimulate all of the senses – taste, smell, touch, hearing and vision – and use music, old photographs or seeing familiar places to stimulate memories.
- Your service user will have fluctuations in their moods. Be sensitive to their needs, as they may not be able to tell you that they are in pain or depressed.

When it all kicks off

Challenging behaviour requires careful management. It is important to ensure the physical safety of all of your residents. If a service user is being aggressive to another service user, do you put the aggressive service user in their bedroom until they calm down?

- It is important to remain calm; shouting or quick movements can exacerbate the situation.
- Call for assistance from another care giver. The service user that is being subjected to the attack should be taken to a safe place, checked for injuries and reassured.
- If it is safe to do so, check to ensure that the aggressive service user is also unharmed. If not, try to ensure that they cannot cause themselves any further harm by removing breakable or sharp objects, where possible.
- You need to try to find out why the service user was being aggressive and whether any steps can be taken to help them to manage their behaviour.

Getting ready for assessment

Tony is working towards a BTEC Extended National Diploma in Health and Social Care. He was given an assignment for Learning aim A with the following title, 'Evaluate how understanding the different types of dementia can have an impact on the quality of patient care'. He had to write a report for a nursing home self-assessment programme. The submission had to:

▶ include a detailed overview of the different types of dementia

▶ evaluate the impact on patient care of being able to differentiate between the different types of dementia, their prognosis and the varying care needs of the service users.

Tony shares his approaches below.

How I got started

First I broke the question down into sections. I like using mind maps and diagrams to help me make sure that I know what areas to research. I wanted to make sure that I understood the differences between the dementia types, the signs and symptoms as well as the prognosis. So I put them in a table and highlighted the similarities.

I looked back at my notes from classroom discussions and found that I was particularly interested in alternative therapies. I decided to go and interview a reflexologist to see if they had helped anyone with dementia.

I gathered all of my research together and I had a separate page for each type of dementia and the needs of the service user. I used highlighters to pick out the key points of my research and I kept checking back to the question to ensure that I was staying on task. I also decided that I needed another perspective on what I was writing, so I got together with some other members of the group and we pooled our research.

How I brought it all together

I decided to write in the third person, past tense, in order to make the piece seem more detached and formal, as I wanted to write in a style that was authoritative and informative. After that I:

▶ created a spidergram of each characteristic of each type of dementia

▶ wrote up my interview with the reflexologist

▶ researched statistical data from reports on the quality of care for individuals with dementia.

I anonymised the anecdotes that I had gained from the reflexologist and referenced my research using the Harvard system. Finally, I wrote a short summary as a conclusion to the article.

What I learned from the experience

I enjoyed speaking to the reflexologist and found the information really interesting but I spent too much time trying to make that information relevant to the assignment. I should have just included it as supporting data in a paragraph in the body of the text. Next time, I'd have a clearer idea of what I hoped to achieve from the interview and have a list of questions, rather than just hoping that my interest in the subject would allow some relevant data to evolve.

I found it really useful to skill share with my classmates, they had so many different perspectives that I found it really opened my eyes to the alternative ways that there are of approaching the same question.

I liked the style of writing that I adopted for the finished piece as I think that it reflected the formality that I was striving for, however, I should have concentrated more on the operative verbs than on my writing style. I struggled to write the conclusion because I was trying so hard to fit all of the information that I'd learned about reflexology into the assignment. Next time, I must be more disciplined in my approach and not allow myself to indulge my personal interests in specific subjects rather than concentrating on the fundamentals of the assignment.

Think about it

▶ Have you written a plan with timings so you can complete your assignment by the agreed submission date?

▶ Do you have notes on the types of dementia and their prognosis?

▶ Is your information written in your own words and referenced clearly where you have used quotations or information from a book, journal or website?

Assessing Children's Development Support Needs

18

Getting to know your unit

Assessment

You will be assessed by a series of assignments set by your tutor.

Knowing about children and how to support them as they grow and develop are important aspects of working with young people. There are many factors that have impact on growth and development and you will have the opportunity to explore and understand this process. In addition, you will learn about assessment methods so that you can ascertain what stage of development the children might have attained and be able to plan accordingly. You will be able to explore some of the theories about the different areas of development and be able to link these to specific areas of your practice. Learning about, and developing, strategies and ways of supporting children, depending on their individual needs is an important part of this unit.

How you will be assessed

This unit will be assessed by a series of internally assessed tasks set by your tutor. Throughout this unit you will find assessment practices that will help you work towards assessment. Completing these activities will not mean that you have achieved a particular grade, but you will have carried out useful research or preparation that will be relevant when it comes to your final assignment. In order for you to achieve the tasks in your assignment, it is important to check that you have met all of the Pass grading criteria. You can do this as you work your way through the assignment.

If you are hoping to gain a Merit or Distinction, you should also make sure that you present the information in your assignment in the style that is required by the relevant assessment criteria. For example, Merit criteria require you to analyse, assess and effectively plan and implement methods of assessment to identify the children's stages of development. The Distinction criteria require you to justify and evaluate.

The assignment set by your tutor will consist of a number of tasks designed to meet the criteria in the table. This is likely to consist of a written assignment but may also include activities such as the following.

▸ A written piece of work linked to an understanding of growth and development, and the associated theories.

▸ Producing a leaflet to explain about factors that might influence learning and development.

▸ Observations of children from your work experience setting, and an understanding of how children's growth and development might be assessed.

Assessment criteria

This table shows what you must do in order to achieve a **Pass**, **Merit** or **Distinction** grade, and where you can find activities to help you.

Pass	Merit	Distinction
Learning aim **A** Understand patterns, principles and theories that contribute to an understanding of growth and development in children from birth to eight years		
A.P1 Explain patterns of growth and development of selected children of different ages. **Assessment practice 18.1**	**A.M1** Analyse stages of growth and development across different areas for selected children of different ages. **Assessment practice 18.1**	**A.D1** Evaluate the extent to which theories of growth and development can be used to support the selected children's growth and development. **Assessment practice 18.1**
A.P2 Explain principles and theories that contribute to an understanding of children's growth and development. **Assessment practice 18.1**	**A.M2** Assess how theories can be used to identify children's stages of growth and development. **Assessment practice 18.1**	
Learning aim **B** Examine factors that may impact on children's growth and development		
B.P3 Discuss the influence of factors on children's growth and development. **Assessment practice 18.2**	**B.M3** Assess how one area of development affected by factors may impact on other areas of development. **Assessment practice 18.2**	**BC.D2** Justify approaches to assessment used for the early recognition and support for children with differing needs. **Assessment practice 18.2**
Learning aim **C** Explore how assessment is used to identify children's stages of growth and development and their support needs		
C.P4 Explain methods used for the assessment of children's growth and development from birth to eight years. **Assessment practice 18.2**	**C.M4** Effectively plan and implement appropriate methods of assessment to identify the children's stages of development. **Assessment practice 18.2**	**BC.D3** Evaluate the extent to which professionals help children to meet their developmental milestones through the application of the theories of growth and development and use of assessment methods. **Assessment practice 18.2**
C.P5 Plan for and observe children to identify their stages of development. **Assessment practice 18.2**	**C.M5** Assess the methods of observation selected for the assessment of each child's growth and development. **Assessment practice 18.2**	

Getting started

Understanding how children grow and develop is important when working with children. At the end of this unit, you will know how you can contribute to and plan for children's further development in specific areas. You will also understand how observation and assessment of development is valuable in caring for children.

Write a list of factors that might influence or affect growth and development.

A Understand patterns, principles and theories that contribute to an understanding of growth and development in children from birth to eight years

Key terms

Growth – increase in size and weight.

Development – the acquisition of skills and abilities over time.

Patterns of growth and development

Definition of growth and development

The terms **growth** and **development** are often linked together when referring to children, and they are both important for assessing whether a child is progressing at a typical rate. You will be able to understand how they interlink as you move through this unit, but you will begin by considering their separate definitions.

Growth

You will probably be aware that people grow from the moment of conception until they reach maturity. The human embryo cells in the uterus increase in number and take on specific tasks. When the baby is born one of the first checks carried out is to weigh the child and measure their length and the circumference of their head. Often the gender and these measurements of the newborn are the immediate information gathered, after checking that physically everything is all right. Growth is determined by a number of factors, such as genetic inheritance, environmental issues and other influences. In some cases, growth does not progress in the typical way and this will be discussed later in the unit. Babies are routinely weighed and measured to check that they are making progress against an agreed set of norms. Every child is an individual but they will all normally increase in length (height) and weight steadily over the following months and years.

Development

When a baby is born it has certain reflex actions – these are inborn and are not part of the developmental process. Such reflexes include:

▶ suckling and swallowing movements that babies need to feed effectively

▶ hand grasp, when you place your finger in the palm of a baby's hand it will grip your finger.

As babies grow, they acquire certain other abilities and skills. These are usually attained at specific times during their development, and usually in a specific order:

▶ from top to bottom (that is, head first – then body before legs and feet)

▶ inside to out (that is, from the centre to the outer extremities – arms before fingers and legs before feet)

▶ simple to complex (that is, from babbling to using single words to speaking in sentences).

Health professionals check a child's development progress (as well as their growth) throughout childhood. Hearing, eyesight, language acquisition, motor skills and cognitive abilities are checked and recorded at regular intervals. This will initially be carried out by the health visitor and then by the doctor and/or nurse, to check that development is following a typical pattern. It is important always to keep in mind that children are individuals and will develop at different rates and at different times. So long as a child is within the range for typical development then no further screening will be necessary.

Developmental milestones for children between birth and eight years

Milestones

Milestones are important reference points when considering the development of children and you will note that many people use these when asking about a baby or toddler. People will ask if a baby is able to sit unaided, is crawling or is walking. This information allows people to make a judgement as to how development is progressing. Each area of development has separate milestones, and children may or may not reach milestones in line with the expected rate of development (**norms of development**). All children are individuals and there will be variations between children in their patterns of growth and development.

You will see that the main milestones for the development of a child between the ages of zero and eight years have a time frame in which they might be observed and these are documented in Tables 18.1–6.

Areas and aspects of development

The areas of development – physical, cognitive/intellectual, speech/language, emotional and social – are often considered separately. However, you should remember that in the holistic development of the child, they all link together.

Physical development

Physical development relates to anything linked with muscle control and is often referred to in distinct areas, such as fine motor development and gross motor development.

Fine motor development

Fine motor development concerns the small muscles that allow finer, more detailed and deliberate movements. The ones that you will notice most are the movements of the hands and how refined and precise they become. Other small muscles will be developing as well and the muscles in the feet will strengthen to deal with balance and walking. Children will progress from holding a toy with both hands to using one hand and eventually to picking up small objects with finger and thumb. They will also develop skills for holding pencils and crayons and will be able to demonstrate skills for drawing and writing.

Gross motor development

Gross motor development concerns the large muscles of the body. These muscles start to develop quickly, and you will have seen babies kicking their legs and moving their arms. They have been doing this during their development before birth and all mothers will be able to tell you about their baby kicking and moving, often quite vigorously, during pregnancy. As the muscles grow stronger and develop, children move through a developmental sequence. First they are able to lift their head. Later they sit, then crawl, then start to pull themselves into a standing position and 'cruise' around the furniture, eventually they start to walk. Table 18.1 shows the approximate ages and accepted norms of fine and gross motor development.

Key terms

Milestone – significant stage in development.

Norms of development – achievement of milestones at approximate and accepted age ranges by the majority of children.

Discussion

Consider what you have observed in your placement. Discuss with your peers whether you feel there is a gender difference in the age when fine motor skills are developed sufficiently to enable letter formation and detailed drawing.

▶ **Table 18.1** Approximate ages for development of motor skills

Age	Fine motor development	Gross motor development
0–3 months	Reflexes: • sucking • rooting	Moves arms and legs randomly
3–6 months	Plays with fingers Watches hands May hold rattle Reaches for toys Moves objects from one hand to the other Puts objects in mouth	Waves arms Lifts head Lifts arms to indicate a wish to be lifted up Rolls over
9 months	Grasps objects Deliberately releases objects and drops them	Sits unaided More mobile – crawling, shuffling
12 months	Uses finger and thumb pincer grip to pick up small objects Points to objects using index finger Builds a tower with three blocks Scribbles Holds a cup	May stand alone Cruising around furniture May walk unaided
18 months	Develops more precise movements Grasps crayon with palmar grip Builds tower with four to six blocks Turns knobs Puts shapes into a sorter	Walks unaided Walks upstairs with help Climbs onto a sit-on toy Squats
2 years	Begins to draw, tries to copy a circle and dots Uses a spoon to feed self effectively Tries to string large beads	Runs Climbs onto furniture Uses sit-and-ride toys
2.5 years	Developing a hand preference Completes simple jigsaws Developing a tripod grasp (first two fingers and thumb) Puts interlocking blocks together	Runs quickly Kicks a ball Throws a ball Jumps with both feet leaving the ground together Rides a tricycle More confident about stairs
3 years	Washes and dries hands Holds a crayon More confident in drawing a circle Has a definite hand preference for most tasks	Steers and pedals a tricycle Runs forwards and backwards Walks upstairs with confidence Aims when throwing and kicking a ball
3–4 years	Fastens some buttons Uses scissors and cuts out simple shapes Draws a person with head, body and legs Builds using interlocking blocks Builds a tower of nine or ten blocks Makes objects, e.g. snakes using modelling medium	Walks along a line Aims and throws a ball Hops
4–5 years	Forms letters Writes own name Colours in pictures Completes 20-piece jigsaw puzzle	Skips using a rope Runs quickly and avoids obstacles Throws and catches a ball accurately
5–8 years	Cuts out shapes accurately Drawings developing more detail Ties shoelaces Executes refined small muscle activities	Hops, skips and jumps with confidence Balances on a beam Chases and dodges others Rides a bicycle and uses roller skates

Locomotion

Locomotion is the ability to move, particularly from one place to another. It begins with arm and leg movements that can be noted during pregnancy and in newborns. This is followed by rolling and crawling during the first months of independent life. The child is mainly using the large muscles and will repeat the processes until they become quite sophisticated. Rolling over at will and raising the head are precursors to crawling. Once crawling has been mastered, it can be used quite speedily and with a definite purpose. The crawling stage varies considerably and may be missed out in some instances, although this is not the usual pattern. Walking with adult help, or pulling themselves to a standing position and 'cruising' around the furniture is the next stage. Eventually, with adult encouragement and assistance, the infant makes their first tentative steps towards independent walking. It is quite usual for infants to revert to crawling at times, and then to try walking again. Over time, they will become independent and competent in development of their locomotor skills. As the muscles develop and the skills are refined, children are able to climb, run, kick a ball, hop and skip. Children enjoy movement and will take any opportunity to run and climb.

▶ Why is this type of play important for child development?

Balance

Balance is linked to the development of the large muscles in the legs and the small muscles in the feet but also the development of other sensory organs such as the ears and the eyes. Balance is needed when you are still and when on the move. They are known as:

▶ static balance, for example standing on a wall or beam, standing on one leg

▶ dynamic balance, for example when throwing or catching, or when kicking a ball.

Balance is an important aspect of development, allowing greater freedom and confidence when performing tasks. In order for balance techniques to be developed, children need to be able to focus on a given task and maintain their concentration. They need to be aware of their body and have a concept of **spatial awareness**. Developing a good sense of balance also ensures certain safeguards, for example being aware that they are not maintaining balance ensures they will put their hands out to ease the effect of a fall. **Hand-eye coordination** is another factor that helps in the development of balance. Children also need to be able to isolate movement of one or two parts of the body in order to compensate or get back to a balanced position, for example moving one or both arms when walking along a wooden beam.

> ### Key terms
>
> **Spatial awareness** – knowing your location, both in relation to a given space and to other objects around you.
>
> **Hand-eye coordination** – the ability of the visual system to use information taken in through the eyes to organise movement of the hands when carrying out a specific task, such as handwriting or catching a ball.

Coordination

The development of good coordination requires a number of elements to be in place and to work together. These include balance, a sense of rhythm, spatial awareness, auditory awareness and visual awareness.

Coordination enables tasks, such as tying shoe laces or walking up and down stairs, to be carried out with ease. Children who have coordination development difficulties may appear to be clumsy, they may regularly drop things, have difficulty with sports and often have poor handwriting.

Some children present themselves with different challenges, such as walking backwards, climbing and jumping, swinging from ropes and developing a sense of rhythm and movement by listening to music and dancing.

Hand-eye coordination

This is the coordination of specific parts of the body. Its development is necessary for many tasks to be carried out with precision. The eye receives information and the brain guides and directs the hands to accomplish the task, for example writing, picking up an object or catching a ball. Hand-eye coordination is a life skill required for almost everything people do, for example reading, writing, drawing, working with interlocking bricks, getting dressed, playing sports, using scissors and many more activities.

Hint

Think about a toddler looking at a book. Note all the aspects of physical development required to do this.

Extend

Many people find it difficult to balance when walking on a beam or plank. List the skills required to do it effectively.

Intellectual/cognitive development

While you may tend to consider each area of development separately, you must remember that they do not occur in isolation. For children to reach the milestones in cognitive/intellectual development it requires maturity in other areas, for example to complete a jigsaw puzzle, children need thinking skills to solve the problem and physical skills to carry it out. In addition, for children to know their colours, someone will have to have taught them colour recognition and encouraged them. Table 18.2 shows the approximate age of intellectual/**cognitive** development. However, you should remember that development is dependent on other factors, and the experiences of the child.

Key terms

Cognitive – ability to learn, to think, to understand and problem-solve.

▶ **Table 18.2** Approximate age of intellectual cognitive development

Age	Intellectual/cognitive and neurological development
0–3 months	Begins to smile Turns towards sounds Follows objects with eyes
4–6 months	Smiles Laughs and gurgles Explores hands and feet Puts objects in mouth Rolls over Develops palmar grasp Listens, and responds when spoken to
7–12 months	Vocalises some words Places objects in containers Recognises own name Sits unaided Pulls up to stand/walk
1–2 years	Imitates others and their actions Walks, climbs and runs Starts to solve problems Begins pretend play Understands ideas Speaks more words
2–3 years	Learns new skills Language and vocabulary increases Greater control of hands and fingers Gains more independence
3–5 years	Longer attention span Asks many questions Develops strong friendships Shares and takes turns
5–8 years	Very curious Develops an interest in numbers, reading and writing Develops greater confidence Plays cooperatively

Neurological and brain development

At birth, a baby's brain has approximately 100 billion brain cells but it will continue to grow and mature as the baby grows and has new experiences. The **neurons** continue to make new pathways and connections. As the brain matures it goes through two types of process. One is the development of new connections, which depends on the child's developmental processes. The other is termed 'pruning', this involves the neurons that are not used being 'pruned' and disappearing. The early years are a period of great growth and development, and many factors influence the connections that are being made. The brain of a typical 3-year-old is twice as active as that of an adult. Poor maternal nutrition during pregnancy and of the child during its early years can detrimentally affect brain development. Extreme stress in early childhood can affect cognitive and emotional development. As children grow and mature they might be encouraged to share and be kind to other children. In such cases, different neural connections are made in the brain than if they had been encouraged to be selfish and needy.

> **Key terms**
>
> **Neuron** – a nerve cell that processes information through electrical and chemical signals.

Development of abstract concepts

Abstract thought develops over time and children develop at different rates. The ability to think about abstract concepts depends on two basic tools.

1 Previous knowledge or 'hooks' to which children can link or attach new knowledge. For example, it is difficult to explain 'snow' to a child who has never seen it – you might say that it is white, powdery and cold. The child may then link that to knowledge about other powders but to fully understand the properties of snow, it needs to be experienced and touched.

2 Patterns. Initially, the child may need to see the actual objects, especially in mathematics. For example, placing five objects in front of the child and asking them to count them, then removing two and allowing a re-count to determine how many are left. This process needs to be practised and a 4-year-old child may always need the objects, but an 8-year-old child is likely to have developed the patterns necessary to carry out this process without needing to see the objects.

There needs to be a balance of knowledge and practice before the process is fully developed.

Thinking skills

Thinking skills are the mental processes used to make sense of experiences, or to solve problems and make decisions.

There are three distinct processes involved.

1 Gathering information. You do this using your senses – seeing, touching, hearing and smelling. You are also able to retrieve information from previous experiences that have been stored in your memory banks.

2 Understanding. You can organise information and form clear concepts, which helps link similar experiences together.

3 Productive thinking. You can then use information and understanding to create, analyse, evaluate and make decisions.

There are thinking skills programmes, and children who are encouraged to develop in this way appear to be more challenged, will work harder and achieve more.

Memory

Memory is vital to intellectual/cognitive development and is fundamental to aspects of emotional and social development, for example self-image and self-esteem. When adults are asked to remember their early childhood, recall tends to be sparse. However, it is obvious that recognition memory is extremely good in very young children. They are accurate in remembering people's faces, especially their main carers, their toys, surroundings and recurring events. Also, memory of familiar things and people tends to be very good. Children cannot read, write or draw without knowing shapes and sounds from their memory. Similarly, you build up memories as to how you act and behave in certain situations.

There are three stages to memory:

1 encoding – organising the information to be stored

2 storage – keeping the information

3 retrieval – the ability to recall the information.

You remember using information from all your senses, and sometimes a particular taste or smell makes you recall events and experiences from your childhood. There are strong links between language and memory and that could explain why people do not seem to be able to recall memories before they developed language.

Speech, language and communication

Very young children learn the rules of **language** and conversation from interaction with adults. Babies cradled in the arms of their carers can be observed to maintain eye contact as their carer talks to them, or makes friendly, soothing noises. When the carer stops, the infant may start making cooing or gurgling noises in return, when the baby stops the adults will often respond and so a sequence of vocalisation takes place. The beginnings and rules of conversation are being formed.

Speech

Children start to speak and use recognisable words at around the one-year stage. Prior to that, children are developing sounds and gaining control of the tongue and mouth (see Table 18.3).

Language

The structure of language falls into three main categories.

1 Phonology – relates to the sounds of language, e.g. c, b, m. It is important to be able to identify the different sounds, as cat, mat and bat all have distinct and different meanings. Phonics is about using the sounds to build up different words.

2 Semantics – relates to the words or units of language, and how meaning can be altered by adding another unit, e.g. adding 'dis' to 'appear' changes the word to its opposite meaning.

3 Syntax – the rules of sentence structure and how words are placed within the sentence. If the words are not in the correct order, it can alter the whole meaning of a sentence, for example 'the boy chased the dog' has a totally different meaning to 'the dog chased the boy'. The same words have been used only their order in the sentence has changed.

Communication

Communication is about receiving information from and transmitting information to other people in a variety of ways. It may be through pictures, symbols, verbally, musically or by touch.

Key terms

Language – the use of words in a structured way.

Communication – the ability to exchange information in a variety of ways, e.g. speaking, writing or using other media.

Speech – the ability to express yourself through clear, distinct and understandable sounds.

▶ **Table 18.3** Approximate age of language development

Age	Language development
Pre-linguistic stage	
6 weeks	Cooing and starting to develop control of lips and tongue.
6–9 months	Babbling – blending vowels and consonants – ba, ma, da.
9–10 months	Echolalia (repetition of speech by a child learning to talk) – mamama, dadada, bababa.
Linguistic stage	
12 months	First words – often unclear.
12–18 months	Holophrases (single words) but tone may denote meaning.
18–24 months	Two word utterances, 'telegraphic speech', using key words, e.g. mama gone.
2–3 years	Rapid development and use of language. Learning many new words. Use of plurals. More complex structure. Use of sentences.
3–4 years	Sentences become more complex and longer. Vocabulary continues to increase.
4–5 years	Mastery and fluency of language – begins to understand the basic rules of grammar for plurals and past tense. Becoming more fluent in speech.
5–6 years	Becomes more fluent and likes to experiment with sounds.
6–8 years	Masters more complex language use and sentence structure. Use of language is a key feature in the development of reading and writing skills.

Ⅱ PAUSE POINT   What are your earliest memories? What was your approximate age?

Hint   List the stages and processes required to remember events from the past.

Extend   Research the link between the use of language and memory.

Emotional

Emotional development is about your feelings and how you express them. It begins at a very young age and develops more positively if good strong attachments have been made. It is often linked to social development but also includes a number of other categories, for example independence, which help to make up your emotional stability and development. Table 18.4 shows the approximate ages and stages of emotional development.

▶ **Table 18.4** Approximate age of emotional development

Age	Emotional development
0–3 months	Emotions initially linked to physical needs, e.g. crying when hungry. Children gradually recognise their carers and stop being distressed when they see, smell or hear them.
3–6 months	Emotional development linked to attachments, children start to develop their self-image. Gain in self-confidence with praise and positive responses.
6–12 months	Infants play more and are more mobile. Become more aware of emotions and interactions with others. Enjoy positive responses from carers and other people.
1–2 years	Realisation of being an individual in their own right, develop self-image. Start to use 'me', 'my' and 'mine' a great deal in language, and refer to themselves by name. May be possessive with toys. Checks adult's face for signs of approval/warning when unsure of actions. Plays alongside other children rather than cooperatively, may start to develop friendships with other children.

Age	Emotional development
2–3 years	Self-image and self-concept continue to develop. Experiences a wide range of emotions – anger, fear, frustration. May have tantrums when tired or frustrated. Starts to imitate others. Wants to 'win', to be first at things. Starts using strategies to control emotions, e.g. favourite toy as a comfort when upset. Increased physical ability aids independence in self-help skills.
4–5 years	Has usually established a secure self-concept. Being accepted by other children is important. May show empathy regarding other people's feelings. Understands many social rules.
6–8 years	Friendships are very important. Becoming better at controlling emotions. Compare themselves to others.

Self-identity

The development of self-image is a gradual process. Children begin to recognise themselves at around 18–24 months of age. They realise that they are individuals in their own right and there is a well-known test that can be carried out to show this. When you place a very young child in front of a mirror they may not realise that they are looking at themselves. If you put a mark on the child's nose using blusher or lipstick and they touch their nose or try to rub the mark off, they have reached the stage when they realise that they are looking at themselves (their own image) in the mirror. **Self-identity** is how they see themselves, for example what they look like, their gender, who they are in relation to other people they know. Children gradually build up a picture of what they look like and the attributes they have.

▶ Is this another baby?

Self-esteem

Self-esteem is linked to self-confidence and comes from several sources, for example friendships, relationships with care-givers, playing with other children, school and own temperament. Children should be presented with activities and tasks that they can

Key terms

Self-identity – awareness of your own unique identity; the potential and qualities you possess.

Self-esteem – respect for own self, self-worth.

carry out and succeed in doing. If a child always fails, then they are likely to develop low self-esteem. Remember that success breeds success. It makes people feel better, and it improves both their self-confidence and their self-esteem.

Peers play a great part in this process. If children are accepted, included and enjoy playing together then their self-esteem will be higher. However, if a child is bullied, teased, belittled and left out, then their self-esteem is likely to be low.

Attachment

Infants form bonds of attachment when they have strong positive feelings for other people. The natural first instance of this is with their mother. There are certain factors that have been found to help with attachment, such as:

▶ skin-to-skin contact – many maternity hospitals and units encourage mothers to lie their newborn baby directly on their skin for at least an hour

▶ eye-to-eye contact – gazing and looking at their parent's face

▶ familiar voices – particularly the mother's voice, even before birth

▶ familiar smells – breast milk and the mother.

This attachment need is so strong that it is linked to the baby thriving and to social development, as children with strong, positive family attachments tend to show affection to others. They will feel secure and know that there are people around them who care for them.

Independence

In order to foster independence in children, there need to be positive attitudes of love and support. Good parenting allows greater freedom, encourages curiosity, helps teach and develop new skills, and provides emotional care. Some very young children can be encouraged to make informed choices, such as about which story they would like, which songs to sing and which T-shirt to wear. Encouraging self-help skills, such as feeding and dressing themselves, also presents children with some responsibility which is closely linked to independence.

Moral development

Moral development is about learning the difference between right and wrong. It is generally thought that the development of morality is based on experiences, the environment in which you live and your emotional, cognitive and social development. Although they do not yet understand right and wrong, between 18 and 24 months of age infants start to be aware that there is a certain degree of disapproval for some types of behaviour. For example, taking a toy from another child is wrong. It is believed that children initially learn to avoid disapproval rather than they understand why it is wrong. Between the ages of 3 and 8 years, children are starting to think about other people and their reactions to what is happening. Children start to empathise with others, and can become upset at what they perceive as unfairness. Praise is very powerful and can be used effectively to develop positive attitudes and behaviour patterns.

Social development

Social development is about relationships with others, how you develop friendships and the attributes that attract you to other people. Individuals require specific skills to relate to other people and to understand them, their motives and intentions, and what is defined as acceptable and unacceptable behaviour. Social development is linked very closely with emotional development. When people are very young they learn about relationships and interactions from those they are very close to and these are very important parts of the developmental process.

▶ **Table 18.5** Approximate age of social development

Age	Social development
0–6 months	Focuses on the human face. Smiles, eye contact. Likes being held and spoken to.
6–12 months	Recognises emotions in others. Likes being held and playing games. Wary of strangers. Imitates actions, e.g. clapping.
1–3 years	Joins in simple games. Likes company – does not like people being out of sight, tries to follow if adult leaves the room.
3–5 years	Friendships begin. Will take turns and share. Will comfort another child in distress. Understands some rules.
5–8 years	Enjoys using rules. Starts to realise difference between purpose and accident. Protective of younger children. Stronger friendship groups.

Friendships

The ability to form friendships is an important aspect of social development, which starts with the relationships with care-givers. Children notice facial expressions and begin to understand body language. These interactions lead children to believe that the experiences are positive, rewarding and enjoyable. They will begin to interact with other children and will imitate, follow and play alongside them. These early interactions form the building blocks for deeper relationships and these emerging friendships are often encouraged by carers. Deeper attachments may develop.

Cooperation

Children develop the skills for working together as they move through different stages of play. They observe interactions and relationships develop and as they move from parallel play (just playing alongside rather than with other children) to more associative and cooperative play, they will explore and interact more actively. They start to work together to solve problems and their play becomes more intense and focused. As active learners, they will develop and learn best when they feel safe and valued, especially when working with someone else towards a common goal. Children learn that there is much to be gained from cooperation, such as sharing and helping each other.

❚❚ PAUSE POINT Why is bonding or attachment so important?

 How might you encourage children to work cooperatively?

  Research and create a list of ways in which you can positively promote self-confidence or self-esteem in a child.

Principles of growth and development

Rates of growth and development vary between children

Growth and development follow a definite sequence but there may be significant variations within that pattern, and the rate of development between children can also vary. When you consider the milestone charts, you will notice that they allow a wide range of time for the development of various skills and abilities. However, significant delay is likely to be investigated and may be monitored over time. There are a number of reasons for variations in growth and development which will be considered in greater detail later. Reasons include genetic inheritance, illness or accident, environmental issues and nutrition.

How growth can impact on each of the areas of development

Growth and development are interrelated and co-dependent. Growth is essential for the development of physical skills and fine muscle control. The ability to crawl is linked to the strength of a child's muscles. Once the children can stand they are able to develop the skills required for walking. Fine motor control is linked to the growth of the bones and muscles in the hands and wrist.

The development of speech is assisted by the development and growth of the tongue as a muscle, the ability to control the movement of the lips and the emergence of the teeth. Once speech and language develops and children can be understood, this is reinforced by positive reactions and so the child continues to vocalise.

Social and emotional development is linked to growth as the child feels secure and capable. Children's development is often associated with what is expected of them, for example there may be greater expectations of taller children who may be expected to dress themselves and fasten shoes as these are skills linked to physical development. Children will act in direct relation to how adults respond to them. It is impossible to separate growth from development.

Patterns of typical development

Typical development follows the milestones in each of the specific areas of development. Most children develop skills and abilities in similar patterns or sequences and at similar ages. It is important to have an understanding of the milestones of development and the order in which they are attained. You will notice that the milestones are presented in general time frames or 'windows' rather than at a specific age. However, as development follows a sequence or pattern it is possible to predict what the next stage is likely to be and you will be able to plan for it and provide appropriate support. For example, when children start to pull themselves into a standing position and 'cruise' round the furniture, the milestone predicts that walking will follow quite soon afterwards.

To encourage the developmental process, it is important that children receive love and attention, that there is interaction through songs and rhymes and stories, and that adults are consistent about behaviour and provide positive attitudes.

> **Key term**
>
> **Typical** – showing the characteristics expected in a particular group of people.

Different areas of development advance at different rates

As a child matures it can be quite noticeable that different areas of development move forward at different rates. This may be gender related, especially towards puberty when girls seem to grow taller and mature more quickly at around 11 years old. Similar rates of development occur in much younger children, and parents and carers will notice rapid improvements or changes in development at different times.

- Physical development – growth spurts are evident and are often more noticeable as clothes cease to fit properly, which is particularly noticeable in boys. Children are generally very active and become expert at dodging obstacles, especially when running.
- Cognitive/intellectual development – the child's brain develops at a rapid rate and is ready to absorb new information. Development depends on the influence of parents and carers and other people and is very much affected by experience.
- Language development – noticeable especially when the social contacts increase, for example at school, and there is a vocabulary explosion around the four to five-year marker. Children enjoy the sounds of language and as they develop friendships the use of language becomes more important.
- Emotional development – closely linked to family life and other experiences. It becomes more obvious that children are coping better with emotional factors and do not have temper and behavioural outbursts linked to tiredness and frustration. Friendships start at around the time a child attends nursery or preschool and flourish in the months leading up to reception intake in school.
- Social development – greatly influenced by contact with others and so improvements in interaction are often more noticeable when children mix with other children and adults, as well as at home.

Development is holistic

It is sometimes helpful to consider the different areas of development separately but you must always look at the child as a whole, not just an accumulation of separate parts. There is a great degree of co-dependence when carrying out the simplest of tasks. For example sorting objects into different colour categories will require:

- fine motor skills to pick up the objects
- cognitive development to realise that all the blue objects need to be together (same for other colours)
- hand-eye coordination to place them appropriately
- appropriate level of language development to explain or talk about the process.

This relationship concerning all areas of development, together with maturity in growth, is vital for the child to develop into an accomplished and well-balanced person.

Key term

Holistic – everything is part of the whole, dealing with the whole not a specific part. (The whole is greater than the sum of its parts.)

Reflect

Remember, do not look at areas of development in isolation but always consider the 'whole' child. This holistic approach will form an important aspect of your work and contact with children.

Case study

Just a quiet activity

Jarinder, who is 6 years old, is sitting quietly in a chair with her favourite book, which she has chosen from her collection of books in her bedroom. She comes downstairs with it and is reading it and smiling at some of the illustrations. Jarinder carefully turns the pages and is obviously enjoying what she is doing. After a while, she gets up to find some paper and coloured pencils, lies on the floor and begins to draw a picture, copying one from her book. She concentrates very hard and is continuously looking from her picture back to the book to check her progress. When she finishes, she tidies everything away. Jarinder shows her mother the finished picture and tells her about her 'quiet time'.

Check your knowledge

1. Which areas of development are required for Jarinder to carry out these tasks?
2. Make a list of the skills Jarinder is using.
3. Is Jarinder within the expected norms of typical development?

Atypical development

You have considered the patterns of typical development but it is essential to note that not all children will follow them exactly. There will be children who require additional and specific support in their development and it is important that **atypical** development is identified quickly so that support can be provided as early as possible.

Atypical development covers both delayed and enhanced development, and includes everything that falls outside the realm of typical development.

> **Key term**
>
> **Atypical** – irregular, not usual for the group or type.

Global delay

Some children have a developmental pattern that shows delay across all areas. When the overall development is mapped against the norms of development and shows a developmental pattern that is of a much younger child in all areas (for example a 5 year old who has a developmental pattern of a 2 year old) then their development is described as globally delayed. The example is an exaggeration as this type of delay would have been identified much earlier.

Specific delay

Some children show delay in one area of development but this may impact on other areas, as Table 18.6 shows.

▶ **Table 18.6** Areas of developmental delay

Area of delayed development	Potential impact on other areas of development
Physical	May result in restricted social contacts, with fewer opportunities to interact. In turn, this may impact on speech and language development.
Emotional	May impact on behaviour and may result in social/emotional insecurity, the child may be less confident and less able to concentrate.
Social	May lead to fewer opportunities to engage in physical play and also fewer opportunities to communicate with others.
Cognitive/intellectual	May struggle with language development as this is closely linked to cognitive development. In turn, this may affect reading, writing and mathematical ability.
Language	May impact on cognitive and social development, as the child may be frustrated due to inability to communicate effectively with peers. May also affect behaviour patterns.

Children who are gifted or talented or able in one or more areas of development

Gifted children show an advanced progression in specific areas, usually intellectual/cognitive and language development. They have an enhanced academic ability and reach the cognitive milestones early. They may also have a greater ability for memory, they may demonstrate early reading and writing development, and have a thirst for knowledge. These children may still need to play and be accepted at their physical stage of development but are often treated as much older. Many children classed as gifted feel isolated as their behaviour and ability levels are different.

Children deemed to be talented have an enhanced ability that relates to skills or practical interests, for example they may be talented in musical ability, in specific sports or in developing artistic abilities. They are often extremely focused and may spend a great deal of time practising and enjoying their given talent.

When you are observing children and assessing their development, it is important that you always check against the norms of development and do not jump to conclusions that are not evidence based.

If a child is showing signs of enhanced or delayed development, it is best for parents and carers to seek advice from professionals such as doctors, health visitors, learning disability coordinators, speech and language therapists or physiotherapists.

PAUSE POINT

Why is it important to recognise delayed or enhanced development early?

Hint Provide some examples that differentiate between gifted and talented.

Extend Why is understanding the milestones in all development areas important? How does this help identify delayed or enhanced development?

Theories of development

There are many theories of how development occurs and how it can be helped and promoted or why and how delay occurs. Some of the more well-known theories are listed below and they may help you understand and plan for the further development of children in your care.

Cognitive development

Jean Piaget (1896–1980)

Piaget suggested that development in children happened in stages (see Table 18.7). He had a great influence on early years and education settings. His theory was based on his beliefs regarding how people's brains process information and how their behaviour changes as a result. He believed that children are active learners and that active play enables children to discover new things and develop new concepts. He also put forward the idea that there are specific processes that children go through in order to learn. These are:

▶ assimilation – new information is absorbed into the child's existing understanding

▶ accommodation – information is modified or adapted to account for the new experiences and knowledge

▶ adaptation – adapting ideas and concepts through assimilation and accommodation

▶ equilibrium – a balance of existing and new concepts as the child makes sense of its environment, linked to the development of schemas (ideas and concepts) and patterns of behaviour.

The development of these schemas may be observed in very young children, for example observing a child painting. The child may produce a series of vertical lines in different colours. If you observe other aspects of their play you may note that they are stacking objects on top of each other, building towers. You may observe other patterns of behaviour with similar themes running through them, for example horizontal lines and placing toys in a line, circular patterns and enclosing objects (placing objects inside each other). Children developing this enclosing schema may paint a picture and then 'enclose' it with more paint over the top.

Piaget suggested that there were certain stages that children moved through as they develop skills and attributes, as shown in Table 18.7.

▶ **Table 18.7** Piaget's stages of development

Age	Stage of development	Characteristics of the stage
0–2 years	Sensorimotor	Children are learning by using their senses and developing greater physical control.
		In the early months, learning is from reflex actions such as grasping and sucking.
		Initially, a child will not look for an object if it is removed but at around six months old, they will search for the object even if it is out of sight. This is known as object permanence.
2–7 years	Pre-operational	During this stage, children start to use symbols – one object taking the place of another, e.g. small toys may be used to represent food in the 'home corner'. This will eventually mean that symbols, such as specific marks on paper, will represent words and a child will be able to develop the skills required for reading and writing.
		Animism is a further example at this stage of development – children attribute feelings to inanimate objects, e.g. 'naughty table', if they bump into it.
		Children are considered to be egocentric and only able to see things from their own point of view – it is difficult for a child at this stage to feel empathy with or sympathy for another person.
		Children are unable to conserve, to recognise a constant factor even if the pattern or shape is different. Conservation only develops towards the end of this stage.
7–11 years	Concrete operational	Children can conserve.
		They can solve mental problems but may occasionally use physical prompts, e.g. counters or fingers.
		They understand and like rules.
11–15+ years	Formal operational	Children engage in abstract thought.
		They work through logical processes.

Research

Research Piaget's conservation experiments for mass and volume. You might like to try these experiments with children aged 3–4 years old. Record your findings.

Piaget carried out many different experiments to substantiate his theories and he firmly believed that children learn best through 'hands on' experiences and discovery play. Readiness is essential as children's thought processes need to be ready before they can move on to the next stage.

Reflect

Encouraging children to discover information and experience things for themselves is much more effective than being told about them.

Lev Vygotsky (1896–1934)

Vygotsky was a social constructivist and, as such, he believed that cognitive development was linked to the role that adults and other children play in children's learning processes. The social environment and the experiences a child has are very important for learning to take place. Being with other people helps children to acquire new skills and concepts. It is important to spend time with children encouraging them, showing them how to do a task, such as doing a simple jigsaw puzzle, talking to them, praising and generally helping them complete the task.

Vygotsky suggested that the stage of ability that a child has attained is the zone of actual development. He also believed that children have skills and concepts that are emerging or almost there. He termed the gap between what they currently can do and what they might be able to achieve with support the zone of proximal development.

Zone of Proximal Development

What might be achieved with adult support and encouragement

Zone of Actual Development

▶ **Figure 18.1** Vygotsky's development zones.

Information processing theory

The information processing theory considers the mental processes of how people learn. There has been much research in this area of study. As children grow older their ability to process information improves, but it is thought that children process information differently from adults. Memory plays an important part in this process, and past experiences enhance their ability to solve new problems as they are able to draw on similar experiences that have already happened. Children do not have a large bank of such experiences and, as a result, the younger the child the longer it takes to process the information and solve new problems. It appears that the time taken to process information is linked to intelligence, and that children with high cognitive levels seem to be good at remembering past events and experiences. You have already looked at the importance that memory plays in intellectual/cognitive development. There is a great deal of ongoing research into this field of work.

PAUSE POINT

When you have been in a work experience placement, have you noticed children engaged in discovery play?

> Hint

See Piaget's pre-operational stage. Observe a group of children within that age range and note if they are using symbols.

> Extend

Research Jerome Bruner's theory of learning and 'scaffolding'. Note any similarities with the work of Vygotsky.

Behaviourism

John B Watson (1879–1958)

Watson applied his theory of behaviourism to child development. He suggested that a child's behaviour is shaped by their environment and nurture rather than by their genetic make-up and genetic inheritance (nature). The nature versus nurture debate is ongoing in child psychology. Watson is famous for stating that he could take a child and train them to become a specialist in any area. He believed that environmental forces and conditioning can greatly influence what type of person the child would become.

> **Key terms**
>
> **Operant conditioning** – learning based on reinforcement following an initial behaviour.
>
> **Reinforcement** – a process of encouraging, strengthening or establishing a pattern of behaviour.

> **Research**
>
> Research Watson's work known as the 'Little Albert' experiment.

Burrhus Frederic (B.F.) Skinner (1904–1990)

Skinner suggested that individuals are all active in the learning process and that they learn by exploring their environment and altering their behaviour patterns based on the consequences of their actions (**operant conditioning**). He believed that the consequences fell into three main categories of **reinforcement**.

1 Positive reinforcers – these are likely to help with the repetition of behaviour intended to gain something that the child wants. He suggested that this was the most efficient way of encouraging new behaviour, and that positive reinforcers could take the form of positive attention, treats, praise or stickers. Attention is very powerful and can inadvertently be used to reinforce undesirable behaviour, for example a child might misbehave to gain attention.

2 Negative reinforcers – these may help with a repeat of behaviour intended to prevent a negative impact, such as using goggles/eye protectors to prevent injury from debris.

3 Punishers – these are likely to stop the child repeating some patterns of behaviour.

A primary reinforcer is one that provides instant gratification, for example praise or a small gift.

A secondary reinforcer is not instant but is something that the child has learned can be beneficial, for example, money or a promise of something they want.

It has also been shown that reinforcers are more powerful if used unpredictably rather than every time a particular behaviour occurs – an exception to this might be the use of praise. Delayed reinforcement is less effective, for example if provided at the end of the week.

Albert Bandura (b. 1925)

Bandura developed his social learning theory as he felt that children learn a great deal by observing what others do and then copying those actions. He carried out a series of experiments to confirm his ideas that children learn a great deal by imitation and that what you observe is more powerful than what you are told. This has far-reaching implications for carers and childcare workers alike. If a child considers that you are a role model they will imitate what you do rather than what you say. For example, if you tell children not to throw rubbish away in the street but then you discard a sweet wrapper, they are more likely to copy your actions than listen to your words. Visual learning has more impact than verbal.

> **Research**
>
> Research Bandura's experiments with Bobo dolls. Make a note about the differences of the three groups he observed.

Emotional and social development

John Bowlby (1907–1990)

Bowlby carried out much of his research into emotional attachment after the Second World War, when he was asked to look at the varying emotional and behavioural effects on children brought up in a range of institutions, such as orphanages. He found that although physical needs were adequately taken care of, there was evidence of psychological damage due to the lack of bonding and **attachment**. He considered the lives of these children and found that most had been separated from their mothers and families at an early age. Bowlby felt that there was a pattern in the way the children reacted. As children grow older and become more mature they are more ready to accept separation and many individuals choose to move away from home in their late teens for a variety of reasons, for example to study at college/university. However, babies and toddlers find separation from their main carer very difficult and traumatic and Bowlby proposed that they were suffering from **separation anxiety**.

> **Key terms**
>
> **Attachment** – a special bond or relationship with other people.
>
> **Separation anxiety** – distress as a result of being absent from someone they are attached to.

Case study

Being nearby

Jamie is 18 months old and loves to explore and play in the garden, especially when his mother is tidying the plants and generally neatening up the area. He is content playing with his toys but likes to be able to see his mother. She keeps an eye on Jamie to ensure that he is safe and enjoys chatting to him while he is playing.

On one occasion, Jamie's mum has to go out for a short while and so she arranges for a neighbour to come to look after Jamie. Jamie knows the neighbour well, as she regularly calls round for coffee and he has always played quite happily while his mother and the neighbour chat.

However, a few moments after his mother leaves, Jamie becomes distressed and starts to cry. He is initially comforted but keeps looking around, crying and asking for his mother. When Jamie's mum returns, he immediately goes to her and wants to be picked up and cuddled. Once this happens, he very quickly settles and continues to play.

Check your knowledge

1 Are there any indications that Jamie is securely attached?

2 Why did he become upset when left with the neighbour?

3 What term is used to explain what happened?

4 What does his reaction on his mother's return tell you about their relationship?

Bowlby believed that babies need to form one main attachment – usually to the mother, but this could also be to a main care-giver. He believed that this attachment needs to be developed and firmly established within the first year. Prolonged separation in infancy from this person could result in psychological damage. This attachment is not only a way of providing for the physical needs of the child but provides the emotional ties for constant and consistent support. He also stated that children separated from their carers might have difficulty forming deep and lasting relationships later in life. Although Bowlby focused mainly on maternal attachment he had not fully considered other and multiple attachments. Work in this area was explored more fully by Michael Rutter.

Michael Rutter (b.1933)

In the 1970s and 80s, Rutter carried out a great deal of research and began to question some of Bowlby's findings. Although he agreed with much of Bowlby's work, he felt it did not go far enough, and was focused mainly on children and adolescents with problems. Rutter's research showed that children are able to form multiple attachments rather than just the main attachment to the mother. He concluded that it was beneficial to form these attachments. In addition, he suggested that the quality of care and the nature of the separation were major factors in the reactions of the child to these events. He believed that forming attachments was a valuable and necessary process for the mental and cognitive stability of the child. However, if this did not happen then compensatory factors could be implemented to improve the wellbeing of individuals. Rutter was very involved with programmes for improving the development of children found in the orphanages of Romania following the Ceausescu regime. Many of these children were exposed to loving relationships and stimulating environments, and as a result their intellectual development improved considerably.

ⅠⅠ PAUSE POINT Have you noticed young children becoming upset when separated from their parents? How does this link to Bowlby's work?

> Hint   Think about the criticisms and limitations of Bowlby's work.
>
> Extend   How did Rutter extend Bowlby's work? What additional evidence did he determine in the process of attachment theory?

Sigmund Freud (1856–1939)

Freud developed the psychosexual stages of development theory. He suggested that there are three parts to the personality: the id, the ego and the superego.

▶ The id – the instinctive part of the personality, it is driven by need or desire and is often thought of as selfish and without thought for others. Meeting the id's need is followed by gratification.

▶ The ego – involved in planning how to meets the id's needs and desires, e.g. an infant smiling or crying.

▶ The superego – develops later and is often thought of as the conscience and is linked to self-esteem.

> **Research**
>
> Research Freud's theories of the id, ego and superego. Do you think these theories can explain behaviour?

As Freud developed the concept of the id, he suggested that people's main drives are sexual and aggressive and that the energy behind these is referred to as the libido. He believed that there are five stages of psychosexual behaviour.

Erik Erikson (1902–1994)

Erikson was influenced by Freud's work but did not feel that people's personalities are fixed but that they change throughout the course of their lives. He suggested that the stages of personality development are life stages, linked to social changes. Erikson proposed that at each stage individuals face a dilemma or conflict and that the outcome will determine how their personality develops.

▶ **Table 18.8** Erikson's stages of personality development

Age	Stage	Description
0–1 years	Basic trust *versus* Mistrust	Trying to decide whether people are safe and friendly or hostile.
2–3 years	Autonomy *versus* Shame	Exploring the environment and trying to do things for themselves. Moving out of nappies.
4–5 years	Initiative *versus* Guilt	Ability to plan and carry out actions. Needing to learn more about their gender role.
6–12 years	Industry *versus* Inferiority	Starting and establishing themselves in school. Starting to compare themselves to others.
13–18 years	Identity *versus* Confusion	Needing to develop their own identity and be seen as separate from their parents.

Abraham Maslow (1908–1970)

Maslow developed a theory that has become known as the hierarchy of needs. He suggested that a person's basic needs must be met before they can move to a higher order of needs. Figure 18.2 shows that physiological and safety needs must be met before social and cognitive needs. Maslow was interested in understanding behaviour and motivation and studied groups of high achievers.. Children cannot learn, that is develop cognitive skills, unless their physical and emotional needs have been met.

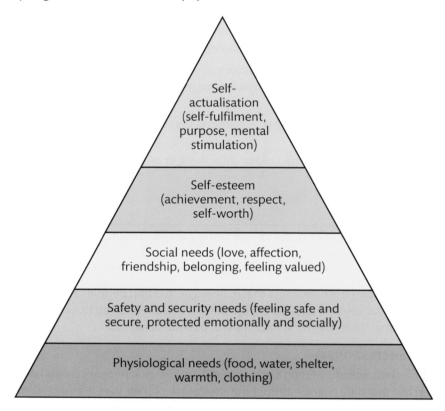

▶ **Figure 18.2** Maslow's hierarchy of needs.

Susan Harter (b. 1939)

Harter carried out research into aspects of social and emotional development, particularly into the concept of self-esteem. Self-image or self-identity is the way a person regards themselves, for example, gender, where they live, height and what they look like. The development of self-image also takes into account the reactions of other people and what is said about us. Children note how people talk to them and how they are treated. If children are liked and loved this helps to promote a positive self-image, whereas if they are continuously criticised they will feel that they are not good enough. It is important for young children to be praised for themselves as well as for their actions.

People also have a view of what they would want to be like – their ideal self. Many individuals desire to be slightly different in some way, for example a bit taller, a bit slimmer, or more active. The concept of the ideal self is developed from the messages they pick up from other people, such as carers, tutors and other children, about what is important and valued. Children also absorb messages from television and other sources that reinforce an image of the 'ideal child'. Harter's model indicates that the closer the self-image is to the ideal self then the higher their self-esteem. It is quite usual and normal for there to be a difference between the self-image and the ideal self.

Moral development

Lawrence Kohlberg (1927–1987)

Kohlberg built on Piaget's theory of moral development and also suggested three levels of moral development, sub-divided into stages (as shown in Table 18.9).

▶ **Table 18.9** Kohlberg's stages of moral development

Stage and age	Example
Pre-conventional level (6–13 years) Stage 1	Punishment and obedience – linked to a behaviourist approach, where actions are followed by consequences, with positive or negative reinforcement.
Stage 2	Individualism, instrumental purpose and change. A realisation that to repeat 'good' actions will lead to reward and to avoid 'bad' actions that will lead to punishment. This leads to wishing to help people and an acceptance that this behaviour might be reciprocated.
Conventional level (13–16 years) Stage 3	This is a development of thought about what is acceptable and what is not. Good child – motives are important and people are meant to help each other.
Stage 4	Law and order, orientation. The child becomes more aware of society and what is right and wrong. Children develop an ideal that they need to keep the law and abide by regulations.
Post conventional level (16–20 years) Stage 5	Social contract – fairness in society, and developing an understanding that rules can sometimes be broken if they are deemed to be unfair.
Stage 6	Not everyone reaches this stage as it relates to people who are extremely principled and will not compromise under any circumstance, even if their lives are threatened, e.g. Mother Teresa of Calcutta or Martin Luther King.

Jean Piaget (1896–1980)

Piaget saw moral development as happening in three stages.

▶ Pre-moral (0–4 years) – children are learning right from wrong and are becoming aware of their own actions. They are also starting to be aware of the reactions of the adults around them.

▶ Moral realism (4–7 years) – moral development is greatly influenced by the adults the child comes into contact with on a regular basis. The child's judgement very much depends on what they think adults would expect.

▶ Moral relativism (8–11 years) – children become preoccupied with justice and following rules. They have a concept of fairness and can become very upset by a sense of perceived unfairness. They become more aware of motives for actions and develop a realisation that treating people the same is not always fair.

According to Piaget, young children believe that the 'size of the crime' is the main aspect rather than the intent, for example accidentally dropping a plate of cakes is much worse than stealing one cake. It takes time for children to develop an awareness of intent.

Language development

There are two main theorists associated with language development, Noam Chomsky and Lev Vygotsky.

▶ **Figure 18.3** How might the child regard this as part of their moral development according to Piaget?

Noam Chomsky (b.1928)

Chomsky believes that the ability to learn language is innate, and is part of people's natural instincts. Other theorists, such as B.F. Skinner, thought that language acquisition comes from the way children are nurtured, and that correct usage is reinforced by praise and repetition.

Chomsky's theory explains how language acquisition follows a set pattern in development. He suggests that people have a non-physical structure in the brain that allows for the development of language. He called this a Language Acquisition Device (LAD). He suggested that the brain is programmed to work out the complexities of language and this would explain how children can learn language quickly and become very efficient in its use. Children can very quickly learn the rules of language, for example children realise that a plural usually requires an 's' to be added to a word, and so they will talk about 'foots' and 'mouses', although they will not have heard them in use. They also quickly adapt when they become used to and hear the more familiar 'feet' and 'mice'.

Lev Vygotsky (1896–1934)

Vygotsky suggested that language and thought begin as two different entities. He believed that a baby's babbling is not linked to thinking. He felt that it is around the age of two that language and thought come together, allowing the child to use language to help them think.

He also suggested that people have two different types of speech:
1 internal speech, which helps them to think by organising patterns of thought (for example 'I'll do that later.')
2 external speech, which is used in communication with others.

Vygostsky felt that between the ages of 2 and 7 years these two types of speech blend together and children will often give running commentaries about what they are doing. He referred to this as egocentric thought and speech.

Ⅱ PAUSE POINT   Have you tried to learn another language? What helped you when you were trying to master it?

> **Hint**   You may see children incorrectly adapting language rules (plurals and past tenses, e.g. sheeps or bringed). Which theorist does this more closely reflect?

> **Extend**   Research Charles Cooley's 'Looking Glass Self' theory and note any links to Susan Harter's work.

Assessment practice 18.1   `A.P1` `A.P2` `A.M1` `A.M2` `A.D1`

You are currently working in an early years centre and your supervisor has asked you to contribute to a portfolio of information that will be available for all new members of staff. He has asked you to produce a document in which you will provide information about different stages of growth and development for identified age ranges. In addition, you will need to add details of related theories and how this can support children's growth and development within the setting.

You will need to produce a document in which you provide information about the milestones of development at three distinct ages, for example 1, 3 and 6 years. You will also need to make reference to appropriate theories and how they might support children's growth and development.

Plan
- What am I being asked to do?
- How will I approach the task?
- Are there any areas I think I may struggle with?

Do
- Have I spent some time planning my approach to the task at hand?
- Can I seek others' opinions?
- Am I utilising all of the support available to me?

Review
- I can describe my thought processes.
- I can explain what success looks like.
- I can identify how this learning experience relates to future experiences in the workplace.

B Examine factors that may impact on children's growth and development

Factors

Personal factors

There are a number of factors that have an impact on growth and development. Some of these have a positive impact and others will have a negative impact. In this section, you will examine a range of them and you will see that they fall into specific categories.

Health

Health is a major factor in how people grow and develop. A healthy lifestyle promotes holistic development. It is important to remember that good health is much more than being free from disease and illness. It includes wellbeing, a positive emotional and social outlook, and being part of the community. In order to maintain good health, a child needs to feel secure, and cared for in positive relationships. Children require their physical needs to be met by a healthy diet, warmth, shelter and provision for movement and exercise. Protection from disease, whenever possible is advantageous and includes healthcare monitoring and screening, taking advantage of immunisation programmes and promoting good hygiene practices.

Some children are at more risk of experiencing development and health issues. For example:

▶ children cared for away from the family home – many have emotional needs that might impact on other developmental areas

▶ children in need of protection (previously known as 'children at risk') – abuse can affect overall development

▶ children of travellers – who are often not in health screening programmes, and their education may be interrupted

▶ children of immigrants (especially illegal immigrants) – may not fully access health and education services, due to language and other barriers

▶ teenage mothers – especially if living on their own

▶ children in families with alcohol and substance abuse problems – care may be lacking and education and health services not fully accessed

▶ children with an inherited genetic condition that might affect development, for example Down's syndrome, cystic fibrosis

▶ children with disabilities – who may need additional support and care, and may lack mobility.

Chronic illnesses in children affect their holistic development. This is especially the case if they are often in hospital, when they are not mixing with their peers and emotional, social, cognitive and physical development is likely to be affected.

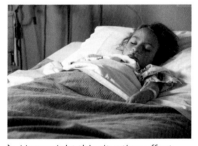

▶ How might this situation affect social development?

Disability

Events or circumstances that result in disability can occur before, during and after birth, and the reasons and causes of these disabilities are vast and complex.

▶ Before birth – some disabilities are caused through genetic inheritance (and these will be covered later in this unit). Some of the causes of disability in the unborn child include alcohol or substance misuse by the mother, certain diseases contracted during the development of the foetus such as rubella (German measles), abnormalities during pregnancy and the mother being physically abused during pregnancy.

▸ During the birth process – this includes lack of oxygen to the child, a prolonged birth process or lack of medical attention.

▸ After the birth – disabilities may be caused by accident, abuse, disease and illness.

Some diseases and conditions are present at or prior to birth, but are not identified until much later. Autism and other conditions may only become evident as the child matures. Many autistic children are highly intelligent, particularly in a specific area, for example art or maths. However, there is often some difficulty in communication, behaviour and some aspects of cognitive development. It is not unusual for children with autism to require specific support, particularly during their developmental years.

There is an increasing number of children who have congenital hearing loss which can be rectified but may create some delay in language and social development.

Genetic inheritance

Children inherit genetic information from both parents. Each cell in the body contains 46 chromosomes that carry genetic material. These chromosomes are made up of 23 pairs and you receive one set of 23 from your biological mother and the other set of 23 from your biological father. These chromosomes contain genes that determine certain features in your make-up, for example, hair, skin and eye colour, height and blood group. Some genes are **dominant** and some are **recessive**. For example, the gene for blue eyes is recessive and the gene for brown eyes is dominant. Therefore, if a child inherits a 'blue-eye gene' from one parent and a 'brown-eye gene' from the other parent, the dominant gene will determine the eye colour as brown. However, a recessive 'blue-eye gene' from each parent will result in blue eyes. It is also possible for two brown-eyed parents to have a blue-eyed child if they each pass on a recessive 'blue-eye gene'. It is not possible for two blue-eyed parents to have a brown-eyed child. Genetic inheritance is complicated and recent research shows that there may be inherited dispositions (tendencies), for example a predisposition to certain cancers or to asthma, which may only develop if other factors are present. There are some diseases and conditions that are genetically inherited, such as haemophilia and cystic fibrosis. These will be considered further as you now look at prenatal factors.

Prenatal factors

Some factors affecting growth and development occur before birth. Where possible, it is vital that the welfare of the child is considered from conception and the best care and attention provided. The mother should maintain a healthy lifestyle and take advantage of the available prenatal care.

Care during pregnancy

During pregnancy, the mother will be supported and advised on how to care for her unborn child. She will be asked about her general health, and whether her vaccinations are up to date as it is vital to avoid certain diseases during pregnancy that could adversely affect the developing foetus, such as rubella (German measles). The baby's health and development will also be monitored with scans and weight checks at various stages of foetal development. It is important that the mother has a healthy, balanced diet and that she does not use pregnancy as an excuse to eat excessively. Obesity during pregnancy reduces mobility and exercise, which affects the oxygen levels and blood flow. It can lead to heart disease in the mother and may affect the foetus. In addition, it is advisable to avoid certain food items, such as raw eggs (and related products such as fresh mayonnaise), liver and liver products such as paté. Expectant mothers are advised strongly not to smoke as this reduces the oxygen available to the unborn child, causing a lower birth weight. Alcohol intake should be reduced or eliminated as it has been shown that the use of alcohol, particularly during

> **Key terms**
>
> **Dominant gene** – produces its coded characteristics in the individual.
>
> **Recessive gene** – coded characteristics are present but may be masked by a dominant gene.

early pregnancy, interferes with the healthy development of foetal brain cells. In severe cases, the baby is born with foetal alcohol syndrome causing learning and behavioural difficulties. Similarly, substance abuse during pregnancy may result in the child being born already addicted to these substances, which may cause developmental delay in all areas.

Genetic disease

You have already considered genetic inheritance but there are a number of conditions that are carried by the genes or are caused by a faulty allocation of genes on the chromosome, for example Down's syndrome is caused by an extra chromosome resulting in characteristic traits of the condition. There are tests available during pregnancy that indicate whether a foetus is carrying a particular disease or syndrome, for example **amniocentesis**. Some conditions are carried by a recessive gene. Someone with that recessive gene but who has no signs or symptoms of the condition is known as a 'carrier'. If both parents carry the recessive gene, it may be passed to the developing child and the condition will manifest itself. For example, there may be several generations in a family with no evidence of cystic fibrosis, and then it may present itself again.

Haemophilia is a genetically inherited condition carried by females but passed on to males. This is known as a 'sex-linked' condition.

Sickle cell anaemia is a condition that only presents in certain ethnic groups, causing the red blood cells to sickle and block small blood vessels, resulting in painful and acute episodes.

> **Key terms**
>
> **Amniocentesis** – taking a sample of amniotic fluid (liquid surrounding the unborn child) to test for chromosomal abnormalities and foetal infections.
>
> **Phenylketonuria** – a rare genetic condition that affects brain development.

> **Research**
>
> Research sickle cell anaemia to find out how it affects individuals, and which groups of people might be at risk.

Phenylketonuria is a genetic condition that affects protein metabolism and causes developmental delays. Babies are tested for this condition just after birth, by pricking their heel and testing the blood. This condition can be alleviated by adherence to a strict diet which must be followed to avoid learning and behavioural difficulties.

▶ When is this type of screening carried out?

Lifestyle of the mother

The ongoing lifestyle of the mother has an impact on the environment that both an unborn baby and its siblings live in. There are some factors that have greater influence than others.

▸ Diet. Maternal diet is important as it will usually determine whether the whole family follows healthy eating patterns. This is particularly important for passing on healthy eating practices to children, which continue into adulthood.

▸ Smoking. You have considered how smoking can affect the unborn child but it is also detrimental to the health of anyone in the smoker's immediate environment. Research has shown that smoking within the home increases the risk of sudden infant death syndrome, as well as causing and aggravating respiratory disorders such as asthma, bronchitis and related chest infections. Smoking pollutes the atmosphere and is now prohibited in cars if there is a child present. It is also against the law to smoke in public buildings and when using public transport.

▸ Use of alcohol. Alcohol use can affect the unborn child in a number of ways but it can also impair the judgement of those taking care of children and babies. It is recommended that intake of alcohol is monitored and limited. Research has shown that alcohol use is a key factor in domestic and child abuse, accidents within the home, aggression and lack of care and attention.

PAUSE POINT	Why is it important that the mother adopts a healthy lifestyle when expecting a baby?
Hint	Why is prenatal care like inoculation against rubella important? List possible effects of not partaking in such a programme.
Extend	Research foetal alcohol syndrome and note some of its effects on the child.

Socio-economic factors

Socio-economic factors, including occupation, education, income, housing and wealth affect the financial wellbeing of the family unit, and impact on children's growth and development.

Poverty

Table 18.10 shows that child poverty has an impact on a number of areas and each will affect development in specific ways.

▸ **Table 18.10** The impact of child poverty

Effects of poverty	Examples
Education	Lack of books, electronic equipment, space or privacy to do homework, fewer educational visits.
Housing	Poor housing in deprived areas, possible overcrowding with damp conditions and in poor repair.
Health	Poor quality food and poor diet, overcrowding may lead to increased spread of illness, dampness might aggravate respiratory conditions, e.g. asthma, bronchitis.
Environment	May be derelict or deprived with poorly maintained play areas. Lack of public amenities, e.g. toddler groups and social meeting places. Central urban areas with poor air quality. Costs of transport.
Mortality rates	Mortality rates are higher in direct relation to child poverty due to an accumulation of factors related to housing, health and the environment.
Sport	Unable to purchase specialist equipment or afford access to sport or activity centres.
Cultural activities/ interests	Cost of entry into activity areas, lack of electronic access, lack of books, lack of equipment or materials.

The effects of poverty might have longer-term impacts, such as:

▸ reduced life expectancy due to ill-health

▸ greater possibility of temporary housing or accommodation

▸ developmental delay as focus is on basic needs of food and shelter, warmth and safety rather than intellectual and social/emotional development

▸ employment disadvantage

▸ cycle of deprivation in which:

  ▸ stress levels are higher

  ▸ diet is unhealthy.

Access to health and education services

Access to health and education services is important but depends a great deal on where people live. If their home is close to their GP, hospital, drop-in-centres, dentist, school, nursery, and library, then the family is more likely to access these services. Knowledge about available services is often by word of mouth, or from posters and notices displayed in the health care or educational facilities. Within the healthcare system, there are many programmes that people can take advantage of. Dieticians provide advice about healthy eating to avoid becoming overweight, which might lead to problems such as lack of mobility, breathing difficulties, heart conditions and general poor health. Education and library services provide storytelling sessions and access to computers and other equipment and materials.

There are a number of barriers that can create difficulties for people in accessing these services, such as:

▸ language – if English is a second or other language then translation may be required

▸ ability or disability might need to be addressed

▸ mobility – transport and costs may pose a problem.

Culture

Culture affects much of what people do and will vary from family to family. Within the family, if there is a culture of valuing education then school will be well-supported and learning attained at school will be reinforced at home. There will be active parental involvement and the children will be encouraged to do well. If education is not valued, the children are less likely to do well due to lack of encouragement and involvement in school activities.

In some cultures, there is a difference between what is expected of boys and girls. As a result, children may not be presented with the same opportunities or attention. Certain subjects may be deemed to be more suitable for boys, for example science subjects and maths, whereas other subjects may be seen as more suitable for girls. In times past, it was extremely difficult for a girl to go to university or to enter a male-dominated profession, such as medicine. Now it is more dependent on academic ability than on gender.

Diet

The food people eat is a major contributor to a healthy lifestyle and it is important to maintain a balanced diet. This will provide the correct proportions of the correct nutrients to keep the body healthy. A healthy diet should include a wide variety of foods, such as:

▸ plenty of fruit and vegetables

▸ carbohydrates, e.g. bread, rice, pasta (wholegrain if possible), potatoes

▸ protein, for example meat, fish, eggs, beans, pulses and other non-dairy sources of protein

▸ milk and dairy foods

▸ small portions of foods and drinks that are higher in fat and sugar.

> **Key term**
>
> **Culture** – the ideas, beliefs, customs and social behaviour of a group of people.

Eating a balanced diet will help prevent children becoming overweight and will provide them with the nutrition they require to grow and develop.

Environmental factors

Environmental factors include home life and conditions within the home and the surrounding area, such as pollution. Each of these has an impact on children's development.

Housing

▶ How might this situation affect development?

The family's accommodation impacts on the growth and development of the children. Certain conditions are required for children to grow, flourish and develop to their full potential.

▶ Light – rooms with adequate access to natural light have a positive effect on an individual's feeling of wellbeing. Light enables children to play, read and work in a comfortable environment. Dark and dingy rooms can seem oppressive and do not lead to a productive, friendly and relaxing atmosphere.

▶ Warmth – adequate warmth is a basic need for all people. Effective heating in the home ensures comfortable surroundings in which children can concentrate on activities such as reading, homework and creative projects and interests. A cold and/or damp home encourages the growth of mould and generally has a negative effect on children's overall health and wellbeing.

▶ Cleanliness – a basic essential in any home, to ensure that children are living in a safe environment, and that food preparation areas are sanitary and hygienic. Insanitary conditions mean a greater chance of infection and illness, which can have a detrimental effect on growth and development.

▶ Space – children require space to spend time alone or for carrying out their own activities. Overcrowded conditions can have an adverse effect on emotional and intellectual development.

In addition, it is advantageous to have an outdoor area where children can play in the fresh air. If this is not possible, there may be a park or playground in the area for outdoor play.

Pollution

Table 18.11 shows the three main types of **pollution** that might affect children's growth and development.

> **Key term**
>
> **Pollution** – presence or introduction into the environment of a harmful or toxic substance.

▶ **Table 18.11** The impact of pollution

Pollutant	Possible impact on people's lives
Air	Particulates in the air, mainly from vehicles and industry, increase the proportions of carbon dioxide, lead and other contaminants in the air. Air pollution is more prevalent in large towns and cities and can lead to aggravation of some respiratory conditions, e.g. asthma and bronchitis, but may also cause skin and eye irritations. These conditions may affect children's health and restrict their energy levels, or attendance at nursery or school.
	Long-term, poor air quality may lead to respiratory conditions becoming chronic, with associated damage to brain, nerves, liver and kidneys and development of lung cancer. Other medical conditions may also be made worse.
Water	If water becomes contaminated, it might result in outbreaks of sickness and diarrhoea, caused by waterborne bacteria or parasites.
Noise	Excessive, loud, disagreeable and unwanted noise can have a harmful effect on the ears and hearing, and can also impact on the whole nervous system. Noise pollution, particularly prolonged, is harmful when it interferes with sleep, the ability to concentrate or talk and may result in headaches and general feelings of being unwell. Using earphones and listening to loud noise on a regular basis can have a detrimental effect. Children can suffer from noise induced hearing loss (NIHL) which can interfere with speech and language development, impairing learning.

Emotional factors

Domestic abuse

Children who live in abusive situations are at great risk as it impacts on all areas of their development, and the effects can carry on into adult life. It also affects their **self-worth** and **self-concept**. Any form of abuse within the home affects everyone living there, even when they are not the targeted individual. To witness and hear abusive behaviour has long-term impacts and may disturb a child's behaviour and outlook into adulthood. The child may experience difficulty in trusting others and in forming meaningful relationships. Some individuals who have been abused become abusers themselves, as this is their mental image of family life. It manifests itself in much the same way as poor attachment (see below) and if the child has been the target of the abuse, other factors may affect their lives, such as physical impairment, low self-esteem or social inadequacy.

> **Key terms**
>
> **Self-worth** – a sense of own value or worth.
>
> **Self-concept** – the way in which you see yourself, a mental image that includes abilities, strengths, weaknesses, status and other characteristics.

> **Link**
>
> See *Unit 7: Principles of Safe Practice in Health and Social Care.*

Poor attachment

If a child does not form an attachment or if the attachment is broken during critical periods, then there may be detrimental consequences, which might include:

▶ delinquency
▶ reduced intellectual or cognitive development
▶ reduced emotional development
▶ increased aggression
▶ depression
▶ inability to show affection for others
▶ difficulty maintaining long-term relationships.

Transitions

Everyone goes through various **transitions** and the way they feel about them may be influenced by how those transitions were handled when they were young. For an adult, some of these transitions might include changing from school to college or university, or training for and starting a new job. Some individuals seem to manage change or transition better than others.

Personal transitions that happen to all children

There are a number of changes that all children might experience, and some will be particular to the circumstances and lifestyle of a family, for example being cared for by a childminder or being in a day nursery. However, the majority of children will experience going to nursery and starting school. Later transitions will include changing tutor and class within the school and other changes that an adult might feel are minor but can upset children. Routines provide a stable base in a child's life and changes to routine might create confusion for a child, for example parties, sports days and outings.

Most children will experience starting school. For the majority of children, it involves being left with other children in the care of an adult they may not know, in a building or room they are unfamiliar with. Adults have the hindsight to know that this can be a very positive experience but it can be quite daunting for some children. Therefore, this transition needs to be approached sensitively and handled carefully. The majority of schools offer visits for parents and children during the term prior to starting school. If the child attends a nursery class or unit linked to the school, they may well have additional visits and, in both cases, they will be with an adult they know and trust. Gradually they will start to familiarise themselves with their surroundings and the new people they meet. Careful handling and consideration for the child's feelings often means that entry into school can be quite smooth, especially if children are with others who they know from nursery or other places. Sensitivity can reduce anxiety and enhance a sense of discovery and adventure.

Particular transitions that children may experience

There are some transitions that are specific and will only happen in the lives of some children. They may include moving house, family breakdown, family illness or death.

Many of these are traumatic in a child's life and will require a great deal of support and care. They may involve other services, such as counselling. Some of the following examples might happen in the life of a child and will have varying effects on their emotional and social development. Some situations will have short-term effects but others will have longer-term effects, and may involve contact with bereavement counsellors or other associated professionals.

▸ Moving house can be exciting, especially if other factors remain stable, for example the house move is in the same area so school and friendship groups may not be affected. However, if a child is moving away from the area it may mean that there will be considerable change with starting a new school, developing new friends and moving further away from relatives.

▸ Family breakdown or divorce will have an impact on a child's development, particularly emotionally and socially. In the majority of cases, there will have been a progressive situation that leads to the eventual breakdown of the parents' relationship. Children may feel that they have been the cause of these difficulties and their loyalty may be torn between their parents.

▸ Family illness, or the death of a main carer, may result in a child having to be cared for away from the family home. This may be by another family member or by a foster family, and may be short-term. However, in some instances the care needs to be long-term and perhaps permanent.

❚❚ PAUSE POINT   Think about some of the transitions that you have experienced. What aspects made them easier or more difficult?

Hint   List some of the transitions that all children will experience and others that only some children might experience.

Extend   How might starting a new school be handled to make it as easy as possible for a young child to adapt?

The impact of factors on growth and development

Short- and long-term impacts on growth and development

Short-term impacts

Some illnesses and injuries might have a relatively short-term impact on growth and development. A child with a broken leg, for example may have impaired physical movement for a limited time, and there may be some effect on their social activity and emotional wellbeing. However, once they recover, the child will quickly absorb any developmental delay. A child may be cared for by others for a variety of reasons, for example parental illness, and this may have an emotional impact on the child. The whole family may need to move due to events out of their control, for example flooding, and there will be some disruption to their normal routine.

Long-term impacts

Long-term impacts require other support mechanisms to be in place. For example, serious accidents resulting in mobility problems may require the use of a wheelchair. This will mean adaptations to whatever setting the child is in to accommodate this. Instances of domestic and violent abuse may have long-term impacts that continue into adult life. Congenital problems might result in developmental delays that have long-term impacts, much depends on the nature of the issue and how soon it is identified and effective support provided. Family bereavement can result in major changes that may be long-term.

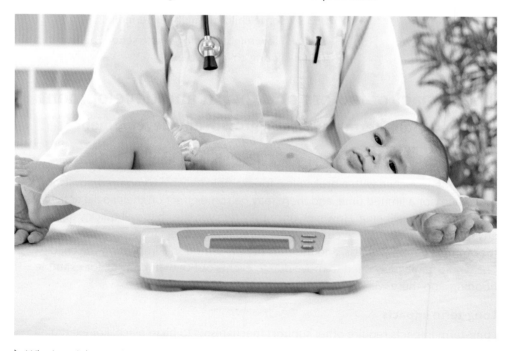

Failure to grow and thrive

Children may be diagnosed as failing to grow and **thrive**, if they fall significantly below the healthy weight for their age. This can be accompanied by some cognitive or emotional delay. There can be a number of reasons for this and it is important that the underlying cause is determined, so that support might be provided and programmes for recovery put in place. Failure to thrive could be caused by conditions such as cerebral palsy, Down's syndrome, infections, allergies, heart disease and metabolic disorders.

There are three main reasons for failure to thrive:

1 inadequate intake of food and nutrition

2 nutrition and calories cannot be absorbed

3 excessive or disproportionate requirements for the nutritional intake.

If a mother attends regular check-ups during pregnancy and the child is checked regularly after birth, then patterns that might lead to failure to thrive can be detected early and preventative measures put in place. Check-ups might include blood and urine tests, X-rays and other screening tests to determine whether or not the cause of the child's failure to thrive is metabolic, or due to parenting practices. Treatment depends mainly on the cause. It may be that special diets and supplements are required or that any organic cause is treated. If failure to thrive is linked to problems in the home, then social services may become involved. If failure to thrive is addressed early, it is possible for the child to have no long-term effects once their weight is maintained. However, if the condition has been prolonged, then there might be long-term effects such as learning difficulties and emotional problems.

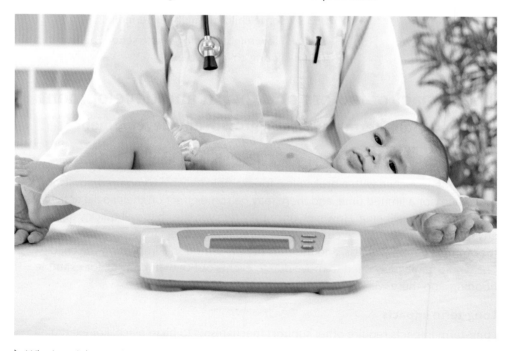

▶ Why is weight monitoring important in infancy?

Delayed or enhanced development

Delayed or enhanced development is atypical development and is when a child does not meet the milestones in a particular area of development within the age range identified for typical development patterns. A child who is not walking by the age of two years, for example, has delayed physical development and this will need to be investigated and monitored to ascertain the underlying cause. Other areas of their development will also be investigated as one area of atypical development can impact on another. Similarly, enhanced development, such as a child walking at six months old, may require monitoring as it can impact on other areas of development, particularly social and emotional. In both cases, there may be a requirement for additional specialist support. Professionals working with young children will carry out detailed observations of the child's development and compare them with the milestones of typical development. In addition, the child may perceive itself as 'different' and its self-esteem may be low, which will impact on its emotional development.

How the impact on one area of development may affect other areas

Early recognition of atypical development in one area is important as it often impacts on other areas of development.

▶ **Table 18.12** Recognition of developmental delay

Area of development	Effect on other areas
Delay in social development	The child may not like being with other people and shows little enjoyment in being in groups. As a result, they may not engage in play at an appropriate level and often refrain from joining in with activities. This will have an adverse effect on emotional development as the child will not use a range of emotions and will be unable to engage fully in experiences and events, e.g. trips, outings and holidays.
Delay in cognitive development	Cognitive and language development are very closely related. Delay in this area may mean that the child struggles to use language, which in turn will have a detrimental effect on reading and writing skills. The printed word is symbolic and the child needs to be able to understand these abstract concepts. Shapes of letters correlate to specific sounds and the child may be unable to make these links. Other areas of cognitive development may be affected, such as colour recognition and problems with mathematical and number development. Play will be affected, which in turn will impact on social development. The child may have low self-esteem and may display behavioural problems if excluded from play by other children.
Delay in language development	People use language to express their feelings and to communicate effectively with others so this will impact social and emotional development, resulting in fewer opportunities to play and interact. The child may then be frustrated and upset. Language development is closely linked to organised thought and, as it is associated with cognitive development, there may be further impacts in that area of development.
Delay in emotional development	Emotional development is linked to recognising feelings, and to developing relationships with other people. If this area of development is delayed, it may mean that children miss out on opportunities to play with other children and develop friendships. It is also linked with the ability to manage behaviour and to develop strategies to deal with anger and frustration. There are strong links between emotions and the ability to concentrate, which may further impact on cognitive development.
Delay in physical development	A child with delayed physical development may have difficulty keeping pace with their peers. They may find it harder to explore and engage in physical play. As a result, they may have fewer opportunities to interact with other children, and there may be some degree of social isolation. This might result in bullying, which can affect a child's behaviour patterns and self-esteem.
Enhanced cognitive and language development	Cognitive and language development are very closely linked and enhanced development is more commonly shown in both these areas together. A child with enhanced development may need additional support as they may find it more difficult to form relationships within their peer group. They may not sustain interest in play activities alongside the other children as it may not challenge their cognitive development. Additionally, these children are often treated as older than their chronological age and may struggle with concepts that are beyond their emotional maturity.

▶ Is this child gifted or talented?

Enhanced or delayed development may affect a child's self-esteem. Childcare workers and other professionals need to be aware of this and provide praise and encouragement to improve a child's confidence and emotional stability.

> **Research**
>
> Research other types of enhanced development and the education services and programmes that can accommodate and provide for these children's needs.

How factors may be counterbalanced by other factors

You have considered a range of factors affecting growth and development including personal, health, environmental and emotional factors. Some of these can be counterbalanced to some extent by other interventions and programmes designed to have positive impact.

Family and friends beyond the immediate family may in some way provide an enriched environment and present the child with opportunities for learning and stimulation. Support for families can vary but trips out to places of interest, swimming and sports events can help provide additional and different experiences.

Tutors and other educational professionals can have a potentially important impact on children's self-esteem and self-belief. It has been said that 'success breeds success', and if a child succeeds on a regular basis then this heightens their self-esteem. Similarly, if a tutor has high expectations, children often have higher achievement rates and the tutor may well help them use appropriate resources to aid their progress.

Local government provides free nursery places for children who meet specific criteria. This is part of a compensatory programme that enables children to receive specific support for all areas of development, as well as having the opportunity to play with a wide range of toys, interact with other children and develop friendships.

There are a number of programmes available to try to improve the health and eating habits of children.

All early years settings and primary schools have policies and guidelines regarding inclusive practice, so that all children are able to access a wide range of activities, programmes and appropriate support to enable them to reach their potential.

> **Discussion**
>
> In small groups, discuss whether compensatory programmes and actions are beneficial and effective.

 PAUSE POINT   Can you explain how short-term impacts on development might be reduced further?

Hint   What might be the long-term impact of failure to thrive?

Extend   Research 'Pygmalion in the Classroom'. How might that idea impact on children's self-esteem and development?

Assessment practice 18.2   `B.P3` `C.P4` `C.P5` `B.M3` `C.M4` `C.M5` `BC.D2` `BC.D3`

You are working in a children's centre and the manager has asked you to develop some materials that will help new members of staff understand the impact that factors might have on children and how assessment can be very supportive.

You will need to produce a report based on observations you have carried out, explaining the impact that factors have on children's growth and development and how assessment supports and promotes children's growth and development. Your report should include plans for observations, records of observations and a reflective account.

Plan
- Do I have any existing knowledge around the task at hand?
- What resources do I need to complete the task? How can I organise them?

Do
- Have I already spent some time on observations that I can use for this task?
- I can set milestones and evaluate my progress and success at these intervals.

Review
- I can draw links between this learning and prior learning.
- I can identify how this learning experience relates to future experiences (that is in the workplace).

C   Explore how assessment is used to identify children's stages of growth and development and their support needs

Assessment methods

There are a number of ways to assess children and each has a different purpose. All forms of assessment are important. Some will be less formal than others, some will be ongoing and some will involve writing reports and developing plans for the future.

Formal, informal, formative, summative

Table 18.13 shows the different types of assessment and the purpose of using each method.

Assessment type	Purpose
Formal	Generally linked to summative assessments. Usually carried out at certain stages during a child's development and passed to others involved in the developmental needs of the child. An example of this may be at the end of the Early Years Foundation Stage (EYFS) in England, when the EYFS Profile is completed for each child and passed to relevant staff as the child moves to Year 1 of the National Curriculum.
Informal	Usually ongoing and more relaxed. Provides a developmental picture of the progress a child is making. Formative, as they are used to plan for the short-term future. Observing a child's development in all areas is the commonest type of informal assessment and is carried out on a daily basis in most early years settings.
Formative	Ongoing during the learning/development process. Looks at the individual child's progress in all areas at different times. May be through observations, which help inform what stage of development the child is at and how to plan for further development in that area. Supports the curriculum in the short term. Many early years settings keep a record of children's progress, with appropriate photographs and reports detailing progress of activities and achievements. This record may be passed to the child's parents at some point.
Summative	Usually formal. Focuses on the outcome of learning, so usually occurs at the end of a period of learning. Considers children's development in all areas. Also used to review the child's progress at certain points in the curriculum, and to inform long-term planning. As with the EYFS Profile, can be shared with other settings at the end of the reception year. Typically used to check that an individual child is progressing at the correct level of development. Will help determine support for a child who is falling behind.

Developmental screening programmes

Antenatal screening helps the mother throughout pregnancy and starts as soon as the pregnancy is confirmed. These checks include:

▶ blood tests – to check for infectious diseases or inherited conditions

▶ urine tests – carried out routinely throughout pregnancy, to check for protein or sugar in the urine

▶ weight – checked routinely to ascertain a healthy weight gain and monitor any loss or rapid gain

▶ ultrasound scans – to check the baby's growth, and for abnormalities (18–21-week scan).

There are a variety of screening checks offered at birth and they form part of the newborn screening programme, which includes the following:

▶ Blood spot screening – a small blood sample is taken from the baby's heel, to test for rare but serious conditions, such as sickle cell disease, phenylketonuria or cystic fibrosis. Early identification of these and other conditions ensures that early treatment is provided, which can dramatically improve a child's health, growth and development.

▶ Physical examination – usually carried out within 72 hours of birth. A second examination is done at around 6–8 weeks after birth. This will include measurements such as weight, head circumference and length, alongside checking the baby's heart, hips, eyes and, in boys, whether the testes have descended.

▶ Hearing test – early identification of hearing loss can help prevent delay in other associated areas of development, such as speech.

Ongoing screening is designed to identify problems or developmental delays throughout childhood, such as:

▶ learning difficulties

▶ emotional and behavioural conditions, including autism

▶ hearing impairment

▶ visual impairment

▶ height and weight

▶ speech and language.

If there are any areas for concern, then early intervention can have positive results for later life.

Growth monitoring

When a child is born, the parents are provided with a Personal Child Health Record Book (PCHR or 'red book') that contains documentation to record the initial information about a child, including height, weight and head circumference. Each of these measurements provides important details from which the potential future development of the child can be determined. Throughout the first years of life growth is monitored and the information recorded in the child's records and in their PCHR.

Measuring and recording growth

A child's birth weight provides a good starting point from which to monitor their growth and progress. The weight and length of newborns have been routinely recorded for many years, so it is possible to predict typical growth rate. For example, a baby is expected to triple its birth weight at around the one-year mark, so a baby weighing 3.2 kg (approx. 7 lbs) at birth should be about 9.5 kg (approx. 21 lbs) at one year old. Periods of ill-health may mean that weight gain is slightly lower, but a child whose weight is significantly below average may require investigation and monitoring. Similarly, a very overweight baby will need to be monitored to determine the cause, as babies usually only feed until they are satisfied. It is also possible to estimate a child's adult height by doubling their height at 2 years old for a boy, or at 18 months for a girl. This only provides a rough estimate, but as height is genetically determined, it is a formula that is often used.

Head circumference provides initial information about possible abnormalities. For example, hydrocephalus is a condition characterised by a large head as there is more cerebrospinal fluid than normal, which can cause pressure and result in brain damage. Microcephaly is a small head circumference and might indicate abnormality in brain development.

Centile charts

Weight, length and head circumference are usually plotted on a centile chart. The centile chart is an ongoing record about an individual child, providing information at a glance and allowing comparisons with the norms of development. The vertical axis shows the types of development. Areas above the centile line indicate good development and those below may indicate areas that require investigation. A dip in weight, for example, might coincide with, and be explained by, a period of illness. The horizontal axis shows age in weeks, up to one year, and weight and length are plotted appropriately.

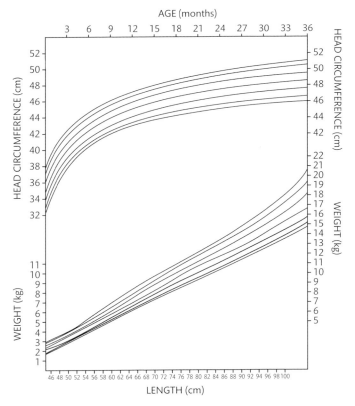

► **Figure 18.4** A centile chart showing head circumference, weight and length

Assessment frameworks

The main purposes for using specific assessment frameworks are to:

▸ ensure that assessment is fair and used by all interested parties
▸ determine if progress and development is within the range of typical development
▸ determine areas where progress and/or development is delayed or enhanced
▸ provide support for the child that is consistent and appropriate to the needs of the child.

Common Assessment Framework (CAF)

The CAF was designed so that anyone working with children across the UK in a range of professions and agencies could work together more effectively. It enables practitioners to have a simple assessment of the whole child, identify their needs and consider how those needs might be met. It is used within health, education, childcare, social care, police, youth services and other services dealing with children and young people. It is designed to help with the implementation of the Every Child Matters agenda. It is primarily used to assess children's additional needs and to be an effective and coordinated method of meeting those needs by working together for the good of the child.

The CAF is for children who have additional needs in certain areas. These needs may not be limited to only one area and include:

▸ growth and development
▸ additional educational requirements
▸ family and environmental issues (and/or any specific needs of the parent or carer).

The reasons for carrying out this assessment can be complex and varied. Children and their families can experience difficult situations that might have a detrimental effect on children and young people. This may result in behavioural or antisocial issues, poor school attendance and truancy, housing issues and other domestic problems. Early intervention programmes can alleviate problems before they become entrenched and established. There are specific steps to the process and simplified examples are provided here.

1 Identify needs and obtain consent to carry out the assessment – check if anyone else is already working with the child. As the CAF is a voluntary assessment, consent must be given at the start of the process and also for information obtained to be shared with people in other services.

2 Assess the needs – discuss with the child and their family the extent and impact of the needs. Gather the information and complete the appropriate parts of the form, which must be signed by the child or their parent.

3 Deliver the service – this may be a multi-agency approach. A team of professionals might work with the child, with a Lead Practitioner.

4 Review – the plan and progress should be reviewed. Further actions may be required to support the child further. If the needs have been met, then the case may be closed.

Curriculum Frameworks

The Early Years Foundation Stage (EYFS) (England)

The EYFS is used in all schools and Ofsted-registered early years' providers. It contains the standards required by the Childcare Act 2006 for children aged 0–5 years. Four guiding principles shape the EYFS, which are listed below.

1 Every child is a unique child, who is constantly learning and can be resilient, capable, confident and self-assured.

2 Children learn to be strong and independent through positive relationships.

3 Children learn and develop well in enabling environments, in which their experiences respond to their individual needs and there is a strong partnership between practitioners and parents and/or carers.

4 Children develop and learn in different ways and at different rates.

Discussion

The aims of the Every Child Matters agenda are for children to:

• stay safe
• be healthy
• enjoy and achieve
• make a positive contribution
• achieve economic wellbeing.

In small groups, discuss what each of these aims might actually mean for children in your care. How can practitioners help children achieve these aims?

The framework is split into seven Areas of Learning, which are further subdivided into the Early Learning Goals.

At the age of two years, there is a progress check but the main assessment is at the end of the EYFS, when the EYFS Profile will be completed. The profile consists of a series of observations and assessments against the Early Learning Goals. It will be shared with parents and passed to the relevant tutors for National Curriculum Year 1.

The National Curriculum (England)

The National Curriculum was introduced in 1988. Although there have been some changes, it has remained much the same. Its introduction meant that all children in local authority maintained schools in England would follow the same programmes of study for the same subjects in an academic year. The programmes of study provide the detail of what must be taught. The National Curriculum documents in each subject provide the statutory guidelines of what must be covered. Children begin studying the National Curriculum the year after their fifth birthday, and this became known as National Curriculum Year 1. All subsequent school years follow this numerical system.

Following the National Curriculum, there are specific times during a child's education when assessment takes place. These are known as Key Stages. Key Stage 1 is towards the end of Year 2 and children are assessed against Attainment Targets through a series of Standard Assessment Tests (SATs). Key Stage 2 is towards the end of Year 6, and Key Stage 3 at Year 9. Key Stage 4 is during Year 11, and at this point many children will be taking GCSE examinations. Assessments at Key Stages 1 and 2 focus on English, Maths and Science, and at each of these assessment stages a written report will be given to the parents or guardians of the child.

Although the National Curriculum was initially introduced and used in England, Wales and Northern Ireland, revisions in each country mean that there are now definite differences. You will need to be aware of the National Curriculum requirements for whichever area of the UK you are working in.

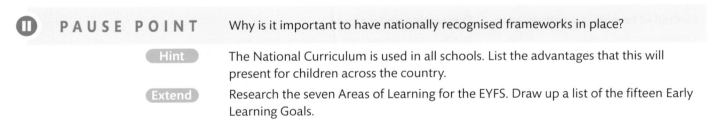

II   PAUSE POINT   Why is it important to have nationally recognised frameworks in place?

> Hint   The National Curriculum is used in all schools. List the advantages that this will present for children across the country.

> Extend   Research the seven Areas of Learning for the EYFS. Draw up a list of the fifteen Early Learning Goals.

How to plan and carry out assessment through observation

In order to plan an observation, you will need to decide which area of development you are interested in. It might be an aspect of social development, and so you will be looking at interactions with other children. If physical development is the focus of your observation, it is useful to narrow the observation to either fine or gross motor skills. When considering observing a baby, then a number of different areas of development might be looked at together. It is important that you know the rationale for your observation. You must then decide how you are going to record your findings, and whether you will be a participant in the activity or not. Look at the types and methods of observation to help you decide. When writing up an observation, there is specific information that should be noted such as the name (or some way to identify the child), the age in years and months, the date of the observation, the start and finish times, the setting, and the aim and objectives of the observation.

> **Research**
>
> Carry out a small research project looking at the purpose and importance of observations when working with young children.

Why observe?

John is a childcare worker. He notices that Tarik (a five-year-old boy) does not talk very much to the other children in the setting. John decides that it might be helpful to carry out an observation to see how Tarik interacts with other children. He positions himself near one of the group activities that Tarik is engaged in and documents what he observes.

Check your knowledge

1 What did John need to consider before carrying out the observation?

2 What information would he need to have noted?

3 What would help him decide whether Tarik's language use is within the expected levels of development?

4 Why is confidentiality important?

5 Who might he share his findings with?

6 What would he need to know in order to plan for Tarik's future development?

Methods of recording

There are a number of different ways to record observations (see Table 18.14) and much depends on the purpose and rationale of your observation. Always keep in mind that any observation only provides a snapshot of what is happening during a very short timescale. In order to assess a child's ability, a number of detailed observations must be carried out over a period of time.

▶ **Table 18.14** Recording observations

Method of recording an observation	Explanation and purpose
Spontaneous description	Anecdotal written account of what happens as it happens.
Structured observation	Observing children taking part in a planned learning activity.
Non-participant observation	The observer watches the children without taking part in the activity or interacting in any way with the children.
Participant observation	The observer takes an active part in an activity and interacts with a child or children to extend their learning.
Structured recording	Using audio or video recordings. The observer must seek specific permission to use audio or video recordings of children.
Checklist or pre-planned schedule	Observing the children's skills by comparing them using a developmental checklist.
Time sample	Observing a child's play or interaction at short intervals over a longer time period.
Event sample	Observing a child's behaviour at certain times, e.g. on arrival at nursery.
Sociogram	Used to show an infant class child's understanding of friendship groups. These are not usually used with younger children as friendship groups have not been established.
Tracking	Establishing which areas of the setting the child moves to, or keeps returning to, and which resources they engage with.

Areas of development

In order to attain a picture of a child's overall development it will be necessary for you to carry out a number of observations of each area of development (physical, intellectual, language, social and emotional), especially if there are concerns about delayed development.

Timing and environmental considerations

The timing of the observation may affect the outcome as children can behave differently at different times, for example from mornings to afternoons. Some children tire easily and are not as engaged later in the day. Very young children may be used to a nap, and become upset if tired. Young children tend to like routines and some can become upset if this is altered or changed.

If a child's environment is secure, rich and varied it will support learning and development, as children play and engage with others better in a friendly interactive setting. If the environment is clinical or strange, they may not interact well. Children are affected by change. If the layout of a setting is changed, for example then children may not react in the same way. It has also been observed that playing outside, particularly in a natural environment, has a positive impact on social interaction and play.

Ethical issues

When working with children you need to be aware of any ethical issues and conflicts of interest. If you have any doubts about what you should do in any given circumstance, you must seek advice from your line manager. Ethical issues might include:

▸ how to challenge anti-discriminatory practice and comments
▸ permission to carry out certain tasks and observations
▸ adherence to a code of confidentiality.

Discriminatory practice must always be challenged, including discriminatory comments. However, it takes tact and diplomacy to do this effectively and without being confrontational. If a child has made an adverse comment to another child, it needs to be challenged in some way. If this is not done, you are in danger of being perceived as condoning it by omission. You may need to seek advice about this from more experienced workers.

Permission is always required for child observations. Most settings get this permission from the parents at the point of a child's admission, so that the correct documentation is in place from the outset. It is good practice to keep parents informed and to share your findings with the family. The only exception may be when safeguarding issues are involved.

Confidentiality is an important aspect of working with children, and all staff and learners must adhere to this at all times. There will be a policy within the setting that provides all the salient details about this. Observations are included within the policy guidelines and should be kept confidential within the setting. Access to findings should only be given to those who have reason to need it (for example your line manager, an educational psychologist, social services, police). All records and reports should contain facts, and not uninformed judgements. In certain circumstances, for example safeguarding or additional support, these may be used later in case conferences, so they should always be dated and signed.

▸ **Figure 18.5** Why is confidentiality important?

Using milestones to compare a child's stage of development against typical development

It is important to compare an individual child's stage of development to the established norms of typical development, rather than making judgements based on your own knowledge. Over the years, researchers have used findings from observing children at different ages to develop lists of typical development at specific ages. These observations showed that although some children have delayed or enhanced development, the majority of children reach milestones at around the same age. For example, by 18 months old most children will be able to walk unaided. Although some children will still be unsteady and others may be very confident, the milestone refers to their ability to walk. You will find many sources of information about milestones, such as the pioneering work carried out by Mary Sheridan and documented in her book – *From Birth to Five Years: Children's Developmental Progress*. You will need to ensure that these sources provide reputable information, and make sure to always use a recognised reference source when stating that a child is within the norms of development.

The involvement of parents in assessment

Assessment of a child's needs must involve their parents in order to gain an accurate overall picture. Parents notice their child's development. Involving and listening to parents helps to ensure that their children's behaviours and abilities are fully understood in all contexts, and develops cooperative relationships with families. In many cases, parents have vital information about the specific needs of their children, and about any problems they may be trying to come to terms with.

The welfare of the child is the most important aspect of care and education. If concerns are raised by other workers, then this too must be shared with the parents. Parental consent must always be sought and received before any referral can be made. The only exception is in the case of child abuse, when the welfare of the child overrides everything else. Parental consent is also required prior to carrying out observations, and it is good to share observational findings with the parents.

When working with children, it is essential to develop supportive relationships. Parents have the greatest influence on children and their support is vital for children to reach their potential. Parental involvement makes a positive difference in behaviour and achievement. It is beneficial to engage with parents in all aspects of development and learning, and work together as partners.

> **Research**
>
> Research the importance and impact of developing a positive partnership with parents regarding all aspects of their child's development.

The importance of sharing information

▶ With colleagues

Within any setting, you will work closely with a number of colleagues and you may need to share information about a child with them. It is necessary for you to ensure that information sharing with colleagues always has a definite purpose for the learning and development of that specific child. Your supervisor or line manager will typically be the first person you approach, but if information is specific to the additional needs of the child or a safeguarding issue, then the information would be given only to those with 'a need to know', such as the Learning Disability Coordinator or the Safeguarding Designated Person.

▶ With other professionals

There are times when a childcare worker is part of a multi-agency team of professionals, for example social workers, nurses, teaching assistants, GPs, and educational psychologists. This will certainly be the case if an assessment has been made under the Common Assessment Framework, as information sharing is part of this process. All people working with children need to have a common core of skills and knowledge, this underpins multi-agency working. This common core of knowledge and skills includes communication, child development, safeguarding, supporting transitions, multi-agency working and information sharing. It is important to be aware of the need for consent, with the exception of safeguarding issues. There are also other professionals who you may be involved with, such as physiotherapists or speech and language therapists, who may come to your setting to see a child and will discuss that child's progress with you. You must remain professional and only pass on pertinent, relevant and factual information, rather than your own point of view.

▶ Who might be involved in planning to support children with additional needs?

▶ With the child and their family

Sharing information with the child and their family is an important aspect of building up a positive relationship and working partnership with them. Parents like to have current details of their child's progress and development. In many settings there are records, for example reading records, of what the child has been doing. Parents are usually encouraged to add notes about other reading activities at home, which provides a more detailed overall picture about a child's interest in reading and looking at books. Most settings will have specific times during the year when parents can speak to their childcare professional, for example the tutor or key worker, about their child's progress within the setting. This encourages a two-way dialogue about the child's learning and development.

❚❚ **PAUSE POINT**   Why is it important to refer to the milestones of development following an observation?

　　　Hint　　Think about the people who should be involved or informed about any assessment process. What can they contribute?

　　　Extend　　Why are there exceptions about who is involved within a setting when there is a safeguarding concern or issue?

The contribution of assessment to the promotion of children's growth and development

Early identification of children failing to grow or thrive

Early identification of failure to grow and thrive is vital as treatment and/or interventions can be put in place that can have a life-changing effect on the child. Early identification has the potential for developmental delay and poor long-term outcomes to be reversed. When weight gain is significantly lower than that of other children of same sex and age, investigation of the underlying cause is necessary as this will also affect growth. If a medical condition is the cause, early diagnosis and treatment is essential.

Early identification of atypical development

You have considered in detail the milestones of typical development and have noted that children's development follows a predictable course. You have also explored some of the factors contributing to atypical development and, as with anything that can affect development, early diagnosis or identification is of prime importance.

It is not always easy to determine atypical development patterns in a baby and it may be that as the child progresses and matures, behaviours are noticed that are outside the expected range of development, for example very late crawling or walking, or very delayed speech or vocalisation. Development may be noticeably at a different pace and late in emerging. It is important to note:

▸ When the skill emerges – is it very late?

▸ In what order the skill emerges – is it out of sequence?

▸ How established is the skill – is the quality as to be expected?

> **Discussion**
>
> Why is it important to identify atypical development as early as possible?

Interventions to support and promote development

Early **interventions** have been shown to have a positive impact on children's individual developmental needs. Much depends on the nature of the need identified, but there are a number of additional support initiatives that might be employed to promote development. Specific plans might be drawn up and implemented, with short- and long-term goals, and programmes to target specific areas of development. Some examples of these are now explained.

Care plans

Care plans are usually created for children in some form of care, who require extra support. It should be noted that not every child needs a care plan. A care plan might result from discussions with parents or carers, medical services or after observations or assessments from those working with the child. The care plan may take different forms but will always include details concerning the child's needs, and how they can be met in both the short- and long-term. It also provides details about the resources required, which may include additional staffing or special equipment and resources. The plan will always be individual, and copies will be provided for parents or carers and other individuals involved in care. The plan will be reviewed at least once a year (or more often, if needed) to ascertain the child's progress, and whether any changes are needed. Parents or carers and members of the multi-agency team will be involved in this process.

> **Reflect**
>
> It is important to remember that premature babies may appear to show some developmental delay, as they have not had as much time developing prior to birth. However, this does not mean that their development is atypical.

> **Key term**
>
> **Intervention** – a plan or act designed to alter the course of a disease, injury or condition by initiating a treatment or programme to aid recovery.

Learning plans

The ideal situation would be for every child to have a learning plan. However, for practical reasons there is usually a general plan for the majority of children within a class or group. Individual Learning Plans (or Individual Education Plans), which take into account a specific child's development and abilities, are created for children with additional or specific needs. The plan shows details of the developmental and learning needs of the child and suggests how these can best be met. As with other plans, ILPs and IEPs are reviewed regularly to ascertain progress, and may be amended in light of the review.

Behaviour plans

Behaviour plans are often known as Behaviour Intervention Plans. They are usually created when a child's behaviour is regularly or consistently undesirable and unacceptable. The plan is for a specific child and the type of unacceptable behaviour is described very precisely. The type of behaviour required is also specified in detail, alongside the reinforcement measures to be used. If the child has other types of unacceptable behaviour, these will be itemised individually with the same detail and the reinforcement measures identified. The plan should be straightforward and simple, so that it is easy for anyone working with the child to remember the stages. This behaviour plan will be reviewed on a regular basis, to check whether the behaviour modification plans are effective.

Specialist support from health professionals

There is a wide range of support mechanisms that can be provided for children requiring additional provision. This might include assistance from specialist professionals in the form of advice, resources or ongoing therapy. Support for children with multiple and varied needs may require input from a number of different services:

- Assistive technology
- Occupational therapy services
- Auditory/hearing services
- Physiotherapy services
- Counselling services
- Psychological services
- Education programmes
- Respite care and services
- Medical services
- Special Educational Needs
- Nutritional/dietary services
- Speech and language therapy (SALT).

The importance of monitoring and reviewing interventions

Any intervention or plan regarding a child's additional needs must be monitored and reviewed on a regular basis to ensure that it continues to meet the child's ongoing needs. In addition, further actions or support may be required and should be added to the plan, with appropriate signatures and dates. This is true for assessments under the CAF and any other type of intervention or plan. Reviews and/or monitoring meetings must happen as often as necessary, but no later than a year after the plan is implemented. The review and monitoring process must be arranged with all interested parties involved, and decisions must be recorded. If the child's needs have been met, then no further intervention will be required and the plan will be completed and closed. However, if the needs are ongoing, then it is important to ascertain whether the intervention is effective, and whether the plan remains in place as it is, or continue with amendments if additional actions have been identified. If it is decided that the intervention will continue, then a further monitoring and review date must be determined and set as appropriate.

PAUSE POINT Can you explain what type of interventions or plans might be used when caring for children in any type of setting?

Hint Why must Behaviour Improvement Plans be very specific and detailed?

Extend Why is it important to regularly review and monitor intervention programmes?

Assessment practice 18.3

C.P4 C.P5 C.M4 C.M5 BC.D2 BC.D3

You are working in a Child Care Centre and you have been asked to develop some materials that will help new members of staff understand the different screening and assessment methods that might be used when working with children and how they might be used to support children.

You will need to produce a report in which you will need to explain a range of screening and assessment methods which might be used from birth to 8 years. You should make reference to developmental screening monitoring programmes and other assessment frameworks such as the EYFS and the National Curriculum. You should then plan to observe children to identify their stage of development, providing a rationale concerning the methods of observation you have selected.

Plan
- How will I approach this task?
- Do I need clarification around anything?
- Do I have any existing knowledge around the task at hand?

Do
- Am I confident that I know what I am doing and that I know what it is I should be achieving?
- Have I already spent some time on observations that I can use for this task?

Review
- I can explain what I have learned and why it is important.
- I can identify how this learning experience relates to future experiences (that is in the workplace).

Further reading

Sharma, A. and Cockerill, H. (2014) *Mary Sheridan's From Birth to Five Years* 4th edition, Abingdon: Routledge Erikson.

Mooney, CG. (2000) *Theories of Childhood: An Introduction to Dewey, Montessori, Erickson, Piaget and Vygotsky*, St Paul, MN: Redleaf Press.

Kellett, M. (2011) *Children's Perspectives on Integrated Services: Every Child Matters in Policy and Practice*, Houndmills: Basingstoke Palgrave Macmillan.

Daniel, B. and Taylor J. (2004) *Child Neglect: Practice Issues for Health and Social Care*, London: Jessica Kingsley Publishers.

Cable, C., Miller L. and Goodliff, G (Eds) (2009) *Working with Children in the Early Years*, Abingdon: David Fulton/Routledge.

Trodd, L. (2013) *Transitions in the Early Years: Working with Children and Families*, London: Sage Publications Ltd.

Websites

www.education.gov.uk
General information about all aspects of education.

www.foundationyears.org.uk
Information about early years education.

www.rospa.com
Information about home safety.

www.nidirect.gov.uk
Information on schools and special educational needs and disabilities.

www.earlychildhoodnews.com
Earlychildhood News – professional resource for tutors and parents.

www.nhs.uk
NHS Choices – information about signs, symptoms and treatments.

THINK ▶FUTURE

Emily Ayrman

Children's nurse

I've been working as a children's nurse for many years but my first serious thoughts about a career within this sector began as a teenager. After completing my BTEC National in Health and Social Care, I applied to university to begin nurse training and thoroughly enjoyed it. I was interested in working with children so I continued training and qualified as a children's nurse, so that I could work specifically with children. Some aspects of training for children's nursing were quite challenging, but I really enjoyed the practice elements. Approximately half of my time was spent in practical training and experience.

I learned to communicate with other people in many different ways. This included talking to the children and their parents, gaining their trust and listening to their concerns. In addition, I learned to comfort and reassure families, demonstrating confidence and authority, so that they would trust me to provide a high standard of care and treatment. I learned to relate to and be open with my colleagues, and to ensure that I understood instructions and treatments, and always to record and check that all details are correct.

Once I'd qualified, I secured a position in a local hospital and I loved working on the children's wards and making a difference in their young lives. All my friends and family kept telling me that I'd find working with the very young too difficult. However, I don't find this and feel that I have a lot to offer the children in my care. For many children being in hospital is quite traumatic and I'm usually able to help them settle by talking to them about their worries, while looking after their health care. I thoroughly enjoy the work I do as I can make such a difference to children's lives.

Focusing your skills

Monitoring and assessing growth and development

It is important to be aware of whether growth and development is progressing within the accepted norms. You will use these skills every day in any role when working with children. This will equip you to provide the best care, attention and resources for them. Think about each of the areas of development (physical, intellectual, language, social and emotional) and consider the value of assessing and monitoring children's progress against developmental milestones.

- What are the implications of making uninformed judgements following an observation? What is the rationale for referencing your findings against the established work of those who have researched child development patterns?

- What type of assessment methods are used in more formal settings, such as primary schools? How does assessment differ in the Early Years Foundation Stage from the National Curriculum assessments?
- What monitoring and assessment programmes are health professionals involved in?

Healthy eating – questions

Observations are part of your daily routine. Consider these questions:
- Why is it important to eat a healthy diet?
- Why should babies and young children not be fed with 'diet' foods?
- Can you name the five items to be included in a balanced diet?
- Why should sugar and saturated fat be limited in a healthy diet?

Getting ready for assessment

Jamila is working towards a BTEC National in Health and Social Care. She was given an assignment for Learning aim A, in which she had to produce a document about different stages of growth and development, with details about how the related theories might support children in a childcare setting. This information would form part of a portfolio that would be available for new members of staff. She was able to use case studies for children aged 1, 3 and 6 years of age. The work had to:

▸ explain whether or not the child in each case study was at the typical stage of development for their age, and relate this to the norms of development.

▸ provide details of the related theories of development and suggest how they might be used to support the child in their childcare setting. Jamila shares her experience below.

How I got started

First I collected all my notes and put them into a folder. I would need to ensure that I had a clear understanding of the work of the different theorists. I'd written up some notes about the milestones of development that I'd used for some observations from my placement. I sorted my information into the different areas of development so that I could clarify my thoughts about each section. I began by looking at the case studies and linking the age of the child in each study to the norms of development. I could then make a judgement about whether the child was at a typical stage of development or not. I then needed to consider how the theories of development linked to the examples from the studies. Once I'd sorted my notes out, the task became much easier.

How I brought it all together

I'd been asked to produce a document to be used in a portfolio, so I decided to make it interesting. I thought it would be better to break up the text by using some appropriate pictures to emphasise certain points. I was aware that confidentiality is important so I didn't use any photos from my placement. I started with an introduction to explain why it's important to be able to recognise typical and atypical development in children.

I then went on to:

▸ Use the case studies to demonstrate how childcare workers might judge whether or not a child is showing typical development patterns. I mapped the behaviour to the appropriate milestone, which provided me with an approximate age for that behaviour. I was then able to state that for the particular case study the child was (or was not) demonstrating typical behaviour for that age.

▸ Determine which of the theorists' works could explain why that behaviour was present for that particular activity and age range.

Finally, I wrote a short summary as a conclusion to the article.

What I learned from the experience

I realised how important observations are when considering the growth and development of a child. If they are carried out at regular intervals they can be very beneficial for informing the next stage for planning activities. I also realised that I need to improve my time management as the work took a little longer than I'd thought.

Think about it

▸ Have you considered writing an action plan with deadlines so you can complete your assignment by the agreed submission date?

▸ Do you have notes on the milestones of children's development and the work of the major theorists? If you start with the milestones, you will have them at hand when writing up your observations and other assignment work.

▸ Is your information written in your own words (to demonstrate your understanding) and referenced clearly?

Nutritional Health 19

Getting to know your unit

Assessment
You will be assessed by a series of assignments set by your tutor.

Good nutrition is widely recognised as being vital for health. Yet, as a nation, there is an increasing incidence of obesity and illnesses, such as type 2 diabetes and heart disease, which can result from poor nutrition.

In addition, a good diet is important for recovery from illness. Past studies have shown that people receiving care have not always received sufficient nutrition, with adverse effects on their recovery.

It is crucial that care workers have a good understanding of nutrition, as well as of the reasons why individuals may not be eating an adequate diet, and how this can be rectified.

How you will be assessed

This unit will be assessed by your tutor, by a series of internally assessed tasks set by them. There are a variety of activities within this unit that will consolidate your knowledge and stimulate your ideas. There are two assessment practices that will enable you to check you have all the knowledge needed to complete the assignment. These give you the opportunity to develop your technique and support you to achieve the higher grades.

When producing work for the final assessment, it is crucial that you check your work thoroughly against the unit specification, to ensure you have not missed anything out. This is important, as the Pass criteria cannot be awarded if the work is incomplete. It also gives you an opportunity to check your work for spelling, punctuation and grammar errors.

If you are hoping to achieve the Merit and Distinction grades, it is important that you pay attention to the descriptor verbs in the task. These are words like 'explain', 'describe', 'analyse' and 'evaluate'.

The assignment set by your tutor will be made up of a number of tasks, which will give you the opportunity to present all the information needed to achieve the Distinction criteria. It will involve a mixture of written answers and activities, including:

▸ a resource for volunteers
▸ an examination of factors affecting two individuals with specific dietary needs
▸ an assessment of the nutritional intake of the two individuals
▸ professionally presented recommendations for improvements to the two individuals' diet.

Assessment criteria

This table shows what you must do in order to achieve a **Pass**, **Merit** or **Distinction** grade, and where you can find activities to help you.

Pass	**Merit**	**Distinction**

Learning aim A Understand concepts of nutritional health and characteristics of essential nutrients

Pass	**Merit**	**Distinction**
A.P1 Explain how the concepts of nutritional health contribute to health and wellbeing. Assessment practice 19.1	**A.M1** Assess the impact of dietary intake and dietary deficiencies on nutritional health. Assessment practice 19.1	**AB.D1** Evaluate the role of nutritional health in maintaining the selected individuals' health and wellbeing, and the impact of influencing factors. Assessment practice 19.1
A.P2 Explain the sources of essential nutrients and their functions in the body. Assessment practice 19.1		

Learning aim B Examine factors affecting dietary intake and nutritional health

Pass	**Merit**	**Distinction**
B.P3 Explain the health, socio-economic and cultural factors that can influence the nutritional health of the selected individuals. Assessment practice 19.1	**B.M2** Assess how the dietary intake and nutritional health of the selected individuals are influenced by their dietary habits and lifestyle choices. Assessment practice 19.1	
B.P4 Compare the dietary intake of the selected individuals with their nutritional requirements. Assessment practice 19.1		

Learning aim C Plan nutrition to improve individuals' nutritional health

Pass	**Merit**	**Distinction**
C.P5 Produce clear plans to improve the nutritional health of two individuals with different dietary needs. Assessment practice 19.2	**C.M3** Produce professionally presented plans to improve the nutritional health of two individuals with different dietary needs. Assessment practice 19.2	**C.D2** Justify the recommendations in the plans in relation to the needs and situations of the selected individuals. Assessment practice 19.2
C.P6 Explain how the recommendations will improve the nutritional health of the selected individuals. Assessment practice 19.2	**C.M4** Analyse how the recommendations will improve the nutritional health of the selected individuals. Assessment practice 19.2	**C.D3** Evaluate the importance of planning nutritional health for selected individuals to ensure their dietary needs are met, and that influencing factors are taken into account. Assessment practice 19.2

 A # Understand concepts of nutritional health and characteristics of essential nutrients

Concepts of nutritional health

To provide nutritious, healthy food and advice on healthy eating, it is important to understand the theory behind the wealth of dietary information that is published. You also need to understand the way that processing can affect the nutritional value of foods, so you can avoid destroying nutrients.

This section looks at the current advice and issues affecting the diet of people who live in the UK.

Healthy eating and a balanced diet

The National Diet and Nutrition Survey, published in May 2014, showed that, on average, the population of the UK is still consuming too much saturated fat, added sugars, salt, and not enough fruit, vegetables, oily fish and fibre. Dietary advice has been available to people in the UK for many decades. During the Second World War the government issued leaflets with recipes for nourishing meals, alongside healthier lifestyles and dietary advice. Current advice has been designed to be easy to understand and hopefully, more likely to be followed.

Eatwell plate and main food groups

The eatwell plate is a visual representation of the proportions of each different type of food you should consume.

The eatwell plate illustrates food in groups as this is a simple way of categorising foods. The five main food groups are:

▸ fruit and vegetables (33 per cent)

▸ bread, other cereals and potatoes (33 per cent)

▸ milk and dairy products (15 per cent)

▸ foods containing fat and foods containing sugar (7 per cent)

▸ meat, fish and alternatives (12 per cent).

It is easier for people to plan a healthy diet if advice is not too complicated. Even children can usually understand these food groups. Anyone on a special diet may need help from a dietician to adapt this to their dietary restrictions.

Malnutrition, including under-nutrition and obesity

You might think of malnutrition as a condition in which people are not getting enough to eat, however, malnutrition is any condition in which the body does not receive sufficient nutrients to function properly. Malnutrition can include both under-nutrition and **over-nutrition**.

> **Key term**
>
> **Over-nutrition** – a condition that results either from eating too much, or eating too many of the wrong types of food, or taking too many vitamins or other dietary supplements.

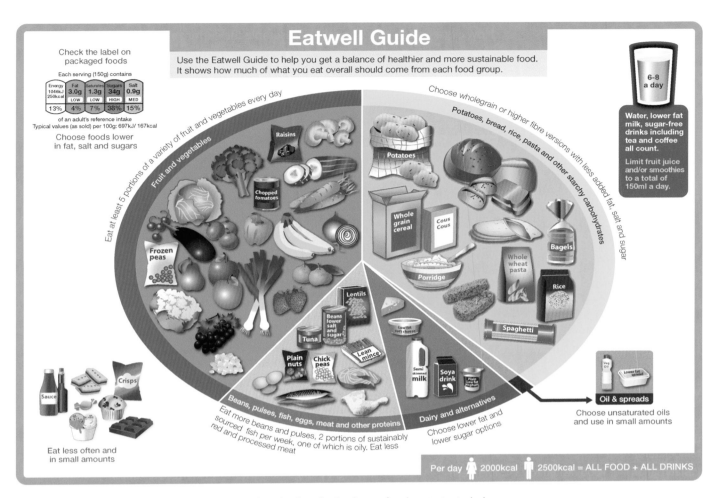

▸ **Figure 19.1** Public Health England promotes this pie chart in the form of a plate to try to help people to visualise the proportion of their daily intake that should come from different types of foods (Source: **www.gov.uk**).

Under-nutrition

Under-nutrition is a **deficiency** of calories, or of one or more essential nutrients, and results from having insufficient food, or a person having a condition where they are unable to digest nutrients from the diet. This might include conditions such as ulcerative colitis, when food passes through the digestive tract very quickly before the nutrients can be absorbed into the bloodstream. The Department of Health considers a person with a body mass index of less than 18.5 to be underweight.

Overweight and obesity

The World Health Organization defines:

▸ Overweight as having a body mass index greater than or equal to 25. Being overweight increases the risk of arthritis, type 2 diabetes and high blood pressure.

▸ Obesity as having a body mass index greater than or equal to 30.

The National Audit Office warns that being obese can take up to nine years off your lifespan. In addition to the health problems linked to being overweight, people who are obese are far more likely to develop health problems such as cancer, heart disease, stroke, infertility and depression.

> **Key term**
>
> **Deficiency** – the absence of a particular nutrient in the body, due to a lack in the diet or conditions that prevent nutrients being absorbed from the diet.

PAUSE POINT How closely does your normal diet resemble the current advice for a healthy diet?

> Hint How does it compare with recommendations illustrated by the eatwell plate?

> Extend If your diet does not resemble the eatwell plate, look at the differences to see if you are at risk of malnutrition.

Effects of food processing methods

In recent years warnings have been given about eating too much processed food. Foods that are processed have been altered in some way, sometimes to make them last longer, or for convenience.

Table 19.1 shows the various methods that food manufacturers use to prevent food from deteriorating. Some methods have a detrimental effect on the nutritional value of foods.

▶ **Table 19.1** Methods used to prevent food from deteriorating

Method		Positive effects	Negative effects
Canning	Cooked and sealed without air to prevent aerobic bacteria from reproducing.	Retains protein and carbohydrate, safe to consume for several years.	Vitamins B complex and C are lost, can be high in salt or sugar.
Freezing	Frozen quickly after harvest or cooking.	Does not usually need additives or preservatives. Vitamins and antioxidants retained.	Some ready meals have additives and can be high in salt and sugar.
Vacuum packed	Air removed as food is sealed in plastic packaging.	Lasts 2–3 weeks in fridge as no air for aerobic bacterial reproduction.	Some foods are salted before sealing, so may have high salt content.
UHT (Ultra-high temperature)	Food is sterilised by heating for 1–2 seconds to above 135 °C.	Heat kills bacteria and spores. Lasts 6–9 months before opening.	Can affect taste, but no effect on nutritional value.
Pasteurisation	Food heated to 73 °C for fifteen seconds.	Food lasts slightly longer and taste is unchanged.	No negative effects.
Additives	Substances are added to foods in addition to the main ingredients.	Improves flavour, taste, colour, or consistency, or improves shelf life.	Some people have reactions to additives.
Curing	Foods are preserved using salt and sodium or potassium nitrite or nitrate, inhibiting growth of micro-organisms.	Increases shelf life without refrigeration.	Makes the salt content very high, which can pose a health risk.
Jams and preserves	Fruits are boiled with sugar and poured into sterilised jars.	Dehydrates bacteria to prevent fruit from rotting.	Little nutritional value as heating destroys vitamins, and very high in sugar.
Smoking	Food is exposed to wood smoke.	Inhibits the growth of bacteria.	Chemicals produced by this method have been linked to cancer.
Pickling	Storing food in acetic acid, for example vinegar.	The acidity prevents the growth of bacteria.	Has been linked to stomach and oesophageal cancers.

Key term

Antioxidant – substances that may prevent or delay some types of cell damage, such as cancer. Antioxidants are found in many foods, including fruits and vegetables and include beta-carotene, lycopene and vitamins A, C and E.

Effect of food preparation methods

The nutritional value of food can be affected by the way food is prepared. Fresh vegetables served raw have a high nutritional value, as long as they are fresh. Cooking vegetables destroys some of the vitamins, but some cooking methods cause less damage than others. When vegetables are boiled, the vitamins are lost into the water, and the longer they are boiled the more vitamins are lost. However, studies have shown that cooked tomatoes contain more lycopene, an **antioxidant** that reduces the risk of heart disease and some types of cancers.

If you use the water from boiling your vegetables to make gravy, you can save some of the vitamins. Or you can steam them instead, to retain much of their nutritional value. Stir-frying is also a good cooking method for retaining vitamins, and only requires a minimal amount of fat. Cooking vegetables in a casserole with meat retains the goodness in the gravy, and roasting vegetables also releases more nutrients than steaming or stir-frying.

Frying food is quick, and retains nutrients, but adds calories to a meal, unless dry frying, frying without adding fat to the pan, is used. Grilling is also quick, and has the added advantage of allowing fat to drip away from the food during the cooking process.

The nutritional value of food is reduced by keeping food hot, so whenever possible food should be served as soon as it is cooked.

II   PAUSE POINT   What advice would you give about the healthiest ways to preserve, store and cook foods?

> **Hint**   Choose methods to maximise nutrition and minimise health risks.
>
> **Extend**   Find out if there is evidence to back up benefits and risks linked to different ways of preserving and cooking food.

Current nutritional issues and effects on health

The food industry is constantly developing. Research results are often summarised in the media, informing us about recent discoveries of harm or benefits from different foods, or substances used in food processing. More efficient methods are discovered to make food production more cost effective.

Self-prescribed health supplements

According to the Food Supplements (England) (Amendment) Regulations 2007, food supplements are sold in dose form and are intended to add to, not replace, the normal diet. Examples include vitamin and mineral tablets. A well-balanced diet should include all the nutrients needed to keep you well. However, some people struggle to consume sufficient amounts of important vitamins and minerals. This includes fussy eaters and those unable to eat certain foods for medical reasons. It also includes people with conditions leading to poor absorption, or who experience frequent diarrhoea. Food supplements can also benefit people who need to consume high quantities of particular substances, for example a woman who suffers from heavy periods may benefit from iron supplements to help replace the iron lost during her period.

Genetically modified foods

According to the World Health Organization, foods are genetically modified (GM) if the DNA of the cells making up that food has been altered.

Genetic modification may be done for several reasons. One is to produce higher yields of crops, which could be vital to avert starvation in developing countries in a world where the population continues to rise.

Crops may be modified to make them poisonous to pests that damage the crop, removing the need to use pesticides. This is better for the environment and reduces the exposure of the farm workers to pesticides.

Some crops are modified to make them more nutritious. For example, a strain of rice has been developed that is richer in vitamin A, a nutrient that can be lacking in some Asian diets.

A further advantage of GM foods is that they last longer before starting to deteriorate, GM tomatoes, bananas and pineapples have all been produced to last longer.

Nutritional measures and recommended dietary intakes

A good understanding of the function of different components of food is useful for care workers, who may need to advise individuals about dietary changes required to improve health.

Balancing energy requirements for protein, fat, carbohydrate (kilocalories and kilojoules)

The body needs energy to function. Even when you are resting, your body uses energy for all the processes going on inside, such as respiration, temperature control, digestion and cell repair. This is known as the basal metabolic rate. The amount of energy you need for this depends on your age, gender, size and the climate you live in. It also depends on your lifestyle. If you have a strenuous job or do a lot of exercise, your energy needs will be greater. It is important to balance the amount of energy being used and the amount of calories eaten. Too many calories will lead to weight gain, and too few, to weight loss.

Of course, it is not just calories that you need to think about, but the type of foods you eat. Energy comes from the carbohydrate, fat and protein in your diet. Nutritional balance means having just the right proportion of different types of food.

If you look at the labels on packaged food, you will notice that energy is measured in two different units, kilocalories and kilojoules. Kilocalories are the units normally referred to as calories, and are the ones normally used to measure and control intake when people are trying to lose or gain weight. Kilojoules are a different measure, mainly used by scientists, 1 kilocalorie equals 4.2 kilojoules.

Measuring body mass index (BMI)

The body mass index is used to decide whether people are the right weight for their height. The ideal BMI is between 18.5 and 24.9.

In recent years, the value of BMI as a tool to identify obesity has been questioned as it does not take into account overall percentages of body fat and muscle. Muscle weighs more than fat, so individuals with a higher percentage of muscle will weigh more. Some practitioners now recommend that waist size is a better predictor of risk to health. Ideally, the waist measurement should not exceed half that of the height.

Worked example: Overweight or obese?

Using the formula BMI = weight in kilograms/(height in metres)^2

The BMI of a person who weighs 60 kg and measures 1.9 m would be:

$$\frac{60}{(1.9)^2} = \frac{60}{3.61} = 16.6$$

This would categorise the person as underweight.

Over to you:

Calculate the BMI of the following individuals:

Stewart – weight 50 kg, height 1.7 m

Shabnum – weight 78 kg, height 1.6 m

Claude – weight 85 kg, height 1.8 m

Weight for height and gender

When monitoring people's weight, it is important to consider their height and gender. A person who weighs 80 kg (12 stone 7 lbs) would be very overweight if they were 1.45 m (4 ft 9 ins) tall, but would be normal weight if they measured 1.9 m (6 ft 2 ins). Men are slightly heavier than women of the same height because they usually have more muscle.

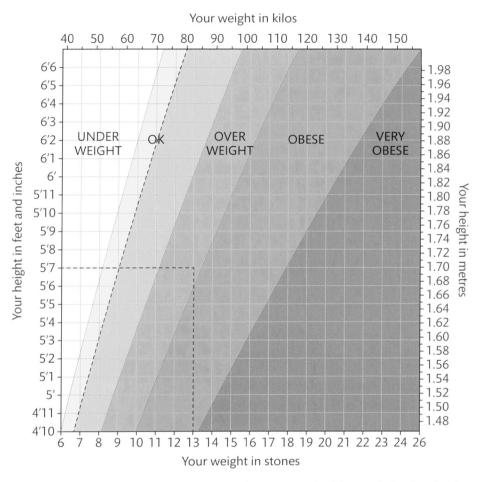

▶ **Figure 19.2** This chart is an easy way to check if a person is a healthy weight for their height (Source: NHS Choices, 2015).

Using growth charts to monitor weight gain

Babies and young children should have their weight regularly monitored, and this is usually done at a special clinic in the local health centre. This is to monitor their weight gain, so that action can be taken if they are not putting weight on or putting weight on too quickly. Their weight is recorded on a chart, which also records their birth weight. There are lines printed on the chart showing the range of weights for children according to their age, so babies can be compared to others of the same age. The normal range is quite large. The most important thing is the rate of increase, and just because a baby is within the normal range for their age does not mean all is well. For example, you may be worried if a baby at the top end of the scale stops putting on weight.

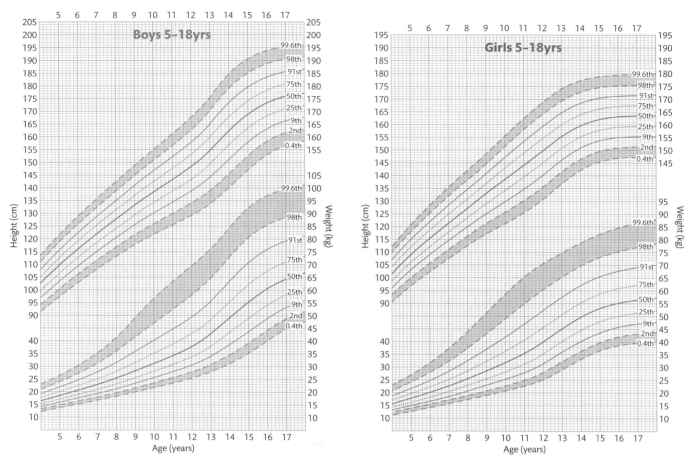

▶ **Figure 19.3** There are different charts for boys and girls, and the normal patterns of gaining weight are different according to gender

Research

Look at the two charts in Figure 19.3. Using the internet, or a child development book, find out what the different lines mean. Compare the difference between the expected height and weight at different ages for boys and girls.

Using and interpreting Dietary Reference Values, Reference Nutrient Intakes, nutrients per portion and per 100 g of food

Dietary Reference Values

Dietary Reference Values (DRVs) are estimates of the amount of energy and nutrients needed for good health. This will vary according to age, size and gender. *Dietary Reference Values for Food Energy and Nutrients for the United Kingdom* has been published by the Department for Health.

Reference Nutrient Intakes

Reference Nutrient Intake (RNI), or Reference Intake (RI) are guidelines used to inform consumers about the amount of protein, vitamins and minerals that should meet the needs of most of the group to which they apply. They are not minimum targets.

According to the UK government, on average the population of the UK meets RIs for all micronutrients (vitamins and minerals) except sodium, which is still too high, and potassium.

Nutrients per portion and per 100 g of food

When buying packaged foods, the nutritional value is usually displayed on the label. From December 2016 this is a legal requirement. The label explains the amount of calories, protein, fat, carbohydrates, sugar and salt provided per 'serving' and per 100 g, and will state how much a 'serving' weighs for that product. Some also list vitamins and minerals found in that food, and the percentage of RI is given. To compare one product with another, you should use the amount per 100 g on each product.

Compare the nutritional information displayed on the packaging of a can of beans and a can of spaghetti hoops.

(Hint)   Compare the amount per 100 g rather than the whole container, so you are comparing like with like.

(Extend)   Research the recommendations for a person with constipation and decide which product to recommend.

Characteristics of essential nutrients

As a future care worker, it is important that you understand the functions of different nutrients in the body, and the effects of dietary deficiency. It will help you to understand what foods are particularly important for individuals. You need to know common sources of particular nutrients to enable you to offer suitable foods to ensure that nutritional needs are met.

Carbohydrates

There are two different types of carbohydrate: simple carbohydrates, which are sugars, and complex carbohydrates, which are starches and fibre.

Carbohydrates provide energy for the body. People need a lot of energy just to exist. Even when you are asleep cells need oxygen and nutrients to function. Your heart needs to beat, your lungs need to take in oxygen and give out carbon dioxide. Additionally, your brain needs energy to maintain your vital functions and you need to replace cells. This is known as **basal metabolism**. When you are active you need energy for movement.

Sugars

Sugars occur naturally in foods, such as fruit and milk, or can be added when you sprinkle sugar on foods, or include it when baking (these are known as **free sugars**). Some of the simplest forms of sugar are glucose and fructose, which are single molecules and are absorbed into the bloodstream and transported around the body to provide energy.

Sugars are added to many types of foods. You will not be surprised to learn that biscuits and cakes contain added sugar, but you may not be aware that there is sugar in ketchup, beer, high-fibre snack bars and some tinned vegetables.

The ingredient listed first on food labels is the main ingredient. It is surprising how many foods list a sugar as the first, or one of the main ingredients. Sometimes sugar is listed as:

- glucose or glucose syrup
- sucrose
- maltose
- dextrose
- invert sugar.

Recently, new evidence has emerged that eating a diet high in free sugars can increase the risk of heart disease, obesity and type 2 diabetes. The current recommendations state that free sugars should not exceed 5 per cent of your total energy intake. This is half of the previous recommendation.

Starch

The Food Standards Agency (FSA) and NHS Choices recommend that a third of the food you eat should come from starchy foods such as pasta, rice, bread, potatoes and chapattis, with wholegrain foods being particularly healthy. Starchy foods are sometimes referred to as complex carbohydrates. Starchy foods release energy more slowly than sugars, so will keep you satisfied longer. Starches are

Key terms

Basal metabolism – the energy necessary to maintain vital body functions, such as respiration and circulation, while fasting and at total rest.

Free sugars – sugars added to foods, including in baking, as opposed to naturally occurring sugars, such as lactose in milk and fructose in fruit.

▶ **Figure 19.4** Sugar is in many foods and drinks, not all of which taste particularly sweet.

Reflect

Look at labels when you are buying snacks. If any of these ingredients appears first or high in the list, see if you can find something else to buy instead that contains less sugar.

polysaccharides, which are made of many **monosaccharide** molecules combined together. In digestion, complex carbohydrates are broken down into glucose, a monosaccharide, for conversion to energy.

If the body does not need all the glucose in the bloodstream, the hormone insulin is released from the pancreas. Insulin converts excess glucose into glycogen, which is stored in the liver and muscles. Excess glucose may also be stored as body fat.

When blood glucose is low another hormone, glucagon, is released from the pancreas. Glucagon converts glycogen back into glucose. When glucose is needed quickly, for example in response to stress or a threat, the adrenal glands release the hormone epinephrine. Epinephrine converts glycogen in the muscles back to glucose so that the body is ready to respond to the threat or stress.

Non-starch polysaccharides

Non-starch polysaccharides, also known as fibre, are an important component of a healthy, balanced diet. They are important in the processes of digestion and elimination.

Proteins

Protein is a vital nutrient and is essential to health. It is used by the body for growth and repair, so it is particularly important for infants and children, and people who are ill or injured. Proteins are made up of amino acids.

There are 20 different amino acids, which can combine to form different polypeptides, nine of which must come from the food you eat. These are known as essential amino acids. The remaining 11 amino acids you can make yourself. These are known as non-essential amino acids. Complete proteins provide all of the nine essential amino acids and include meat, fish, poultry, eggs, milk, soya and cheese.

Protein is used in the body in a variety of ways. All tissues in the body contain protein, including muscle, hair and bone. Enzymes and hormones are also proteins. Proteins are used in all activities taking place inside the body, such as messages travelling along nerves, digesting food, and muscles contracting.

The recommended daily intake of protein varies according to age, size, gender and how active a person is. For example, a baby boy weighing 4 kg needs approximately 10 g of protein per day – about 2.5 g per kg body weight. An adult only needs about 0.75 g of protein per kg body weight, so if you weigh 60 kg you need about 45 g of protein a day.

It is unusual for people in the UK to lack protein in their diet. In fact, the average daily intake of protein in the UK, according to the British Nutrition Foundation, is 88 g for men and 64 g for women, which is more than sufficient. It certainly should not be the case in a residential care setting that individuals are not receiving adequate protein, although people receiving day care may not receive an adequate diet at home.
This should be identified by a good care worker, so that support with meals can be initiated. If someone is following a vegan or vegetarian diet you must make sure it is varied, so that all the nine essential amino acids are eaten. Do not worry too much as the body can store amino acids for a short time, so as long as the diet is varied and well-balanced there should not be a problem. Good vegan sources of protein include nuts, seeds, lentils, beans, and soya. In fact, 2 oz of kidney beans, chick peas or lentils contain as much protein as 3 oz of steak. They are low in fat, and these nutritious foods are loaded with fibre so will keep a person feeling full for a long time.

Fats and oils

In 2013, the Family Food Survey estimated the average energy intake of fat in the UK was 35 per cent higher than the recommended maximum. The current government recommendation is that average (population) intake of total fat should account for no more than 35 per cent and saturated fatty acids no more than 11 per cent of food energy intake. On average, this is 30 g per day for men and 20 g per day for women.

Another word for fats and oils is lipids. Lipids are insoluble in water. A high percentage (95 per cent) of lipids in your diet is triglycerides, which are made up of three fatty acids attached to glycerol. Bile, secreted from the gall bladder into the digestive tract, and lipase, secreted from the pancreas into the jejunum, starts the digestion of lipids by splitting the fatty acids and glycerol apart.

Fatty acids can be used as energy in most cells. Glycerol can be converted into glucose by the liver and can be used for cellular respiration. It is important to have some fat in your diet, as it is an important source of vitamins A, D, E and helps you to absorb vitamin K. You also need to eat fat to make hormones, to keep your skin healthy and to prevent loss of body heat. Fat is high in calories, so provides energy, although current recommendations say you should get most of your energy from carbohydrates. Eating too much fat for your nutritional and energy needs can contribute to the development of obesity.

Monounsaturates, polyunsaturates, and saturates

Fatty acids are made up of carbon, hydrogen and oxygen. There are two main types of fat: saturated and unsaturated. Monounsaturated and polyunsaturated fats have fewer hydrogen atoms than saturated fats.

Most saturated fat comes from animal sources, such as lard, cream, butter and the fat on meat. One exception is coconut oil, which is 90 per cent saturated. Saturated fat is generally solid at room temperature. Most unsaturated fat is from vegetable sources and is usually liquid at room temperature.

Unsaturated fats contain essential fatty acids that cannot be manufactured by the body so that you need to get them from food. Unsaturated fat in the diet can lower the levels of low-density lipoproteins (LDLs), known as 'bad' cholesterol in the blood, and raise the levels of high-density lipoproteins (HDLs), known as 'good' cholesterol. HDLs protect against heart disease. Saturated fat has long been blamed for the high rate of heart disease and strokes in the UK. Research is ongoing but the current advice remains to limit consumption of saturated fat. There is also some evidence that a diet high in saturated or unsaturated fat can increase the risk of cancer.

Cis and trans fats

Unsaturated fats can exist in two different forms, as cis fats or trans fats. Most of the fats found in animals and plants exist in the form of cis fats. Cis fats are monounsaturated or polyunsaturated, but have a short shelf life. Hydrogenation is a process of adding hydrogen to cis fats to change them into trans fats, which makes them saturated. This increases their shelf life, but the resulting products are thought to increase the risk of heart disease. Many food manufacturers have stopped using them in their products.

Cholesterol

You naturally make a certain amount of cholesterol yourself, and some people make more than others. Cholesterol can build up in the artery walls, narrowing the lumen (the central cavity). If this happens in the coronary arteries it may eventually lead to angina or a heart attack. If arteries in the brain are affected, the risk of having a stroke is increased.

People who naturally make a high amount of cholesterol need to be particularly careful to eat a diet low in saturated fat. They can be prescribed medication, called statins, which reduce the cholesterol in the blood, thus reducing the chances of a heart attack or stroke. Some people are lucky to have a naturally low cholesterol level.

It is recommended that everyone, except children under five years of age, have a diet low in saturated fat. Children under five years of age may struggle to take in sufficient calories to meet their energy needs, if their diet is low in fat. While you cannot dictate to adults what they eat, it is important to offer healthier alternatives and ensure that service users are aware of healthy eating advice, so they can make an informed choice.

PAUSE POINT   Next time you eat a meal, identify the protein, carbohydrate and fat in the food you are eating.

Hint   Some foods contain more than one food group.

Extend   Compare your meal to Figure 19.1. Try to adjust your meals so that your diet matches the eatwell plate.

Vitamins

Vitamins are essential nutrients that your body needs in small amounts to work properly. There are two types of vitamins: fat-soluble and water-soluble. Excess fat-soluble vitamins can be stored in the body and, therefore, do not have to be eaten daily, whereas excess water-soluble vitamins are excreted in the urine, so a daily intake is necessary. Soaking vegetables in water for long periods before cooking them, results in vitamins being lost into the water. If you boil vegetables, use the water to make gravy. Chopping vegetables too small creates a larger surface area, and more nutrients will be lost. Vitamins are also lost when food is kept hot after cooking.

Table 19.2 shows the daily requirements for the main vitamins, food sources and deficiency diseases associated with a dietary lack. The table uses the most recently published recommendations for adults for the daily amounts of vitamins and mineral required in the diet (Food Labelling (Nutrition Information) (England) Regulations 2009).

▶ **Table 19.2** The daily requirements of the main vitamins as recommended by food labelling regulations

Vitamin	Function	Food sources	Effects of shortage	Water-/fat-soluble	Notes
A	Night vision, keeps skin and linings of nose, mouth, lungs and gut healthy. Antioxidant.	Oily fish, liver, butter, cheese, eggs, milk, fruit and vegetables.	Night blindness, itching, dry and thickened skin.	Fat-soluble	Stored in liver, excess can be harmful.
D	Absorption of calcium in intestine, regulates calcium and magnesium in bone tissue.	Fish liver, oily fish, eggs, margarine, sunlight.	**Rickets** and **osteomalacia** leading to soft bones. Children may develop bow legs. **Osteoporosis**, leading to fractures.	Fat-soluble	Produced in skin by sun, stored in liver.
E	Maintains healthy muscles, antioxidant, protects cell membranes, helps to maintain healthy skin, eyes and strengthens the immune system.	Eggs, cereal oils, veg oils, nuts, seeds.	Poor muscle, circulatory and nerve performance.	Fat-soluble	
K	Blood clotting.	Leafy vegetables (especially spinach and celery), cheese and liver, asparagus, coffee, bacon and green tea.	Rare, bleeding into brain in newborn babies.	Fat-soluble	Widely given by injection to babies at birth. Can be made by intestinal bacteria.
B group	Release of energy from carbohydrates. Metabolism of fats and proteins, health and maintenance of nervous system.	Liver, yeast, leafy green vegetables, nuts, milk and whole grains.	B_1, beri-beri; B_3, pellagra; B_9, **megaloblastic anaemia**, **neural tube defects**; aB_{12} pernicious anaemia.	Water-soluble	
C	Formation of bones, teeth, and blood, wound healing, fighting infection, healthy skin and gums. Antioxidant.	Blackcurrants, citrus fruits, green veg, peppers, tomatoes.	**Scurvy**, leading to bleeding gums and poor healing, easy bruising.	Water-soluble	Not stored in body, so daily dose needed. Lost in cooking.

Key terms

Rickets – condition in which children's bones are soft and deformed. Tends to affect the leg bones, which bear most of the child's body weight, but can also affect the spine. There is a risk of bone fractures, and children with rickets are more prone to tooth decay.

Osteomalacia – or soft bones, is vitamin D deficiency in adults. It causes bone pain, muscle weakness and an increased risk of fractures.

Osteoporosis – a condition, typically as a result of hormonal changes or deficiency of calcium or vitamin D, in which there is loss of bone tissue, weakening the bones and making them fragile, and more likely to break.

Megaloblastic anaemia – type of anaemia characterised by red blood cells that are larger than normal. There are also fewer red blood cells, so body tissues and organs do not get enough oxygen.

Neural tube defects – abnormalities of the brain, spine, or spinal cord that can happen in the first month of pregnancy. The commonest is spina bifida, where the spinal column does not close properly.

Scurvy – a rare condition caused by lack of vitamin C, which affects the body's ability to form collagen. Symptoms include tiredness, shortness of breath, pain in the limbs, swollen and bleeding gums, delayed wound healing and bruising easily.

Minerals

There are seven major minerals and nine trace minerals found in food. The main minerals to consider when planning diet are calcium, iron and sodium. Minerals have an important role in the healthy functioning of the body. Even though some are only required in tiny amounts, your health will suffer if you do not get what your body needs. Minerals are known as trace elements and are needed for three main reasons:

1 building strong bones and teeth

2 controlling body fluids inside and outside of cells

3 converting food eaten into energy.

Calcium

Adequate calcium intake is needed to develop strong bones and teeth. Vitamin D is required for the absorption of calcium from the small intestine. Calcium is laid down in the bones from birth up to early adulthood. It is particularly important for young people, especially females, to eat lots of calcium-rich foods to reduce the risk of osteoporosis in later life. Calcium is also essential for blood clotting, and helps the heart, muscles and nerves to work properly. Calcium activates certain enzymes. Good sources of calcium include milk, bread, flour, cheese, skimmed milk, green vegetables, sardines (with bones) and tofu. Insufficient calcium or vitamin D in the diet causes rickets in children or osteomalacia in adults. Bones become unusually soft and children with rickets tend to develop bow legs.

Osteoporosis is a fairly common condition in post-menopausal women and also occurs, but less commonly, in older men. The density of the bones is low, making them brittle, and vulnerable to fractures. Building bone density in the teens and early twenties by ensuring a good intake of calcium and vitamin D can protect against osteoporosis, as can treatment with hormone replacement therapy after the menopause. Weight-bearing exercise, such as skipping, walking or running is also very useful in maintaining bone density.

▶ Rickets in childhood is caused by insufficient calcium in the diet, or insufficient vitamin D, which is needed to absorb calcium.

Iron

Iron is essential for the production of haemoglobin in red blood cells. Haemoglobin is the oxygen carrying part of the cell. Lack of iron in the diet leads to iron deficiency anaemia. Symptoms include breathlessness, rapid pulse rate, feeling tired and cold, dizziness, headaches and lack of concentration. Iron also helps the immune system to function and is important for growth in childhood.

Good sources of iron in the diet are dark green leafy vegetables, red meat, liver, apricots and dried fruit. Many breakfast cereals are fortified with iron. Vitamin C increases absorption of iron. Taking iron supplements can cause constipation, nausea, vomiting and stomach ache. Taking iron supplements causes the faeces (stools) to be black, so people should be warned of this to avoid alarm.

The recommended intake of iron in men is 8.7 mg per day. After periods start and before the menopause, women require 14.8 mg per day, to compensate for blood loss during menstruation.

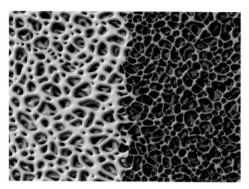

▶ You can see the effect of osteoporosis on bone density, causing bones to be brittle and break more easily; the bones on the right are more brittle.

Sodium

Sodium is an important mineral, as it helps to maintain fluid balance. Sodium works with potassium to regulate the blood pressure. Sodium also helps with muscle contraction and transmission of nerve impulses. Good sources of sodium are eggs, meat, and bread. In the UK, people are unlikely to lack sodium in their diet, as salt (sodium chloride) is used in food processing. Bacon, ham, tinned vegetables and crisps can all contain high levels of salt, and therefore sodium. You are more likely to be getting too much sodium in your diet than too little. It is recommended that adults do not consume more than 6 g of salt per day.

The most likely time that a person may lack sodium is during illness. If a person has diarrhoea, or has been perspiring heavily due to a high fever, for example, they will lose sodium. This sometimes needs to be replaced, either orally, by drinking a rehydration solution, or by intravenous drip. Signs of low sodium include dizziness, confusion, and muscle cramps.

Water

Water is not only found in drinks, but is also a component of many foods. Most of the fluid you consume comes from drinks, but you also get fluid from foods, such as lettuce and cucumber, soups and jelly. For example, fresh celery is 94 per cent water.

The average adult male is about 60 per cent water. The average adult woman is about 55 per cent water. It is very important that people have an adequate intake of fluids because most of the chemical reactions that take place in the cells of the body need water. Water is also needed to carry nutrients around the body.

Water has several very important functions including:

▶ regulating body temperature

▶ improving bowel function

▶ enabling chemical reactions to take place inside cells

▶ helping the exchange of oxygen and carbon dioxide in the lungs

▶ aiding the action of medicines.

There is medical evidence to show that water is helpful in preventing or reducing the effects of a wide variety of conditions, including:

▶ pressure ulcers   ▶ diabetes

▶ constipation   ▶ confusion

▶ kidney stones   ▶ mouth health

▶ heart disease   ▶ skin conditions

▶ urinary tract infections ▶ headaches

▶ incontinence   ▶ blood clots.

▶ low blood pressure

In recent years, advice has been to drink between six and eight glasses of water a day, in addition to drinks such as tea, coffee, soft drinks and alcohol. However, there is little scientific evidence to support this, and studies such as Valtin (2002) say that six to eight cups of any fluid are sufficient. The main signs of dehydration are feeling thirsty and dark-coloured urine, instead of pale yellow. There are groups of people who need to be observed carefully, such as children and older people, who may not recognise the sensation of thirst. People with dementia may not respond to feeling thirsty by taking a drink, even if one is nearby. Additionally, older people often restrict their fluid intake, wrongly assuming that this will reduce the likelihood of incontinence.

Dietary fibre

Dietary fibre comes from plant-based foods, such as vegetables and cereals, and is not absorbed by the body. This means that fibre is not a nutrient, and contains no useable calories or vitamins. It is very important, however, because it helps the gut to process food and absorb nutrients. It lowers blood cholesterol and helps to control blood sugar levels, which in turn control appetite.

There are two types of fibre, soluble and insoluble. Soluble fibre can be partially digested and is important in reducing cholesterol in the blood. Pulses, such as peas, beans and lentils, are a good source of soluble fibre, as are oats. Insoluble fibre is contained in vegetable stalks, wholemeal cereal and brown rice, for example. It is also known as cellulose. It is important because it forms the bulk in faeces, preventing constipation, and is thought by some experts to help prevent bowel cancer and other bowel disorders. Fibre makes people feel full, so they are less likely to overeat.

Dietary sources and deficiencies

As we have seen, all the nutrients above are essential components of a healthy diet. A diet that is lacking in any of these nutrients can cause deficiencies that may be harmful to a person's overall health and well-being. The table below summarises the main dietary sources of each group of nutrients and gives examples of the symptoms that might occur if the diet is deficient in this area.

Can you name all six components of food, and the sources of each?

 Hint   Look at the eatwell plate to refresh your memory.

Extend   What advice would you give to a friend who has become a vegan, to ensure they have a balanced diet?

▶ **Table 19.3** Dietry sources of essential nutrients and symptoms of deficiency

Nutrient	Dietary Sources	Effects of Deficiency
Protein	• Complete proteins – meat, fish, eggs, poultry, milk, soya, cheese	• Muscle wasting, hair loss, delayed wound healing. • Severe lack of protein causes marasmus or kwashiorkor. Symptoms include diarrhoea, fatigue, limited growth in children, cognitive impairment. In kwashiorkor individuals also develop fluid in the abdomen.
Carbohydrate	• Sugars – honey, granulated sugar, cakes, biscuits, fruit, milk • Starches – flour, bread, potato, rice • Fibre – leafy veg, whole wheat, dried fruit	• Insufficient intake of starchy carbohydrates causes ketosis, where fat is broken down to supply energy, and ketones build up in the blood stream as a by-product. Symptoms of ketosis are dehydration, chemical imbalance, characteristic breath odour. • Insufficient fibre leads to constipation.
Fats	• Saturated – butter, cream, meat • Unsaturated – olive oil, rapeseed oil, avocado, nuts and seeds	• Insufficient intake of fats could mean that the intake of fat-soluble vitamins A, D, E and K is also inadequate. This can affect night vision, skin and epithelial cells, the immune response, bone strength, the nervous system and blood clotting.
Vitamins (fat soluble)	• Vitamin A – fish oil, liver, butter, cheese, eggs, milk • Vitamin D – oily fish, liver, eggs, milk, margarine • Vitamin E – eggs, cereal, vegetable oils, nuts and seeds • Vitamin K – green leafy vegetables, cheese, vegetable oils, coffee, bacon and green tea	• Insufficient vitamin A affects the ability to see in low light, and increases the risk of death from infectious diseases. • Insufficient vitamin D affects bone strength, leading to rickets in children and osteomalacia or osteoporosis in adults. Rickets causes bowing of legs, osteomalacia causes bone cracks and muscle weakness, and osteoporosis causes bones to become brittle and an increase in risk of fractures. • Vitamin E deficiency can cause involuntary movements and a loss of feeling in the lower legs and feet. • Vitamin K deficiency causes bleeding disorders, with blood slow to clot. Bruising is another sign.
Vitamins (water soluble)	• B Group – liver, yeast, leafy green vegetable, nuts, milk and whole grains • Vitamin C – oranges, blackcurrants, potatoes	• B_1 (Thiamine) deficiency affects the heart and circulation, or nerve and muscle weakness. • B_3 (Niacin) deficiency, known as pellagra, causes mental confusion, diarrhoea, nausea, inflamed mucous membranes and scaly skin • B_9 (folic acid) deficiency is linked with neural tube defects in unborn children, and megoblastic anaemia in adults. • B_{12} (folate) deficiency causes anaemia, as vitamin B_{12} is used in the production of red blood cells. • Deficiency of vitamin C is called scurvy. Signs of scurvy are bleeding gums, poor healing, increased incidence of infection.
Minerals	• Calcium – milk, cheese, white flour, sardines, green vegetables, tofu • Iron – eggs, liver, green vegetables, dried fruit • Sodium – bacon, ham, tinned veg, crisps, table salt	• Signs of calcium deficiency include rickets in children, osteomalacia and osteoporosis in adults, numbness or tingling in fingers, muscle cramps, abnormal heartbeat and high blood pressure. • Iron deficiency leads to anaemia, a low level of red blood cells. A person with iron deficiency anaemia will be pale, have a fast pulse and may feel dizzy and lack of concentration. • Signs of sodium deficiency include headache, nausea, vomiting, tiredness, muscle spasms and seizures. Sodium deficiency is called hyponatraemia.

B　Examine factors affecting dietary intake and nutritional health

Dietary needs of individuals

Although there is general guidance for healthy eating, dietary needs do change as you grow, develop and age.

Children and young people

During childhood, growth and development is rapid, and children are, or should be, very active. An adequate intake of protein and carbohydrates is, therefore, very important.

The NHS publishes advice on healthy eating for children who are a healthy weight, underweight or overweight to support parents in making healthy choices. A child of a healthy weight should be encouraged to eat five portions of fruit and vegetables, and to base their diet on starchy foods. High sugar or high fat foods, such as sweets, cakes, sugary drinks and biscuits should be limited to occasional treats rather than forming their main diet. This will reduce the risks of obesity and tooth decay. Some children are sensitive to additives in food, particularly some artificial colours, which can make some children show signs of hyperactivity. Artificial colours are given E numbers, and these are listed on the label of foods and drink, to enable parents to identify those their child is sensitive to. Cooking using raw ingredients will eliminate these from a child's diet.

The eatwell plate continues to provide a good basis for diet in the teenage years, but there are a few particular points to note. Iron is particularly important for young women once menstruation has started. This is a crucial time for maximising bone density to reduce the risk of osteoporosis in later life, as there is a rapid increase in muscle and bone mass during growth spurts for both genders. This means that protein, calcium and vitamin D are important dietary components. It is recommended that no more than 11 per cent of calories during adolescence are obtained from added sugars, so young people need to limit the amount of high sugar foods and drinks.

Adults

Once growth has stopped, adults need to maintain their weight, and try to avoid putting on extra weight, by basing their diet on the eatwell plate guidance. Being overweight increases the chances of developing arthritis, diabetes, and cancer. To reduce the risk of developing high blood pressure, salt should be limited to 6 g (about one teaspoonful) per day. High sugar foods should be a treat rather than a regular part of the diet. In 2016, the four UK Chief Medical Officers issued new recommendations that adults should have several alcohol-free days a week, and that both men and women should limit their weekly consumption of alcohol to 14 units. Drinking more than this amount has been linked with Alzheimer's disease and several cancers, including breast cancer. Previous claims that moderate drinking provides some protection against heart disease are no longer promoted. The British Heart Foundation recommends exercise, a healthy diet and not smoking as safer ways to protect the heart.

Eating at home allows you control over what you eat. Cooking from raw ingredients can be a real eye-opener when you find out exactly what goes into particular recipes, and is likely to help you eat a healthier diet.

Minimising obesity and monitoring calorie intake

It is not desirable for people to become obsessed with their weight, but it is sensible to weigh yourself every few months, just to be aware if your weight is starting to increase or decrease. It is much easier to lose a few pounds occasionally than wait until you are severely overweight. It is also important to notice any unintentional weight loss, which should be discussed with your doctor.

In 2013, Defra (the Department for Environment, Food and Rural Affairs) classified 37 per cent of adults as overweight, with a further 25 per cent classified as obese.

As people move through adulthood, they tend to increase a little in weight, due to changes in body composition. Muscle mass tends to decline after 30 years of age, and fat mass tends to increase. In addition, many people reduce their physical activity as they age.

In order to reduce the risk of obesity, it is important that there is a balance between the calories eaten and the energy being used in day-to-day life. If a person needs to lose weight, it can be helpful to monitor the calories in food, by reading the nutritional information on food packaging, and choosing foods that are low in calories but which contain the essential balance of nutrients.

Older people

According to the World Health Organization, the energy requirement per kilogram of body weight reduces in later life. Older people should still follow the basic guidelines for a healthy diet, to avoid poor nutrition. However, as people become less active they usually require fewer calories to maintain their weight, although vitamin and mineral requirements remain the same.

Older people may be less mobile and drink less water, and so have a tendency to become constipated. An adequate intake of fibre is important to prevent this. Fluid intake is crucial to reduce the risk of urinary tract infections. People who are struggling with continence problems are often reluctant to drink, however, this can make incontinence issues worse as their urine becomes more concentrated, and urinary tract infections are more likely to develop.

Osteoporosis is caused by depletion of calcium, resulting in low bone density. Although the calcium content of bone cannot be increased in later life, the loss of calcium can be reduced by ensuring that the diet contains sufficient calcium and vitamin D.

Case study

Albert

Albert is 80 years old. He lost his wife suddenly a month ago, when she had a stroke and died. They had been married for 55 years, and he had previously been fit and well. Albert looks very frail, and is very unsteady on his feet. He has not eaten anything substantial since being admitted to the hospital ward 24 hours ago, following a fall at home.

Check your knowledge

1 As a group, discuss the factors that have led to Albert's decline following the death of his wife.
2 If you were looking after Albert in hospital, what measures would you put in place to prevent a further decline in his nutritional state?
3 How would you tempt Albert to eat more?
4 What would be your priorities when planning his dietary intake?

Pregnant women

The NHS provides dietary advice leaflets to pregnant women. Additionally, women can get dietary advice from their midwife, and from the NHS Choices website. The basics of healthy eating do not change, with plenty of starchy foods for energy.

Pregnant women are advised to avoid raw or undercooked meat, patés and liver. Liver is high in vitamin A, and too much vitamin A can harm an unborn child. Protein is important to support the growing foetus, with lean meat and fish being good sources. However, tuna should be restricted to 140 g per week (for canned tuna, no more than four cans of tuna, based on a medium-sized can of tuna with a drained weight of 140 g per can). Shark, swordfish and marlin should be avoided, as they can contain high levels of mercury, which may harm the nervous system of the developing baby. Shellfish should be cooked, as raw shellfish can contain harmful bacteria and viruses.

Dairy foods are important, as these contain calcium, which supports the bone formation of the developing foetus. If insufficient calcium is consumed, the developing foetus will usually take what it needs, and this can increase the risk of dental problems in the mother. Milk and yoghurts should be made from pasteurised milk, as unpasteurised dairy produce is more likely to contain listeria, a bacterium that can cause miscarriage and stillbirth.

Pregnant women are advised to eat plenty of fruit and vegetables, which are high in vitamins and minerals, to support the growing baby. Vitamin D and folic acid are particularly important. Vitamin D supports bone development, and folic acid is recommended to reduce the risk of spina bifida and **hydrocephalus**. Fruit and vegetables are also high in fibre, to prevent constipation, a common problem in pregnancy. Dark green vegetables are high in iron, which will help to prevent iron deficiency anaemia.

Women are advised to avoid alcohol from the time they start trying to conceive (get pregnant) until after the baby is born, or until they are no longer breast feeding.

During the last three months of pregnancy, a woman needs about an extra 200 calories a day.

> **Key term**
>
> **Hydrocephalus** – a condition where cerebrospinal fluid builds up in the skull, which can cause brain damage without treatment. Treatment is by insertion of a shunt in early infancy, to drain the excess fluid into another part of the body, usually the abdominal cavity.

Breastfeeding mothers

Breastfeeding mothers need an extra 500 calories a day. A normal, healthy diet should provide sufficient nutrients to support milk production. It is important to increase fluid intake, and ensure that vitamin D intake is good, using supplements if necessary.

Alcohol and highly spiced foods should be avoided, as these will pass through to the baby. If the baby develops loose stools it is worth monitoring the mother's diet, as it may be that particular foods, such as tomatoes, are the cause.

 **PAUSE POINT**   Compare recommended diets of people at different life stages: a child, an adolescent, a pregnant woman, an active adult male and an elderly woman. Identify similarities and differences.

Hint   Identify which components support growth and development, and which increase and decrease risks of disease.

Extend   Research the risks linked to alcohol, salt, or sugar to review evidence supporting advice to avoid excessive consumption of these substances.

Factors affecting nutritional health

Dietary habits

Meal patterns

'Meal patterns' refers to the timing and the way in which a person takes their food. Some people stick to the traditional three meals a day – breakfast, lunch and dinner. However, there are many possible variations to that pattern. Some households eat together. However, in an increasingly busy world, individual family members may eat separately, and people may eat frequent snacks and microwave meals. In 2012, a study completed by Meaghen Christian, and others at the University of Leeds found that children who eat meals with their family consume more fruit and vegetables, and are more likely to develop good eating habits.

One in six meals is now eaten outside the home, contributing to 20 per cent of women's, and 25 per cent of men's total intake. Many food chains have responded to the pressure to display nutritional information on the menu, making it easier for people to make healthier choices when eating out.

Snacking

Eating between meals, once discouraged, is now normal behaviour in the UK. If the snacks consist of healthy foods and do not push the daily calorie intake above energy use, then there is no problem with this. However, there are many opportunities to purchase foods high in fat, salt and sugar from vending machines and fast food outlets, and it is these snacks that can cause a problem. Occasionally eating unhealthy foods is of no consequence, but people who consume lots of high-fat, high-sugar foods, such as crisps, chocolate and fizzy drinks, are significantly increasing their risk of obesity, high blood pressure and heart disease as they age.

Personal preferences

Most people have foods they like and foods they dislike, very few people like absolutely every food offered to them. Some people are described as fussy eaters, disliking a lot of foods. Other people feel it is morally wrong to eat animals, or think a **vegetarian** or **vegan** diet is healthier. When giving food and drink to service users, these considerations need to be taken into account, as you also need to ensure that the diet provided is nutritionally balanced. So it is not enough to serve the same meal to everyone while omitting the unwanted foods, these must be substituted with something of equal nutritional value.

> **Key terms**
>
> **Vegetarian** – a diet that does not include meat, poultry or fish, but does include eggs and dairy products.
>
> **Vegan** – a diet that excludes all meat, poultry, fish, eggs and dairy produce.

Lifestyle factors

Social eating and drinking

In 2013, Defra reported that the average energy intake from eating out was 220 kcal per person per day, accounting for 10 per cent of the total energy intake. When eating out, your diet tends to be higher in fat and protein, and lower in carbohydrates than when you eat at home.

Consumption of alcohol is another activity associated with social situations. The NHS recommends that adults do not drink more than 14 units a week, spread over three or more days. Many people are unaware of the long-term health risks of regularly exceeding recommended limits. Regular drinking raises the body's tolerance to alcohol, meaning that a person will not feel drunk as quickly, and might, therefore, gradually increase the amount of alcohol consumed.

The organ most at risk from regular over-consumption of alcohol is the liver, but the risk of cancer, strokes and heart attacks is also increased.

In 2010, a survey in the UK by YouGov on drinking habits concluded that 7.5 million people may be unaware that their drinking habits are putting them at risk.

The NHS reports that approximately 15,000 people in England die from alcohol-related causes each year, 32 per cent from liver disease, 21 per cent from cancer and 17 per cent from heart disease and strokes.

Research

As an individual, or in a group, research the long-term risks associated with alcohol.

1 How does alcohol-related liver disease (ARLD) affect the liver?

2 What are the early- and late-stage signs and symptoms of ARLD?

3 How does alcohol affect the body's cells, leading to cancer?

4 How does alcohol affect the cardiovascular system?

Useful websites: **www.nhs.uk/livewell, www.drinkaware.co.uk**

Exercise/activity levels

People who participate in strenuous activity will have different dietary needs. Professional sportspeople usually have a dietician to advise them on the most appropriate diet for their sport.

Elite athletes may eat as many as 6000 calories a day, eating lots of carbohydrate-rich food for energy. Carbohydrate is an important nutrient for athletes as it provides fuel. It is stored in the liver and muscles as glycogen, and released when needed during exercise. Carbohydrate can be quickly broken down to provide energy, but only limited amounts can be stored, so during prolonged periods of exercise glycogen will become depleted leading to an increased risk of injury. The other source of energy is fat, but this cannot be converted into energy as quickly as glycogen.

Protein-rich foods are also very important to help build and repair muscles.

The other crucial component of the diet for sportspeople is fluids. Water is usually adequate, but for intense activity isotonic (containing similar concentrations of salt and sugar to the human body) and hypotonic (less concentration of salt and sugar) drinks are useful to speed up the process of water transferring into the bloodstream.

Theory into practice

Calorie counter

There are several websites that enable you to calculate how many calories are burnt up by doing different types of exercise.

This is one of them: **www.weightlossforgood.co.uk/calorie_calculator.htm**

Experiment with all the different types of sports and fitness activities you participate in to see which ones burn the most calories.

Socio-economic factors

Cost of food

Many people think that a healthy diet costs more than an unhealthy one, but this is not necessarily true. Supermarkets are criticised for focusing on high fat, salt and sugar foods when running promotions. This is often given as the reason why people on low incomes tend to eat a less healthy diet than better off people.

Cheaper foods often have more calories, so are seen to be better value for money. However, they are often lacking in nutritional value, especially vitamins and minerals. In addition, some cheap foods do not keep you feeling full for long, and can increase the risk of over-eating and consequent obesity.

Many healthy foods are not particularly expensive. Chicken, pork, carrots, porridge oats, pasta, and lentils can all be bought cheaply and made into delicious, healthy meals.

The NHS Eat4Cheap Challenge publishes advice about how people can cut down on their food bills without compromising on the healthiness of their diet.

Some ways to reduce the cost of food include cooking from basic ingredients, making sure that leftovers are used up safely and experimenting with swapping branded foods for supermarket own brands. As a rule, unprocessed foods, such as raw meat and vegetables, from the budget range are a good buy.

Theory into practice

Comparing foods for nutrition and value

Look at a range of similar foods to compare the nutritional value. For example, three different types of biscuits, including a packet claiming to be a healthy option. Look at the values for 100 g for a fair comparison. Look at the fat content – both saturated and unsaturated – and the carbohydrate content, including sugars.

Did your findings surprise you?

Compare the price and nutritional value of three similar products from different ranges of food, economy, own label and branded.

Do you think that budget foods are less healthy? It may depend on the food you have chosen.

Access to shopping facilities

The cost of food is almost always lower at large supermarkets. This can have an impact on those not living in close proximity to one, or those who do not have access to a car to transport large shopping bags home. There are often shoppers' buses that serve rural communities once or twice a week, and, of course, people can use taxis to get home, which may be cheaper than owning a car. If people are relying on local, smaller shops, it is likely that this will increase the cost of their weekly food bill. Those who have the access and skills to use a computer and the internet, can shop online and have it delivered, or friends and family can order on behalf of a person without these skills.

Cultural factors

One of the biggest influences on your diet is your family. You will have developed your first eating habits from your primary carers, and it is they who have guided you about what you should and should not eat. This may have been directly, through teaching you about healthy eating or religious rules, or indirectly through the foods that you have been served and your carers' own food preferences.

Fasting and feasting are features of many religions, along with beliefs about certain animals being sacred or unclean. You should always respect people's religious rules on eating, even when they cannot see you preparing their meals. If a person discovers they have accidentally broken their religion's rules it can cause them great distress.

> **Discussion**
>
> Do you have people in your group who are from different cultures, or who follow different religions? If so, as a group, discuss any rules and practices about eating, drinking and mealtimes. Find out why these differences occur.

Being a guest at another family's mealtime can be awkward for young children, as they are faced with unfamiliar foods. However, it is an opportunity to introduce children to a variety of foods and to encourage them to taste new foods.

PAUSE POINT   Find out about the dietary restrictions for different religions – you could make yourself a chart.

Hint   Some religions have different dietary rules at certain times of the week or year.

Extend   Find out why these rules are important to people of different religions.

Education

A substantial amount of money is spent on educating the population about healthy eating, and food hygiene, and this education has had a considerable influence over the foods people choose to eat, and how they prepare it.

Public health and food hygiene

The local environmental health department is responsible for monitoring anyone preparing food for public consumption to ensure that the food they serve is fit to eat, and prepared in a hygienic way. If unsafe food hygiene practice is identified, improvement notices are issued, and organisations can be temporarily or permanently closed. Inspections are carried out both with and without warning, and good practice is rewarded by awarding up to five stars.

In recent years, there have been a number of prominent campaigns to improve public awareness about healthy eating. The 5 A DAY campaign began in 2003, when a £150,000 Big Lottery grant was awarded to 66 Primary Care Trusts to improve the consumption of fruit and vegetables in their local communities.

In 2013, Defra reported that 16 per cent of children were achieving five portions, having been 18 per cent in 2011, and over 20 per cent in 2007.

Change4Life, launched in 2009, inspires a range of organisations to work with families and individuals to engage in healthier lifestyles. Strategies include activity and cooking sessions in local community settings, and information stands in shopping centres. There is a range of resources, such as booklets on healthy eating, gadgets to suggest healthy food swaps, and web-based resources. The important element is that the ideas promoted are easy to incorporate into busy family lives.

A new healthy eating campaign called Sugar Smart, launched in January 2016, is focusing on the need to reduce the amount of sugar in children's diets.

Supporting change

Bethan is 26 years old. She is a lone parent of two children, Ailsa and Toby. Bethan works 25 hours a week, in a low paid job. All three members of the family are overweight. Bethan always feels tired, and justifies using local takeaways several nights a week to save her having to cook the evening meal. Evenings are mainly spent watching television, or playing board games with the children once their homework is complete. Housework is done at the weekend, as well as the grocery shopping. The family live in an inner city area, and have a very small garden, which is mainly grass.

Check your knowledge

1 Using the internet, look at the resources for the Change4Life campaign.

2 Imagine you were working in a community health centre in the area where Bethan, Ailsa and Toby, and similar families, live. How could you use the Change4Life resources to support local families to improve their wellbeing?

3 Think of some of your own ideas to add to the existing resources. Produce an outline plan to show how you could promote wellbeing to families at risk of future ill-health due to their lifestyle choices.

4 Obtain some of the Change4Life resources (**www.nhs.uk/change4life**) and plan a campaign stand for your school or college.

Marketing foods

Marketing campaigns have been blamed for poor nutritional intake. You will almost certainly have bought or eaten food because you have seen it advertised on television, billboards or in magazines. You may have also noticed food advertisements pop up when you are using the internet. There has been much media coverage on the topic of obesity, and food advertising has been heavily criticised for influencing people to buy unhealthy foods.

Research published in *The Lancet* online, in February 2015, concluded that efforts should be made to protect older children from advertisements for foods that are high in calories and low in essential nutrients, as this encourages them to develop a sweet tooth. If this could be prevented, it might be possible to reverse the obesity trend.

In 2003, Ofcom, responsible for standards on TV and radio, was asked to consider proposals to restrict the advertising of junk food during children's programmes. As a result, since December 2008 foods containing high levels of fat, salt and sugar may not be advertised at times when children are likely to be watching TV.

Restrictions on advertising in non-broadcast media, such as children's magazines, are even stricter, and only fresh fruit and vegetables may be promoted in this way. It is also not permitted to use recognised cartoon characters to promote unhealthy foods.

Of course, this only applies to children. Adults are expected to be able to understand the basics of healthy eating and to not be so easily influenced by advertisements.

Case study

Changing shopping habits

Courtney McMahon works at a community project set up in a former mining village in South Yorkshire. The obesity rates in the village are much higher than average and Courtney has been researching the eating habits of the local community. She was not surprised to find that there is a high consumption of high-fat, high-sugar foods, and a poor intake of fruit and vegetables.

Courtney decided to try to gain more understanding about the psychology used by shops to persuade customers to buy certain goods. The project is planning to open a community shop in the centre, so they could try the same techniques to persuade people to buy healthy foods.

Courtney found out that retailers have become very skilled at persuading consumers to spend their money.

- In supermarkets, the smell of freshly-baked bread is often pumped out to draw people to the in-store bakery, or just to make shoppers feel hungry.
- Products the retailer is trying to persuade shoppers to buy on impulse are placed at the entrance and at the ends of aisles.
- The large supermarket chains produce own-brand products, which have a higher profit margin than branded ones, so they often position them near well-known brands, hoping the consumer will buy the cheaper alternative.
- The products that give the highest profit are often stacked at eye-level, as it is known that consumers are more likely to buy products in their line of sight.

Check your knowledge

1 What are the major influences on your own family's food consumption? Think about the last week. Why did your family buy the food they did?

2 Discuss with other people in your group reasons for making particular food purchases.

3 Devise a plan for Courtney to use in the new community shop. Think about different types of consumers, including children, adolescents, adults and older people, males and females.

Food labelling

Food labels allow people to make choices about the food they eat. If a person is trying to choose a healthy diet they need to know whether food has a high or low content of different components.

The information printed on food packaging is governed by the European Food Information to Consumers Regulation No. 1169/2011 (FIC), which became a legal requirement in the UK in December 2014. From December 2016, an additional nutrition declaration is required providing the consumer with information about energy, fat, saturated fat, carbohydrates, sugar, protein and salt content per 100 g, and per portion. Labels must be accurate, clear and easy to understand.

Many food labels indicate the contents are healthy options. There are rules governing this. Manufacturers cannot call foods 'low fat', for example, unless the food has less than 3 g of fat per 100 g. A food cannot be labelled as a source of vitamin C unless a portion contains at least 15 per cent of the recommended daily intake. If a specific health claim is made, there must be scientific evidence to back this up. For example, there is plenty of evidence that high fibre foods are good for a healthy gut, and calcium will strengthen bones in young adults, so these claims can be made.

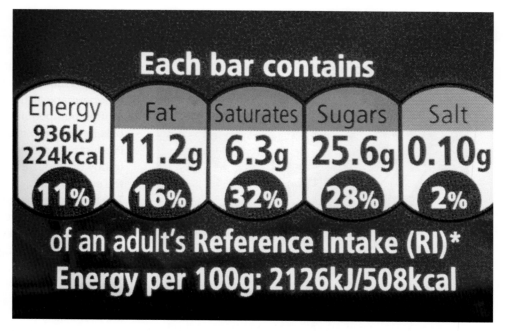

Each bar contains

Energy 936kJ 224kcal	Fat	Saturates	Sugars	Salt
11%	11.2g 16%	6.3g 32%	25.6g 28%	0.10g 2%

of an adult's Reference Intake (RI)*
Energy per 100g: 2126kJ/508kcal

▶ **Figure 19.5** The Department of Health and the FSA recommend 'at a glance' information on food packaging, giving consumers information about the nutritional content of foods through the use of traffic light colours.

Discussion

Look in the supermarket for foods using this system. You may find that you can identify the recommended daily amount of the ingredients, and what proportion of this is included in that particular product.

Do you think this has any influence on what people choose to eat? Discuss with your friends and family what they consider when choosing food products.

Role of health professionals

Health professionals have a duty to ensure that the service users in their care receive the correct type of diet for their needs.

▶ Dieticians work with people who are having difficulty in maintaining a nutritious balanced diet. This may be because of a medical condition, such as diabetes mellitus, or coeliac disease, which means that the service user's diet is restricted. They also work with people whose health is at risk because of their diet. This might include people who are obese, or who eat a really limited range of foods, putting them at risk of deficiencies in essential nutrients. Dieticians also advise people who are not eating sufficient nutrients, such as frail elderly people, those being treated for cancer, or those with swallowing disorders.

▶ Public health nutritionists are concerned with the health of the population rather than that of individuals. They advise the government about current research findings on healthy eating, to be used in public health campaigns.

▶ Doctors, in particular (GPs), are ideally placed to discuss diet during consultations. Many of the people they see do not come into regular contact with any other health professionals. The individual may have come to discuss a minor ailment, but the GP can take the opportunity to check their weight, or blood pressure, or order tests for diabetes or cholesterol levels. Advice about avoiding saturated fat or high salt foods can be given, and a referral made to a dietician, if necessary.

▶ Nurses also need a good understanding both of healthy diets and of special diets. They should be able to advise service users about which foods to choose, and which to avoid, for a range of medical conditions. Nurses are involved in administering feeds by nasogastric tube and ensuring that those who are unable to eat independently receive adequate food and drink. During protected mealtimes, all the nurses on a hospital ward are expected to concentrate on ensuring that all the patients are receiving sufficient food and fluids, particularly those who have been identified as being at risk of malnutrition. If a patient does not want to eat the meal they have been offered, alternatives, such as soup or toast, should always be available, 24 hours a day.

▶ Sports nutritionists work with athletes to devise diets that maximise their strength, stamina and fitness enabling athletes to perform at their best. The sports nutritionist prepares a diet plan that considers different needs according to whether the sports performer is training for an event, recovering from an event or injury, or resting. The diet usually includes powder supplements as well as normal foods, to match the requirements for the particular sport in which the performer participates.

⏸ **PAUSE POINT**   What obstacles might health professionals face when trying to persuade people to follow their nutritional advice?

Hint   Think about how people respond when faced with change.

Extend   Research theories about supporting people to make changes to their behaviour.

Relevant legislation

Legislation

The Food Standards Act 1999 resulted in the establishment of the FSA, a government department whose main purpose is to protect the public from risks associated with the consumption of food. The FSA advises government ministers on matters relating to food safety and standards. It provides guidance to the public about healthy eating, and carries out surveys on diet to monitor whether eating habits are changing as a result of public health advice. The FSA also works with the food industry on topics such as food labelling, to make it easier for the public to make healthy choices. In addition the FSA works with farmers to ensure that meat, poultry and crops are produced safely.

The Food Safety Act 1990 governs food hygiene. Environmental health departments, part of the local council, carry out unannounced inspections of all premises selling food, to ensure that good food hygiene practice is carried out. This is essential to reduce the risk of food poisoning.

Policies

The UK government publishes a huge range of policies around food production and consumption. There are policies around farming practices, school lunches, food labelling, reduction of consumption of sugar and salt, obesity, and high blood pressure to name a few.

Government guidance

There have been several attempts to improve the diet of the population through social policy. This is a different approach to health education, and involves creating more opportunities for people to choose healthy foods.

In 2014, Public Health England published three guidance documents in a series entitled *Healthier and More Sustainable Catering*. This included one setting out the most recent nutrition principles, and two toolkits, one for the catering industry serving food to adults, and one aimed at staff providing food to older people in residential care.

These guidance documents provide detailed, scientific and evidence-based information to set out the issues people face around nutrition, clear advice about nutrition, good practice in providing meals that are well balanced, and take account of religious and cultural influences on diet. The version relating to older people in residential care includes information about assessing individuals to identify those at risk of malnutrition, so measures can be put in place to supplement the diet, if necessary.

> **Research**
>
> News reports often promote the idea that children need a healthy diet to reach their potential at school. In 2005, Jamie Oliver highlighted the poor quality of school dinners, and much improvement has been seen since. Uptake of school dinners has increased, and children in Reception, Y1 and Y2 now get free lunches.
>
> As a group, research whether there is any evidence that the nutritional value of food does improve attainment at school.

Other initiatives include:

▶ The School Food Plan, published in 2013 by the founders of Leon Restaurants on the request of the then Secretary of State for Education, Michael Gove.

▶ The Children's Food Trust is a national charity that aims for all children in the UK to eat well. Evidence supports the theory that children who eat a healthy diet are healthier and more successful than their less well-nourished peers. It provides training for staff involved in providing meals for children.

 Its Eat Better, Start Better campaign provides schools and early years' providers with ready-made weekly menus for staff to use, so they can be quickly put into practice. There are two sets of menus, one for autumn/winter, the other for spring/summer, to give some variety. The menus include vegetarian options and portion sizes for children of different ages.

 The Children's Food Trust also promotes children's cookery sessions in collaboration with the Tesco Eat Happy Project.

▶ Encouraging children to enjoy cooking at school can have a positive impact on healthy eating at home

Factors affecting dietary intake

Specific conditions

Diabetes mellitus

Diabetes mellitus is usually just called diabetes. There is another condition, diabetes insipidus, so it is important to be sure that you know which one you are dealing with. There are two types of diabetes mellitus, known as type 1 and type 2.

Type 1 diabetes usually develops in childhood or early adulthood. The hormone insulin is not being produced by the pancreas. If left untreated, this would lead to certain death due to lack of glucose in the cells and vital organs. Type 1 diabetes is treated with insulin injections, once or more each day. To maintain a healthy blood glucose level, it is important that the carbohydrate consumed by the individual balances their insulin injections. If an individual with type 1 diabetes does not eat sufficient carbohydrate to balance their insulin injection, they can develop hypoglycaemia, too little glucose in the bloodstream. They will need to take glucose quickly, such as a sugary drink. Without treatment, hypoglycaemia can rapidly lead to confusion and loss of consciousness and could be fatal. If the person regularly eats too much carbohydrate, however, their blood glucose will be consistently high. This can lead to some very serious complications including blindness, kidney failure, stroke, and gangrene, which may require amputation of their lower limbs.

▶ Blood glucose is monitored by regular testing. Just one drop of blood is needed.

Prediabetes is a condition in which an individual's blood glucose levels are raised above normal, but not sufficiently high to be diagnosed as diabetic. In the UK, around 7 million people are thought to have prediabetes. During this phase, there is an opportunity for the individual to slow down, or even stop, the development of type 2 diabetes, by making lifestyle changes to increase exercise and follow a healthy diet.

Type 2 diabetes is a condition in which some insulin is still being produced, but the body has developed resistance to it, meaning that the insulin is not used properly. Some individuals with type 2 diabetes can control their blood glucose levels by eating a healthy diet and increasing their exercise levels. If this does not restore the blood glucose to normal levels, the individual will need to take medication to increase the amount of insulin being produced and to improve the responsiveness of the cells to insulin. Some individuals may also need to have insulin injections.

Anyone with diabetes should see a registered dietician.

Coronary heart disease (CHD)

CHD is a condition where one or more of the arteries that supply the heart muscle with oxygenated blood have become narrowed. This can cause **angina** or even a **heart attack**.

The narrowing of the arteries is usually caused by atherosclerosis, the build-up of fatty deposits, atheroma, in the walls of the arteries. Atheroma are made of cholesterol, lipids and waste materials.

Many people think that foods high in saturated fat contain cholesterol. However, cholesterol is made by the liver from saturated fat in the diet, and is essential for healthy cells. In the bloodstream, you have molecules called lipoproteins. There are two main types of lipoproteins, low density lipoproteins (LDL) and high density lipoproteins (HDL). LDLs take cholesterol to the cells and HDLs take cholesterol from the cells back to the liver to be broken down, so LDLs tends to be responsible for the development of atheroma.

A blood test can measure the levels of cholesterol, LDL and HDL in the bloodstream, and identify people at risk of atherosclerosis.

The diet recommended to reduce blood cholesterol levels is:

▸ high in wholegrain carbohydrates, fruit and vegetables

▸ low in saturated fats.

Foods thought to be particularly good at lowering cholesterol include soya, nuts, oats, barley, olive oil, sunflower oil, and plant sterols and stanols. Sterols and stanols mimic cholesterol, causing the body to absorb them rather than cholesterol. As a result, less bile is absorbed into the bloodstream and the body is tricked into making more bile by removing more cholesterol from the blood circulation, which lowers cholesterol levels in the blood.

People who have high blood cholesterol levels are often prescribed statins (lipid-lowering medications) to block cholesterol production in their liver.

Digestive disorders

Irritable bowel syndrome

Irritable bowel syndrome (IBS) is a condition where the bowel function is easily disturbed, causing abdominal pain, flatulence, bloating and either constipation or diarrhoea, or sometimes both. However, on examination there is no apparent abnormality in the bowel. The cause is not clear, but there appears to be overactivity in the nerves in the gut, and some people can identify particular foods that seem to trigger their symptoms. Sometimes IBS develops following a bout of diarrhoea caused by an infection, and continues after the infection has gone. Some people find that they have these symptoms after a course of antibiotics, which kill the normal bacteria that should be present in the bowel. There is much varied advice given to people with IBS, but the best thing is to experiment with the diet to try to identify which foods make it worse, and avoid them. Probiotic yogurt drinks might also help, as they contain specific live bacteria that may help restore the balance of healthy gut bacteria.

Key terms

Angina – chest pain caused by inadequate oxygen supply to the heart muscle when it is under stress, usually relieved by rest or taking tablets to dilate the arteries.

Heart attack – chest pain, similar to angina but usually more severe, caused by blockage of the artery supplying oxygen to the heart muscle. This pain is not relieved by rest or angina tablets, and is a medical emergency.

Crohn's disease

Crohn's disease is an inflammatory condition of the alimentary canal. It can affect any part, from the mouth to the anus, and occurs in patches, with sections of normal tissue in between. It is a lifelong condition, but tends to flare up intermittently, causing symptoms such as diarrhoea, abdominal pain, fatigue, weight loss and anaemia, and then go into a period of **remission**.

> **Key term**
>
> **Remission** – a period of time when a disease is inactive, but is not considered cured.

The main treatment for Crohn's disease is medication with steroids, which reduce inflammation, and immunosuppressants, which reduce the immune system attack on the healthy bacteria in the gut. There is no particular diet recommended for individuals with Crohn's disease, but some people find that particular foods trigger attacks. During flare ups, some people change their diet to special liquid feeds, which may be delivered straight into the veins to give the gut a rest.

Food allergies and intolerances

Food allergies and **food intolerances** are very different. If someone is allergic to a food they experience a reaction, usually within seconds of eating the food. The reaction can be extremely serious and life threatening, with swelling of the mouth and throat blocking the airway. In addition, the heart rate may increase and the blood pressure fall, they may lose consciousness. Other symptoms can include a raised itchy rash (hives), abdominal pain, vomiting, and diarrhoea. Common causes of food allergy include peanuts (which are legumes), nuts, shellfish, eggs, soy and milk. Anyone with a severe food allergy should be issued with an **epipen**, which both they and close contacts should know how to use.

> **Key terms**
>
> **Food intolerance** – symptoms such as diarrhoea, bloating and wind, caused by eating specific foods. It is not the same as an allergic reaction and is not usually life threatening.
>
> **Epipen** – a device delivering a rapid injection of adrenaline to quickly control symptoms of anaphylactic shock, which in severe cases cause the throat and tongue to swell, blocking the airway.

Coeliac disease

Coeliac disease is an autoimmune disease caused by an intolerance to the protein gluten, which is found in wheat, barley and rye. The gluten causes the immune system to produce antibodies, which attack the lining of the bowel. This can affect the ability of the body to absorb nutrients from food, and can lead to anaemia and osteoporosis. It can also increase the risk of bowel cancer.

Some people are diagnosed in childhood, others not until much later, owing to the symptoms being similar to many other bowel disorders. Symptoms include abdominal pain – particularly after eating foods containing gluten – diarrhoea, constipation, bloating, failure to gain weight in childhood, weight loss in adulthood, and anaemia leading to tiredness.

People with coeliac disease need to eliminate all foods containing wheat, rye and barley from their diet. Gluten-free products, such as breads, biscuits and cakes are available, but can be very expensive to buy. If a person has been medically diagnosed with coeliac disease some gluten-free products can be obtained on prescription. Food lists are available from Coeliac UK, and some information is available on their website.

> ### Theory into practice
>
> **Avoiding gluten**
>
> Make a list of foods that contain gluten.
>
> Design a menu for one day for a person who has to avoid gluten. Try to make it as tasty as possible.
>
> Next time you are in a supermarket look at the range of foods available to customers who are intolerant to particular food components. It is useful to see what you can buy in case you ever need to get some at short notice. Compare the prices to other foods in the supermarket.

Lactose intolerance

Lactose, the natural sugar in milk, is a common dietary intolerance. It can be mild or severe. Children who are lactose intolerant do not produce lactase, an enzyme that breaks down lactose into glucose and galactose during digestion before it can be absorbed. Children with this condition in its severest form have difficulty putting on weight and suffer from diarrhoea. The lactose ferments inside the bowel causing bloating. Lactose is present in a wide variety of foods, including chocolate, cheese, ice cream, mayonnaise and cakes. Anyone eliminating all these products from their diet is at risk of calcium deficiency. The following foods are a good source of calcium:

▶ sardines (with the bones mashed in)

▶ broccoli

▶ celery

▶ soya beans.

 **PAUSE POINT**   Can you remember what conditions are caused by lack of calcium in children and adults?

 Hint   Think about the function of calcium in the diet.

Extend   Why is it important to have an adequate calcium intake during childhood and early adulthood?

Loss of ability to feed independently

Some people are unfortunately unable to feed themselves independently. This may be throughout their lives or following an accident, such as a spinal injury to the neck, or development of a debilitating condition, such as following a stroke.

Paralysis

If the spinal cord is severely damaged, due to injury or degeneration at the neck, little or no movement beyond this point is possible. This is known as either quadriplegia or tetraplegia (inability to move all four limbs). In this case, the individual must rely on a carer to feed them. It is important that this is done in a relaxed way so that meals can be enjoyed, without the person feeling they need to eat quickly. If the carer can eat their meal at the same time, sitting next to the person at a dining table, this will be a more natural and relaxed situation.

People who are paralysed can become underweight due to muscle loss and a poor appetite. If this is the case, the person may be prescribed fortified drinks containing calories, protein, vitamins and minerals to boost intake. Conversely, they may start to gain weight due to lack of exercise, and need to reduce their calorie intake. Another common problem is constipation, as lack of mobility causes the bowels to become sluggish. A diet high in fibre, along with plenty of fluids, should help this, although laxatives may also be needed.

Stroke

A stroke (or cerebrovascular accident) can affect any part of the brain. You may know that the left side of the brain controls the right side of the body, and vice versa. Typically, following a stroke, the individual will have weakness down one side of their body. Whether it is the dominant or non-dominant side that is weak, or paralysed, it may be difficult to feed independently. Cutting food and picking food up often requires two hands. In addition, people who have had a stroke experience perception problems. The brain may not register half of the field of vision, meaning that the person may ignore half of their plate of food, unless you turn it round during the meal.

Following a stroke, about 50 per cent of people will experience difficulty with swallowing. This can result in choking, and aspiration pneumonia (caused by inhaling food). Foods can be pureed to make them easier to swallow, and fluids can be mixed with a thickening powder to reduce the risk of choking. If necessary, a nasogastric tube can be passed into the individual's stomach for a few days, so the person can be fed safely.

If some degree of independence can be maintained, then it should be. There are a wide variety of gadgets available to assist people who are having difficulty in feeding themselves. Some of these include wide handled cutlery, plate guards and non-slip mats.

▶ What problems do you think these items could help with?

Another way of maintaining independence is to cut food up before serving it, enabling the service user to manage by themselves.

If there is no possibility of an individual feeding themself, then it is important that meals are given while their food is still hot. The service user should not feel a nuisance, so you should sit down and create a relaxed situation where the meal can be enjoyed. Make sure you protect the individual's clothing with a napkin. Offer drinks frequently, do not over-fill the service user's mouth, and let them swallow one mouthful before offering more. Ensure they are offered sufficient to food eat. It may be necessary to tell the person what you are going to feed them, especially if they have a visual impairment or are confused. It is also an opportunity for social conversation.

The service user's face and hands should be washed at the beginning and at the end of the meal.

Alternative methods of feeding

Nasogastric tube (NGT)

Some service users may need to be fed via a tube into their stomach. There are several reasons why service users may need to be fed this way. Swallowing difficulties, known as dysphagia, may mean that the service user chokes frequently, or is unable to eat sufficient food to maintain their nutritional health. A stroke, or cancer of the oesophagus, can cause dysphagia. Sometimes a tube is passed up the service user's nose, down the throat and into their stomach to enable liquid feed to be given straight into the stomach.

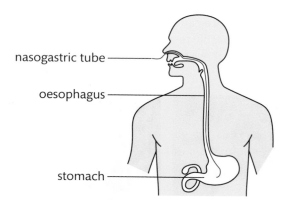

nasogastric tube

oesophagus

stomach

▶ **Figure 19.6** Diagram showing how a nasogastric tube allows food to be delivered directly to the stomach

Percutaneous endoscopic gastrostomy (PEG)

If swallowing is a permanent problem, or the oesophagus has been surgically removed due to disease, a gastrostomy can be created. This is a hole made through the service user's abdomen straight into their stomach. You might hear these called a PEG or MIC-KEY button. Sometimes a jejunostomy tube is inserted into part of the small intestine rather than into the stomach, for example if the stomach has been surgically removed.

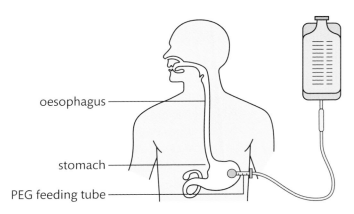

oesophagus

stomach

PEG feeding tube

▶ **Figure 19.7** A gastrostomy may be created for someone who has problems swallowing food

Tube feeding is potentially unsociable. Children may be happy to be fed at the table and play with utensils, but teenagers and adults may be self-conscious, and prefer to do this somewhere private. You should always respect the service user's privacy and dignity.

Intravenous infusions (IVI)

An IVI, or 'drip', is used to get fluids into the body, to prevent or treat dehydration due to inadequate fluid intake. Dehydration can be caused by a number of factors including:

▶ gastroenteritis (diarrhoea and sickness)

▶ untreated or uncontrolled diabetes mellitus

▶ heatstroke

▶ being 'nil by mouth' in hospital, as part of treatment.

Total parenteral nutrition (TPN)

TPN provides all the service user's nutritional needs. It bypasses the digestive system and delivers the nutrient solution directly into a vein (this may be a peripheral vein but is more usually directly into a large central vein. There are several types of service users who might receive nutrition in this way, including those:

▶ who are unconscious, such as patients in intensive therapy units (ITU)

▶ who are not able to absorb nutrients properly from the gut

▶ with certain types of cancer.

Thickened fluids

If an individual is at risk of choking, they will be prescribed thickened fluids to reduce this risk. Xanthan gum (a starch powder) is used to thicken fluids without affecting the taste.

Safety tip

Choking can cause aspiration pneumonia, when food or fluids are inhaled into the lungs. It is important to ensure that you are aware if a patient or service user needs their fluids thickening.

You have started a new job at a family centre in an inner city area of Middlesbrough. Data from the Office for National Statistics has revealed that the healthy life expectancy is 58.6 years for men and 60.1 years for women, the worst in the UK.

You have been employed as part of a new project to tackle this by improving nutrition in the local area.

Your first task is to create a resource pack for volunteers who will be recruited to support the initiatives. Your resource pack should include:

1 an explanation of how the concepts of nutritional health contribute to health and wellbeing

2 an explanation of the sources of essential nutrients and their function in the body

3 an assessment of the impact of dietary intake and dietary deficiencies on nutritional health.

Your team leader explains that each member of staff will have a caseload of families identified as needing targeted support to improve their dietary intake, and reduce their risk of developing illnesses associated with poor nutrition. Two of the people on your caseload are described below.

Ahmed is a 56-year-old Muslim man who lives alone. He is 170 cm tall and weighs 86.4 kg. His doctor has tested his fasting blood glucose level and found it to be 6.5 mmol. He has recently been discharged from hospital following a stroke, and is still having difficulties with swallowing. Carers visit four times a day. They leave Ahmed cheese sandwiches on white bread for lunch, and a piece of cake to eat for tea. They make him a drink at each visit, but later often find it has not been drunk. Ahmed suffers from irritable bowel syndrome.

Felicity is a 13-year-old girl who is pregnant. She lives in a chaotic household. Her dad does not work, and struggles with depression. Food shopping tends to be disorganised, with the family often eating takeaway meals while watching television.

For Ahmed and Felicity:

1 explain the health, socio-economic and cultural factors that influence their nutritional health

2 compare the dietary intake of Ahmed and Felicity with their nutritional requirements

3 assess how the dietary intake and nutritional health of Ahmed and Felicity are influenced by their dietary habits, personal circumstances and lifestyle choices

4 evaluate the role of nutritional health in maintaining Ahmed and Felicity's health and wellbeing, and the impact of influencing factors.

Plan

- I have read the question and know what I need to do.
- I have looked through the unit specification and am clear about what I need to include.
- I have asked for clarification about anything I am unsure about.

Do

- I know how to complete the task fully.
- I can see where I have not done enough, and know where to look for more information.
- I am spending enough time to ensure the task is completed on time.

Review

- I have proofread the work and checked against the assessment criteria and unit content.
- I can see how this relates to the assessment criteria and how this activity will help me to achieve the learning outcomes.
- I have identified areas I need to improve on.
- I am confident that this will achieve the merit and distinction criteria.

C Plan nutrition to improve individuals' nutritional health

Assessment of nutrient intake

How to record food intake

If there are real concerns about an individual's dietary intake, an accurate record is needed of all food and drink consumed over a period of a few days. All food eaten must be included, such as meals, snacks, sweets, drinks and food supplements, and the portion size should be indicated. This might be used, for example, for individuals with anorexia nervosa, or those who have lost their appetite. This can be a real revelation, and many people are surprised when they see exactly what, and how much or how little they have been consuming.

It enables a dietician to assess accurately the actual daily intake, and plan how to improve nutrition.'

Maintaining nutritional needs

The Health and Social Care Act 2008 requires every organisation providing health or social care to make sure that individuals in their care have enough to eat and drink, and that service users are well nourished and hydrated. To achieve this, service users need to have a nutritional needs assessment. Following this, if necessary, a plan is implemented to ensure that support is in place so that service users are well nourished.

Nutritional assessment score

The 'Malnutrition Universal Screening Tool' ('MUST') has been used by health professionals, such as nurses and dieticians, since 2003. It was developed by the Malnutrition Advisory Group, a committee of the British Association for Parenteral and Enteral Nutrition (BAPEN). It is the most commonly used nutritional assessment tool in the UK and is supported by the Royal College of Nursing and the British Dietetic Association.

Step by step: 'MUST'   BAPEN

5 Steps

1 Measure the individual's height and weight to calculate their BMI[1]
BMI greater than 20 = 0
BMI between 18 and 20 = −1
BMI less than 18 = 2

▼

2 Find out if there has been unplanned weight loss in the last 3–6 months.
Less than 5% of total body weight lost = 0
5–10% weight loss = 1
More than 10% weight loss = 2

▼

3 If the person has been acutely ill **and** there has been or is likely to be no nutritional intake for >5 days, score 2.[2]

4 Add total score from steps 1 to 3.
Score 0 = low risk
Score 1 = medium risk
Score 2 or more = high risk

▼

5 Once a person has been identified as at risk of malnutrition, a care plan should be developed to inform carers about the strategies that should be used to reduce this risk, which might include:
- referral to a dietician
- referral to a speech and language therapist, for swallowing assessment
- food supplements
- special dietary considerations, personal preferences, and familiar foods.

[1]If unable to obtain height and weight, see 'MUST' Explanatory Booklet for alternative measurements and use of subjective criteria.
[2]Acute disease effect is unlikely to apply outside hospital. See 'MUST' Explanatory Booklet for further information.
The 'MUST' Explanatory Booklet is available at **http://www.bapen.org.uk/screening-and-must/must/must-toolkit/the-must-explanatory-booklet**

Calculating 'MUST' score

Maimura is 44 years old and was diagnosed with stomach cancer three months ago. She has been admitted to hospital as she has been vomiting for five days and is unable to keep any food down. Looking at Maimura's patient record you can see that three months ago she weighed 57 kg. As she entered the emergency department, her trolley was wheeled over the trolley scales and her weight was recorded as 48 kg. Maimura is very unwell, so rather than disturb her to measure her height, the nurse estimates this from Maimura's demispan, the distance between the base of her middle finger to the sternal notch, which is 78 cm. Maimura's height is estimated to be 1.63 m.

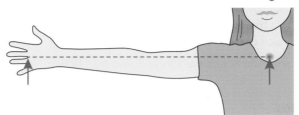

Height (m)	Men (18–54 years)	1.75	1.73	1.72	1.71	1.69	1.68	1.67	1.65	1.64	1.63	1.62	1.60	1.59	1.58	1.56	1.55	1.54
	Men (>55 years)	1.69	1.68	1.76	1.66	1.65	1.64	1.62	1.61	1.60	1.59	1.57	1.56	1.55	1.54	1.53	1.51	1.50
	Demispan (cm)	82	81	80	79	78	77	76	75	74	73	72	71	70	69	68	67	66
Height (m)	Women (18–54 years)	1.69	1.67	1.66	1.65	1.63	1.62	1.61	1.59	1.58	1.57	1.56	1.54	1.53	1.52	1.50	1.49	1.48
	Women (>55 years)	1.65	1.64	1.63	1.62	1.61	1.59	1.58	1.57	1.56	1.55	1.54	1.52	1.51	1.50	1.49	1.47	1.46

▶ **Figure 19.8** Measuring demispan

Using the information above calculate Maimura's 'MUST' score.

Do you think Maimura is at low, medium or high risk of malnutrition?

Fluid balance

The fluid content of the body is regulated by hormones in the process of homeostasis. Antidiuretic hormone is released by the pituitary gland to decrease the amount of fluid the kidneys produce, and the adrenal glands produce aldosterone to stimulate the reabsorption of sodium in the kidneys, which causes water to be reabsorbed, maintaining homeostasis. Sometimes fluid balance can become disturbed causing dehydration or water retention. Medical causes of dehydration include diarrhoea and vomiting, heatstroke, high blood glucose levels, and high temperature. Fluid retention can occur in heart failure, kidney failure, alcoholic cirrhosis of the liver and obstruction of the lymphatic system.

A useful tool to help diagnose these conditions is to measure all fluid entering and leaving the body:

▶ fluids enter the body in foods; and, in hospital, via intravenous drips and nasogastric tube feeding

▶ fluids leave the body through sweating, breathing out, in faeces and vomit, and in urine.

It is impossible to measure all of these accurately, but you would expect slightly less fluid to be excreted than taken in. In a 24-hour period, the volume of drinks, feeds, soups and intravenous infusion would be recorded, and any urine passed would be measured, and bowel and vomit output would also be measured. At the end of the 24-hour period, the volumes in and out would be added up and the difference calculated. This information is then shared with the medical team.

Time	IV (ml)	Oral (ml)	Hourly intake (ml)	Cumulative intake (ml)	Cumulative output (ml)	Hourly output (ml)	Urine (ml)	Vomit (ml)
Carried forward	499.2	500		999.2	875			
12:00 – 13:00	41.6	200	241.6	1240.8	1030	155	155	
13:00 – 14:00	41.6		41.6	1282.4	1160	130	130	
14:00 – 15:00	41.6	200	241.6	1524	1430	270	95	175
15:00 – 16:00	41.6		41.6	1565.6	1545	115	115	
16:00 – 17:00	41.6	150	191.6	1757.2	1670	125	125	
17:00 – 18:00	41.6	100	141.6	1898.8	1780	110	110	

▶ **Figure 19.9** An example of a fluid balance chart.

Food charts

Food charts are used to record intake where there are concerns about whether a person is taking in an adequate diet. A good example can be found in the Department of Health, Social Services and Public Safety (Northern Ireland) publication entitled *Promoting Good Nutrition: Guidance and resources to support the use of 'MUST' across all care settings*.

Sources of nutritional information

Food analysis tables

Public Health England use *McCance and Widdowson's The Composition of Foods Integrated Dataset 2015* as a reference for the nutritional content of foods. Several organisations collaborate to collate this information, including the British Nutrition Foundation.

Charts relating to portion sizes

One of the main factors identified as a concern in regards to increasing levels of obesity is portion sizes. Good sources of charts indicating portion sizes are provided by Bupa UK, the NHS Choices website, the British Nutrition Foundation and the British Heart Foundation.

Information on food packaging (especially for processed foods)

The NHS Choices website Live Well webpage provides a useful source of information for interpreting food labels, which helps the general public to make informed choices about the food they buy and its health risks and benefits.

Quantitative analysis

To assess whether a person is eating a healthy diet, a quantitative analysis can be carried out. To do this accurately, you need to know the weight of the food that has been consumed. The quantity of energy (calories), protein, fat, iron, vitamin C and fibre in the diet can then be calculated. It is easier to record this information on a chart.

Assessment of analysis

Once the diet analysis has been completed, the individual's intake can be compared with recommended intake. For a healthy adult without any specific dietary needs, this would be the RNI values. If the individual has a medical condition that requires a special diet, this needs to be considered. For example, an individual with a kidney disorder might need a low protein diet.

Your analysis should highlight any nutrients the person is lacking, or over-consuming.

Nutritional health improvement plan

Nutritional health improvement plans might be put in place for a variety of reasons. It may be because a health risk has been identified that could be avoided with changes to the diet. It may be as a result of a person making a conscious decision to improve their diet, either as a lifestyle change, or in preparation for a specific event, such as training for a sporting event.

Recommendations for meals, snacks, drinks, portion size, cooking methods

When devising an improved menu for a person you should include their total intake for the day, including drinks and snacks, and give advice on the portion size. It is important that the diet takes into consideration any medical conditions, such as allergies and intolerances, and cultural preferences.

Cooking methods should also be included in your recommendations. Look back at learning aim A to review the health benefits of different cooking methods.

Recommendations for activity level, daily exercise and energy expenditure

The Chief Medical Officers of all four UK countries agree that physical activity is important for people of all ages. Long sedentary periods should be avoided by everyone.

Adults aged 19–64 years should aim to be active every day, with muscle strengthening activity on at least two days each week. The recommendations are either for 30 minutes of moderate intensity activity five days a week, or for 75 minutes of intense activity spread across the week, or a combination of the two.

Children and young people aged 5–18 years should aim for 60 minutes or more of moderate activity daily, with vigorous activity on three days of the week.

Part of your nutritional health improvement plan should focus on recommendations for exercise, especially if an individual is not very active. Recommendations for exercise need to tap into the individual's interests, time availability and family circumstances, or the chances are that the changes will not be sustainable.

You can include time spent walking, for instance to and from the bus stop, on housework and gardening, and on hobby activities such as dancing and ice skating. Not all exercise needs to be in a gym, or in a formal exercise setting.

If the individual is doing a significant amount of exercise, this can be taken into account when deciding on their daily calorie intake. This could be an incentive to increase activity levels if the individual is not normally very active.

▶ People who exercise a lot will need more calories than those with sedentary lifestyles

Recommendations relating to lifestyle and personal food preferences

Finally, in order to create a realistic diet plan, you need to know about the individual's lifestyle. Your recommendations should take account of their likes and dislikes, whether their religion has dietary restrictions, their budget and time available for shopping and cooking and any cultural factors that may affect their food choices. Someone who is busy, for example, may need advice about choosing suitable ready meals, whereas others may be happy to cook from raw ingredients. You should discuss these factors with the individual before making recommendations.

If your diet plan is going to include the weekend, you may need to consider differences in the individual's weekend lifestyle compared to weekdays. For example, they may have more time at the weekend, or wish to eat out.

How the plan will be monitored

You will need to agree a date to meet the individual again, to see how they are progressing. To get useful information, it would help if the individual kept a diary of their food and fluid intake, and activity levels. You could use the same chart for food and drink as you used for the quantitative analysis, as it would make the comparison easier. The individual will also need a chart to record their activity.

Assessment practice 19.2

(This activity is based on Ahmed and Felicity, the same characters in Assessment practice 19.1.)

For Ahmed and Felicity:

- produce professionally presented plans to improve the nutritional health of both Ahmed and Felicity
- explain, analyse and justify your recommendations to improve the health of Ahmed and Felicity
- evaluate the importance of planning nutritional health for Ahmed and Felicity to ensure their dietary needs are met, and all influencing factors are taken into account.

Plan

- I have read the question and know what I need to do.
- I have looked through the unit specification so I am clear about what I need to include.
- I have asked for clarification about anything I am unsure about.

Do

- I know how to complete the task fully.
- I can see where I have not done enough, and know where to look for more information.
- I am spending enough time to ensure the task is completed on time.

Review

- I have proofread the work and checked against the assessment criteria and unit content.
- I can see how this relates to the assessment criteria and how this activity will help me to achieve the learning outcomes.
- I have identified areas I need to improve on.
- I am confident that this will achieve the merit and distinction criteria.

Further reading

Aldworth, C. (2008) *Knowledge Set Nutrition and Well-being*, Harlow: Pearson.

Dimbleby, H. and Vincent J. (2013) *The School Food Plan*, available at: **www.schoolfoodplan.com/wp-content/uploads/2013/07/School_Food_Plan_2013.pdf**

Department of Health, Social Services and Public Safety (2015) *Promoting Good Nutrition Guidance and resources to support the use of 'MUST' across all care settings*, available at: **www.dhsspsni.gov.uk/sites/default/files/publications/dhssps/pgn-must_0.pdf**

Public Health England (2015) *McCance and Widdowson's The Composition of Foods Integrated Dataset 2015: user guide*, available at: **www.gov.uk/government/uploads/system/uploads/attachment_data/file/417175/McCance___Widdowson_s_Comp_of_Foods_Integrated_Dataset_User_Guide.pdf**

Websites

Age UK: **www.ageuk.org.uk**

British Association for Parenteral and Enteral Nutrition: **www.bapen.org.uk**

British Heart Foundation: **www.bhf.org.uk**

British Nutrition Foundation: **www.nutrition.org.uk**

Bupa: **www.bupa.co.uk**

Crohn's and Colitis UK: **www.crohnsandcolitis.org.uk**

Coeliac UK: **www.coeliac.org.uk**

Diabetes UK: **www.diabetes.co.uk**

Heart UK: **http://heartuk.org.uk**

NHS Choices Live Well: **www.nhs.uk/livewell**

Stroke Association: **www.stroke.org.uk**

Patient: **www.patient.co.uk**

World Health Organization: **http://www.who.int/en/**

THINK ▶FUTURE

Alexis Bukowski

Catering manager at a specialist residential home for people with dementia

I've been working in the catering sector since leaving school, firstly in a restaurant, where I trained as a sous chef. I became interested in moving into the care sector after my grandmother was diagnosed with Alzheimer's disease in 2012, and I observed the effect it had on her eating and drinking.

I applied for a catering post in a care home in 2012, and was successful. I started to research the effect diet can have on the development of Alzheimer's, and attended the Alzheimer's Society Conference in 2014, where one of the speakers talked about the way lifestyle can affect dementia. I was promoted to manager in early 2015, and am now responsible for planning menus, ordering food and providing nutritious, appetising meals. I've got to know all the residents well, and I also make time to speak to relatives to find out the sort of food their loved ones enjoy. I also make sure that there are always plenty of snacks and soups available, in case anyone doesn't feel like eating at mealtimes. As a team, we've adopted the same approach as hospitals, where everyone available helps at mealtimes, to ensure that each resident gets help, and meals are eaten when they are fresh. Of course I'm also responsible for food hygiene, making sure all our food is stored and prepared correctly, and that all the staff have the right training. I'm pleased to say we got a 5-star rating last time the food hygiene inspectors came!

Focusing your skills

Planning a menu

It is important to plan thoroughly when planning a menu for 30 people in a care setting. Here are some things you would need to consider.

- You need to consider all the special dietary needs of the residents to make sure everyone is going to receive a nutritious meal.
- You need to make sure the different needs are met but you are still working economically. You might add sauces as you serve, for example, so you would not have to make a completely different meal for someone intolerant to gluten.
- You need to make sure that the menu is nutritionally balanced. You could use the eatwell plate to estimate this.
- Have a go at planning a menu for one day, with three meals, and three choices for the main meal.

Maintaining a 5-star food hygiene rating

- You need to use different chopping boards for different types of foods – raw meat, vegetables, dairy, fish and bread.
- You need to monitor the temperatures in fridges and freezers, and when keeping food hot until ready to be eaten. Do you know what temperatures are necessary for this?
- Storage of foods is also crucial. Do you know which foods need to be kept separately? How should you organise a fridge?
- You need to ensure there is no risk of vermin or flies contaminating the food preparation areas, and that hand hygiene is maintained.

Getting ready for assessment

Saeed is working towards a BTEC National in Health and Social Care. He was given an assignment with the title 'Improving nutritional health' for Learning aim C. He had to meet two people to assess their current diet, and work with them to devise a realistic plan for improvement. The plan had to:

▶ use information obtained in a previous assignment to plan a nutritional improvement plan

▶ show the individuals that the plan had been devised based on knowledge of nutritional theory.

Saeed shares his experience below.

How I got started

I'd already met the two people I was basing my plans on, as I used them for my first assignment for learning aim B. One person was a friend of mine, Charlie, who I noticed always seemed to be eating junk food. He is the same age as me, 17, but is already overweight. The other person is my dad, Hamid, who works long hours and often grabs food when he can. They both completed a food diary for me.

First I looked through all my notes on recommended healthy diets, and the food diaries that Charlie and my dad completed. I decided to use the eatwell plate to compare their current intake to the recommended intake, to see if I could identify whether there were any imbalances. I also found *McCance and Widdowson's The Composition of Foods Integrated Dataset* on the internet. I bookmarked it so I could refer to it to calculate Charlie and my dad's intake of different components to compare to RIs, which are listed in the textbook. Once I'd identified what needed to improve in each diet, I arranged time to speak to both of them to discuss what I'd found. I needed to know what they would, and would not be prepared to eat, as well as whether they'd want to continue to buy most food ready to eat, or if they had time or opportunity to cook at home.

How I brought it all together

I decided to use a variety of fonts, colours and pictures to make the plan look interesting and professional. To start, I wrote a short summary about the health risks each of my chosen individuals faced with their current diet. For each person:

▶ I created a table for each component showing their current intake compared to recommendations.

▶ I created a suggested menu for a week for breakfast, lunch, dinner, snacks and drinks.

▶ I added an explanation about how the suggested menu would improve their health, both now and in the future. I referenced this in a numbered style and printed the list of references on the back page of the booklet.

Finally, I wrote an evaluation to hand in to my tutors, to evaluate the importance of nutritional planning, and how I'd taken into account the lifestyle, preferences, and interest in cooking when planning the menus.

What I learned from the experience

I wish I'd started analysing the food diaries earlier, as I hadn't realised how long it would take. I'd also present the plan on A4 single sheets in a folder rather than trying to present it as an A5-booklet, as I spent a long time fiddling with the layout trying to ensure my work looked professional for the Merit grading criterion. I was glad I'd chosen two people I knew well, as this meant that I could keep going back to them to clarify things without feeling too self-conscious. I had to do this several times, so if I'd used a person I didn't know, I would have needed to have planned my information gathering better.

Think about it

▶ Have you written a plan with timings so you can complete your assignment by the agreed submission date?

▶ Do you have *McCance and Widdowson's The Composition of Foods Integrated Dataset* saved somewhere, as well as a list of RIs?

▶ Is your information written in your own words, and referenced clearly where you have used information from a book, journal or website?

Biochemistry for Health 24

Getting to know your unit

This unit is useful for anyone wishing to enter a career in health or food technology. It will provide you with a good knowledge of the structures and functions of biological molecules, the principles of metabolism and the characteristics of enzymes that catalyse all metabolic reactions. You will also learn about the importance of nucleic acids and the uses of biochemistry in industrial and clinical settings.

How you will be assessed

This unit will be assessed by a series of internally assessed tasks set by your tutor. Throughout this unit there are assessment practices that will help you to work towards your assessment. Completing these activities will not mean that you have achieved a particular grade, but that you will have carried out useful research or preparation for your assessment tasks.

In order to succeed in the tasks of your assignments, it is important that you meet all of the Pass grading criteria. You can do this as you work your way through the assignment.

If you are hoping to achieve a Merit or Distinction, you should also ensure that you present the information in your assignment in the style that is required by the relevant assessment criterion. For example, Merit criteria require you to assess and analyse and Distinction criteria require you to evaluate and justify.

The assessment set by your tutor will consist of a number of tasks designed to meet the criteria in the table. This is likely to consist of a written assignment but may also include activities such as:

▶ producing display materials to explain the structures and importance to living organisms of some inorganic elements and key organic molecules

▶ carrying out and writing reports on practical activities, such as investigations into enzyme activity or extracting DNA.

Assessment criteria

This table shows what you must do in order to achieve a **Pass**, **Merit** or **Distinction** grade, and where you can find activities to help you.

Pass	Merit	Distinction

Learning aim **A** Explore how the structure of biological molecules affects metabolism

A.P1

Explain the structures of carbon, hydrogen, nitrogen and oxygen, and how they produce organic and inorganic biological molecules.

Assessment practice 24.1

A.M1

Assess the relevance of the structure of carbon, hydrogen, nitrogen and oxygen to the metabolism of biological molecules, proteins, fats, carbohydrates and haemoglobin.

Assessment practice 24.1

A.D1

Evaluate the structure, function and role of inorganic and organic molecules, and their impact on metabolism.

Assessment practice 24.1

A.P2

Investigate the nature, function and role of atoms, and the structure and function of organic and inorganic molecules and their impact on metabolism.

Assessment practice 24.1

Learning aim **B** Explore the action of biological molecules in metabolic processes

B.P3

Explain the structure, and physical and chemical properties of biomolecules and nucleic acids.

Assessment practice 24.2

B.M2

Assess the impact of factors affecting enzyme activity on metabolic processes and metabolic rates.

Assessment practice 24.2

B.D2

Evaluate how the structure, functions and action of biomolecules affect metabolic rates.

Assessment practice 24.2

B.P4

Investigate the factors affecting enzyme activity, and the enzymatic extraction of DNA.

Assessment practice 24.2

Learning aim **C** Examine the principles of biochemistry in industry

C.P5

Explain the aetiology of metabolic disorders of genetic and endocrine origins.

Assessment practice 24.3

C.M3

Assess the impact of DNA sequencing in the development of treatment/ therapy for metabolic disorders.

Assessment practice 24.3

C.D3

Evaluate how biological molecules and their role in metabolism influence current research and development of techniques and technology in treating metabolic disorders.

Assessment practice 24.3

C.P6

Explain the concept and uses of enzymes in biochemistry in the diagnosis and treatment of metabolic disorders and diseases, including DNA profiling and sequencing.

Assessment practice 24.3

Getting started

Do you know what the following terms mean: metabolism, catabolism, anabolism, polymer, hydrogen bonds, glycolysis?

Do you understand the principles behind scientific methodology?

Keep a record of what you know now and then see how well you can answer these questions when you have completed this unit.

 A

Explore how the structure of biological molecules affects metabolism

Reflect

All the chemical reactions that make and maintain living organisms are carried out at cellular level. It is important to revise what you have already learned about cells and organelles. Remind yourself about the physiological processes that maintain life – including respiration, protein synthesis, cell division, the action of hormones, how molecules pass across cell membranes and the importance of nucleic acids.

All living and non-living things consist of matter. Matter is made of chemical **elements**, which are made up of atoms. Inside atoms are smaller, subatomic, particles. It is the proportions of the various particles that give atoms, and therefore their elements, their specific characteristics and properties. It also enables different elements to react together to form **molecules**.

The structure of atoms

Atoms

Atoms are the building blocks of molecules. Every solid, liquid or gas is made of neutral or ionised (electrically charged) atoms. Atoms are very small. If two million of the largest atoms were placed end to end, they would occupy just 1 mm in diameter.

Atoms consist of a nucleus and **electrons**.

The centrally located nucleus makes up most of the atomic mass. It contains positively charged particles, called **protons**, and particles with no charge, called **neutrons**. Electrons are negatively charged particles that move around the nucleus. Electrons are much smaller than either protons or neutrons.

The number of electrons in a particular type of atom equals the number of protons in the atom. Thus, atoms have no overall electrical charge; they are electrically neutral.

Key terms

Element – a substance made up of atoms, all of the same type.

Molecule – the smallest part of a compound.

Atom – the smallest unit of matter with the properties of a chemical element and that can enter into chemical reactions.

Electron – negatively charged subatomic particle.

Proton – positively charged subatomic particle.

Neutron – subatomic particle that has no electric charge.

Electronic configuration

Figure 24.1 shows a representation of the atomic structure of carbon, hydrogen, oxygen and nitrogen. This is a very simplified model but one that can be used to explain how atoms interact.

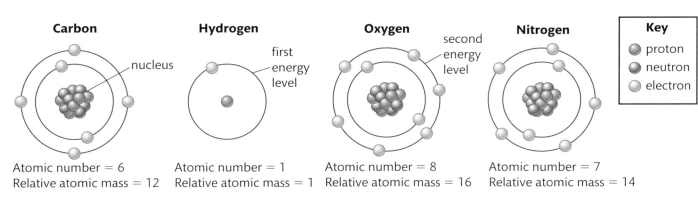

Carbon	Hydrogen	Oxygen	Nitrogen
Atomic number = 6	Atomic number = 1	Atomic number = 8	Atomic number = 7
Relative atomic mass = 12	Relative atomic mass = 1	Relative atomic mass = 16	Relative atomic mass = 14

▶ **Figure 24.1:** Highly simplified representations of some atoms

The concentric circles, where the electrons are at varying distances from the nucleus, represent energy levels. The first energy level can only hold *up to* two electrons. The second and third energy levels can hold *up to* eight electrons and the fourth can hold up to 18 electrons.

The nucleus of a carbon atom contains six protons, and six neutrons. The 6 electrons orbit the nucleus at different energy levels, two at the first level and four at the second level.

An atom always 'attempts' to fill its outermost energy level with the maximum number of electrons for that level; it does this by either gaining, losing or sharing electrons.

Link

See the sections on the Structure and function of organic molecules and the Structure and function of inorganic molecules, for more about atomic configuration.

Despite atoms being so small, they are largely empty space because the distance between the electron orbitals and the nucleus is relatively large. Protons and neutrons have a mass of one. Electrons are 1800 times smaller than both protons and neutrons.

Hydrogen atoms are the smallest. Each consists of one electron orbiting the nucleus, which contains just one proton.

Figure 24.1 shows the atomic structure of carbon, hydrogen, nitrogen and oxygen. These elements are important for carbon-based living organisms on Earth. All the important biological molecules contain carbon, hydrogen and oxygen and some (for example amino acids and nucleic acids) also contain nitrogen. Water consists of hydrogen and oxygen, and is vital to life.

Link

See the section on Structure and function of inorganic molecules, for more about the properties of water and its importance for life.

Chemistry of elements, ions and electrolytes in living cells

The atoms of elements may exist in slightly different forms, including **ions** (charged particles). Liquids that contain ions are called electrolytes. Electrolytes are important in the body. There are many different elements on Earth, some that are important to living organisms include carbon, hydrogen, oxygen, nitrogen, sodium, potassium, calcium, magnesium, sulfur, phosphorus and chlorine.

Ions

If an atom gains one or more extra electrons it now carries an overall negative charge. It is a negative **ion**, also called an **anion**. For example, a chlorine atom has seven electrons in its outer energy level, which is the third energy level. It needs one more electron to complete this shell and make it stable. If it gains an electron (from another atom that wants to lose one) it becomes a negative ion, chloride, Cl^-.

If an atom loses an electron it now carries an overall positive charge. It is now a positive ion, also called a **cation**. For example, a sodium atom has 11 electrons, so in the outer energy level there is one electron. If a sodium atom loses this outer electron, its outer energy level (now the second level) is full, and the sodium atom has an overall positive charge. It is a positive ion, Na^+.

Ions in watery solution, such as the extracellular fluid (fluid outside of the cells) in your body, are called electrolytes (see below).

There are also organic ions. For example lactic **acid**, $CH_3CH(OH)CO_2H$ is an **organic compound** with covalent bonds but which can ionise to lactate, $CH_3CHOHCOO^-$ and a hydrogen ion, H^+. Hydrogen ions are vital in living cells as proton gradients power many processes (see below).

> **Key terms**
>
> **Ion** – atom or molecule with an unequal number of electrons and protons, which means it has either a net positive or negative electric charge, due to its having lost or gained one or more electrons.
>
> **Anion** – negatively charged ion.
>
> **Cation** – positively charged ion.
>
> **Acid** – substance that dissociates into one or more hydrogen ions (H^+) and one or more anions.
>
> **Organic molecules (compounds)** – molecules of life; they are built around chains of carbon atoms. There are four main groups – carbohydrates, lipids, proteins and nucleic acids.

Hydrogen ions

A hydrogen ion, H^+, is formed when a hydrogen atom loses its single electron. It is, therefore, just a proton. Proton gradients across membranes in living cells are a source of potential energy. They generate a chemiosmotic potential, also known as the proton motive force. This is important for cellular functions in the body. There is more about this in the section on the Principles of metabolism, glucose metabolism.

Electrolytes

When molecules of inorganic acids, **bases** or **salts** dissolve in the water in body cells or tissue fluid they undergo dissociation (separation) into ions. Such ions are also called electrolytes because the resulting solution will now conduct an electrical current. Acids, bases and salts are all electrolytes.

As water is the major constituent of living cells, and chemical reactions take place in solution in this water, the electrolyte balance in living organisms is very important. Electrolytes:

▶ are essential minerals

▶ control **osmosis** of water between body compartments – cells and body fluids

> **Key terms**
>
> **Base** – substance that dissociates into one or more hydroxyl ions (OH^-) and one or more cations.
>
> **Salt** – substance that dissolves in water into anions and cations, neither of which is a hydrogen or hydroxyl ion.
>
> **Osmosis** – the passage of water from an area of high water potential to one of low water potential across a partially permeable membrane.

▶ help maintain the acid-base balance needed for normal cellular activities, by acting as buffer systems and preventing sudden changes in pH of body fluids such as blood

▶ allow nerve impulses to be transmitted.

Case study

Holiday ills

Ajani is on holiday and suffers a bad attack of traveller's diarrhoea and vomiting. Although she cannot eat, she makes sure she drinks plenty of water to replace what she is losing in vomit and watery stools. She adds a sachet of salts and glucose, which she bought from a pharmacy before leaving home, to the water to replace lost electrolytes. The glucose in the sachet helps to keep her blood glucose level in balance and provides a source of energy. If she had not taken the special sachets with her on holiday, adding six level teaspoons of sugar and a half a level teaspoon of table salt and sugar to a litre of clean water is a viable alternative for adults, rather than just drinking clean water. (However, for babies, small children and the elderly, there is a risk that these quantities are not suitable or safe. It is always advisable for these individuals to carry the recommended oral rehydration remedies.)

In many less economically developed countries, diarrhoea is a major cause of death in infants, as the water they drink is not treated to remove micro-organisms such as bacteria and viruses.

Check your knowledge

1 How could water be made safer to drink in less economically developed countries?

2 What simple treatment can be used to treat infants suffering from diarrhoea?

Nature of bonds in biological molecules

Biological molecules contain different elements joined by chemical bonds, such as ionic or covalent bonds.

Link

See the sections on Covalent bonds and Ionic bonds for more about these bonds.

Isotopes

Some chemical elements can have variant forms of atoms, with a different neutron number. These are called isotopes. The number of protons (the atomic number) is the same but because there are more neutrons, the isotope has a heavier relative atomic mass. Some isotopes are unstable and emit their extra neutrons as radioactivity. Radioactive isotopes have been a useful research tool for biochemists when working out sequences or reactions during metabolic pathways. Radioactive carbon dating uses radioactive isotopes of carbon, ^{14}C, to date fossils.

Isomers

Whereas alternative forms of an atom are called isotopes, alternative structural forms of molecules are called isomers. Certain compounds with the same molecular formula have slightly different arrangements of the atoms within each molecule. The spatial arrangement of atoms within a molecule can influence the shape of the molecule and in turn this affects how that molecule functions in the body.

Link

See the section on the Structure of organic molecules for more about isomers.

PAUSE POINT Draw diagrams to show the atomic structure of carbon, hydrogen, oxygen and nitrogen atoms – all important in your body.

Hint Remember that the atomic number of an element shows the number of protons in its nucleus. The relative atomic mass of an element tells you how many protons and neutrons are in its nucleus. You can then deduce the number of electrons and work out how many electrons are at each energy level.

Extend Consider why people with anorexia or bulimia might be advised to drink a lot – especially fluids with added salt and sugar.

Structure and function of inorganic molecules

Valence

Valence, or valency, indicates the combining capacity of atoms. It refers to the number of extra or deficient electrons in the element's atomic outermost energy level.

Sodium and chlorine both have a valence of one. One atom of sodium reacts with one atom of chlorine to form a molecule of sodium chloride (table salt).

Carbon atoms have four electrons in their outermost energy level. It is difficult to gain or lose four electrons so they share electrons to obtain the extra four. If each carbon atom shares its four electrons in the outer energy level with other atoms, which also share their electrons in their outer energy levels with the carbon, then each carbon atom now has access to eight electrons in its outer energy level. See Figure 24.2 for an example. Carbon has a valence of four.

Covalent bonds

Covalent bonds between atoms within a molecule involve shared electrons. Covalent bonds are strong.

In some cases, for example a hydrogen molecule, H_2, molecular oxygen, O_2 and molecular nitrogen, N_2, the electrons are shared between the same types of atom.

In other cases, for example, water and carbon dioxide, the atoms are shared between different types of atoms.

Carbon always forms covalent bonds and can share four pairs of electrons. It can share the four electrons in its outer energy level with the electrons of four hydrogen atoms. Carbon–hydrogen bonds are present in all biological organic molecules.

Carbon dioxide

Figure 24. 2 shows the covalent bonds formed by electron sharing between one atom of carbon and two atoms of oxygen to form carbon dioxide.

Inorganic carbon dioxide is the main source of carbon in organic molecules, as it is the source of carbon fixation during photosynthesis by producers. Once the plants have synthesised organic carbon-based molecules, other organisms can obtain these molecules by eating and digesting the producers, or by eating the primary consumers. Living organisms produce carbon dioxide as a by-product of respiration and this enters the atmosphere, replacing that taken out by photosynthesis.

The carbon dioxide you produce during respiration enters your blood and lowers its pH. This triggers faster ventilation and expulsion of this potentially harmful carbon dioxide.

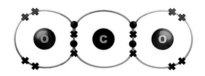

▶ **Figure 24.2:** Bond formation in a molecule of carbon dioxide; two pairs of electrons are shared between the carbon atom and each oxygen atom

PAUSE POINT   Which of these biological molecules contain nitrogen? Amylase, DNA, ATP, antibodies, glycogen, table sugar, urea, haemoglobin, water.

> Hint   Think about which of the above is a protein, nucleic acid or derived from proteins or nucleic acids.

> Extend   The atomic number for nitrogen is 7 and the relative atomic mass is 14. The radioactive isotope of nitrogen, ^{15}N is used in biochemical research. How does the atomic structure of ^{15}N differ from the atomic structure of normal nitrogen and how does this difference make ^{15}N radioactive?

Water consists of one molecule of oxygen covalently bonded with two molecules of hydrogen. Figure 24.3 shows the structure of a molecule of water. The shared electrons are unevenly distributed forming a polar covalent bond; the shared electrons spend more time orbiting the oxygen atom than around each hydrogen atom, which gives each molecule of water polarity (each end of the molecule has a different charge).

▶ **Figure 24.3:** A molecule of water

Characteristics of water

Water is the most abundant and important of all inorganic molecules on Earth. Water is the most abundant material in your cells and tissues. Without water there is no life.

Universal solvent

Water is an excellent solvent and dissolves most substances, which are called solutes when in solution. Due to its polarity, water is a universal solvent. When substances dissolve in water and dissociate into ions, water molecules surround both the positive and negative ions.

Water is also a good suspending medium, and many molecules can be suspended in it. Many large organic molecules are suspended in the watery cytoplasm of cells. Consequently these molecules can come together and react with each other.

Lubricant

Water forms the basis of lubricants in the body, such as mucus, which helps food pass smoothly through the gut, and synovial fluid, which lubricates your joints.

Hydrogen bonds

There is a weak attraction between the positive hydrogen ends of one water molecule and the more negatively charged oxygen end of another water molecule. These attraction forces between water molecules are called hydrogen bonds.

Hydrogen bonds are weaker than covalent bonds, so they do not bind atoms into molecules. They serve as bridges between different molecules. Polarity and hydrogen bonds in water give water some unusual but vital-for-life properties, such as its boiling point and freezing point.

Because water molecules have a high attraction (cohesion) for one another, water has the following properties.

▶ A high specific heat capacity, which means it takes a lot of heat energy to warm up but a long time to cool down. This makes it able to resist sudden changes in temperature. As living organisms consist of about 80 per cent water, if water did not resist sudden temperature changes, they would overheat very quickly when outside on a hot day.

▶ A high latent heat of vaporisation – because water needs a lot of energy to evaporate, it is useful for cooling; when you sweat the water evaporates, taking a lot of heat from the blood flowing through vessels in the skin.

- Small molecules with a low molecular mass of 18. Unexpectedly, water has a high boiling point of 100 °C. This is because it takes a lot of heat energy to make the water molecules separate from one another and move far enough apart for water to become gaseous vapour. If this was not the case, most water on Earth would not be in liquid form and, therefore, there would not be the huge diversity of living organisms that exist. Liquid water:
  - provides aquatic habitats
  - makes up the bulk of living cells and tissues
  - provides an internal transport medium (for example blood and lymph)
  - provides the medium for metabolic reactions in cells.
- A high surface tension. A drop of water on a flat surface does not spread out because the hydrogen bonds pull molecules together. Surface tension also allows some insects, for example pond skaters, to walk across the surface of the water. Water forms drops on waxy surfaces, such as leaves and bird feathers, rolling off them rather than wetting them. The same happens on waterproof clothing. Because of surface tension and cohesion, in plants columns of water are pulled from their roots up the xylem tissue to the leaves.
- A low freezing point of 0 °C. As water temperature lowers, its molecules become closer together until at 4 °C water is at its densest. As the temperature drops below 4 °C, the water molecules move apart and a lattice-like, crystalline structure forms. The density of ice is less than that of water, so ice floats on water. At the North Pole, where there is no land mass, the polar ice cap forms on the ocean surface, allowing polar bears to live and hunt. In winter, as ponds cool, the densest water at 4 °C goes to the bottom of the pond, thus leaving enough liquid water for pond inhabitants to survive (even if the top is frozen). If water did not behave in this way, all the oceans would be largely ice as they would freeze from the bottom up, leaving little room for living organisms. Ice melts at 0 °C and changes to liquid water.

Water can be split into hydrogen ions and hydroxyl ions. This is used on the International Space Station (ISS) to generate oxygen from water. Every drop of water, from sweat to urine, is recycled in the ISS. Plants growing on the ISS also generate oxygen and absorb carbon dioxide.

Buffers and pH

Aqueous (watery) solutions of weak acids and bases resist changes of pH when a stronger acid or base is added. Such solutions are called buffers. Free hydrogen ions (H^+) can 'mop up' negative ions and free hydroxyl ions (OH^-) can 'mop up' positive ions. Buffers are used in many laboratory investigations to keep the pH constant. In living organisms, buffers help to keep pH levels fairly constant and resist changes in pH that would disrupt protein structure and **denature** enzymes and other proteins.

> **Key term**
>
> **Denature** – destroy structure and, therefore, ability to function.

Ionic bonds

Ionic bonds are chemical bonds that involve the electrostatic attraction between oppositely charged ions. The resulting compounds are ionic compounds. An example is sodium chloride, where the single electron in the outermost energy level of the sodium atom leaves and completes the outer energy level of the chlorine atom. The resulting Na^+ and Cl^- ions attract each other. When in water, many salts formed by ionic bonding dissociate into their cations and anions to form electrolytes.

▶ Hydrochloric acid, HCl, made in the stomach, contains ionic bonding between one hydrogen ion and one chloride ion.

▶ Sodium ethanoate, CH_3COONa, is the sodium salt of ethanoic acid, formed by reacting ethanoic acid and sodium hydroxide. For some patients, a solution of sodium ethanoate can be used in intravenous injections instead of sodium chloride, to restore electrolyte balance. The bond between Na^+ and CH_3COO^- is ionic.

Where there are differences in ion concentrations across cell membranes, an electrochemical gradient forms across such membranes. This leads to movement of ions, and such movement is vital to many physiological processes, such as nerve impulse conduction and proton movements involved in generating ATP. You will learn more about these and about electron transport in the section on Principles of metabolism.

⏸ PAUSE POINT   Explain the following terms: valence, covalent bonds, ionic bonds, hydrogen bonds.

(Hint)   Imagine you are explaining these terms to someone who knows very little chemistry.

(Extend)   Explain how hydrogen bonds give water some of its unusual properties.

Structure and function of organic molecules

All organic molecules, which form the basis of life on Earth, contain carbon. Carbon has a valance of four and can form single, double and triple covalent bonds with other atoms. Hence there is a wide range of organic molecules found within living organisms. Organic molecules are also important for pharmaceutical products, for example in antibiotics, statins, antibodies and in hormone replacement such as insulin, thyroxine and oestrogen.

The main groups of organic molecules of interest to biochemists and biologists are amino acids, proteins (polypeptides), carbohydrates, lipids and nucleic acids.

Carbohydrates

Carbohydrates contain carbon, hydrogen and oxygen in their molecules. Carbohydrates are the most abundant molecules on Earth and the bulk of human diets, the staple foods, consist of carbohydrates. Carbohydrates have three main functions:

▶ as an energy source – for example, glucose is respired to release energy and make ATP

▶ as an energy store – starch is stored in plants and glycogen is stored in animal cells and in some bacteria

▶ structural – cellulose forms plant cell walls; chitin is present in fungal cell walls and insects' exoskeletons. RNA, ATP and the hydrogen carrier NAD contain the pentose (5-carbon) sugar ribose and DNA contains the pentose sugar, deoxyribose; glycoproteins (proteins with sugar attached) form some cell membrane proteins, antibodies and bacterial cell walls.

Monosaccharides

Monosaccharides are the simplest carbohydrate molecules. They are sugars and they:

▶ taste sweet

▶ are soluble in water.

Different sugars have different numbers of carbon atoms in each molecule. Triose sugars have three, tetrose sugars have four, pentose sugars have five and hexose sugars have six.

Triose and tetrose sugars in solution have straight chain molecules, whereas the other forms in solution have ring structures.

Monosaccharide hexose sugars, such as glucose, are the **monomers** that bond together by condensation reactions to form disaccharides, and then large polymer molecules (polysaccharides) such as starch and glycogen.

Glucose molecules can exist as different isomers.

Alpha glucose (α-glucose) has an –OH group at C_1 (carbon atom number 1) below the plane of the ring whereas beta glucose (β-glucose) has the –OH group at C_1 above the plane of the ring. This may not seem a very big difference but it affects the way two molecules of β-glucose can bond together and greatly influences the structure and properties of cellulose, which is a polymer of β-glucose. Table 24.1 shows the molecular formulae and molecular structures of some monosaccharides.

▶ **Table 24.1:** Molecular structure and formula of some monosaccharides

Name of sugar	Molecular formula	Structural formula	Type of sugar	Role in organisms
triose	$C_3H_6O_3$		triose	Intermediate in the glycolysis pathway (see the section Principles of metabolism)
α-glucose	$C_6H_{12}O_6$		hexose	Energy source; monomer of the energy stores starch and glycogen; two molecules joined together form the disaccharide maltose
β-glucose	$C_6H_{12}O_6$		hexose	Energy source; monomer of the polymer cellulose, which forms plant cell walls
fructose	$C_6H_{12}O_6$		hexose	Energy source; together with glucose forms the disaccharide sucrose
galactose	$C_6H_{12}O_6$		hexose	Energy source; with glucose forms the disaccharide lactose

▶ **Table 24.1:** *continued*

Name of sugar	Molecular formula	Structural formula	Type of sugar	Role in organisms
ribose	$C_5H_{10}O_5$		pentose	Component of RNA, ATP, NAD (a coenzyme), and some vitamins
deoxyribose	$C_5H_{10}O_4$		pentose	Component of DNA

Disaccharides

Disaccharides are also sweet-tasting, water-soluble sugars. Alpha maltose (α-maltose – malt sugar) is formed when a **condensation reaction** takes place between two molecules of α-glucose. The reaction is between two –OH groups, one on C_1 of one glucose molecule and the other on C_4 of the other glucose molecule (see Figure 24.4). Between them, a 1,4 glycosidic bond is formed. With the addition of a molecule of water, maltose can be **hydrolysed** back to two molecules of glucose.

> **Key terms**
>
> **Condensation reaction** – reaction to join two or more smaller molecules to make a larger molecule, involving the elimination of one or more molecules of water; the reverse of hydrolysis.
>
> **Hydrolysis** – breaking of a larger molecule, by the addition of water, into smaller molecules.

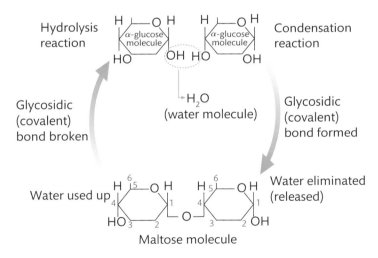

▶ **Figure 24.4:** Formation of maltose from glucose by condensation and hydrolysis of maltose to glucose

The equation shows the formation of a disaccharide from two monosaccharides:

$$C_6H_{12}O_6 + C_6H_{12}O_6 \rightarrow C_{12}H_{22}O_{11} + H_2O$$

Other disaccharides are:

▶ sucrose (cane sugar), made from one molecule of glucose and one of fructose

▶ lactose (milk sugar), made from one molecule of glucose and one of galactose.

Shapes of molecules

Mirella Albescu is a midwife. She recently had to advise a mother whose newborn baby was not thriving, and was often sick after being breastfed. Tests showed that the baby had galactosaemia.

Normally, enzymes in the gut hydrolyse lactose sugar in milk to glucose and galactose. Another enzyme, glucose isomerase, then changes galactose (an isomer of glucose) to glucose for respiration. Respiration releases the energy from the glucose that the baby needs to grow and live. Babies with galactosaemia do not have glucose isomerase enzymes, or the enzyme is not quite the right shape and does not work properly. As a result, these babies cannot get enough energy from breast milk or formula feed and they have to be given special formula feed.

Mirella has lactose intolerance. She lacks the enzyme lactase that digests lactose to glucose and galactose, so she avoids eating many dairy products. Mirella's son is diabetic and Mirella has recently found out that he should not have drinks containing artificial sweeteners, because receptors in the gut sense the sweetness of these artificial sweeteners, which triggers a response from the pancreas to produce insulin.

Check your knowledge

1   How do you think the formula feed for babies with galactosaemia differs from breast milk or normal formula feed?

2   Explain why Mirella cannot eat dairy products such as cheese and milk chocolate.

3   Why should people with diabetes not have drinks that contain artificial sweeteners?

Polysaccharides

Polysaccharides are polymers of monosaccharides. They are made of many thousands of glucose monomers bonded together.

Glycogen and starch are polysaccharides of α-glucose. They are each stored within large granules inside cells. They are both excellent energy stores because:

▸ they are compact, and being in dense granules means they do not occupy as much space in the cell as would the many glucose molecules from which they are made

▸ they are both insoluble in water, so they do *not* create any osmotic effects in the cell; sugar would dissolve, lower the water potential and cause water to enter cells by osmosis, and this would cause animal cells to burst

▸ enzymes in cells can 'snip off' a few glucose monomers at a time from the large glycogen or starch molecules; these glucose molecules can then be respired to release energy.

Fats (lipids)

Lipids are also known as fats, they:

▸ contain large amounts of carbon and hydrogen and smaller amounts of oxygen in their molecules

▸ are insoluble in water, because they are not polar and do not attract water molecules

▸ are soluble in alcohol and in other fats.

▸ The most important types of lipids in living organisms are triglycerides, fatty acids, glycerol, phospholipids and cholesterol, which is a **steroid** derived from **isoprene** units. Some **terpenes**, such as vitamin A, are also important.

Lipids have many functions in the body, including the following examples.

▸ Energy source. Triglycerides are hydrolysed to fatty acids and glycerol and can then be respired aerobically to release energy to make ATP; the by-products are carbon dioxide and water. Respiration of 1 kg lipid produces 1 kg metabolic water – far more than is produced when 1 kg carbohydrate is respired. Lipids release just over twice as much energy per unit mass as do carbohydrates, because they have many more hydrogen atoms bonded to carbon atoms, and very little oxygen.

Steroid – chemical substance with a specific four-ring carbon structure, related to cholesterol.

Isoprene – organic compound with the formula $H_2C=C-CH=CH_2$ produced by many plants; may help stabilise cell membranes against increased temperatures.

Terpenes – organic compounds made of chains of isoprene units, also known as isoprenoids.

▶ Energy store. Triglycerides, or white fat, are insoluble in water and can be stored in cells without causing any osmotic effects. Fat is stored in special cells in adipose tissue. It is also stored in yellow bone marrow. Brown fat is stored in adipose tissue between the shoulder blades and in a few other areas. Brown fat cells contain many mitochondria. Newborn babies contain a lot of brown fat that can be easily respired to generate heat and protect them from hypothermia (low body temperature). Adults contain some brown fat. In response to prolonged extreme cold, brown fat cells appear in adult white fat tissue. Men should have between 3 and 20 per cent of their body mass as fat. Women store more fat in preparation for pregnancy and breast feeding and should have between 12 and 33 per cent of their body mass as fat. Hibernating and migrating animals also accumulate large fat stores.

▶ Insulation and protection. Subcutaneous (under skin) fat acts as a heat insulator. It also cushions against knocks.

▶ Nerve conduction. The fatty myelin sheath around neurones prevents loss and leakage of ions and enables fast nerve conduction. (Multiple sclerosis is a neurological condition that occurs when this myelin sheath is damaged or destroyed by the body's immune system.)

▶ Brain development. Foetuses and children need a constant supply of fatty acids to support the growth of their nerve cells (neurones) in the brain. In adulthood the fatty acids are still needed to maintain the myelin around neurones.

Triglycerides

Triglycerides are dietary fats made of one molecule of glycerol bonded to three fatty acids. They are macromolecules (large molecules) but *not* polymers as each molecule is made from condensation reactions between more than one type of smaller molecule. A condensation reaction happens between each –OH group of the glycerol and the –COOH group of each fatty acid. Three water molecules are produced and three covalent ester bonds form (see Figure 24.5).

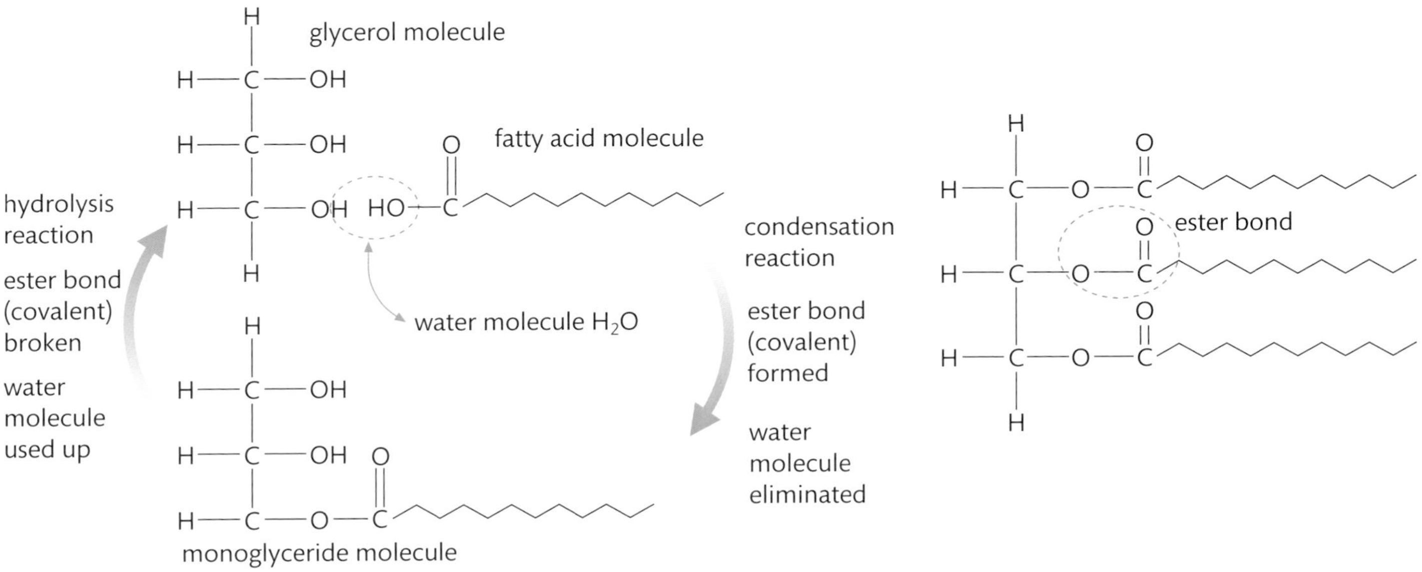

▶ **Figure 24.5:** Formation of a triglyceride

Triglycerides are a source of energy and required for energy storage. They are found in meats, dairy produce and cooking oils; your liver also makes triglycerides.

Fatty acids are components of triglycerides. They are long chain hydrocarbons with a carboxylic acid (–COOH) group at one end. They can be respired to release energy; some are used to make phospholipids – constituents of cell membranes.

There are many different fatty acids. Some of them can be synthesised by humans and some, called essential fatty acids, have to be obtained in the diet. Alpha linoleic acid (α-linolenic acid), which is an **omega-3 fatty acid**, and linoleic acid, which is an **omega-6 fatty acid**, are essential dietary fatty acids for humans.

The essential fatty acids are needed for:

▶ healthy growth

▶ good functioning of the immune system

▶ development and maintenance of the nervous system.

Case study

Fish oils

James Mackintosh is a nutritionist. He has a BSc degree and is also studying for his Master's degree. He is researching to find out more about fish oils, which are rich in essential fatty acids. James has found that fish obtain these essential fatty acids by eating algae, which make them. He has also learned that some staple crops, such as wheat, may be genetically modified to contain the essential fatty acids that humans need in their diet.

Check your knowledge

1 From which organisms do you think the gene for essential fatty acids, to be inserted into wheat plants, would be obtained?

Fatty acids have a carboxyl (–COOH) group at one end of a long-chain hydrocarbon tail, made only of carbon atoms bonded covalently to hydrogen atoms. Because the carboxyl group ionises by losing a hydrogen ion and becoming –COO⁻ and H⁺, it is an acid, as it produces free hydrogen ions (protons).

▶ If every carbon atom in the hydrocarbon chain bonds with two (or three) hydrogen atoms, with only single bonds, C–C (one shared pair of electrons between adjacent carbon atoms), the fatty acid is described as saturated. Saturated fats, for example animal fats such as butter and lard, are generally solid at room temperature and have high melting points.

▶ If the hydrocarbon chain contains fewer hydrogen atoms, adjacent carbon atoms need to share two pairs of electrons and form a double bond (–C=C). These fatty acids are unsaturated.

▶ If there is one double bond between two adjacent carbon atoms, the fatty acid is monounsaturated.

▶ If there is more than one double bond between adjacent carbons in the hydrocarbon chain, the fatty acid is described as polyunsaturated.

▶ Unsaturated fatty acids have a kink where there is a double bond. These kinks push the molecules apart slightly and make them more fluid. Unsaturated fatty acids have a higher melting point. Consequently they are generally liquid at room temperature and are called oils.

Glycerol

Glycerol (glycerine) is a component of triglycerides. When your body respires stored fat for energy, glycerol and fatty acids are released into the blood stream. Your liver and fat cells can use glycerol to make phospholipids – constituents of cell membranes.

Every glycerol molecule contains three carbon atoms. Glycerol is an alcohol as the molecule contains free –OH groups.

As there are *three* –OH groups one glycerol molecule can react with *three* fatty acids, forming a *tri*glyceride.

Phospholipids

The molecular structure of phospholipids resembles that of triglycerides, except that one fatty acid is replaced by a phosphate group, see Figure 24.6.

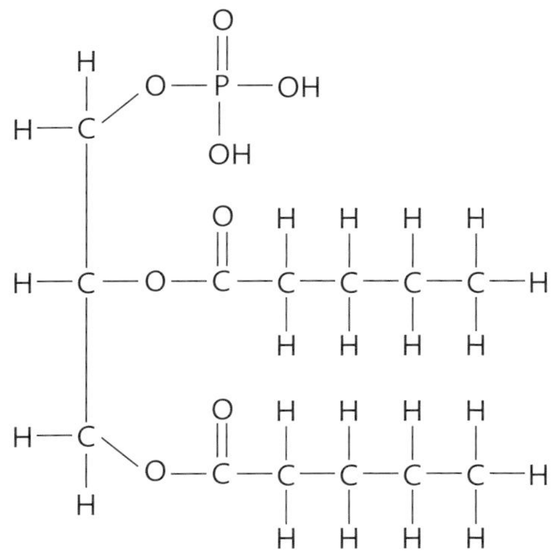

▶ **Figure 24.6:** Molecular structure of a phospholipid

The phosphate group can become ionised by losing a hydrogen ion and leaving a negatively charged oxygen ion. The presence of this charge gives phospholipid molecules polarity and makes the phosphate head hydrophilic (attracted to water) and miscible (able to mix with) with water. The two fatty acid chains left are hydrophobic and do not mix with water. If phospholipids are spread onto a watery surface, they form a bilayer with hydrophilic heads facing into the water and hydrophobic tails tucked inside. This arrangement is found in the phospholipid bilayer of cell surface membranes, separating watery cytoplasm form the watery extracellular fluid. It is also found in membranes surrounding organelles inside cells.

Phospholipids can also form micelles – tiny balls of phopsholipid. These can be used to deliver certain large molecules, such as genes during gene therapy, into cells as the micelle dissolves in and passes through the lipid bilayer of cell membranes.

Cholesterol

Cholesterol is a type of lipid called a sterol (a steroid alcohol) that is *not* made from glycerol or fatty acids. It is an essential substance in the body. Cholesterol is a vital component of animal cell membranes and is the main constituent of myelin sheaths around nerve cells. The steroid hormones testosterone, oestrogen, progesterone, aldosterone and vitamin D are all made from cholesterol.

Each cholesterol molecule consists of four carbon-based rings, derived from four isoprene (C_5H_8) units. Because it is a small hydrophobic molecule, it can fit between phospholipids in animal cell membranes, making them stronger. Humans make cholesterol in the liver, from saturated fats in the diet. Cholesterol is needed by most body cells and is transported to and from the liver in the blood. To make it miscible with the watery blood, it is combined with proteins, to form high density lipoproteins (HDLs) and low density lipoproteins (LDLs). HDLs contain relatively more protein and are sometimes called 'good cholesterol'. LDLs contain relatively more cholesterol and are sometimes called 'bad cholesterol'. LDLs may deposit cholesterol as fatty plaques in artery walls; HDLs remove the fatty plaques from artery walls. The build-up of fatty plaques inside artery walls leads to atherosclerosis, increasing a person's risk of heart attack or stroke.

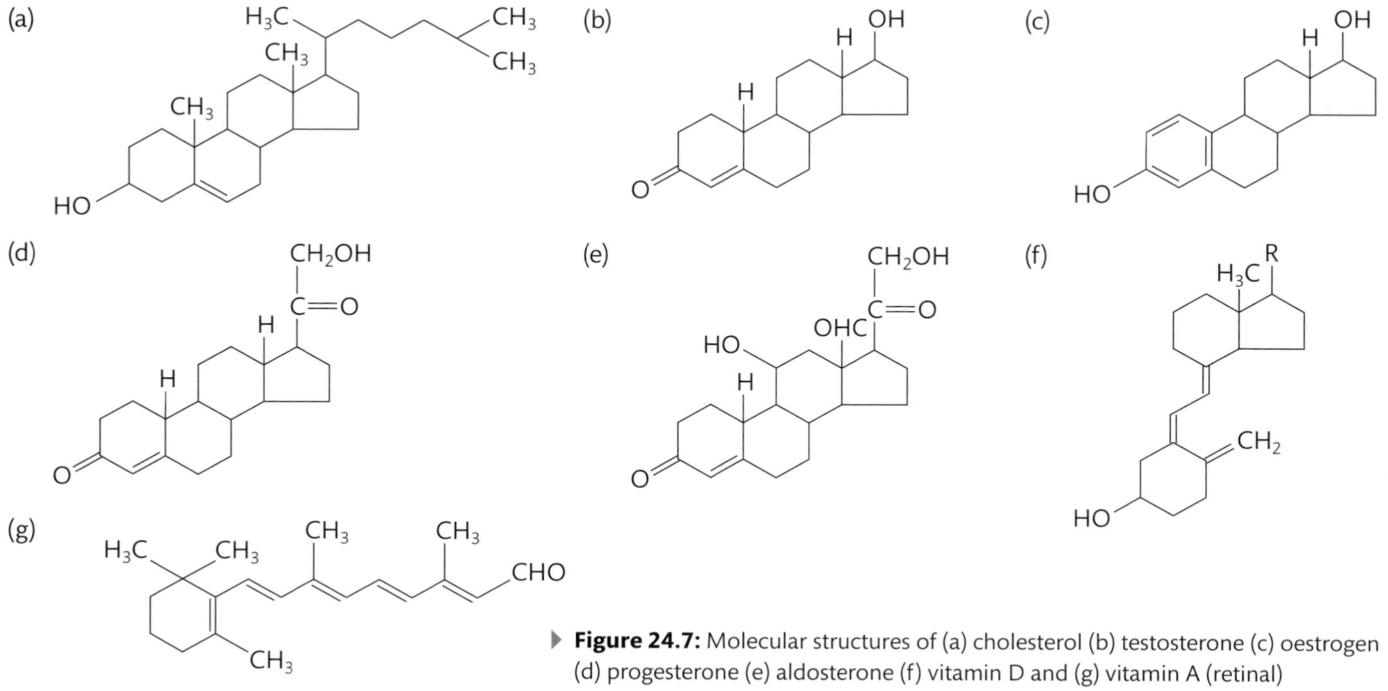

Figure 24.7: Molecular structures of (a) cholesterol (b) testosterone (c) oestrogen (d) progesterone (e) aldosterone (f) vitamin D and (g) vitamin A (retinal)

PAUSE POINT

Make a list to show all the uses of various types of fats in the body. What sorts of foods are rich in fats?

Hint — Include terpenes, cholesterol and phospholipids as well as triglycerides.

Extend — Explain why people need some cholesterol in their bodies. Why do you think measuring someone's blood levels of HDL and LDL may be included in a medical examination?

Proteins

Proteins are large polymers made of long chains of amino acids (see below). Proteins make up about 75 per cent of an organism's dry mass. Some are structural, for example collagen in connective tissue, bones and tendons, proteins in muscle and those within cell membranes. Others form part of a living organism's 'toolkit' and, because they each fold into a specific shape, they function as enzymes, antibodies, receptors, channels for transporting ions across membranes, and haemoglobin that transports oxygen to cells. Some hormones are small proteins (peptides). Some proteins act as buffers, because when they dissolve in water they ionise. COOH dissociates to COO⁻, producing hydrogen ions, lowering the pH; and NH_2 groups can accept hydrogen ions, becoming NH_3^+ and raising the pH.

Amino acids

Amino acids are the monomers of proteins. There are many hundreds of amino acids but only 20 different amino acids are involved in protein synthesis. Each contains carbon, hydrogen, oxygen and nitrogen. Some also contain sulfur. They all have a backbone, an amino group (NH$_2$) and a carboxyl (COOH) group. Each also has a side chain (R) that is different for each amino acid. Figure 24.8 shows the general molecular structure for an amino acid.

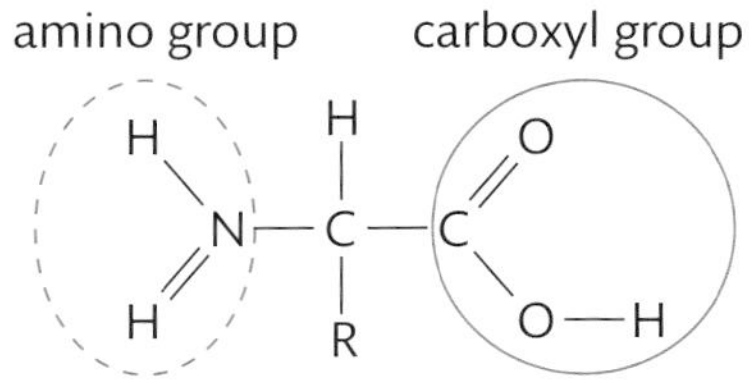

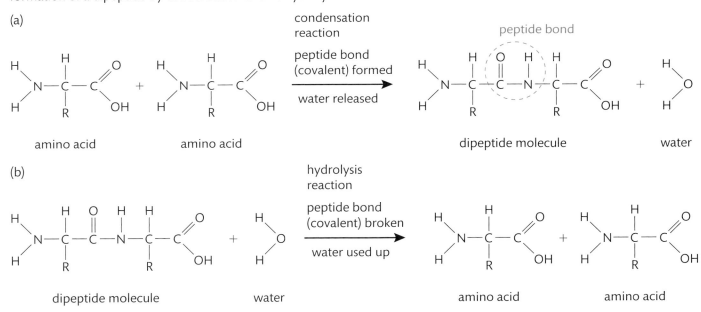

▶ **Figure 24.8:** Molecular structure of an amino acid

Glycine is the simplest amino acid, where R is one atom of hydrogen. In alanine, R is CH$_3$; and in cysteine R is CH$_3$S. R groups vary in size, electric charge and polarity. Some are hydrophobic (water-hating) and some are hydrophilic (water-loving).

Humans need to obtain ten amino acids from their diet. These are called essential amino acids. From these ten, they can synthesise the other ten, when necessary.

Amine bonds (Peptide bonds)

Amino acids are joined together by covalent peptide (amine) bonds. The formation of a peptide bond involves a condensation reaction between the amino group of one amino acid and the carboxyl group of another amino acid. Figure 24.9 shows the formation of a dipeptide by condensation and its hydrolysis back to two amino acids.

▶ **Figure 24.9:** (a) Formation of a peptide bond by condensation and (b) the breaking of a peptide bond by hydrolysis

The structure of amino acids

▶ Primary structure. The sequence of amino acids in the polypeptide chain is the primary structure of a protein. It is determined by the sequence of nucleotide bases on a length of DNA (a gene).

▶ Secondary structure. Once the chain of amino acids has been assembled it twists into coils, called alpha helices or zig-zag structures called beta pleated sheets. These are held together by hydrogen bonds between –NH groups of one amino acid and the –CO group of another amino acid at a different position within the coil or pleat.

Link

Further information about nucleotide bases and DNA sequencing can be found in the section on Nucleic acids.

▶ Tertiary structure. The coiled or pleated protein folds into a specific 3D shape, held together by hydrogen bonds and ionic bonds between amino acids that are close to each other. Hydrogen bonds form between hydrogen atoms with a small positive charge and nitrogen atoms with a weak negative charge. Some proteins coil into fibrous proteins, such as collagen in bones and tendons; keratin in skin, hair and nails; elastin in ligaments and blood vessel walls. Others, such as enzymes, haemoglobin and insulin, fold into globular (spherical) shapes. Figure 24.10 shows how hydrogen bonds and ionic bonds form within protein molecules.

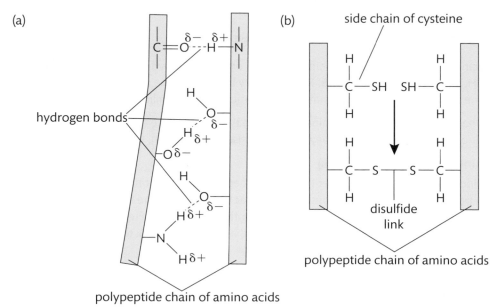

▶ **Figure 24.10:** (a) Hydrogen bonds and (b) disulfide bonds within protein molecules

Disulfide bonds between R groups of two adjacent cysteine amino acids within a protein are strong, heat-resistant covalent bonds.

▶ Hydrophobic and hydrophilic interactions. Hydrophobic parts of the R groups associate together at the centre of the polypeptide, thus avoiding contact with water. Hydrophilic parts are at the edge of the polypeptide, where they are close to water. Hydrophobic and hydrophilic interactions cause twisting of the amino acid chain, which changes the shape of the protein.

▶ Quaternary structure. Many proteins are made of more than one polypeptide chain and they therefore have a quaternary structure. Insulin and haemoglobin have quaternary structures.

Haemoglobin

Haemoglobin is the oxygen-carrying protein found in red blood cells. It is made of four polypeptide chains – two alpha chains and two beta chains. Each chain has its own tertiary structure, but when they join together they form one haemoglobin molecule. The bonds and interactions within this molecule give it a very specific shape. At one position on the outside of each chain is a non-protein haem group. In each haem group is an iron ion (see Figure 24.11).

Haemoglobin could not function without haem groups. When blood is in the lungs, iron ions inside haemoglobin in the red blood cells combine with oxygen and become the oxygenated form, oxyhaemoglobin. The molecule changes shape, and changes colour from purple/red to bright red. When blood arrives at respiring tissue, where the oxygen concentration is low, oxygen dissociates from oxyhaemoglobin, which becomes deoxygenated. The oxygen diffuses into the mitochondria inside muscle cells for aerobic respiration.

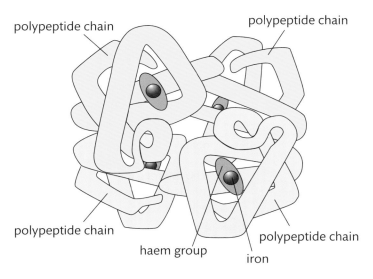

polypeptide chain

polypeptide chain

polypeptide chain

polypeptide chain

haem group

iron

▶ **Figure 24.11:** The structure of haemoglobin

Case study

Sickle cell anaemia

Jayden Winfrey suffers from sickle cell anaemia. His parents were both symptomless carriers of this condition, so he inherited two mutated alleles of the gene for haemoglobin. Two protein strands of each haemoglobin molecule have a different amino acid than usual at position 6 in the chain. This small change causes the haemoglobin to have a different shape. At tissues where the level of oxygen is low, the haemoglobin inside Jayden's red blood cells is stringy and not round. This makes his red blood cells sickle shaped, instead of being round; the sickled cells block his capillaries.

This prevents enough red blood cells and oxygen reaching his respiring tissues, causing a painful crisis. Jayden's condition means that he has a blood transfusion every three months, when he is given blood of the same blood group as his own but with normal haemoglobin content.

Check your knowledge

1   Why is the level of oxygen at tissue lower than the level of oxygen in lungs?

2   Why do you think Jayden needs blood transfusions as frequently as every three months?

Membrane proteins

According to the fluid mosaic model, which is the accepted model used to explain cell membrane structure, various protein molecules float in the phospholipid bilayer that makes up the fabric of the cell membrane. Some of these proteins act as receptors, some as channels and some as carriers.

Membrane receptors

Proteins on the outer side of the cell surface membrane, next to the extracellular fluid, each have a specific shape. These proteins are receptors. Certain molecules such as peptide hormones, which act as chemical messengers for cells to signal to each other, can each fit into specifically shaped receptors, because the shapes of receptor and messenger molecules are complementary to each other. When the signalling molecule has docked with its receptor, this can initiate a reaction inside the cell.

Channels

Channel proteins span the whole membrane. The amino acids making up their structure are positioned in such a way that hydrophilic ones are lining the channel pore. This allows particular ions surrounded by water molecules to pass through these specific channels down their concentration gradient by facilitated diffusion, using only their own kinetic energy. Figure 24.12 shows the structure of a cell membrane with receptors and channels.

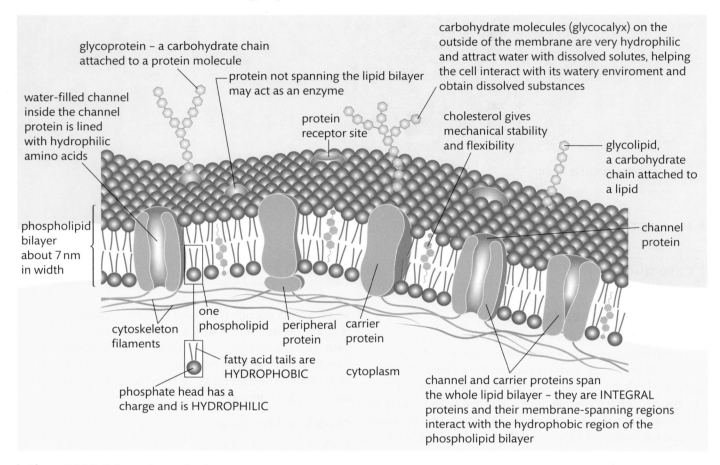

glycoprotein – a carbohydrate chain attached to a protein molecule

carbohydrate molecules (glycocalyx) on the outside of the membrane are very hydrophilic and attract water with dissolved solutes, helping the cell interact with its watery enviroment and obtain dissolved substances

protein not spanning the lipid bilayer may act as an enzyme

water-filled channel inside the channel protein is lined with hydrophilic amino acids

protein receptor site

cholesterol gives mechanical stability and flexibility

glycolipid, a carbohydrate chain attached to a lipid

phospholipid bilayer about 7 nm in width

channel protein

cytoskeleton filaments

one phospholipid

peripheral protein

carrier protein

cytoplasm

fatty acid tails are HYDROPHOBIC

phosphate head has a charge and is HYDROPHILIC

channel and carrier proteins span the whole lipid bilayer – they are INTEGRAL proteins and their membrane-spanning regions interact with the hydrophobic region of the phospholipid bilayer

▶ **Figure 24.12:** Cell membrane structure

Carrier proteins and protein pumps

When molecules move across membranes, against the concentration gradient, they require more energy than that associated with their own kinetic energy. Carrier proteins embedded in the membrane are associated with ATPase enzymes that hydrolyse the ATP (adenosine triphosphate) molecule, releasing cellular energy, which moves the molecules across the membrane from low to high concentration. The carrier protein is sometimes called a protein pump and its configuration changes as it transports molecules across the cell membrane.

Hormones

Hormones are chemical messengers made in endocrine glands. These glands have no ducts and the hormones are secreted straight into the blood flowing through them. The hormones, many of which govern long-term changes to do with growth and maturity, are then transported around the body in the blood stream. When they meet and fit into complementary-shaped receptor proteins on the cell surface membranes of their target tissue:

▶ If they are peptides (small proteins) such as insulin, which regulates blood sugar, they stay attached to the receptor and this initiates a series of events inside the cell.

▶ If they are steroids such as the sex hormones testosterone or oestrogen, or aldosterone, which regulates salt content in the body, they are all derived from cholesterol (see Figure 24.7). Because they are fat soluble, they pass through the lipid bilayer of the cell surface membrane, combine with a receptor in the cytoplasm and then pass through the nuclear envelope into the nucleus, where they initiate a reaction by activating genes. This photograph shows the molecular structure of insulin.

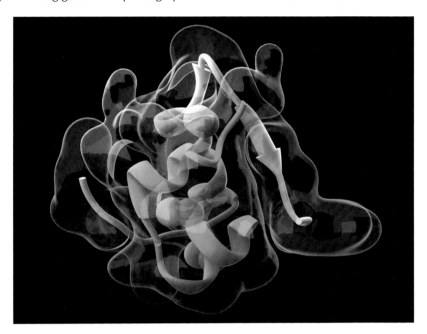

▶ Molecular structure of insulin

> **Link**
>
> To find out more about the endocrine system, see the section on the Aetiology of metabolic disorders.

Principles of metabolism

Metabolism

Metabolism refers to all the chemical reactions and processes that occur in living cells and organisms to maintain life. These vital processes include:

▶ movement

▶ nutrition (obtaining food)

▶ respiration

▶ growth

▶ perception and response to stimuli

▶ excretion of toxic metabolic waste

▶ reproduction.

Some metabolic reactions, called **catabolic** reactions, involve breaking down larger molecules, which provide the energy for vital processes. **Anabolic** reactions use energy and may involve synthesising large molecules or structures from smaller ones.

> **Key terms**
>
> **Metabolism** – the chemical reactions that take place inside living cells to maintain life.
>
> **Catabolism** – metabolic reactions that involve splitting large molecules into smaller ones, often with the release of energy.
>
> **Anabolism** – metabolic reactions that involve synthesising large molecules from smaller ones, using energy.

Metabolic pathways

The metabolism of particular substances occurs in a series of separate reactions, each catalysed (enabled and speeded up) by a different enzyme. These series of reactions are called metabolic pathways.

In a metabolic pathway the initial chemical, called the metabolite, is modified by a series of enzyme-catalysed reactions where the product from one reaction is the **substrate** for the next reaction. Sometimes the subsequent reactions take place immediately and in some cases the product may:

▶ start another metabolic pathway
▶ be stored for later metabolism.
▶ Within a living cell there are many different metabolic reactions taking place at the same time forming an elaborate network of interconnected pathways.
▶ Because each is catalysed by a specific enzyme these reactions can occur independently.
▶ Some enzymes require activators, such as inorganic ions, to help them catalyse their reaction. Some enzymes also need cofactors, such as certain vitamins or their derivatives, to help them function properly (see the section: Characteristics of biomolecules).
▶ In **eukaryotic cells**, the organelles inside cells divide cells into discrete compartments. Certain reactions take place within specific organelles. This gives a division of labour and ensures that the different reactions going on, some of which may be anabolic and some catabolic, do not interfere with each other.
▶ Metabolic reactions are reversible and can proceed in two directions. The direction in which any reaction proceeds at any given time is determined by the needs of the cell. In many reactions, the end product can inhibit the enzyme catalysing the final reaction; consequently the cell does not overproduce any products. As the product is used, the enzyme inhibition stops and the reaction proceeds again.
▶ Metabolic pathways are regulated by feedback inhibition.
▶ Some metabolic pathways flow in a cycle, such as the stage of aerobic respiration called the Krebs cycle (see the section on Glucose metabolism and cellular respiration).
▶ Metabolic reactions are also crucial for maintaining homeostasis (a steady state).

Aerobic respiration (respiration using oxygen) involves a series of metabolic pathways, glycolysis, the link reaction, the Krebs cycle and oxidative phosphorylation (addition of phosphate). Anaerobic (without oxygen) respiration involves glycolysis and either the lactate pathway or the ethanol pathway (see the section on Glucose metabolism and cellular respiration).

Glycolysis pathway and mitochondrial oxidation

Glycolysis was the first metabolic pathway discovered by scientists. The glycolysis pathway is a metabolic pathway that generates ATP (adenosine triphosphate - the universal energy currency for use in cells for anabolism). It is the first stage of respiration. It involves oxidation reactions that take place in cell organelles called mitochondria.

Sodium-potassium pumps

In the cell surface membranes of most cells are special protein carriers called sodium-potassium pumps. These use energy from the hydrolysis of ATP to actively transport three sodium ions (Na^+) out of the cell, while at the same time actively transporting two potassium ions (K^+) into the cell. These sodium-potassium pumps make sure that the concentration of sodium ions inside cells does not increase, as this would cause water to enter the cells by osmosis. In animal cells, this would cause the cells to swell and burst as they do not have a rigid cell wall. In neurones (nerve cells), the sodium-potassium pumps maintain the resting potential (when neurones are not sending impulses).

Assessment practice 24.1   A.P1 A.P2 A.M1 A.D1

You have been asked to produce display material to help explain to learners studying health care the importance of understanding some basic biochemistry.

1 Produce a large, illustrated and annotated poster to:
   (a) explain the atomic structures of some elements important for living organisms: carbon, hydrogen, oxygen and nitrogen
   (b) show the molecular structure of some inorganic molecules – water and carbon dioxide – important to living organisms
   (c) show the molecular structure of the organic molecules amino acids, proteins, triglycerides, monosaccharides, disaccharides and polysaccharides.

2 Add annotations to your poster to indicate how the inorganic and organic molecules you have shown affect the metabolism of living organisms.

3 Indicate, on a separate poster or leaflet, how the atomic structures of the key elements, C, H, O and N, enable them to react together to make the organic molecules proteins, fats and carbohydrates. You should also show how the presence of an inorganic element, iron, within the protein haemoglobin enables haemoglobin to perform its function.

Plan
- Do I know what I am being asked to do?
- Do I have enough information or should I extend my research?

Do
- Do I know what I want to achieve?
- Can I check my work to see where I have gone off task and can make changes to put this right?

Review
- Can I instruct someone else on how to complete the task more efficiently?
- Do I know what I would do differently next time and the approach I would take with the parts that I found difficult this time?

B Explore the action of biological molecules in metabolic processes

The chemical properties and the shapes (configuration) of biological molecules determine how they will react with other molecules within metabolic pathways.

Configuration of biomolecules

The configuration of biomolecules refers to the 3D shape of the molecules that allows them to carry out their functions and to interact with other molecules. Many important biomolecules are macromolecules, for example triglycerides, or polymers such as polysaccharides, proteins and nucleic acids.

Condensation

Polymers are formed by bonds forming between monomers during condensation reactions. (See the section on the Structure and function of organic molecules.)

Condensation reactions also occur between glycerol and fatty acids to make the macromolecules, triglycerides. Triglycerides are not polymers as they are formed by condensation reactions between two different types of molecules. Three ester bonds are formed.

Condensation reactions produce the peptide bonds linking amino acids in a protein chain.

α- glucose molecules undergo condensation to form α-maltose, where the bond joining the two glucose residues is an α--1,4 glycosidic bond (see the section on Structure and function of organic molecules, sub-section Disaccharides); and then further condensation reactions produce starch. Starch contains α-amylose (a linear polymer of several thousand glucose residues linked by α-1,4 glycosidic bonds) and amylopectin. Amylopectin is also made from many α-glucose residues joined by α-1,4 glycosidic bonds but the polymer is branched with α-1,6 branch points every 24–30 glucose residues.

Hydrolysis

Hydrolysis of organic polymers produces their monomers.

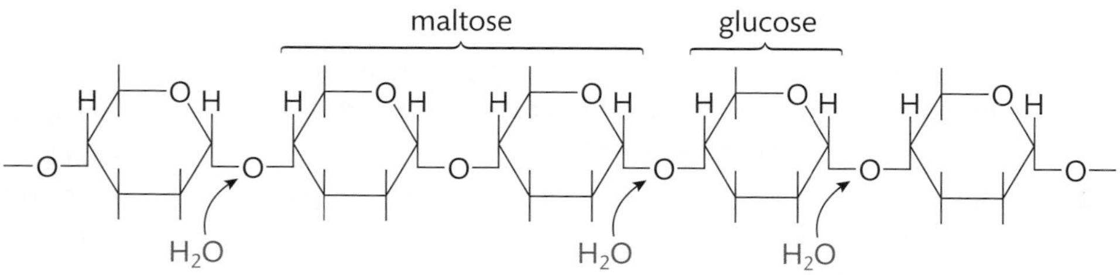

▶ **Figure 24.13:** Hydrolysis of starch to produce α-maltose and α-glucose

Starch is a food reserve in plants and a major nutrient in animals. Glycogen is a food reserve in animals. Starch and glycogen are both hydrolysed to glucose, which is the main respiratory substrate.

Cellulose is a structural polysaccharide, made from repeating units of β-glucose, making up plant cell walls. Humans and other mammals do not make enzymes that digest cellulose, they rely on some of the micro-organisms in their gut to make cellulose enzymes and digest cellulose. Cellulose is, therefore, an important source of dietary fibre for humans.

> **Discussion**
>
> Why do you think the enzyme that digests α-amylase cannot also digest cellulose?

Glucose metabolism and cellular respiration

Respiration is the release of energy from food, usually from glucose, which is the chief respiratory substrate, although fats and amino acids can also be respired. The energy stored in these complex macromolecules comes originally from sunlight, trapped during the process of photosynthesis. Respiration takes place in a series of metabolic pathways, each consisting of several stages, so that the energy is released in small,

Biochemistry for Health

manageable amounts that will not damage cells. This released energy is used to make ATP from **ADP** and **P$_i$** and some is converted to heat which may be lost to the environment or help regulate the organism's temperature. You have probably seen an overall equation representing aerobic respiration.

$$C_6H_{12}O_6 + 6O_2 \rightarrow 6H_2O + 6CO_2 + energy$$

This is an oversimplified view, although it summarises the process.

ATP is a small soluble molecule that can diffuse easily within a cell. When hydrolysed by an enzyme, ATPase, it releases small amounts of energy to drive anabolic reactions. It is known as the universal energy currency as it occurs in all types of cells and because it releases small amounts of energy at a time. Figure 24.14 shows the formation and hydrolysis of ATP.

Key terms

ADP – adenosine diphosphate, an important organic compound in metabolism.

P$_i$ – inorganic phosphate, the appropriate concentration of intracellular inorganic phosphate (P$_i$) is required for cellular metabolism.

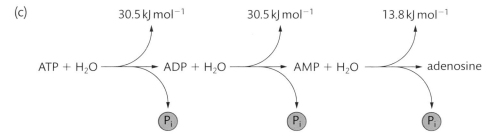

▶ **Figure 24.14:** (a) the structure of ATP (b) formation and hydrolysis of ATP (c) the chemical energy released form the hydrolysis of ATP

Biological processes requiring energy from the hydrolysis of ATP include:

▶ active transport
▶ endocytosis – the transport of large substances into a cell
▶ exocytosis – the transport of large substances out of a cell
▶ synthesis of polymers and macromolecules
▶ DNA replication
▶ protein synthesis
▶ cell division
▶ movement.

Activation of chemicals, such as the phosphorylation (addition of phosphate) of glucose at the beginning of respiration so that it becomes more reactive, also requires ATP.

The enzymes involved in the oxidation and reduction reactions of glucose metabolism need the help of coenzymes, such as NAD and FAD. NAD, nicotinamide adenine dinucleotide, is a non-protein molecule, derived from vitamin B_3 and ribose sugar. It helps dehydrogenase enzymes carry out oxidation reactions:

▶ NAD oxidises substrate molecules by accepting two hydrogen atoms from them, and becomes reduced NAD

▶ NAD oxidises substrate molecules during glycolysis, the link reaction and the Krebs cycle, and delivers hydrogen atoms (protons and electrons) to the inner membranes of mitochondria to be used in oxidative phosphorylation for the generation of ATP from ADP and P_i

▶ when reduced NAD gives up its hydrogen atoms it becomes reoxidised and can continue to oxidise more substrate molecules.

Figure 24.15 summarises the stages of respiration, both aerobic and anaerobic.

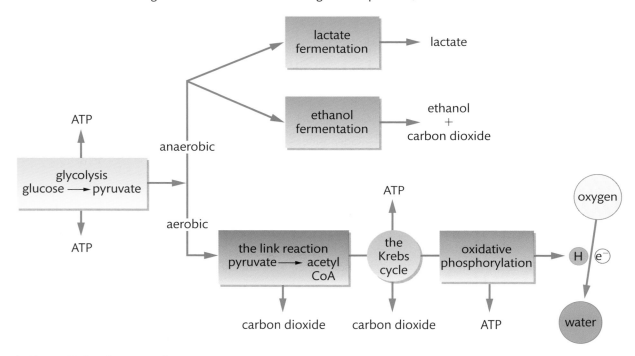

▶ **Figure 24.15:** The stages of respiration

Glycolysis

Glycolysis is the first stage of respiration – common to both aerobic and anaerobic respiration. It occurs in the cytoplasm of living cells. It is an ancient metabolic pathway occurring in many bacteria as well as all eukaryotic cells.

▶ There are ten reactions in this pathway; each catalysed by a different enzyme that changes each molecule of glucose (6C) to two molecules of a 3-carbon compound, pyruvate.

▶ In the process, two molecules of ATP are used and four generated; giving a net production of two molecules of ATP per molecule of glucose.

▶ Most reactions in this pathway can be reversed to produce glucose-6-phosphate, which can then be synthesised into glycogen or starch.

Four atoms of hydrogen (protons and electrons) are removed per molecule of glucose. This dehydrogenation is catalysed by dehydrogenase enzymes, aided by two molecules of NAD, each of which accepts two hydrogen atoms, becoming reduced NAD (NADH$_2$).

Although glycolysis is anaerobic and occurs without oxygen, it involves **oxidation** of the substrate by removing hydrogen atoms. It also involves making ATP by substrate level phosphorylation.

Glycolysis produces two molecules of ATP, two molecules of pyruvate and two **reduced** NAD per molecule of glucose. Pyruvate is now actively transported into the mitochondria of eukaryotic cells for aerobic respiration. Three stages occur in mitochondria:

▸ the link reaction and the Krebs cycle both happen in the mitochondrial matrix

▸ oxidative phosphorylation, involving the electron transport chain occurs on the folded inner mitochondrial membrane, the cristae, and also involves the intermembrane space.

Figure 24.16 shows the structure of a mitochondrion.

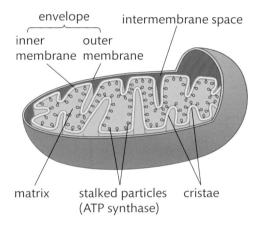

▸ **Figure 24.16:** Structure of a mitochondrion

The link reaction

The link reaction occurs in the mitochondrial matrix. A large enzyme, pyruvate dehydrogenase, catalyses both the **dehydrogenation** and **decarboxylation** of pyruvate. There is no ATP produced during the link reaction. Two molecules of NAD become reduced as two molecules of pyruvate are oxidised by dehydrogenation. The two carboxyl groups produced, one from each pyruvate during decarboxylation, are the origin of some of the carbon dioxide produced during respiration.

The three-carbon pyruvate molecules are changed to two-carbon acetate molecules. These molecules each combine with a coenzyme A (CoA) molecule to become acetyl coenzyme A (acetyl CoA) which carries the acetate on to the Krebs cycle.

> **Key terms**
>
> **Dehydrogenation** – removal of hydrogen atoms from substrate molecules.
> **Decarboxylation** – removal of a carboxyl (COO$^-$) group from substrate molecules.

This equation summarises the link reaction:

2 pyruvate + 2NAD + 2CoA → 2CO$_2$ + 2 reduced NAD + 2 Acetyl CoA

> **Key terms**
>
> **Oxidation** – removal of hydrogen atoms or removal of electrons from substrate molecules.
>
> **Reduction** – addition of hydrogen atoms or addition of electrons to substrate molecules.

The Krebs cycle

The Krebs cycle also takes place within the mitochondrial matrix.

▶ The Krebs cycle (Figure 24.17) is a series of enzyme-catalysed reactions that oxidise each acetate molecule to two molecules of carbon dioxide, by decarboxylation. Dehydrogenase enzymes also remove hydrogen atoms from substrate molecules and reduce NAD and another coenzyme FAD (flavine adenine dinucleotide – derived from vitamin B2).

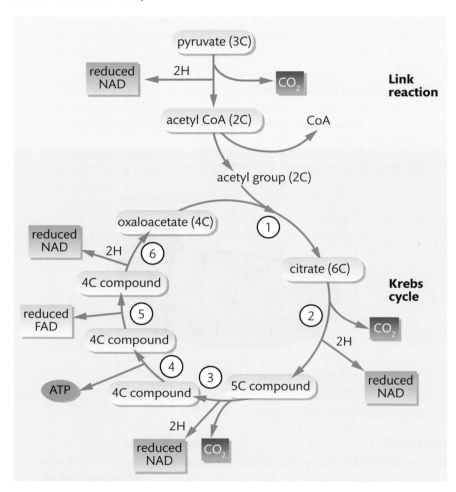

▶ **Figure 24.17:** Krebs cycle

▶ Acetate released from acetyl CoA combines with a four-carbon compound, oxaloacetate, to form a six-carbon **compound**, citrate.

▶ Each molecule of citrate is decarboxylated to produce one molecule of carbon dioxide and a five-carbon compound.

▶ This five-carbon compound is further decarboxylated and dehydrogenated, producing a four-carbon compound, one molecule of carbon dioxide and one molecule of reduced NAD. One molecule of ATP is produced.

▶ The four-carbon compound is dehydrogenated, producing a different four-carbon compound and a molecule of reduced FAD.

▶ Rearrangement of the atoms in the four-carbon molecule, catalysed by an isomerase enzyme, followed by further dehydrogenation, regenerates a molecule of oxaloacetate, so the cycle can continue.

For every molecule of glucose there are two turns of the Krebs cycle.

Table 24.2 shows the products of the link reaction and the Krebs cycle.

▶ **Table 24.2:** The products of the link reaction and the Krebs cycle

Product per molecule of glucose	The link reaction	The Krebs cycle
Molecules of reduced NAD	2	6
Molecules of reduced FAD	0	2
Molecules of carbon dioxide	2	4
Molecules of ATP	0	2

The reduced NAD and FAD coenzymes carry hydrogen atoms to the electron transport chain on the inner mitochondrial membrane for oxidative phosphorylation.

Although oxygen is not directly used in either the link reaction or the Krebs cycle, neither would run in the absence of oxygen as the reduced coenzymes could not be reoxidised at the electron transport chain, so both of these processes are aerobic.

Other substrates besides glucose can be respired aerobically:

▶ fatty acids are broken down to many molecules of acetate that enter the Krebs cycle via acetyl CoA

▶ glycerol may be converted to pyruvate and enter the Krebs cycle via the link reaction

▶ amino acids may be deaminated (the amino group (NH_2) is removed) and the rest of the molecule can enter the Krebs cycle directly, or be changed to pyruvate or acetate.

Discussion

In your body at any one time you have about 5 g ATP. However, throughout a 24-hour period, you make and break down about 25–50 kg of ATP. How do you think this happens?

 **PAUSE POINT**   In your cells, you have very small amounts of oxaloacetate but every day you use a great deal of it. Suggest why there are only small amounts of oxaloacetate in your cells. Where, in your cells, is oxaloacetate found?

Hint   Think of how ATP is made and then broken down. Look at Figure 24.18, think about how oxaloacetate is regenerated.

Extend   Explain why each step of the Krebs cycle has to be catalysed by a different enzyme.

Case study

Sudden infant death

Both Elizabeth's baby sons died from SIDS – sudden infant death syndrome, sometimes called cot death. Scientists have found that SIDS may be caused by a deficiency of an enzyme, acyl coenzyme A dehydrogenase that catalyses the breakdown of medium length fatty acids into acetyl CoA for entering the Krebs cycle for respiration. If the baby's blood sugar has dropped, possibly after vomiting or a period of fasting, fats cannot be respired and the low blood sugar may cause sudden death. Newborn babies are now screened for the presence or absence of this enzyme. The lack of a functioning enzyme is a genetic condition.

Check your knowledge

1   If a family has experienced one child dying from SIDS, is it more or less likely that if they have other children these children may also die from SIDS? Explain your answer.

Oxidative phosphorylation

This is the final stage of aerobic respiration.

▶ It involves the generation of ATP in the presence of oxygen.

▶ It occurs on the mitochondrial inner membranes, the cristae, which give a large surface area for the electron transport and ATP synthase proteins embedded in it, both of which are involved in the synthesis of ATP.

▶ It involves direct use of oxygen and produces water.

Figure 24.18 summarises oxidative phosphorylation.

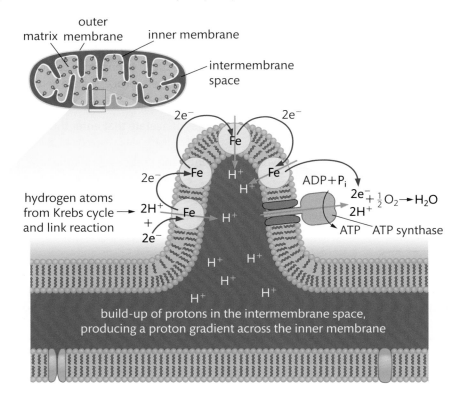

▶ **Figure 24.18:** Oxidative phosphorylation

1 Reduced NAD and reduced FAD bring hydrogen atoms to the cristae.
2 The hydrogen atoms dissociate into protons and electrons.
3 The electrons are accepted by special electron transport proteins in the cristae. Each protein contains an iron ion inside it which can accept an electron to become reduced and then lose the electron becoming reoxidised.
4 The electrons are passed along a chain of the electron carrier proteins – the electron transport chain (ETC).
5 As electrons pass along the chain they lose some of their energy and this energy is used to pump the protons into the intermembrane space between the inner and outer mitochondrial membranes. This is not the same as active transport and does not use ATP.
6 As protons accumulate in the intermembrane space, a proton gradient (which is also an electrochemical gradient) forms across the cristae (inner membrane).
7 Protons flow down their electrochemical gradient, through special channels associated with ATP synthase enzymes, through the inner membrane and into the matrix.
8 The electrons coming off the ETC combine with oxygen (the final electron acceptor) to form oxygen ions (O^{2-}) that then combine with protons to form water.

How much ATP is made, per molecule of glucose, during oxidative phosphorylation?

Table 24.3 shows the number of reduced coenzymes formed during respiration.

▶ **Table 24.3:** The number of reduced coenzymes formed during respiration

The number of molecules made from one molecule of glucose			
Name of molecule produced	Stage of respiration		
	Glycolysis	The link reaction	The Krebs cycle
Reduced NAD	2	2	6
Reduced FAD	0	0	2

The protons and electrons from the 10 molecules of reduced NAD can theoretically produce 25 molecules of ATP.

The protons and electrons from the two molecules of reduced FAD can theoretically produce three molecules of ATP.

So during oxidative phosphorylation 28 molecules of ATP may be produced per molecule of glucose.

What is the total number of ATP molecules made per molecule of glucose during respiration?

In addition to the 28 molecules of ATP made during oxidative phosphorylation, four are made, but two used, during glycolysis and two are made during the Krebs cycle. Therefore, in total, a maximum of 32 molecules of ATP are made per molecule of glucose, during aerobic respiration. If glucose is respired anaerobically, only four molecules of ATP are made but two are used, during glycolysis, giving a total of two molecules of ATP per molecule of glucose. Because the anaerobic respiration happens very swiftly, many molecules of ATP can be made, but the glucose is only partially oxidised.

❚❚ PAUSE POINT Explain why the pH in the intermembrane space in a mitochondrion is lower than the pH of the mitochondrial matrix.

Hint Think about what accumulates in the intermembrane space.

Extend Suggest how the oxygen used as the final electron acceptor at the end of the ETC reached the mitochondria.
Cyanide inhibits an enzyme at the end of the ETC. Suggest why cyanide is a deadly poison.

Anaerobic respiration

In the absence of oxygen, in human cells the reduced NAD produced during glycolysis is reoxidised via the lactic acid pathway. The pyruvate (pyruvic acid) accepts hydrogen atoms from the reduced NAD, forming lactic acid and reoxidised NAD.

 $NADH_2 + CH_3COCOOH \rightarrow NAD + CH_3CHOHCOOH$

 pyruvic acid   lactic acid

This reaction does not make any ATP but it allows the NAD to be reoxidised, so glycolyis can continue to run. When you are exercising and in oxygen deficit, your muscles respire anaerobically but you cannot sustain this for very long as lactic acid build-up causes muscle fatigue. The lactic acid is carried away from the muscles in the bloodstream to the liver, where it can be recycled to glucose and then to glycogen.

Fats and amino acids *cannot* be respired anaerobically as they do not undergo glycolysis. They enter the Krebs cycle directly. This is why aerobic exercise, like swimming, cycling and walking or running, is better for weight loss than anaerobic exercise, such as weight-lifting. However, the liver can convert amino acids and glycerol to glucose; this is called gluconeogenesis. Stored glycogen in the liver can be hydrolysed to glucose; this is glycogenolysis. These ways of making glucose are important, as the blood glucose level has to be maintained within narrow limits to supply cells with glucose for respiration to release energy. This is especially important to brain tissue, which can use *only* glucose for respiration. Other types of cells can respire amino acids or fatty acids, if necessary.

Plants and yeast can also respire anaerobically as well as aerobically. They use a different metabolic pathway for anaerobic respiration. The pyruvate is decarboxylated to produce carbon dioxide and then accepts hydrogen atoms from reduced NAD to make ethanol.

$$NADH_2 + CH_3COCOOH \rightarrow NAD + CO_2 + CH_3CHOH$$
$$\text{pyruvic acid} \qquad\qquad\qquad \text{ethanol}$$

Investigation

Food analysis

You can carry out investigations to find out if foods contain carbohydrate (sugars and starch), fat and protein. Table 24.4 shows some food analysis tests.

▶ **Table 24.4:** Some food analysis tests

Macronutrient	Test	Positive result
Starch	Add iodine in KI (potassium iodide) solution.	Colour changes from brown to blue/black.
Protein	Add biuret reagent (dilute sodium hydroxide and dilute copper sulfate).	Colour changes from blue to mauve/purple.
Lipids	Shake food with ethanol. Allow to settle and pour ethanol into a test tube containing distilled water.	A white milky emulsion is seen near the top of the water.
Reducing sugars	Add Benedict's reagent and heat.	Colour changes from blue to green/yellow/brick red.
Non-reducing sugars	If testing for reducing sugar is negative, hydrolyse any sucrose in the food by heating with dilute hydrochloric acid. Cool and add sodium hydrogen carbonate to neutralise. Now add Benedict's reagent and heat.	First Benedict's test: no colour change. After heating with acid and carrying out second Benedict's test there is a colour change from blue to red.

> **Safety tip**
>
> Take care when heating Benedict's reagent, and use a thermostatically controlled water bath set at 80 °C. If you heat Benedict's reagent in a test tube it may overheat, spurt out and burn you.

Energy conversion

A piece of apparatus called a calorimeter measures the heat energy given off when food is burned. The heat from the burning food is transferred to water and the temperature rise of the water is measured. You know that the specific heat capacity of water is 4.2 kJ per kg, which means that it takes 4.2 kJ energy to heat 1 kg water by 1 °C. If 1 g of pure carbohydrate (such as flour or sugar) is burned and the heat from it used to heat a known mass of water, M kg, then the formula below can be used to calculate the energy in the gram of carbohydrate.

Energy in 1 g carbohydrate = $(4.2 \times M \times \text{temperature rise})$ kJ

If the investigation is repeated using 1 g of fat instead of carbohydrate, the temperature rise of the same mass of water is just over twice that produced with 1 g of carbohydrate.

Fat molecules contain more energy than carbohydrate molecules as there are more C–H bonds to be broken, releasing energy. Table 24.5 shows the energy values of fat, carbohydrate and protein.

▶ **Table 24.5:** Energy values of fat, carbohydrate and protein

Type of food	Energy value (kJ g^{-1})
Fat	37
Carbohydrate	17
Protein	17

Characteristics of biomolecules

Many of the biomolecules in your body are made in your body cells. Proteins are encoded directly by lengths of DNA called genes. Genes also govern the synthesis of non-protein molecules as genes encode enzymes and enzymes catalyse the anabolic reactions in the metabolic pathways to synthesise these non-protein molecules.

Enzymes

Enzymes:

▶ are globular proteins that are soluble in water

▶ are biological catalysts that speed up metabolic reactions but are unchanged at the end of the reaction

▶ are specific – each type only catalyses a specific reaction

▶ have a cleft in their molecule, called the active site; the specific 3D shape of the active site is crucial to the enzyme's specificity, as only the substrate molecule should fit into the enzyme's active site as their shapes are complementary to each other, just as a key only fits a specific lock – Figure 24.19 shows the lock and key hypothesis and the induced fit hypothesis of enzyme action

▶ reduce the activation energy needed to start a metabolic reaction, which means that metabolic reactions can proceed at the relatively cool temperatures found inside living cells.

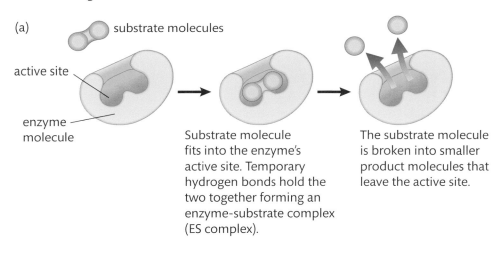

(a) substrate molecules

active site

enzyme molecule

Substrate molecule fits into the enzyme's active site. Temporary hydrogen bonds hold the two together forming an enzyme-substrate complex (ES complex).

The substrate molecule is broken into smaller product molecules that leave the active site.

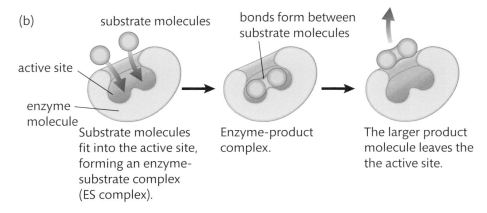

(b) substrate molecules

bonds form between substrate molecules

active site

enzyme molecule

Substrate molecules fit into the active site, forming an enzyme-substrate complex (ES complex).

Enzyme-product complex.

The larger product molecule leaves the the active site.

▶ **Figure 24.19:** (a) The lock and key and (b) induced fit hypotheses of enzyme action

The activity of enzymes, and hence their rates of reaction are affected by temperature, pH, cofactors (see section on Cofactors) such as activators and coenzymes, inhibitors and concentrations of enzymes or substrate molecules.

You have probably learned about many of the enzymes involved in digesting food and Table 24.6 shows the functions of some of the digestive enzymes.

▶ **Table 24.6:** The functions of some digestive enzymes

Enzyme	Location in body	Substrate	Products	Notes
Salivary amylase	Made in the salivary glands, acts in the mouth	Cooked starch	Maltose	Carbohydrase that works best at pH6.8, and will only work if chloride ions are present as cofactors. Calcium ions may also affect the rate of reaction of α-amylase by acting as cofactors.
Pepsin	Made in chief cells in the stomach; acts in the stomach	Proteins	Peptides	Proteolytic enzyme; works best in low pH, 1–2, so needs hydrochloric acid (HCl), which is also made in the stomach. Released as inactive form, pepsinogen, activated by HCl to active pepsin.
Lipase	Made in the pancreas, acts in the small intestine	Fats, e.g. triglycerides	Monoglycerides and two fatty acids	Needs optimum pH around 7.8 to work.

Nucleic acids (genes) are also digested as many foods contain cells and, therefore, their nuclei and nucleic acids. Nucleases hydrolyse nucleic acids to nucleotides, and nucleotidases hydrolyse nucleotides to their constituents: sugars, phosphates and organic bases.

There are many metabolic reactions occurring in cells and many of these are involved in synthesising large molecules from smaller ones. Each step of the many metabolic pathways occurring in cells is catalysed by a different enzyme. You have already learned about the pathways in respiration and seen how many enzymes are involved, including ATP synthase.

Denaturation

As enzymes are proteins they have a tertiary structure, held together by hydrogen bonds, ionic bonds, disulfide bonds and other molecular forces and interactions. High temperatures and extreme changes in pH can break those bonds and disrupt the shape of the enzyme molecule. If the active site shape changes, so it is no longer complementary to that of the substrate molecules, then the reaction slows and eventually stops. The enzyme is denatured. This change is irreversible and the enzyme can no longer function.

Cofactors

Some enzymes, particularly those involved in catalysing oxidation-reduction reactions, such as those involved in respiration, can only work if another small non-protein molecule is attached to them. These small molecules are called **cofactors**.

▶ Some cofactors, called prosthetic groups, are part of the enzyme structure.
▶ Others, for example mineral ion cofactors and organic coenzymes, form temporary associations with the enzyme.

The enzyme carbonic anhydrase, in red blood cells, which catalyses the interconversion of water and carbon dioxide to carbonic acid, has a zinc-based prosthetic group permanently attached to its active site.

$$CO_2 + H_2O \longleftrightarrow H_2CO_3 \longleftrightarrow H^+ + HCO_3^-$$

Carbonic anhydrase

The enzyme catalase, which quickly breaks down toxic hydrogen peroxide produced during respiration, contains iron.

Coenzymes

Coenzymes are small, organic, non-protein molecules that bind temporarily to the active site of enzyme molecules, either just before or at the same time that the substrate binds. The coenzymes are chemically changed during the reaction and need to be recycled to their original state, sometimes by a different enzyme.

Many coenzymes are derived from water-soluble vitamins. Dietary deficiency of these vitamins can result in disorders and diseases, as shown in Table 24.7.

▶ **Table 24.7:** Examples of coenzymes, the vitamins they are derived from, and deficiency diseases resulting from dietary lack

Vitamin	Coenzyme derived from it	Deficiency disease
B12	Cobalamin coenzymes	Pernicious anaemia (a progressive anaemia, which can be fatal if untreated)
Folic acid	Tetrahydrafolate	Megaloblastic anaemia (large, irregularly shaped erythrocytes)
Nicotinamide, B3	NAD	Pellagra (diarrhoea, dermatitis and dementia)
Pantothenate, B6	Coenzyme A	Elevated blood plasma triglyceride levels
Thiamine, B1	Thiamine pyrophosphate	Beriberi (mental confusion, irregular heartbeat, muscular weakness, paralysis and heart failure)

Case study

Vitamin B12 deficiency

Mary is 95 years old and generally in good health. She gets tired and is sometimes a little confused. Her GP sent a blood sample to be tested for vitamin B12 levels. As these were low, he decided to give Mary an injection of vitamin B12 every twelve weeks, as recent medical research has shown that dementia-like symptoms and tiredness can result from lack of vitamin B12. Elderly people cannot absorb as much of this vitamin from their food as younger people do. Mary says she feels much better after having her vitamin B12 injection.

Check your knowledge

1 Which coenzyme is derived from vitamin B12?

2 Why do you think it would be cost effective for the NHS to give all elderly people who are becoming confused and forgetful a vitamin B12 injection at 12-week intervals?

Inhibitors

Inhibitors are substances that reduce the activity of an enzyme. They do this by combining with the enzyme molecule, which in turn influences the way in which the substrate binds to the enzyme:

▶ some may block the active site and some change the shape of the active site

▶ both of these will inhibit the formation of enzyme-substrate (ES) complexes and, therefore, product formation.

Competitive inhibitors

Competitive inhibitors are substances whose molecules have a similar shape to the enzyme's substrate molecules.

▶ They compete directly with substrate molecules for a position on the enzyme's active site, forming an enzyme-inhibitor complex that is catalytically inactive.

▶ However, once on the active site, the inhibitor is not changed by the enzyme, as the normal substrate molecule would be.

- The presence of the inhibitor on the enzyme's active site prevents the substrate molecule from joining the active site. This reduces the rate of formation of ES complexes and of product molecule formation.
- Most enzyme inhibition by competitive inhibitors is reversible. As collisions between enzyme, substrate or inhibitor molecules is random, increasing the concentration of substrate would reduce the effect of reversible competitive inhibition, as there is more chance of an enzyme molecule colliding with a substrate molecule than with an inhibitor molecule.

If the competitive inhibitor binds irreversibly to the enzyme's active site it is called an inactivator.

Figure 24.20 shows how a competitive inhibitor works.

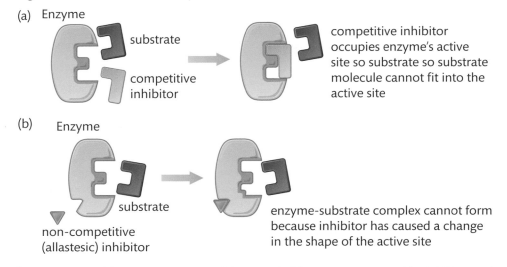

(a) Enzyme

substrate

competitive inhibitor

competitive inhibitor occupies enzyme's active site so substrate so substrate molecule cannot fit into the active site

(b) Enzyme

substrate

non-competitive (allastesic) inhibitor

enzyme-substrate complex cannot form because inhibitor has caused a change in the shape of the active site

▶ **Figure 24.20:** (a) How a competitive inhibitor works (b) How a non-competitive inhibitor works

Non-competitive inhibition

If free enzyme molecules can bind to inhibitor molecules, then this type of inhibition is called non-competitive inhibition.

- Non-competitive inhibitors do not compete with substrate molecules for a place on the enzyme's active site. They attach to the enzyme molecule in a region (an allosteric site) away from the active site and disrupt the enzyme's tertiary structure, changing its shape.
- This distortion changes the shape of the active site so that it is no longer complementary to the shape of the substrate molecule and the substrate molecule can no longer bind to the enzyme's active site. ES complexes cannot form.
- The more inhibitor molecules are present, the greater the degree of inhibition, because more enzyme molecules are distorted and either cannot form ES complexes or cannot complete the catalytic reaction involving ES complexes.
- Adding more substrate molecules usually has no effect as most allosteric inhibitors bind irreversibly to the enzyme, permanently distorting its 3D shape.

End-product inhibition

One way in which enzyme-catalysed reactions may be regulated is by end-product inhibition.

- After the catalysed reaction has reached completion, product molecules may stay tightly bound to the enzyme and keep it in an inactive form. For example, the active site may not be exposed.

In this way the enzyme cannot form more of the product than the cell needs. Such regulation is an example of negative feedback.

⏸ PAUSE POINT   Clearly explain the difference between competitive and non-competitive enzyme inhibitors.

   Hint   Think about whether they are competing with the substrate for the enzyme's active site.

   Extend   Explain the importance of end product inhibition in metabolic pathways.

Investigation

Enzyme properties

You can investigate the specificity of enzymes and the factors that affect the rate of enzyme-catalysed reactions.

Research

Visit **www.saps.org.uk** and search for phosphatase enzymes. You can carry out practical investigations on the effects of temperature, pH, and inhibition using phosphatase enzymes extracted from mung beans.

Phosphatase enzymes remove phosphate groups from a range of organic phosphates, making a pool of phosphates available for metabolic reactions, such as forming ATP and nucleic acids. The substrate used is phenolphthalein phosphate (PPP), which is broken down by the enzyme to free phenolphthalein, which becomes pink in alkaline solution, as sodium carbonate is added to it. The darker the pink colour the greater the enzyme activity so the rate (amount of susbstrate converted per unit time) can be quantified using colorimetry. You can also plan and carry out investigation into the effect of enzyme and substrate concentration using this enzyme.

Nucleic acids

Nucleic acids occur in all living organisms on Earth – in prokaryotic and eukaryotic cells, as well as in viruses. Both DNA (deoxyribose nucleic acid) and RNA (ribose nucleic acid) are polymers. In this case the monomers are nucleotides. Nucleic acids are polynucleotides.

Structure of nucleic acids

Nucleotides are joined together by condensation reactions.

Figure 24.21 shows three nucleotides joined together.

▶ There are five different nucleotide bases:

▶ adenine (A) and guanine (G), which have a double ring structure; these are purines

▶ cytosine (C), thymine (T) and uracil (U), which have a single ring structure; these are pyrimidines.

▶ DNA contains the bases A, T, G and C, RNA contains the bases A, U (instead of T), G and C.

Figure 24.22 shows the molecular structures of the nucleotide bases.

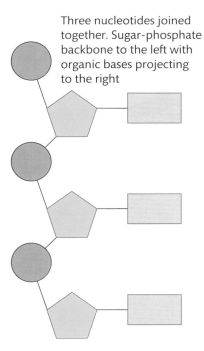

Three nucleotides joined together. Sugar-phosphate backbone to the left with organic bases projecting to the right

▶ **Figure 24.21:** Three nucleotides joined together, the sugars (orange) and phosphate groups (red) form the backbone and the organic nitrogenous bases are shown in green

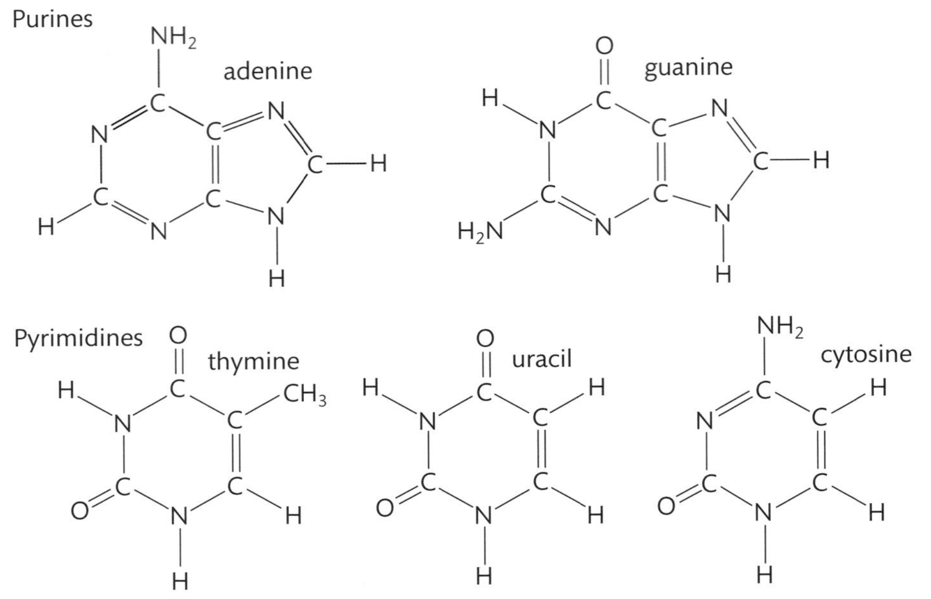

Purines

adenine

guanine

Pyrimidines thymine   uracil   cytosine

▶ **Figure 24.22:** Purine and pyrimidine nucleotide bases

Structure of DNA

DNA is a double helix. Each DNA molecule consists of:

▶ two backbone chains of deoxyribose sugars and phosphate groups; described as antiparallel as they each run in opposite directions

▶ pairs of nitrogenous bases joining the backbones together:

  ▶ the base pairs join to each other by hydrogen bonds (H bonds)

  ▶ a purine base always joins with a pyrimidine base, so the 'rungs of the ladder' are always the same size. Adenine joins by two H bonds with cytosine; thiamine joins by three H bonds with cytosine. This type of specific base pairing is called complementary base pairing.

The hydrogen bonds make each molecule of DNA very strong and stable, while enabling it to unzip in order to copy itself before cell division; or for part of it (a gene) to unzip before transcription prior to assembly of a new protein.

The sequence of base pairs form coded information, which is protected from corruption by the base pairs being inside the backbones.

The genetic code

On each chromosome there are specific lengths of DNA, called genes. Genes carry the code for making proteins, many of which form the structure of an organism, or cellular tools such as enzymes and antibodies, and some of which are **transcription factors** that activate or suppress the expression of other genes.

Triplet codes

The sequence of amino acids in the protein is determined by the sequence of base triplets on the coding strand of the DNA molecule. Hence the genetic code is a triplet code. It is near universal because in almost all living organisms the same DNA base triplet codes for the same amino acid.

The genetic code is also **degenerate**, which means that for all amino acids except methionine and tryptophan, there is more than one base triplet. This may reduce the effect of point mutations, as a change of one base triplet could produce another base triplet that still codes for the same amino acid.

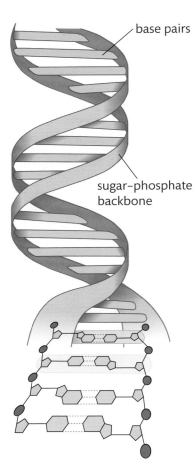

base pairs

sugar–phosphate backbone

▶ **Figure 24.23:** The DNA double helix

The genetic code is also non-overlapping. It is read from a fixed point in groups of three bases (triplets) that do not overlap. Figure 24.24 shows the standard DNA triplet code.

> **Key terms**
>
> **Transcription factor** – protein that binds to a specific DNA sequence and which controls the rate of transcription of genetic information from DNA to mRNA.
>
> **Degenerate** – code in which many code words have the same meaning: describes the genetic code because, in many instances different base triplets/codons specify the same amino acid; some amino acids are, therefore, coded for by more than one base triplet/codon.

First position	Second position				Third position
	T	C	A	G	
T	Phe	Ser	Tyr	Cys	T
	Phe	Ser	Tyr	Cys	C
	Leu	Ser	STOP	STOP	A
	Leu	Ser	STOP	Trp	G
C	Leu	Pro	His	Arg	T
	Leu	Pro	His	Arg	C
	Leu	Pro	Gln	Arg	A
	Leu	Pro	Gln	Arg	G
A	Ile	Thr	Asn	Ser	T
	Ile	Thr	Asn	Ser	C
	Ile	Thr	Lys	Arg	A
	Met	Thr	Lys	Arg	G
G	Val	Ala	Asp	Gly	T
	Val	Ala	Asp	Gly	C
	Val	Ala	Glu	Gly	A
	Val	Ala	Glu	Gly	G

Key:

Asp	Aspartic acid	Lys	Lysine	Cys	Cysteine
Glu	Glutamic acid	Gly	Glycine	Phe	Phenylalanine
His	Histidine	Asn	Asparagine	Leu	Leucine
Ile	Isoleucine	Gln	Glutamine	Met	Methionine
Arg	Arginine	Trp	Tryptophan	Pro	Proline
Thr	Threonine	Tyr	Tyrosine	Val	Valine
Ser	Serine	Ala	Alanine		

▶ **Figure 24.24:** The standard DNA triplet code

DNA replication

Before a cell divides, each DNA molecule replicates.

1 The double helix of the entire DNA molecule unwinds, a bit at a time, and the hydrogen bonds between complementary base pairs break. This is catalysed by the enzyme helicase.

2 The nucleotide bases are exposed.

3 Free DNA nucleotides within the nucleus, bond onto the exposed nucleotide bases, by forming hydrogen bonds following complementary base-pairing rules, A with T and C with G. This is catalysed by the enzyme DNA polymerase.

4 Covalent bonds form between the sugar of one nucleotide and the phosphate group of the adjacent nucleotide, forming the new backbones. This is catalysed by the enzyme ligase.

5 Figure 24.25 summarises how DNA replicates.

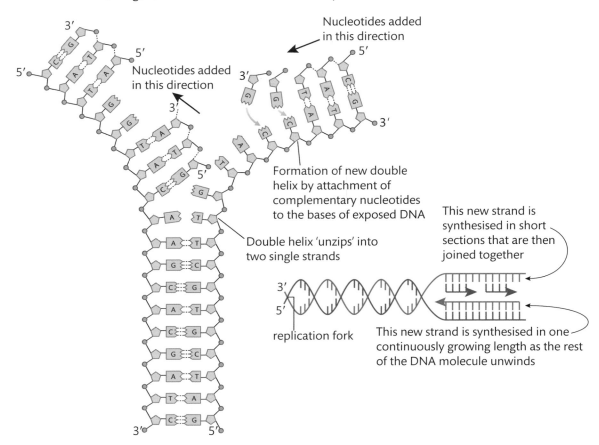

▶ **Figure 24.25:** DNA replication

At the end of replication, two new molecules of DNA, both identical to each other and to the parent molecule, are made. Each new molecule contains one old strand and one new strand, so this type of replication is described as semi-conservative.

RNA is structurally different from DNA

As you have learned, DNA and RNA are structurally different. Table 24.8 compares RNA with DNA.

▶ **Table 24.8:** Comparison of DNA and RNA

Nucleic acid	Sugar	Nitrogenous bases	Number of polynucleotide strands	Location in prokaryotic cells	Location in eukaryotic cells
DNA	deoxyribose	A, T, G and C	Usually two	Free in cytoplasm as nucleoid and plasmids	Nucleus, chloroplasts and mitochondria
RNA	ribose	A, U, G and C	Usually one	Ribosomes	Nucleus and ribosomes

Types of RNA

▶ Messenger RNA (mRNA) carries the genetic code of a gene from the nucleus into the cytoplasm to ribosomes, where the information is translated and proteins are assembled from amino acids.

▶ ncRNAs, which are non-coding RNA molecules. They do not convey information for protein synthesis but some are involved in regulating other genes. Others are involved in protein synthesis:

  ▶ transfer RNAs (tRNA), each carry a specific amino acid to the ribosomes for assembly into proteins

  ▶ ribosomal RNA (rRNA), each ribosome is made of RNA and protein. They are nucleoproteins. The rRNA is the catalyst in ribosomes, enabling protein assembly.

Protein synthesis

Protein synthesis is the assembly of amino acids into proteins, which takes place in two main stages: transcription and translation.

Transcription

Transcription is the process where the instructions on the coding strand of the length of DNA are copied onto a messenger molecule – a length of mRNA. Transcription occurs in the cell nucleus.

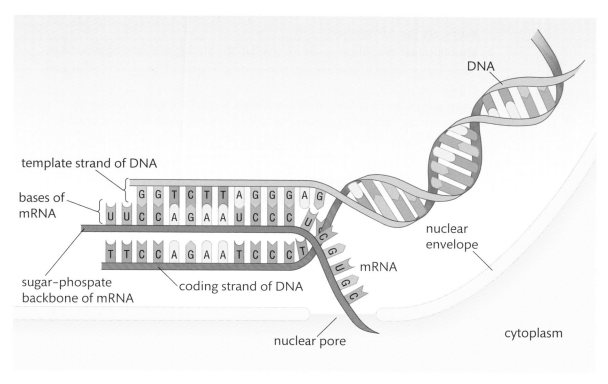

▶ **Figure 24.26:** Transcription of a gene

1 The part of the chromosome with the relevant gene dips into the nucleolus, which is a dense area of the nucleus containing lots of RNA nucleotides. The gene (length of DNA) unwinds and unzips as the hydrogen bonds between the nitrogenous bases break.

2 The DNA bases on the nucleotides are exposed.

3 Free RNA nucleotides line up along the template strand of the DNA and make temporary hydrogen bonds with their complementary bases. Adenine, from an RNA nucleotide base, pairs with thymine on the DNA template strand. Uracil on a strand of RNA pairs with the base adenine on the DNA template strand. Cytosine pairs with guanine and guanine with cytosine. The enzyme RNA polymerase catalyses these reactions.

4 Sugars and phosphate groups of adjacent RNA nucleotides bond together.

5 This forms a single polynucleotide chain that is *complementary* to the DNA *template* strand of the gene. It is, therefore, a copy of the coding strand of the gene.

6 Each codon (triplet of nucleotide bases) on the mRNA codes for a specific amino acid.

7 The pre mRNA can now break away from the gene, which winds up again.

Before this can act as mRNA during the next stage of protein synthesis (translation) it has to be edited, by splicing out the introns.

Introns, exons and splicing

Within a length of DNA that forms a gene, there is a specific sequence of base triplets that determines the sequence of amino acids in the protein encoded by that gene. However, within a gene there are non-coding regions of DNA called introns. These are not expressed. They separate the coding or expressed regions of the gene, which are called exons.

1 The entire DNA of a gene, both introns and exons, is transcribed and the resulting mRNA is called premature or pre mRNA.

2 This pre mRNA is then edited and the RNA introns, lengths corresponding to the DNA introns, are removed; the remaining mRNA exons, corresponding to the DNA exons, are joined together.

3 Endonuclease enzymes may be involved in the editing and splicing processes.

4 Some introns may become short, non-coding lengths of RNA involved in gene regulation.

5 Some genes can be spliced in different ways, so that a length of DNA with its introns and exons can, according to how it is spliced, encode more than one protein.

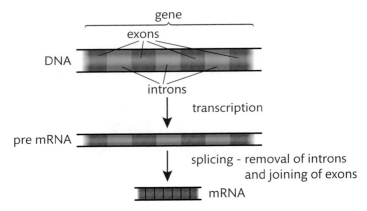

▶ **Figure 24.27:** Removal of introns and joining of exons during splicing of pre mRNA to produce mRNA that will be translated into a protein

Translation

Transfer amino acid molecules

Transfer RNA molecules (tRNAs) are made in the nucleolus and then pass out of the nucleus into the cytoplasm. Each is a single stranded polynucleotide but can twist into hairpin shapes. At one end is a trio of nucleotide bases, which recognises and attaches to a specific activated amino acid. At the loop of the hairpin is another triplet of bases called an anticodon, which is complementary to a specific codon on the mRNA, see Figure 24.28 (a).

Translation at the ribosome

Ribosomes catalyse the synthesis of polypeptides (proteins). Ribosomes are made of two subunits (a larger and a smaller one) that are made within the nucleus and pass out into the cytoplasm where they join together.

(a)

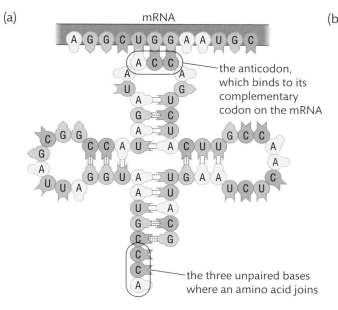

(b)

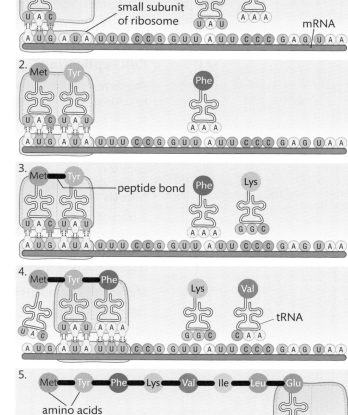

▶ **Figure 24.28:** (a) A tRNA molecule
(b) translation at a ribosome

1 The length of mRNA binds to a ribosome, so that two of its codons are attached to the small ribosomal subunit.

2 The first exposed codon is always AUG. A tRNA with the corresponding anticodon, UAC, and holding the amino acid methionine, forms hydrogen bonds with this codon. Energy from ATP and a catalyst (ribosomal RNA) allow this reaction to happen.

3 A second tRNA molecule brings a different amino acid and binds to the second codon.

4 Now two amino acids are side by side and a peptide bond forms between them.

5 The ribosome now moves along the mRNA so that codons 2 and 3 are exposed to the subunit.

6 A third tRNA brings a third amino acid and binds to its codon. The first tRNA molecule leaves and is free to collect and bring another amino acid of the same type to the ribosome.

7 This continues until the ribosome reaches a base triplet that does not code for an amino acid but codes for 'stop'.

Chaperone proteins

Chaperone proteins assist the synthesised protein chain to fold into its correct shape. This tertiary structure is held by disulfide bonds, hydrogen bonds, ionic bonds and weak ionic forces provided that, when folded, certain amino acids are brought close together so these bonds can form. Hence the sequence of amino acids is very important for protein function. Mutations – changes to the genetic material of a cell – can alter the sequence of amino acids in a protein. This would alter the protein's shape and prevent it from functioning.

PAUSE POINT   Make a table to compare transcription with DNA replication.

Hint   Remember to look at ways in which the two are similar and also how they differ.

Extend   Explain the difference between transcription and translation.

Cell replication

You have seen how DNA replicates before a cell divides. Once each molecule of DNA has duplicated itself, the chromatin (DNA and the histone proteins it is wound around) condenses and coils very tightly into visible chromosomes. Each chromosome is made of two identical sister chromatids, joined at the centromere. In this supercoiled state, the genes within them cannot be transcribed, so cannot express the proteins they code for.

Mitosis

Eukaryotic cells divide by mitosis to produce two daughter cells, genetically identical to each other and to the parent cell. Mitosis is used for growth, repair, replacement of certain cells (such as skin, blood and bone), cloning of B and T cells during the immune response and, in some organisms, asexual reproduction.

Mitosis is a continuous process but scientists describe four stages as outlined in Figure 24.29.

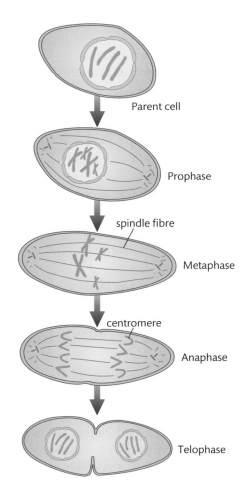

▶ **Figure 24.29:** The stages of mitosis

Step by step: Mitosis

- During prophase, the nuclear envelope breaks down and a spindle forms from protein threads.
- At metaphase, the chromosomes (each made of two identical chromatids) join to the spindle along the equator.
- At anaphase, the spindle thread shortens and pulls the chromatids of each chromosome apart and towards opposite ends (poles) of the cell.
- At telophase, two new nuclear envelopes form around the sets of chromosomes and the cell divides into two daughter cells, genetically identical to each other and to the parent cell.

Cell death

Cells should divide about 50 times before undergoing a process called apoptosis – programmed cell death. This is not the same as death by trauma; it is an orderly and tidy process.

Investigation DNA extraction and electrophoresis

You can extract DNA from many types of plant material, such as cress leaves, onions or kiwi fruits.

> **Safety tip**
>
> Take care with ethanol as it is highly flammable and skin contact may be harmful.
>
> Wear eye protection, and immediately wash off any protease that gets onto your skin. If using kiwi fruits, you may not need to use protease as kiwi fruits contain protease enzymes.

Step by step: Extracting DNA from kiwi fruits

- Skin a kiwi fruit and place it in a mortar with a pinch of salt and some cold water. Using the pestle, create a runny paste.
- Strain the paste through a fine-mesh tea strainer into a beaker.
- Add 30 cm^3 detergent, mix and leave to settle.
- Pour this mixture into test tubes, so that each one is one third full.
- Add a pinch of protease enzyme (such as meat tenderising powder) to each test tube. This digests the proteins associated with DNA in chromatin and produces a purer sample.
- Now carefully pour ice-cold 90 per cent ethanol down the inside of the test tubes containing the treated kiwi fruit paste, tilted at 45°, so that the ethanol forms a layer on top. The salted DNA is insoluble in ethanol and precipitates out at the junction of the ethanol and DNA extracted from the paste.
- Dip a glass rod into the test tube and twirl it to spool the DNA onto it. Place the spooled DNA into ethanol to preserve it. Keep in a lidded container.

Step by step: Gel electrophoresis

Electrophoresis is used to separate different sized fragments of DNA. It can separate fragments that differ by only one base pair and is widely used in gene technology to separate DNA fragments for identification and analysis.

- Incubate DNA samples with restriction enzymes at 25–40 °C for up to an hour. These enzymes digest the DNA samples – each cuts the DNA sample into fragments of particular lengths because each restriction enzyme has an active site that fits a specific recognition site on a length of DNA – a particular base pair sequence.
- Set up an electrophoresis tank and, with combs in place, pour in molten agarose gel. When the gel has set, carefully remove the comb; this leaves wells at one end of the agarose gel.
- Pour in buffer solution so that the gel is covered.
- Take your small tubes of digested DNA and add a dense loading dye to each. You should also have a control tube of undigested DNA, and you need to add loading dye to that tube as well.
- Using a different pipette for each sample, add each sample of DNA and dye to one of the wells in the agarose gel. Carefully position the pipette just above the well and allow the dye and DNA to fall into the well. If you place the pipette into the well, the DNA will go underneath the gel and the investigation will not work.
- Place electrodes at each end of the tank. The positive electrode is at the end of the tank furthest from the wells. The electrodes should be in the buffer solution but outside of the area with the gel.
- Connect the electrodes to the power supply. As current flows, the DNA fragments migrate towards the anode (positive electrode) because DNA has an overall negative charge, due to its many phosphate groups. Allow the process to run for two to four hours.
- The DNA fragments migrate towards the anode (positive electrode). Fragments of DNA all have a similar surface charge regardless of their size. Smaller DNA fragments pass more easily through the gel and travel further.
- Switch off the power. Drain the tank of buffer and add a dye that stains the DNA bands within the gel.

You can carry out this process in your school or college. Figure 24.30 shows the apparatus for gel electrophoresis of DNA.

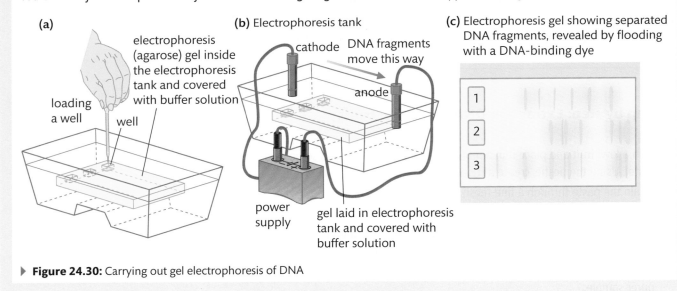

(a)

electrophoresis (agarose) gel inside the electrophoresis tank and covered with buffer solution

loading a well

well

(b) Electrophoresis tank

cathode DNA fragments move this way

anode

power supply

gel laid in electrophoresis tank and covered with buffer solution

(c) Electrophoresis gel showing separated DNA fragments, revealed by flooding with a DNA-binding dye

1
2
3

▶ **Figure 24.30:** Carrying out gel electrophoresis of DNA

DNA sequencing

In 1975, the British biochemist Fred Sanger developed a method to sequence the nucleotide bases in lengths of DNA (genes). His method has since been superseded but it led to the work carried out on the Human Genome Project – an international collaborative project to sequence the entire DNA in the human genome.

Second generation sequencing machines used today are very fast.

Step by step: DNA sequencing

- A long length of DNA is mechanically cut, using a nebuliser, into fragments of 300–800 base pairs.
- Each length is broken into single-stranded DNA (ssDNA).
- One ssDNA is incubated with activated nucleotides (nucleotides with two extra phosphate groups, e.g. adenosine triphosphate, which is adenine, a sugar and three phosphates), in the sequence TTP, ATP, CTP and GTP. The enzymes DNA polymerase, ATP sulfurylase and luciferase are added.
- As the DNA polymerase incorporates the correct complementary activated nucleotide onto the ssDNA, two phosphate groups are released.
- The enzyme ATP sulfurylase catalyses their conversion to ATP.
- The enzyme luciferase converts this ATP to luciferin and a photon of light.
- The intensity of the light emitted can be detected by a computer and can show if one, two or three of these nucleotides was incorporated adjacently into the double stranded DNA.

One million reads can occur simultaneously so a 10 hour run generates 400 million bases of sequencing information. Special software packages assemble these sequences into longer sequences.

Biochemical investigation

Scientific methodology

Science builds on previous knowledge and tries to improve people's understanding of the world. It seeks to give rational explanations of observed phenomena, so that humans can understand the nature of the world and the universe. Science relies on evidence rather than on beliefs or opinions.

The scientific method is meant to be self-correcting and prevent publication of data based on fraudulent or careless practices. It is also supposed to prevent scientists' personal and cultural beliefs influencing their selection of data and to prevent them from actively trying to support their hypothesis. In other words, scientists are encouraged to be objective.

In 1934, the concept of falsification was introduced. This means that scientists attempt to disprove their hypothesis rather than to prove it. If they fail to disprove it, they can say that the evidence supports it. Hence science cannot prove anything, it can only gather evidence to support a hypothesis, or not, as the case may be. It is also never possible to prove a negative – absence of evidence is not evidence of absence!

With enough supporting evidence, the hypothesis becomes a theory. Scientific theories are based on practical investigations and observations and represent the best model or theory you have to explain something at the time. However, at any stage any theory may need to be modified, in the light of new evidence, which may not support it.

The scientific method may have some variation in its approaches to problems but all variations depend on gathering empirical evidence (information obtained by observation and experimentation). Hence observation and practical experimentation are key to this process. Many scientific studies begin with some anecdotal evidence – observations that have been noted and are deemed worthy of further investigation.

> ### Step by step: The scientific method
>
> - Observe a phenomenon and ask a question.
> - Research, using sources of information such as books and websites, to find out about the phenomenon/question you have asked.
> - Make a prediction based on what you have found out.
> - Design (plan) and carry out an experiment to test the prediction. This includes stating which equipment and techniques are needed.
> - Carry out the investigation.
> - Keep a written record of your method, as step-by-step instructions, so that someone else can replicate the experiment.
> - Repeat your experiment to see if you get the same/similar results. This tells you whether your data are reliable or not.
> - Present your data, using tables and graphs.
> - Analyse your data, which may involve a statistical test.
> - Draw conclusions.
> - Evaluate your methodology, identifying sources of errors and limitations. Make suggestions to improve the method.
> - Communicate your findings to others – this may be discussing class results or publishing in a peer-reviewed journal.
> - Identify further research questions arising from the investigation.
> - Archive your findings.

Factors affecting scientific research and investigation

When you are planning an investigation you need to clearly understand what your independent variable and dependent variable are. For example if you are investigating how changing temperature affects the rate of an enzyme-controlled reaction, temperature is the independent variable – the factor that causes the change in the dependent variable, which is the rate of reaction. The rate of reaction depends on the temperature.

There are also control variables. These are factors that could also affect the rate of reaction. They have to be kept constant so that the only factor changing the rate of reaction is the independent variable.

In some studies ethical considerations have to be taken into account. People taking part in clinical trials need to give their informed consent. Children cannot do this so there are few trials involving the effects of treatments on children. Animals also cannot give consent and many people object to testing medicines and treatments on animals. Sometimes a trial shows such a marked positive effect on those receiving the new medicine that the trial is stopped for ethical reasons so that the control group can also be given the treatment.

Health and safety

Many scientific investigations involve potential hazards. Exposure to a hazard is a risk. Before carrying out an investigation a risk assessment is carried out to reduce potential risks and comply with health and safety requirements.

Link

For further information about health and safety issues see *Unit 13: Scientific Techniques for Health Science.*

Communicating investigative outcomes using scientific reports

It is important that scientists publish their findings for others to read. In this way, society builds a large body of knowledge to inform policy making and healthcare practices.

In the 1970s, a scientist in China systematically researched a traditional cure for malaria. She tested *Artemesia* (sweet wormwood) plants and found that particular leaves picked at a specific time during the plants' life cycle produced a chemical, artemisinin. At that time, scientists in China were not allowed to publish their findings so scientists in the rest of the world did not have access to this information. The information is now in the wider domain and artemisinin is the most effective drug available to treat malignant (falciparum) malaria.

Scientists publish their results in peer-reviewed journals. All sources of information used to inform the research have to be referenced, so that anyone reading the article can go to the original sources of information and find out more. At the beginning of each article there is a brief synopsis, outlining the method and findings. The synopsis helps scientists undertaking literature research for their project to decide whether the article is appropriate for them to read in full. Table 24.9 shows the conventions about how to reference sources of information.

▶ **Table 24.9:** Referencing sources of information

Source of information	Details to note	Examples of how to present the reference
Books	Author names, date of publication, title of the publication, publisher.	Carey, N. (2012) *The Epigenetics Revolution*, Icon Books Ltd.
Journals, magazines	Names of the authors, the title of the article, title of the journal/magazine, volume number and page references for the article within the journal, date.	Shirvani, T. et al, Life cycle energy and greenhouse gas analysis for algae-derived biodiesel. *Energy Environmental Science* Vol. 4 pp 3773-3778 (2011).
Websites	Names of the authors, the title of the article, date, URL.	Lundquist, T.J. et al, A Realistic Technology and Engineering Assessment of Algae Biofuel Production. Energy Biosciences Institute (2010). http://works.bepress.com/tlundqui/5

Information sources are usually listed in author alphabetical order at the end of an article.

It is important that scientists also publish investigations that give unexpected results, as this is still informative and may lead to further studies.

1 Produce a large poster to show the molecular structures, and explain the physical and chemical properties, of carbohydrates (sugars and starches), fats – including triglycerides, phospholipids and cholesterol, proteins and nucleic acids.

2 Carry out practical investigations into two factors that affect enzyme activity. Write a plan for your investigation, including a clearly stated hypothesis, the background science, independent (the factor that changes) and dependent (the factor that changes when the independent variable changes) variables, a list of equipment, a list of control variables (and statements as to why each needs to be controlled, and how each will be controlled), and a risk assessment. Once your plan has been approved, carry out the investigations and write a report on them. Analyse and present your data, and evaluate your investigations in terms of errors, limitations and improvements. Include references. Share your findings with others in your class.

3 Carry out and write a brief report on the extraction of DNA.

4 Write an article for a health magazine explaining the importance of enzymes in metabolic processes and the factors that affect rates of enzyme activity.

5 In your article, you should also show how the structure of enzyme molecules and their substrate molecules affect metabolic rates. Explain the importance of coenzymes and cofactors. Include some evaluation of how certain medicines act as enzyme inhibitors, for example ACE inhibitors.

Plan
- Do I know what I am being asked to do?
- Do I have enough information or should I extend my research?

Do
- Do I know what I want to achieve?
- Can I check my work to see where I have gone off task and can make changes to put this right?

Review
- Can I instruct someone else on how to complete the task more efficiently?
- Do I know what I would do differently next time and the approach I would take with the parts that I found difficult this time?

C   Examine the principles of biochemistry in industry

An understanding of the biochemical processes that take place in living cells can help scientists understand certain diseases that are the result of metabolic disorders, and inform the research into their diagnosis and treatment. It can also lead to important uses of enzymes in biotechnology.

Aetiology of metabolic disorders

Aetiology is the study of the origins and causes of diseases. This includes studying the factors that may contribute to a disease, or predispose someone to a certain condition.

There are many different kinds of diseases, including infections. In this unit, you are concerned with metabolic disorders, some of which have an underlying genetic cause.

Disorders of the endocrine system

The endocrine system is a collection of the glands that secrete hormones. Besides the endocrine glands, some organs, such as bone, skin and the kidneys, also secrete hormones. Kidneys make a hormone that stimulates the production of red blood cells, and the skin makes vitamin D (which is a hormone). Hormones are chemicals, either protein or steroid (lipid) molecules, that regulate metabolism, growth, development, mood, sleep and reproduction. The hormones are secreted directly into the bloodstream, which carries them to their target organs. Hormone molecules fit into complementary shaped receptor molecules on the cell surface membranes of the target organ cells and initiate metabolic reactions inside the target cells. Hormone imbalances (too much or too little) cause disorders. You will only consider two examples here, diabetes and disorders of the thyroid gland.

Diabetes mellitus (sugar diabetes)

The pancreas secretes two hormones, insulin and glucagon, that regulate blood glucose level. Your blood glucose level must be maintained within narrow limits, at around 90 mg per 100 cm^3 blood, so that respiring cells receive enough glucose to carry out respiration. Prolonged high blood sugar levels are harmful to body organs and are a feature of a group of metabolic disorders, collectively called diabetes mellitus. Diabetes occurs if:

▶ the beta cells of the pancreas do not produce enough insulin

▶ body cells do not respond properly to the insulin produced, usually leading to insufficient insulin secretions as the cells cannot continue to produce insulin.

There are four main types of diabetes as shown in Table 24.10.

▶ **Table 24.10:** Types of diabetes – causes, characteristics and treatments

Type of diabetes	Causes and characteristics	Prevention and treatment
Type 1 – previously called insulin-dependent or juvenile-onset diabetes	Autoimmune disease; the body mistakenly identifies beta cells as foreign and mounts an immune response, destroying beta cells of the pancreas. Symptoms include increased urination, hunger and thirst. Develops quickly, and is sudden onset.	Treated with insulin injections following monitoring of blood glucose levels; controlled diet and exercise to maintain healthy weight; often require medication to control blood pressure.
Type 2 – previously called adult or maturity onset diabetes; accounts for 90% of worldwide diabetes cases	Strong genetic predisposition; associated with obesity, particularly abdominal fat, and with hypertension (high blood pressure). Symptoms include increased urination, hunger and thirst. Develops slowly.	Medication to stimulate beta cells to make more insulin; increased exercise, diet regulation and maintenance of healthy weight, avoidance of alcohol and smoking.
Gestational	Glucose intolerance during pregnancy, particularly in the third trimester (6–9 months). Symptoms include recurrent infections, blurred vision, increased urination, hunger and thirst.	Treated with insulin and careful regulation of diet during pregnancy. Although disappears after giving birth, about 40–60% of women will develop type 2 diabetes within 15 years after the pregnancy.
Defects in beta cells or insulin production	May be due to genetic defects or destruction of beta cells by certain viruses; may be associated with other genetic conditions such as Down's, Turner or Klinefelter syndromes. Symptoms include increased urination, thirst and hunger.	Treated with insulin as well as blood glucose level monitoring, diet and exercise.

Diabetes can shorten a person's life expectancy and can lead to many complications. The high levels of glucose in the blood damage blood vessels, which leads to bleeding, tissue and organ damage. Complications of diabetes include blindness due to retinal damage, foot and leg ulcers, which may lead to gangrene and potentially loss of lower limbs, sensory and motor disturbances of the nervous system, kidney disease, muscle weakness and atrophy, decline in cognitive function and increased risk of heart attack and stroke. In the twenty-first century, the incidence of type 2 diabetes has been increasing greatly in developed countries. This is associated with lifestyle changes such as eating increased amounts of processed foods, more sugar in the diet and higher levels of obesity.

Disorders of the thyroid gland

The thyroid gland is a bow-tie shaped organ at the front of the neck (see Figure 24.31). It secretes the hormones thyroxine and calcitonin. The four small parathyroid glands attached to the dorsal surface of the thyroid gland secrete parathyroid hormone.

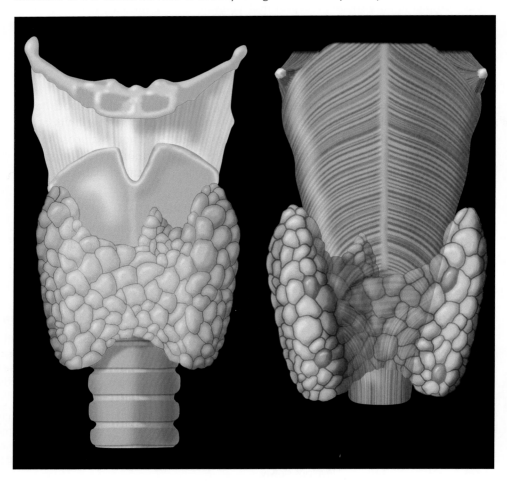

▶ **Figure 24.31:** Location of the thyroid and parathyroid glands; the front view on the left shows the thyroid in relation to the larynx and trachea and the back view on the right shows the position of the parathyroid glands (shown in red)

Thyroxine is an iodine-containing hormone, it:

▶ regulates metabolic rate
▶ affects body temperature
▶ regulates catabolism of protein, carbohydrate and fat
▶ maintains the secretion of growth hormone
▶ regulates maturation of the skeleton and development of the nervous system
▶ regulates heart rate.

Calcitonin stimulates deposition of calcium in bone and regulates blood calcium ion levels.

Parathyroid hormone regulates the calcium ion levels in blood and extracellular fluid, the absorption of calcium from food in the gut, the movement of calcium ions into and out of bones and the excretion of calcium into breast milk, urine, sweat and faeces. Table 24.11 shows the consequences of some of the disorders of the thyroid and parathyroid glands.

▶ **Table 24.11:** Disorders of the thyroid and parathyroid glands

Disorder	Cause and Symptoms	Treatment
Acute/infectious thyroiditis	Infection by, for example, staphylococcal and streptococcal bacteria. Symptoms include inflammation and swelling of the thyroid gland, pain in the throat, generally feeling unwell.	Antibiotics
Chronic thyroiditis – Hashimoto's disease (underactive thyroid)	Common autoimmune condition in which lymphocytes and plasma cells infiltrate the gland and destroy cells, leading to hypothyroidism (underactive thyroid gland). Genetic factors may be involved. Symptoms include slowing of the metabolic rate causing cold intolerance, weight gain, dry skin and hair; goitre – swelling of the thyroid gland.	Lifelong thyroxine hormone supplements
Grave's disease – hyperthyroidism (overactive thyroid gland)	Autoimmune disease that is the commonest cause of hyperthyroidism. Genetic factors may be involved. Symptoms include an enlarged thyroid gland; excess hormone secretion leads to an increased metabolic rate causing hunger, weight loss, fatigue and heat intolerance. Can lead to heart failure and death if untreated.	Surgery or radioactivity to ablate the thyroid gland, followed by lifelong thryoxine hormone supplements
Excess calcitonin	May be due to a tumour in thyroid gland. Disruption of calcium ion metabolism, which may affect bone building, muscle contraction and blood clotting.	Treatment of the tumour or supplements of calcitonin hormone
Hypoparathyroidism	Parathyroid glands may be removed during surgery to ablate an overactive thyroid gland; leads to low blood calcium leading to tetany (muscle spasms) anorexia, seizures and death.	Lifelong parathyroid hormone supplements

Case study

Thyroid storm

Kelly gave birth to her second baby when she was aged 35. Very soon afterwards, while she was still in hospital, she suffered a thyroid storm.

Thyroid storms may occur after severe emotional distress. Kelly's thyroid gland suddenly started to secrete huge amounts of thyroxine, causing her heart rate to soar, and fever, sweating, shaking, agitation, high blood pressure. This led to a heart attack. Fortunately, as Kelly was still in hospital, she received prompt treatment for the heart attack and was given medication to reduce the production of thyroxine. As she had recently given birth and wanted to breastfeed her baby, her thyroid gland was removed surgically rather than by radioactive iodine treatment.

Kelly now takes a daily dose of thyroxine hormone, which she must do for the rest of her life. Mother and baby are both doing well.

Check your knowledge

1 Why do you think radioactive isotopes of iodine are used to treat Grave's disease?
2 Why do you think pregnant and breastfeeding women who have an overactive thyroid gland are not treated with radioactive iodine?

A lack of dietary iodine is the main cause of goitre (enlarged thyroid gland) in less economically developed countries. The thyroid gland enlarges as it tries to compensate by producing more thyroxine. This condition is rare in developed countries where food, such as table salt, has iodine added.

❚❚ PAUSE POINT   Compare types 1 and 2 diabetes.

Hint   Think about causes, symptoms and treatments. Include similarities as well as differences.

Extend   Explain, with reference to named examples, how autoimmunity can cause hormone imbalances.

Disorders due to genetic defects

There are several thousand metabolic disorders due to genetic abnormalities. Two are outlined here, glycogen storage disease and phenylketonuria.

Glycogen storage disease

Glycogen storage disease refers to a group of inherited disorders of glycogen metabolism, resulting in the storage of abnormally large levels of glycogen in the liver, muscles and other parts of the body. There are 11 types, each one caused by a specific defective enzyme involved in a particular stage of glycogen metabolism. Symptoms include growth failure, muscle weakness, cramps, delayed motor development, renal failure, haemolytic anaemia and heart failure. Clinical trials are currently investigating gene therapy as a treatment.

Phenylketonuria

Phenylketonuria (PKU) is the result of a mutation in the gene coding for an enzyme, phenylalanine hydroxylase, which is involved in the metabolism of the amino acid phenylalanine. Normally, phenylalanine should be changed to tyrosine and then to melanin, which is the pigment of hair, skin and eyes. People with PKU are, therefore, often very fair complexioned. The build-up of phenylalanine causes irreparable brain damage, with severe learning difficulties and behavioural problems. Although PKU is rare, because of its devastating effects all newborn babies are screened for PKU, between seven and ten days after birth. If the test is positive, the baby's diet is regulated to include only low amounts of phenylalanine, preventing brain damage and allowing them to live a normal life.

Case study

PKU

Aziz Gorshani is a children's nurse. He is looking after a young boy, Sol, who was diagnosed with PKU soon after birth. The child's parents were told that their child would need a special diet. However, they thought that because the disease was genetically inherited, the diet would not make any difference and they ignored the advice. Sol is now 10 years old. He has severe learning difficulties, and he is very aggressive and difficult to manage.

Check your knowledge

1   PKU is rare so why are all newborn babies screened for it?

2   Why do you think that it is recommended that people with PKU have diets with low amounts, rather than no amounts of the amino acid phenylalanine?

Uses of biotechnology

Biotechnology is the use of living organisms and systems to develop or make products. The earliest forms, developed thousands of years ago, include making cheese, bread, beer, wine and yoghurt. In 1917 the bacterium *Clostridium acetobutylicum* was used to make acetone needed to make explosives during the First World War. In the 1940s penicillin, made by the fungus *Penicillium gryseum*, discovered twenty years previously, was produced and used to treat bacterial infections.

Enzymes in biotechnology

Many biotechnology processes rely on enzymes and three of these will be discussed here.

Biological detergents

Enzymes in biological detergents break down proteins, starches and fats in the dirt and stains on clothing. These stains may originate from blood, sweat, urine and faeces, food and soil. Biological detergents may contain α-amylase, cellulose, lipase and protease. The enzymes hydrolyse their substrate molecules and digest stains at lower temperatures, maximum 50°C, than non-biological detergents do.

Discussion

What are the substrates for each of the enzymes used in biological detergents? Why do you think these detergents do not work so well at temperatures above 50°C?

Glucose isomerase

Glucose isomerase catalyses the conversion of glucose to another hexose sugar, fructose. (See the section on Disaccharides.) Fructose tastes much sweeter than sucrose (table sugar) or glucose and is used to sweeten drinks and other products. Glucose isomerase enzymes are obtained from bacteria.

Streptokinase

Streptokinase is an enzyme secreted by several species of *Streptococcus* bacteria. If used within 90 minutes following a heart attack, stroke or pulmonary embolism, it can break down the clot, reducing damage to the heart or brain. Streptokinase is on the list developed by the World Health Organization of essential medicines needed in basic healthcare systems.

Research

Research how enzymes are used in diagnostic tests. For example, biosensors used to detect blood and urine glucose levels for diagnosing and monitoring diabetes. For information about how glucose meters work and how people with diabetes can manage their condition with the help of glucose meters, go to:

www.diabetes.org.uk/Guide-to-diabetes/Monitoring/Testing/?gclid=CLKikb_tlcsCFQUq0wodpy8MGQ

DNA fingerprinting

Modern biotechnology encompasses recombinant DNA technology and is underpinned by a wide knowledge of microbiology and genetics. One well-known example is the use of DNA profiling.

Paternity testing

In 1978, the British biochemist Alec Jeffreys was locating tandem repeat sequences of DNA. (Tandem repeats are repetitive non-coding segments of DNA, between 10–100 base pairs long.) Jeffreys obtained DNA from his laboratory technician and her parents, and analysed it. He found that although the DNA profile for each family member was unique, the tandem repeats showed a family resemblance. He realised this technique could be used to confirm or refute maternity and paternity, as half the child's tandem repeats match those of the mother and half match those of the father.

DNA profiling

DNA profiling is used to identify criminals – if the suspect's DNA profile matches specimens left at the scene of a crime, such as semen in a rape victim's body. It has also been used to:

- show when people have been wrongly convicted, to secure their release
- confirm that medieval human remains found in Leicester in 2012 were those of Richard III
- identify bodies after a terrorist attack or a disaster
- identify previously unknown remains; for example, matching profiles of soldier's descendants with the remains of First World War soldiers found on French battlefield sites.

The procedure

There are slightly different procedures for profiling DNA, but the principles underlying them all are outlined here.

- DNA is obtained from the individual – either by a mouth swab, from saliva on a toothbrush, from blood or hair or, in the case of ancient remains, from bone.
- The DNA is then digested with restriction enzymes. These enzymes cut the DNA at specific recognition sites. The enzymes cut the DNA into fragments, which will vary in size from individual to individual.
- These fragments are separated by gel electrophoresis and stained. Larger fragments travel the shortest distance in the gel.
- A banding pattern can be seen.
- The DNA to which the individual's is being compared is treated with the same restriction enzymes, and also subjected to electrophoresis.
- The banding patterns of the DNA samples can then be compared.

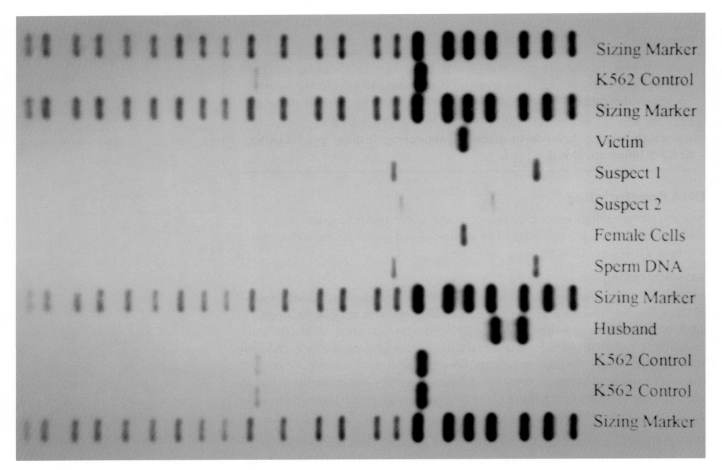

▶ DNA profile from a rape investigation showing that Suspect 1 is a match to DNA in the sperm found in the victim's body

In 1986, DNA profiling was used for the first time to solve some murders in Leicestershire. Professor (now Sir) Alec Jeffreys compared the suspect's DNA against crime scene samples and established that the suspect was not guilty. The police then took samples from more than 5000 local men; none matched the crime scene DNA. However, a man (Colin Pitchfork) was overheard boasting that a friend had given DNA on his behalf. Colin Pitchfork was arrested and his DNA was found to match the DNA found at the crime scene.

Research into the use of biochemistry

Clinical biochemistry involves using biochemistry to diagnose and treat metabolic disorders, as well as the development of new drugs. Many hospitals have a biochemistry laboratory where tests requested by doctors help diagnose patients' conditions and monitor the effectiveness of their treatment. Many of the tests are carried out on body fluids such as blood, urine and cerebrospinal fluid. Some are used to detect raised levels in the blood of specific enzymes, which have been released from damaged cells of particular organs. This indicates which organs are damaged. Biochemical tests may also be used for screening the population for certain diseases, such as bowel and breast cancer.

Hospital biochemistry laboratories are also involved in research into the biochemical bases of diseases such as obesity, osteoporosis and diabetes, and the clinical trials of new drugs.

The Biotechnology and Biological Sciences Research Council (BBSRC), created in 1994, is a UK Research Council that funds scientific research institutes and university departments in the UK. Its head office is in Swindon and BBSRC is a government-funded organisation.

Link

For further information about the use of clinical biochemistry, see *Unit 15: Microbiology for Health Science*.

Assessment practice 24.3   C.P5 C.P6 C.M3 C.D3

You have been asked to write an article about the use of biochemistry in metabolic disorders for the health section of your local newspaper.

1 In your article, explain the aetiology (causes) of metabolic disorders, including gene mutations and hormone imbalances.

2 Explain how enzymes are used in the diagnosis and treatment of metabolic disorders. Refer to specific examples, such as the use of enzymes in biosensors for reading blood glucose levels, and in test strips to find levels of glucose in urine. Explain which enzymes are used in DNA profiling and DNA sequencing.

3 Assess the impact of DNA sequencing of the human genome on the development of treatment/therapy for metabolic disorders.

4 Evaluate how biological molecules and their role in metabolism influences current research, and the development of treatments for metabolic disorders.

Plan
• Do I know what I am being asked to do?
• Do I have enough information or should I extend my research?

Do
• Do I know what I want to achieve?
• Can I check my work to see where I have gone off task and can make changes to put this right?

Review
• Can I instruct someone else on how to complete the task more efficiently?
• Do I know what I would do differently next time and the approach I would take with the parts that I found difficult this time?

Further reading and resources

Books

Voet, D. and Voet, J. (2011) *Biochemistry*, Hoboken, NJ: John Wiley and Sons.

Hemsworth, Dr H. (2015) *Ace Biochemistry!: The EASY Guide to Ace Biochemistry*, self-published: Dr Holden Hemsworth.

Rennenberg, R., Berkling, V. et al. (2016) *Biotechnology for Beginners*, 2nd edition, Cambridge, MA: Academic Press Inc.

Websites

www.biologyreference.com/Bl-Ce/Carbohydrates.html
Biology Reference: Information about carbohydrates.

www.sciencegeek.net/Chemistry/chempdfs/ProteinCarbsFat.pdf
ScienceGeek: Information about the structure of proteins, carbohydrates and fats.

www.chem4kids.com/files/bio_nucleicacids.html
Chem4Kids.com: Information about nucleic acids.

www.sciencemuseum.org.uk/whoami/findoutmore/yourbody/ whatdoyourcellsdo/whatisacellmadeof/whyareenzymesimportant
Science Museum: Information about why enzymes are important.

THINK ▶▶FUTURE

Ariana Llywelyn
Clinical biochemist

I got my first degree, a BSc in Biochemistry from the University of Liverpool. I'm now a clinical biochemist, and I work in a large teaching hospital.

I spend quite a lot of my time in a laboratory, analysing blood and urine samples and interpreting the results to help the clinicians diagnose patients' illnesses. I also spend time in clinics and operating theatres, to help support the team investigating patients' conditions and monitoring the progress of their treatments.

Part of my work involves evaluating the quality and effectiveness of the tests, as well as developing and implementing new techniques and tests; for example, looking for better and more specific markers (chemicals secreted by cells) for particular diseases. The tests my team carry out are used to investigate levels of a patient's electrolytes, and how well their heart, liver and kidneys are working.

I advise clinical staff on the correct use of tests and the necessary follow-up investigations that they should ask for. I often participate in conferences for clinicians, where I present information about new analytical tests that are being developed.

Focusing your skills

Health and Safety

Large laboratories receive many hundreds of samples each day for testing so systems must be in place to document all samples and ensure they are dealt with promptly. It would be very distressing to a patient if they received a wrong diagnosis, so it is important to know the reasons for these procedures.

- Why are samples not stored for long? Why must they be stored under the correct conditions?
- Why should samples be labelled clearly?
- How could you ensure that the correct results go with the appropriate sample to the right clinical department?

Scientific skills

When you manage laboratory projects you will need the ability to liaise with a wide variety of technical colleagues, such as microbiologists, biomedical scientists and pathologists. You will also need the following skills and attributes:

- an investigative mind
- analytical skills
- good organisational skills
- ability to use scientific methodology
- self-motivation, self-direction
- ability to work individually or as part of a team.

Getting ready for assessment

Atash Karzai is studying for a BTEC National in Health and Social Care. He has been given an assignment to carry out a practical task of separating DNA by gel electrophoresis. Atash shares some aspects of his experience below.

How I got started

I asked my tutor if there was an electrophoresis kit in college – and found we had one. This had come from an organisation called SAPS (Science and Plants for Schools). I visited their website (**www.saps.org.uk**) to find out more about the protocol. I also spoke to our lab technician to find out if I could use the kit, and to see if we had all the materials I would need.

Think about it

I familiarised myself with all the parts of the kit and thought about how the practical would be carried out. I studied the instructions. I also thought about how I could show my results to others in my class and how I had to make sure I understood everything.

How I brought it all together

I drew up a plan, had it checked and then ordered the equipment and chemicals I needed. I made sure that I had enough time to carry out the protocol and to come back into the lab to switch off the batteries. Lastly, I wrote up all the notes from my experiment.

What I learned from the experience

I learned a lot. This is a really cool experiment and I made a DNA profile. Next time I might try it with some DNA I have extracted from onions.

Think about it

▸ Have you written a plan with timings, so you can complete your assignment by the agreed submission date?

▸ Do you have notes on the principles behind and uses of gel electrophoresis?

▸ Do you fully understand how to carry out the protocol and what is happening at each stage?

▸ Can you present your findings to others in your class and explain what you did, and what you found?

▸ Is your information written in your own words and referenced clearly where you have used quotations or information from a book, journal or website?

Glossary

Accountable: required to explain actions or decisions to someone.

Acid: substance that dissociates into one or more hydrogen ions (H+) and one or more anions.

Action research: systematic study, usually on a small scale, that investigates the impact of a specific activity that is carried out as a part of a normal work role. Action research is particularly practised in education and in health and social care contexts.

Addison's disease: a rare disorder of the adrenal glands that causes low blood pressure, generalised weakness, progressive anaemia and bronzed skin.

ADP: adenosine diphosphate, an important organic compound in metabolism.

Adsorbent: able to hold on to (absorb) substances.

Advocate: a person speaking on behalf of someone else, who puts their case forward, especially where an individual is unable to speak for themself.

Aerobic: requiring oxygen.

Aggressive: behaving in a forceful way, ready to attack or confront.

Aim: an overall goal or target to be achieved. An aim should relate to a defined purpose.

Akaryotic: having no cell structure, no cytoplasm and no organelles. Consists of nucleic acid and a protein coat.

Allele: alternative forms of a gene, found at the same place on a chromosome arising from mutation.

Amniocentesis: taking a sample of amniotic fluid to test for chromosomal abnormalities and foetal infections.

Anabolism: metabolic reactions that involve synthesising large molecules from smaller ones using energy.

Anaerobic: not requiring oxygen.

Analyte: a substance whose chemical constituents are being identified and measured.

Angina: chest pain caused by inadequate oxygen supply to the heart muscle when it is under stress, usually relieved by rest or taking tablets to dilate the arteries.

Angioplasty: a procedure that uses a balloon to widen blocked or narrow coronary arteries. Angioplasty is now a common and routine operation in heart surgery.

Anion: negatively charged ion.

Ankylosing spondylitis: a form of spinal arthritis seen mostly in young males, causing immobility and fusion of the vertebral and sacroiliac joints.

Anonymity: ensuring that any data associated with an individual collected for research purposes is documented and stored in such a way that it cannot be traced back to the individual by name.

Antibodies: proteins produced by B lymphocytes that respond to antigens.

Antigen: a molecule, usually a protein that may stimulate an immune response or be recognised as 'self' by the immune system. Cell surface membranes contain antigens.

Antigen presenting cell (APC): a cell that displays an antigen (derived from a pathogen) on its surface, presenting it to a B cell or T-cell to stimulate the immune response.

Antimicrobial: substance that kills or prevents the growth of micro-organisms.

Antioxidant: substances that may prevent or delay some types of cell damage such as cancer. Antioxidants are found in many foods including fruits and vegetables and include beta-carotene, lycopene and vitamins A, C and E.

Antiseptic: substance that can be applied to skin or other living tissues such as teeth to kill micro-organisms or to inhibit their growth.

Arguments: contrasting lines of reasoning that are synthesised systematically to develop a conclusion.

Artificial selection: selective breeding, where humans select plants or animals for their desired characteristics and breed only from those chosen specifications.

Aseptic technique: practices and procedures performed under carefully controlled conditions to minimise contamination by micro-organisms.

Aspergillosis: disease caused by a mould fungus, *Aspergillus spp* which usually affects the respiratory system.

Aspiration: using suction to remove fluid from a body cavity.

Assertive: being confident and assured.

Assistive technology: devices for people with disabilities that help them to maintain or improve their ability to perform daily living activities.

Atherosclerosis: a disease of the arteries in which fatty material deposits build up on their inner walls damaging them causing narrowing and hardening of the affected arteries.

Atom: the smallest unit of matter which the properties of a chemical element and can enter into chemical reactions.

Attachment: a special bond or relationship with other people.

Attribute: a quality which contributes to who you are, helps form your personality.

Atypical: irregular, not usual for the group or type.

Autopsy: post mortem examination of a body to find out the cause(s) of death.

Average: a measure of a usual, common amount or rate, a norm.

Basal metabolism: the energy necessary to maintain vital body functions such as respiration and circulation while fasting and at total rest.

Base: substance that dissociates into one or more hydroxyl ions (OH$^-$) and one or more cations.

Beliefs: strongly held opinions stored in the subconscious mind.

Bibliography: a list of published sources relevant to the topic that have been read to increase knowledge and understanding, but which are not necessarily specifically referred to in an essay or research paper.

Bilirubin: waste product made from the breakdown of bile salts.

Binge drinking: drinking heavily in one session leading to symptoms such as speech slurring, loss of balance, slowing of mental processes or behavioural changes, e.g. violence or aggression.

Biofilms: thin layers of mucilage (slime) adhering to a surface and containing bacteria which make the slime. Biofilms may alter bacterial metabolism and make it harder for antibacterial medicines to work.

Bioinformatics: interdisciplinary field of science (includes maths, statistics, computer science and engineering) that develops methods and software for understanding biological data.

Biological agent: a micro-organism, cell culture or human endoparasite that may cause infection, allergy, toxicity or create another hazard to human health.

Biomarkers: certain proteins that are produced in abnormal amounts by cells and under certain pathological circumstances can be used to diagnose specific conditions.

Biopsy: pathology examination of body tissues taken from a living patient to find the cause of a disease or illness.

Body image: how a person sees their physical self, including their thoughts and feelings about their body.

Cardiovascular: the heart and blood vessels.

Cardiovascular system: body system consisting of veins, venules, capillaries, arteries, arterioles, the heart and blood, which facilitates gas exchange and the transport of nutrients to and waste from the cells.

Catabolism: metabolic reactions that involve splitting large molecules into smaller ones, often with the release of energy.

Cation: positively charged ion.

Citation: the process of quoting evidence from other sources.

Clinical: the observation and treatment of a person rather than looking at theories or laboratory research.

Clone: a group of cells (or organisms) that are genetically identical to each other.

Closed question: requires the respondent to select a response from a given menu of possible answer options.

Code of practice: written statements that set out how members of a particular profession should conduct themselves.

Cofactor: substance that has to be present to make sure an enzyme-catalysed reaction takes place at the appropriate rate.

Cognitive: mental processes of the brain that help you understand and comprehend; your memory and your reasoning.

Cognitive behavioural therapy (CBT): a practical talking therapy used to improve an individual's state of mind, helping them to manage problems by changing the way they think or behave. CBT focuses on current problems or issues rather than on what happened to an individual in the past.

Collation: the process of systematically organising data from research in preparation for analysis and evaluation of data.

Colonoscopy: an endoscopy specifically used to look at the inner lining of the large intestine (rectum and colon) using a thin flexible tube (a colonoscope).

Communication: the ability to exchange information in a variety of ways, e.g. speaking, writing or using other media.

Competence: the ability to do something successful or efficiently.

Compound: chemical made from two or more elements, which are chemically combined.

Conclusion: a concise statement based on evidence and reasoned arguments that summarises key findings from an investigation.

Condensation: reaction to join two or more smaller molecules to make a larger molecule, involving the elimination of one or more molecules of water, the reverse of hydrolysis.

Confidence: how you feel about your ability to perform certain roles or tasks.

Confidential: information that is secret and should not be shared without permission.

Confidentiality: ensuring that personal information relating to any individual including all data collected for a research study is shared only with those whom the individual has consented to being informed.

Continuing Professional Development: the process of taking part in a range of learning activities to update, increase and improve your knowledge and skills throughout your working life.

Control group: group of individuals participating in research but who are not exposed to the health or care intervention being investigated.

Control test: a scientific test in which each variable is tested alone without the influence of the variables being investigated to check that any change observed in the experiment is not due to either the independent variable or the dependent variable on its own.

Creatinine: breakdown product of creatine phosphate found in muscles, removed via kidneys; elevated levels in blood indicate renal failure/kidney disease.

Creutzfeldt-Jakob disease: condition caused by an abnormally shaped protein called a prion, infecting the brain. New variant CJD is believed to be caused by consuming meat from cattle infected with bovine spongiform encephalopathy (BSE).

Culture: the beliefs, language, styles of dress, ways of cooking, religion, ways of behaving shared by a particular group of people.

Cushing's syndrome: a rare disorder which is more common in women, involving over production of corticosteroid hormones (stress hormones) by the adrenal cortex causing weight gain and obesity, high blood pressure, high blood glucose levels, tiredness and generalised weakness.

Cytoplasm: gel-like substance enclosed by the cell surface membrane about 80% water; medium in which many metabolic reactions take place. Organelles are suspended in the cytoplasm.

Data: information that could be measurements, opinions or concepts. It is a plural word but its singular, datum is rarely used.

Data set: a large number of values of the same measure from different individuals/tests.

Decarboxylation: removal of a carboxyl (COO-) group from substrate molecules.

Deficiency: the absence of a particular nutrient in the body due to a lack in the diet or conditions that prevent nutrients being absorbed from the diet.

Degenerate: code in which many code words have the same meaning, describes the genetic code because, in many instances different base triplets/codons specify the same amino acid, some amino acids are therefore coded for by more than one base triplet/codon.

Dehydrogenation: removal of hydrogen atoms from substrate molecules.

Demographics: statistics about the population and particular groups within it, for example age, income and education.

Denatured: having the molecular shape permanently changed leading to the molecules not being able to function.

Denature: destroy structure and therefore ability to function.

Dependency: relying on another person, object or routine in order to cope with daily living activities.

Dependent variable: a variable relating to a phenomenon whose value is dependent of another variable, for example respiration rate and pulse rate.

Development: the acquisition of skills and abilities over time.

Diagnose: identify the nature of an illness or other medical condition by examination of the symptoms.

Diagnostic procedures: techniques used to identify a specific illness or medical condition.

Differential staining: process using more than one chemical to stain tissues, cells or structures showing differences between them.

Dignity: worthy of respect, a pride in oneself.

Dilemma: a situation requiring a difficult choice to be made between two or more alternatives because the advantages and disadvantages between each of the alternatives is finely balanced.

Discrimination: an unjust or prejudicial judgement about a person; treating another person differently on the grounds of their age, race or gender.

Disinfectant: substance that can be applied to surfaces to kill micro-organisms or to inhibit their growth.

Direct carer: someone who provides care for a service user, such as a doctor or social worker.

Disulfide bond: a chemical bond between two sulfur atoms within a molecule. These bonds are very strong and not broken by heat.

Diversity: variety or range.

Dominant gene: produces its coded characteristics in the individual.

Double blind clinical trial: a research technique for testing the effectiveness of a new drug in which patients taking part are allocated at random to one of two groups: one given the test drug and the other a placebo. Neither the patients taking part in the trial nor the doctors and professionals caring for them know whether they are receiving the placebo or the test drug.

Droplets: tiny drops of moisture produced when a person breathes out or sneezes. If that person is infected, these droplets may contain bacteria or virus particles that could infect another person.

Electron: negatively charged subatomic particle.

Element: a substance made up of atoms, all of the same type.

Eluate: a solution obtained by elution – the process of extracting one material from another by washing with a solvent.

Empirical data: verifiable data obtained by observation, measurement or from experiences.

Endoscope: a narrow tubular instrument used to examine inside the body; may have an instrument attached to enable a biopsy to be taken or for surgery to be performed.

Endoscopy: examination of inside the body using a specialised tube (an endoscope).

Epidemiologist: scientist who studies patterns of diseases within populations by analysing data to find out what causes disease outbreaks (epidemics).

Epipen: a device delivering a rapid injection of adrenaline to quickly control symptoms of anaphylactic shock which, in severe cases, cause the throat and tongue to swell blocking the airway.

Ethics: written statements relating to what is acceptable and unacceptable that reflect the morals of a society.

Eukaryotic: cells that contain a nucleus and membrane bound organelles; organism made of eukaryotic cells.

Eukaryotic cells: contain a nucleus and other organelles enclosed within membranes.

Event sampling: recording behaviours at a specific moment in time, for example the key features of a child's behaviour during their first week attending a nursery.

Evidence based practice: in health and social care practice that is informed by reliable research data that enables the most appropriate care to be provided in the specific context of the circumstances.

Evolution: appearance of new species as the result of a gradual change over many generations in the genetic make- up of existing species.

Experiment: specifically designed test to assess the validity of a hypothesis.

Experimental learning: information or skills acquired through experience and observation while working.

Fact: a phenomenon that is known for example children grow into adults or can be proven to be true, for example people affected by dementia lose aspects of their memory.

Feedback: reaction from other people about your performance which can be used to inform improvement.

Findings: the knowledge and understanding gained from a piece of research or a research study.

Fluorescence: a form of light emission by a substance that has absorbed light or another part of the electromagnetic spectrum. The

emitted light has a longer wavelength than the absorbed electromagnetic radiation.

Fomites: objects or substances that carry infecting agents and transfer them from one person to another.

Food intolerance: symptoms such as diarrhoea, bloating and wind, caused by eating specific foods. It is not the same as having an allergic reaction and is not usually life threatening.

FRANK: national drug education service set up in 2003 by the DH and Home Office to provide education to reduce the use of both legal and illegal drugs through its website and media campaigns.

Free sugars: sugars added to foods, including baking as opposed to naturally occurring sugars such as lactose in milk and fructose in fruit.

Fybromyalgia: a condition in which there is widespread pain as a joint, part of the body or the entire body becomes extra sensitive to pain. There is no cure and treatment aims to ease some of the symptoms.

Gene: length of DNA that codes for one or more proteins or that codes for a regulatory length of RNA.

Genetically modified: altering the DNA of an organism to create something that does not occur through natural reproduction.

Genome: all the genetic material in a cell/organism.

Genomics: a science discipline that sequences and analyses the functions of genomes.

Gillick competence: a term used to decide whether a child (aged 16 and under) is considered able to consent to their own medical treatment without the need for parental permission or knowledge. The term originates from a legal case about contraception.

Glycoproteins: molecules consisting primarily of protein with a sugar molecule attached.

Goal: an aim or desired result.

Graticule: measuring device used in an eyepiece of a microscope. Once calibrated it can be used to measure dimensions of objects viewed with a microscope.

Growth: increase in size and weight.

Hand-eye coordination: the ability of the visual system to use information taken in through the eyes to organise movement of the hands when carrying out a specific task, such as handwriting or catching a ball.

HDL: high density lipoproteins, these protein and lipid complexes carry cholesterol in the blood and sweep some cholesterol off the artery walls; also called 'good cholesterol'.

Health surveillance: a system of checks which may be required by law, to detect ill effects of hazards to health, provide data

and monitor control systems (and check for lapses) to provide protection against hazards to health and wellbeing.

Heart attack: chest pain, similar to angina but usually more severe caused by a blockage of the artery supplying oxygen to the heart muscle. This pain is not relieved by rest or angina tablets and is a medical emergency.

Herd immunity: protection of a population from infectious disease that occurs following a large percentage of the population being made immune to the infection.

Histamine: chemical released by some cells in the immune system in response to injury or infection.

Holistic: everything is part of the whole, dealing with the whole not a specific part. The whole is greater than the sum of its parts.

Host: organism in or on which a parasite lives and from which the parasite obtains its nutrients and shelter, an organism infected by an infecting agent or pathogen.

Human papilloma virus (HPV): causes many skin and moist membrane infections including premalignant lesions that may develop into cancer of the cervix.

Hydrocephalus: a condition where cerebrospinal fluid builds up in the skull which can cause brain damage without treatment. Treatment is by insertion of a shunt in early infancy to drain the excess fluid into another part of the body usually the abdominal cavity.

Hydrolysis: breaking of a larger molecule by the addition of water into smaller molecules.

Hypothesis: statement that predicts the relationship between two variables.

Immunity: the ability of an organism to resist an infecting agent due to the presence of memory cells.

Immunocompromised: having a weakened/less efficient immune system for example due to being HIV+, taking immunosuppressant drugs following a transplant surgery, treatment with chemotherapy with cancer, following another infection or having neutropenia (lack of certain white blood cells).

Impairment: mental or physical weaknesses. For example a visual impairment means that an individual is unable to see clearly.

Inclusion: being part of an institution, event or culture.

Independent variable: a phenomenon not dependent on the value of another variable for example time or temperature.

Indirect care: providing a service that helps direct carers look after a person, provided by people such as GP receptionists or hospital chefs.

Infarct: obstruction of the blood supply to an organ or area of tissue causing tissue death (necrosis) usually caused by a thrombus (blood clot) or an embolus (a thrombus that has moved).

Infecting agent: an organism that infiltrates another living organism (the host) and causes an infectious disease. Infecting agents may be a virus, bacterium, fungus or parasite.

Infective dose: amount of pathogen needed to cause an infection in the host.

Inherited: people inherit things from their parents through genes as the baby is growing in the womb. Eye and hair colour, height and build are a few examples of things a person inherits.

Initiative: doing something to solve a problem before others do.

Inoculation: the introduction of micro-organisms such as bacteria, into/onto the liquid or solid media.

Intervention: a plan or act designed to alter the course of a disease, injury or condition by initiating a treatment or programme to aid recovery.

In vitro: in glass, for example in a test tube.

In vivo: in living cells/tissues.

Ion: atom or molecule with an unequal number of electrons and protons, which means it has either a net positive or negative electric charge due to its having lost or gained one or more electrons.

Isoprene: organic compound with the formula $H_2C=C-CH=CH_2$ produced by many plants; may help stabilise cell membranes against increased temperatures.

Key words: a single word or a short string of words that indicate the content of a piece of text for example health and social care.

Key worker: a healthcare professional who is the main contact person for a team, an individual being cared for and their family.

Kilograms (kg) or grams (g): units for measuring mass.

Language: the use of words in a structured way.

LDL: low density lipoproteins, these protein and lipid complexes carry cholesterol in the blood and 'dump' cholesterol into the artery walls causing fatty plaques that increase the risk of artery disease; also called 'bad cholesterol'.

Learning objective: a statement of the steps to be taken to gain the knowledge and skills needed to accomplish a goal.

Line of enquiry: a specific focus for research that relates directly to a larger topic or issue.

Line of reasoning: systematic exploration of reasons to support the development of an argument or point of view.

Lipid: fats or their derivatives, including fatty acids, oils, waxes or steroids. Insoluble in water but soluble in organic solvents such as ethanol.

Literature search: a process involving a planned thorough and systematic exploration of a range of published material in order to gain a broader understanding of an issue.

Litre (L): unit of volume equal to 1 cubic decimetre (1 dm^3) which is a cube of 10 cm × 10 cm × 10cm equal to 1000 cm^3.

Lymphocytes: a type of white blood cell. They are small and each contains a large nucleus. There are two types – B-lymphocytes and T-lymphocytes.

Macrophage: a large phagocytic white blood cell in tissues. Many accumulate at the site of infection.

Mast cells: type of white blood cell found in connective tissue, that releases histamine during inflammatory reactions.

Mean: the arithmetical average; the total of all the values divided by the number of values.

Median: the middle value of a data set in which all the values are placed in ascending or descending order.

Megaloblastic anaemia: type of anaemia characterised by red blood cells that are larger than normal. There are also fewer red blood cells so body tissues and organs do not get enough oxygen.

Memory cell: B or T cells that remain in the body for a long time giving an immunological memory and enabling faster immune response when next infected by the same pathogen.

Mentor: a person who gives advice and help to a younger or less experienced colleague.

Merozoites: a stage in the life cycle of a plasmodium that can start a new cycle of development.

Metabolism: the chemical reactions that take place inside living cells to maintain life.

Microbiome: all the genes of the microbiota, the products of many of which are essential for a person's wellbeing.

Microbiota: all the micro-organisms in a particular habitat such as in a human body.

Microlitre (μL): unit of volume; 10^{-3}mL; 10^{-6}L.

Micro-organism: a microbiological entity which may be single-celled or multicellular that is capable of replication or of transferring genetic material, for example fungi, bacteria, viruses and some protoctists.

Milestone: significant stage in development.

Millilitre (mL): unit of volume; 1cm^3, 10^{-3}L

Millimole (mmol): 10^{-3} mole, 1 mmol glucose is 0.18 g.

Mode: the single value in a data set that occurs most frequently.

Molarity: the number of moles per solute per litre of solution.

Mole (mol): the amount of a chemical substance that contains as many atoms/molecules as these are atoms in 12g carbon which is 6 × 10^{23}. It is the equivalent to the gram molecular mass, for example a mole of glucose molecular mass 180, is 180 g.

Molecule: the smallest part of a compound.

Monoclonal antibodies: a clone of identical antibody molecules.

Monomer: a molecule that is able to bond in long chains.

Monosaccharide: the simplest form of carbohydrate, it is a building block for more complex carbohydrates.

Morals: unwritten codes of what a society considers to be acceptable or unacceptable behaviours.

Nanometre (nm): unit of linear measurement; 10^{-9} metre (or one billionth of a metre).

Narrative: verbal description of events in the order in which they happen, for example recording the details where the events occurred, who was involved, what was said, what happened.

Natural selection: a mechanism for evolution. All species overproduce young and there is a struggle for existence as they compete for resources. Individuals differ from each other and those individuals best adapted survive longer producing more young, many of whom inherit the more favourable characteristics. The frequency of the favourable characteristic within the population gradually changes.

Neural tube defects: abnormalities of the brain, spine or spinal cord that can happen in the first month of pregnancy. The commonest is spina bifida where the spinal column does not close properly.

Neurone: a nerve cell that processes information through electrical and chemical signals.

Neutron: subatomic particle that has no electric charge.

NICE: the National Institute for Health and Care Excellence; the government organisation that defines the standard expected for health and social care.

Non-fluent aphasia: condition in which damage to the left frontal area of the brain, associated with ability to use and understand language, causes the individual to struggle to speak, omit words and use very short sentences. Also called Broca aphasia.

Non-participant observer: an observer removed from the context of the activity in which the participant behaviour is being observed. The observer is an onlooker only, for example an early years practitioner observing how a group of three year olds play together.

Norms of development: achievements or milestones at approximate and accepted age ranges by the majority of children.

Notifiable disease: a medical condition required by law to be reported to government authorities.

Nursing process: a method of delivering a high standard of nursing care which involves assessing needs, planning and implementing care, evaluating whether the care delivered has been effective and reassessing needs.

Objective: a statement of an intended outcome from an action. An objective should relate to an overall aim but be more specific.

Objectivity: maintaining a neutral or open minded perspective to ensure that ensure that any conclusions are based on impartially obtained evidence, which takes full account of all the data collected in the research.

Omega-3 fatty acid: fatty acid where the first double bond in the hydrocarbon chain is at carbon number 3.

Omega-6 fatty acid: fatty acid where the first double bond in the hydrocarbon chain is at carbon number 6.

Open question: allows the respondent to provide an answer in their own words.

Operant conditioning: learning based on reinforcement following an initial behaviour.

Opinion: a personal judgement, perspective or interpretation which is not necessarily based on fact or knowledge, for example private health care is better than the health care provided by the NHS.

Organelle: organised and specialised structure within a cell. Some, e.g. mitochondria, are membrane bound and are found only in eukaryotic cells. Ribosomes are not bound by a membrane and occur in prokaryotic and eukaryotic cells.

Organic molecules (compounds): molecules of life; they are built around chains of carbon atoms. There are four main groups – carbohydrates, lipids, proteins and nucleic acids.

Osmosis: the passage of water from an area of high water potential to one of low water potential across a partially permeable membrane.

Osteomalacia: or soft bones is vitamin D deficiency in adults. It causes bone pain, muscle weakness and an increased risk of fractures.

Osteoporosis: a condition typically as a result of hormonal changes or deficiency of calcium or vitamin D in which there is loss of bone tissue, weakening of the bones and making them fragile and more likely to break.

Outcome: the actual outcome from an activity.

Over-nutrition: a condition that results from either eating too much or eating too many of the wrong types of food or taking too many vitamins or other dietary supplements.

Oxidation: removal of hydrogen atoms or removal of electrons from substrate molecules.

Palpitations: rapid, strong, or irregular heart beat that may be caused by agitation exertion or illness, usually only lasting for a few seconds.

Pathogenic: capable of causing disease.

Pathology: the science of the causes and effects of disease.

Parasite: an organism that lives in or on another organism (host) from which it obtains nourishment; the host is harmed in the process.

Parkinson's disease: a disorder characterised by slow movements, rigidity and tremors, caused by an insufficient amount of dopamine in the brain due to the death of brain cells.

Participant: an individual who contributes data to research, for example by submitting responses to a questionnaire, taking part in an interview or focus group or by agreeing that their personal data can be used by researchers for a particular research project.

Participant observer: an observer who actively engages in the activity context of the observation alongside the individuals or individual who are being observed, for example a play therapists stimulating play in order to observe the behaviour of an emotionally disturbed child.

Passive: accepting or allowing what happens without offering any resistance or response.

Passive smoking: inhalation of smoke from tobacco products smoked by another person particularly in a closed environment.

Personal development goal: a goal that you aim for to improve some aspect of your skills and attributes to develop you as a person.

Personal responsibility: by choosing their own actions a person is accountable for them.

Phagocytic leucocyte: a white blood cell that can engulf and ingest micro-organisms or other harmful material.

Phenomenon (plural is phenomena): event or observation in relation to the physical world.

Phenylketonuria: a rare genetic condition that affects brain development.

Photosynthesis: process by which plants, algae or some bacteria use sunlight as a source of energy to synthesise organic molecules from carbon dioxide and water; chlorophyll traps the light energy and enables the process to be carried out.

P_i: inorganic phosphate the appropriate concentration of intracellular inorganic phosphate (P_i) is required for cellular metabolism.

Pilot study: small scale, preliminary study used prior to undertaking a research project to evaluate whether the proposed study will be feasible and also improve its design.

Placebo: a medical prescription deliberately made to look like and be administered identically to a real drug but which contains no medically active ingredients.

Plasma cell: a cell derived from a B-lymphocyte cell, which is stimulated by antigen presentation to divide. Plasma cells secrete many antibodies.

Pollution: presence or introduction into the environment of a harmful or toxic substance.

Polysaccharides: three or more monosaccharides combined together to form complex carbohydrates.

Power of attorney: legal right given to someone to act for another individual, and to make decisions about financial, health and social care matters on their behalf.

Primary research: data contributing to the conclusions drawn is generated as a consequence of scientific method, or by the researcher obtaining personal information directly from the individuals.

Proactive: making something happen rather than responding to a situation after it has happened, e.g. having a flu jab rather than getting the flu and having to take flu remedies.

Professional: belonging to an occupation that needs special training or education.

Professional development goal: the aim to improve some aspect of your skills and attributes as part of your professional development.

Progressive: symptoms will gradually get worse.

Prognosis: a practitioner's opinion or judgement about how an individual will recover from an illness or injury or the likely outcome of a medical condition.

Prokaryotic: cells that have cell surface membranes, cytoplasm and a cell wall but do not have a proper nucleus containing DNA. Their DNA floats free in the cell's cytoplasm.

Prophylactic: preventive measure.

Proprioception: unconscious awareness of movement and spatial orientation that comes from within the body which informs the individual for example if they are upright or prone.

Prosthesis: an artificial part that is used to replace a missing or diseased body part, could be external (a missing limb) or internal (a pacemaker used to stimulate heart beat).

Proton: positively charged subatomic particle.

Radioactive isotope: version of a chemical element whose atoms have unstable nuclei with more neutrons than the normal isotope they emit radiation.

Range: the difference between the largest and smallest value in the data set or the spread of the data.

Rapport: an understanding relationship between two people that allows communication between them.

Rationale: a statement justifying a course or action.

Recessive gene: coded characteristics are present but may be masked by a dominant gene.

Recommendations: specific suggestions for future actions.

Reduction: addition of hydrogen atoms or addition of electrons to substrate molecules.

Reference: a source referred to in an essay or research paper.

Reflect: look back on actions and events and learn from them.

Reinforcement: a process of encouraging, strengthening or establishing a pattern of behaviour.

Reliability: a measure of the quality of the methods used to obtain data and the extent to which the same result would be obtained if someone else repeated the research using an identical method.

Remission: a period of time when a disease is inactive, but is not considered cured.

Research: a planned process in which information is gathered systematically for a specific purpose in a context of existing knowledge and understanding with the data obtained then analysed and evaluated to enable conclusions to be drawn regarding the new knowledge and understanding acquired.

Reservoir of infection: principal habitat where an infectious agent lives and proliferates, includes humans, animals, plants, soil or other substances such as biofilms.

Respondents: individuals from the selected sample who submit a completed questionnaire to the researcher.

Response frame: menu of answer options provided for a closed question.

Response rate: percentage representing the proportion of completed questionnaires returned to the researcher relative to the total number of questionnaires distributed. A high response rate increases the reliability and validity of the data gathered from a questionnaire.

Responsibility: a duty you are required or expected to do because it is morally right or legally required.

Rickets: condition in which children's bones are soft and deformed. Tends to affect the leg bones which bear most of the child's weight but can also affect the spine. There is a risk of bone fractures and children with rickets are more prone to tooth decay.

Safeguard: protect from harm.

Safe sex: for example, avoiding risky situations such as when large amounts of alcohol or drugs have been consumed and using a condom.

Salt: substance that dissolves in water into anions and cations, neither of which is a hydrogen or hydroxyl ion.

Sample: group of individuals selected to participate in a particular health and social care research investigation.

Sample population: group of individuals targeted for investigation on the basis that they share the characteristics being investigated.

Scurvy: a rare condition caused by a lack of vitamin C which affects the body's ability to form collagen. Symptoms include tiredness, shortness of breath, pain in the limbs, swollen or bleeding gums, delayed wound healing and bruising easily.

Secondary data: data contributing to the conclusions drawn is retrieved from previously published sources.

Self-concept: the way in which you see yourself, a mental image that includes abilities, strengths, weaknesses, status and other characteristics.

Self-esteem: respect for own self, self-worth.

Self-identity: awareness of your own unique identity, the potential and qualities you possess.

Self-worth: a sense of own value or worth.

Separation anxiety: distress as a result of being absent from someone they are attached to.

Signs: observable physical features of a medical condition, which can be seen or felt by a medical practitioner or healthcare worker, for example a lump or bruise; as opposed to symptoms such as a headache, which are subjective and reported by an individual and may or may not be observable.

Skill: the ability or talent to do something well.

Social construct: an idea or notion of any given society that may not represent reality by appears to be natural and obvious to the people who accept it.

Sociogram: record the interactions one individual makes with other people, for example they are used in childcare to document a child's social development as they learn and play with other children and interact with adults. Sociograms are often recorded as a chart.

Spatial awareness: knowing your location, both in relation to a given space and to other objects around you.

Specialists: people trained to a very high standard in a specialist subject who have studied a curriculum set and recognised by a university or other accredited institution, and passed the relevant exams so that they can work in that specialism.

Speech: the ability to express yourself through clear, distinct and understandable sounds.

Sporozoites: a motile, spore like stage in the lifecycle of some parasites/pathogens such as *Plasmodium sp* that causes malaria.

Standardisation: formal process to ensure that individuals performing the same qualitative task in different situations do so far as possible in exactly the same way. Standardisation involves the individuals being trained for the task then completing an identical task under the same controlled conditions. A standardisation process should be repeated regularly if the task is being performed repeatedly over a long period of time.

Standards of practice: conditions set by central government, local government and local health authorities that care providers must follow.

Stereotyping: an oversimplified idea that a particular type of person or group are all the same because they share one characteristic, for example all people with blue eyes are well behaved.

Steroid: chemical substance with a specific four-ring carbon structure, related to cholesterol.

Stock solution: a concentrated solution that can be diluted to lower concentrations for actual use.

Strategy: a statement of key priorities for change with associated outcomes that will result from the changes to be achieved within defined timescales.

Stump: a part of the limb that is left beyond the healthy joint following an amputation.

Subjective norm: a perceived social pressure that arises from an individual's perception of what other people would think or do in similar circumstances.

Substrate: molecule that an enzyme acts on.

Supervision: directing and overseeing someone's (a learner's) work.

Supervisor: a person who directs and oversees the work of a learner.

Survey: systematic process of gathering information from several individuals, often using a questionnaire.

Symbiotic: interdependent relationship between organisms of different species.

Symptoms: physical or mental features of a medical condition which can be seen or felt by a patient, for example, a headache or redness of the skin. They are often subjective and may not be visible in other people.

Team: a group of people working together towards the same goal.

Terpenes: organic compounds made of chains of Isoprene units, also known as isoprenoids.

Thrive: grow well or flourish.

Time sampling: series of observations made at a regular predetermined time interval for a predetermined fixed amount of time, for example every hour for the duration of a particular finite activity.

Tissue fluid: extracellular fluid that bathes cells. It comes from the fluid part of the blood that has been forced out of the blood capillaries and later goes back into the blood capillaries or the lymph system.

Titration: a technique where a solution of known concentration is used to determine the concentration of another solution with which it reacts.

Transcription factor: protein that binds to a specific DNA sequence and which controls the rate of transcription of genetic information from DNA to mRNA.

Transcripts: exact, word for word written record of what is said by both the interviewee and the interviewer usually taken from an audio or video recording.

Transient ischaemic attack (TIA): sometimes called a mini stroke and is caused by a temporary disruption to the blood supply to part of the brain. Symptoms are similar to those of a stroke but a TIA only lasts for a few minutes or hours and is usually over within 24 hours.

Transition: the process of change.

Translocation: a chromosome abnormality caused by rearrangement of parts between chromosomes. In Down's syndrome an extra piece of chromosome 21 attaches itself to another chromosome.

Triangulation: the circumstances where two or more sources agree with regard to trends in data gathered and or conclusions drawn.

Typical: showing the characteristics expected in a particular group of people.

Unit of alcohol: 10 ml or 8 g of pure alcohol; standard guidance is that this is equal to 250 ml of 4 per cent beer, 76 ml of 13 per cent wine or 40 per cent whiskey, for example.

Validation: recognising or affirming that something is based on the truth or fact, or the worth of a person or their feelings or opinions, making the person feel valued or worthwhile.

Validity: a measure of the quality of data, information and concepts and how well any claims made are supported by evidence.

Variable: entity or factor that can have a range of measurable values, a factor that will affect the results.

Vector: an organism that transmits a pathogen from one organism to another.

Vegan: a diet that excludes all meat, poultry, fish, eggs and dairy produce.

Vegetarian: a diet that does not include meat, poultry or fish but does include eggs and dairy products.

Virus: a submicroscopic infective agent consisting of a protein coat and nucleic acid – either RNA or DNA but not both.

Visuospatial: perception of how far away objects are from each other or how close together they are.

Work shadowing: observing a person doing their job to learn about their role.

Index

Page numbers in italics indicate diagrams.